AF668182

NCERT PHYSICS

REVISION WORK BOOK

Most Effective Revision
& Concept Zipper for >>>>

JEE, NEET & CUET

Vol. 2 CLASS XII

Authors
Dharmendra Singh *(B.Tech)*
Avinash Kumar *(B.Tech)*

Super 6

ADVANTAGES OF REVISION WORK BOOKS

1. Learn with fun while practicing with Self Assessment.
2. Different question types are helpful in increasing the learning and understanding about **Core Concepts** and **Conceptual Applications**.
3. Figure based small methodical questions also help in increasing **figure visualisation**.
4. Innovative style of practice in Workbook manner helps in breaking the monotonicity of subject.
5. Complete sync with NCERT along with **Competition Connect** and **Competition Edge Up** helps in building the foundation for the preparation of competitions like JEE, NEET and CUET.
6. Questions with one word or maximum one sentence long answers are very helpful in **Faster Revision** and **Confidence Boost Up**.

ARIHANT PRAKASHAN (SERIES), MEERUT

All Rights Reserved

© Publisher

No part of this publication may be re-produced, stored in a retrieval system or by any means, electronic, mechanical, photocopying, recording, scanning, web or otherwise without the written permission of the publisher. Arihant has obtained all the information in this book from the sources believed to be reliable and true. However, Arihant or its editors or authors or illustrators don't take any responsibility for the absolute accuracy of any information published and the damage or loss suffered thereupon.

All disputes subject to Meerut (UP) jurisdiction only.

卐 **Administrative & Production Offices**

Regd. Office
'Ramchhaya' 4577/15, Agarwal Road, Darya Ganj, New Delhi -110002
Tele: 011- 47630600, 43518550

卐 **Head Office**
Kalindi, TP Nagar, Meerut (UP) - 250002
Tel: 0121-7156203, 7156204

卐 **Sales & Support Offices**
Agra, Ahmedabad, Bengaluru, Bareilly, Chennai, Delhi, Guwahati, Hyderabad, Jaipur, Jhansi, Kolkata, Lucknow, Nagpur & Pune.

卐 **PRICE** ₹310.00

卐 PO No. : TXT-59-T064205-04-25

Published by Arihant Publications (India) Ltd.

For further information about the books published by Arihant, log on to www.arihantbooks.com or e-mail at info@arihantbooks.com

Follow us on   

FAB 4 Features

TOPIC 1

Electric Charge NCERT Pg 1-3

NCERT Tracker

Every topic is tagged with NCERT page numbers for better syncing with NCERT.

1. Name the property which differentiates two types of charges.

____

2. As per convention, the charge on the glass rod or cat's fur is __(A)__ and that on plastic rod or silk is __(B)__ . If an object possesses an electric charge, it is said to be __(C)__ and if it has no charge, it is said to be __(D)__ . Here, (A), (B), (C) and (D) respectively refer to

(a) negative, positive, electrically neutral, electrically charged ☐

(b) positive, negative, electrically charged, electrically neutral ☐

(c) electrical charged, electrically neutral, negative, positive ☐

(d) None of the above ☐

***18.** Two point charges A and B, having charges $+Q$ and $-Q$ respectively, are placed at certain distance apart and force acting between them is F. If 25% charge of A is transferred to B, then force between the charges becomes

(a) $\frac{9F}{16}$ ☐ (b) $\frac{16F}{9}$ ☐

(c) $\frac{4F}{3}$ ☐ (d) F ☐

Important Concept Tagging

Every question which is based on the important concept from JEE/NEET/CUET point of view is marked with *.

COMPETITION CONNECT

Topic Eddy Current [NCERT (Old) Pg. 218-219]

1. Eddy currents are produced when

(a) a metal is kept in varying magnetic field

(b) a metal is kept in steady magnetic field

(c) a circular coil is placed in a magnetic field

(d) current is passed through a circular coil

2. When bulk iron piece is subjected to changing magnetic field, the current induced on the surface of piece is called ________________ (eddy current/direct current).

3. In transformer, eddy currents produce ______ (heat/sound)in the core of transformer.

4. To reduce eddy current, the laminations of metal are separated by using

(a) lacquer ☐ (b) canada balsam ☐

(c) Both (a) and (b) ☐ (d) None of these ☐

Competition Connect

Supplement containing related portions of old NCERT which are present in NEET/JEE/CUET syllabus but removed from latest NCERT.

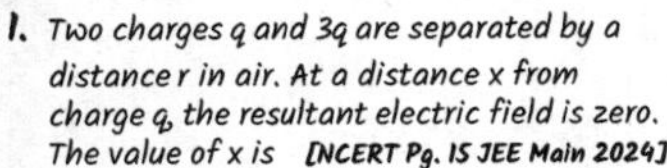

1. Two charges q and $3q$ are separated by a distance r in air. At a distance x from charge q, the resultant electric field is zero. The value of x is **[NCERT Pg. 15 JEE Main 2024]**

(a) $\frac{r}{(1+\sqrt{3})}$ ☐

(b) $r(1+\sqrt{3})$ ☐

(c) $\frac{r}{3(1+\sqrt{3})}$ ☐

(d) $\frac{(1+\sqrt{3})}{r}$ ☐

2. An infinitely long positively charged straight thread has a linear charge density λ Cm^{-1}. An electron revolves along a circular path having axis along the length

4. σ is the uniform surface charge density of a thin spherical shell of radius R. The electric field at any point on the surface of the spherical shell is **[NCERT Pg. 35 JEE Main 2024]**

(a) $\frac{\sigma}{4\varepsilon_0}$ ☐ (b) $\frac{\sigma}{\varepsilon_0}$ ☐

(c) $\frac{\sigma}{\varepsilon_0 R}$ ☐ (d) $\frac{\sigma}{2\varepsilon_0}$ ☐

5. A charge q is placed at the centre of one of the surface of a cube. The flux linked with the cube is **[NCERT Pg. 29 JEE Main 2024]**

(a) $\frac{q}{8\varepsilon_0}$ ☐ (b) zero ☐

(c) $\frac{q}{2\varepsilon_0}$ ☐ (d) $\frac{q}{4\varepsilon_0}$ ☐

Competition Edge Up

Selected PYQs in Sync with NCERT Chapter.

CONTENTS

Chapter 1

Electric Charges and Fields

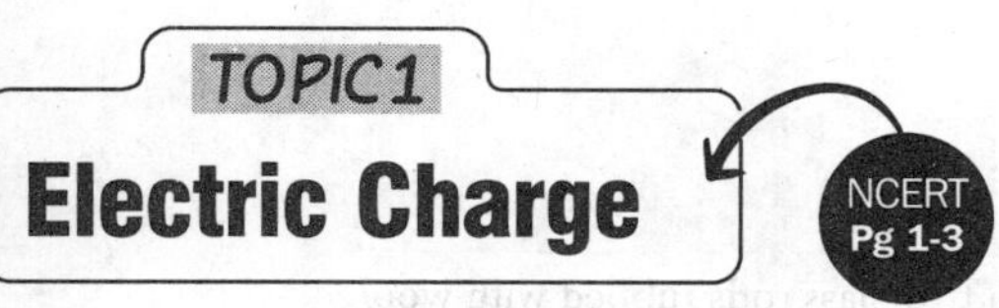

1. Name the property which differentiates two types of charges.

---

2. As per convention, the charge on the glass rod or cat's fur is __(A)__ and that on plastic rod or silk is __(B)__ . If an object possesses an electric charge, it is said to be __(C)__ and if it has no charge, it is said to be __(D)__ . Here, (A), (B), (C) and (D) respectively refer to

(a) negative, positive, electrically neutral, electrically charged ☐

(b) positive, negative, electrically charged, electrically neutral ☐

(c) electrical charged, electrically neutral, negative, positive ☐

(d) None of the above ☐

3. If a plastic rod rubbed with fur is made to touch two small pith balls suspended nearby, then which figure shows their final configuration ?

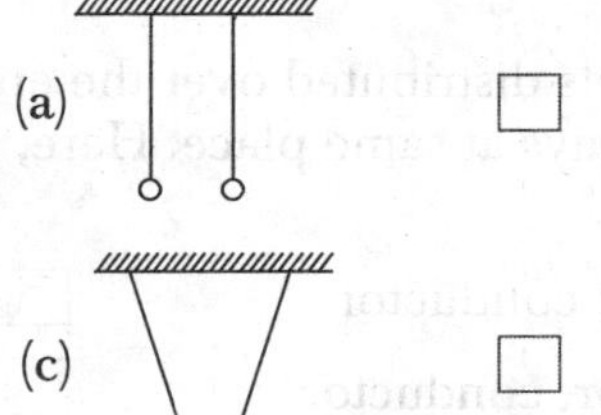

(a) ☐ (b) ☐

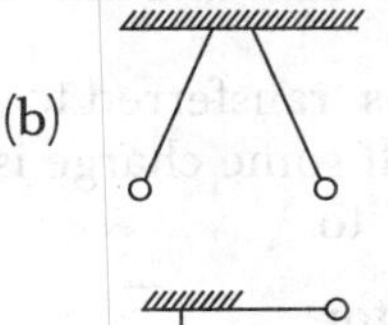

(c) ☐ (d) ☐

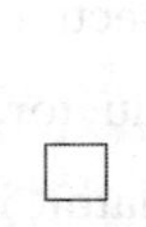

4. If two bodies are rubbed and one of them acquires q_1 charge and another acquires q_2 charge, then ratio of q_1 and q_2 is

(a) 1: 2 ☐ (b) 2 : 1 ☐

(c) 2: 3 ☐ (d) −1 : 1 ☐

Concepts of all questions bearing * are important for JEE/NEET/CUET.

5. Match the figures given in Column I with their respective description given in Column II.

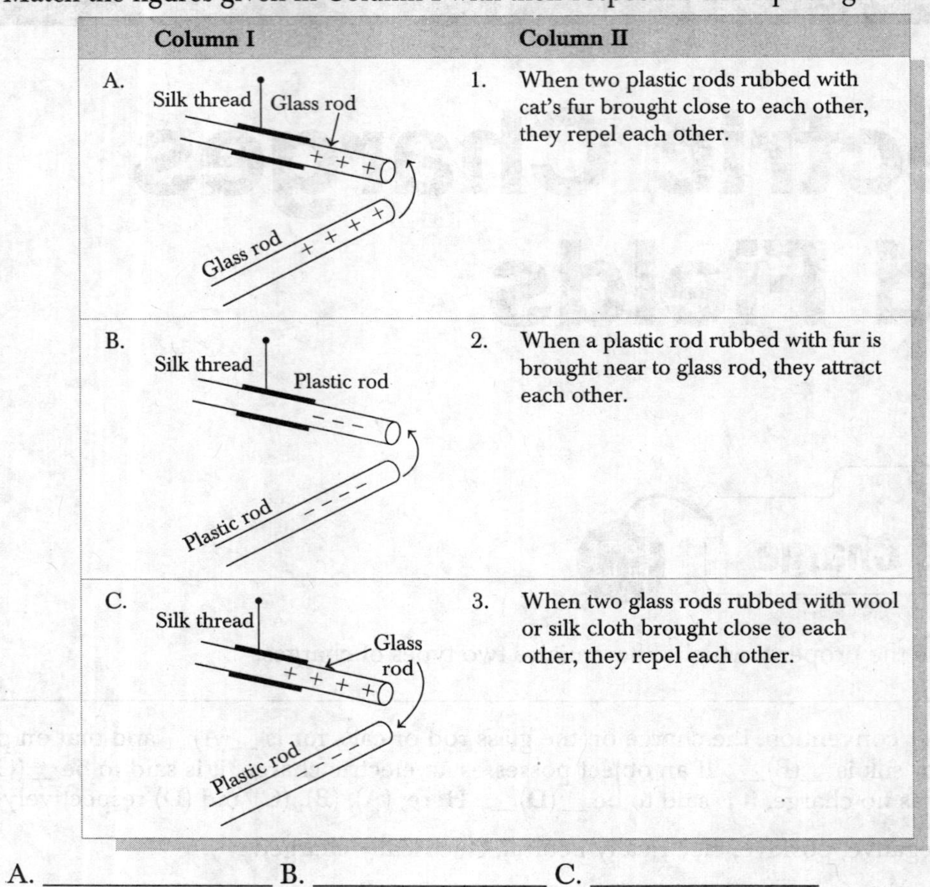

Column I	Column II
A. Silk thread, Glass rod, + + +, Glass rod, + + + +	1. When two plastic rods rubbed with cat's fur brought close to each other, they repel each other.
B. Silk thread, Plastic rod, – – –, Plastic rod, – – – –	2. When a plastic rod rubbed with fur is brought near to glass rod, they attract each other.
C. Silk thread, Glass rod, + + + +, Plastic rod, – – – –	3. When two glass rods rubbed with wool or silk cloth brought close to each other, they repel each other.

A. ________________ B. ________________ C. ________________

TOPIC 2

Conductors and Insulators

NCERT Pg 3-4

6. When some charge is transferred to __(A)__, it readily gets distributed over the entire surface of __(A)__ . If some charge is put on __(B)__, it stays at same place. Here, (A) and (B) respectively refer to

(a) conductor, insulator ☐ (b) insulator, conductor ☐

(c) insulator, insulator ☐ (d) conductor, conductor ☐

7. A cylindrical conductor is placed near another positively charged conductor. The net charge acquired by the cylindrical conductor will be

(a) positive only ☐ (b) negative only ☐

(c) zero ☐ (d) Either positive or negative ☐

TOPIC 3

Basic Properties of Electric Charge and Coulomb's Law

***8.** If a body contains n_1 electrons and n_2 protons, then the total amount of charge on the body is __________ $[(n_2 - n_1)e/(n_1 + n_2)e]$.

9. The number of electrons that must be removed from an electrically neutral silver dollar to give it a charge of $+2.4$ C is 1.5×10^{-19}.

Yes ☐ No ☐

10. An object of mass 1 kg contains 4×10^{20} atoms. If one electron is removed from every atom of the solid, the charge gained by the solid of 1 g is $x \times 10^{-y}$ C. Find x/y.

____

11. If 10^9 electrons move out of a body to another body every second, then how much time is required to get a total charge of 1 C on the other body?

____

***12.** How much is the positive and negative charges in a cup containing 250 g water?

(a) 1.20×10^6 C, 1.20×10^6 C ☐

(b) 1.34×10^7 C, 1.34×10^7 C ☐

(c) 2.60×10^8 C, 2.95×10^7 C ☐

(d) 3.56×10^9 C, 3.56×10^9 C ☐

13. A charged metallic sphere with charge q is put in contact with an identical uncharged sphere. What is the charge on both the spheres?

____

***14.** Force between two charges varies with distance between them as

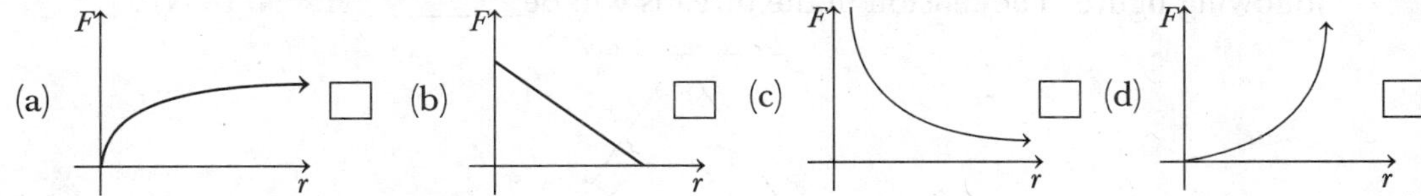

***15.** 1 C is the charge that when placed at a distance of 1 m from another charge of the same magnitude in vacuum experiences an electrical repulsion of magnitude $x \times 10^y$ N. Find the value of xy.

____

***16.** Two charged particles, placed at a distance d apart in vacuum, exert a force F on each other. Now, each of the charges is doubled. To keep the force unchanged, the distance between the charges should be changed to

(a) $4d$ ☐ (b) $2d$ ☐ (c) d ☐ (d) $\frac{d}{2}$ ☐

***17.** Each of the point charges are doubled and their distance is halved. Force of interaction becomes n times. What is the value of n?

____

***18.** Two point charges A and B, having charges $+Q$ and $-Q$ respectively, are placed at certain distance apart and force acting between them is F. If 25% charge of A is transferred to B, then force between the charges becomes

(a) $\frac{9F}{16}$ ☐ (b) $\frac{16F}{9}$ ☐

(c) $\frac{4F}{3}$ ☐ (d) F ☐

***19.** There are two charges q_1 and q_2 located at r_1 and r_2, respectively. The force between them can be represented in vector form as follows

$$F_{21} = \frac{1}{4\pi\varepsilon_0} \frac{q_1 q_2}{r_{21}^2} \cdot \hat{\mathbf{r}}_{21}$$

Now, consider this equation and answer the following in Yes/No.

(a) If in given equation, q_1 and q_2 are of same sign, will F_{21} act along $\hat{\mathbf{r}}_{21}$? ☐

(b) Can force F_{12} on charge q_1 due to charge q_2 be obtained by just interchanging 1 and 2 in given equation? ☐

(c) Does Coulomb's law agree with the Newton's third law? ☐

***20.** Two small spheres each having charge $+Q$ are suspended by insulating threads of length L from a hook. This arrangement is taken in space, where there is no gravitational effect. The angle between the two suspensions and tension in each will be

(a) 180°, $\frac{1}{4\pi\varepsilon_0} \frac{Q^2}{(2L)^2}$ ☐ (b) 90°, $\frac{1}{4\pi\varepsilon_0} \cdot \frac{Q^2}{L^2}$ ☐

(c) 180°, $\frac{1}{4\pi\varepsilon_0} \frac{Q^2}{2L^2}$ ☐ (d) 180°, $\frac{1}{4\pi\varepsilon_0} \cdot \frac{Q^2}{L^2}$ ☐

***21.** Two small spherical balls carrying a charge $Q = 10\,\mu\text{C}$ are suspended by two insulating threads of equal lengths 1 m each, from a fixed point in the ceiling. It is found that in equilibrium, threads are separated by an angle 60° between them as shown in the following figure. The tension in the threads will be ________ (1.8 N/18 N).

60°

Q Q

22. Coulomb's law for electrostatic force between two point charges and Newton's law for gravitational force between two stationary point masses, both have inverse-square dependence on the distance between the charges and masses, respectively.

(i) The strength of these forces by determining the ratio of their magnitude for an electron and a proton will be ____________ ($2.4 \times 10^{39}/4.4 \times 10^{39}$).

(ii) The accelerations of electron and proton due to the electrical force of their mutual attraction when they are 1 Å apart, will be

(a) 2.5×10^{22} ms^{-2}, 3×10^{17} ms^{-2} ☐ (b) 2.5×10^{22} ms^{-2}, 1.4×10^{19} ms^{-2} ☐

(c) 1.9×10^{22} ms^{-2}, 3×10^{19} ms^{-2} ☐ (d) 1.9×10^{22} ms^{-2}, 2.8×10^{38} ms^{-2} ☐

TOPIC 4

Force Between Multiple Charges

NCERT Pg 11-14

23. Three charges $+Q$, q, $+Q$ are placed respectively at distances 0, $\frac{d}{2}$ and d from the origin on the X-axis. If the net force experienced by $+Q$ placed at $x = 0$ is zero, then value of q is ________ $\left(\frac{-Q}{4} / \frac{Q}{2}\right)$.

24. If two point charges of value q and $2q$ are kept at a distance d apart from each other in air and a third charge Q is to be kept along same line in such a way that the net force acting on q and $2q$ is zero, then what will be the position of third charge in terms of q and d?

____

25. Two equal negative charges $-q$ are fixed at points $(0, a)$ and $(0, -a)$ on the Y-axis. A positive charge Q is released from rest at the point $(2a, 0)$ on the axis. The charge Q will

(a) execute simple harmonic motion about the origin ☐

(b) move to the origin and remain at rest ☐

(c) move to infinity ☐

(d) execute oscillatory but not simple harmonic motion. ☐

26. Consider a system of three charges q_1, q_2 and q_3 as shown in the following figure. The force on charge q_1 due to other charges q_2 and q_3 can therefore be obtained by performing a vector addition of the forces due to each one of these charges.

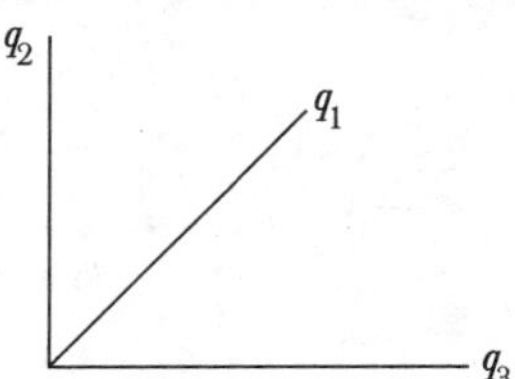

On the basis of above given information, match the items given in Column I with those given in Column II.

Column I	Column II
A. Force on charge q_1 due to charge q_2 can be given as	1. $F_1 = F_{12} + F_{13} + \ldots + F_{1n} = \frac{1}{4\pi\varepsilon_0}\left[\frac{q_1 q_2 \hat{\mathbf{r}}_{12}}{r_{12}^2} + \frac{q_1 q_3 \hat{\mathbf{r}}_{13}}{r_{13}^2} + \ldots + \frac{q_1 q_n \hat{\mathbf{r}}_{1n}}{r_{1n}^2}\right]$
B. Force on charge q_1 due to charge q_3 can be given as	2. $F_{12} = \frac{1}{4\pi\varepsilon_0} \frac{q_1 q_2 \hat{\mathbf{r}}_{12}}{r_{12}^2}$
C. Total force on charge q_1 due to charges q_2 and q_3 will be	3. $F_{13} = \frac{1}{4\pi\varepsilon_0} \frac{q_1 q_3 \hat{\mathbf{r}}_{13}}{r_{13}^2}$
D. If there are $q_1, q_2, \ldots, q_n$ system of charges, then force on q_1 due to all other charges will be	4. $F_1 = F_{12} + F_{13} = \frac{1}{4\pi\varepsilon_0}\left[\frac{q_1 q_2 \hat{\mathbf{r}}_{12}}{r_{12}^2} + \frac{q_1 q_3 \hat{\mathbf{r}}_{13}}{r_{13}^2}\right]$

A. ________ B. ________ C. ________ D. ________

***27.** If three charges q_1, q_2 and q_3, each equal to q are placed at the vertices of an equilateral triangle of side l, then what is the force on charge Q (with same sign as q) placed at the centroid of the triangle?

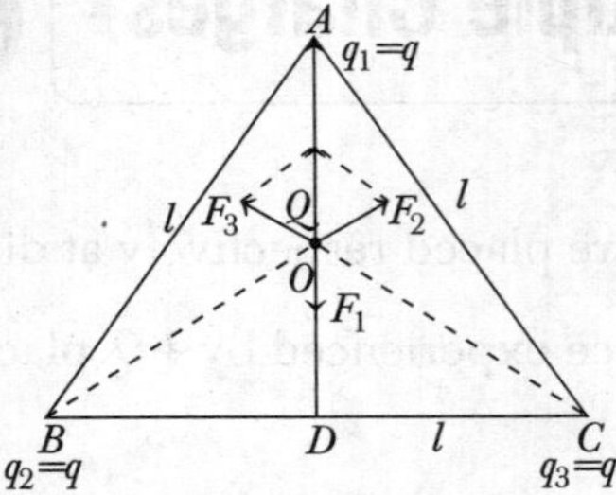

***28.** If charges q, q and $-q$ are placed at the vertices of an equilateral triangle (as shown in the given figure), then what is the force on each charge?

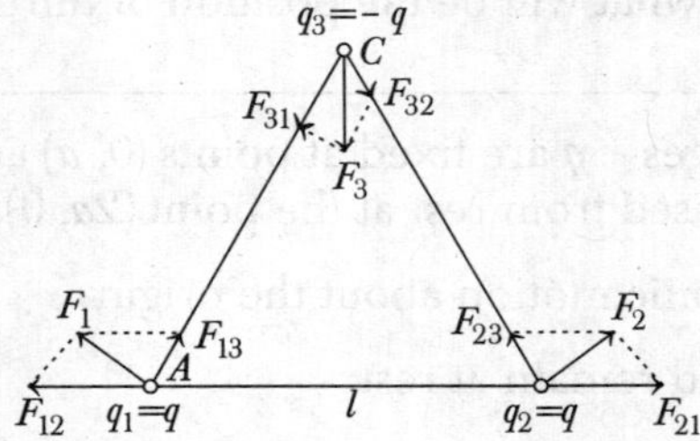

29. In the following figures, two positive charges q_2 and q_3 fixed along the Y-axis, exert a net electric force in the $+x$-direction on a charge q_1 fixed along X-axis. If a positive charge Q is added at $(x, 0)$, the force on q_1 shall

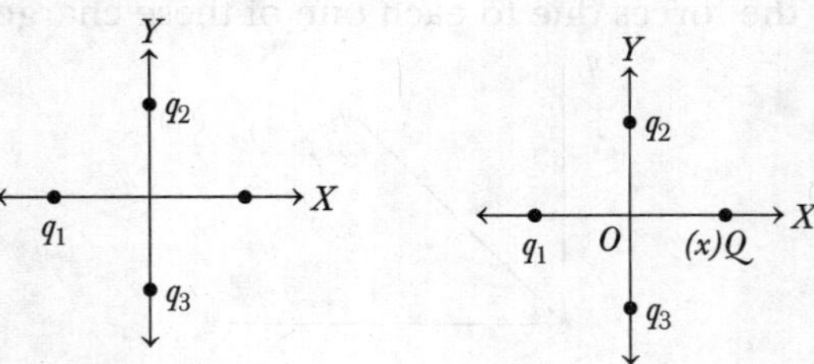

(a) decrease along positive X-axis

(b) increase along positive X-axis

(c) point along the negative X-axis

(d) increase but direction changes because of the intersection of Q with q_2 and q_3

30. A charge Q produces an electric field everywhere in the surrounding. When another charge q is brought at some point P, the field there acts on it and produces a force. So, the electric field produced by the charge Q at a point r will be given as ______ $\left(\frac{kQ}{r^2} / \frac{kq}{r^3}\right)$.

31. The electric field in a certain region is acting radially outward and is given by $E = Aa$. A charge contained in a sphere of radius a centred at the origin of the field will be

(a) $4\pi\varepsilon_0 Aa^2$ ☐ (b) $A\varepsilon_0 a^2$ ☐

(c) $4\pi\varepsilon_0 Aa^3$ ☐ (d) $\varepsilon_0 Aa^3$ ☐

***32.** An unknown charge is contained in a conducting sphere. If the electric field at distance of 20 cm from the sphere is 1.5×10^3 NC^{-1} and points radially inward, then what is the net charge on the sphere?

____

33. In the expression $F = qE$, if q is unity, it means that electric field due to charge Q is numerically equal to the force exerted by it. So, does it mean that, "Electric field due to a charge Q at a point in space may be defined as the force that a unit positive charge would experience, if placed at that point"?

Yes ☐ No ☐

34. The force F on the charge q due to the charge Q depends upon the location of charge q which may take any value in space around the charge Q, so does it mean that electric field due to Q is dependent on the space coordinate r?

Yes ☐ No ☐

35. By superposition principle, the electric field E at r due to the system of charges is

$$E(r) = \frac{1}{4\pi\varepsilon_0}\left(\frac{q_1 \cdot \hat{\mathbf{r}}_{1p}}{r_{1p}^2} + \frac{q_2 \cdot \hat{\mathbf{r}}_{2p}}{r_{2p}^2} + \ldots + \frac{q_n \cdot \hat{\mathbf{r}}_{np}}{r_{np}^2}\right)$$

Here, $\hat{\mathbf{r}}_{np}$ is a unit vector in the direction from __________ (q_n to p/p to q_n) and r_{np} is the __________ (distance/displacement) between q_n and p.

***36.** Charges q, $2q$, $3q$ and $4q$ are placed at the corners A, B, C and D of a square as shown in the following figure. Is the direction of electric field at the centre of the square along CB?

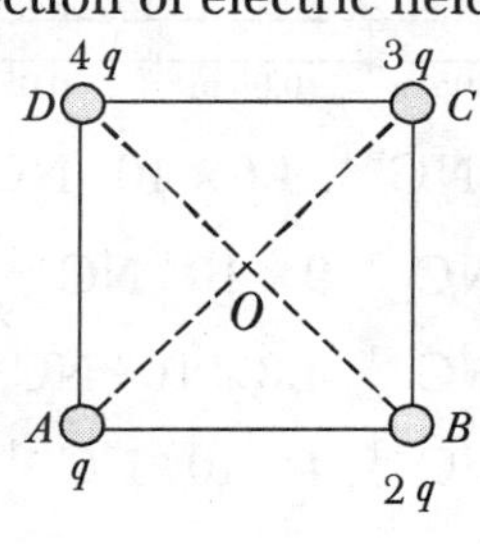

Yes ☐ No ☐

37. Three identical positive point charges, as shown are placed at the vertices of an isosceles right-angled triangle. Which of the numbered vectors coincides in the direction with the electric field at the mid-point M of the hypotenuse?

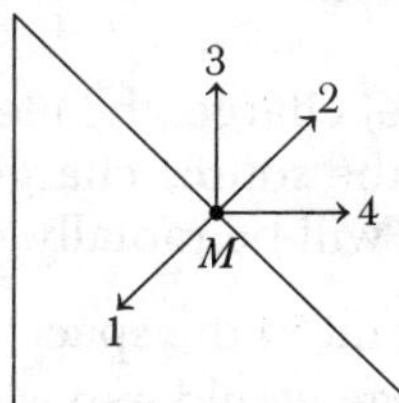

____

***38.** The following figures are regular hexagons with charges at the vertices. In which of the following cases, the electric field at the centre is not zero?

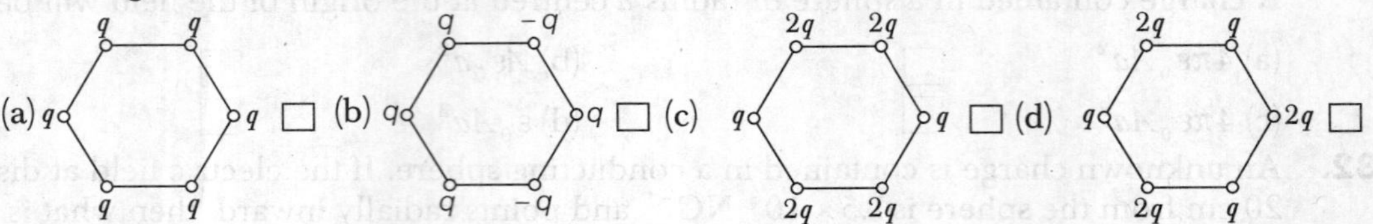

39. An electron falls through a distance of 1.5 cm in a uniform electric field of magnitude 2.0×10^4 NC^{-1}. The direction of field is reversed keeping its magnitude unchanged and a proton falls through a same distance. What will be the time of fall in each case?

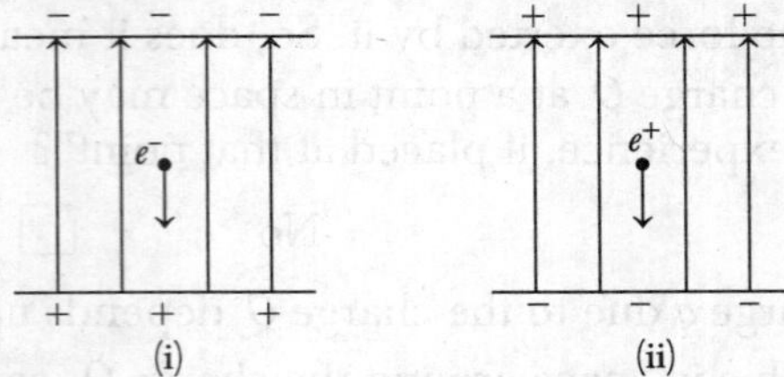

***40.** Two point charges q_1 and q_2 of magnitude $+10^{-8}$ C and -10^{-8} C are placed 0.1m apart. What will be electric fields at points A, B and C as shown in the given figure?

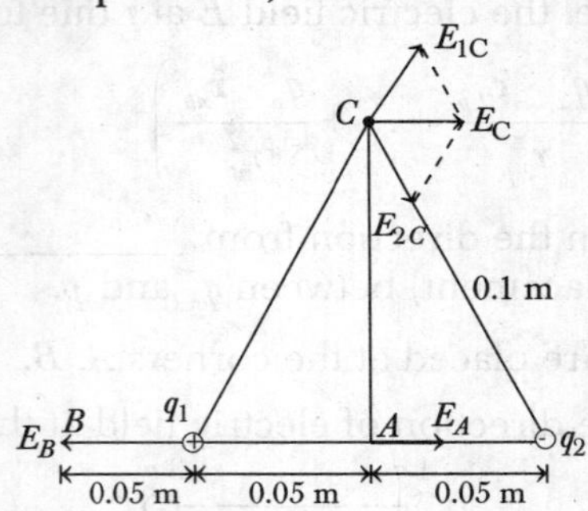

(a) 7.2×10^4 NC^{-1}, 3.2×10^{-5} NC^{-1}, 4.6×10^9 NC^{-1}

(b) 7.2×10^4 NC^{-1}, 3.2×10^4 NC^{-1}, 9×10^3 NC^{-1}

(c) 3.6×10^2 NC^{-1}, 2.1×10^3 NC^{-1}, 4.8×10^6 NC^{-1}

(d) 1.2×10^3 NC^{-1}, 2.3×10^2 NC^{-1}, 4×10^5 NC^{-1}

TOPIC 6

Electric Field Lines

NCERT Pg 19-21

41. For a ________ (positive/negative) charge, the electric field will be directed radially outwards from the charge and if the source charge is ________ (positive/negative), the electric field vector at each point will be radially inwards.

42. **Statement I** Electric field at a point in the space around a system of charges tells us about the force that a unit positive charge would experience, if placed at that point.

Statement II Electric field is a characteristic of the system of charges and is independent of test charge that we place at a point to determine the field.

Which of the following statement(s) is/are correct?

(a) Only Statement I □

(b) Only Statement II □

(c) Both Statement I and Statement II □

(d) Neither Statement I nor Statement II □

43. Consider the given figure and answer the following questions.

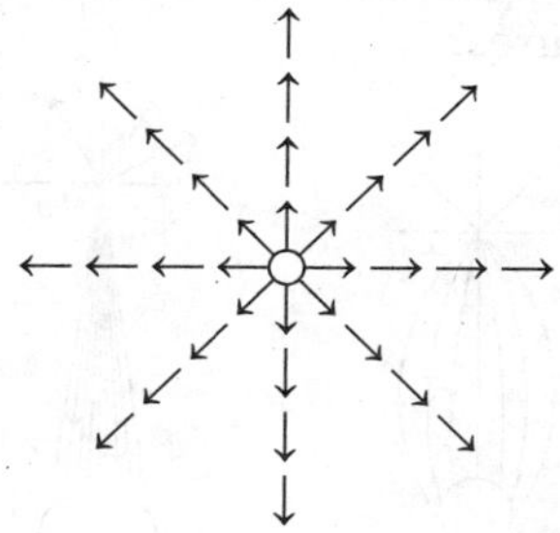

(i) Is the electric field shown in the figure due to a positive point charge?

Yes □ No □

(ii) Is the magnitude of field (in the above figure) represented by the density of field lines?

Yes □ No □

(iii) E is ______ (strong/weak) near the charge, so the density of field lines is ______ (less/more) near the charge. Similarly, the electric field gets ______ (weaker/stronger) away from the charge and the density of field lines is ______ (less/more).

***44.** Match the items given in Column I with those given in Column II.

Column I		Column II
A.	Electric field lines due to single positive charge	1. 
B.	Electric field lines due to single negative charge	2. 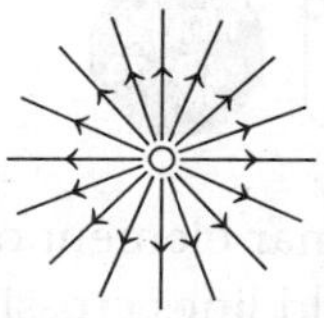
C.	Electric field lines due to two equal charges	3. 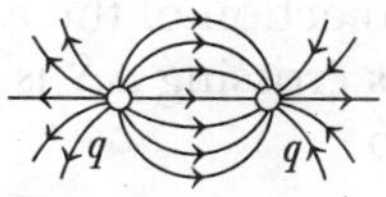
D.	Electric field lines due to two opposite charges	4. 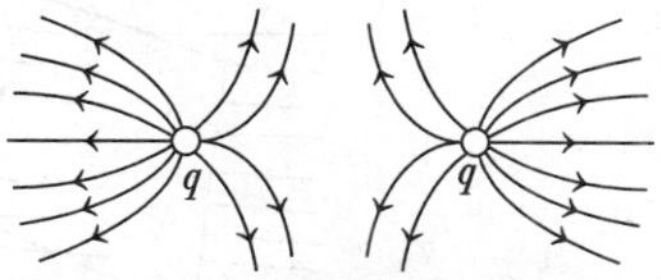

A. ______________ B. ______________ C. ______________ D. ______________

45. Answer the following in Yes or No.

(i) Field lines start from positive charges and end at negative charges. ☐

(ii) If there is a single charge, field lines can start or end at infinite. ☐

(iii) In a charge free region, electric field lines can be taken to be continuous curves without any breaks. ☐

(iv) Electric field lines form closed loops. ☐

46. A positive point charge is brought near an isolated conducting sphere. It is best depicted by which of the following figures?

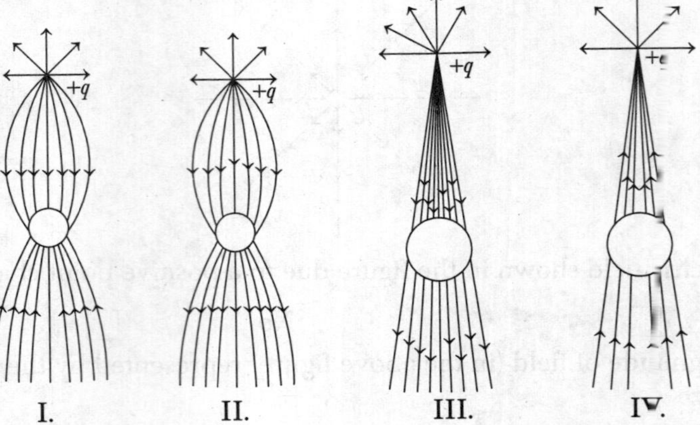

47. The following figure is representing a metallic solid sphere placed in a uniform electric field. The lines of force that follow the path will be ________.

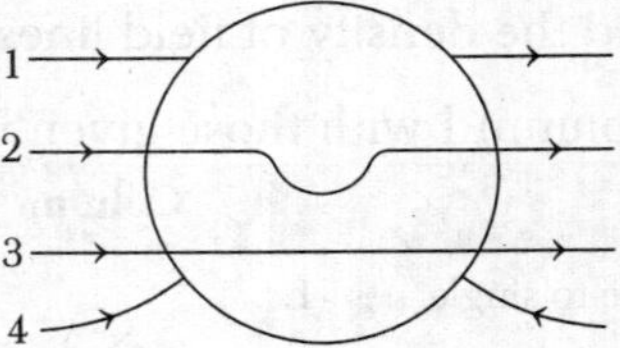

TOPIC 7 Electric Flux

NCERT Pg 21-23

***48.** If we place a small planar element of area ΔS normal to E at a point [as shown in Fig. (a)], then the number of field lines crossing it is proportional to __(A)__ . If the area element be at angle θ, the projection of the area element normal to E is __(B)__ . Therefore, the number of field lines crossing ΔS is proportional to __(C)__ . Here, (A), (B) and (C) respectively refers to

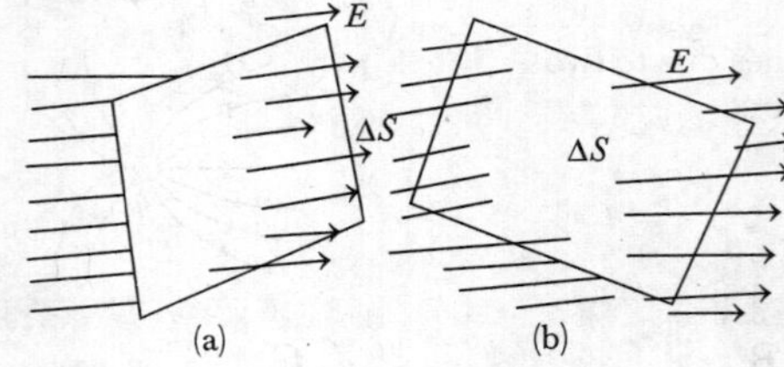

(a) $\frac{E}{\Delta S}$, $\Delta S \sin\theta$, $E\Delta S \sin\theta$ ☐ (b) $E\Delta S$, $\Delta S \sin\theta$, $E\Delta S \sin\theta$ ☐

(c) $\frac{E}{\Delta S}$, $\Delta S \cos\theta$, $E\Delta S \cos\theta$ ☐ (d) $E\Delta S$, $\Delta S \cos\theta$, $E\Delta S \cos\theta$ ☐

***49.** A closed cylinder is placed in an uniform electric field. The electric flux passing through the cylinder is

(a) ES ☐ (b) $-ES$ ☐

(c) zero ☐ (d) $\frac{ES}{2}$ ☐

***50.** The electric field in a region is given by $\mathbf{E} = \frac{E_0}{a} x\hat{\mathbf{i}}$. The electric flux passing through a cubical volume bounded by the surfaces $x = 0$, $x = a$, $y = 0$, $y = a$, $z = 0$ and $z = a$, will be

(a) $E_0 a$ ☐ (b) $E_0 a^2$ ☐

(c) $\frac{E_0 a}{2}$ ☐ (d) $\frac{E_0 a^2}{2}$ ☐

TOPIC 8

Electric Dipole

NCERT Pg 23-27

***51.** For an electric dipole, solve the given analogy for electric field.

E_{axial} (for $r >> a$) : $2\frac{kp}{r^3}$: : $E_{\text{equatorial}}$ (for $r >> a$) : ?

____

52. State whether the given statements are True or False.

(i) The dipole field falls off as $\frac{1}{r^2}$. ☐

(ii) The magnitude and the direction of the field depend on the distance r and the angle between the position vector r and the dipole moment p. ☐

53. Will the ratio of electric fields on the axis and at equator of an electric dipole be 2 : 1?

Yes ☐ No ☐

54. Calculate the electric field (in N/C) due to an electric dipole of length 2 cm having charge 4 μC at an angle 60° from the direction of electric dipole moment, 1 m from the centre of electric dipole.

____

***55.** Two charges ± 10 μC are placed 5.0 mm apart. What will be the electric field (in NC^{-1}) at a point P on the axis of dipole 15 cm away from its centre O on the side of positive charge as shown in following figure?

A O B
−10 μC +10 μC P

____

***56.** Two charges $\pm 10\,\mu C$ are placed 5.0 mm apart. What will be the electric field (in N/C^{-1}) at a point Q, 15 cm away from centre O and normal to the axis of dipole as shown in the following figure?

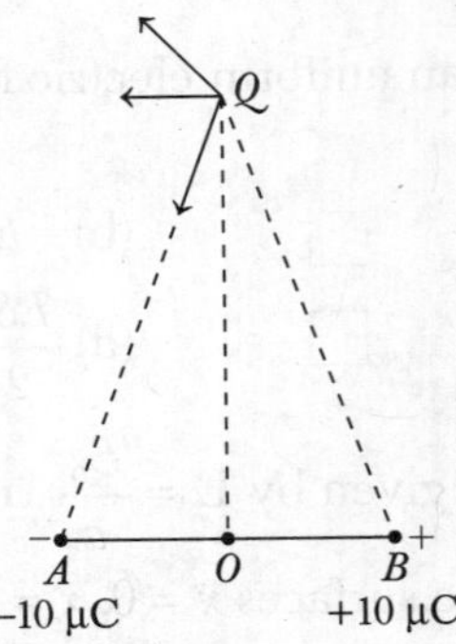

***57.** Three point charges $+q$, $-2q$ and $+q$ are placed at points $(x = 0, y = a, z = 0)$, $(x = 0, y = 0, z = 0)$ and $(x = a, y = 0, z = 0)$, respectively. The magnitude and direction of the electric dipole moment vector of this charge assembly are

(a) $\sqrt{2}\,qa$ along + y-direction ☐

(b) $\sqrt{2}\,qa$ along the line joining of points (0,0,0) and $(a,a,0)$ ☐

(c) qa along the line joining points (0,0,0) and $(a,a,0)$ ☐

(d) $\sqrt{2}\,qa$ along + x-direction ☐

TOPIC 9

Dipole in a Uniform External Field

58. An electric dipole is placed in a uniform electric field with the dipole axis making an angle θ with the direction of the electric field. The orientation of the dipole for stable equilibrium is

(a) $\pi/6$ ☐ (b) $\pi/3$ ☐

(c) 0 ☐ (d) $\pi/2$ ☐

***59.** Consider the following diagram and answer the following questions.

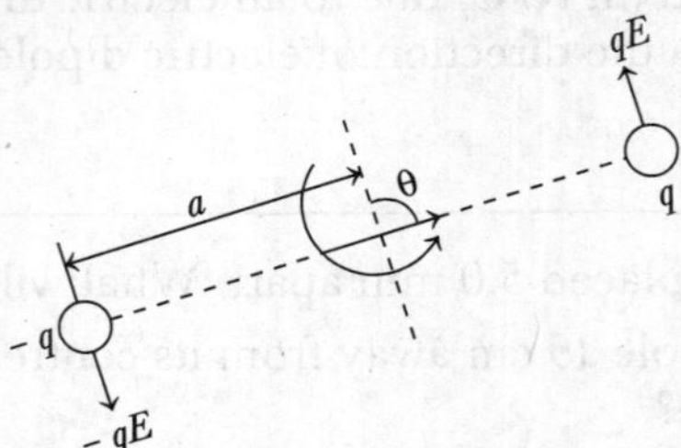

(i) What is the net force on a dipole when it is placed in a uniform external field?

____

(ii) As the charges are separated, so the force starts acting at different points. Does it result in torque?

Yes ☐ No ☐

(iii) In case of zero net force, is this torque independent of origin?

Yes ☐ No ☐

(iv) What will be the magnitude and direction of this torque?

____

60. The following figure is representing electric field lines in which an electric dipole is placed as shown below. Which one of the following options is correct?

(a) The dipole will experience a force towards right. ☐

(b) The dipole will experience a force towards left. ☐

(c) The dipole will not experience any force. ☐

(d) The dipole will experience a force upwards. ☐

61. Assume that an electric dipole is placed at an angle of 30° to a non-uniform electric field, so the dipole will experience a

(a) torque only ☐

(b) torque as well as translational force ☐

(c) translational force only in the direction normal to the direction of field ☐

(d) translational force only in the direction of field ☐

62. An electric dipole is placed at an angle of 30° with an electric field intensity 2×10^5 N/C. It experiences a torque equal to 4 N-m. What will be the charge Q on the dipole, if the dipole length is 2 cm?

____

***63.** An electric dipole consists of two charges of 0.1 μC separated by a distance of 2.0 cm. The dipole is placed in an external field of 10^5 N/C. What maximum torque does the field exert on the dipole?

____

TOPIC 10

Continuous Charge Distribution and Gauss's Law

64. Consider a non-spherical conductor shown in the following figure, which is given a certain amount of positive charge.

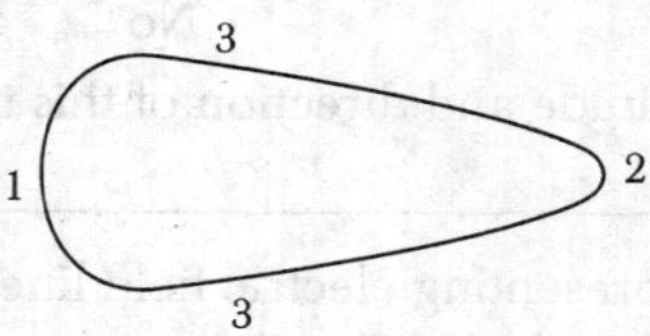

The charge distributes itself on the surface such that the charge densities are σ_1, σ_2 and σ_3 at the regions 1, 2 and 3, respectively. Arrange these charge densities in decreasing order.

____

65. A uniformly charged conducting sphere of 2.4 m diameter has a surface charge density of 80 μCm^{-2}. What is the charge on the sphere?

____

66. If net electric flux through a closed surface is zero, does it mean that the total charge contained in the closed surface is zero?

Yes ☐ No ☐

67. **Statement I** Gauss' law is true for any closed surface, no matter what is its shape or size.

Statement II The term q on the right side of equation of Gauss' law $\left(\frac{q}{\varepsilon_0}\right)$ includes the sum of all charges enclosed by the surface.

Which of the following statement(s) is/are correct?

(a) Only statement I ☐ (b) Only statement II ☐

(c) Both statements I and II ☐ (d) Neither statement I nor II ☐

68. If a surface is chosen such that there are some charges present inside and outside it, then the term q on the right side of Gauss' law represents only the total charge inside the surface.

Yes ☐ No ☐

***69.** Consider the following figures. The electric flux through the surface

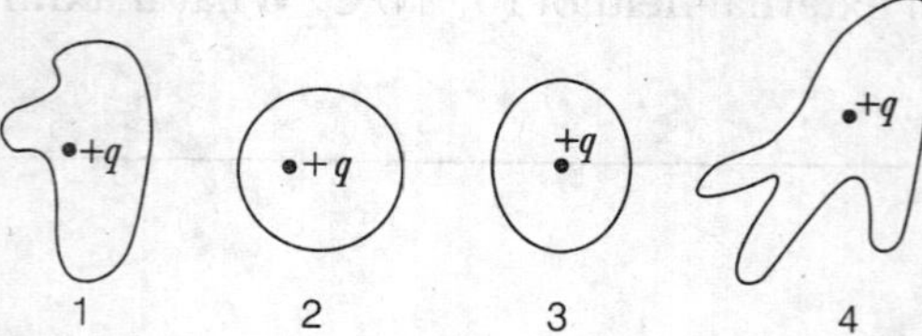

(a) in Fig. 3 is the least. ☐

(b) in Fig. 4 is the largest. ☐

(c) is same for all the figures. ☐

(d) in Fig. 2 is same as in Fig. 3 but is smaller than in Fig. 4. ☐

70. A point charge $+10\,\mu C$ is at a distance of 5 cm directly above the centre of a square of side 10 cm as shown in the given figure. The magnitude of electric flux through the square will be __________ $N\text{-}m^2C^{-1}$ $(1.88 \times 10^5/11.28 \times 10^5)$.

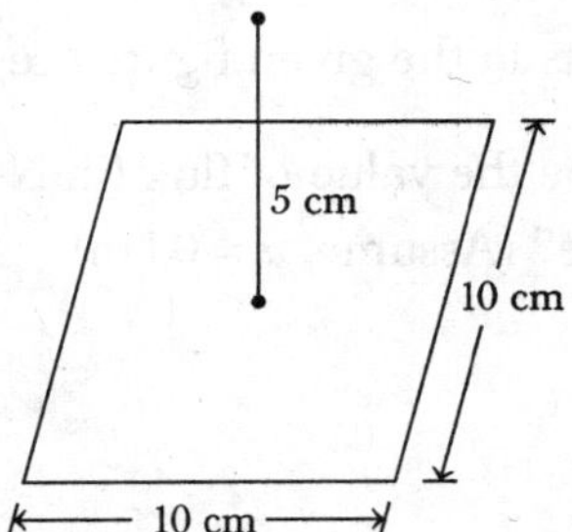

71. A charged particle q is placed at the centre O of cube of length L. Another same charge q is placed at a distance L from O. Find the electric flux through $EFGH$.

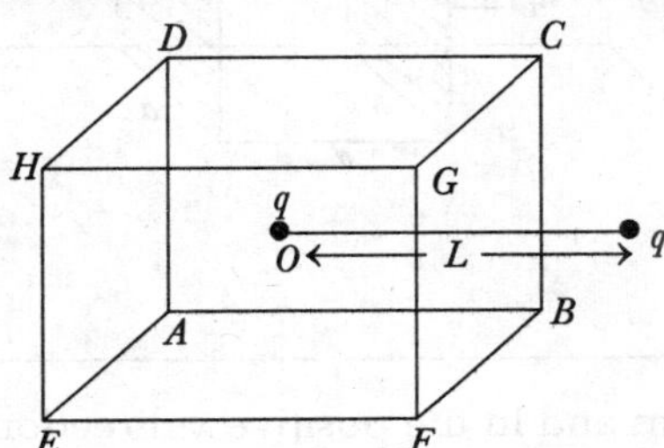

72. A sphere encloses an electric dipole with charge $\pm 3 \times 10^{-6}$ C. What is the total electric flux across the sphere?

(a) -3×10^{-6} N-m²/C ☐ (b) Zero ☐

(c) 3×10^{6} N-m²/C ☐ (d) 6×10^{-6} N-m²/C ☐

73. Consider the charge configuration and spherical Gaussian surface as shown in the following figure. While calculating the flux of electric field over the spherical surface, will the electric field be zero?

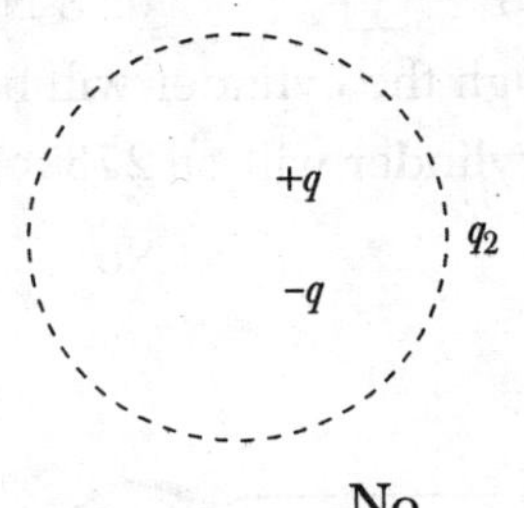

Yes ☐ No ☐

74. What is the value of electric flux for Gaussian surface A that encloses the charged particles in free space? (Take, $q_1 = -14$ nC, $q_2 = 78.85$ nC, $q_3 = -56$ nC)

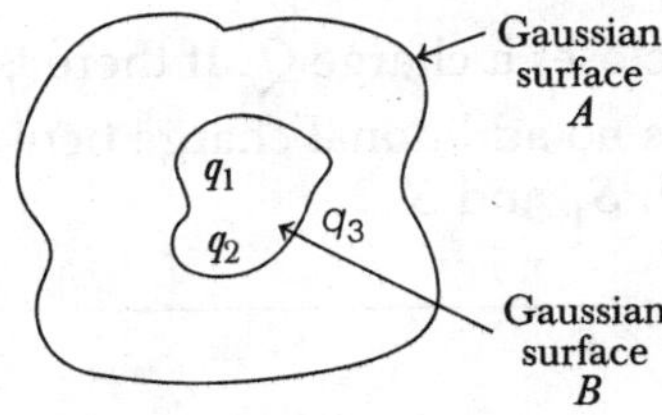

(a) 10^3 N-m^2 C^{-1} ☐ (b) 10^3 CN^{-1} m^{-2} ☐
(c) 6.32×10^3 N-m^2 C^{-1} ☐ (d) 6.32×10^3 CN^{-1} m^{-2} ☐

***75.** The electric field components in the given figure are $E_x = \alpha x^{\frac{1}{2}}$, $E_y = E_z = 0$, in which $\alpha = 800\ \text{N/cm}^{\frac{1}{2}}$. What will be the value of flux (in N-m^{2}C^{-1}) through the cube and the charge (in C) within the cube? (Assume, $a = 0.1$ m)

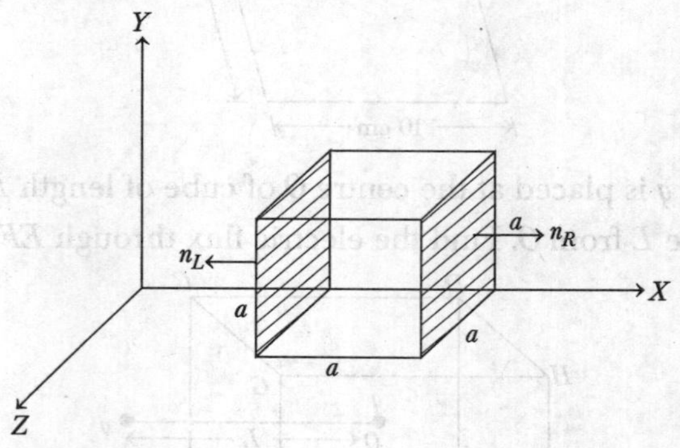

---

76. An electric field is uniform and in the positive x-direction for positive x with the same magnitude but in negative x-direction for negative x. It is given that $E = 200\,\hat{\mathbf{i}}$ N/C for $x > 0$ and $E = -200\,\hat{\mathbf{i}}$ N/C for $x < 0$. A right circular cylinder of length 20 cm and radius 5 cm has its centre at the origin along the X-axis, so that one face is at $x = +10$ cm and the other is at $x = -10$ cm.

Now, answer the following questions on the basis of above passage.

(i) What is the net outward flux through each flat face?

(ii) What is the flux through the side of cylinder?

(a) 2 N-m^{2}C^{-1} ☐ (b) Zero ☐ (c) 3 N-m^{2}C^{-1} ☐ (d) 4.5 N-m^{2}C^{-1} ☐

(iii) The net outward flux through the cylinder will be ______ (1.732/3.14) N-m^{2}C^{-1}.

(iv) The net charge inside the cylinder will be 2.78×10^{-11} C.

Yes ☐ No ☐

TOPIC 11

Applications of Gauss's Law

NCERT Pg 33-37

77. A sphere S_1 of radius r_1 encloses a charge Q. If there is another concentric sphere S_2 of radius $r_2\ (r_2 > r_1)$ and there is no additional charge between S_1 and S_2, then what is the ratio of electric flux through S_1 and S_2?

---

78. Match the items given in Column I (Conductor) with the items given in Column II (Electric field).

Column I		Column II
A.	1.	The electric field inside a uniformly charged thin spherical shell is always zero.
B.	2.	The electric field due to an infinitely long straight uniformly charged wire can be given as $E = \frac{\lambda}{2\pi\varepsilon_0 r}$.
C.	3.	The electric field due to a uniformly charged infinite plane sheet can be given as $E = \frac{\sigma}{2\varepsilon_0}$.
D.	4.	The electric field outside uniformly charged thin spherical shell can be given as $E = \frac{q}{4\pi\varepsilon_0 r^2}$.

A. ______ B. ______ C. ______ D. ______

***79.** Electric charge is uniformly distributed along a long straight wire of radius 1mm. The charge per cm length of the wire is Q coulomb. Another cylindrical surface of radius 50 cm and length 1m symmetrically encloses the wire as shown in the following figure. What will be the total electric flux passing through cylindrical surface?

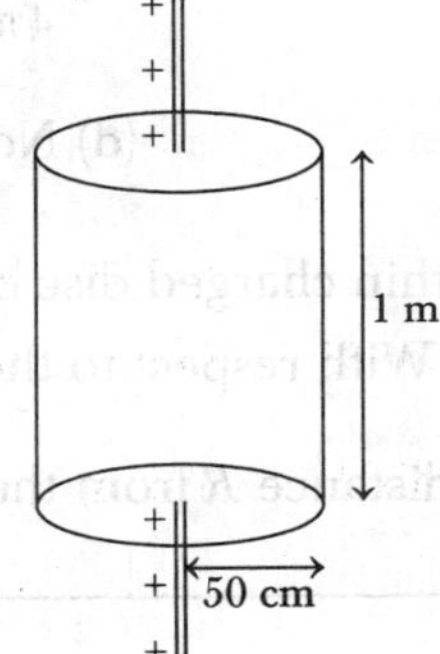

____

80. The electric field near a conducting surface having a uniform surface charge density σ is given by ________ $\left(\frac{2\sigma}{\varepsilon_0}/\frac{\sigma}{\varepsilon_0}\right)$ and it is ________ (normal/parallel) to the surface.

81. Two large, thin metal plates are parallel and close to each other. On their inner faces, the plates have surface charge densities of opposite signs and of magnitude 17.0×10^{-22} Cm^{-2}. What is **E** in the outer region of the first plate?

(a) 17×10^{-22} N/C ☐
(b) 1.5×10^{-15} N/C ☐
(c) 1.9×10^{-10} N/C ☐
(d) Zero ☐

***82.** Shown in the figure is a shell made of a conductor. It has inner radius *a* and outer radius *b* and carries charge *Q*. At its centre, a dipole **p** as shown.
In this case,

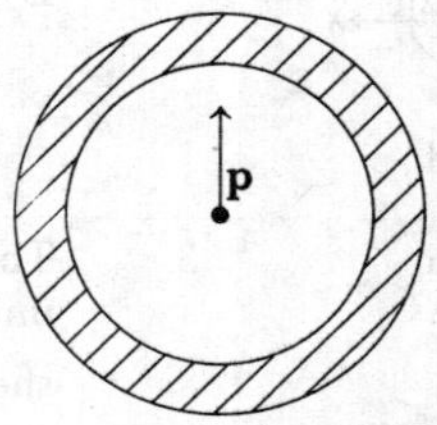

(a) surface charge density on the inner surface is uniform and equal to $\frac{(Q/2)}{4\pi a^2}$ ☐
(b) electric field outside the shell is the same as that of a point charge at the centre of the shell ☐
(c) surface charge density on the outer surface depends on $|\mathbf{p}|$ ☐
(d) surface charge density on the inner surface of the shell is zero everywhere ☐

***83.** An early model for an atom considered it to have a positively charged point nucleus of charge *Ze*, surrounded by a uniform density of negative charge upto a radius *R*. The atom as a whole is neutral. For this model, what is the electric field at a distance $r > R$ from the nucleus?

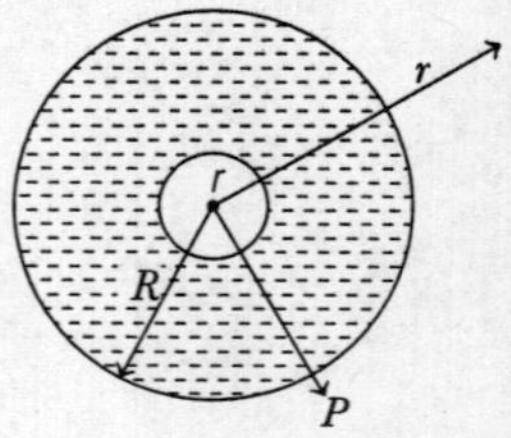

____

84. A solid conducting sphere of radius *a* has a net positive charge 2*Q*. A conducting spherical shell of inner radius *b* and outer radius *c* is concentric with the solid sphere and has a net charge − *Q*. The surface charge density on the inner and outer surfaces of the spherical shell will be

(a) $0, \frac{Q}{4\pi c^2}$ ☐
(b) $\frac{-Q}{4\pi b^2}, \frac{Q}{4\pi c^2}$ ☐
(c) $\frac{-2Q}{4\pi b^2}, \frac{Q}{4\pi c^2}$ ☐
(d) None of these ☐

85. The surface charge density of a thin charged disc of radius *R* is σ. The value of electric field at the centre of disc is $\frac{\sigma}{2\varepsilon_0}$. With respect to the field at the centre, what will be the electric field along the axis at a distance *R* from the centre of the disc?

____

86. A solid sphere of radius R_1 and volume charge density $\rho = \frac{\rho_0}{r}$ is enclosed by a hollow sphere of radius R_2 with negative surface charge density σ, such that the total charge in the system is zero. ρ_0 is a positive constant and r is the distance from the centre of the sphere. The ratio of radii $\frac{R_2}{R_1}$ is

(a) $\frac{\rho_0}{\sigma}$ ☐ (b) $\frac{\sigma}{\rho_0}$ ☐ (c) $\sqrt{\frac{2\sigma}{\rho_0}}$ ☐ (d) $\sqrt{\frac{\rho_0}{2\sigma}}$ ☐

Assertion-Reason Questions

Direction (Q. Nos. 1-10) *In the following questions, a statement of Assertion is followed by a corresponding statement of Reason. From the following options, choose the correct one.*

(a) Both Assertion and Reason are correct and Reason is the correct explanation of Assertion.
(b) Both Assertion and Reason are correct but Reason is not the correct explanation of Assertion.
(c) Assertion is correct but Reason is incorrect.
(d) Assertion is incorrect but Reason is correct.

1. **Assertion** (A) If there exists Coulomb attraction between two bodies, both of them may not be charged.
Reason (R) In Coulomb attraction, two bodies are oppositely charged.

(a) ☐ (b) ☐ (c) ☐ (d) ☐

2. **Assertion** (A) When a neutral body acquires positive charge, its mass decreases.
Reason (R) A body acquires positive charge when it loses electrons.

(a) ☐ (b) ☐ (c) ☐ (d) ☐

3. **Assertion** (A) No two electric field lines of force can intersect each other.
Reason (R) Tangent at any point of electric line force gives the direction of electric field.

(a) ☐ (b) ☐ (c) ☐ (d) ☐

4. **Assertion** (A) Though the electric field due to charge Q is defined in terms of test charge q, but it is independent of q.
Reason (R) F is proportional to q, so the ratio $\frac{F}{q}$ is independent of q.

(a) ☐ (b) ☐ (c) ☐ (d) ☐

***5.** **Assertion** (A) On moving a distance two times the initial distance away from an infinitely long straight uniformly charged wire, the electric field reduces to one-third of the initial value.
Reason (R) The electric field is inversely proportional to the distance from an infinitely long straight uniformly charged wire.

(a) ☐ (b) ☐ (c) ☐ (d) ☐

6. **Assertion** (A) Three equal charges are placed equidistant from each other on a circle. Net field charges at centre is zero.

Reason (R) Force on unit positive charge at centre can be represented by three sides of a triangle, taken in same order.

(a) ☐ (b) ☐ (c) ☐ (d) ☐

7. **Assertion** (A) On going away from a point charge or a small electric dipole, electric field decreases at the same rate in both the cases.
Reason (R) In case of a point charge, electric field is inversely proportional to square of distance from the charge.

(a) ☐ (b) ☐ (c) ☐ (d) ☐

8. **Assertion** (A) Electric force on a proton and an electron, moving in a uniform electric field is same.
Reason (R) Electron is lighter than proton.

(a) ☐ (b) ☐ (c) ☐ (d) ☐

*9. **Assertion** (A) The positive charge particle is placed in front of a spherical uncharged conductor. The number of lines of forces terminating on the sphere will be more than those emerging from it.
Reason (R) The surface charge density at a point on the sphere nearest to the point charge will be negative and maximum in comparison to other points on the sphere.

(a) ☐ (b) ☐ (c) ☐ (d) ☐

10. **Assertion** (A) A metallic shield in form of a hollow shell may be build to block an electric field.

Reason (R) Field lines are reflected from the metallic surface.

(a) ☐ (b) ☐ (c) ☐ (d) ☐

Case Based Questions

1. Smallest charge that can exist in nature is the charge of an electron. During friction it is only the transfer of electrons which makes the body charged. Hence, net charge on any body is an integral multiple of charge of an electron [1.6×10^{-19} C] i.e., $q = \pm ne$
Where $n = 1, 2, 3, 4, \ldots\ldots$

Hence, no body can have a charge in form of a fraction as 1. $1e$, $2.7e$ $\frac{3}{5}e$, etc.

Recently, it has been discovered that elementary particles such as protons or neutrons are composed of more element units called quarks.

(i) Which of the following properties is not satisfied by an electric charge?

(a) Total charge conservation ☐

(b) Quantization of charge ☐

(c) Two types of charge ☐

(d) Circular line of force ☐

(ii) If a charge on a body is 1 nC, then how many electrons are present on the body?

(a) 6.25×10^{27} (b) 1.6×10^{19}

(c) 6.25×10^{28} (d) 6.25×10^{9}

(iii) A polythene piece rubbed with wool is found to have a negative charge of x coulombs and the number of electrons transferred is 2×10^{12}. Then, find the value of x.

(a) 3.2×10^{-7} (b) 2.3×10^{-12}

(c) 2×10^{-14} (d) 1.3×10^{-14}

(iv) On charging a soap bubble, its size

(a) increases (b) decreases

(c) remains same (d) Cannot be said

2. Net electric flux through a cube is the sum of fluxes through its six faces. Consider a cube as shown in the figure, having sides of length $L = 10.0$ cm. The electric field is uniform, has a magnitude $E = 4.00\times 10^{3}\ \text{NC}^{-1}$ and is parallel to the xy-plane at an angle of 37° measured from the $+x$-axis towards the $+y$-axis.

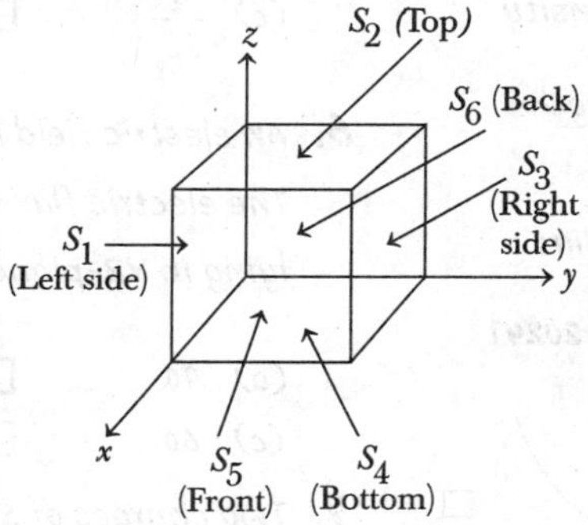

(i) Electric flux passing through surface S_6 is

(a) $-24\ \text{Nm}^2\ \text{C}^{-1}$ (b) $24\ \text{Nm}^2\ \text{C}^{-1}$

(c) $32\ \text{Nm}^2\ \text{C}^{-1}$ (d) $-32\ \text{Nm}^2\ \text{C}^{-1}$

(ii) Electric flux passing through surface S_1 is

(a) $-24\ \text{Nm}^2\ \text{C}^{-1}$ (b) $24\ \text{Nm}^2\ \text{C}^{-1}$

(c) $32\ \text{Nm}^2\ \text{C}^{-1}$ (d) $-32\ \text{Nm}^2\ \text{C}^{-1}$

(iii) The total net electric flux through all faces of the cube is

(a) $8\ \text{Nm}^2\ \text{C}^{-1}$ (b) $-8\ \text{Nm}^2\ \text{C}^{-1}$

(c) $24\ \text{Nm}^2\ \text{C}^{-1}$ (d) zero

(iv) Choose the wrong statement about electric flux.

(a) Flux is positive if the field lines come out of the surface.

(b) Flux is negative if the field lines come out of the surface

(c) Flux is equal to the product of magnitude of the electric field and the projection of area perpendicular to the field.

(d) None of the above

COMPETITION EDGE UP

1. Two charges q and $3q$ are separated by a distance r in air. At a distance x from charge q, the resultant electric field is zero. The value of x is **[NCERT Pg. 15, JEE Main 2024]**

(a) $\dfrac{r}{(1+\sqrt{3})}$ ☐

(b) $r(1+\sqrt{3})$ ☐

(c) $\dfrac{r}{3(1+\sqrt{3})}$ ☐

(d) $\dfrac{(1+\sqrt{3})}{r}$ ☐

2. An infinitely long positively charged straight thread has a linear charge density $\lambda\ \text{Cm}^{-1}$. An electron revolves along a circular path having axis along the length of the wire. The graph that correctly represents the variation of the kinetic energy of electron as a function of radius of circular path from the wire is **[NCERT Pg. 33, JEE Main 2024]**

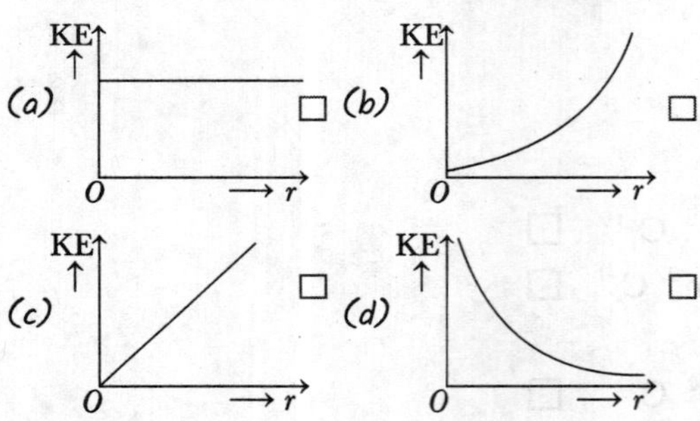

3. Five charges $+q$, $+5q$, $-2q$, $+3q$ and $-4q$ are situated as shown in the figure. The electric flux due to this configuration through the surface S is **[NCERT Pg. 24, JEE Main 2024]**

+5q S +q −2q +3q −4q

(a) $\dfrac{3q}{\varepsilon_0}$ ☐ (b) $\dfrac{5q}{\varepsilon_0}$ ☐

(c) $\dfrac{4q}{\varepsilon_0}$ ☐ (d) $\dfrac{q}{\varepsilon_0}$ ☐

4. σ is the uniform surface charge density of a thin spherical shell of radius R. The electric field at any point on the surface of the spherical shell is **[NCERT Pg. 35, JEE Main 2024]**

(a) $\dfrac{\sigma}{4\varepsilon_0}$ ☐ (b) $\dfrac{\sigma}{\varepsilon_0}$ ☐

(c) $\dfrac{\sigma}{\varepsilon_0 R}$ ☐ (d) $\dfrac{\sigma}{2\varepsilon_0}$ ☐

5. A charge q is placed at the centre of one of the surface of a cube. The flux linked with the cube is **[NCERT Pg. 29, JEE Main 2024]**

(a) $\dfrac{q}{8\varepsilon_0}$ ☐ (b) zero ☐

(c) $\dfrac{q}{2\varepsilon_0}$ ☐ (d) $\dfrac{q}{4\varepsilon_0}$ ☐

6. An electric field is given by $(6\hat{i} + 5\hat{j} + 3\hat{k})$ N/C. The electric flux through a surface area $30\hat{i}\ \text{m}^2$ lying in YZ-plane (in SI unit) is **[NCERT Pg. 21, JEE Main 2024]**

(a) 90 ☐ (b) 150 ☐

(c) 60 ☐ (d) 180 ☐

7. Two charges of $5Q$ and $-2Q$ are situated at the points $(3a, 0)$ and $(-5a, 0)$, respectively. The electric flux through a sphere of radius $4a$ having centre at origin is **[NCERT Pg. 29, JEE Main 2024]**

(a) $\dfrac{7Q}{\varepsilon_0}$ ☐ (b) $\dfrac{2Q}{\varepsilon_0}$ ☐

(c) $\dfrac{3Q}{\varepsilon_0}$ ☐ (d) $\dfrac{5Q}{\varepsilon_0}$ ☐

8. C_1 and C_2 are two hollow concentric cubes enclosing charges $2Q$ and $3Q$ respectively as shown in figure. The ratio of electric flux passing through C_1 and C_2 is **[NCERT Pg. 29, JEE Main 2024]**

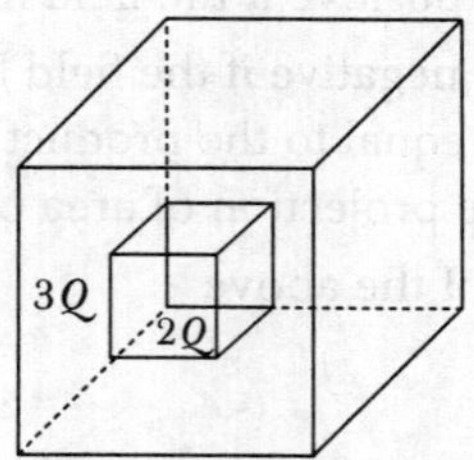

(a) 2 : 3 ☐ (b) 3 : 2 ☐

(c) 5 : 2 ☐ (d) 2 : 5 ☐

9. If $\oint \mathbf{E} \cdot d\mathbf{S} = 0$ over a surface, then

[NCERT Pg. 29, NEET 2023]

(a) the magnitude of electric field on the surface is constant. ☐

(b) all the charges must necessarily be inside the surface. ☐

(c) the electric field inside the surface is necessarily uniform. ☐

(d) the number of flux lines entering the surface must be equal to the number of flux lines leaving it. ☐

10. Two point charges $-q$ and $+q$ are placed at a distance of L, as shown in the figure.

$-q$ •————————• $+q$
←——L——→

The magnitude of electric field intensity at a distance $R(R >> L)$ varies as

[NCERT Pg. 24, NEET 2022]

(a) $\frac{1}{R^3}$ ☐ (b) $\frac{1}{R^4}$ ☐

(c) $\frac{1}{R^6}$ ☐ (d) $\frac{1}{R^2}$ ☐

11. The acceleration of an electron due to the mutual attraction between the electron and a proton when they are 1.6 Å apart is ($m_e \simeq 9 \times 10^{-31}$ kg, $e = 1.6 \times 10^{-19}$ C)

$\left(\text{Take, } \frac{1}{4\pi\varepsilon_0} = 9 \times 10^9 \text{ Nm}^2\text{C}^{-2}\right)$

[NCERT Pg. 08, NEET (Oct.) 2020]

(a) 10^{24} m/s^2 ☐

(b) 10^{23} m/s^2 ☐

(c) 10^{22} m/s^2 ☐

(d) 10^{25} m/s^2 ☐

12. A spherical conductor of radius 10 cm has a charge of 3.2×10^{-7} C distributed uniformly. What is the magnitude of electric field at a point 15 cm from the centre of the sphere?

[NCERT Pg. 14, NEET (Sep.) 2020]

$\left(\frac{1}{4\pi\varepsilon_0} = 9 \times 10^9 \text{ Nm}^2/\text{C}^2\right)$

(a) 1.28×10^5 N/C ☐

(b) 1.28×10^6 N/C ☐

(c) 1.28×10^7 N/C ☐

(d) 1.28×10^4 N/C ☐

Chapter 2

Electrostatic Potential and Capacitance

1. Tick (✓/×) for correct/incorrect statements in given boxes.

(i) When an external force does work in taking a body from one point to another against a force like spring force or gravitational force, that work gets stored as the potential energy of the body. ☐

(ii) In bringing the charge q from the point R to P, we apply an external force F_{ext} just enough to counter the repulsive electric force F_E (i.e. $F_{ext} = -F_E$). This means that, there is no net force on or acceleration of charge q when it is brought from R to P. ☐

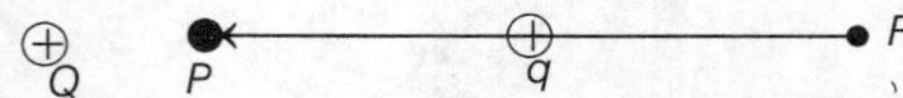

***2.** A point charge (+ q) is taken along two different paths say AMB (path 1) and ACB (path 2) such that A, M and B lie on the circle and + q (another charge) is placed at the centre (as shown in the figure). Are the work done along path ACB and path AMB equal?

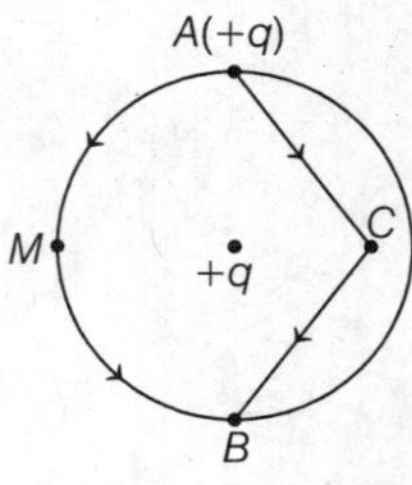

Yes ☐ No ☐

*Concepts of all questions bearing * are important for JEE/NEET/CUET.*

3. A uniform electric field E exists between two charged plates. What would be the work done in moving a charge q along the closed path $ABCDA$?

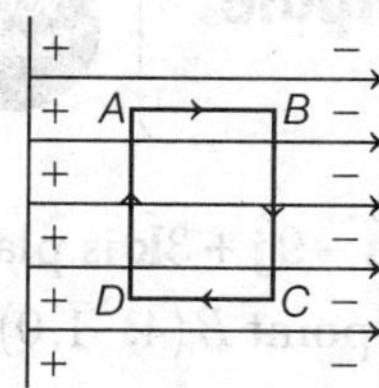

TOPIC 2

Potential due to a Point Charge

NCERT Pg 48-49

4. Answer the following questions in Yes/No.

I. Can the following figure be used for determining the potential due to a point charge? ☐

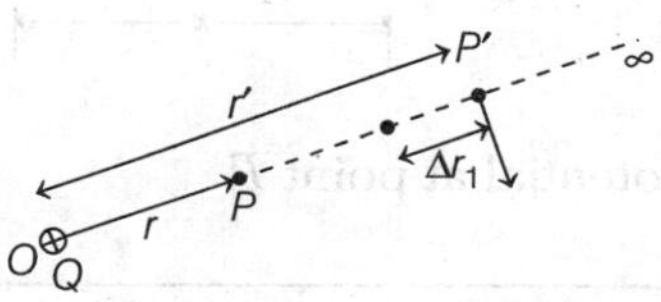

II. If potential is to be determined at point P, then we need to calculate the work done in bringing a unit positive charge from infinity to point P. ☐

III. For $Q > 0$, is the work done against the repulsive force on the test charge negative? ☐

***5.** If 100 J of work has to be done in moving an electric charge of 4 C from a place, where potential is – 10 V to another place, where potential is V volt, find the value of V.

***6.** Which one of the following options depicts the correct relation between V and r due to point charge?

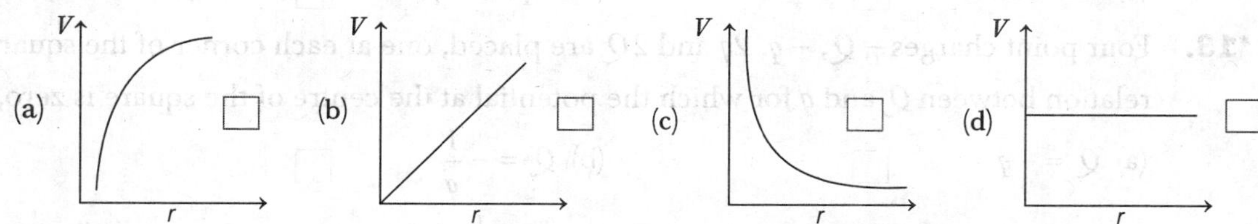

7. What will be the value of electric potential at a point P due to charge of 4×10^{-7} C located 9 cm away?

TOPIC 3

Potential due to an Electric Dipole and a System of Charges

***8.** A dipole of dipole moment $\mathbf{p} = 5\hat{\mathbf{i}} - 9\hat{\mathbf{j}} + 3\hat{\mathbf{k}}$ is placed at point $A(2,-3,1)$. The electric potential due to this dipole at the point $B(4,-1,0)$ is equal to (All the parameters specified here are in SI units.

(a) 2×10^9 ☐ (b) -3.66×10^9 ☐
(c) 3×10^9 ☐ (d) -3×10^9 ☐

9. A short electric dipole has a dipole moment of 16×10^{-9} C-m. The electric potential due to dipole at a point at a distance of 0.6 m from the centre of dipole situated on the line making an angle of 60° with dipole axis will be ____________ (200 V/100 V).

10. An electric dipole consists of two charges of equal magnitude and opposite sign separately by a distance $2a$ as shown in figure. The dipole is along the X-axis and is centred at the origin.

(i) Calculate the electric potential at point P.

____

(ii) Calculate V at a point far from the dipole.

____

11. The potential at a point due to an electric dipole will be maximum and minimum when the angles between the axis of the dipole and the line joining the point to the dipole are respectively

(a) 90° and 180° ☐ (b) 0° and 90° ☐
(c) 90° and 0° ☐ (d) 0° and 180° ☐

12. The potential in the equatorial plane of a dipole of a dipole moment p is

(a) infinite ☐ (b) zero ☐
(c) maximum ☐ (d) equal to p ☐

***13.** Four point charges $-Q$, $-q$, $2q$ and $2Q$ are placed, one at each corner of the square. The relation between Q and q for which the potential at the centre of the square is zero, is

(a) $Q = -q$ ☐ (b) $Q = -\frac{1}{q}$ ☐

(c) $Q = q$ ☐ (d) $Q = \frac{1}{q}$ ☐

***14.** Consider the figure given below. Match the items given in Column I (electric potential at different points) with those given in Column II (relative formulae).

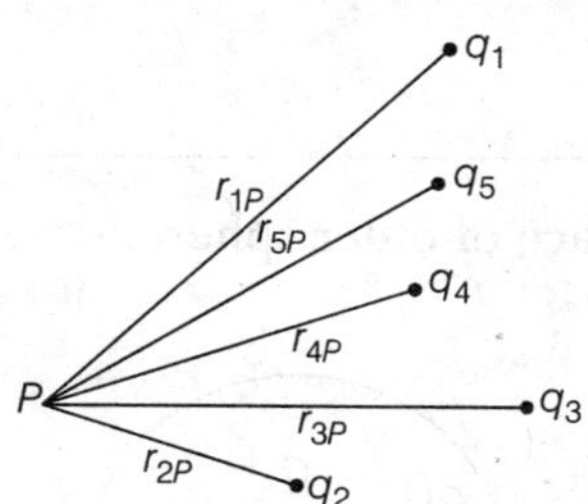

Column I	Column II
A. Electric potential V_1 at P due to charge q_1	1. $\frac{1}{4\pi\varepsilon_0}\cdot\frac{q_3}{r_{3P}}$
B. Electric potential V_2 at P due to charge q_2	2. $\frac{1}{4\pi\varepsilon_0}\left[\frac{q_1}{r_{1P}}+\frac{q_2}{r_{2P}}+\frac{q_3}{r_{3P}}+\frac{q_4}{r_{4P}}+\frac{q_5}{r_{5P}}\right]$
C. Electric potential V_3 at P due to charge q_3	3. $\frac{1}{4\pi\varepsilon_0}\cdot\frac{q_1}{r_{1P}}$
D. Potential V at P due to the total charge configuration	4. $\frac{1}{4\pi\varepsilon_0}\cdot\frac{q_2}{r_{2P}}$

A. ______________ B. ______________ C. ______________ D. ______________

15. Tick (✓/×) for correct/incorrect statements in given boxes.

(i) The electric potential outside the shell is given by $V=\frac{1}{4\pi\varepsilon_0}\cdot\frac{q}{r}(r\geq R)$. ☐

(ii) The electric field inside the shell is zero. This implies that the potential is constant inside the shell whose value is $V=\frac{1}{4\pi\varepsilon_0}\cdot\frac{q}{R}$. ☐

***16.** Two charged metallic spheres with radii R_1 and R_2 are brought in contact and then separated. The ratio of final charges Q_1 and Q_2 on the two spheres respectively will be

(a) $\frac{Q_1}{Q_2}=\frac{R_2}{R_1}$ ☐ (b) $\frac{Q_1}{Q_2}<\frac{R_1}{R_2}$ ☐ (c) $\frac{Q_1}{Q_2}>\frac{R_1}{R_2}$ ☐ (d) $\frac{Q_1}{Q_2}=\frac{R_1}{R_2}$ ☐

***17.** A conducting sphere of radius R is given a charge Q. The electric potential and the electric field at the centre of the sphere respectively, are

(a) zero and $\frac{Q}{4\pi\varepsilon_0 R^2}$ ☐ (b) $\frac{Q}{4\pi\varepsilon_0 R}$ and zero ☐

(c) $\frac{Q}{4\pi\varepsilon_0 R}$ and $\frac{Q}{4\pi\varepsilon_0 R^2}$ ☐ (d) Both are zero ☐

***18.** Three concentric metal shells A, B and C of respective radii a, b and c $(a<b<c)$ have surface charge densities $+\sigma$, $-\sigma$ and $+\sigma$, respectively. The potential of shell B is

(a) $\frac{\sigma}{\varepsilon_0}\left(\frac{a^2-b^2}{a}+c\right)$ ☐ (b) $\frac{\sigma}{\varepsilon_0}\left(\frac{a^2-b^2}{b}+c\right)$ ☐ (c) $\frac{\sigma}{\varepsilon_0}\left(\frac{b^2-c^2}{b}+a\right)$ ☐ (d) $\frac{\sigma}{\varepsilon_0}\left(\frac{b^2-c^2}{c}+a\right)$ ☐

***19.** Two charges 3×10^{-8} C and -2×10^{-8} C are located 15 cm apart. At what point on the line joining the two charges is electric potential zero in between them? (Take, potential at infinity to be zero.)

____

***20.** Find the potential at the surface of outer sphere.

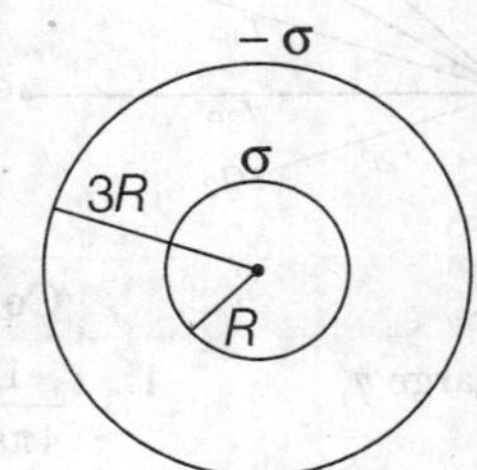

(a) $\frac{3\sigma R}{\varepsilon_0}$ ☐ (b) $\frac{-4\sigma R}{\varepsilon_0}$ ☐ (c) $\frac{-8\sigma R}{3\varepsilon_0}$ ☐ (d) Zero ☐

21. Two metallic spheres of radii 1 cm and 3 cm are given charges of -1×10^{-2} C and 5×10^{-2} C, respectively. If these are connected by a conducting wire, the final charge on the bigger sphere is $x \times 10^{-2}$ C. What is the value of x here?

____

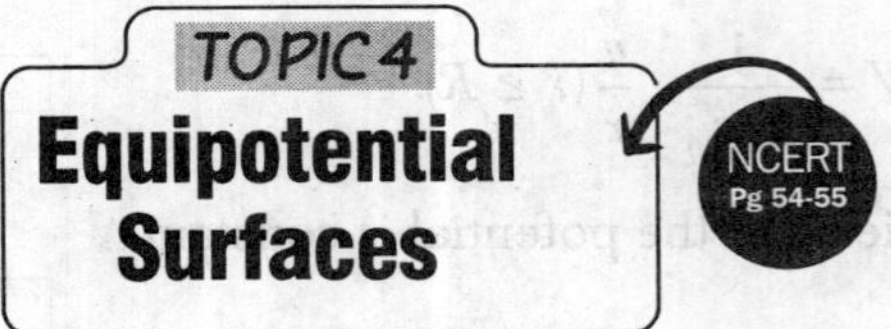

22. Choose the diagram showing the correct representation of equipotential surfaces for a single point charge.

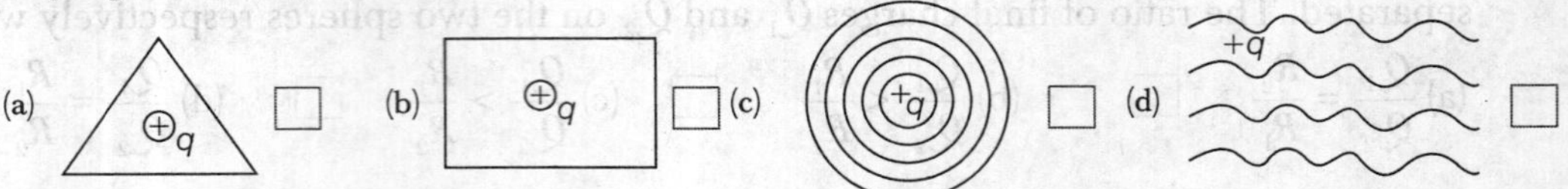

23. A, B and C are three points in a uniform electric field. The electric potential is

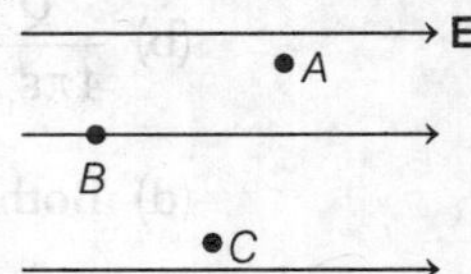

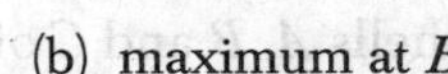

(a) maximum at A ☐ (b) maximum at B ☐

(c) maximum at C ☐ (d) same at all the three points A, B and C ☐

24. The __(A)__ field lines for a single charge q are __(B)__ lines starting from or ending at the charge, depending on whether q is positive or negative. It means that __(C)__ field is normal to __(D)__ surface passing through that point. Here, (A), (B), (C) and (D) are respectively, refer to

(a) electric, radial, electric, equipotential ☐
(b) magnetic, curved, magnetic, plane ☐
(c) electric, curved, magnetic, equipotential ☐
(d) magnetic, radial, electric, plane ☐

25. The figure given below is representing the equipotential surface for ____________ (uniform/non-uniform) electric field.

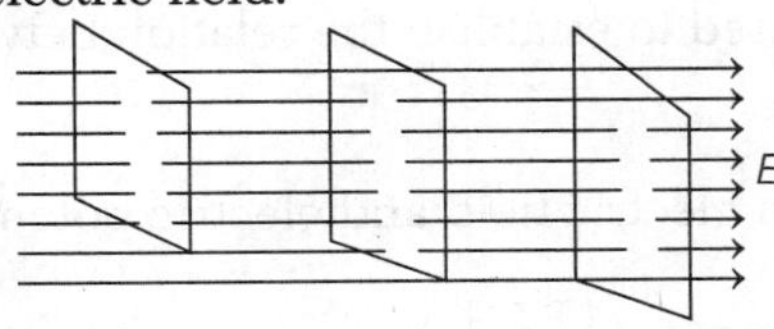

26. Equipotential surface between two equal and opposite charges passing through the middle point is a plane.

True ☐ False ☐

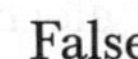

27. There is a uniform electric field of intensity E which is as shown below. How many labelled points have the same electric potential as the fully shaded point?

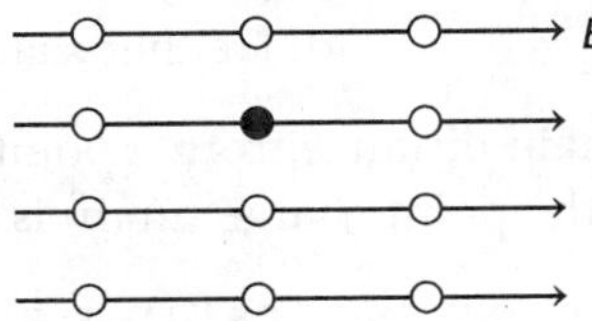

____

28. The figure given below shows various equipotential surfaces.

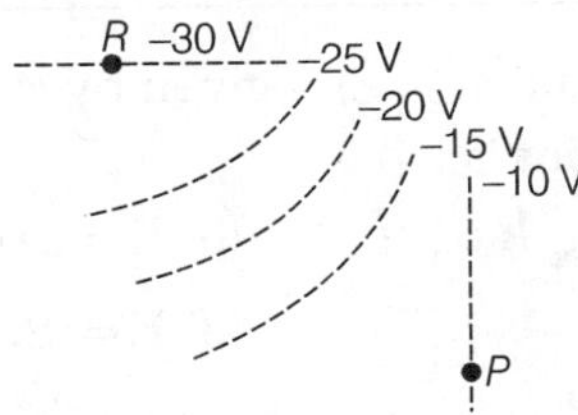

What is the direction of electric field **E** at points P and R?

____

29. The diagrams below show regions of equipotentials.

(i) 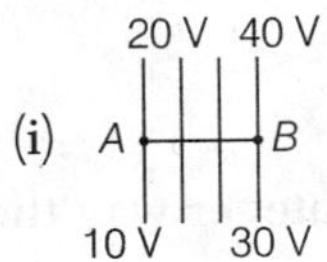

(ii) 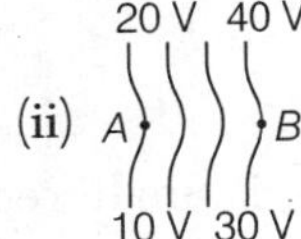

(iii) 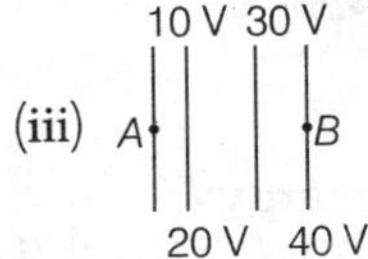

(iv) 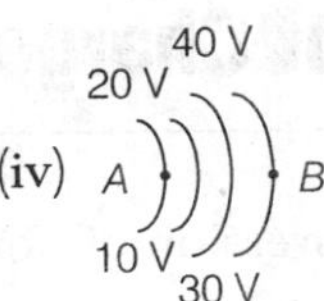

A positive charge is moved from A to B in each diagram, then

(a) maximum work is required to move q in Fig. (iii). ☐
(b) in all the four cases, the work done is the same ☐
(c) minimum work is required to move q in Fig. (i). ☐
(d) maximum work is required to move q in Fig. (ii). ☐

30. Consider the given diagram and answer the following questions in (Yes/No).

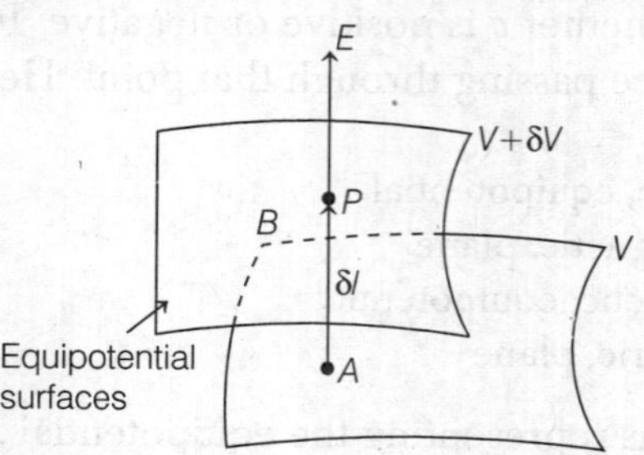

(i) Can this diagram be used to establish the relation between electric potential and electric field? ☐

(ii) Is the relation between electric field and electric potential given by $|E| = +\dfrac{|\delta V|}{\delta l}$? ☐

***31.** **Statement I** Equation $|E| = +\dfrac{|\delta V|}{\delta l}$ tells that the electric field is in the direction in which the potential decreases steepest.

Statement II The magnitude of electric field is given by the change in the magnitude of potential per unit displacement normal to the equipotential surface at that point.

Which of the following statement(s) is/are correct?

(a) Only statement I ☐ (b) Only statement II ☐

(c) Both statements I and II ☐ (d) Neither statement I nor II ☐

32. The electric potential at a certain distance from a point charge is 600 V and the electric field is 200 NC^{-1}. The distance of the point charge (in m) is ________ (2/3).

***33.** If potential (in V) in a region is expressed as $V(x, y, z) = 6xy - y + 2yz$, then find electric field (in N/C) at point (1, 1, 0).

---

34. The electric potential at a point (x, y, z) is given by $V = -x^2y - xz^3 + 4$. The electric field **E** at that point is

(a) $\mathbf{E} = (2xy + z^3)\hat{\mathbf{i}} + x^2\hat{\mathbf{j}} + 3xz^2\hat{\mathbf{k}}$ ☐ (b) $\mathbf{E} = 2xy\hat{\mathbf{i}} + (x^2 + y^2)\hat{\mathbf{j}} + (3xz - y^2)\hat{\mathbf{k}}$ ☐

(c) $\mathbf{E} = z^3\hat{\mathbf{i}} + xyz\hat{\mathbf{j}} + z^2\hat{\mathbf{k}}$ ☐ (d) $\mathbf{E} = (2xy - z^3)\hat{\mathbf{i}} + xy^2\hat{\mathbf{j}} + 3z^2 x\hat{\mathbf{k}}$ ☐

TOPIC 5 Potential Energy of a System of Charges

NCERT Pg. 55-58

35. The expression of potential energy $U = \dfrac{1}{4\pi\varepsilon_0} \cdot \dfrac{q_1 q_2}{r_{12}}$, is unaltered whatever way the charges are brought to the specified locations.

True ☐ False ☐

36. Can we define electric potential energy between the two points as the work required to be done by an external force in moving (without accelerating) charge q from one point to another for electric field of any arbitrary charge configuration?

Yes ☐ No ☐

37. What is the work done in moving a $2\mu C$ point charge from corner A to corner B of a square $ABCD$ in figure, when a $10\mu C$ charge exists at the centre of the square?

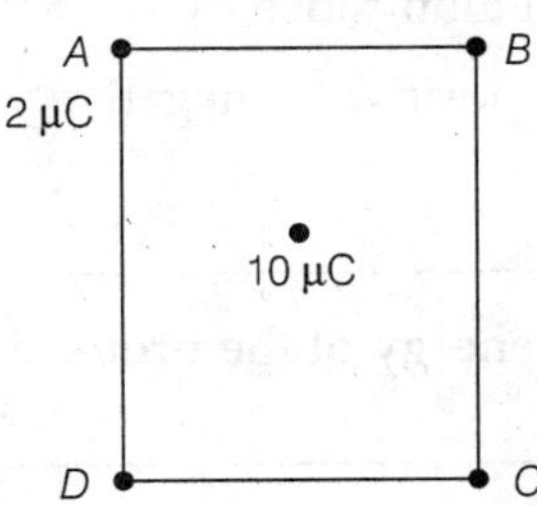

***38.** Three charges Q, $+q$ and $+q$ are placed at the vertices of a right angle isosceles triangle as shown alongside. The net electrostatic energy of the configuration is zero, if the value of Q is

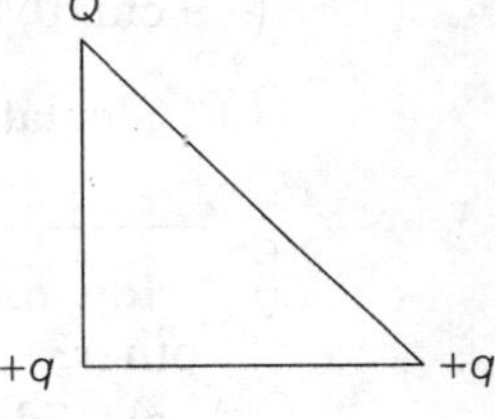

(a) $-2q$ ☐ (b) $\frac{-q}{1+\sqrt{2}}$ ☐

(c) $+q$ ☐ (d) $\frac{-\sqrt{2}q}{\sqrt{2}+1}$ ☐

39. Four charges are arranged in the respective order at the corners of a square $ABCD$ of side d as shown in the given figure. Match the work done at each point in Column I with its value in Column II.

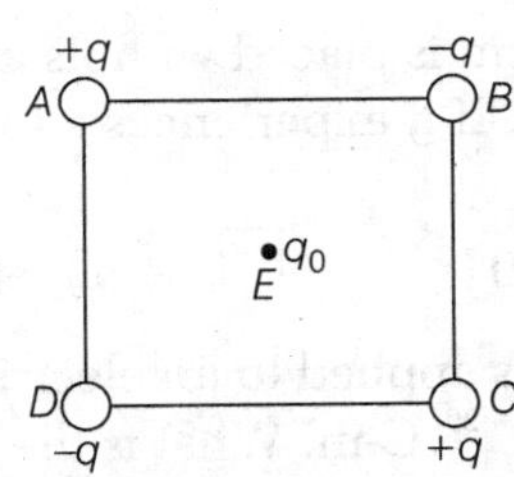

	Column I		Column II
A.	W_A	1.	$\frac{-q^2}{4\pi\varepsilon_0 d}\left(2-\frac{1}{\sqrt{2}}\right)$
B.	W_B	2.	$-q^2/4\pi\varepsilon_0 d$
C.	W_C	3.	zero
D.	W_D	4.	$\frac{-q^2}{4\pi\varepsilon_0 d}\left(1-\frac{1}{\sqrt{2}}\right)$

A. ________ B. ________ C. ________ D. ________

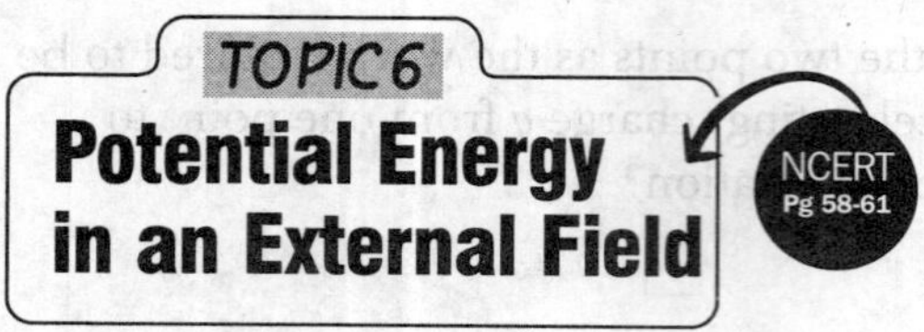

40. In the figure, proton moves a distance d in a uniform electric field E as shown in the figure given alongside.

(i) Does the electric field do a positive or negative work on the proton?

(ii) Does the electric potential energy of the proton increase or decrease?

---

41. A system consist of two charges 7 μC and – 2μC (and with no external field) placed at (– 9 cm, 0, 0) and (9 cm, 0, 0), respectively.

(i) Calculate electrostatic potential energy of the system.

(ii) How much work is required to separate the two charges infinitely away from each other?

(a) 0.7 J ☐ (b) 6.5 J ☐ (c) 3.5 J ☐ (d) 4.8 J ☐

(iii) Assume that the same system of charges (considered above) is now placed in an external electric field $E = A\left(\frac{1}{r^2}\right)$; $A = 9 \times 10^5$ NC^{-1} m^2, so the electrostatic energy of the configuration will be x joules. What is the value of x here?

***42.** An electric dipole of length 2 cm is placed with its axis making an angle of 30° to a uniform electric field 10^6 N/C. If it experiences a torque of $20\sqrt{3}$ N m, then potential energy of the dipole is

(a) −10J ☐ (b) −20J ☐ (c) −60J ☐ (d) −40J ☐

43. An electric field of 1000 V/m is applied to an electric dipole at an angle of 45°. The value of electric dipole moment is 10^{-29} C-m. What is the potential energy of the electric dipole?

(a) -9×10^{-20} J ☐ (b) -10×10^{-29} J ☐
(c) -20×10^{-18} J ☐ (d) -7×10^{-27} J ☐

***44.** An electric dipole is placed at an angle of 30° with an electric field intensity 2×10^5 N/C. It experiences a torque equal to 4 N-m. The charge on the dipole, if the dipole length is 2 cm, will be x mC. What will be the value of x ?

***45.** A molecule of a substance has a permanent electric dipole moment of magnitude 10^{-29} C- m. A mole of this substance is polarised (at low temperature) by applying a strong electrostatic field of magnitude 10^6 Vm^{-1}. The direction of field is suddenly changed by an angle of 60°. What will be the amount of heat released by the substance in aligning the dipoles along the new direction of field?

(a) 8 J ☐ (b) 15 J ☐ (c) 3 J ☐ (d) 20 J ☐

TOPIC 7

Electrostatics of Conductors

NCERT Pg 61-65

46. When the conductor is charged, the excess charges can reside only on the surface in the static situation. Does it mean that the interior of a conductor can have no excess charge in the static situation?

Yes ☐ No ☐

47. The radii of two metallic spheres ar 5 cm and 10 cm and both carry equal charges of 150 μC. If the two spheres are shorted, then charge will be transferred

(a) 50 μC from smaller to bigger ☐ (b) 100 μC from bigger to smaller ☐
(c) 0 μC from smaller to bigger ☐ (d) 50 μC from bigger to smaller ☐

48. Consider the given diagram and answer the following questions.

Conducting body

E

E

E

(i) Is the electric field outside the conductor, normal to the surface with magnitude E?

Yes ☐ No ☐

(ii) Will the total contribution to the flux come only from the outside cross-section of the above figure?

Yes ☐ No ☐

(iii) What will be the value of electric field at the surface of the charge conductor (given in the figure)?

(a) $\sigma \times \varepsilon_0$ ☐ (b) $\frac{|\sigma|}{\varepsilon_0}$ ☐ (c) $\frac{\sigma}{2\varepsilon_0}$ ☐ (d) $\frac{3\sigma}{2\varepsilon_0}$ ☐

49. If any cavity in a conductor remains shielded from outside electric influence, the field inside the cavity is always ________(zero/maximum).

50. A bird perches on a bare high power line and nothing happens to the bird. A man standing on the ground touches the same line and gets a fatal shock. This is because current passes only when there is a difference in potential.

Is the above paragraph technically correct?

Yes ☐ No ☐

TOPIC 8

Dielectrics and Polarisation

NCERT Pg 65-67

51. In a non-polar molecule, the centre of positive and negative charges ________ (coincide/separated). The molecule has no ________ (permanent/temporary) dipole moment. ________(Oxygen/Chloride) and ________ (hydrogen/carbon) are the examples of ________ (polar/non-polar) molecule. Because of their symmetry, they have ________ (no/infinite) dipole moment.

52. Match the Column I with Column II.

Column I	Column II
A. Conductor	1. O C O
B. Dielectric	2. H, CL, P, HCL
C. Polar molecule	3. E_0, σ_{free}, E_{in}, $E_0+E_{in}=0$
D. Non-polar molecule	4. E_0, σ_p, $E_0+E_{in}\neq 0$

A. ________ B. ________ C. ________ D. ________

53. **Statement I** In an external electric field, the positive and negative charges of a non-polar molecule are displaced in opposite directions.

Statement II The non-polar molecule develops an induced dipole moment.

Which of the following statement(s) is/are correct?

(a) Only statement I (b) Only statement II

(c) Both statements I and II (d) Neither statement I nor II

54. When a slab of insulating material 4 mm thick is introduced between the plates of a parallel plate capacitor of separation 4 mm, it is found that the distance between the plates has to be increased by 3.2 mm to restore the capacity to its original value. The dielectric constant of the material is

(a) 2 (b) 5 (c) 3 (d) 7

55. When a dielectric is placed in an electric field, the electric field inside the dielectric –

(a) increase (b) decrease

(c) constant (d) zero

56. Inside the dielectric, the volume element ΔV has some net charge. This is because, the positive charge of one dipole sits close to the negative charge of the adjacent dipole.

Yes No

TOPIC 9
Capacitor, Capacitance & the Parallel Plate Capacitor

57. The electric field in the region between the conductors is proportional to the charge Q. It means, if the charge on the capacitor is doubled, then electric field will be _________ (halved/doubled) .

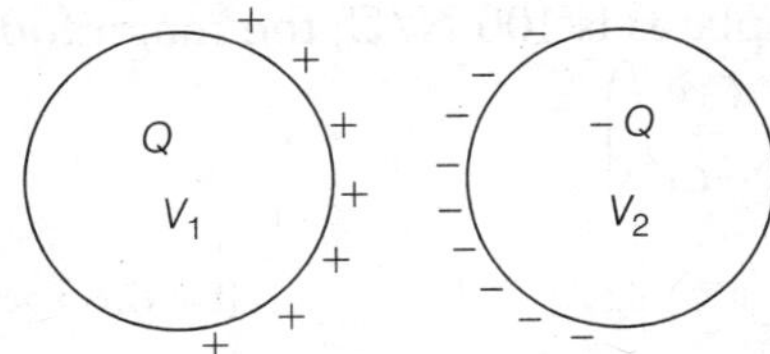

***58.** Consider the given figure and answer the following questions.

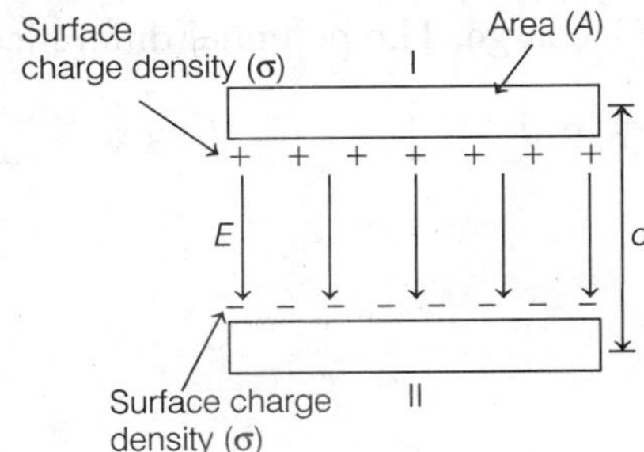

(i) What does the above figures represent?

____

(ii) What will be the value of electric field in outer region I?

____

(iii) What will be the value of electric field in outer region II?

____

(iv) What will be the value of electric field in the inner region between the plates I and II?

____

59. A capacitor is connected across a battery and a plate separation of capacitor is increased without removing the battery, then capacitance will __________(increase/decrease).

***60.** A parallel plate capacitor has capacity C, distance of separation between plates is d and potential difference V is applied between the plates. Force of attraction between the plates of the parallel plate air capacitor is $\frac{CV^2}{xd}$. Here, the value of x will be _______ (2/4).

***61.** The graph shows the variation of voltage V across the plates of two capacitors A and B *versus* increase of charge Q stored in them. Which of the capacitors has higher capacitance?

V
B
A
V_B
V_A
Q
Q

____

62. A parallel plate capacitor with plates of area 1 m^2 each, are at a separation of 0.1 m. If the electric field between the plates is 100 N/C, the magnitude of charge on each plate is $\left(\text{Take, } \varepsilon_0 = 8.85 \times 10^{-12} \frac{C^2}{N\text{-}m^2}\right)$

(a) 9.85×10^{-10} C ☐ (b) 8.85×10^{-10} C ☐
(c) 7.85×10^{-10} C ☐ (d) 6.85×10^{-10} C ☐

63. A parallel plate capacitor has 1μF capacitance. One of its two plates is given + 2 μC charge and the other plate + 4 μC charge. The potential difference developed across the capacitor is

(a) 1V ☐ (b) 2 V ☐ (c) 3 V ☐ (d) 2.5 V ☐

TOPIC 10

Effect of Dielectric on Capacitance

NCERT Pg 69-71

64. If dielectric constant and dielectric strength be denoted by K and X respectively, then a material suitable for using it as a dielectric in a capacitor must have ________ (high/low) K and __________ (high/low) X.

65. A capacitor connected to a 10 V battery collects a charge of 40 μC with air as dielectric and 100 μC with a given oil as dielectric. The dielectric constant of the oil is

(a) 1.5 ☐ (b) 2.0 ☐ (c) 2.5 ☐ (d) 3.0 ☐

66. __(A)__ of a substance is the factor by which the capacitance __(B)__ from its vacuum value when the dielectric is fully inserted between the plates of capacitor. Here, (A) and (B) respectively refers to

(a) Dielectric constant, increases ☐ (b) Dielectric strength, increases ☐
(c) Dielectric strength, decreases ☐ (d) Dielectric constant, decreases ☐

***67.** A dielectric is placed in between two parallel plates of a capacitor. The dielectric constant of dielectric is K. If the initial capacity is C, then the new capacity will be ________ $\left(KC/\frac{C}{K}\right)$.

68. A parallel plate capacitor is made of two circular plates separated by a distance of 5 mm and with a dielectric of dielectric constant 2.2 between them. When the electric field in the dielectric is 3×10^4 V/m, the charge density of the positive plate will be closed to $x \times 10^{-7}\,\text{Cm}^{-2}$. The value of x is

(a) 3.8 ☐ (b) 5.8 ☐ (c) 5.2 ☐ (d) 4.5 ☐

***69.** A parallel plate air capacitor has a capacitance 18 μF. If the distance between the plates is tripled and a dielectric medium is introduced, the capacitance becomes 72 μF. The dielectric constant of the medium is

(a) 4 ☐ (b) 9 ☐ (c) 12 ☐ (d) 2 ☐

***70.** A slab of material of dielectric constant K has the same area as the plates of a parallel plate capacitor but has a thickness $\left(\frac{3}{4}\right)d$, where d is the separation of plates. By what value will the capacitance change, if the slab is inserted between the plates?

____

71. The capacitance of a parallel plate capacitor with air as medium is 6 μF. With the introduction of a dielectric medium, the capacitance becomes 30 μF. The permittivity of the medium is (Take, $\varepsilon_0 = 8.854 \times 10^{-12}\ \text{C}^2\text{N}^{-1}\text{m}^{-2}$)

(a) $1.77 \times 10^{-12}\ \text{C}^2\text{N}^{-1}\text{m}^{-2}$ ☐ (b) $0.44 \times 10^{-10}\ \text{C}^2\text{N}^{-1}\text{m}^{-2}$ ☐
(c) $5.00 \times 10^{0}\ \text{C}^2\text{N}^{-1}\text{m}^{-2}$ ☐ (d) $0.44 \times 10^{-13}\ \text{C}^2\text{N}^{-1}\text{m}^{-2}$ ☐

72. Two capacitors C_1 and C_2 are charged to 120 V and 200 V, respectively. It is found that by connecting them together, the potential on each one can be made zero. Then, C_1 / C_2 is

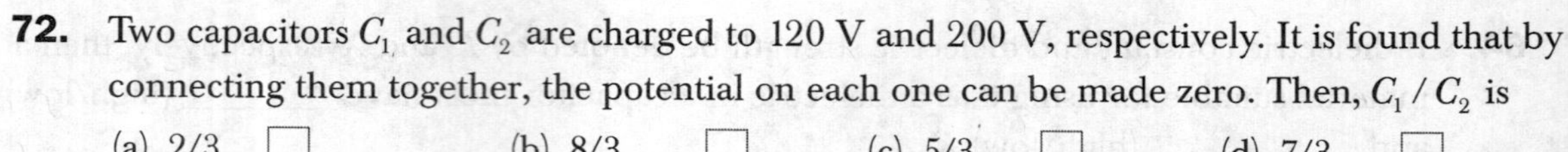

(a) 2/3 ☐ (b) 8/3 ☐ (c) 5/3 ☐ (d) 7/3 ☐

***73.** Find the capacitance of the parallel plate capacitor as shown in the figure below.

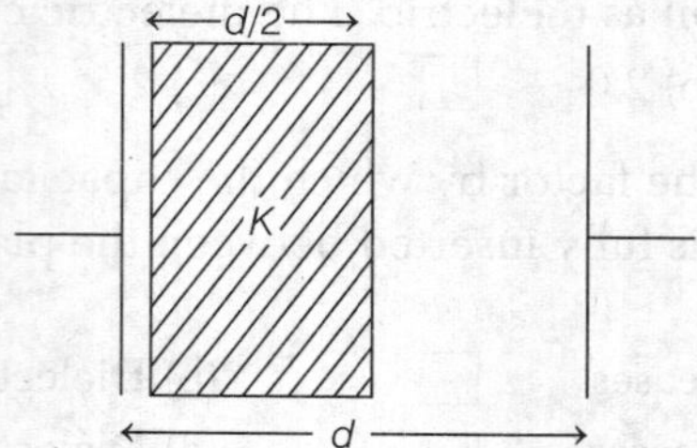

74. Across each of two capacitors of capacitance 1μF and a potential difference of 10 V is applied, then positive plate of one is connected to the negative plate of the other and negative plate of one is connected to the positive plate of the other. After contact,

(a) charge on each is zero ☐
(b) charge on each is same but non-zero ☐
(c) charge on each is different but non-zero ☐
(d) None of the above ☐

***75.** Four parallel plates of equal area A and spacing d are arranged as shown in the following figure. The effective capacitance between a and b is $\frac{n\varepsilon_0 A}{d}$. What is the value of n?

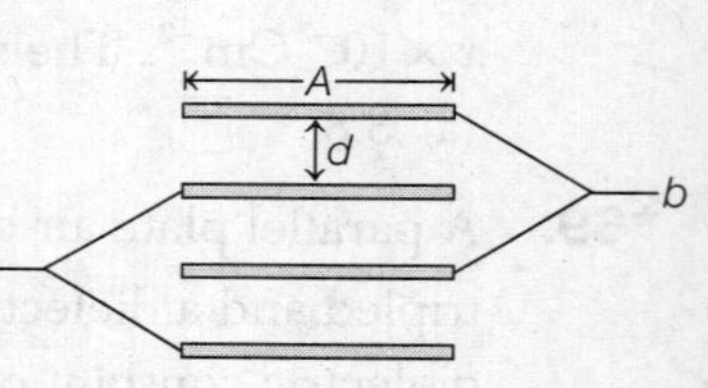

76. Determine the equivalent capacitance between the points A and B in the following circuits.

(i)

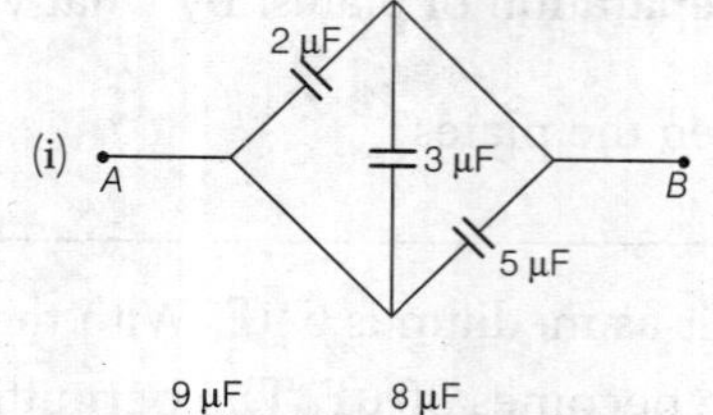

(ii)

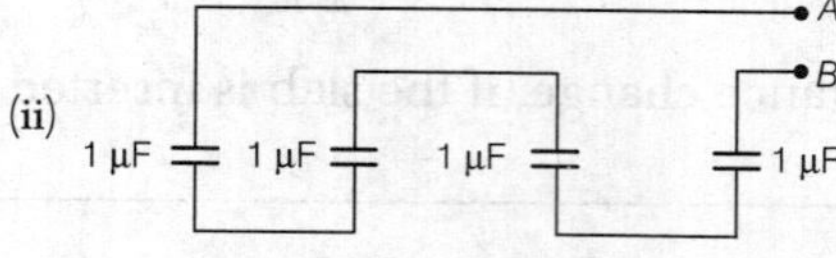

(iii)

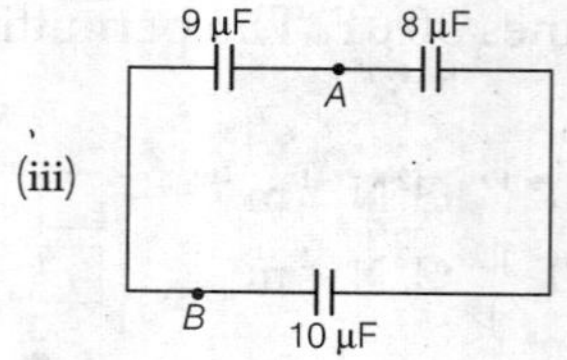

77. If the equivalent capacitance between points P and Q of the combination of the capacitors is 30 μF shown in figure below, then the capacitor C is 60 μF.

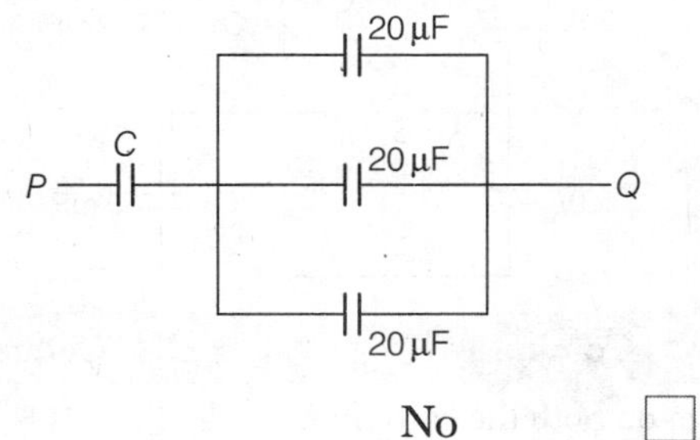

Yes ☐ No ☐

78. How many 1 μF capacitors must be connected in parallel to store a charge of 1 C with a potential of 110 V across the capacitors?

____

***79.** Effective capacitance between A and B in the figure shown below, is (all capacitances are in μF)

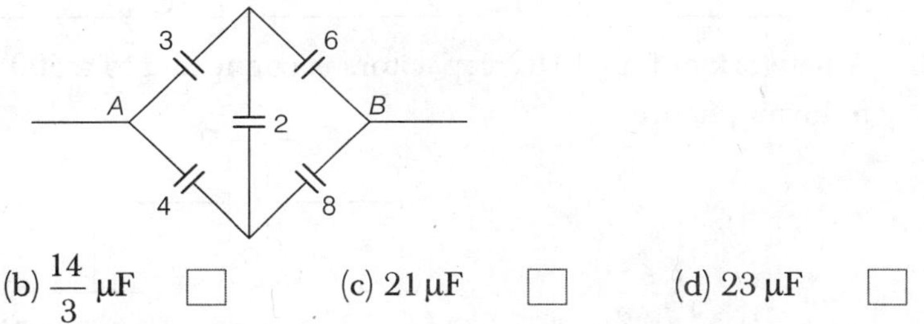

(a) $\frac{3}{14}$ μF ☐ (b) $\frac{14}{3}$ μF ☐ (c) 21 μF ☐ (d) 23 μF ☐

***80.** An infinite number of identical capacitors each of capacitance 1 μF are connected as shown in the figure. The equivalent capacitance between A and B is ________ (2 μF/1 μF).

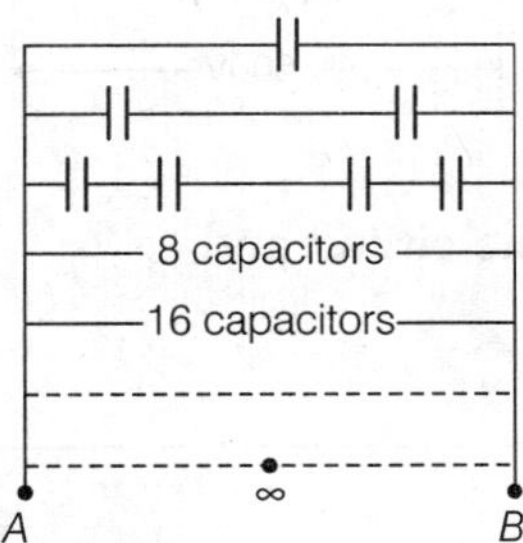

81. In the circuit shown in the figure, will the potential difference across the 4.5 μF capacitor be 8 V?

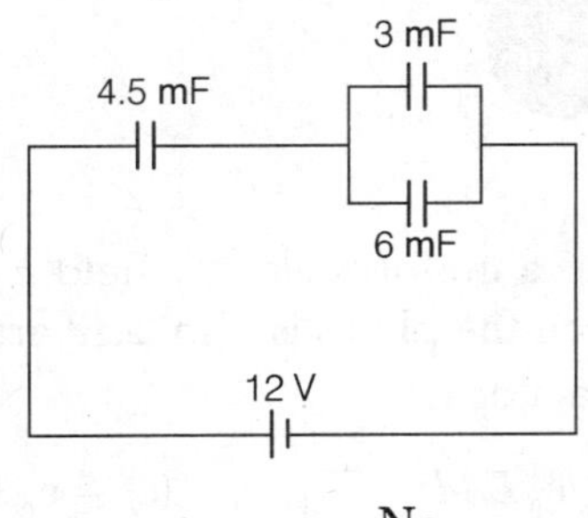

Yes ☐ No ☐

82. Match the Column I (charge on capacitor) with Column II (value).

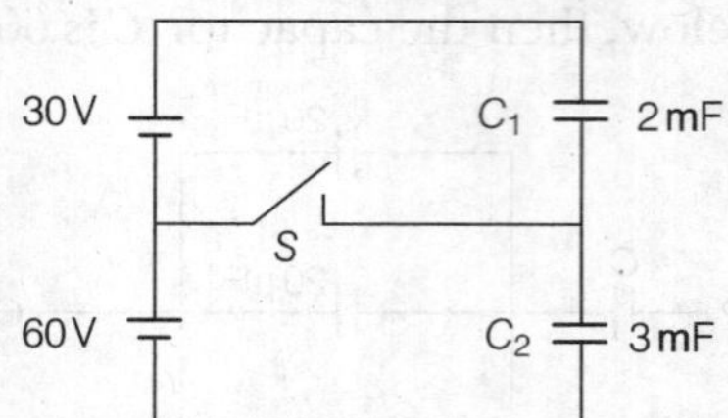

Column I		Column II
A. Charge on both the capacitors (*S* open)	1.	108 μC
B. Charge on C_2 (*S* closed)	2.	240 μC
C. Charge on C_1 (*S* closed)	3.	60 μC
D. Charges on C_1 and C_2 (*S* closed)	4.	180 μC

A. ________ B. ________ C. ________ D. ________

83. A network of four 10 μF capacitors is connected to a 500 V supply as shown in the following figure.

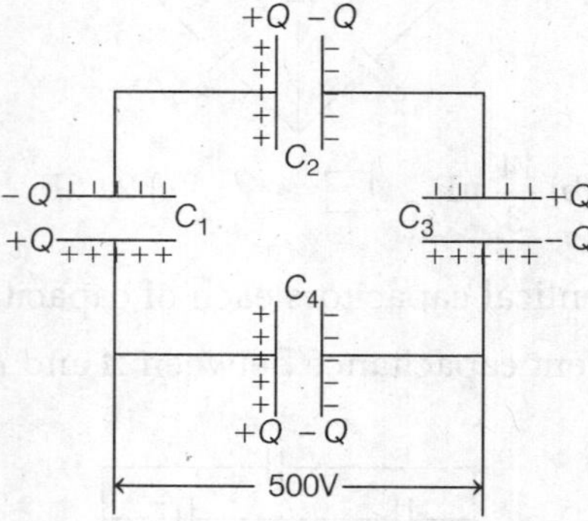

Find

(i) equivalent capacitance of the circuit and

(ii) charge on each capacitor.

TOPIC 12

Energy Stored in a Capacitor

NCERT Pg 73-76

***84.** A parallel plate capacitor has a uniform electric field E (Vm^{-1}) in the space between the plates. If the distance between the plates is d(m) and area of each plate is $A(\text{m}^2)$, the energy (J) stored in the capacitor is

(a) $\frac{1}{2}\varepsilon_0 E^2$ ☐ (b) $\varepsilon_0 EAd$ ☐ (c) $\frac{1}{2}\varepsilon_0 E^2 Ad$ ☐ (d) $E^2 Ad/\varepsilon_0$ ☐

85. A parallel plate capacitor is connected to a 5 V battery and charged. The battery is then disconnected and a glass slab is introduced between the plates, then the quantities that decrease are

I. charge
II. potential difference
III. capacitance
IV. energy stored

***86.** A 900 pF capacitor is charged by 100 V battery as shown in the following figure. How much electrostatic energy is stored by the capacitor?

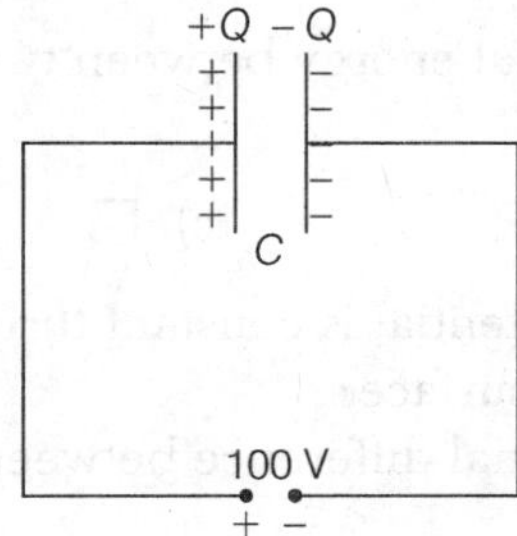

***87.** In the above question, if the capacitor is disconnected from the battery and connected to another 900 pF capacitor as shown in the figure. The electrostatic energy stored by the system will be $x \times 10^{-6}$ J. Here, the value of x will be ________ (2.25/4.50).

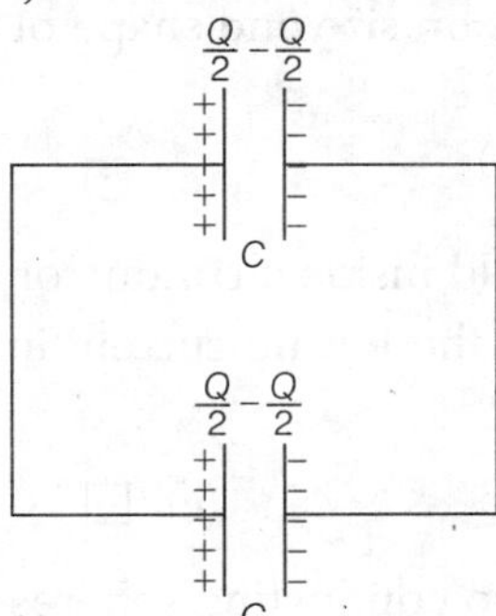

***88.** A capacitor is charged by a battery. The battery is removed and another identical uncharged capacitor is connected in parallel. The total electrostatic energy of the resulting system is

(a) increases by a factor of 4 ☐ (b) decreases by a factor of 2 ☐
(c) remains same ☐ (d) increases by a factor of 2 ☐

89. Two identical capacitors C_1 and C_2 of equal capacitance are connected as shown in the following circuit. Terminals a and b of the key K are connected to charge capacitor C_1 using a battery of emf V volt. Now, disconnecting a and b terminals, terminals b and c are connected. Due to this, the percentage loss of energy will be n%. What is the value of n here?

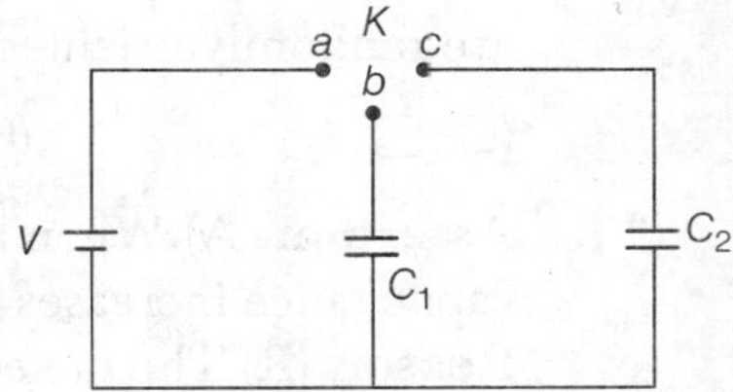

Assertion-Reason Questions

Direction (Q. Nos. 1-10) *In the following questions, a statement of Assertion is followed by a corresponding statement of Reason. From the following options, choose the correct one.*

(a) Both Assertion and Reason are correct and Reason is the correct explanation of Assertion.

(b) Both Assertion and Reason are correct but Reason is not the correct explanation of Assertion.

(c) Assertion is correct but Reason is incorrect.

(d) Assertion is incorrect but Reason is correct.

1. **Assertion** (A) When two positive point charges move away from each other, then their electrostatic potential energy decreases.

Reason (R) Change in potential energy between two points is equal to the work done by electrostatic forces.

(a) ☐ (b) ☐ (c) ☐ (d) ☐

2. **Assertion** (A) Electrostatic potential is constant throughout the volume of the conductor and has the same value on its surface.

Reason (R) There is no potential difference between any two points inside or on the conductor surface.

(a) ☐ (b) ☐ (c) ☐ (d) ☐

3. **Assertion** (A) The capacity of a conductor, under given circumstances, remains constant irrespective of the charge present on it.

Reason (R) Capacity depends on size and shape of conductor and also on the surrounding medium.

(a) ☐ (b) ☐ (c) ☐ (d) ☐

4. **Assertion** (A) Electrostatic field inside a conductor is zero.

Reason (R) In static situation, there is no current inside or on the surface of the conductor.

(a) ☐ (b) ☐ (c) ☐ (d) ☐

5. **Assertion** (A) A and B are two conducting spheres of same radius. A being solid and B hollow. Both are charged to the same potential, then charge on A = charge on B.

Reason (R) Potentials on both are same.

(a) ☐ (b) ☐ (c) ☐ (d) ☐

***6.** **Assertion** (A) An electric field can polarize the polar dielectric material.

Reason (R) In polar dielectrics, each molecule has a permanent dipole moment but these are randomly oriented in the absence of an externally applied electric field.

(a) ☐ (b) ☐ (c) ☐ (d) ☐

***7.** **Assertion** (A) When a dielectric medium is placed between the plates of a condenser, its capacitance increases K times, where K is the dielectric constant of the medium.

Reason (R) The dielectric medium reduces the potential difference between the plates of the condenser.

(a) ☐ (b) ☐ (c) ☐ (d) ☐

8. **Assertion** (A) If the distance between parallel plates of a capacitor is halved and dielectric constant is made three times, then the capacitance becomes 6 times.
Reason (R) Capacity of the capacitor depends upon the nature of the material between the plates.

(a) ☐ (b) ☐ (c) ☐ (d) ☐

9. **Assertion** (A) Only a limited quantity of charge can be given to a capacitor.
Reason (R) A capacitor in an arrangement, which can store sufficient quantity of charge.

(a) ☐ (b) ☐ (c) ☐ (d) ☐

***10.** **Assertion** (A) A parallel plate capacitor is connected across battery through a key. A dielectric slab of dielectric constant K is introduced between the plates. The energy which stored becomes K times.
Reason (R) The surface density of charge on the plate remains constant or unchanged.

(a) ☐ (b) ☐ (c) ☐ (d) ☐

Case Based Questions

1. Electrtic potential energy possessed by a system of charges is by virtue of their positions. When two like charges lie infinite distance apart, their potential energy is zero because no work has to be done in moving charge at inifinite distance from the other.
In carrying a charge q from point A to point B, work done $W = q(V_A - V_B)$. This work may appear as change in KE/PE of the charge. The potential energy of two charges q_1 and q_2 at a distance r in air is $\frac{q_1 q_2}{4\pi\varepsilon_0 r}$. It is measured in joule. It may be positive, negative or zero depending on the signs of q_1 and q_2.

(i) Four equal charges q each are placed at four corners of a square of side 'a' each. Work done in carrying a charge '$-q$' from its centre to infinity is

(a) zero ☐ (b) $\frac{\sqrt{2}q^2}{\pi\varepsilon_0 a}$ ☐

(c) $\frac{\sqrt{2}q}{\pi\varepsilon_0 a}$ ☐ (d) $\frac{q^2}{\pi\varepsilon_0 a}$ ☐

(ii) Two points A and B are located in diametrically opposite directions of a point charge of $+2\ \mu C$ at distance 2 m and 1 m respectively, from it. The potential difference between A and B is

(a) 3×10^3 V ☐ (b) 6×10^4 V ☐

(c) -9×10^3 V ☐ (d) -3×10^3 V ☐

(iii) Two point charges $A = +3$ nC and $B = +1$ nC are placed 5 cm apart in air. The work done to move charge B towards A by 1 cm is

(a) 2×10^{-7} J ☐ (b) 1.35×10^{-7} J ☐

(c) 2.7×10^{-7} J ☐ (d) 12.1×10^{-7} J ☐

(iv) Work done in moving a charge of 5 C across two points having a potential difference of 16 V is

(a) 65 J ☐ (b) 45 J ☐
(c) 40 J ☐ (d) 80 J ☐

2. A dielectric slab is a substance, which does not allow the flow of charges through it but permits them to exert electrostatic forces on one another.
When a dielectric slab is placed between the plates, the field E_0 polarises the dielectric. This induces charge Q_P on the upper surface and $+Q_P$ on the lower surface of the dielectric. These induced charges set up a field E_P inside the dielectric in the opposite direction of $\mathbf{E}_0$ as shown.

+Q
Q_P
E_P
$E - E_0 - E_P$
Dielectric slab
Q_P
–Q

(i) In a parallel plate capacitor, the capacitance increases from 5 μF to 50 μF, on introducing a dielectric medium between the plates. What is the dielectric constant of the medium?

(a) 10 ☐ (b) 50 ☐
(c) 70 ☐ (d) 30 ☐

(ii) A parallel plate capacitor with air between the plates has a capacitance of 10 pF. The separation between the plates is now reduced half and the space between them is filled, with a medium of dielectric constant 5. Calculate the value of capacitance of the capacitor in second case.

(a) 8 pF ☐ (b) 10 pF ☐
(c) 80 pF ☐ (d) 100 pF ☐

(iii) A dielectric introduced between the plates of a parallel plate capacitor

(a) increases the capacity of the capacitor. ☐
(b) decreases the electric field between the plates. ☐
(c) increases the charge stored in the capacitor. ☐
(d) decreases the capacity of the capacitor. ☐

(iv) A capacitor plates are charged by a battery with V volts. After charging battery is disconnected and a dielectric slab with dielectric constant K is inserted between its plates, the potential across the plates of a capacitor will become

(a) zero ☐ (b) $\frac{V}{2}$ ☐
(c) $\frac{V}{K}$ ☐ (d) KV ☐

COMPETITION EDGE UP

1. The electrostatic potential due to an electric dipole at a distance r varies as **[NCERT Pg. 49, JEE Main 2024]**

(a) $1/r$ ☐ (b) $1/r^3$ ☐

(c) r ☐ (d) $1/r^2$ ☐

2. An electric charge 10^{-6} μC is placed at origin (0, 0) m of x-y coordinate system. Two points P and Q are situated at $(\sqrt{3}, \sqrt{3})$ m and $(\sqrt{6}, 0)$ m, respectively. The potential difference between the points P and Q will be **[NCERT Pg. 51, JEE Main 2024]**

(a) 3V ☐ (b) 0 V ☐

(c) $\sqrt{3}$ V ☐ (d) $\sqrt{6}$ V ☐

3. Two identical capacitors have same capacitance C. One of them is charged to the potential V and other to the potential 2V. The negative ends of both are connected together. When the positive ends are also joined together, the decrease in energy of the combined system is **[NCERT Pg. 73, JEE Main 2024]**

(a) $\frac{3}{4}CV^2$ ☐ (b) $\frac{1}{4}CV^2$ ☐

(c) $\frac{1}{2}CV^2$ ☐ (d) $2\ CV^2$ ☐

4. In the following circuit, the equivalent capacitance between terminal A and terminal B is **[NCERT Pg. 71, NEET 2024]**

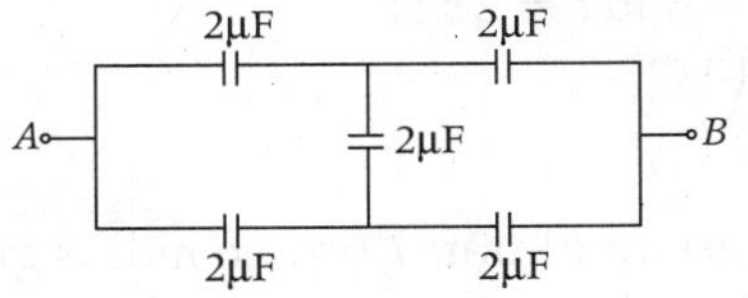

(a) 2 μF ☐ (b) 1 μF ☐

(c) 0.5 μF ☐ (d) 4 μF ☐

5. A thin spherical shell is charged by some source. The potential difference between the two points C and P (in V) shown in the figure is **[NCERT Pg. 51, NEET 2024]**

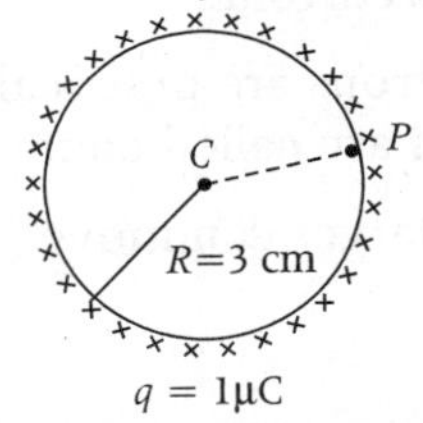

(Take, $\frac{1}{4\pi\varepsilon_0} = 9 \times 10^9$ SI units)

(a) 3×10^5 ☐ (b) 1×10^5 ☐

(c) 0.5×10^5 ☐ (d) zero ☐

6. The equivalent capacitance of the system shown in the following circuit is **[NCERT Pg. 71, NEET 2023]**

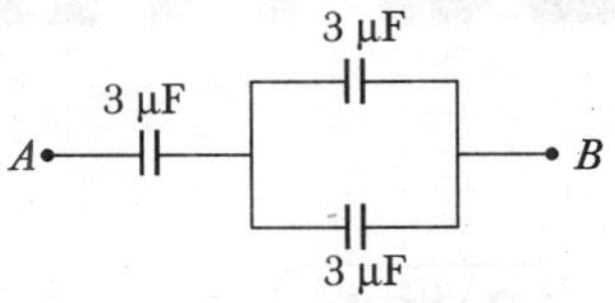

(a) 3 μF ☐ (b) 6 μF ☐

(c) 9 μF ☐ (d) 2 μF ☐

7. Two hollow conducting spheres of radii R_1 and R_2 ($R_1 > R_2$) have equal charges. The potential would be **[NCERT Pg. 52, NEET 2022]**

(a) more on smaller sphere ☐

(b) equal on both the spheres ☐

(c) dependent on the material property of the sphere ☐

(d) more on bigger sphere ☐

8. A parallel-plate capacitor of area A, plate separation d and capacitance C is filled with four dielectric materials having dielectric constants K_1, K_2, K_3 and K_4 as shown in the figure below. If a single dielectric material is to be used to have the same capacitance C in this capacitor, then its dielectric constant k is given by **[NCERT Pg. 70, NEET 2021]**

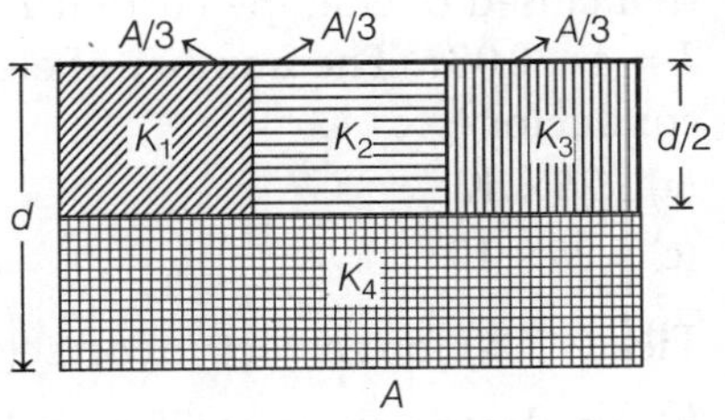

(a) $K = K_1 + K_2 + K_3 + 3K_4$ ☐

(b) $K = \frac{2}{3}(K_1 + K_2 + K_3) + 2K_4$ ☐

(c) $\frac{2}{K} = \frac{3}{K_1 + K_2 + K_3} + \frac{1}{K_4}$ ☐

(d) $\frac{1}{K} = \frac{1}{K_1} + \frac{1}{K_2} + \frac{1}{K_3} + \frac{3}{2K_4}$ ☐

Chapter 3

CURRENT ELECTRICITY

TOPIC 1

Electric Current & Electric Current in Conductors and Ohm's Law

1. In a given time interval t, if q_+ is the net amount of positive charge that flows in the forward direction and q_- is the net amount of negative charge flowing in the forward direction across the area, then the net amount of charge flowing across the area in the forward direction in time interval t, will be given by

(a) $q = q_- - q_+$ ☐
(b) $q = \frac{q_+}{q_-}$ ☐
(c) $q = \frac{q_-}{q_+}$ ☐
(d) $q = q_+ - q_-$ ☐

2. The current flowing through a wire depends on time as $i = 3t^2 + 2t + 5$. The charge flowing the cross-section of the wire in time from $t = 0$ to $t = 2$ s is

(a) 21 C ☐
(b) 10 C ☐
(c) 22 C ☐
(d) 1 C ☐

3. In a closed circuit, the current I (in ampere) at an instant of time t (in second) is given by $I = 4 - 0.08t$. The number of electrons flowing in 50 s through the cross-section of the conductor is

(a) 1.25×10^{19} ☐
(b) 6.25×10^{20} ☐
(c) 5.25×10^{19} ☐
(d) 2.25×10^{20} ☐

4. Tick (✓/✕) for correct/incorrect statement in given boxes.

(i) An electric charge will experience a force, if an electric field is applied. If it is free to move, it will thus move contributing to a current. ☐

(ii) In some materials, especially metals, some of the electrons are practically free to move within the bulk material. These materials are called conductors. ☐

(iii) In electrolytic solutions, both positive and negative charges can move. ☐

*Concepts of all questions bearing * are important for JEE/NEET/CUET.*

***5.** Suppose there is a piece of conductor in the shape of cylinder of radius R (as shown in the following figure) and an electric field is applied in it. Now, we take two thin circular discs of a dielectric of same radius and distribute $+Q$ over one disc and similarly $-Q$ over the other disc. If we attach the two discs on the two flat surfaces of the cylinder, then which of the following option is correct?

$+Q \longrightarrow$ [+ disc] $E \longrightarrow$ [− disc] $\longrightarrow -Q$

(a) An electric field will be created and is directed from the positive to negative end. ☐
(b) The electrons will be accelerated due to this field towards $+Q$. They will move to neutralise the charges. ☐
(c) The electrons as long as they are moving, will constitute an electric current. ☐
(d) All of the above ☐

6. The resistance R not only depends on the material of the conductor but also on the dimensions of the conductor.

Yes ☐ No ☐

7. Two identical slabs each of length l and cross-sectional area A are joined together side-by-side, so that the length of combination is $2l$. The current flowing through the combination is same as that flowing through the each of the slabs.

True ☐ False ☐

***8.** Suppose a slab is divided into two parts by cutting it lengthwise, so that the slab can be considered as a combination of the two identical slabs of length l, each having a cross-sectional area of $\frac{A}{2}$. For a given voltage, if $\frac{I}{2}$ is the current through each slab, then the resistance of each half slab will be

(a) $\frac{R}{2}$ ☐ (b) $\frac{R}{4}$ ☐ (c) $2R$ ☐ (d) $4R$ ☐

9. Two wires A and B made of copper have equal masses and lengths are 10 cm and 20 cm, respectively. If resistance of A be R_A and B be R_B, then the value of $\frac{R_A}{R_B}$ is $\frac{1}{x}$. The value of x here is

(a) 3 ☐ (b) 4 ☐ (c) 5 ☐ (d) 2 ☐

10. Two solid conductors are made up of same material, have same length and same resistance. One of them has a circular cross-section of area A_1 and the other one has a square cross-section of area A_2. What will be the ratio of A_1 / A_2?

____

***11.** The resistance of a wire is R ohm. If it is melted and stretched to n times its original length, its new resistance will be __________ $(n^2/n^3)R$.

***12.** A cylindrical wire of radius 0.5 mm and conductivity 5×10^7 S/m is subjected to an electric field of 10 mV/m. The expected value of current in the wire will be $x^3\pi$ mA. Find the value of x.

____

TOPIC 2

Drift of Electrons and the Origin of Resistivity

NCERT Pg 85-89

13. The expression of drift velocity tells us that the ________ (electrons/protons) move with an average velocity is ________ (dependent/independent) of ________ (time/velocity).

14. Match quantities given in Column I with their appropriate relations given in Column II.

	Column I		Column II
A.	Drift velocity	1.	$m / ne^2\rho$
B.	Electrical resistivity	2.	nev_d
C.	Relaxation period	3.	$\frac{eE}{m}\tau$
D.	Current density	4.	v / J

A. ________ B. ________ C. ________ D. ________

***15.** In the given figure, a battery of emf E is connected across a conductor PQ of length l and different area of cross-sections having radii r_1 and r_2 ($r_2 < r_1$).

Choose the correct option as one moves from P to Q.

(a) Drift velocity of electron increases ☐
(b) Electric field decreases ☐
(c) Electron current decreases ☐
(d) All of these ☐

***16.** A metal wire is subjected to a constant potential difference. When the temperature of the metal wire increases, the drift velocity of the electron in it

(a) increases, thermal velocity of the electrons decreases ☐
(b) decreases, thermal velocity of the electrons decreases ☐
(c) increases, thermal velocity of the electrons increases ☐
(d) decreases, thermal velocity of the electrons increases ☐

***17.** What will be the average drift speed of conduction electrons in a copper wire of cross-sectional area $1 \times 10^{-7}\ \text{m}^2$ carrying a current of 1.5 A? (Assume that, each copper atom contributes roughly one conduction electron. The density of copper is $9.0 \times 10^3\ \text{kg/m}^3$ and its atomic mass is 63.5 u.)

____

18. A straight conductor of uniform cross-section carries a current i. If s is the specific charge of an electron, then momentum of all the free electrons per unit length of the conductor, due to their drift velocity only is

(a) is ☐
(b) $\sqrt{i/s}$ ☐
(c) i/s ☐
(d) $(i/s)^2$ ☐

19. **Statement I** The electron drift arises due to the force experienced by electrons in the electric field inside the conductor.

Statement II Each free electron accelerates in electric field, which increases its drift speed, until it collides with a positive ion of the metal.

Which of the following statement(s) is/are correct?

(a) Only Statement I ☐ (b) Only Statement II ☐
(c) Both Statements I and II ☐ (d) Neither Statement I nor II ☐

20. Suppose the drift speed of electron is small and electron's charge is also small. Can we still obtain the large amount of current in a conductor?

Yes ☐ No ☐

21. When electrons drift in a metal from lower to higher potential, it means that all free electrons of the metal are moving in the same direction.

True ☐ False ☐

22. The paths of electrons between successive collisions in the absence of electric field is $\underline{A}$ and in the presence of electric field, is $\underline{B}$. Here, A and B respectively, refers to

(a) straight lines, curved lines ☐ (b) curved lines, straight lines ☐
(c) straight lines, straight lines ☐ (d) curved lines, curved lines ☐

23. Match the Column I with Column II.

Column I	Column II
A. Mobile charge carriers in metals	1. Positive and negative ions
B. Mobile charge carriers in an ionised gas	2. Electrons and positive charged ions
C. Mobile charge carriers in an electrolyte	3. Electrons

A. ________ B. ________ C. ________

24. ______ (Density/Mobility) is defined as the magnitude of the drift velocity per unit electric field. Its SI unit is ______ $\left(\frac{m^2}{V\text{-}s} \Big/ \frac{V\text{-}s}{m^2}\right)$ and its order is of ____ $(10^6/10^4)$ in practical units.

25. Tick the correct expression for calculating mobility.

I. $\mu = \frac{v_d}{E} = \frac{e\tau}{m}$ ☐ II. $\mu = \frac{E}{v_d} = \frac{e}{\tau m}$ ☐

***26.** Which one of the following graph represents the correct variation of mobility μ of electrons with applied electric field E in a metallic conductor?

(a) 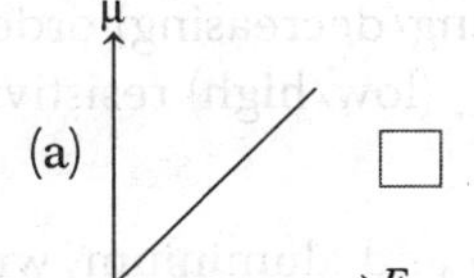

☐ (b) 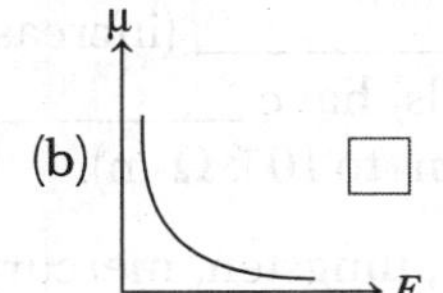

☐ (c) 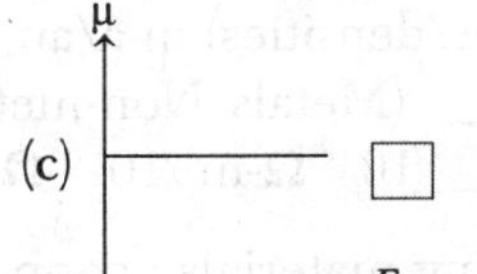

☐ (d) 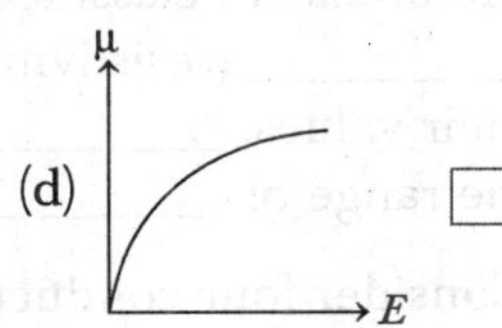

☐

27. How does the mobility of electrons in a conductor change, if the potential difference applied across the conductor is doubled, keeping the length and temperature of the conductor constant?

____

TOPIC 3

Limitations of Ohm's Law & Resistivity of Various Materials

28. Draw a graph, which correctly represents V *versus* I graph for a good conductor.

29. From the graph between current I and voltage V shown in the following figure, identify the portion corresponding to negative resistance.

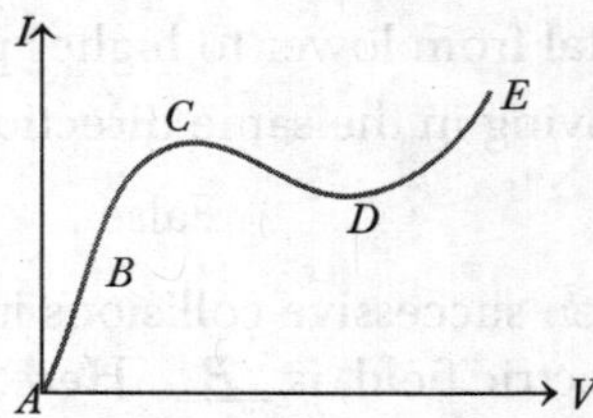

30. If I is the current for a certain V and its direction is reversed keeping its magnitude fixed, will it produce a current of the same magnitude?

Yes ☐ No ☐

31. **Statement I** Ohm's law has been found inconsistent for a large class of materials and devices used in electric circuits.

Statement II The variation in V and I are broadly one or more of the following types.

(i) V increases to be proportional to I.

(ii) The relation between V and I depends on the sign of V.

(iii) The relation between V and I is not unique.

Which of the following statement(s) is/are correct?

(a) Only statement I ☐ (b) Only statement II ☐

(c) Both statements I and II ☐ (d) Neither statement I nor II ☐

32. Which one of the following metals or compounds do not follow Ohm's law?

(a) Au ☐ (b) Ag ☐ (c) Cu ☐ (d) GaAs ☐

33. Materials are classified as conductors, insulators and semiconductors depending on their __________ (resistivities/densities) in a/an __________ (increasing/decreasing) order of their values. __________ (Metals/Non-metals) have __________ (low/high) resistivities in the range of __________ (10^{-8} Ω-m /10^{-5} Ω-m to 10^{-6} Ω-m).

34. Consider four conducting materials : copper, tungsten, mercury and aluminium with resistivity ρ_C, ρ_T, ρ_M and ρ_A, respectively. Then,

(a) $\rho_A > \rho_T > \rho_C$ ☐ (b) $\rho_A > \rho_M > \rho_C$ ☐ (c) $\rho_C > \rho_A > \rho_T$ ☐ (d) $\rho_M > \rho_A > \rho_C$ ☐

***35.** The resistivity of iron is 1×10^{-7} Ω-m. The resistance of iron wire of particular length and thickness is 1 Ω. If the length and diameter of wire both are doubled, then the resistivity (in Ω-m) will be______________ (2×10^{-7} / 1×10^{-7}).

36. Tick (✓/×) for correct/incorrect statement in given boxes.

(i) Insulators like ceramic, rubber and plastics have resistivities 10^{18} times greater than metals or more. ☐

(ii) Semiconductors have resistivities characteristically decreasing with a rise in a temperature. ☐

TOPIC 4

Temperature Dependence of Resistivity

37. As temperature rises, the resistivity of a copper wire ________ (increases/decreases).

38. A wire of a certain material is stretched slowly by 10 percent. Its new resistance and specific resistance become respectively

(a) 1.2 times, 1.1 times ☐ (b) 1.21 times, same ☐
(c) Both remain the same ☐ (d) 1.1 times, 1.1 times ☐

39. The temperature at which the resistance of a copper conductor become double of its value at 0°C is ($\alpha_{Cu} = 4 \times 10^{-3}$/°C)

(a) 300°C ☐ (b) 250°C ☐
(c) 270°C ☐ (d) 220°C ☐

40. Tick (✓) for the correct relation of resistivity of a metallic conductor at temperature T.

I. $\rho_T = \rho_0[1 + \alpha(T - T_0)]$ ☐ II. $\rho_T = \rho_0[1 + \alpha(T_0 - T)]$ ☐

***41.** Which one of the following graph represents the resistivity *versus* temperature for a conductor?

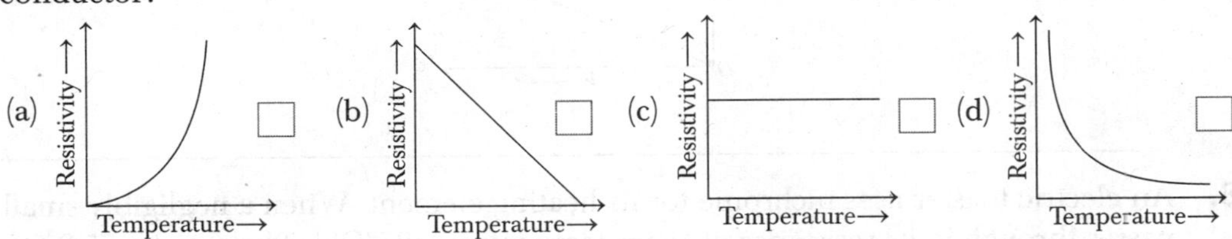

42. Draw a graph that correctly shows the resistivity of nichrome as a function of absolute temperature T.

---

43. The temperature dependence of resistances of Cu and undoped Si in the temperature range 300 K-400 K, is best described by

(a) linear increase for Cu, linear increase for Si ☐
(b) linear increase for Cu, exponential increase for Si ☐
(c) linear increase for Cu, exponential decrease for Si ☐
(d) linear decrease for Cu, linear decrease for Si ☐

44.

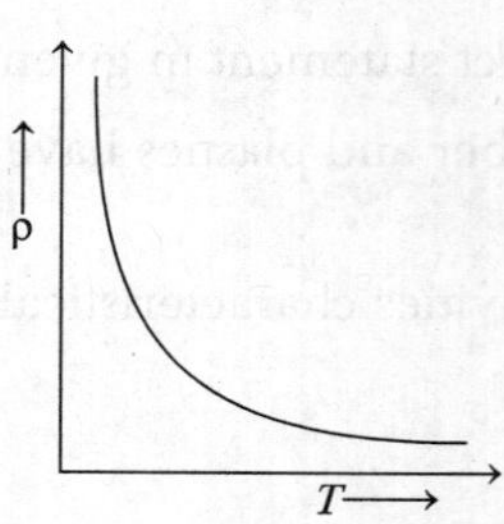

Above figure represents the temperature dependence of resistivity for a typical ______ (conductor/semiconductor/insulator).

45. Is the resistivity of a semiconductor increase or decrease with increase in temperature?

______

46. **Statement I** The temperature dependence of resistance is usually given as $R = R_0(1+\alpha\Delta T)$. The resistance of a wire changes from 100 Ω to 150 Ω when its temperature is increased from 27°C to 227°C. This implies that $\alpha = 2.5\times 10^{-3}$ /°C.

Statement II $R = R_i(1+\alpha\Delta T)$ is valid only when the change in the temperature ΔT is small and $\Delta R = (R - R_0) << R_0$.

Which of the following statement(s) is/are correct?

(a) Only Statement I ☐ (b) Only Statement II ☐

(c) Both Statements I and II ☐ (d) Neither Statement I nor II ☐

47. *I-V* graph for a metallic wire at two different temperatures T_1 and T_2 are as shown in the figure given below. Which of the two temperature is lower ?

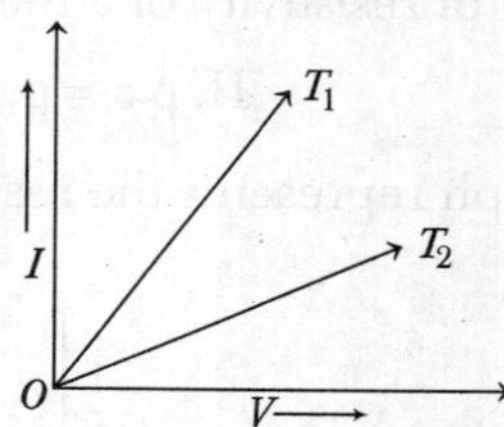

______

***48.** An electric toaster uses nichrome for its heating element. When a negligibly small current passes through it, its resistance at room temperature (27°C) is found to be 75.3 Ω. When the toaster is connected to a 230 V supply, the current settles, after a few seconds, to a steady value of 2.68 A.

If the temperature coefficient of resistance of nichrome averaged over the temperature range involved is $1.7\times 10^{-4}\,°C^{-1}$, then the steady temperature of the nichrome element will be ______ °C.

49. The resistance of the platinum wire of a platinum resistance thermometer at the ice point is 5 Ω and at the steam point is 5.23 Ω. When the thermometer is inserted in hot bath, the resistance of the platinum wire is 5.795 Ω. The temperature of the bath will be 345.65°C.

Yes ☐ No ☐

TOPIC 5

Electrical Energy and Power

NCERT Pg 92-93

50. A hot electric iron has resistance of 100 Ω and is used on a 200 V source. The electrical energy spent if it is used for 2 hr, will be

(a) 800 Wh (b) 1000 Wh (c) 750 Wh (d) 1200 Wh

51. Water boils in an electric kettle in 20 minutes after switching on. If the length of the heating wire is increased to 3/4 of its initial value, then the same amount of water will boil with the same supply voltage in

(a) 35 minutes (b) 12 minutes (c) 10 minutes (d) 8 minutes

52. Two bulbs consume same power when operated at 200 V and 300 V, respectively. When these bulbs are connected in series across a DC source of 500 V, then

(a) ratio of potential differences across them is 3/2

(b) ratio of potential differences across them is 9/4

(c)ratio of powers consumed across them is 4/9

(d) ratio of powers consumed across them is 2/3

***53.** If voltage across a bulb rated 220 V-100 Watt drops by 5% of its rated value, the percentage of the rated value by which the power would decrease is

(a) 5% (b) 10% (c) 20% (d) 2.5%

54. Power of a heater is 500 W at 800°C. What will be its power at 200°C, if $\alpha = 4 \times 10^{-4}$ per °C?

(a) 484 W (b) 672 W (c) 526 W (d) 620 W

55. Two cities are 150 km apart. Electric power is sent from one city to another city through copper wires. The fall of potential per km is 8 V and the average resistance per km is 0.5 Ω. The power loss in the wire is

(a) 19.2 W (b) 19.2 kW (c) 19.2 J (d) 12.2 kW

56. An electric bulb is marked 100 W, 230 V. If the supply voltage drops to 115 V, what is the heat and light energy produced by the bulb in 20 min?

(a) 20000 J (b) 25000 J (c) 30000 J (d) 35000 J

TOPIC 6

Cells, emf, Internal Resistance & Cells in Series and Parallel

NCERT Pg 93-95

57. A cell has ________ (two/three) electrodes, called ________ (positive/neutral) and ________ (negative/neutral). They are immersed in an ________ (electrolytic /concentrated) solution. Dipped in the solution, the electrode exchange ________ (particles/charges) with electrolyte.

58. If E is the emf of a cell of internal resistance r and external resistance R, then potential difference across R is given as

(a) $V = \frac{E}{(R+r)}$ ☐ (b) $V = E$ ☐ (c) $V = \frac{E}{\left(1+\frac{r}{R}\right)}$ ☐ (d) $V = \frac{E}{\left(1+\frac{R}{r}\right)}$ ☐

59. The current through a $\frac{4}{3}\,\Omega$ external resistance connected to a parallel combination of two cells of 2 V and 1 V emf and internal resistance of 1 Ω and 2 Ω respectively is

(a) 1 A ☐ (b) $\frac{2}{3}$ A ☐ (c) $\frac{3}{4}$ A ☐ (d) $\frac{5}{6}$ A ☐

60. Emf is the potential difference between the positive and negative electrodes in an open circuit, i.e. when no current is flowing through the cell.

True ☐ False ☐

61. For what value of I and R, maximum current can be drawn from the cell?

____

62. Two batteries A and B each of emf 2V are connected in series to an external resistance $R = 1\,\Omega$. If the internal resistance of battery A is 1.9 Ω and that of B is 0.9 Ω, then what is the potential difference between the terminals of battery A?

(a) 2 V ☐ (b) 3.8 V ☐
(c) zero ☐ (d) 4.8 V ☐

***63.** The potential difference between A and B in the given figure will be

(a) $(E_1 - E_2) + I(r_1 + r_2)$ ☐ (b) $(E_1 + E_2) - I(r_1 + r_2)$ ☐
(c) $(E_1 + E_2) + I(r_1 - r_2)$ ☐ (d) $(E_1 - E_2) - I(r_1 + r_2)$ ☐

***64.** Is the value of voltage between points A and B in the given circuit equivalent to $\frac{E_1 r_2 + E_2 r_1}{r_1 + r_2} - I\left(\frac{r_1 r_2}{r_1 + r_2}\right)$?

Yes ☐ No ☐

65. Two batteries E_1, E_2 and internal resistances r_1, r_2 are connected in parallel as shown in the figure given alongside. The effective emf of the circuit across A and B is______________ $\left(\frac{E_1 r_2 + E_2 r_1}{r_1 + r_2} / \frac{E_2 r_2 + E_1 r_2}{r_1 + r_2}\right)$.

66. A battery consists of a variable number n of identical cells (having internal resistance r each) which are connected in series. The terminals of the battery are short-circuited and the current I is measured. Which of the graphs shows the correct relationship between I and n?

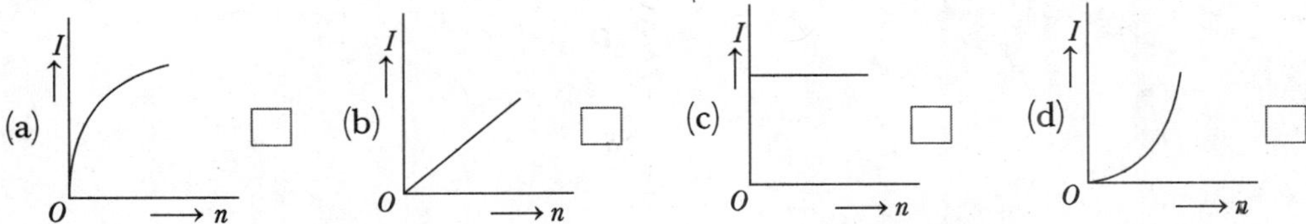

67. There are $n\ (n > 2)$ cells, each of emf E and internal resistance r, connected in series with an external resistance R. One of the cells is wrongly connected, so that it sends current in the opposite direction. The current flowing in the circuit is

(a) $\dfrac{(n-1)\,E}{(n+1)\,r+2}$ ☐ (b) $\dfrac{(n-1)\,E}{nr+R}$ ☐

(c) $\dfrac{(n-2)\,E}{nr+R}$ ☐ (d) $\dfrac{(n-2)\,E}{(n-2)\,r+R}$ ☐

TOPIC 7

Kirchhoff 's Rules

NCERT Pg 97-100

68. In the circuit given here, the points A, B and C are 70 V, zero and 10 V, respectively. Then,

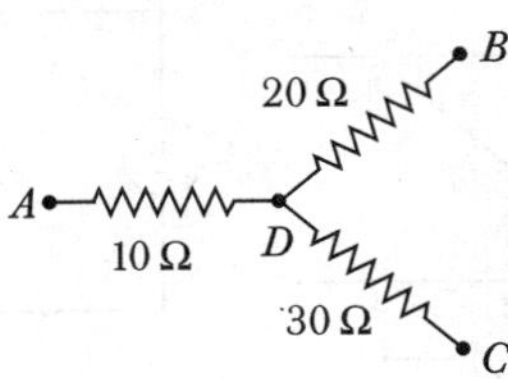

(a) the point D will be at a potential of 60 V ☐
(b) the point D will be at a potential of 20 V ☐
(c) currents in the paths AD, DB and DC are in the ratio of 1 : 2 : 3 ☐
(d) currents in the paths AD, DB and DC are in the ratio of 3 : 2 : 1 ☐

***69.** The value of I in the following circuit will be__________ (0.2/1.2)A.

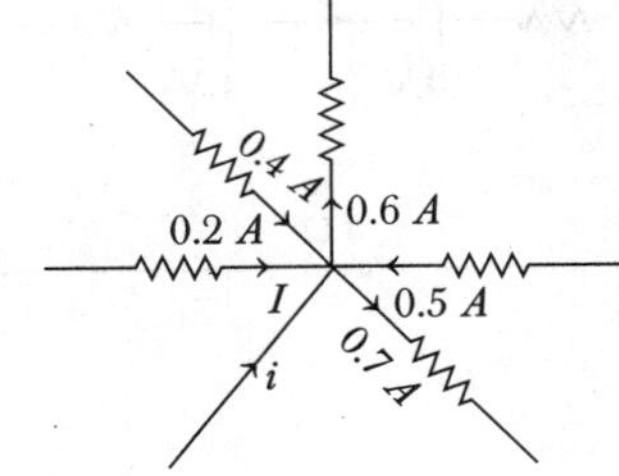

***70.** As the switch S is closed in the circuit shown in figure, current passing through it is

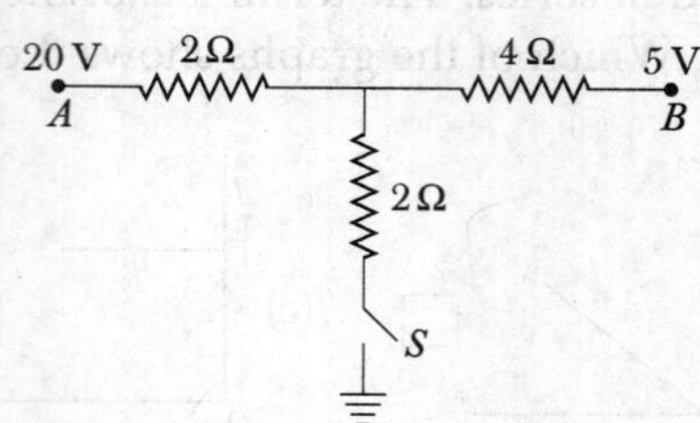

(a) 4.5 A ☐ (b) 6.0 A ☐

(c) 3.0 A ☐ (d) zero ☐

***71.** For the circuit shown in the figure, the value of R must be ________ (5 Ω/ 6 Ω) for circuit (i) and ________ (5 Ω/ 6 Ω) for circuit (ii).

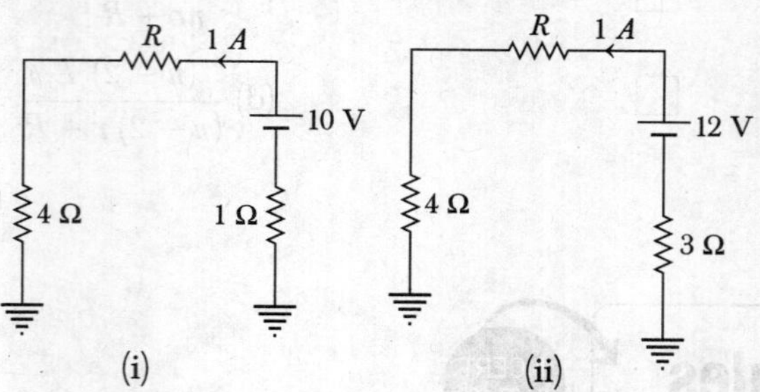

72. For the circuit shown below, the value of current at time t = 3.2 s. What will be the magnitude of current?

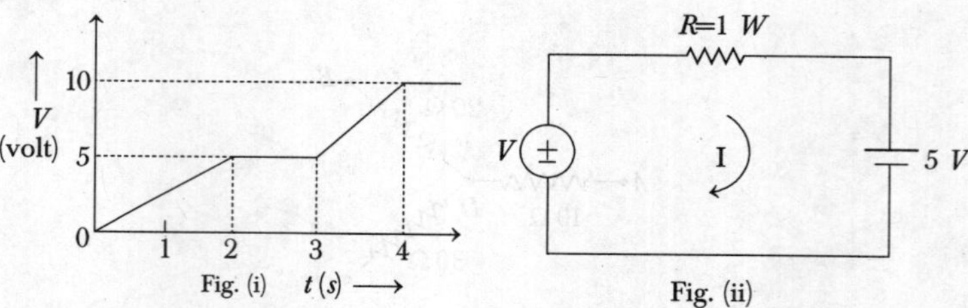

[Voltage distribution $V(t)$ is shown by Fig. (i) and the circuit is shown in Fig. (ii).]

____

***73.** The magnitude and direction of the current in the circuit shown will be ________ ________ (1 A from b to a through e/1 A from a to b through e).

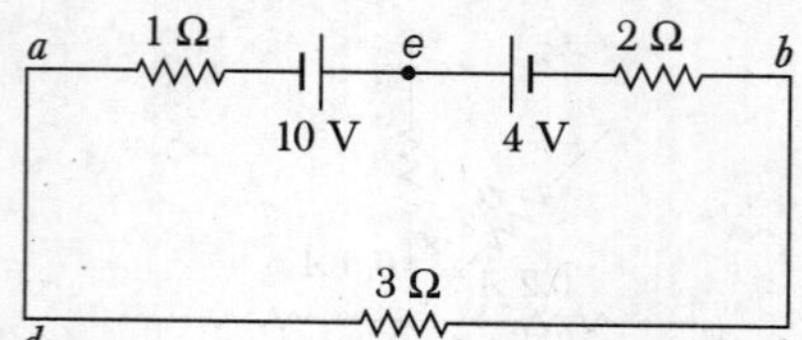

***74.** What will be the value of current (in the given figure) that flows in the 1 Ω resistor?

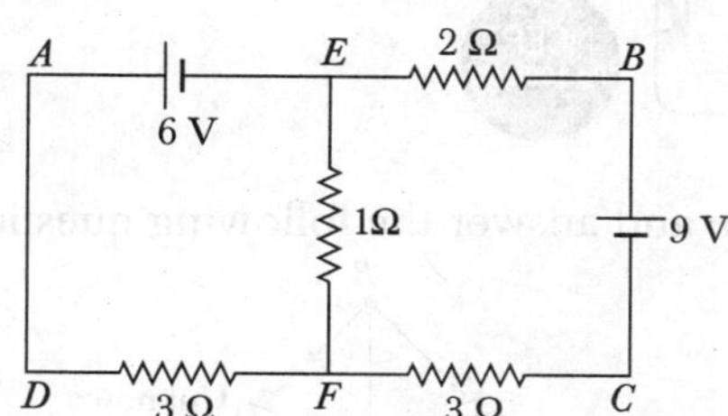

(a) 0.39 A ☐ (b) 1.4 A ☐ (c) 0.13 A ☐ (d) 8.5 A ☐

***75.** A battery of 10 V and negligible internal resistance is connected across the diagonally opposite corners of a cubical network consisting of 12 resistors each of resistance 1 Ω. Calculate the

(i) equivalent resistance of network and

(ii) current in the circuit.

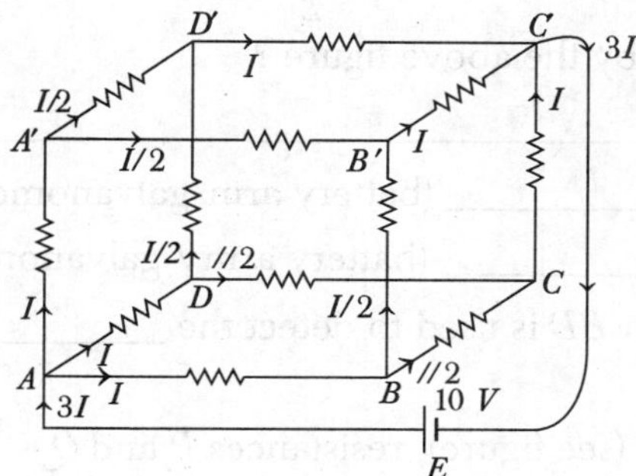

***76.** Consider the following figure.

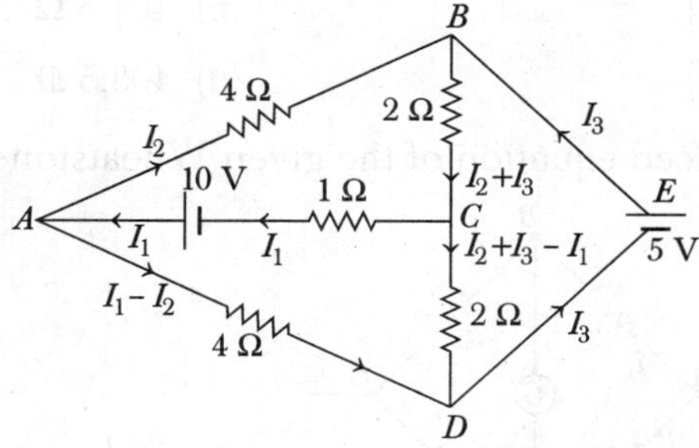

Fill in the blanks to complete the sentence.

Current through arm

AB ________	*CA* ________	*DEB* ________
AD ________	*CD* ________	*BC* ________

***77.** Consider the given figure and answer the following questions.

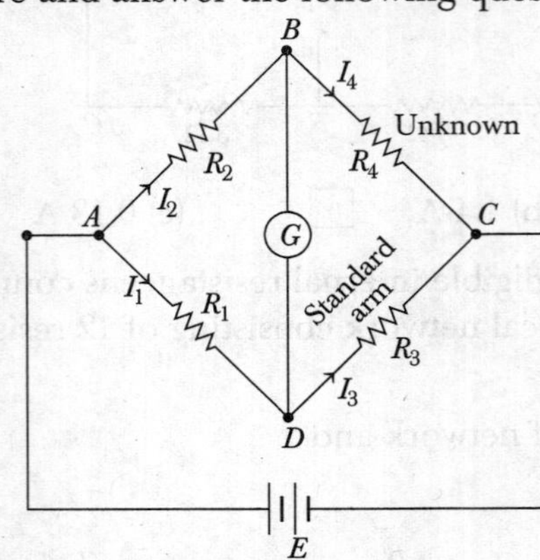

(i) What is represented by the above figure ?

____

(ii) AC is called ______________ (battery arm/galvanometer arm).

(iii) BD is called ______________ (battery arm / galvanometer arm).

(iv) Galvanometer in arm BD is used to detect the ____________(current/potential difference).

***78.** In a Wheatstone bridge (see figure), resistances P and Q are approximately equal. When $R = 400\ \Omega$, the bridge is balanced. On interchanging P and Q , the value of R for balance is $405\,\Omega$. The value of X is close to

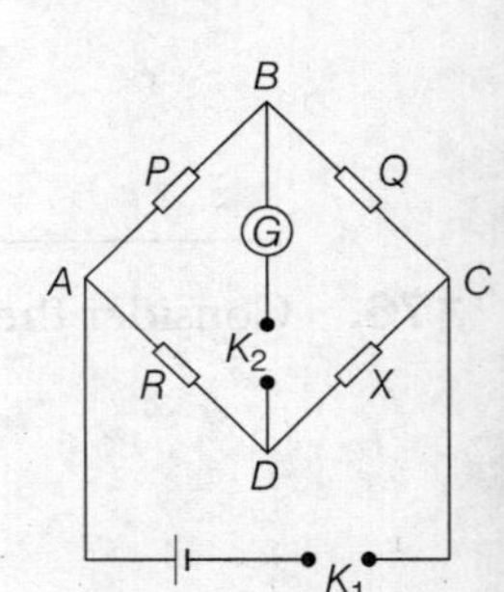

(a) $404.5\ \Omega$ ☐ (b) $401.5\ \Omega$ ☐

(c) $402.5\ \Omega$ ☐ (d) $403.5\ \Omega$ ☐

***79.** What will be the balanced equation of the given Wheatstone bridge?

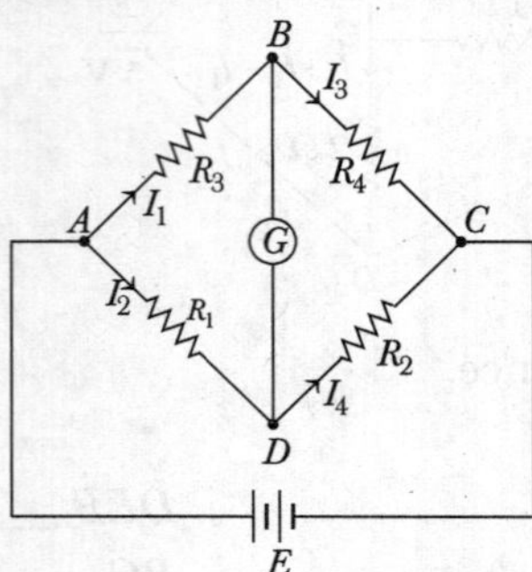

____

80. The magnitude of resistance X in the circuit shown in figure, when no current flows through the 8 Ω resistor is

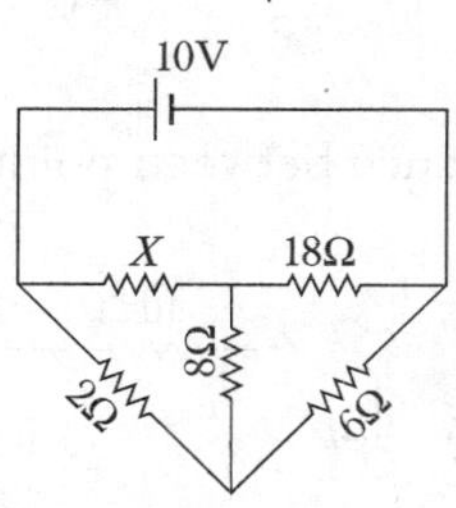

(a) 8 Ω ☐ (b) 6 Ω ☐ (c) 4 Ω ☐ (d) 7 Ω ☐

***81.** The four arms of a Wheatstone bridge have the following resistances, $AB = 100\ \Omega$, $BC = 10\ \Omega$, $CD = 5\ \Omega$ and $DA = 60\ \Omega$. A galvanometer of 15 Ω resistance is connected across BD. The current through the galvanometer when a potential difference of 10 V is maintained across AC, will be ________ (4.87/5.52) mA.

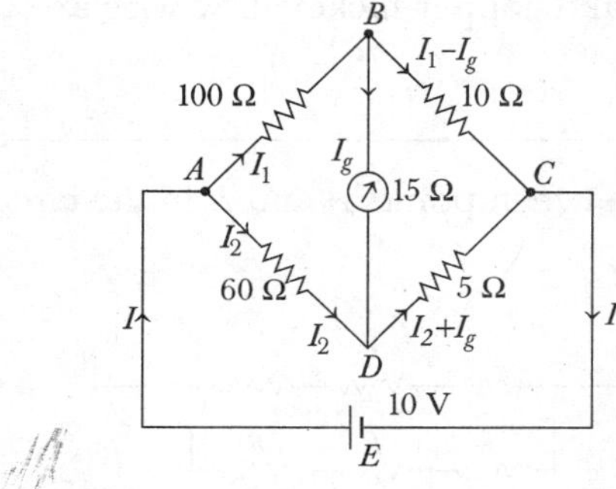

***82.** P, Q, R and S are four wires of resistances 3 Ω, 3 Ω, 3 Ω and 4 Ω respectively. They are connected to form the four arms of a Wheatstone bridge circuit. The resistance with which S must be shunted in order that the bridge may be balanced is .... Ω.

COMPETITION CONNECT

Topic 1. Combinations of Resistors-Series and Parallel [NCERT (Old) Pg. 107-109]

1. For the given mixed combination of resistors, calculate the total resistance between points and B.

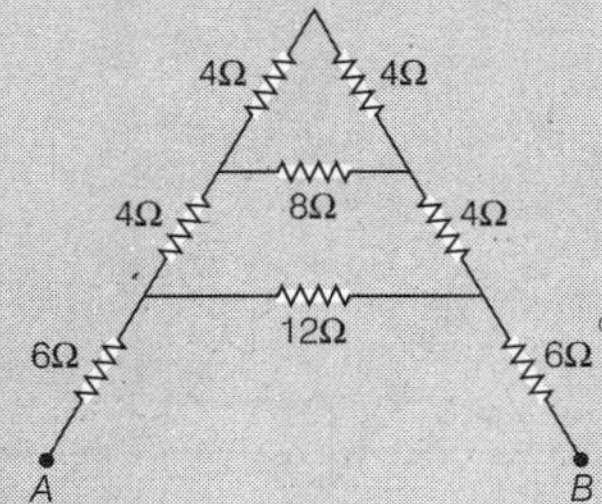

Choose the correct answer from the options given below.

(a) 9 Ω ☐ (b) 18 Ω ☐ (c) 4 Ω ☐ (d) 14 Ω ☐

2. $A \xrightarrow{I} R_1 \xrightarrow{I} R_2 \; B : R_{eq} = R_1 + R_2 :: A \xrightarrow{I} R_1 \xrightarrow{I} R_2 \xrightarrow{I} R_3 \; B : R_{eq} = ?$

Here ? refers to __________ .

3. Determine the equivalent resistance between points A and B in the following circuits.

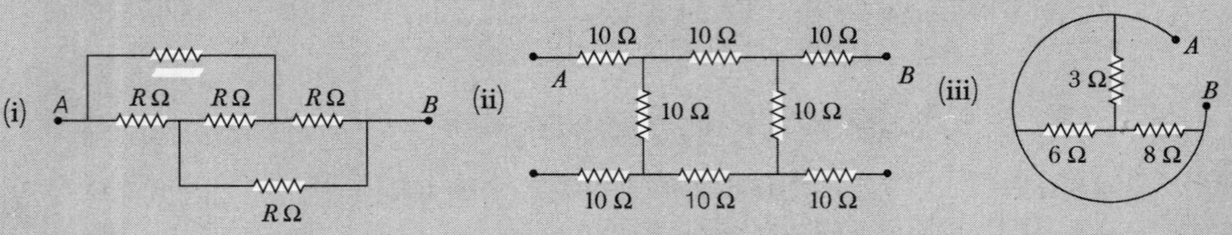

---

4. What equal length of an iron wire and a copper-nickel alloy wire, each of 2 mm diameter should be connected in parallel to give an equivalent resistance of 3 Ω?
(Given, resistivities of iron and copper-nickel alloy wire are 12 μΩ cm and 51 μΩ cm, respectively)

---

5. The equivalent resistance between points A and B in the circuit shown in the following figure is $\frac{x}{5}R$.

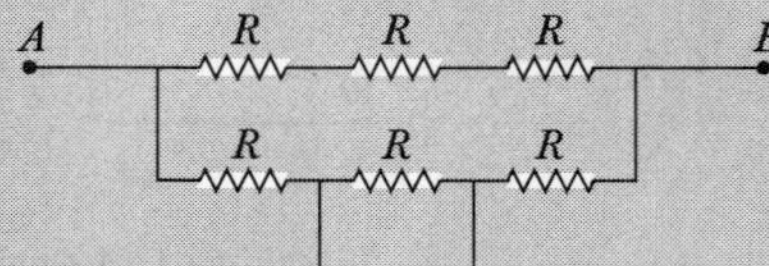

The value of x is __________ .

6. The equivalent resistance of the given circuit between the terminals A and B is

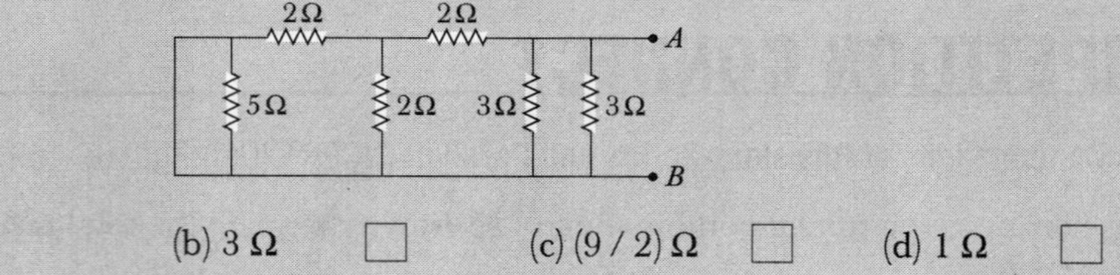

(a) 0 ☐ (b) 3 Ω ☐ (c) (9 / 2) Ω ☐ (d) 1 Ω ☐

7. What will be the resistance across P and Q in the following figure?

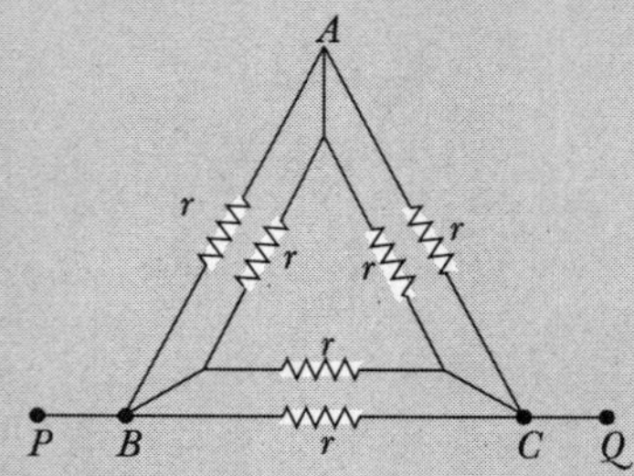

---

8. A ring is made of a wire having a resistance $R_0 = 12\,\Omega$. Find the ratio of lengths between points A and B as shown in the following figure, at which a current-carrying conductor should be connected, so that the resistance R of the sub-circuit between these points is equal to (8/3) Ω.

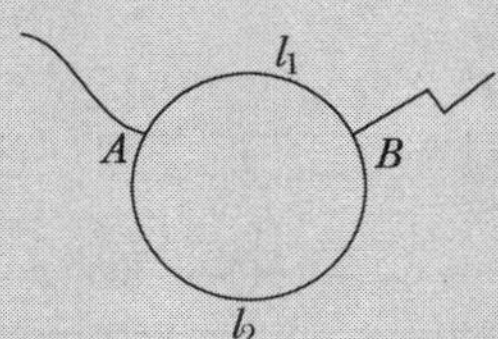

9. A, B and C are voltmeters of resistance R, $1.5\,R$ and $3R$ respectively as shown in the following figure. When some potential difference is applied between X and Y, the voltmeter readings are V_A, V_B and V_C, respectively. Then,

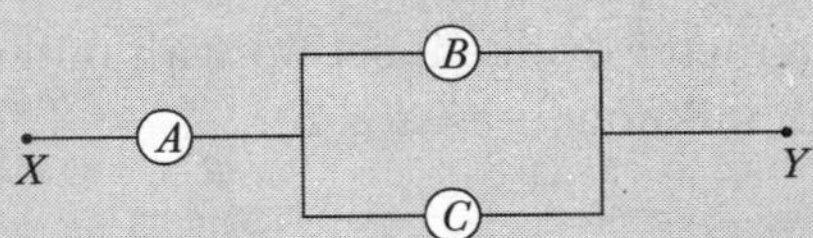

(a) $V_A = V_B = V_C$ ☐

(b) $V_A \neq V_B = V_C$ ☐

(c) $V_A = V_B \neq V_C$ ☐

(d) $V_A \neq V_B \neq V_C$ ☐

10. In the given circuit, find

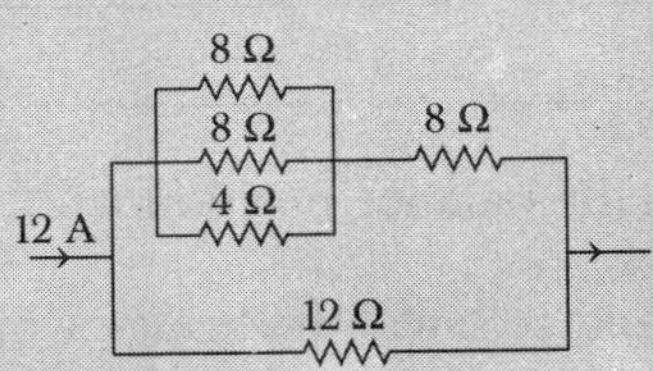

(i) current through 12 Ω resistor and

(ii) voltage through 12 Ω resistor.

---

11. A network of resistors is connected to a 16 V battery with an internal resistance of 1 Ω as shown in the given below. Find

(i) the total resistance of the network and

(ii) the current in the circuit.

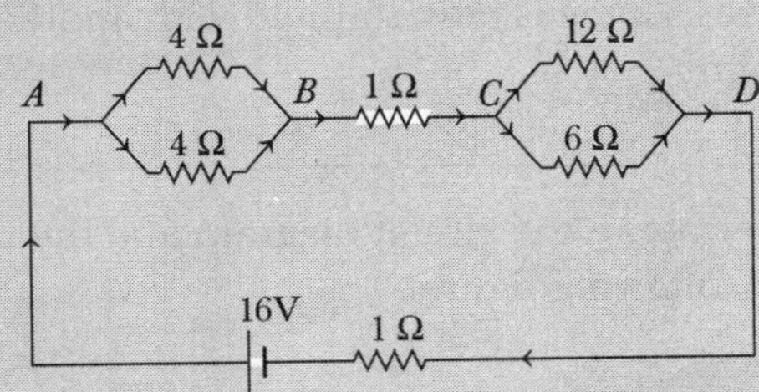

Topic 2. Meter Bridge [NCERT (Old) Pg. 120-121]

12. If the distance of the jockey from end A at the balance point be $l = l_1$ and the four resistances of the bridge at the balance point are R, S, $R_{CM}\ l_1$ and $R_{CM}\ (100 - l_1)$, then write the balance condition of given meter bridge.

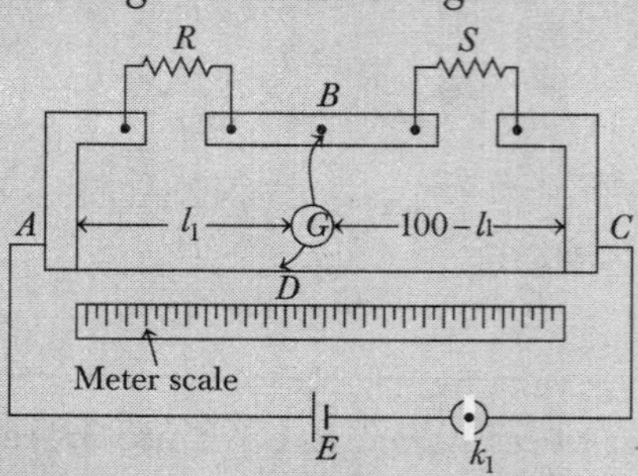

13. In the following figure, a meter bridge is set-up with null deflection in the galvanometer. What will be the value of unknown resistor R ?

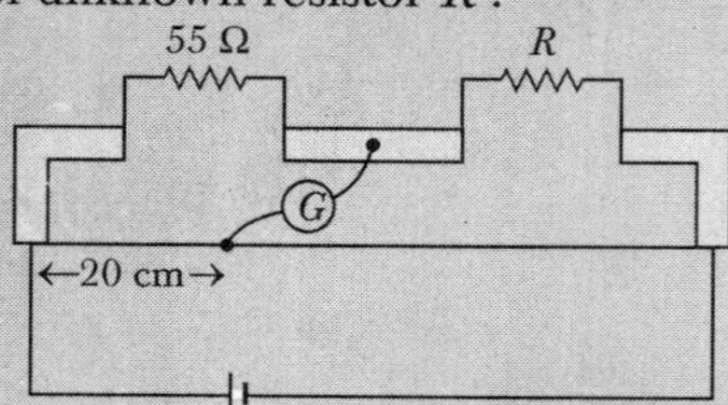

14. The meter bridge shown in the balance position with $\frac{P}{Q} = \frac{l_1}{l_2}$. If we now interchange the positions of galvanometer and cell, will the bridge work? If yes, what will be balanced condition?

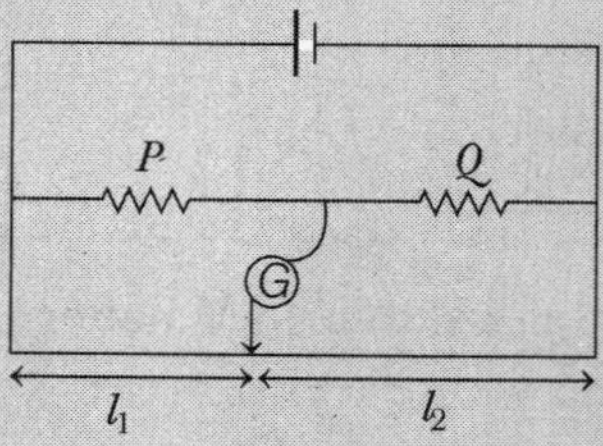

15. A meter bridge is balanced with a 20 Ω resistance in the left gap and a 30 Ω resistance in the right gap. If 20 Ω resistance is now shunted with another 20 Ω resistance, what will be the shift in the null point?

16. In a meter bridge experiment, the circuit diagram and the corresponding observation table are shown in the following figure.

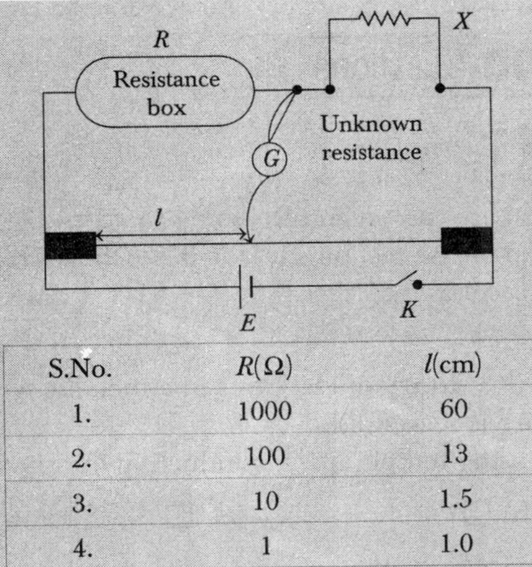

S.No.	$R(\Omega)$	l(cm)
1.	1000	60
2.	100	13
3.	10	1.5
4.	1	1.0

Which of the readings is inconsistent ?

(a) 3 ☐ (b) 2 ☐ (c) 1 ☐ (d) 4 ☐

17. In meter bridge, the percentage error of R can be minimised by adjusting the balance point near the middle of the bridge, i.e. when l_1 is close to 50 cm. Is the given information about meter bridge correct?

Yes ☐ No ☐

18. In the given meter bridge, the null point is found at a distance of 33.7 cm from A. If now a resistance of $12\,\Omega$ is connected in parallel with S, the null point occurs at 51.9 cm. What will be the value of R and S? Tick (✓) on correct values.

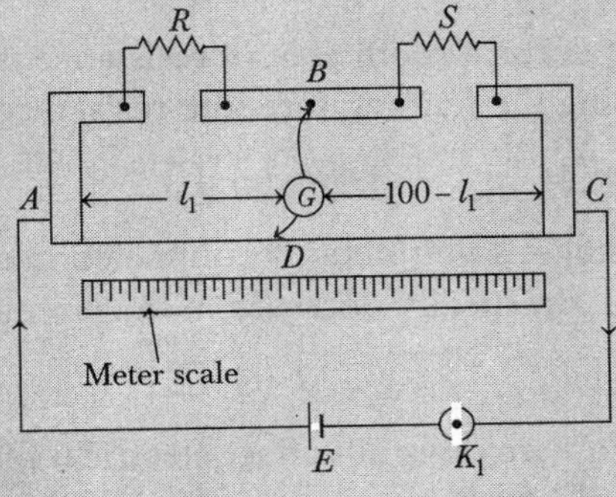

(i) $R = 6.86\ \Omega,\ \ S = 13.5\ \Omega$ ☐ (ii) $R = 4.59\ \Omega,\ \ S = 56.5\ \Omega$ ☐

19. A meter bridge is set-up to determine unknown resistance X using a standard of $10\ \Omega$ resistor. The galvanometer shows the null point when the tapping key is at a 52 cm mark. End corrections are 1 cm and 2 cm respectively, for ends A and B. Find the value of X.

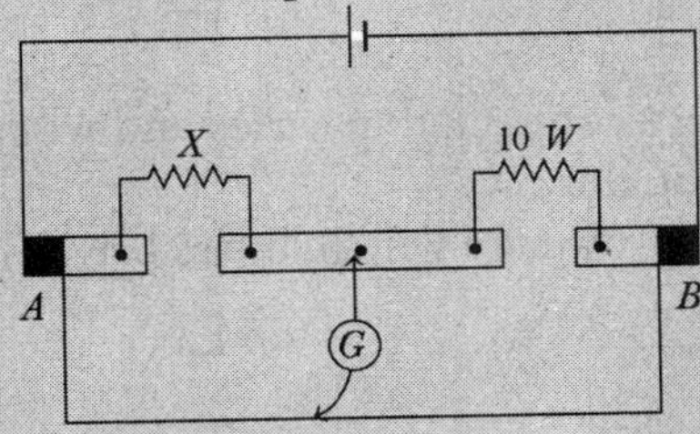

Assertion-Reason Questions

Direction (Q. Nos. 1-10) *In the following questions, a statement of Assertion is followed by a corresponding statement of Reason. From the following options, choose the correct one.*

(a) Both Assertion and Reason are correct and Reason is the correct explanation of Assertion.
(b) Both Assertion and Reason are correct but Reason is not the correct explanation of Assertion.
(c) Assertion is correct but Reason is incorrect.
(d) Assertion is incorrect but Reason is correct.

***1.** **Assertion** (A) The drift velocity of electrons in a metallic wire will decrease, if the temperature of the wire is increased.
Reason (R) On increasing temperature, conductivity of metallic wire decreases.

(a) ☐ (b) ☐ (c) ☐ (d) ☐

***2.** **Assertion** (A) On an average, charge carriers do not move with acceleration but with a steady drift velocity.
Reason (R) This is because of the collisions with ions and atoms during transit. During collisions, the energy gained by the charges is shared with atoms, due to which the atoms vibrate more vigorously and it got heat up.

(a) ☐ (b) ☐ (c) ☐ (d) ☐

3. **Assertion** (A) The current flowing though a conductor is directly proportional to the drift velocity.
Reason (R) As the drift velocity increase the current flowing through the conductor decreases.

(a) ☐ (b) ☐ (c) ☐ (d) ☐

4. **Assertion** (A) The temperature coefficient of resistance is always positive for metals.
Reason (R) On increasing the temperature, the resistance of metal and alloys increases.

(a) ☐ (b) ☐ (c) ☐ (d) ☐

***5.** **Assertion** (A) If by mistake, a voltmeter is connected in series, then circuit will burn.
Reason (R) Current will drastically decrease in the circuit.

(a) ☐ (b) ☐ (c) ☐ (d) ☐

6. **Assertion** (A) Bending a wire does not affect electrical resistance.
Reason (R) Resistance of wire is proportional to resistivity of material.

(a) ☐ (b) ☐ (c) ☐ (d) ☐

7. **Assertion** (A) Heater wire must have high resistance and high melting point.
Reason (R) If resistance is high, then electrical conductivity will be less.

(a) ☐ (b) ☐ (c) ☐ (d) ☐

8. **Assertion** (A) 10 bulbs are connected in series and when one bulb fused then the remaining 9 bulbs will not glow.
Reason (R) Bulb of higher wattage will give less bright light.

(a) ☐ (b) ☐ (c) ☐ (d) ☐

***9.** **Assertion** (A) Terminal voltage of a cell is greater than emf of the cell, during charging of the cell.
Reason (R) The emf of a cell is always greater than its terminal voltage.

(a) ☐ (b) ☐ (c) ☐ (d) ☐

10. **Assertion** (A) Current between two points in an electrical circuit always flows higher potential to lower potential.
Reason (R) During charging of a battery current inside the battery flows from positive terminal to negative terminal.

(a) ☐ (b) ☐ (c) ☐ (d) ☐

Case Based Questions

1. According to Ohm's law, the current flowing through a conductor is directly proportional to the potential difference across the ends of the conductor i.e., $I \propto V \Rightarrow \frac{V}{I} = R$, where R is resistance of the conductor. Electrical resistance of a conductor is the obstruction posed by the conductor to the flow of electric current through it. It depends upon length, area of cross-section, nature of material and temperature of the conductor. We can write, $R \propto \frac{l}{A}$ or $R = \rho \frac{l}{A}$, where ρ is electrical resistivity of the material of the conductor.

(i) The current density of a copper wire of cross-sectional area 2.0 mm^2 carrying a current of 1 A is, (Conductivity of copper is 6.25×10^7 Sm^{-1})

(a) 2.8×10^6 Am^{-2} ☐ (b) 3×10^5 Am^{-2} ☐
(c) 0.5×10^6 Am^{-2} ☐ (d) 1×10^5 Am^{-2} ☐

(ii) The resistance of a 10 m long wire is 100 Ω. Its length is increased by 25% by stretching the wire uniformly. The resistance of wire will change to (approximately).

(a) 156.25 Ω ☐ (b) 155.25 Ω ☐
(c) 158.25 Ω ☐ (d) 160.25 Ω ☐

(iii) If 2 μA current flows through a conductor when potential difference of 6 volt is applied across its ends, then the resistance of the conductor is

(a) 2×10^6 Ω ☐ (b) 3×10^6 Ω ☐
(c) 1.5×10^5 Ω ☐ (d) 5×10^7 Ω ☐

(iv) Choose the correct statement regarding Ohm's law.

(a) It is valid for any circumstances, i.e., independent of temperature. ☐
(b) Ohm's law is valid for all conducting materials. ☐
(c) The temperature must be constant for validation of this law. ☐
(d) None of the above ☐

2. In 1942, a German physicist Kirchhoff extended Ohm's law to complicated circuits and gave two laws, which enables us to determine current in any part of such a circuit. According to Kirchhoff's first rule, the algebraic sum of the currents meeting at a junction in a closed electric circuit is zero. The current flowing in a conductor towards the junction is taken an positive and the current flowing away from the junction is taken as negative.

According to Kirchhoff's second rule, in a closed loop, the algebraic sum of the emf's and algebraic sum of the products of current and resistance in the various arms of the loop is zero. While transversing a loop, if negative pole of the cell is encountered first, then its emf is negative, otherwise positive.

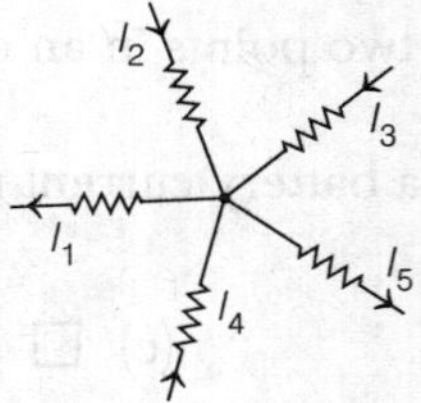

(i) The value of current I in the given circuit is

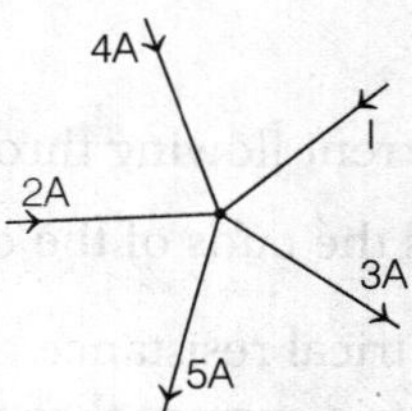

(a) 4.5 A ☐ (b) 3.7 A ☐ (c) 2.0 A ☐ (d) 2.5 A ☐

(ii) Potential difference between A and B in the circuit shown below is

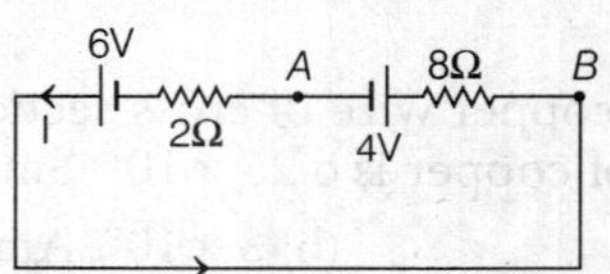

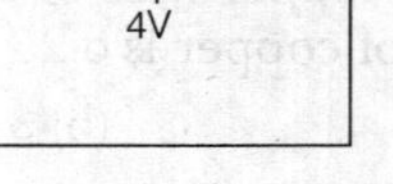

(a) 4 V ☐ (b) 5.6 V ☐ (c) 2.8 V ☐ (d) 6 V ☐

(iii) In the circuit shown the current through 2 Ω resistance is

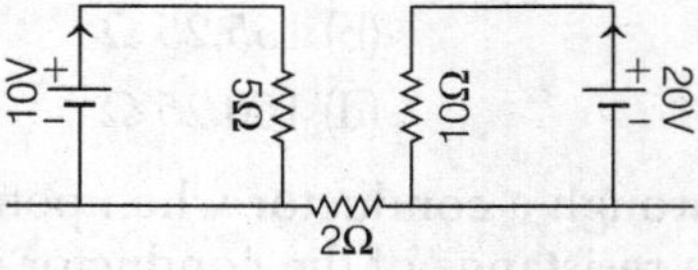

(a) 5 A ☐ (b) 2 A ☐ (c) 0 A ☐ (d) 4 A ☐

(iv) The value fo current i is

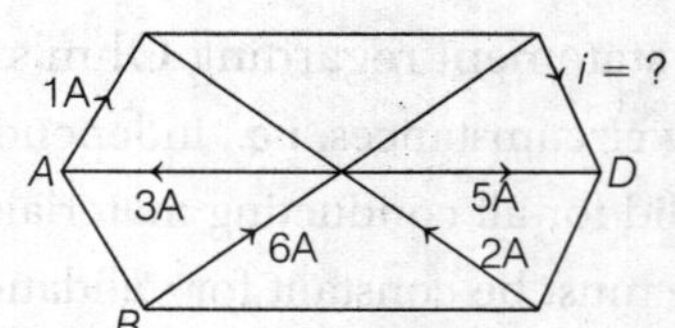

(a) 2 A ☐ (b) 3 A ☐ (c) 1 A ☐ (d) 5 A ☐

COMPETITION EDGE UP

1. Water boils in an electric kettle in 20 min after being switched on. Using the same main supply, the length of the heating element should be _______ to _________ times of its initial length if the water is to be boiled in 15 min.

[NCERT Pg. 92, JEE Main 2024]

(a) increased, 3/4 ☐
(b) decreased, 4/3 ☐
(c) decreased, 3/4 ☐
(d) increased, 4/3 ☐

2. The number of electrons flowing per second in the filament of a 110 W bulb operating at 220 V is (Given, $e = 1.6 \times 10^{-19}$ C)

[NCERT Pg. 92, JEE Main 2024]

(a) 1.25×10^{19} ☐
(b) 6.25×10^{17} ☐
(c) 31.25×10^{17} ☐
(d) 6.25×10^{18} ☐

3. An electric bulb rated 50 W-200 V is connected across a 100V supply. The power dissipation of the bulb is

[NCERT Pg. 92, JEE Main 2024]

(a) 50 W ☐ (b) 100 W ☐
(c) 25 W ☐ (d) 12.5 W ☐

4. The reading in the ideal voltmeter (V) shown in the given circuit diagram is

[NCERT Pg. 95, JEE Main 2024]

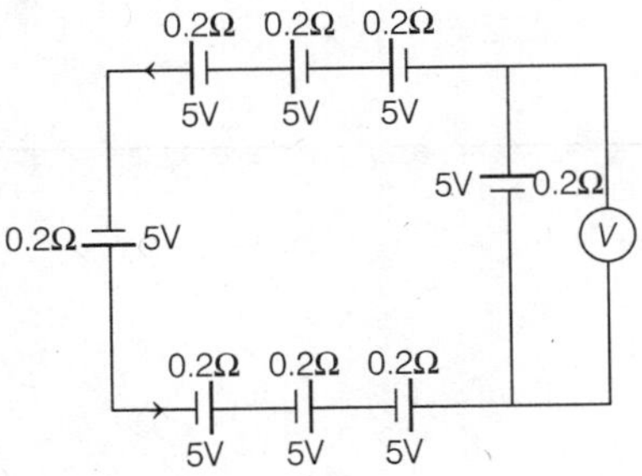

(a) 10 V ☐
(b) 0 V ☐
(c) 5 V ☐
(d) 3 V ☐

5. By what percentage will the illumination of the lamp decrease, if the current drops by 20%?

[NCERT Pg. 92, JEE Main 2024]

(a) 26% ☐ (b) 46% ☐
(c) 36% ☐ (d) 56% ☐

6. Wheatstone bridge principle is used to measure the specific resistance S_1 of given wire, having length L, radius r. If X is the resistance of wire, then specific resistance is, $S_1 = X\left(\frac{\pi r^2}{L}\right)$. If the length of the wire gets doubled then the value of specific resistance will be

[NCERT Pg. 100, JEE Main 2024]

(a) $\frac{S_1}{4}$ ☐ (b) $2S_1$ ☐
(c) S_1 ☐ (d) $\frac{S_1}{2}$ ☐

7. The terminal voltage of the battery, whose emf is 10 V and internal resistance 1Ω when connected through an external resistance of 4 Ω as shown in the figure is

[NCERT Pg. 94, NEET 2024]

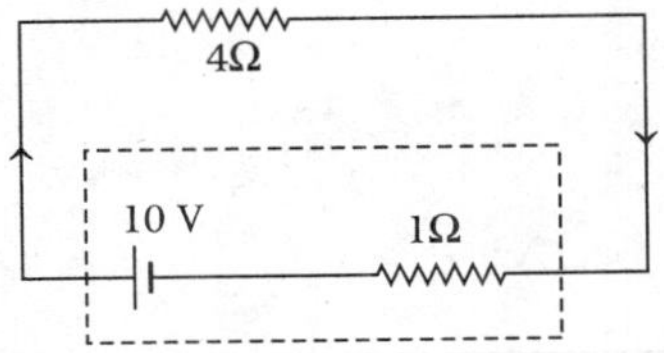

(a) 4 V ☐
(b) 6 V ☐
(c) 8 V ☐
(d) 10 V ☐

8. Two heaters A and B have power rating of 1 kW and 2 kW, respectively. Those two are first connected in series and then in parallel to a fixed power source. The ratio of power outputs for these two cases is **[NCERT Pg. 92, NEET 2024]**

(a) 1 : 1 ☐ (b) 2 : 9 ☐
(c) 1 : 2 ☐ (d) 2 : 3 ☐

9. The resistance of platinum wire at 0°C is 2 Ω and 6.8 Ω at 80°C. The temperature coefficient of resistance of the wire is **[NCERT Pg. 90, NEET 2023]**

(a) 3×10^{-3} °C^{-1} ☐
(b) 3×10^{-2} °C^{-1} ☐
(c) 3×10^{-1} °C^{-1} ☐
(d) 3×10^{-4} °C^{-1} ☐

10. If the galvanometer G does not show any deflection in the circuit shown, the value of R is given by **[NCERT Pg. 98, NEET 2023]**

400 Ω, G, 10 V, R, 2 V

(a) 50 Ω ☐
(b) 100 Ω ☐
(c) 400 Ω ☐
(d) 200 Ω ☐

11. The magnitude and direction of the current in the following circuit is **[NCERT Pg. 98, NEET 2023]**

A, 2Ω, 10 V, E, 5 V, 1Ω, B, D, 7Ω, C

(a) 0.5 A from A to B through E ☐
(b) 5/9 A from A to B through E ☐
(c) 1.5 A from B to A through E ☐
(d) 0.2 A from B to A through E ☐

12. A copper wire of length 10m and radius $(10^{-2}/\sqrt{\pi})$ m has electrical resistance of 10 Ω. The current density in the wire for an electric field strength of 10(V/m) is **[NCERT Pg. 86, NEET 2022]**

(a) 10^4 A/m² ☐
(b) 10^6 A/m² ☐
(c) 10^{-5} A/m² ☐
(d) 10^5 A/m² ☐

Chapter 4

Moving Charges and Magnetism

Scan and take Chapter Test

TOPIC 1 Magnetic Force

NCERT Pg 108-111

1. A proton enters a magnetic field of flux density 1.5 Wbm^{-2} with a velocity of 2×10^7 ms^{-1} at an angle of 30° with the field. The force on the proton will be

(a) 2.4×10^{-12} N ☐
(b) 0.24×10^{-12} N ☐
(c) 24×10^{-12} N ☐
(d) 0.024×10^{-12} N ☐

2. When an electron is kept in a strong magnetic field, then electron moves in opposite direction of applied magnetic field .

True ☐ False ☐

3. In the given figure, if we adjust the value of E and B in such a way that the magnitudes of two forces are equal, then what will be the total force on the charge?

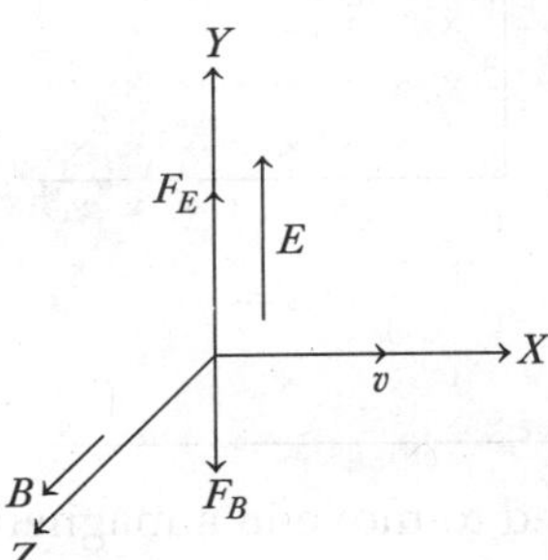

____

4. **Statement I** Just as static charges produce an electric field, the currents or moving charges also produce a magnetic field.
Statement II The magnetic field has several basic properties identical to electric field.

*Concepts of all questions bearing * are important for JEE/NEET/CUET.*

It is defined at each point in space.
Which of the following statement(s) is/are correct?

(a) Only statement I ☐
(b) Only statement II ☐
(c) Both statements I and II ☐
(d) Neither statement I nor II ☐

5. The magnitude of magnetic force per unit length on a wire carrying a current of 8 A and making an angle of 30° with the direction of a uniform magnetic field of 0.15 T is 0.6 Nm^{-1}.

Yes ☐ No ☐

6. A straight wire of mass 200 g and length 1.5 m carries a current of 2A. It is suspended in mid air by a uniform horizontal magnetic field B as shown below. The magnitude of the magnetic field will be xT. What is the value of x here?

***7.** If the magnetic field is parallel to the positive Y-axis and the charged particle is moving along the positive X-axis as shown below, then in which direction, the Lorentz force will act
(i) for an electron
(ii) and for a positive charge (proton)?

***8.** If a charged particle is allowed to move in a magnetic field and the magnetic force is perpendicular to the velocity of the particle, then no work is done and no change in the magnitude of the velocity is produced.

True ☐ False ☐

TOPIC 2

Motion in a Magnetic Field

9. If the velocity of particle moving in a uniform magnetic field is perpendicular to B, then the perpendicular force will act as ____________ (centripetal/centrifugal) force and the particle produces a ____________ (linear/circular) motion ____________ (parallel/perpendicular) to the magnetic field.

10. In a uniform magnetic field, if the velocity of the particle has a component along B, will the motion of the particle along the magnetic field be affected by the magnetic field?

Yes ☐ No ☐

11. What kind of path will the motion of particle describe when the velocity of the particle has a component along B ?

____

***12.** A particle is moving in a uniform magnetic field, describing a circular path of radius r. If the force of mv^2/r acts perpendicular to the path towards the centre of circle, velocity v is perpendicular to B and the magnetic force is perpendicular to both v and B, then which one of the following relation is correct?

(a) $\frac{mv^2}{r} = Bqv$ ☐ (b) $mv^2 r = \frac{Bq}{v}$ ☐ (c) $\frac{mv^2}{r} = \frac{Bq}{v}$ ☐ (d) $mv^2 r = Bqv$ ☐

13. If the momentum of the charged particle will be larger in a magnetic field, then the circle described by the particle will be ____________ (bigger/smaller).

14. Ionised hydrogen atoms and α-particles with same momenta enters perpendicular to a constant magnetic field B. The ratio of radii of their paths $r_H : r_\alpha$ will be

(a) 1 : 2 ☐ (b) 4 : 1 ☐ (c) 1 : 4 ☐ (d) 2 : 1 ☐

15. A proton, a deuteron and an α-particle enter a region of perpendicular magnetic field (to their velocities) with same kinetic energy. If r_p, r_d and r_α are the radii of circular paths of these particles, then find the relation between them.

____

***16.** If there is a component of the velocity parallel to the magnetic field, then it will make the particle move along the field and the path of the particle would be a helical one as shown below.

Match the quantities in Column I with the relation in Column II.

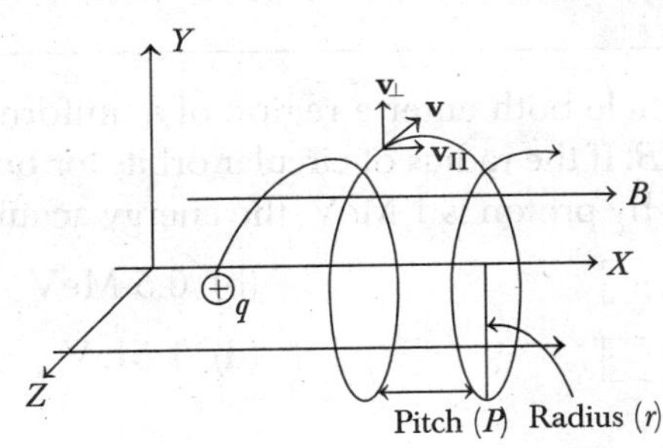

Column I	Column II
A. $v_\perp$	1. $\frac{mv_\perp}{qB}$
B. $v_{\parallel}$	2. $2\pi mv_{\parallel} / qB$
C. Pitch (P)	3. P/T
D. Radius (r)	4. $\frac{Bqr}{m}$

A. ________ B. ________ C. ________ D. ________

17. If an electron with mass 9×10^{-31} kg and charge 1.6×10^{-19} C is moving at a speed of $3 \times 10^7 \text{ ms}^{-1}$ in a magnetic field of 6×10^{-4} T perpendicular to it, then find
(i) the radius of the path of an electron,
(ii) its frequency and
(iii) its energy.

***18.** An electron of mass 0.90×10^{-30} kg under the action of magnetic field moves in a circle of 2.0 cm radius at a speed of $3.0 \times 10^6 \text{ ms}^{-1}$. If a proton of mass 1.8×10^{-27} kg was to move in a circle of the same radius in the same magnetic field, then its speed will be

(a) $3 \times 10^6 \text{ ms}^{-1}$ ☐ (b) $1.5 \times 10^3 \text{ ms}^{-1}$ ☐
(c) $6.0 \times 10^4 \text{ ms}^{-1}$ ☐ (d) Cannot be estimated ☐

19. If the total force on the charge will be zero, then the charge will move in the fields ________ (deflected/undeflected).

20. Ratio of charges on positron to mass of positron (in C kg^{-1}) is approximately

(a) $+2 \times 10^{11}$ ☐ (b) $+5 \times 10^{12}$ ☐
(c) -2×10^{11} ☐ (d) -5×10^{11} ☐

21. An electron is moving in a circular path under the influence of a transverse magnetic field of 3.57×10^{-2} T. If the value of e/m is $1.76 \times 10^{11} \text{ C kg}^{-1}$, the frequency of revolution of the electron is

(a) 1 GHz ☐ (b) 100 MHz ☐
(c) 62.8 MHz ☐ (d) 6.28 MHz ☐

22. A proton of energy 1 MeV describes a circular path in plane at right angles to a uniform magnetic field of 6.28×10^{-4} T. The mass of proton is 1.67×10^{-27} kg. Find the frequency of proton.

***23.** A proton and an α-particle both enter a region of a uniform magnetic field B, moving at right angles to the field B. If the radius of circular orbits for both the particles is equal and the kinetic energy acquired by proton is 1 MeV, the energy acquired by the α-particle will be

(a) 4 MeV ☐ (b) 0.5 MeV ☐
(c) 1.5 MeV ☐ (d) 1 MeV ☐

TOPIC 3

Magnetic Field due to a Current Element, Biot-Savart Law

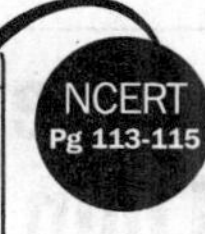

24. Vector form of Biot-Savart's law is

(a) $d\mathbf{B} = \frac{\mu_0}{4\pi} \cdot \frac{I \times d\mathbf{l}}{r^2}$ ☐ (b) $d\mathbf{B} = \frac{Id\mathbf{l} \times \mathbf{r}}{r^3}$ ☐

(c) $d\mathbf{B} = \frac{\mu_0}{4\pi} \cdot \frac{Id\mathbf{l} \times \mathbf{r}}{r^3}$ ☐ (d) $d\mathbf{B} = \frac{\mu_0}{4\pi} \cdot \frac{Id\mathbf{l} \times \mathbf{r}}{r^2}$ ☐

25. A current of i ampere is flowing through each of the bent wires as shown in the figure. The magnitude of magnetic field at O is

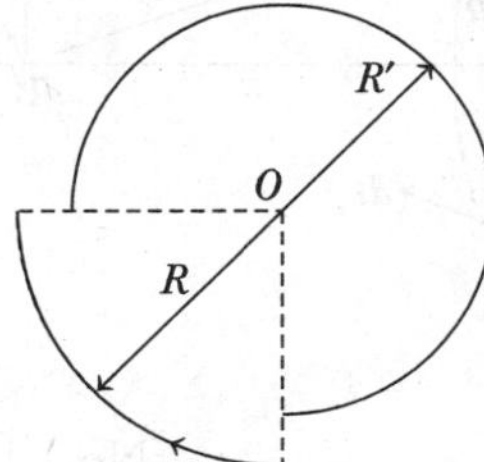

(a) $\frac{\mu_0 i}{4}\left(\frac{1}{R} + \frac{2}{R'}\right)$ ☐ (b) $\frac{\mu_0 i}{4}\left(\frac{1}{R} + \frac{3}{R'}\right)$ ☐

(c) $\frac{\mu_0 i}{8}\left(\frac{1}{R} + \frac{3}{2R'}\right)$ ☐ (d) $\frac{\mu_0 i}{8}\left(\frac{1}{R} + \frac{3}{R'}\right)$ ☐

26. There is a thin conducting wire carrying current. The value of magnetic field induction at any point on the conductor itself is zero.

True ☐ False ☐

27. An element $\Delta\mathbf{l} = \Delta x\hat{\mathbf{i}}$ is placed at the origin and carries a large current $I = 10\text{A}$ as shown in the following figure. What is the magnitude of magnetic field on the Y-axis at a distance of 0.5 m ($\Delta x = 1\text{ cm}$) ?

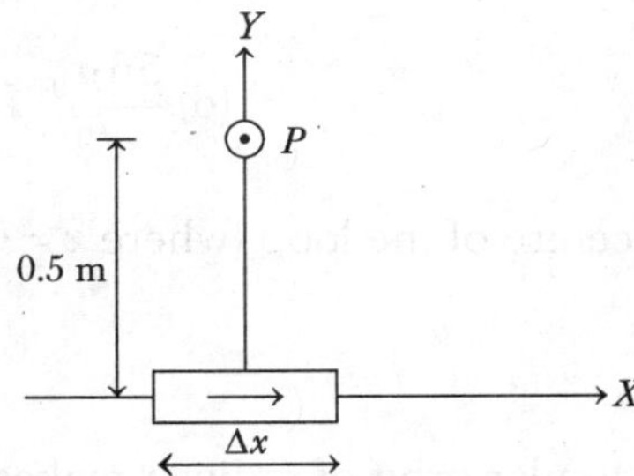

TOPIC 4

Magnetic Field on the Axis of a Circular Current Loop

28. The magnetic field on the axis of a circular current loop is given by

$$d\mathbf{B}_x = \frac{\mu_0 I d\mathbf{l}}{4\pi} \frac{R}{(x^2 + R^2)^{\frac{3}{2}}}.$$

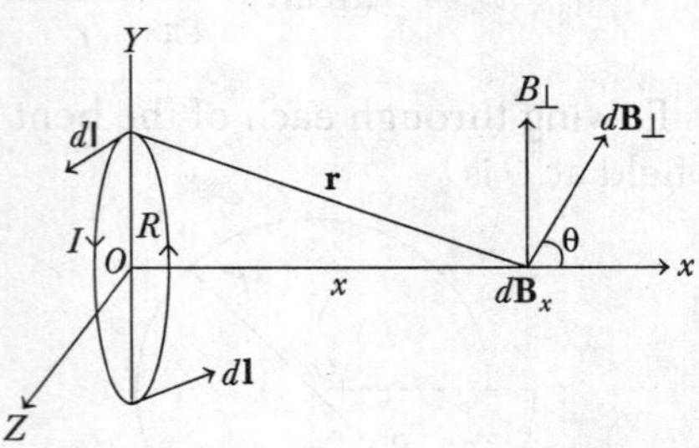

Is the given statement correct?

Yes ☐ No ☐

29. Two circular loops having same radius ($R = 10$ cm) and same current ($I = 7/2$ A) are placed along same axis as shown below. If the distance between their centres is 10 cm, then find net magnetic field at point P.

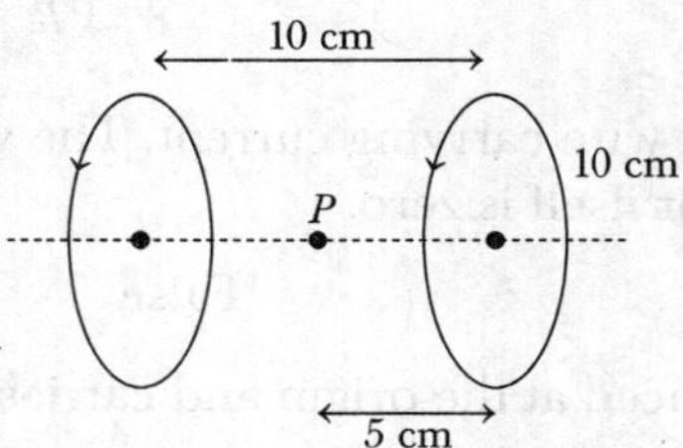

(a) $\frac{50\mu_0}{\sqrt{5}}$ T ☐ (b) $\frac{28\mu_0}{\sqrt{5}}$ T ☐

(c) $\frac{56\mu_0}{\sqrt{5}}$ T ☐ (d) $\frac{56\mu_0}{\sqrt{3}}$ T ☐

30. The magnetic field at the centre of the loop (where $x = 0$) will be given by B_0 = ________ $\left(\frac{\mu_0 I}{2R} / \frac{\mu_0 I}{8R}\right)$.

31. An electron moving in a circular orbit of radius r makes n rotations per second. The magnetic field produced at the centre has magnitude

(a) $\frac{\mu_0 ne}{2\pi r}$ ☐ (b) zero ☐ (c) $\frac{\mu_0 n^2 e}{r}$ ☐ (d) $\frac{\mu_0 ne}{2r}$ ☐

***32.** A straight wire carrying a current of 12 A is bent into a semi-circular arc of radius 2.0 cm as shown in the given figure.

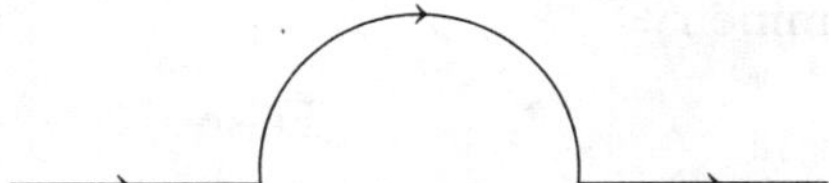

Consider the magnetic field B at the centre of the arc. Answer the following questions.

(i) What is the magnetic field due to the straight segments?

____

(ii) What is difference in the contribution to B from the semi-circle to that of a circular loop?

____

(iii) What will happen, if the wire is bent into a semi-circular arc of the same radius but in opposite way as shown in the figure given below.

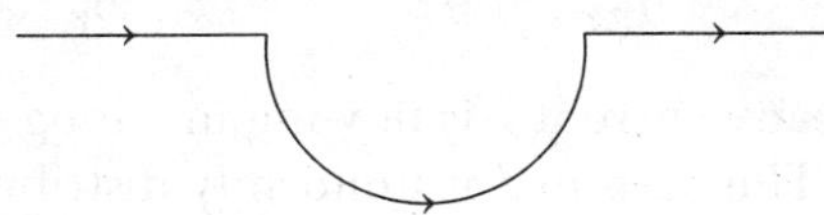

(a) The magnitude of B will remain same but opposite in direction. ☐

(b) The magnitude will become zero. ☐

(c) The magnitude of B will get changed. ☐

(d) None of the above ☐

***33.** Consider a tightly wound 100 turn coil of radius 10 cm, carrying a current of 1 A. The magnitude of the magnetic field at the centre of the coil will be $x \times 10^{-4}$ T. What is the value of x here?

____

TOPIC 5

Ampere's Circuital Law

NCERT Pg 117-120

34. What condition can we assume while choosing an Amperian loop?

(a) At every point on loop, **B** is tangential to the loop and is a non-zero constant B. ☐

(b) At every point on loop, **B** is normal to the loop. ☐

(c) At every point on loop, **B** vanishes. ☐

(d) Anyone of the above ☐

***35.** The magnetic field due to an infinite current-carrying wire at a distance r outside the wire is ________ (parallel/tangential) and given as B = __________ $\left(\frac{\mu_0 I}{2\pi r} / \frac{\mu_0 I}{4\pi r}\right)$.

36. The expression $B = \dfrac{\mu_0 I}{2\pi r}$ implies that the magnetic field at every point on a circle of radius r, (with wire along the axis) is same in magnitude, which means that the magnetic field possesses cylindrical symmetry.

True ☐ False ☐

***37.** The following figure shows a long straight wire of a circular cross-section (radius a) carrying a steady current I. The current I is uniformly distributed across the cross-section. The magnetic field in the region $r > a$ will be

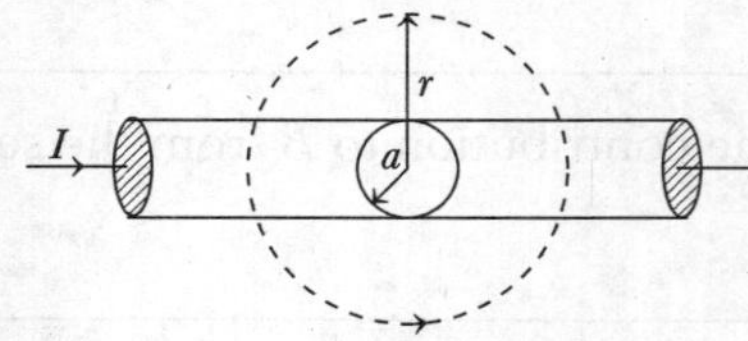

(a) $B = \dfrac{\mu_0 I}{4\pi r}$ ☐ (b) $B = \dfrac{\mu_0 I}{2\pi r}$ ☐ (c) $B = \dfrac{\mu_0 I}{2r}$ ☐ (d) None of these ☐

***38.** In the given figure, a steady current I is flowing in a long straight wire of a circular cross-section (radius a). The current I is uniformly distributed across this cross-section. The value of magnetic field in region $r < a$ will be $\left(\dfrac{\mu_0 I}{x\pi a^2}\right) r$. What is the value of x here?

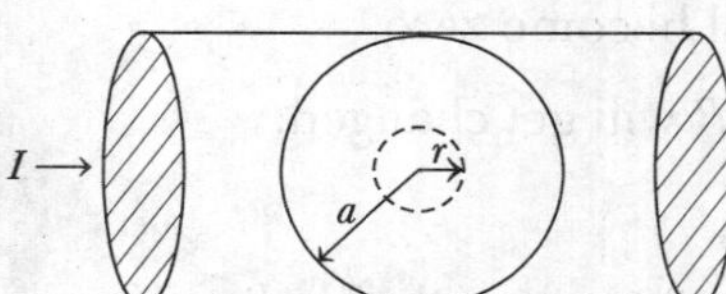

39. A hollow cylinder having infinite length and carrying a uniform current per unit length λ along the circumference as shown in the figure. Magnetic field inside the cylinder is

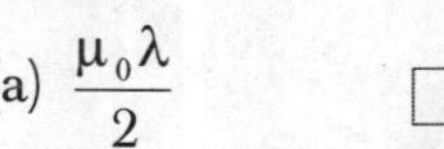

(a) $\dfrac{\mu_0 \lambda}{2}$ ☐ (b) $\mu_0 \lambda$ ☐

(c) $2\mu_0 \lambda$ ☐ (d) None of these ☐

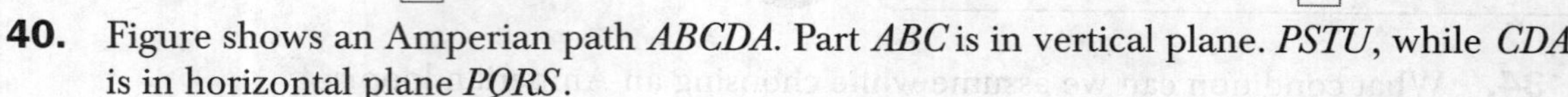

40. Figure shows an Amperian path $ABCDA$. Part ABC is in vertical plane. $PSTU$, while CDA is in horizontal plane $PQRS$.

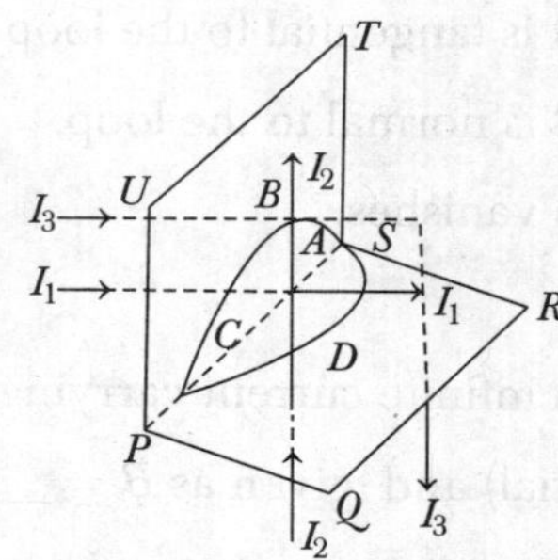

The direction of circulation along the path is shown by an arrow near points B and D. $\oint \mathbf{B} \cdot d\mathbf{l}$ for this path according to Ampere's law will be

(a) $(I_1 - I_2 + I_3)\mu_0$ ☐ (b) $(-I_1 + I_2)\mu_0$ ☐
(c) $I_3 \mu_0$ ☐ (d) $(I_1 + I_2)\mu_0$ ☐

41. A long straight wire of radius a carries a steady current i. The current is uniformly distributed across its cross-section. The ratio of the magnetic field at $a/2$ and $2a$ is

(a) 1/2 ☐ (b) 1/4 ☐ (c) 4 ☐ (c) 1 ☐

42. A current I flows along the length of an infinitely long, straight, thin walled pipe. Then,

(a) the magnetic field at all points inside the pipe is the same, but not zero ☐
(b) the magnetic field is zero only on the axis of the pipe ☐
(c) the magnetic field is different at different points inside the pipe ☐
(d) magnetic field at any point inside the pipe is zero ☐

43. The figure below shows a section of solenoid in an enlarged manner. What is the field between two neighbouring turns?

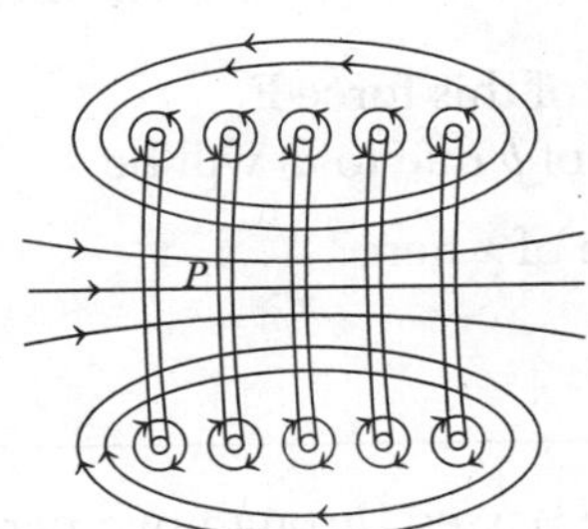

____

44. Consider the given figure and answer the following questions.

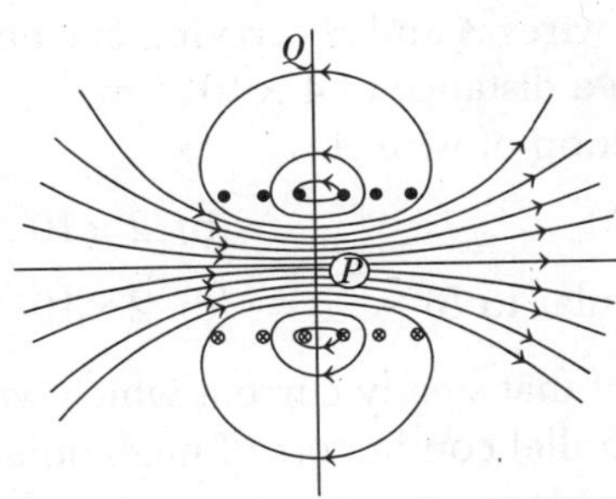

(i) Magnetic field at interior mid-point P is __________ (uniform/non-uniform) and __________ (strong/weak) along the axis of solenoid.

(ii) Is the magnetic field weak at the exterior mid-point Q?

Yes ☐ No ☐

***45.** A long solenoid has 20 turns cm^{-1}. The current necessary to produce a magnetic field of 20 mT inside the solenoid is approximately

(a) 1A ☐ (b) 2 A ☐
(c) 4 A ☐ (d) 8 A ☐

***46.** A solenoid of length 0.5 m has a radius of 1 cm and is made up of 500 turns. It carries a current of 5 A. The magnitude of the magnetic field inside the solenoid will be $x \times 10^{-3}$ T. What is the value of x here?

____

TOPIC 7

Force between Two Parallel Currents, the Ampere

NCERT Pg 122-124

***47.** In the given figure, the conductor b carrying a current I_b experience a sideways force due to the field $\mathbf{B}_a = \frac{\mu_0 I_a}{2\pi d}$. The direction of this force is towards the conductor a. The magnitude of this force $\mathbf{F}_{ba}$ (i.e. the force on segment L of b due to a) will be $\frac{\mu_0 I_a I_b}{x\pi d} \cdot L$. What is the value of x here?

d, a, b, $\mathbf{F}_{ba}$, L, I_a, $\mathbf{B}_a$, I_b

____

48. Currents of 10 A and 2 A are passed through two parallel wires A and B respectively, in opposite directions. If the wire A is infinitely long and length of the wire B is 2 m, then find the force acting on the conductor B which is situated at 10 cm distance from A.

____

***49.** Two long parallel straight wires A and B carrying currents of 4.0 A and 5.0 A in same direction are separated by a distance of 4×10^{-2} m.
The force on a 0.20 m section of wire A is

(a) 2×10^{-5} N (towards B) ☐ (b) 2×10^{-5} N (away from B) ☐
(c) 2×10^{-5} N (perpendicular to B) ☐ (d) 2×10^{-5} N (parallel to B) ☐

50. One ampere is the value of that steady current which when maintained in each of the two very long, straight, parallel conductors of negligible cross-section; placed one metre apart in vacuum, would produce on each of these conductors a force equal to 2×10^{-7} N/m of length.
Is this the correct definition of one ampere?

Yes ☐ No ☐

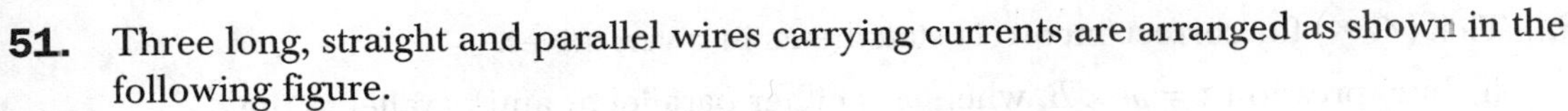

51. Three long, straight and parallel wires carrying currents are arranged as shown in the following figure.

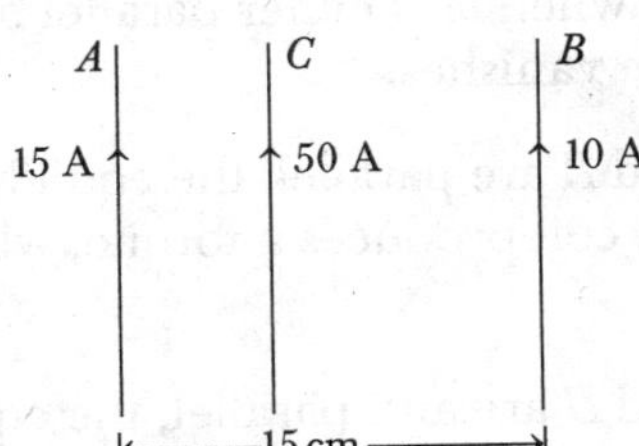

The wire C which carries a current of 50 A is so placed that it experiences no force. Find the distance of wire C from wire A.

____

52. The horizontal component of earth's magnetic field at a certain place is 3×10^{-5} T and the direction of field is from geographic South to the geographic North. A very long straight conductor is carrying a steady current of 1 A.

Answer the following questions, considering the given situation.

(i) What is the force per unit length on it when it is placed on a horizontal table and the direction is from East to West?

(a) 3×10^{-5} Nm^{-1} ☐ (b) 8×10^{-4} Nm^{-1} ☐

(c) 6×10^{-2} Nm^{-1} ☐ (d) 4×10^{-2} Nm^{-1} ☐

(ii) The force per unit length on it, when it is placed on a horizontal table and the direction of current is from South to North, will be x newton. What is the value of x here?

____

TOPIC 8

Torque on Current Loop, Magnetic Dipole

53. A current-carrying square loop is suspended in a uniform magnetic field acting in the plane of the loop. If the force on one arm of the loop is **F**, then the net force on the remaining three arms of the loop is

(a) 3 **F** ☐ (b) –**F** ☐ (c) –3 **F** ☐ (d) **F** ☐

***54.** A square loop with each side 1 cm, carrying a current of 10 A, is placed in a magnetic field of 0.2 T. The direction of magnetic field is parallel to the plane of the loop. The torque experienced by the loop is

(a) zero ☐ (b) 2×10^{-4} Nm ☐ (c) 2×10^{-2} Nm ☐ (d) 2 Nm ☐

55. Area enclosed by a planar loop is 2×10^{-3} m^2. If the loop carries a current of 2 A, then magnitude of magnetic dipole moment of the loop is 4×10^{-3} JT^{-1}.

True ☐ False ☐

56. Tick (✓/✗) for correct/incorrect statements in given boxes.

(i) In expression $\tau = m \times B$, when m is either parallel or anti-parallel to the magnetic field, the torque vanishes. ☐

(ii) In $\tau = m \times B$, when m and B are parallel, the equilibrium is a stable one. Any small rotation of the coil produces a torque, which brings it back to its original position. ☐

(iii) In $\tau = m \times B$, when m and B are anti-parallel, the equilibrium is unstable as any rotation produces a torque which increases with the amount of rotation. ☐

57. A circular coil of 25 turns and radius 12 cm is placed in a uniform magnetic field of 0.5 T normal to the plane of the coil. Is no torque act on it when a current of 6 A flows through it?

Yes ☐ No ☐

58. A 100 turns closely wound circular coil of radius 10 cm carries a current of 3.2 A, then answer the following questions.

(i) What is the magnetic field at the centre of the coil?

____

(ii) What is the magnetic moment of the coil?

____

59. The coil of magnetic moment 10 A-m^2 is placed in a vertical plane and is free to rotate about a horizontal axis which coincides with its diameter. A uniform magnetic field of 2 T in the horizontal direction exists such that initially the axis of the coil is in the direction of field. The coil rotates through an angle of 90° under the influence of the magnetic field.

(i) What are the magnitudes of torques on the coil in the initial and final positions?

____

(ii) What is the angular speed acquired by the coil, when it has rotated by 90°? The moment of inertia of the coil is 0.1 kg-m^2.

____

60. A current-carrying circular loop lies on a smooth horizontal plane. Can a uniform magnetic field be set-up in such a manner that the loop turns around itself?

____

61. A current-carrying circular loop is located in a uniform external magnetic field. If the loop is free to turn, then the orientation of the stable equilibrium will be in the direction of _______________ (external field/internal field).

***62.** The correct expression for calculating magnetic field due to a dipole is $\mathbf{B} = \frac{\mu_0}{4\pi} \cdot \frac{2\mathbf{m}}{x^3}$. It is similar to the expression obtained for the electric field of a dipole. Which of the following is the incorrect match for substitution ?

(a) $\mu_0 \rightarrow \varepsilon_0$ ☐ (b) $\mathbf{m} \rightarrow \mathbf{P}_e$ ☐

(c) $\mathbf{B} \rightarrow \mathbf{E}$ ☐ (d) None of these ☐

TOPIC 9

The Moving Coil Galvanometer

NCERT Pg 129-132

***63.** A galvanometer of resistance 70 Ω is converted into an ammeter by a shunt resistance $r_s = 0.03\ \Omega$. The value of its resistance will become

(a) 0.025 Ω ☐ (b) 0.022 Ω ☐
(c) 0.035 Ω ☐ (d) 0.030 Ω ☐

64. To overcome the large value of current in the circuit, a small resistance called ________ (series/shunt) resistance is connected in parallel with the galvanometer coil, so that most of the current passes through the ____________ (series/shunt).

***65.** Which instrument is shown in the given figures?

I. 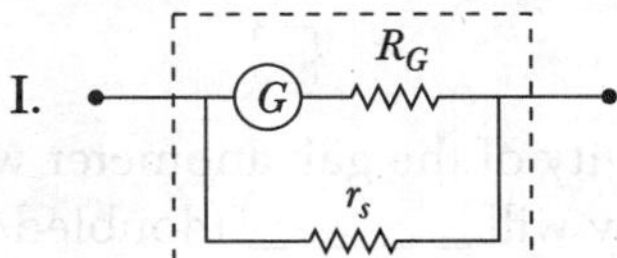

II. 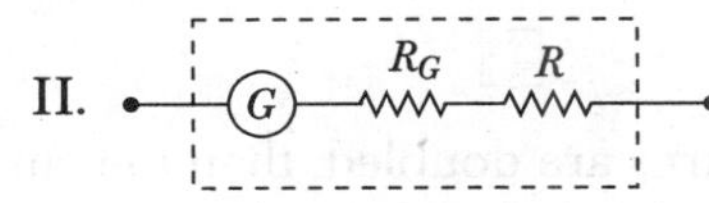

____

66. The following figure shows the construction details of a moving coil galvanometer.

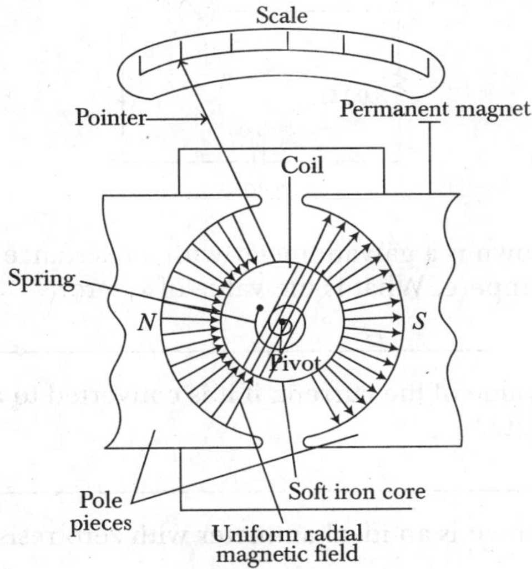

Match the part in Column I with its function in Column II.

Column I	Column II
A. Soft iron core	1. produces deflecting torque
B. Pole pieces	2. produces restoring torque
C. Spring	3. produces radial field
D. Coil	4. increases field strength

A. ______________ B. ______________ C. ______________ D. ______________

***67.** A galvanometer of 50 Ω resistance has 25 divisions. A current of 4×10^{-4} A gives a deflection of one division. To convert this galvanometer into a voltmeter having a range of 25 V, it should be connected with a resistance of

(a) 2500 Ω as a shunt ☐ (b) 245 Ω as a shunt ☐

(c) 2550 Ω in series ☐ (d) 2450 Ω in series ☐

68. The coil of a galvanometer consists of 100 turns and effective area of 1 cm^2. The restoring couple is 10^{-8} N- m rad^{-1}. The magnetic field between poles is of 5 T. What is the current sensitivity of this galvanometer?

____

***69.** Current sensitivity of a moving coil galvanometer is 5 div/mA and its voltage sensitivity (angular deflection per unit voltage applied) is 20 div/V. The resistance of the galvanometer is

(a) 250 Ω ☐ (b) 25 Ω ☐

(c) 40 Ω ☐ (d) 500 Ω ☐

70. If number of turns are doubled, then the current sensitivity of the galvanometer will be ________ (doubled /halved) and the voltage sensitivity will ________ (doubled/remain same).

***71.** In the given figure, the current is to be measured.

(i) If the ammeter shown is a galvanometer with a resistance $R_G = 60\,\Omega$, then the value of current will be x ampere. What is the value of x here?

____

(ii) What will be the value of the current, if it is converted to an ammeter by a shunt resistance $r_s = 0.02\Omega$?

____

(iii) If the ammeter shown is an ideal ammeter with zero resistance, then its value will be ________ (1/2) A .

Assertion-Reason Questions

Direction (Q. Nos. 1-10) *In the following questions, a statement of Assertion is followed by a corresponding statement of Reason. From the following options, choose the correct one.*

(a) Both Assertion and Reason are correct and Reason is the correct explanation of Assertion.
(b) Both Assertion and Reason are correct but Reason is not the correct explanation of Assertion.
(c) Assertion is correct but Reason is incorrect.
(d) Assertion is incorrect but Reason is correct.

***1.** **Assertion** (A) The vector product $q(\mathbf{v} \times \mathbf{B})$ makes the force due to magnetic field zero, if velocity and magnetic field are parallel or anti-parallel.
Reason (R) The force acts in a (sideways) direction perpendicular to both velocity and the magnetic field.

(a) ☐ (b) ☐ (c) ☐ (d) ☐

***2.** **Assertion** (A) Force experienced by moving charge will be maximum, if direction of velocity of charged particle is parallel to applied magnetic field.
Reason (R) Force on moving charge depends on the direction of applied magnetic field.

(a) ☐ (b) ☐ (c) ☐ (d) ☐

3. **Assertion** (A) A magnetic field interacts with a moving charge and not with a stationary charge.
Reason (R) A moving charge produce a magnetic field.

(a) ☐ (b) ☐ (c) ☐ (d) ☐

4. **Assertion** (A) When observation point lies along the length of the current element, magnetic field is zero.
Reason (R) Magnetic field close to current element is zero.

(a) ☐ (b) ☐ (c) ☐ (d) ☐

***5.** **Assertion** (A) The lines of constant magnitude of magnetic form concentric circles.
Reason (R) The direction of field at any point on circle is tangential to it.

(a) ☐ (b) ☐ (c) ☐ (d) ☐

6. **Assertion** (A) For a point on the axis of a circular coil carrying current, magnetic field is maximum at the centre of the coil.
Reason (R) Magnetic field produced by circular current loop does not depend on the distance of point from the circular coil.

(a) ☐ (b) ☐ (c) ☐ (d) ☐

7. **Assertion** (A) A solenoid tends to contract when current passes through it.
Reason (R) Two straight parallel metallic wires carrying current in same direction repel each other.

(a) ☐ (b) ☐ (c) ☐ (d) ☐

8. **Assertion** (A) The magnetic field at the ends of a very long current-carrying solenoid is half of that at the centre.
Reason (R) If the solenoid is sufficient long, the field within it is uniform.

(a) ☐ (b) ☐ (c) ☐ (d) ☐

9. **Assertion (A)** No net force acts on a rectangular coil carrying a steady current when suspended freely in a uniform magnetic field.
Reason (R) Forces acting on each pair of the opposite sides of the coil are equal and opposite.

(a) ☐ (b) ☐ (c) ☐ (d) ☐

10. **Assertion** (A) If we increase the current sensitivity of a galvanometer by increasing number of turns, its voltage sensitivity also increases.
Reason (R) Resistance of a wire also increases with N.

(a) ☐ (b) ☐ (c) ☐ (d) ☐

Case Based Questions

1. Ampere's law gives a method to calculate the magnetic field due to given current distribution. According to it, the circulation $\oint \mathbf{B} \cdot d\mathbf{l}$ of the resultant magnetic field along a closed plane curve is equal to μ_0 times the total current crossing the area bounded by the closed curve provided the electric field inside the loop remains constant. Ampere's law is more useful under certain symmetrical conditions. Consider one such case of a long straight wire with circular cross-section (radius R) carrying current I uniformly distributed across this cross-section.

(i) If two infinitely long wires, carrying currents 30 A and 10 A respectively are placed along X and Y-axes. The equation of zero magnetic field points will be

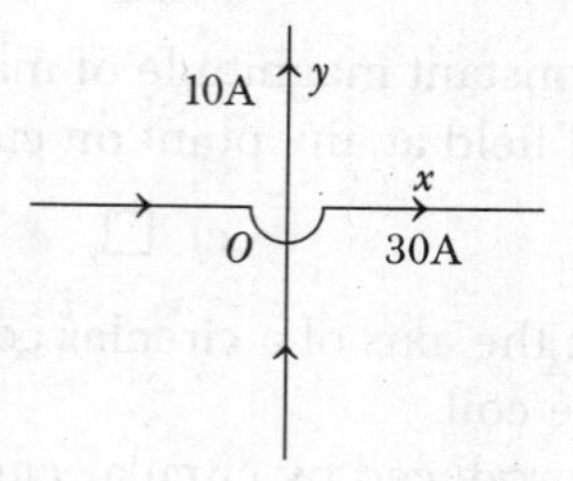

(a) $y = 3x$ ☐ (b) $y = -3x$ ☐

(c) $x = 3y$ ☐ (d) $x = -3y$ ☐

(ii) A long straight wire of a circular cross-section of radius a carries a steady current I and the current I is uniformly distributed across the cross-section. Which of the following plot represents the variation of magnitude of magnetic field B with distance r from the centre of the wire?

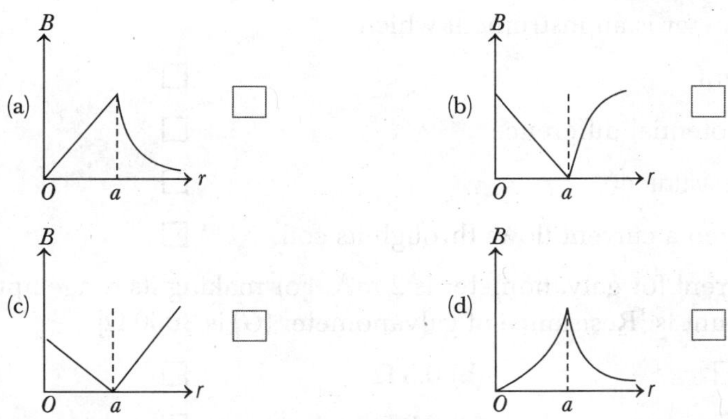

(iii) Rule used to determine the direction of magnetic field due to a long wire is

(a) right hand thumb rule ☐

(b) left hand thumb rule ☐

(c) Fleming's right hand rule ☐

(d) Fleming's left hand rule ☐

(iv) A long wire carrying a certain current produces a magnetic field of 0.8 T at a distance 0.5 cm, then magnetic field at a distance of 1 cm is

(a) 0.16 T ☐ (b) 0.2 T ☐

(c) 0.8 T ☐ (d) 0.4 T ☐

2. Moving coil galvanometer operates on Permanent Magnet Moving Coil (PMMC) mechanism and was designed by the scientist D'arsonval.
Moving coil galvanometers are of two types

I. Suspended coil

II. Pivoted coil type or tangent galvanometer

Its working is based on the fact that when a current-carrying coil is placed in a magnetic field, it experiences a torque. This torque tends to rotate the coil about its axis of suspension in such a way that the magnetic flux passing through the coil is maximum.

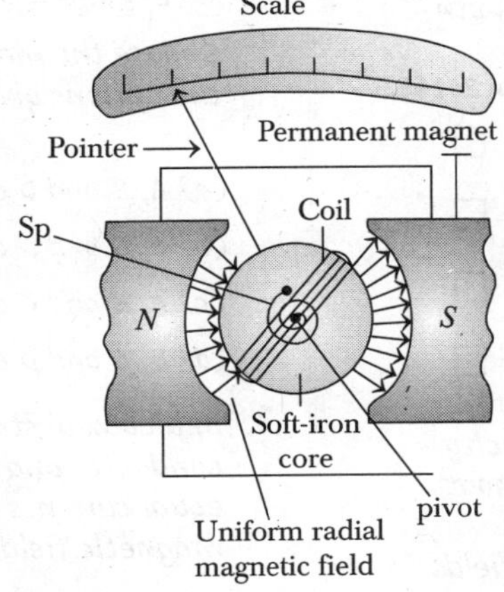

(i) A moving coil galvanometer is an instrument which

(a) is used to measure emf ☐

(b) is used to measure potential difference ☐

(c) is used to measure resistance ☐

(d) gives a deflection when a current flows through its coil ☐

(ii) Full scale deflection current for galvanometer is 2 mA. For making its range upto 30 A, the required value of shunt is [Resistance of galvanometer (G) is 3000 Ω]

(a) 0.1 Ω ☐ (b) 0.3 Ω ☐

(c) 0.4 Ω ☐ (d) 0.2 Ω ☐

(iii) The sensitivity of a moving coil galvanometer can be increased by

(a) decreasing the number of turns in the coil ☐

(b) decreasing the strength of magnetic field ☐

(c) decreasing the area of the coil ☐

(d) decreasing the value of torsional constant ☐

(iv) To convert a galvanometer into an ammeter, one should connect

(a) high resistance in series with galvanometer ☐

(b) low resistance in series with galvanometer ☐

(c) low resistance in parallel with galvanometer ☐

(d) None of the above ☐

COMPETITION EDGE UP

1. *The electrostatic force* $\mathbf{F}_1$ *and magnetic force* $\mathbf{F}_2$ *acting on a charge q moving with velocity v can be written*

[NCERT Pg. 109, JEE Main 2024]

(a) $\mathbf{F}_1 = q\mathbf{E}, \mathbf{F}_2 = q(\mathbf{B} \times \mathbf{v})$ ☐

(b) $\mathbf{F}_1 = q\mathbf{v}, \mathbf{E} \cdot \mathbf{F}_2 = q(\mathbf{B} \cdot \mathbf{v})$ ☐

(c) $\mathbf{F}_1 = q\mathbf{E}, \mathbf{F}_2 = q(\mathbf{v} \times \mathbf{B})$ ☐

(d) $\mathbf{F}_1 = q\mathbf{B}, \mathbf{F}_2 = q(\mathbf{B} \times \mathbf{v})$ ☐

2. *A proton moving with a constant velocity passes through a region of space without any change in its velocity. If E and B represent the electric and magnetic fields respectively, then the region of space may have*

A. $E = 0, B = 0$ B. $E = 0, B \neq 0$

C. $E \neq 0, B = 0$ D. $E \neq 0, B \neq 0$

Choose the most appropriate answer from the options given below.

[NCERT Pg. 109, JEE Main 2024]

(a) A, B and D only ☐

(b) A, C and D only ☐

(c) A, B and C only ☐

(d) B, C and D only ☐

3. *In a coaxial straight cable, the central conductor and the outer conductor carry equal currents in opposite directions. The magnetic field is zero*

[NCERT Pg. 117, JEE Main 2024]

(a) outside the cable ☐
(b) in between the two conductors ☐
(c) inside the inner conductor ☐
(d) inside the outer conductor ☐

4. A uniform magnetic field of 2×10^{-3} T acts along positive y-direction. A rectangular loop of sides 20 cm and 10 cm with current of 5A is in YZ-plane. The current is in anti-clockwise sense with reference to negative X-axis. Magnitude and direction of the torque is **[NCERT Pg. 124, JEE Main 2024]**

(a) 2×10^{-4} N-m along positive z-direction ☐
(b) 2×10^{-4} N-m along negative z-direction ☐
(c) 2×10^{-4} N-m along positive x-direction ☐
(d) 2×10^{-4} N-m along positive y-direction ☐

5. A current of 200 μA deflects the coil of a moving coil galvanometer through 60°. The current to cause deflection through $\pi/10$ rad is **[NCERT Pg. 129, JEE Main 2024]**

(a) 180 μA ☐ (b) 120 μA ☐
(c) 30 μA ☐ (d) 60 μA ☐

6. A galvanometer has a coil of resistance 200 Ω with a full scale deflection at 20 μA. The value of resistance to be added to use it as an ammeter of range 0-20 mA is **[NCERT Pg. 129, JEE Main 2024]**

(a) 0.40 Ω ☐ (b) 0.20 Ω ☐
(c) 0.50 Ω ☐ (d) 0.10 Ω ☐

7. A galvanometer of resistance 100 Ω when connected in series with 400 Ω measures a voltage of upto 10 V. The value of resistance required to convert the galvanometer into ammeter to read upto 10 A is $x \times 10^{-2}$ Ω. The value of x is **[NCERT Pg. 129, JEE Main 2024]**

(a) 800 ☐ (b) 20 ☐
(c) 2 ☐ (d) 200 ☐

8. A tightly wound 100 turns coil of radius 10 cm carries a current of 7 A. The magnitude of the magnetic field at the centre of the coil is (Take, permeability of free space as $4\pi \times 10^{-7}$ SI units) **[NCERT Pg. 116, NEET 2024]**

(a) 44 mT ☐ (b) 4.4 T ☐
(c) 4.4 mT ☐ (d) 44 T ☐

9. A wire carrying a current I along the positive X-axis has length L. It is kept in a magnetic field $\mathbf{B} = (2\hat{i} + 3\hat{j} - 4\hat{k})$ T. The magnitude of the magnetic force acting on the wire is **[NCERT Pg. 128, NEET 2023]**

(a) $\sqrt{5}$ IL ☐ (b) 5 IL ☐
(c) $\sqrt{3}$ IL ☐ (d) 3 IL ☐

10. A long solenoid of radius 1 mm has 100 turns per mm. If 1A current flows in the solenoid, the magnetic field strength at the centre of the solenoid is **[NCERT Pg. 122, NEET 2022]**

(a) 12.56×10^{-2} T ☐
(b) 12.56×10^{-4} T ☐
(c) 6.28×10^{-4} T ☐
(d) 6.28×10^{-2} T ☐

11. From Ampere's circuital law for a long straight wire of circular cross-section carrying a steady current, the variation of magnetic field in the inside and outside region of the wire is **[NCERT Pg. 118, NEET 2022]**

(a) a linearly increasing function of distance upto the boundary of the wire and then linearly decreasing for the outside region. ☐
(b) a linearly increasing function of distance r upto the boundary of the wire and then decreasing one with 1 / r dependence for the outside region. ☐
(c) a linearly decreasing function of distance upto the boundary of the wire and then a linearly increasing one for the outside region. ☐
(d) uniform and remains constant for both the regions. ☐

12. In the product $\mathbf{F} = q(\mathbf{v} \times \mathbf{B})$

$= q\mathbf{v} \times (B\hat{i} + B\hat{j} + B_0\hat{k})$

For $q = 1$ and $\mathbf{v} = 2\hat{i} + 4\hat{j} + 6\hat{k}$

and $\mathbf{F} = 4\hat{i} - 20\hat{j} + 12\hat{k}$

What will be the complete expression for $\mathbf{B}$? **[NCERT Pg. 109, NEET 2021]**

(a) $-8\hat{i} - 8\hat{j} - 6\hat{k}$ ☐
(b) $-6\hat{i} - 6\hat{j} - 8\hat{k}$ ☐
(c) $8\hat{i} + 8\hat{j} - 6\hat{k}$ ☐
(d) $6\hat{i} + 6\hat{j} - 8\hat{k}$ ☐

Chapter 5

Magnetism and Matter

TOPIC 1

The Bar Magnet and Gauss's Law

1. The magnetic field due to a bar magnet is given in the figure. Which point denotes a Gaussian surface?

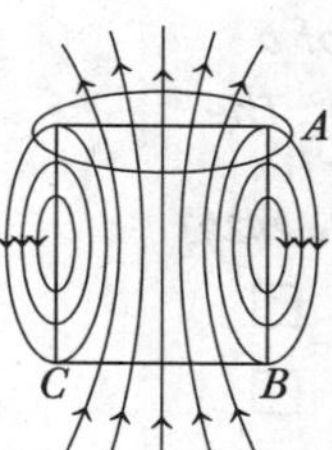

---

2. Arrange the magnetic field lines (A, B, C) in the increasing order of their magnitude of magnetic field.

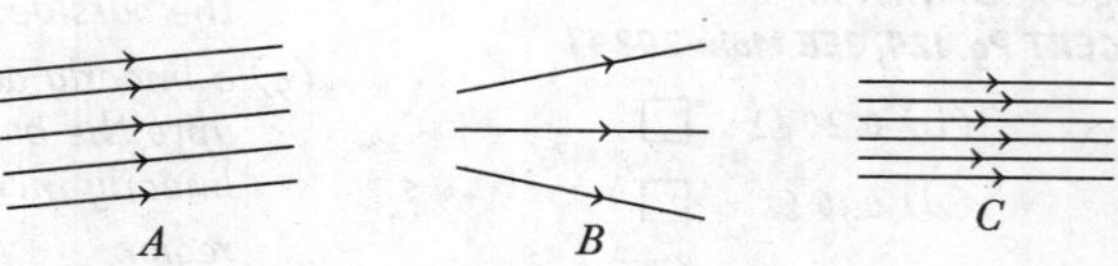

---

3. At the point of intersection of two magnetic field lines, the magnetic needle will align in two directions periodically.

True ☐ False ☐

4. The ratio of strength of North pole to the strength of South pole in a magnet is

(a) 1 : 1 ☐ (b) 1 : 2 ☐ (c) 2 : 1 ☐ (d) 2 : 3 ☐

5. Two magnets have the same length and the same pole strength as shown below.

N S

N S

Hole

*Concepts of all questions bearing * are important for JEE/NEET/CUET.*

Do both the magnets have same magnetic moment?

Yes ☐ No ☐

6. The area of cross-section of three magnets of same lengths are A, $2A$ and $6A$ respectively, then what will be the ratio of their magnetic moments?

____

7. Rate of change of torque τ with deflection θ is maximum for a magnet suspended freely in a uniform magnetic field of induction B. What will be the value of θ in this case?

____

8. Suppose a magnetic needle is oscillating inside a magnetic field. If I denotes the moment of inertia of coil needle, then angular frequency is given by ____________ $\left(\sqrt{\frac{mB}{I}} / \sqrt{\frac{mI}{B}}\right)$.

***9.** A bar magnet suspended freely in a uniform magnetic field is vibrating with a time period of 3s. If the field strength is increased to 4 times of the earlier field strength, then what will be the change in the time period?

____

10. Choose the incorrect statement(s).

(i) Magnetic potential energy is always positive.

(ii) Restoring torque on the magnet placed in a magnetic field is given by $mB \cos \theta$.

(iii) Magnetic field for an oscillating magnetic needle having magnetic moment m and inertia I is given by $B = \frac{4\pi^2 I}{mT^2}$.

(iv) The dipole placed in a magnitude is at stable equilibrium when it makes 180° angle with magnetic field.

____

***11.** Match the following columns, in context when a bar magnet is in influence of magnetic field.

Column I	Column II
A. Maximum torque	1. $\theta = 0°$
B. Unstable equilibrium	2. $\theta = 90°$
C. Stable equilibrium	3. $\theta = 180°$
D. Maximum potential energy	4. mB

A. ________ B. ________ C. ________ D. ________

***12.** A dipole or current-carrying loop is placed in a uniform magnetic field in four different orientations as shown in the following figures. Write the increasing order of potential energy in given figures.

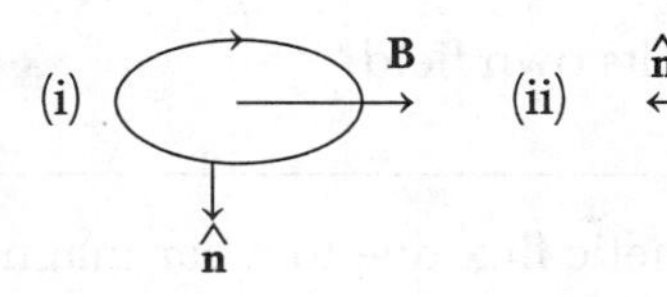

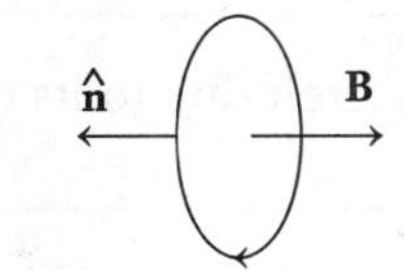

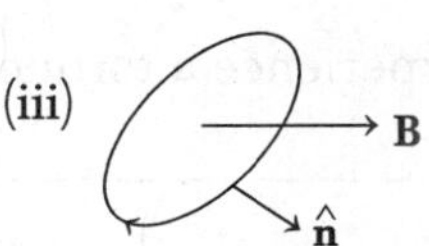

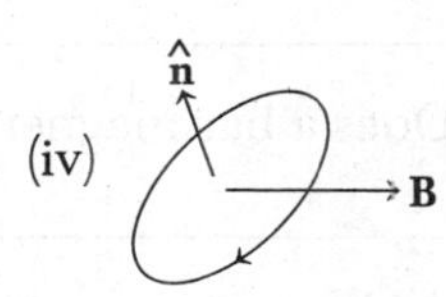

____

13. You have two similar bars A and B. You cut both bars by half and B resist to reunification. Which of the following statement is correct?

(i) Bar B is made of iron (ii) Bar B is magnet

(iii) Bar A is magnet

____

14. In magnetostatics, the ratio of magnetic field on equatorial line and at axial line for a short bar magnet will be ________ (1: 2/2 : 1).

15. A magnetic substance experiences greater magnetic attraction on the axial line of the magnet as compared to the equatorial line of the magnet.

True ☐ False ☐

***16.** Match the physical quantities given in Column I with their respective expression in Column II.

Column I	Column II
A. Magnetic field at axial line of dipole	1. $\mathbf{m} \times \mathbf{B}$
B. Magnetic field at equatorial line of dipole	2. $-\mathbf{m} \cdot \mathbf{B}$
C. Torque acting on a dipole	3. $\dfrac{-\mu_0 m}{4\pi r^3}$
D. Energy in rotating a dipole in a magnetic field	4. $\dfrac{\mu_0 m}{2\pi r^3}$

A. ________ B. ________ C. ________ D. ________

***17.** Four magnets are placed in a square shape facing their opposite pole to each other. The dipole moment in this case will be

(a) m ☐ (b) $4m$ ☐ (c) zero ☐ (d) $\dfrac{m}{4}$ ☐

18. For which configuration of the corresponding dipoles, the potential energy is lowest?

B

A O C

D

(Arrow represents the direction of magnetic moment and A, B, C, D, O represent magnetic dipoles.)

____

19. Does a bar magnet experience a torque on itself due to its own field?

____

20. A sheet of paper is folded to form a cylinder. The magnetic flux due to a bar magnet placed inside this cylinder is ________ (zero/unity).

TOPIC 2

Magnetisation and Magnetic Intensity

***21.** A paramagnetic substance in the form of a cube with sides 1cm has a magnetic dipole moment of 20×10^{-6} J/T when a magnetic intensity of 60×10^{3} A/m is applied. Its magnetic susceptibility is

(a) 3.3×10^{-4} ☐ (b) 3.3×10^{-2} ☐ (c) 4.3×10^{-2} ☐ (d) 2.3×10^{-2} ☐

22. An iron rod of 0.2 cm^2 cross-sectional area is subjected to a magnetising field of 1200 Am^{-1}. The susceptibility of iron is 599. The permeability will be __________ $(7.5/8) \times 10^{-4}$ TmA^{-1}.

***23.** Magnetic field and magnetic intensity of a material are 1.8 T and 1000 A/m respectively. Find magnetic susceptibility of the material used.

____

24. A solenoid having 1000 turns per metre carries a current 2A in its coil. The magnetic intensity due to this solenoid is __________ (2000/4000)A/m.

25. Magnetic field due to a solenoid is 1 T and magnetic intensity is 2000 Am^{-1}. The magnetic permeability of the material used is

(a) 100 ☐ (b) 200 ☐ (c) 300 ☐ (d) 400 ☐

26. A solenoid of 2000 turns produces a magnetic field of 1 T when magnetic intensity is 2×10^{3} A/m.
Choose the correct statement(s).

I. Magnetisation produced is 8×10^{5} A/m, if core material has 400 magnetic permeability.

II. If 2 A current produces 1 T magnetic field, then 794 A current is needed, if core material is removed to produce same magnetic field.

III. Magnetisation produced becomes double when core material is removed.

____

***27.** The magnetic moment produced in a substance of 1 g is 6×10^{-7} Am^2. If is density is 5 g/cm^3, then the intensity of magnetisation in A/m will be

(a) 8.3×10^{6} ☐ (b) 3.0 ☐ (c) 1.2×10^{-7} ☐ (d) 3×10^{-6} ☐

28. If a small magnet intensity at a distance x in the end on position is 9 gauss, what will be the intensity at a distance $\frac{x}{2}$ on broadside on position?

(a) 9 gauss ☐ (b) 4 gauss ☐
(c) 36 gauss ☐ (d) 4.5 gauss ☐

TOPIC 3

Magnetic Properties of Materials

NCERT Pg 147-149

29. Which of the following figure represents diamagnetic material correctly?

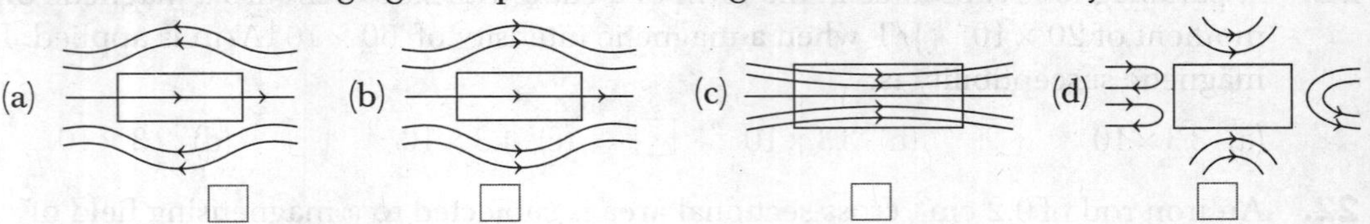

30. The relative permeability of a substance X is slightly less than the unity and that of substance Y is slightly more than the unity. Which type of materials are X and Y?

31. What happens to the magnetisation of a paramagnetic material when absolute temperature decreases?

***32.** As temperature is lowered, magnetisation increases and saturates in paramagnetic materials. It is because

(a) all dipoles are perfectly oriented
(b) magnetic energy becomes maximum
(c) no electron transfer takes place
(d) magnetising intensity decreases

33. The macroscopic volume of dimension 1 nm^3, which is aligned in common direction to produce strong magnetic effect are called ________ (domain/magneton).

COMPETITION CONNECT

Topic 1. Bar Magnet [NCERT (Old) Pg. 176-179]

1. If the bar magnet of magnetic moment 0.40 A-m^2 is replaced by a solenoid of cross-sectional area 2×10^{-4} m^2 and 1000 turns but of the same magnetic moment, then the current flowing through the solenoid is ________ (1A/2A).

2. A bar magnet of length 6 cm is placed in a magnetic field of strength $B = 2 \times 10^{-4}$ T with its axis 45°. If it experiences a torque of 1.6 N-m, then the magnetic moment will be

(a) 1.13×10^4 A-m^2
(b) 1.5×10^5 A-m^2
(c) 2.5×10^4 A-m^2
(d) 0.5×10^4 A-m^2

3. A magnetic needle of magnetic moment 6.7×10^{-2} A-m^2 and moment of inertia 7.5×10^{-6} kg-m^2 is performing simple harmonic oscillations in a magnetic field of 0.01T. Time taken for 10 complete oscillations is

(a) 8.89 s
(b) 6.98 s
(c) 8.76 s
(d) 6.65 s

4. A short bar magnet of magnetic moment $m = 0.32\ \text{JT}^{-1}$ is placed in a uniform magnetic field of 0.15 T. If a bar is free to rotate in the plane of the field, then the potential energy which would corresponds to its unstable equilibrium is

(a) 4.8×10^{-2} J ☐ (b) -4.8×10^{-2} J ☐ (c) 7.5×10^{-2} J ☐ (d) 3.6×10^{5} J ☐

5. When the current is switched ON, a magnetic needle completes one round per second in a toy model. If moment of inertia of needle is 7.5×10^{-6} kg-m^2 and magnetic moment is 6.7×10^{-2} A-m^2, then the correct pair regarding magnetic field for the information provided will be

(a) $+44$ G $\rightarrow$ towards the centre ☐ (b) -44 G $\rightarrow$ towards the centre ☐

(c) $+49$ G $\rightarrow$ outwards from centre ☐ (d) -49 G $\rightarrow$ towards the centre ☐

6. A short bar magnet having dipole moment m is placed with its axis at 30° with uniform magnetic field of 800×10^{-4} T, experiences a torque of 0.016 N-m.

Mark the correct/incorrect (✓/✗) statement.

(i) Work done in bringing the bar magnet from most stable position to most unstable position is 0.064 J. ☐

(ii) Magnetic moment of given magnet is 0.4 A-m^2. ☐

(iii) Maximum torque acting on the magnet is 0.32 J. ☐

(iv) Magnetic moment of given magnet is 0.16 A-m^2. ☐

7. The magnitude of magnetic field at axial line of a bar magnet having magnetic moment 0.40 A-m^2 of length 5.0 cm at a distance of 50 cm from its mid-point is ____________ (6.4/4.6) $\times 10^{-7}$ T.

8. The magnitude of magnetic field strength on axial line of bar magnet at a distance of 0.4 m from its centre having dipole moment 50 A-m is $x \times 10^{-4}$ T. Find the value of x.

____

9. A bar magnet is given below.

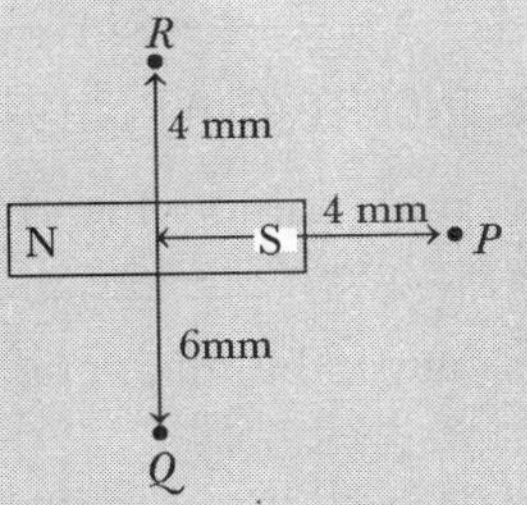

R
4 mm
N S
4 mm
P
6mm
Q

Arrange the magnetic field at points P, Q and R in increasing order.

____

10. The magnetic susceptibility of a paramagnetic substance at −73°C is 0.0060, then its value at −173°C will be

(a) 0.0030 ☐ (b) 0.0120 ☐ (c) 0.0180 ☐ (d) 0.0045 ☐

11. At 280 K, for aluminium, magnetic susceptibility $\chi = 2.4 \times 10^{-5}$ and magnetic intensity H is 2000 Am^{-1}. What will be the magnetisation at 320 K?

____

12. Tick (✓) in front of correct and (✗) in front of incorrect sentences about ferromagnetic substances.

I. In a ferromagnetic substance, magnetic field lines are highly concentrated. ☐

II. In some ferromagnetic materials, magnetisation persists. ☐

III. In ferromagnetic phase, magnetic susceptibility is given by $\chi = \frac{C}{T - T_C}$ $(T > T_C)$. ☐

IV. Ferromagnetic materials are used to make hard magnets. ☐

13. At which temperature, ferromagnet becomes paramagnet ?

____

14. Match the magnetic substances in Column I with the χ-T graphs in Column II.

Column I	Column II
A. Diamagnetic	1. 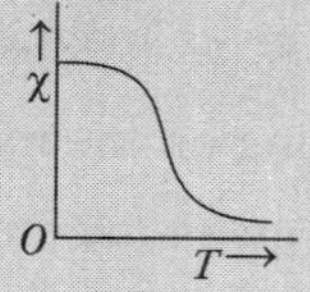 (χ vs T graph)
B. Paramagnetic	2. 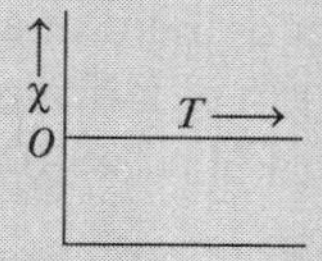 (χ vs T graph)
C. Ferromagnetic	3. 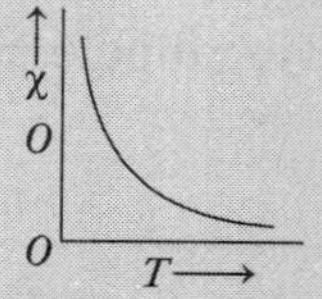 (χ vs T graph)

A. ______________ B. ______________ C. ______________

Topic 2. Magnetic Properties of Materials [NCERT (Old) Pg. 194-196]

15. The property of ferromagnetic material in which magnetic field exist even after reducing the magnetic intensity to zero is called ______________ (retentivity/coercivity).

16. **Assertion** (A) In a hysteresis curve, the magnetic material do not repeat its original initial curve.

Reason (R) For a given value of H, B is not unique but depends on the previous history of sample.

(a) Both A and R are true and R is the correct explanation of A. ☐

(b) Both A and R are true but R is not the correct explanation of A. ☐

(c) A is true but R is false. ☐

(d) A is false but R is true. ☐

17. The figure given below shows the variation of B and H in a magnetic substance.

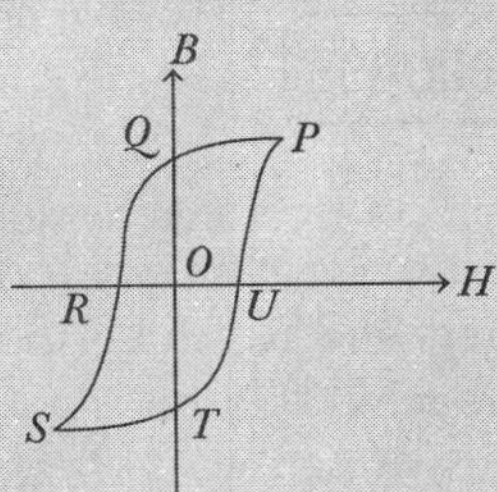

For the substance to be suitable for making a hard magnet,

(a) OQ should be large, OR should be small ☐

(b) OQ and OR both should be large ☐

(c) OS should be large ☐

(d) OU should be small ☐

18. Permanent magnets can be synthesised by placing magnetic materials into solenoid.

True ☐ False ☐

19. ________ (Soft iron/Steel)is used to make permanent magnets because it has high coercivity.

20. Some of the material mentioned below are used for magnetisation purposes. Pick the odd one out on the basis of their uses.

____

21. An electromagnet is made of material that is suitable for magnetisation purposes. Which of the following pair is wrongly matched for the respective properties?

(a) Soft iron → ferromagnetic → high magnetic permeability ☐

(b) Soft iron → diamagnetic → low retentivity ☐

(c) Steel → paramagnetic → high retentivity ☐

(d) Steel → ferromagnetic → high retentivity ☐

22. A solenoid having a soft iron core attains magnetic field, $B = 4\text{T}$ when current, I flows through it. What will be the value of magnetic field B when current through the solenoid is zero?

____

23. Hysteresis curves for two materials are given below.

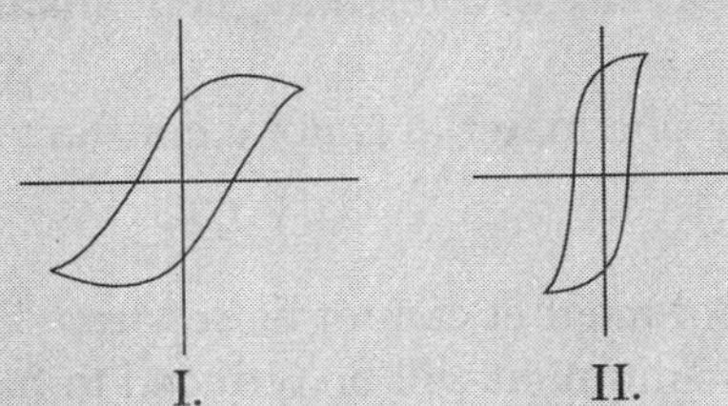

Which of these is suitable for transformer core?

____

Assertion-Reason Questions

Direction (Q. Nos. 1-10) *In the following questions, a statement of Assertion is followed by a corresponding statement of Reason. From the following options, choose the correct one.*

(a) Both Assertion and Reason are correct and Reason is the correct explanation of Assertion.
(b) Both Assertion and Reason are correct but Reason is not the correct explanation of Assertion.
(c) Assertion is correct but Reason is incorrect.
(d) Assertion is incorrect but Reason is correct.

1. **Assertion** (A) A magnetic needle aligns itself along direction of magnetic field when placed near a bar magnet.
Reason (R) In this state/configuration, potential energy is minimum.

(a) ☐ (b) ☐ (c) ☐ (d) ☐

***2.** **Assertion** (A) Ferromagnetic substances are those which gets strongly magnetised when placed in an external magnetic field.

Reason (R) Ferromagnetic substances have strong tendency to move from a region of weak magnetic field to strong magnetic field, i.e. they get strongly attracted to a magnet.

(a) ☐ (b) ☐ (c) ☐ (d) ☐

3. **Assertion** (A) Basic difference between an electric line and magnetic line of force is that former is discontinuous and the latter is continuous or endless.
Reason (R) No electric lines of force exist inside a charged body but magnetic lines do exist inside a magnet.

(a) ☐ (b) ☐ (c) ☐ (d) ☐

4. **Assertion** (A) Paramagnetic substances get poorly attracted in magnetic field.

Reason (R) Because magnetic dipoles are weakly aligned along external magnetic field.

(a) ☐ (b) ☐ (c) ☐ (d) ☐

***5.** **Assertion** (A) A paramagnetic sample displays greater magnetisation when cooled.
Reason (R) The magnetisation does not depend on temperature.

(a) ☐ (b) ☐ (c) ☐ (d) ☐

6. **Assertion** (A) When a magnetic dipole is placed in a non-uniform magnetic field, only a torque acts on the dipole.
Reason (R) Force acts on dipole is zero, if magnetic field were uniform.

(a) ☐ (b) ☐ (c) ☐ (d) ☐

***7.** **Assertion** (A) The permeability of a ferromagnetic material is independent of magnetic field.
Reason (R) Permeability of a material is not a constant quantity.

(a) ☐ (b) ☐ (c) ☐ (d) ☐

8. **Assertion** (A) The poles of magnet cannot be separated by breaking into two pieces.
Reason (R) The magnetic moment will be reduced to half when a magnet is broken into two equal pieces.

(a) ☐ (b) ☐ (c) ☐ (d) ☐

9. **Assertion** (A) Susceptibility is defined as the ratio of intensity of magnetisation M to magnetic intensity H.
Reason (R) Greater the value of susceptibility, smaller is the value of intensity of magnetisation M.

(a) ☐ (b) ☐ (c) ☐ (d) ☐

***10.** **Assertion** (A) For a perfectly diamagnetic substance, permeability is always 1.
Reason (R) The ability of a material to permit the passage of magnetic lines of force through it, is called magnetic permeability.

(a) ☐ (b) ☐ (c) ☐ (d) ☐

Case Based Questions

1. Magnetic materials are broadly classified as diamagnetic, paramagnetic and ferromagnetic. For diamagnetic materials, χ is negative and small, and for paramagnetic materials it is positive and small. Ferromagnetic materials have large χ and are characterised by non-linear relation between B and H.

(i) The magnetic susceptibility is negative for
(a) diamagnetic material only ☐
(b) paramagnetic material only ☐
(c) ferromagnetic material only ☐
(d) paramagnetic and ferromagnetic materials ☐

(ii) The magnetic moment of a diamagnetic atom is
(a) much greater than one ☐
(b) equal to one ☐
(c) between zero and one ☐
(d) equal to zero ☐

(iii) Substance which magnetic susceptibility does not depend on temperature is
(a) diamagnetism ☐ (b) paramagnetism ☐
(c) ferromagnetism ☐ (d) ferrite ☐

(iv) For protecting a magnetic needle, it should be placed in
(a) iron box ☐ (b) wooden box ☐
(c) metallic box ☐ (d) None of these ☐

2. When a ferromagnetic sample is heated, its magnetisation decreases due to increase in the randomisation of its domains. At a sufficiently high temperature, the domain structure disintegrates and the ferromagnetic substance becomes paramagnetic.

(i) Curie temperature is the temperature above which
(a) ferromagnetic material becomes diamagnetic ☐
(b) ferromagnetic material becomes paramagnetic ☐
(c) faramagnetic material becomes diamagnetic ☐
(d) faramagnetic material becomes ferromagnetic ☐

(ii) Nickel shows ferromagnetic property at room temperature. If the temperature is increased beyond curie temperature, then it will show

(a) anti-ferromagnetism ☐ (b) no magnetic property ☐

(c) diamagnetism ☐ (d) paramagnetism ☐

(iii) The susceptibility of ferromagnetic substance is

(a) positive and very large ☐ (b) negative and vergy large ☐

(c) negative and very small ☐ (d) positive and very small ☐

(iv) Ferromagnetic materials in which the magnetisation disappears instant on removal of the external field is

(a) soft iron ☐ (b) alnico ☐

(c) ferrite ☐ (d) Both (b) and (c) ☐

COMPETITION EDGE UP

1. A straight magnetic strip has a magnetic moment of 44 Am^2. If the strip is bent in a semicircular shape, its magnetic moment will be .... Am^2. (Given, $\pi = 22/7$)
[N CERT Pg. 140, JEE Main 2024]

2. The coercivity of a magnet is 5×10^3 A/m.
The amount of current required to be passed in a solenoid of length 30 cm and the number of turns 150, so that the magnet gets demagnetised when inside the solenoid is .... **[NCERT Pg. 138, JEE Main 2024]**

3. Paramagnetic substances
A. align themselves along the directions of external magnetic field.
B. attract strongly towards external magnetic field.
C. has susceptibility little more than zero.
D. move from a region of strong magnetic field to weak magnetic field.
Choose the most appropriate answer from the options given below.
[NCERT Pg. 148, JEE Main 2024]
(a) B, D Only ☐
(b) A, C Only ☐
(c) A, B, C, D ☐
(d) A, B, C Only ☐

4. A coil having 100 turns, area of 5×10^{-3} m^2, carrying current of 1 mA is placed in uniform magnetic field of 0.20 T such a way that plane of coil is perpendicular to the magnetic field. The work done in turning the coil through 90° is .... μJ.
[NCERT Pg. 139, JEE Main 2024]

5. A circular coil having 200 tuns, 2.5×10^{-4} m^2 area and carrying 100 μA current is placed in a uniform magnetic field of IT. Initially the magnetic dipole moment **M** was directed along **B**. Amount of work, required to rotate the coil through 90° from its initial orientation such that **M** becomes perpendicular to **B** is .... μ J.
[NCERT Pg. 139, JEE Main 2024]

6. The magnetic moment of a bar magnet is 0.5 Am^2. It is suspended in a uniform magnetic field of 8×10^{-2} T. The work done in rotating it from its most stable to most unstable position is
[NCERT Pg. 139, JEE Main 2024]
(a) 8×10^{-2} J ☐ (b) 4×10^{-2} J ☐
(c) 16×10^{-2} J ☐ (d) zero ☐

7. Match List-I with List-II.

	List-I (Material)		List-II (Susceptibility (χ))
A	Diamagnetic	I.	$\chi = 0$
B	Ferromagnetic	II.	$0 > \chi \geq -1$
C	Paramagnetic	III.	$\chi >> 1$
D	Non-magnetic	IV.	$0 < \chi < \varepsilon$ (a small positive number)

Choose the correct answer from the options given below. **[NCERT Pg. 147, NEET 2024]**

(a) A → II, B → III, C → IV, D → I

(b) A → II, B → I, C → III, D → IV

(c) A → III, B → II, C → I, D → IV

(d) A → IV, B → III, C → II, D → I

8. An iron bar of length L has magnetic moment M. It is bent at the middle of its length such that the two arms make an angle 60° with each other. The magnetic moment of this new magnet is **[NCERT Pg. 139, NEET 2024]**

(a) M

(b) $\frac{M}{2}$

(c) 2M

(d) $\frac{M}{\sqrt{3}}$

9. The net magnetic flux through any closed surface is **[NCERT Pg. 142, NEET 2023]**

(a) positive

(b) infinity

(c) negative

(d) zero

10. An iron rod of susceptibility 599 is subjected to a magnetising field of 1200 A m^{-1}. The permeability of the material of the rod is (Take, $\mu_0 = 4\pi \times 10^{-7}$ T m A^{-1}) **[NCERT Pg. 146, NEET (Sep.) 2020]**

(a) 8.0×10^{-5} T m A^{-1}

(b) $2.4\pi \times 10^{-5}$ T m A^{-1}

(c) $2.4\pi \times 10^{-7}$ T m A^{-1}

(d) $2.4\pi \times 10^{-4}$ T m A^{-1}

Chapter 6

Electromagnetic Induction

Scan and take Chapter Test

TOPIC 1

The Experiments of Faraday and Henry

1. Name the phenomenon in which electric current is generated by varying magnetic fields.

____

2. Tick (✓/×) for correct/incorrect statement in given boxes.

(i) Induced electric field is a non-conservative field. ☐

(ii) Induced electric field lines always form closed loops. ☐

(iii) When there is no relative motion between a coil and a bar magnet, there will be no induced current in the coil. ☐

☐

3. Arrange the magnitude of induced current in increasing order in given cases , if bar magnet is moving towards stationary coil with different speeds.

I. 2 m/s ← N S II. 4 m/s → N S III. 3 m/s ← S N IV. 5 m/s → N S

____

4. When a current carrying coil is moving towards a stationary coil, current is induced in stationary coil.

Yes ☐ No ☐

5. A constant magnetic field through a coil can induce a current in the coil.

True ☐ False ☐

*Concepts of all questions bearing * are important for JEE/NEET/CUET.*

6. Observe the movement of bar magnet with respect to coil and match the following columns.

Column I	Column II
A. (N S)	1. No current is induced in the coil.
B. (N S ←)	2. Number of field lines through the loop increases.
C. (N S →)	3. Number of field lines through the loop decreases.

A. ________ B. ________ C. ________

TOPIC 2
Magnetic Flux

NCERT Pg 156-157

7. A long solenoid of diameter 0.1 m has 2×10^4 turns per meter. At the centre of the solenoid, a coil of 100 turns and radius 0.01 m is placed with its axis coinciding with the solenoid axis. The current in the solenoid reduces at a constant rate to 0 A from 4 A in 0.05 s. If the resistance of the coil is $10\pi^2 \Omega$, then the total charge flowing through the coil during this time is

(a) 16 μC ☐ (b) 32 μC ☐ (c) 16π μC ☐ (d) 32π μC ☐

8. In the shown diagram when tapping key is pressed, the flux through the coil C_1 ________ (increases/decreases).

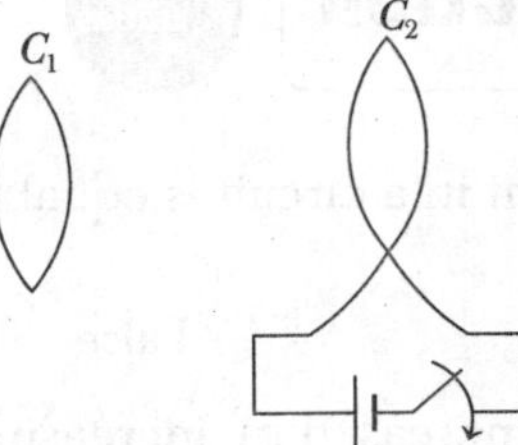

9. Read the analogy and then complete it.
Electric flux : Gauss law : : Magnetic flux : ?

____

***10.** In a region, area vector **A** and magnetic field **B** are given as
$\mathbf{A} = 2\hat{\mathbf{i}} + 3\hat{\mathbf{j}} - 4\hat{\mathbf{k}}$ and $\mathbf{B} = \hat{\mathbf{i}} + \hat{\mathbf{j}} - \hat{\mathbf{k}}$. So, the magnitude of magnetic flux will be

(a) 5 Wb ☐ (b) 1 Wb ☐ (c) 9 Wb ☐ (d) 4 Wb ☐

11. If a coil is placed in uniform magnetic field at some angle, then match the following columns.

Column I	Column II
A. 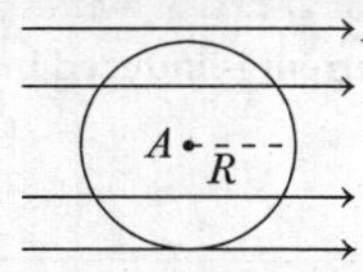 B, A, R	1. Flux through circular loop is BA.
B. R, A, B 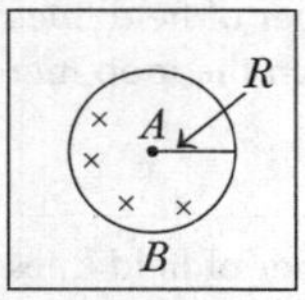	2. Flux through circular loop is $BA \cos 37°$.
C. 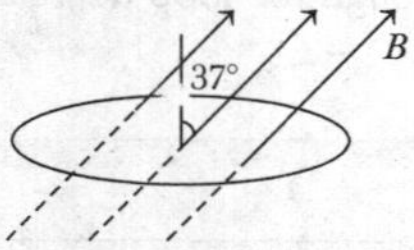 37°, B	3. Flux through circular loop is zero.

A. ________________ B. ________________ C. ________________

***12.** A circular disc of radius 0.2 m is placed in a uniform magnetic field of induction $\frac{1}{\pi}\left(\frac{\text{Wb}}{\text{m}^2}\right)$ in such a way that its axis makes an angle of 60° with **B**. What will be the magnitude of magnetic flux linked with the disc?

____

***13.** A circular coil enclosing an area of 10 cm^2 is placed with its plane making an angle of 30° with the magnetic field of strength 10^4 T. The value of magnetic flux associated with coil is 5 Wb.

True ☐ False ☐

TOPIC 3
Faraday's Law of Induction

NCERT Pg 157-159

14. The magnitude of induced emf in a circuit is equal to the time rate change of magnetic flux through the circuit.

True ☐ False ☐

15. Induced emf in a coil can be increased by increasing number of turns.

Yes ☐ No ☐

16. A vertical metallic pole falls down through the plane of the magnetic meridian. Will any emf be induced between its ends?

Yes ☐ No ☐

17. A wire loop is rotated in a magnetic field. The frequency of change of direction of the induced emf is

(a) once per revolution ☐
(b) twice per revolution ☐
(c) four times per revolution ☐
(d) six times per revolution ☐

18. The total charge induced in a conducting loop when it is moved in magnetic field depends on

(a) the rate of change of magnetic flux ☐ (b) initial magnetic flux ☐

(c) the total change in magnetic flux ☐ (d) final magnetic flux ☐

19. Identify the case in which bulb will glow.

(a) 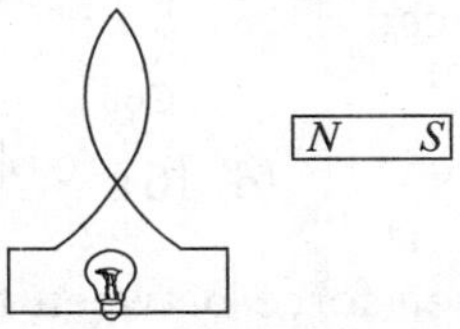 N S ☐ (b) 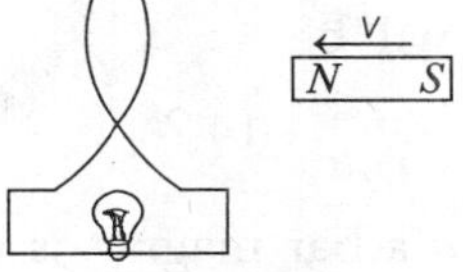 V N S ☐

(c) 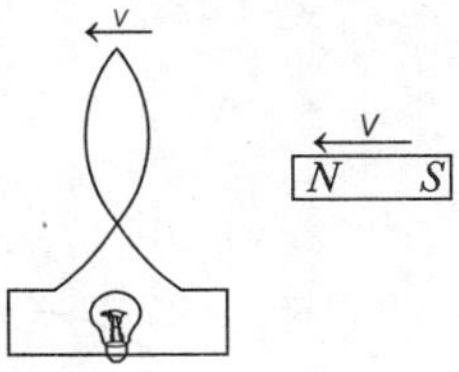 V V N S ☐ (d) 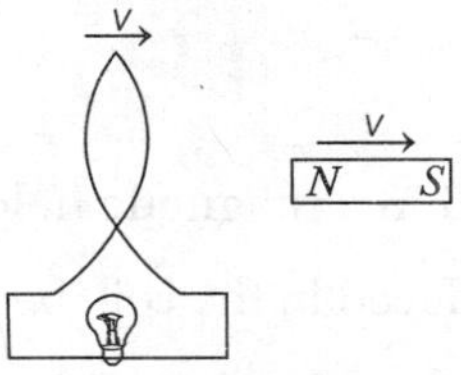 V V N S ☐

20. The magnetic flux linked with a coil satisfies the relation $\phi = (4t^2 + 6t + 9)$ Wb, where t is the time in seconds. The emf induced in the coil at $t = 2$ s is _______ (22/44)V.

***21.** A uniform magnetic field of 0.2 T is set-up perpendicular to the plane of coil of square shape having side 20 cm. If magnetic field becomes zero in 0.5 s at a steady state, then calculate the value of induced emf.

____

22. A field of 4×10^{-2} T is acting perpendicular to the coil of area 10^{-2}m^2 having 100 turns. What will be the time required to remove the coil, if the average value of induced emf is 0.2 V ?

____

23. A circular coil of radius 2 cm is placed perpendicular to a magnetic field of 6×10^3 T. If the induced emf is 44 V when the magnetic field is changed to 10^3 T in 4 s, then the number of turns in the coil is

(a) 14 ☐ (b) 21 ☐ (c) 28 ☐ (d) 35 ☐

24. The magnetic flux through a coil perpendicular to the plane is varying according to the relation ($\phi = 2t^2 - 3t + 4$) Wb. The value of induced current through the coil after 1s is found to be 1 A, if the resistance of the coil is 1 Ω.

Yes ☐ No ☐

***25.** A square coil of length 10 cm, 200 turns and resistance 2 Ω is placed in uniform magnetic field of 10^{-3} T. The plane of coil is perpendicular to magnetic field. If field becomes zero in 1 ms, the induced current in the coil is

(a) 1A ☐ (b) 10 μA ☐ (c) 10 A ☐ (d) 10 nA ☐

26. The magnetic flux linked with a coil at any instant t is given by $\phi = 5t^4 - 100t^2 + 300$, the emf induced in the coil at $t = 1$ s is

(a) 200 V ☐ (b) 220 V ☐ (c) 180 V ☐ (d) 160 V ☐

TOPIC 4

Lenz's Law and Conservation of Energy

NCERT Pg 160-162

27. In the following figure, the magnet is moved towards the coil with speed v and induced emf is ε. If magnet and coil recede away from one another each moving with speed $2v$, the induced emf in the coil will be

(a) ε ☐ (b) 2ε ☐ (c) 4ε ☐ (d) $16\,\varepsilon$ ☐

28. If north pole of a bar magnet is moving towards a coil, then force between them will be attractive.

Yes ☐ No ☐

29. A coil is placed in a magnetic field **B** as shown in figure.

A current is induced in the coil, because **B** is

(a) outward and decreasing with time ☐

(b) parallel to the plane of coil and decreasing with time ☐

(c) outward and increasing with time ☐

(d) parallel to the plane of coil and increasing with time ☐

30. The direction of induced current in shown deformed wire is ________ (anti-clockwise/clockwise).

***31.** Predict the direction of induced current and match the following columns.

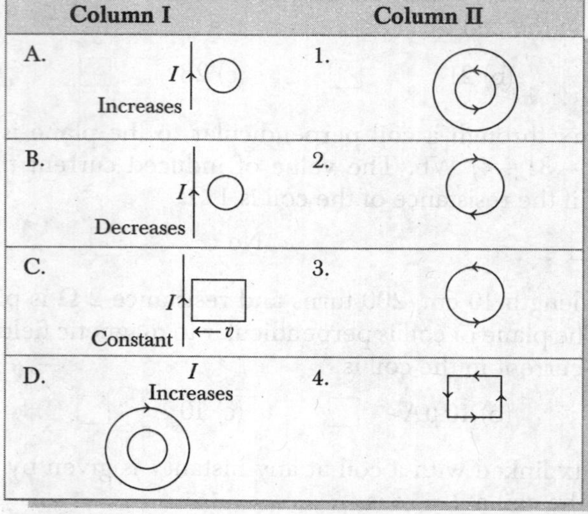

Column I	Column II
A. I Increases	1.
B. I Decreases	2.
C. I Constant v	3.
D. I Increases	4.

A. ________ B. ________ C. ________ D. ________

32. An electron moves on a straight line path *XY* as shown. The *abcd* is a coil adjacent in the path of electron. What will be the direction of current, if any induced in the coil?

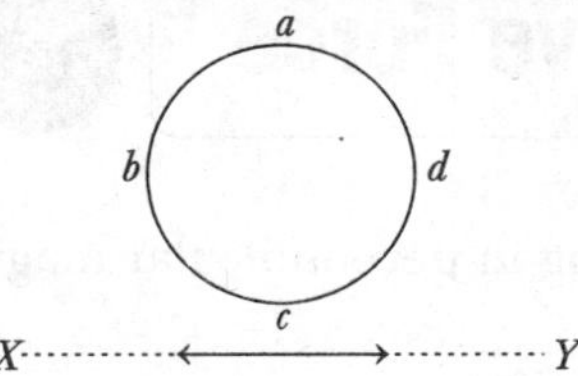

(a) *abcd* ☐

(b) *adcb* ☐

(c) The current will reverse its direction as the electron goes past the coil ☐

(d) No current induced ☐

33. Identify the direction of induced current in the coil and match the following columns.

Column I	Column II
A.	1. No induced current
B.	2. Counter-clockwise
C.	3. Clockwise

A. ________ B. ________ C. ________

34. Which of the following loops results constant induced emf when moving out from a magnetic field region?

(a) Only rectangular loop ☐ (b) Only circular loop ☐

(c) Both (a) and (b) ☐ (d) None of these ☐

35. The polarity on the lower plate of capacitor is

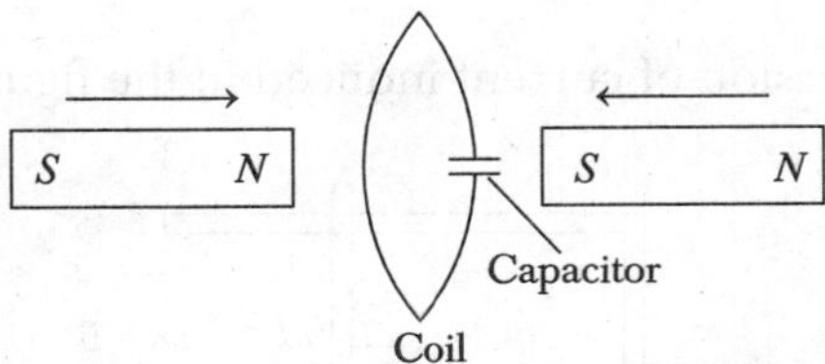

(a) positive ☐ (b) negative ☐

(c) neutral ☐ (d) None of these ☐

TOPIC 5

Motional Electromotive Force

NCERT Pg 162-165

36. If a conducting rod is moving in perpendicular magnetic field, an emf is induced across its ends.

True ☐ False ☐

37. If a metallic rod of length l is moving with speed v perpendicular to magnetic field B. The motional emf in vector form can be written as

(a) $(\mathbf{v} \times \mathbf{B}) \cdot \mathbf{l}$ ☐ (b) $(\mathbf{v} \times \mathbf{B}) \times \mathbf{l}$ ☐

(c) $(\mathbf{v} \cdot \mathbf{B}) \times \mathbf{l}$ ☐ (d) $(\mathbf{v} \cdot \mathbf{B}) \cdot \mathbf{l}$ ☐

38. Due to translatory motion of a straight conductor in perpendicular magnetic field, the induced emf is called ____________ (motional emf/rotational emf).

39. A rod of length 1 m is falling with speed 2 m/s in perpendicular magnetic field of 1 T. The emf induced across the ends of the rod is 2 V.

True ☐ False ☐

40. A conductor of length 0.4 m is moving with a speed of 7 m/s perpendicular to a magnetic field of intensity 0.9 Wb/m^2. Find the induced emf across the conductor.

____

***41.** A bird is flying with speed 2 m/s in earth's magnetic field of 2 μT. If end-to-end length of bird's wings is 2 cm and all three quantities are perpendicular to each other, then emf induced across the wings is $A \times 10^{-8}$ V. Find the value of A.

____

42. A bar magnet of length l is passing through a conducting loop of radius R with velocity v. The radius of the bar magnet is such that it passes through the loop. Draw the emf *versus* l/v graph for the configuration given below.

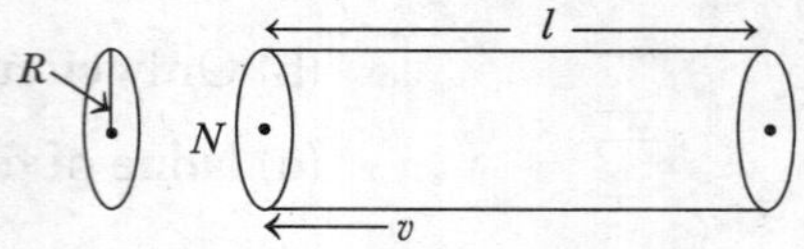

R N S l v

____

***43.** What will be the expression of current induced in the figure given below?

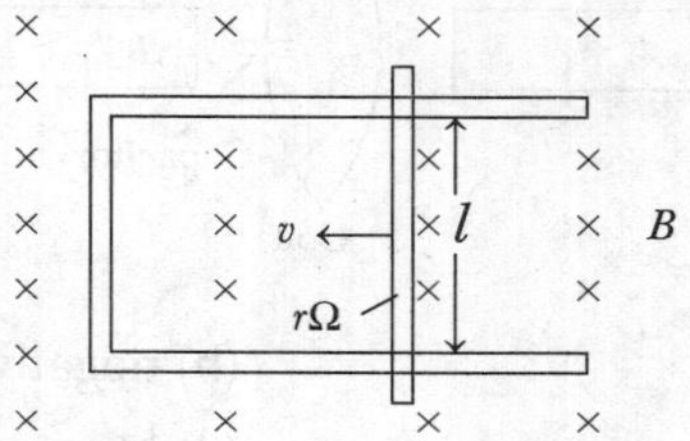

v l B rΩ

____

44. A 10 m long horizontal wire extends from north-east to south-west. It is falling with a speed of 5.0 ms^{-1} at right angles to the horizontal component of the earth's magnetic field of 0.3×10^{-4} Wb/m^2. The value of the induced emf in wire is 1.5×10^{-3} V.

True ☐ False ☐

45. The following figure shows a conducting rod PQ in contact with metal rails RP and SQ, which are 25 cm apart in a uniform field of flux density 0.4 T acting perpendicular to the plane of the paper. Ends R and S are connected through a 5 Ω resistance. If the rod moves to the right with a velocity of 5 ms^{-1}, then find

(i) emf induced, (ii) magnitude of induced current

(iii) direction of induced current through 5 Ω resistor.

***46.** A conducting rod of length l, hinged at one end, is rotating with angular speed ω in uniform magnetic field B. The emf induced in the rod is

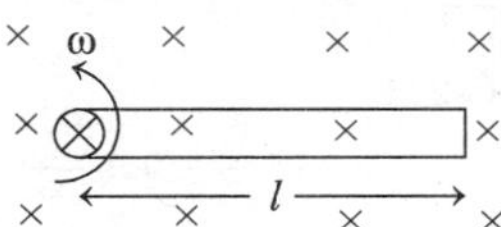

(a) $\frac{B\omega l^2}{2}$ ☐ (b) $\frac{B\omega l^2}{4}$ ☐ (c) $B\omega l$ ☐ (d) $\frac{B^2\omega l}{2}$ ☐

47. A vertical disc of diameter 0.1 m makes 20 rev/s about a horizontal axis passing through its centre. A uniform magnetic field of 0.1 T acts perpendicular to the plane of the disc. The potential difference between its centre and rim is found to be 1.5×10^{x} V. Here, the value of x is ________ (–2 / 4) .

48. A conducting rod of length $2l$ is rotating with angular velocity ω about the centre of rod. A constant magnetic field B is applied perpendicular to the plane of rod.
Match the following columns.

	Column I		Column II
A.	emf across AC is	1.	zero
B.	emf across AE is	2.	$\frac{B\omega l^2}{2}$
C.	emf across BC is	3.	$\frac{3B\omega l^2}{8}$
D.	emf across DE is	4.	$\frac{B\omega l^2}{8}$

A. ________ B. ________ C. ________ D. ________

***49.** In a wheel with 5 metallic spokes each 0.2 m long is rotating with speed 100 rev/min. A constant magnetic field of 10^{-4} T is acting perpendicular to the plane of wheel. The magnitude of induced emf between axle and the rim of wheel is

(a) 2.09×10^{-5} V ☐ (b) 2.09×10^{-3} V ☐

(c) 1.3×10^{-2} V ☐ (d) 1.3×10^{-3} V ☐

50. When a conducting rod of length l, resistance r is sliding on two parallel conducting rails and system is placed in perpendicular magnetic field B, the heat dissipated in rod is $\frac{B^2 l^2 v^2}{r}$.

Yes ☐ No ☐

51. In perpendicular magnetic field of 2 mT, a 0.2 m long conductor having current 40 A is placed. To move the conductor with speed 2 m/s, the power required is

(a) 32 mW ☐ (b) 320 mV ☐

(c) 3.2 mV ☐ (d) 0.32 mW ☐

***52.** A loop is moving according to figure shown below.

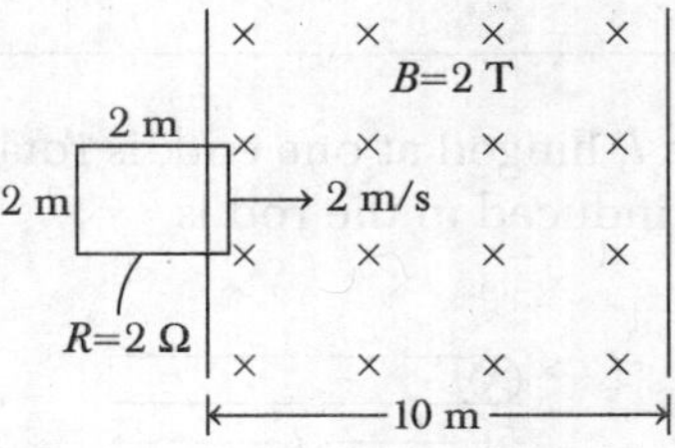

The current-time graph will look like

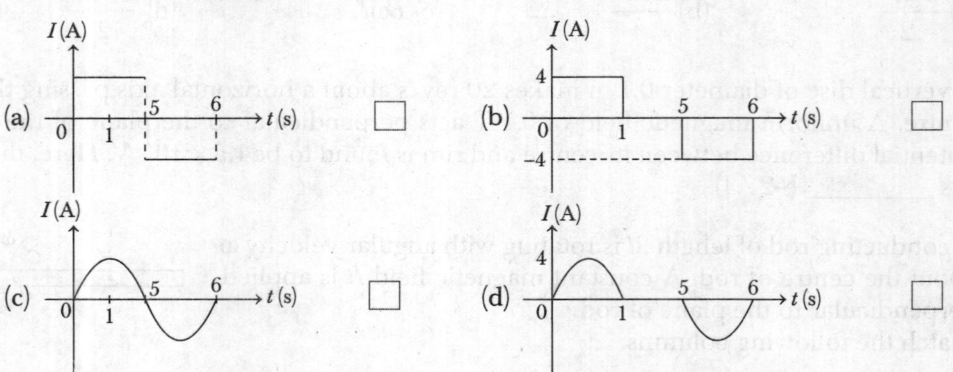

53. A square loop of side a is moving with speed v in perpendicular magnetic field B as shown in figure below.

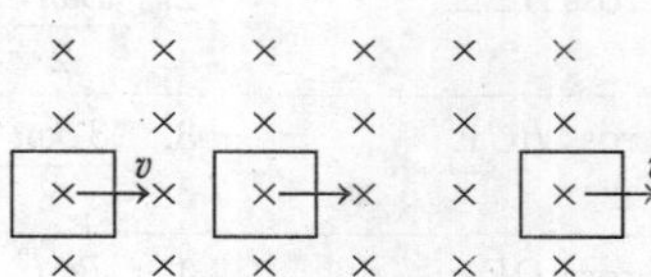

The graph between flux and distance is

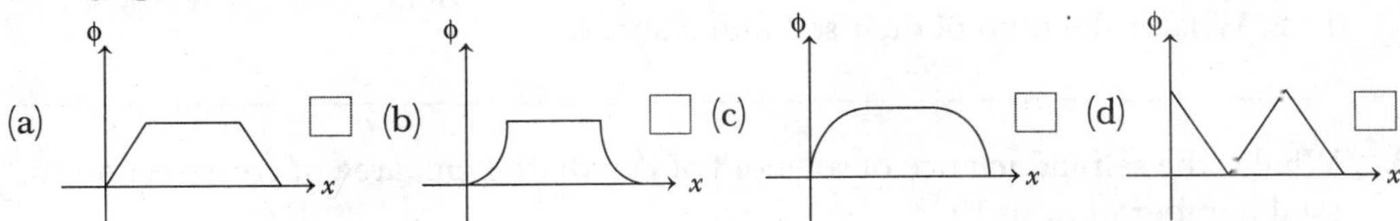

***54.** Two coils of same length are arranged co-axially as shown in the following figure, if radius of inner coil is r_1 and number of turns per unit length is n_1. The radius of outer coil is r_2 with number of turns per unit length n_2. The mutual inductance of the system is

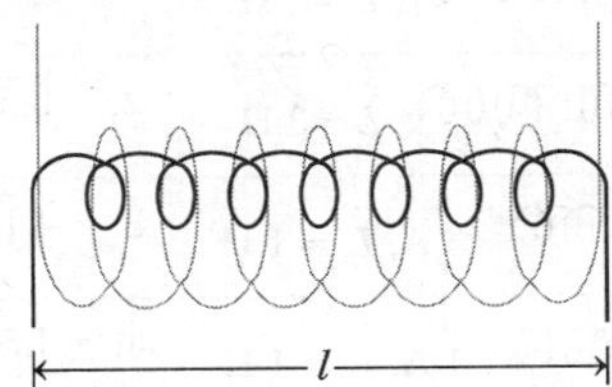

(a) $\mu_0 n_1 n_2 \pi r_1^2 l$ ☐ (b) $\mu_0 n_1 n_2 \pi r_2^2 l$ ☐ (c) $\mu_0 n_1 n_2 r_1^2 l$ ☐ (d) $\mu_0 n_1 r_2 r_2^2 l$ ☐

***55.** A conducting ring of radius r is placed in a varying magnetic field perpendicular to the plane of the ring. If the rate at which the magnetic field varies is x, the electric field intensity at any point of the ring is _______ .

56. Two circular coils are arranged co-axially, one of small radius r_1 and other with r_2, such that $r_1 >> r_2$. Mutual inductance of the coils is proportional to

(a) $\frac{r_1^2}{r_2}$ ☐ (b) $\frac{r_2^2}{r_1}$ ☐ (c) $\frac{r_1}{r_2}$ ☐ (d) $\frac{r_2}{r_1}$ ☐

57. The coefficient of mutual inductance is _______ (4 H/8 H) when magnetic flux changes by 4×10^{-2} Wb and change in current is 10^{-2} A.

58. The current in one coil changes from 5 A to 0 in 0.1 s. If the mutual inductance of pair of coils is 2 H, the emf induced in other coil is

(a) 10 V ☐ (b) 100 V ☐ (c) 0.10 V ☐ (d) 10 mV ☐

***59.** When the current changes from + 2 A to – 2 A in 0.05 s, an emf of 8 V is induced in a coil. The coefficient of self-induction of the coil is

(a) 0.2 H ☐ (b) 0.4 H ☐ (c) 0.8 H ☐ (d) 0.1 H ☐

60. What is the self-inductance of a coil which produces 5 V when the current changes from 3 A to 2 A in 1 ms?

____

***61.** In a solenoid, if number of turns doubled, then self-inductance will increase by _______ times. (2/4)

62. Two solenoids of equal number of turns have their lengths and the radii in the same ratio 1 : 2. What is the ratio of their self-inductances?

___

***63.** What is the self-inductance of solenoid of length 31.4 cm, area of cross-section 10^{-3} m^2 and total number of turns 10^3?

___

64. A 100 mH coil carries a current of 1 A. Energy stored in its magnetic field is ______ (0.5 / 0.05) J.

65. Match the Column I for different inductors of respective current values with the energy stored in them in Column II

	Column I		Column II
A.	2 A, $L = 2$ H	1.	4.5 J
B.	1 A, $L = 3$ H	2.	0.5 J
C.	3 A, $L = 1$ H	3.	4 J
D.	1 A, $L = 1$ H	4.	1.5 J

A. ______ B. ______ C. ______ D. ______

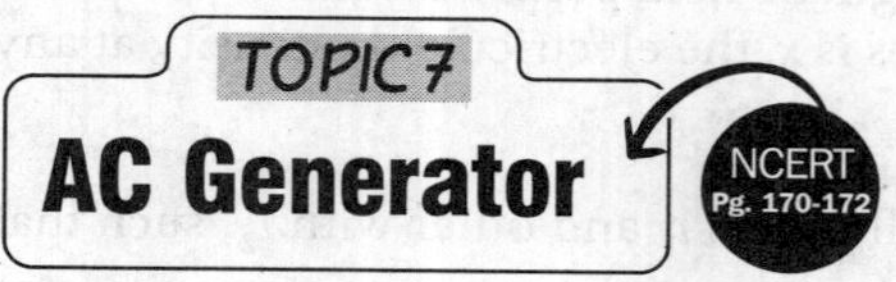

66. Tick the correct expression of instantaneous emf produced in the electric generator.

(i) $NBA \sin \omega t$ ☐ (ii) $E_0 \sin 2\pi \nu t$ ☐

***67.** The variation of emf with time for four types of generators are shown in the figures. Which amongst them can be called AC?

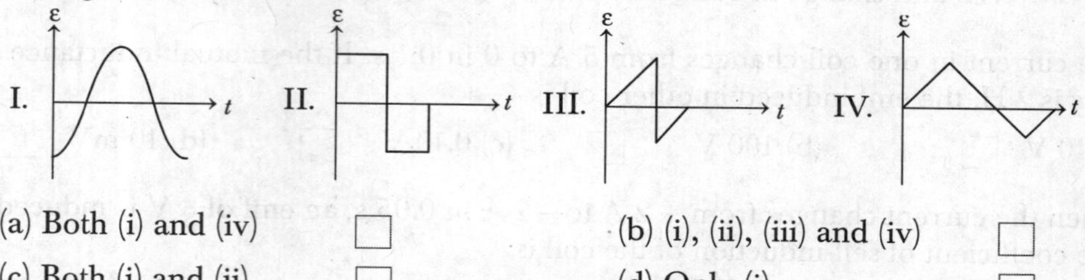

(a) Both (i) and (iv) ☐ (b) (i), (ii), (iii) and (iv) ☐

(c) Both (i) and (ii) ☐ (d) Only (i) ☐

68. Kamla paddles a stationary bicycle, the paddles of the bicycle are attached to a 100 turns coil of area $0.10\ m^2$. The coil rotates at 1/2 rev/s and it is placed in a uniform magnetic field of 0.01 T perpendicular to the axis of rotation of the coil. What is the maximum voltage generated in the coil?

___

COMPETITION CONNECT

Topic Eddy Current [NCERT (Old) Pg. 218-219]

1. Eddy currents are produced when

(a) a metal is kept in varying magnetic field ☐

(b) a metal is kept in steady magnetic field ☐

(c) a circular coil is placed in a magnetic field ☐

(d) current is passed through a circular coil ☐

2. When bulk iron piece is subjected to changing magnetic field, the current induced on the surface of piece is called ______________ (eddy current/direct current).

3. In transformer, eddy currents produce ______ (heat/sound)in the core of transformer.

4. To reduce eddy current, the laminations of metal are separated by using

(a) lacquer ☐ (b) canada balsam ☐

(c) Both (a) and (b) ☐ (d) None of these ☐

5. The plane of the laminations must be arranged parallel to the magnetic field to reduce eddy currents.

True ☐ False ☐

6. A coil is suspended in a uniform magnetic field with the plane of the coil parallel to the magnetic lines of force. When a current is passed through the coil, it starts oscillating; it is very difficult to stop. But, if an aluminium plate is placed near the coil, it stops. This is due to

(a) development of air current when the plate is placed ☐

(b) induction of electrical charge on the plate ☐

(c) shielding of magnetic lines of force as aluminium is a paramagnetic material ☐

(d) electromagnetic induction in the aluminium plate giving rise to electromagnetic damping ☐

7. A bar magnet is dropped in two pipes of same length. One pipe is made up of PVC and other one with aluminium. Through which pipe magnet will take less time?

____

Assertion-Reason Questions

Direction (Q. Nos. 1-10) *In the following questions, a statement of Assertion is followed by a corresponding statement of Reason. From the following options, choose the correct one.*

(a) Both Assertion and Reason are correct and Reason is the correct explanation of Assertion.

(b) Both Assertion and Reason are correct but Reason is not the correct explanation of Assertion.

(c) Assertion is correct but Reason is incorrect.

(d) Assertion is incorrect but Reason is correct.

1. **Assertion** (A) The relative motion between a bar magnet and a coil produces current in the coil.

Reason (R) The magnitude of current depends on resistance of the coil.

(a) ☐ (b) ☐ (c) ☐ (d) ☐

2. **Assertion** (A) A constant magnetic field cannot induce emf in a coil.

Reason (R) Induced emf in a coil is the time rate of change of magnetic flux through the coil.

(a) ☐ (b) ☐ (c) ☐ (d) ☐

***3.** **Assertion** (A) An induced emf of 2 V is developed in a circular loop, if current in the loop is changed at a rate of 4 As^{-1}. If 4 A of current is passed through this loop, then flux linked with this coil will be 2 Wb.

Reason (R) Flux linked with the coil is

$$|\phi| = \left|\frac{e}{di/dt}\right| i$$

(a) ☐ (b) ☐ (c) ☐ (d) ☐

4. **Assertion** (A) The induced emf and current will be same in two identical loops of copper and aluminium when rotated with same speed in the same magnetic field.

Reason (R) Induced emf is proportional to rate of change of magnetic field while induced current depends on resistance of wire.

(a) ☐ (b) ☐ (c) ☐ (d) ☐

5. **Assertion** (A) Induced emf will always occur whenever there is change in magnetic flux.

Reason (R) Current always induces whenever there is change in magnetic flux.

(a) ☐ (b) ☐ (c) ☐ (d) ☐

***6.** **Assertion** (A) Lenz's law violates the principle of conservation of energy.

Reason (R) Induced emf always opposes the change in magnetic flux responsible for its production.

(a) ☐ (b) ☐ (c) ☐ (d) ☐

7. **Assertion** (A) Figure shows a metallic conductor moving in magnetic field. The induced emf across its end is zero.

B, v, l

Reason (R) The induced emf across the ends of a conductor is given by $e = Bvl \sin \theta$.

(a) ☐ (b) ☐ (c) ☐ (d) ☐.

8. **Assertion** (A) To move a rod on two parallel conducting rails with constant speed, mechanical energy is required.

Reason (R) This mechanical energy first converted into electrical energy and then to thermal energy.

(a) ☐ (b) ☐ (c) ☐ (d) ☐

9. **Assertion** (A) If current shown in the figure is increasing, then

$$V_A > V_B$$

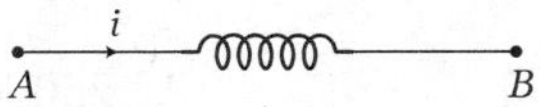

Reason (R) If current passing through an inductor is constant, then both ends of the inductor are at same potential.

(a) ☐ (b) ☐ (c) ☐ (d) ☐

***10.** **Assertion** (A) Mutual inductance of two coils depends on the distance between the coils and their orientation.

Reason (R) It does not depend on the magnetic material filled between the coils.

(a) ☐ (b) ☐ (c) ☐ (d) ☐

Case Based Questions

1. When a current I flows through a coil, flux linked with it is $\phi = LI$, where L is a constant known as self inductance of the coil.

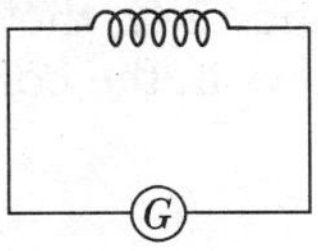

Any change in current sets up an induced emf in the coil. Thus, self inductance of a coil is the induced emf set up in it when the current passing through it changes at the unit rate. It is a measure of the opposition to the growth or decay of current flowing through the coil. Also, value of self inductance depends on the number of turns in the solenoid, its area of cross section and permeability of its core material.

Answer the following questions

(i) The inductance in a coil plays the same role as

(a) inertia in mechanics ☐

(b) energy in mechanics ☐

(c) momentum in mechanics ☐

(d) force in mechanics ☐

Or The unit of self-inductance is

(a) weber-ampere ☐ (b) weber/ampere ☐

(c) ohm-second ☐ (d) farad ☐

(ii) A current of 2.5 A flows through a coil of inductance 5 H. The magnetic flux linked with the coil is

(a) 0.5 Wb ☐ (b) 12.5 Wb ☐
(c) zero ☐ (d) 2 Wb ☐

(iii) The inductance L of a solenoid depends upon its radius R as

(a) $L \propto R$ ☐ (b) $L \propto \frac{1}{R}$ ☐
(c) $L \propto R^2$ ☐ (d) $L \propto R^3$ ☐

(iv) The induced emf in a coil of 10 henry inductance in which current varies from 9 A to 4 A in 0.2s is

(a) 200 V ☐ (b) 250 V ☐
(c) 300 V ☐ (d) 350 V ☐

2. The magnitude of the induced emf in a circuit is equal to the rate of change of magnetic flux through the circuit. Mathematically, Faraday's second law can be expressed as,

Induced emf $\propto$ Rate of change of magnetic flux $e = \frac{-d\phi_B}{dt}$

$$\left[\because \text{rate of change of magnetic flux} = \frac{\phi_2 - \phi_1}{t_2 - t_1}\right]$$

The negative sign in above relation indicates that the induced emf in the loop due to changing flux always opposes the change in the magnetic flux.

Answer the following questions

(i) The direction of induced emf during electromagnetic induction is given by

(a) Faraday's law ☐ (b) Lenz's law ☐
(c) Maxwell's law ☐ (d) Ampere's law ☐

(ii) In a circuit with a coil of resistance 2 Ω, the magnetic flux changes from 2.0 Wb to 10.0 Wb in 0.2 s. The charge that flows in the coil during this time is

(a) 5.0 C ☐ (b) 4.0C ☐
(c) 1.0 C ☐ (d) 0.8 C ☐

(iii) The unit of magnetic flux is

(a) Wbm^{-2} ☐ (b) Wb ☐
(c) H ☐ (d) Am^{-1} ☐

Or

The dimensions of magnetic flux are

(a) $[MLT^{-2}A^{-2}]$ ☐ (b) $[ML^2T^{-2}A^{-2}]$ ☐
(c) $[ML^2T^{-1}A^{-2}]$ ☐ (d) $[ML^2T^{-2}A^{-1}]$ ☐

(iv) The magnetic flux linked with a coil, in webers is given by the equation $\phi = 3t^2 + 4t + 9$. Then, the magnitude of induced emf at $t = 2$ s will be

(a) 2 V ☐ (b) 4 V ☐
(c) 8 V ☐ (d) 16 V ☐

COMPETITION EDGE UP

1. A square loop PQRS having 10 turns, area 3.6×10^{-3} m^2 and resistance 100 Ω is slowly and uniformly being pulled out of a uniform magnetic field of magnitude B = 0.5 T as shown. Work done in pulling the loop out of the field in 1.0 s is ..... $\times 10^{-6}$ J.

[NCERT Pg. 160, JEE Main 2024]

P Q S R v

2. The current in an inductor is given by I = (3 t + 8) where t is in second. The magnitude of induced emf produced in the inductor is 12 mV. The self-inductance of the inductor is .... mH.

[NCERT Pg. 168, JEE Main 2024]

3. A rod of length 60 cm rotates with a uniform angular velocity 20 rad s^{-1} about its perpendicular bisector. in a uniform magnetic field 0.5 T. The direction of magnetic field is parallel to the axis of rotation. The potential difference between the two ends of the rod is......V.

[NCERT Pg. 163, JEE Main 2024]

4. The magnetic flux ϕ (in weber) linked with a closed circuit of resistance 8 Ω varies with time (in seconds) as $\phi = 5t^2 - 36t + 1$. The induced current in the circuit at t = 2 s is .... A.

[NCERT Pg. 158, JEE Main 2024]

5. A ceiling fan having 3 blades of length 80 cm each is rotating with an angular velocity of 1200 rpm. The magnetic field of earth in that region is 0.5 G and angle of dip is 30°. The emf induced across the blades is N$\pi \times 10^{-5}$ V. The value of N is ....

[NCERT Pg. 163, JEE Main 2024]

6. A rectangular loop of length 2.5 m and width 2 m is placed at 60° to a magnetic field of 4 T. The loop is removed from the field in 10 s. The average emf induced in the loop during this time is

[NCERT Pg. 157, JEE Main 2024]

(a) – 2 V ☐ (b) – 1 V ☐

(c) + 2 V ☐ (d) + 1 V ☐

7. The magnetic energy stored in an inductor of inductance 4 μH carrying a current of 2 A is

[NCERT Pg. 169, NEET 2023]

(a) 4 mJ ☐ (b) 8 mJ ☐

(c) 8 μJ ☐ (d) 4 μJ ☐

8. A square loop of side 1 m and resistance 1 Ω placed in a magnetic field of 0.5 T. If the plane of loop is perpendicular to the direction of magnetic field, the magnetic flux through the loop is

[NCERT Pg. 157, NEET 2022]

(a) 0.5 Wb ☐ (b) 1 Wb ☐

(c) zero Wb ☐ (d) 2 Wb ☐

9. A big circular coil of 1000 turns and average radius 10 m is rotating about its horizontal diameter at 2 rad s^{-1}. If the vertical component of earth's magnetic field at that place is 2×10^{-5} T and electrical resistance of the coil is 12.56 Ω, then the maximum induced current in the coil will be

[NCERT Pg. 158, NEET 2022]

(a) 0.25 A ☐ (b) 1.5 A ☐

(c) 1 A ☐ (d) 2 A ☐

10. Two conducting circular loops of radii R_1 and R_2 are placed in the same plane with their centres coinciding. If $R_1 >> R_2$, the mutual inductance M between them will be directly proportional to **[NCERT Pg. 167, NEET 2021]**

(a) $\frac{R_1}{R_2}$ ☐ (b) $\frac{R_2}{R_1}$ ☐

(c) $\frac{R_1^2}{R_2}$ ☐ (d) $\frac{R_2^2}{R_1}$ ☐

11. A wheel with 20 metallic spokes each 1 m long is rotated with a speed of 120 rpm in a plane perpendicular to a magnetic field of 0.4 G. The induced emf between the axle and rim of the wheel will be (1 G = 10^{-4} T)

[NCERT Pg. 162, NEET (Oct) 2020]

(a) 2.51×10^{-4} V ☐

(b) 2.51×10^{-5} V ☐

(c) 4.0×10^{-5} V ☐

(d) 2.51 V ☐

Chapter 7

Alternating Current

Scan and take Chapter Test

TOPIC 1

AC Voltage Applied to a Resistor

1. Consider a source which produces sinusoidally varying potential difference across a resistor. This potential difference is called ________ (AC/DC) voltage and given by the expression ________ (V_m sin ωt/V_m tan ωt).

2. The Ohm's law works equally well for both AC and DC voltages.

True ☐ False ☐

***3.** In a purely resistive AC circuit, the current

(a) lags behind the emf in phase ☐

(b) is in phase with the emf ☐

(c) leads the emf in phase ☐

(d) leads the emf in half the cycle behind it in the other half ☐

4. The sum of the instantaneous current values over one complete cycle is ________ (zero/unity) and the average current is ________ (zero/unity).

5. Alternating current cannot be measured by DC ammeter, because

(a) AC cannot pass through DC ammeter ☐

(b) AC changes its direction ☐

(c) average value of current in complete cycle is zero ☐

(d) DC ammeter will get damaged ☐

6. The average current for an AC voltage is zero. It means that the average power consumed is zero and there is no dissipation of electrical energy.

True ☐ False ☐

7. Name the special value of current, which is used to express AC power in the same form as DC power.

____

*Concepts of all questions bearing * are important for JEE/NEET/CUET.*

8. An alternating current is given by the equation $I = I_1 \cos \omega t + I_2 \sin \omega t$. The rms current is given by $\frac{1}{\sqrt{2}}(I_1^2 + I_2^2)^{\frac{1}{2}}$.

True ☐ False ☐

***9.** A resistance of 20 Ω is connected to a source of an alternating potential, $V = 220 \sin(100\pi t)$. What will be the time taken by current to change from its peak value to rms value?

____

10. If an AC main supply is given to be 220 V. The average emf during a positive half-cycle will be ________ (240 V/198 V).

11. The frequency of an alternating voltage is 50 cycles/s and its amplitude is 120 V. Find the rms value of voltage.

____

12. The household line voltage of 220 V is a rms value with a peak voltage of ______ $\left(220\sqrt{2} / \frac{220}{\sqrt{2}}\right)$.

***13.** The voltage of an AC source varies with time according to equation $V = 100 \sin \pi t \cos 100\pi t$, where t is in seconds and V is in volts. Then,

(a) the peak voltage of the source is 100 V ☐
(b) the peak voltage of the source is 50 V ☐
(c) the peak voltage of the source is $\frac{100}{\sqrt{2}}$ V ☐
(d) the peak voltage of the source is 100 V ☐

14. A generator produces a voltage that is given by $V = 240 \sin 120\, t$, where t is in seconds. Which of the following pairs is correctly matched for given equation?

I. Frequency ⟶ 19 Hz

II. rms voltage ⟶ 240 V

____

15. A light bulb is rated at 100 W for a 220 V supply.
Match the Column I (quantities) with the Column II (value in SI unit).

Column I	Column II
A. Resistance of bulb	1. 311
B. Peak voltage	2. 484
C. rms current	3. 0.454

A. __________ B. __________ C. __________

TOPIC 2

Representation of AC Current and Voltage by Rotating Vectors-Phasors

16. Tick (✓/×) for correct/incorrect statement for the phasor diagram shown below.

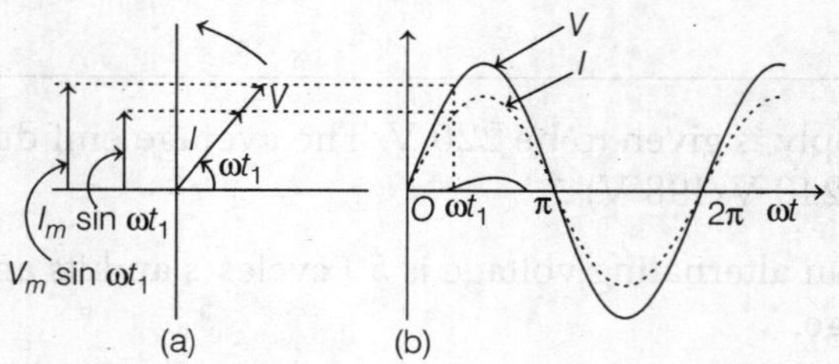

(i) The vertical components of phasors V and I represent the sinusoidally varying quantities V and I. ☐

(ii) The magnitudes of phasors V and I represent the amplitudes or the peak values V_m and I_m of these oscillating quantities. ☐

(iii) The projection of voltage and current phasors on vertical axis, i.e. $V_m \sin \omega t$ and $I_m \sin \omega t$ respectively, represent the value of voltage and current at that instant. ☐

***17.** Match the components of an AC circuit in Column I with the phasor diagram in Column II.

Column I	Column II
A. Resistor only	1.
B. Inductor only	2.
C. Capacitor only	3.

A. ______________ B. ______________ C. ______________

TOPIC 3

AC Voltage Applied to an Inductor

18. When AC voltage is applied to an inductor, the current is obtained as

$$I = \frac{V_m}{L}\int \sin \omega t \, dt = -\frac{V_m}{\omega L}\cos \omega t + \text{constant}$$

where, the integration constant has the dimensions of ________ (current/voltage).

19. The current I in the inductor is varying with time according to the plot shown in figure.

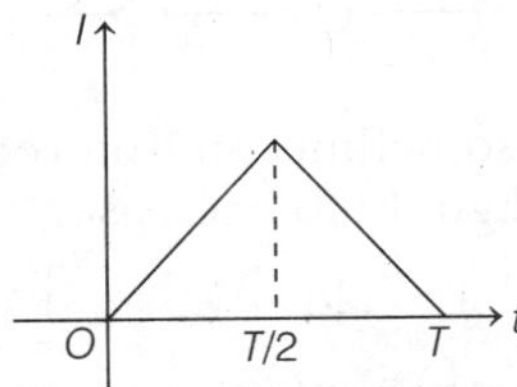

Which one of the following is the correct variation of voltage with time in the inductor coil?

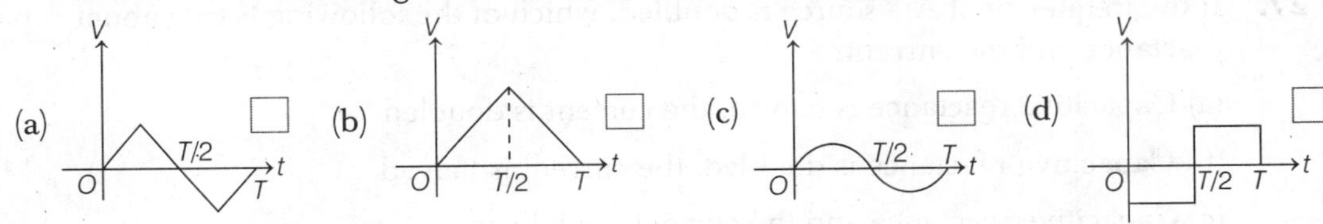

***20.** Two inductors L_1 (inductance 1mH, internal resistance 3 Ω) and L_2 (inductance 2 mH, internal resistance 4 Ω) and a resistor R (resistance 12 Ω) are all connected in parallel across a 5 V battery. The circuit is switched ON at time $t = 0$. The ratio of the maximum to the minimum current (I_{max} / I_{min}) drawn from the battery is ________ .

21. In a purely inductive AC circuit, L is 30 mH, rms voltage is 150 V and frequency is 50 Hz. The inductive reactance is ________ (9.42 Ω / 5.4 Ω) .

22. An inductance of negligible resistance having reactance of 120 Ω at 200 Hz is connected to a 240 V, 60 Hz power line. Then, which of the following pairs is not correctly matched?

I. $L \longrightarrow \frac{3}{\pi}$ H II. X'_L (at 60 Hz) $\longrightarrow$ 36 Ω III. $I_{rms} \longrightarrow$ 6.66 A

____

23. In a purely inductive AC circuit, the current reaches its maximum value ________ (earlier/later) than the voltage by ________ (one-half/one-fourth) of a period.

***24.** A pure inductor of 25 mH is connected to a source of 220 V. If the frequency of the source is 50 Hz, then find the value of inductive reactance and driven current.

____

TOPIC 4

AC Voltage Applied to a Capacitor

25. A light bulb and an open coil inductor are connected to an AC source through a key as shown in the following figure.

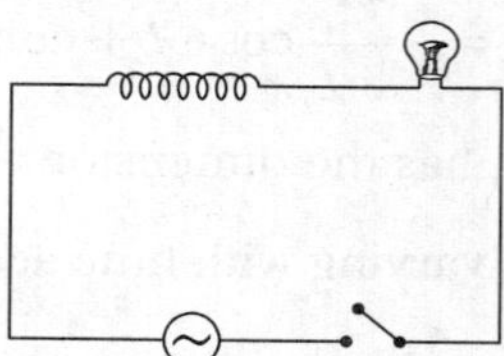

The switch is closed and after sometime, an iron rod is inserted into the interior of the inductor. Will the glow of the light bulb decrease?

Yes ☐ No ☐

26. The amplitude of the oscillating current in a purely capacitive AC circuit is ________ (ωCV_m / ωCI_m).

27. If the frequency of AC source is doubled, which of the following is true about capacitive reactance and the current?

(a) Capacitive reactance is halved, the current is doubled. ☐

(b) Capacitive reactance is doubled, the current is halved. ☐

(c) Capacitive reactance and the current are halved. ☐

(d) Capacitive reactance and the current are doubled. ☐

28. Tick (✓/✗) for correct/incorrect statement in given boxes.

(i) When a capacitor is connected to voltage source in a DC circuit, current will flow for the short time required to charge the capacitor. ☐

(ii) A capacitor in a DC circuit will limit or oppose the current as it charges. ☐

(iii) When a capacitor is fully charged, the current in the circuit falls to zero. ☐

29. In capacitive AC circuit, the current reaches its maximum value ________ (earlier/later) than the voltage by________ (one-half/one-fourth) of a period.

30. Match the relation of voltage (in different circuit elements) in Column I with the current in Column II.

Column I	Column II
A. V_R	1. $\frac{\pi}{2}$ ahead of I
B. V_C	2. Parallel to I
C. V_L	3. $\frac{\pi}{2}$ behind I

A. ________ B. ________ C. ________

31. A 60 μF capacitor is connected to a 110 V, 60 Hz AC supply. Which of the following is the correctly matched pair from given below?

I. $X_C \longrightarrow 44.2\,\Omega$ II. $I_{rms} \longrightarrow 2.49\,\text{A}$

____

32. (i) If a lamp is first connected to a DC source and its capacitance is reduced, then the brightness of the lamp will be __________ (zero/reduced).

(ii) If the same lamp is connected to an AC source and it capacitance is reduced, then the brightness of the lamp will be __________ (zero/reduced).

33. A 15.0 μF capacitor is connected to a 220 V, 50 Hz source.
Match the Column I (quantity) with Column II (value in SI unit).

Column I	Column II
A. X_C (in Ω)	1. 212
B. I_m (in A)	2. 1.04
C. I_{rms} (in A)	3. 1.47

A. ______________ B. ______________ C. ______________

34. An alternating voltage $E = 200\sqrt{2}\sin(100t)$ is connected to a 1 μF capacitor through an AC ammeter. The reading of the ammeter will be ______________ (10 mA/20 mA).

TOPIC 5

AC Voltage Applied to a Series *L-C-R* Circuit

NCERT Pg 186-190

***35.** An AC source of angular frequency ω is fed across a resistor R and a capacitor C in series. The current registered is I. Now, if the frequency of source is changed to $\frac{\omega}{3}$ (for same voltage), the current in the circuit is halved. The ratio of reactance to resistance at the original frequency ω is __________ .

***36.** A resistance of 300 Ω and an inductance of $\frac{1}{\pi}$ H are connected in series to an AC voltage of 20 V and 200 Hz frequency. Calculate the phase angle between the voltage and current ____.

37. (i) If $X_C > X_L$, φ is positive and the circuit is predominantly __________ (capacitive/inductive). The current in the circuit __________ (leads/lags) the source voltage.

(ii) If $X_C < X_L$, φ is negative and the circuit is predominantly inductive. The current in the circuit __________ (leads/lags) the source voltage.

38. When a system is driven by an energy source at a frequency that is near the natural frequency, the amplitude of oscillation will be __________ (large/small).

***39.** An *R-L-C* series circuit contains $L = 1\,\text{mH}$, $C = 1\,\text{nF}$ and two parallel resistors of 100 Ω and 200 Ω. For the source applied with $V_m = 100$ V, the resonant frequency is ________ ($1 \times 10^6\,\text{rad s}^{-1} / 2 \times 10^6\,\text{rad s}^{-1}$).

40. In non-resonant circuit, for the frequencies higher than the resonant frequency, the nature of circuit is ________ (inductive/capacitive).

41. A circuit contains 0.02 μF capacitor and 8 μH inductor in series. It radiates radio waves from a radio-station. Find the frequency of circuit and also calculate wavelength of radio wave.

____

42. An inductor and a capacitor are connected in the circuit as shown in the following figure. The frequency of the voltage supply is equal to the resonant frequency of the circuit. Which ammeter will read 0A current?

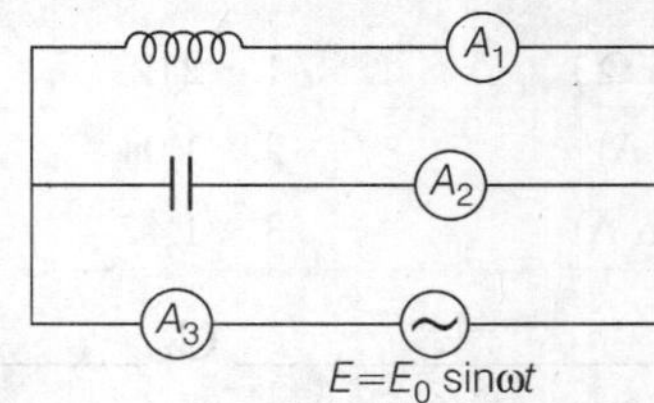

____

***43.** In a series *L-C-R* circuit, the voltage across *R* is 100 V, $R = 1\,\Omega$ and $C = 2\,\mu\text{F}$. The resonant frequency ω is 200 rad/s. At resonance, the voltage across *L* is *x*. Find the value of *x*.

____

44. An *L-C-R* series circuit consists of a resistance of 10 Ω, a capacitor of reactance 60 Ω and an inductor coil. The circuit is found to resonate when put across a 300 V, 100 Hz supply. Find the (Take, π = 3)

(i) resonant frequency of the circuit,

(ii) the capacitance of capacitor and

(iii) the inductance of inductor coil.

____

45. For an *R-L-C* circuit driven with voltage of amplitude V_m and frequency $\omega_0 = \frac{1}{\sqrt{LC}}$, the current exhibits resonance. The quality factor *Q* is given by

(a) $\frac{CR}{\omega_0}$ ☐ (b) $\frac{\omega_0 L}{R}$ ☐ (c) $\frac{\omega_0 R}{L}$ ☐ (d) $\frac{R}{\omega_0 C}$ ☐

***46.** A 100 V, AC source of frequency 500 Hz is connected to an *L-C-R* circuit with $L = 8.1\,\text{mH}$, $C = 12.5\,\mu\text{F}$ and $R = 10\,\Omega$. All connected in series as shown in the following figure.

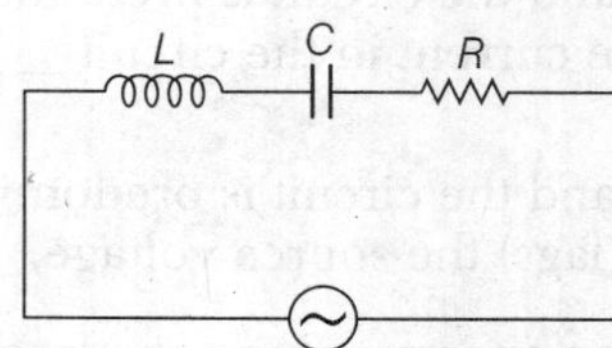

What is the quality factor of the circuit?

____

47. Which of the following combinations should be selected for better tuning of an L-C-R circuit used for communication?

(a) $R = 20\Omega$, $L = 1.5$ H and $C = 35\ \mu$F ☐

(b) $R = 25\Omega$, $L = 2.5$ H and $C = 45\ \mu$F ☐

(c) $R = 15\Omega$, $L = 3.5$ H and $C = 30\ \mu$F ☐

(d) $R = 25\Omega$, $L = 1.5$ H and $C = 45\mu$F ☐

48. Tick (✓/×) for correct/incorrect statement in given boxes.

(i) If the resonance is less sharp, not only is the maximum current less but also the circuit is close to resonance for a larger range ($\Delta\omega$) of frequencies and the tuning of the circuit will not be good. ☐

(ii) Less sharp the resonance, less is the selectivity of the circuit or *vice-versa.* ☐

(iii) If quality factor is large, i.e. R is low or L is large, the circuit is more selective. ☐

49. When a person carrying a metal object walk through a metal detector, it emits a sound. On which principle, it is based?

____

50. A charged 30 μF capacitor is connected to a 27 mH inductor. What is the angular frequency of free oscillation of the circuit?

____

51. Consider the following figure. The resistor, inductor and capacitor are in series.

The AC current in each element is ________ (same/different) at any time, having the ________ (same/different) amplitude and phase.

52. Which of the following statement is correct about the series L-C-R circuit?

I. Applied emf and potential difference across resistance are in same phase.

II. Applied emf and potential difference across inductor coil have phase difference of $\frac{\pi}{2}$.

III. Potential difference across capacitor and inductor have phase difference of $\frac{\pi}{2}$.

IV. Potential difference across resistance and capacitor have phase difference of π.

(a) I and II ☐ (b) II and III ☐

(c) I and IV ☐ (d) All of these ☐

***53.** In an L-C-R series AC circuit, the voltage across each of the components is 50 V. The voltage across the C-R combination will be ____________ $(50/50\sqrt{2})$ V.

54. In a series R-L-C circuit, the voltage across resistor, inductor and capacitor are 8 V, 16 V and 10 V, respectively. Find the resultant emf in the circuit.

____

55. In an L-C-R series AC circuit, the voltage across each of the components L, C and R is 50 V. The voltage across the L-C combination will be zero.

True ☐ False ☐

***56.** In an L-C-R series circuit, the potential difference across the terminals of the inductor is 60 V, across capacitor is 30 V and across the resistance is 40 V.

Will the supply voltage be 50V ?

Yes ☐ No ☐

57. A resistor of 200 Ω and a capacitor of 15 μF are connected in series to a 220 V, 50 Hz AC source. Which of the following pairs is correctly matched?

I. $Z \longrightarrow 280.5\,\Omega$ ☐ II. $I \longrightarrow 0.755$ A ☐

58. In a series L-C-R circuit, the frequency of 10 V AC voltage source is adjusted in such a way that the reactance of the inductor measures 15 Ω and that of the capacitor is 11 Ω. If $R = 3\Omega$, then find

(i) current in circuit and

(ii) voltage across resistor, inductor and capacitor each.

---

59. A sinusoidal voltage of peak value 300 V and an angular frequency $\omega = 400$ rad s^{-1} is applied to series L-C-R circuit, in which $R = 3\Omega$, $L = 20$ mH and $C = 625\,\mu$F. Match the Column I (quantity) with Column II (value in SI unit).

	Column I		Column II
A.	X_L (in Ω)	1.	8
B.	X_C (in Ω)	2.	4
C.	Z (in Ω)	3.	60
D.	I (in A)	4.	5

A. ________ B. ________ C. ________ D. ________

***60.** In the given circuit, the AC source has $\omega = 100$ rad/s. Considering the inductor and capacitor to be ideal, find

(i) current in circuit, (ii) voltage across 100 Ω and (iii) voltage across 50 Ω.

***61.** In a circuit, L, C and R are connected in series with an AC source of frequency f. The current leads the voltage by 45°. The value of C is

(a) $\dfrac{1}{2\pi f(2\pi fL + R)}$ ☐ (b) $\dfrac{1}{\pi f(2\pi fL + R)}$ ☐

(c) $\dfrac{1}{2\pi f(2\pi fL - R)}$ ☐ (d) $\dfrac{1}{\pi f(2\pi fL - R)}$ ☐

***62.** Which of the following graph of voltage and current *versus* ωt is correct for a series L-C-R circuit, if $X_C > X_L$?

(a)
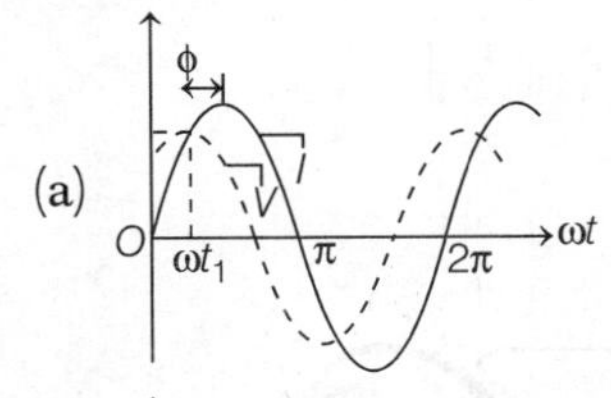

☐

(b)
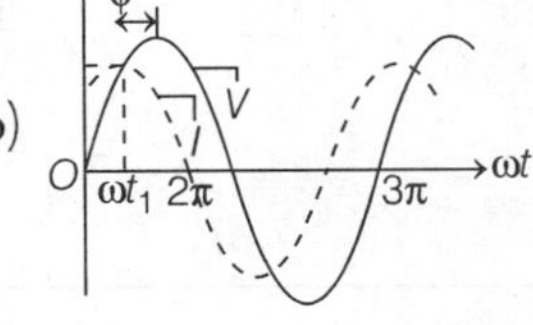

☐

(c)
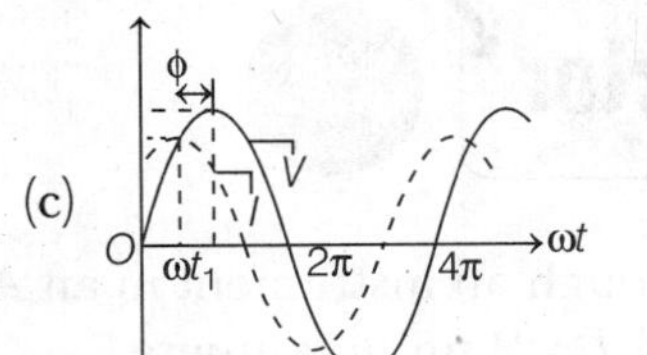

☐

(d) ϕ, V, I, O, ωt_1, π, 2π, ωt ☐

63. Figure shows a series L-C-R circuit, connected to a variable frequency source of 200 V. Here, $C = 80\,\mu\text{F}$, $R = 40\,\Omega$ and $L = 5\text{H}$. Is the source frequency which drives the circuit at resonance $\dfrac{25}{\pi}$ Hz?

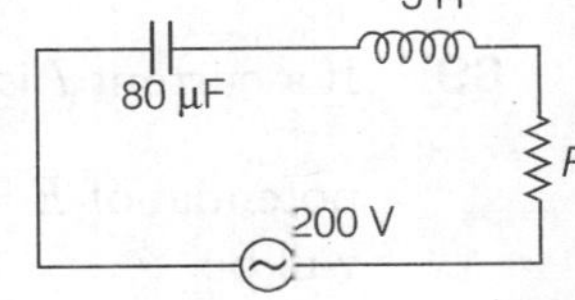

Yes ☐ No ☐

64. In an L-C-R circuit, capacitance is changed from C to $2C$. For the resonant frequency to remain unchanged, the inductance should be changed from L to $\dfrac{L}{2}$.

True ☐ False ☐

65. At resonant frequency, the amplitude of current in an L-C-R series circuit is ____________ (minimum/maximum).

***66.** In the given circuit, the reading of voltmeters V_1 and V_2 is 300 V each. What will be the correct reading of V_3 and ammeter A? (Assume L and C to be ideal)

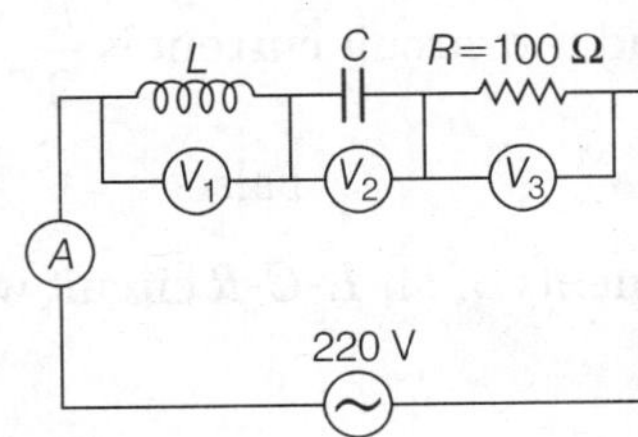

***67.** A series *L-C-R* circuit is shown in the figure below.

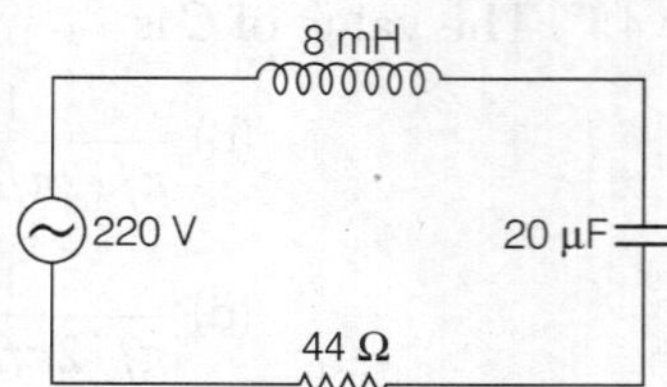

Which of the following pairs is correctly matched for the angular resonant frequency and amplitude of current at the resonating frequency?

I. $\omega \longrightarrow 2000 \text{ rad s}^{-1}$ ☐ II. $I_r \longrightarrow 5 \text{ A}$ ☐

TOPIC 6

Power in AC Circuit : The Power Factor

***68.** The potential difference *V* and the current *I* flowing through an instrument in an AC circuit of frequency *f* are given by $V = 5 \cos \omega t$ volt and $I = 2 \sin \omega t$ ampere (where, $\omega = 2\pi f$). The power dissipated in the instrument is ________ (zero/unity).

69. If a current *I* is given by $I_0 \sin\left(\omega t - \frac{\pi}{2}\right)$ flows in an AC circuit across which an AC potential of $E = E_0 \sin \omega t$ has been applied, then the power consumption *P* in the circuit will be

(a) $\frac{EI_0}{\sqrt{2}}$ ☐ (b) $\sqrt{2}E_0 I_0$ ☐

(c) $\frac{E_0 I_0}{2}$ ☐ (d) zero ☐

70. In an AC circuit, the instantaneous values of emf and current are $\varepsilon = 200 \sin(314)t$ V and $I = \sin\left(314t + \frac{\pi}{3}\right)$ A. Calculate the average power consumed.

____

***71.** If a lamp consumes only 50% of peak power in an AC circuit, then the phase difference between the applied voltage and the circuit current is $\frac{\pi}{3}$.

True ☐ False ☐

72. Which of the following components of an *L-C-R* circuit with AC supply, do not dissipate energy?

____

***73.** In an AC circuit, the instantaneous emf and current are given by $\varepsilon = 100 \sin 30t$, $I = 20 \sin\left(30t - \frac{\pi}{4}\right)$. In one cycle of AC, the average power consumed by the circuit and the wattless current are, respectively

(a) 50 W, 0 A ☐ (b) 50 W, 10 A ☐ (c) $\frac{1000}{\sqrt{2}}$ W, 10 A ☐ (d) $\frac{50}{\sqrt{2}}$ W, 0 A ☐

74. Match the circuits given in Column I with their respective power dissipation in Column II.

	Column I	Column II
A.	Resistive circuit	1. No power dissipation
B.	Purely inductive or capacitive circuit	2. Maximum power dissipation as $X_C = X_L$
C.	*L-C-R* series circuit	3. Power dissipated only in *R*
D.	Power dissipation at resonance in *L-C-R* circuit	4. Maximum power dissipation

A. ________ B. ________ C. ________ D. ________

75. Can power factor be improved by the use of a capacitor of appropriate capacitance in the circuit ?

Yes ☐ No ☐

***76.** A coil of inductive reactance 31 Ω is connected in series to a resistance of 8 Ω. It is placed in series with a condenser of capacitive reactance 25 Ω. The combination is connected to an AC source of 110 V. The power factor of the circuit is ________ (0.64/0.80).

77. A sinusoidal voltage at peak value 283 V and frequency 50 Hz is applied to a series *L-C-R* circuit in which $R = 3\ \Omega$, $L = 25.48$ mH and $C = 796\ \mu$F.

Find
(i) the impedance of the circuit
(ii) the phase difference between *V* and *I*
(iii) the power dissipated in the circuit
(iv) the power factor

TOPIC 7

Transformers

NCERT Pg 194-196

***78.** In a step-up transformer, the turns ratio is 1 : 2. A Leclanche cell (emf = 1.5 V) is connected across the primary. The voltage developed in the secondary would be

(a) 3 V ☐ (b) 0.75 V ☐ (c) 1.5 V ☐ (d) zero ☐

79. A 50 Hz AC current of crest value 1 A flows through the primary of a transformer. If the mutual inductance between the primary and secondary be 0.5 H, the crest voltage induced in the secondary is________ V.

***80.** A power transmission line feeds input power at 2300 V to a step-down transformer with its primary winding having 4000 turns. What should be the number of turns in the secondary winding in order to get output power at 230 V?

____

81. A transformer steps-down 220 V to 22 V to operate a device with an impedance of 220 Ω. Which of the following pairs is correctly matched?

I. $I_s \longrightarrow 0.1$ A ☐ II. $I_p \longrightarrow 0.1$ A ☐

***82.** A 60 W load is connected to the secondary coil of a transformer whose primary coil draws line voltage of 220 V. If a current of 0.54 A flows in the load, then what is the current in the primary coil?

____

***83.** A step-down transformer is used on a 1000 V line to deliver 20 A at 120 V in the secondary coil. If the efficiency of transformer is 80%, will the current drawn from the line be 3 A?

Yes ☐ No ☐

84. A transformer having efficiency of 90% is working on 200 V and 3 kW power supply. If the current in the secondary coil is 6 A, then match the Column I (quantity) with Column II (value in SI unit)

	Column I	Column II
A.	Final power	1. 15
B.	Secondary coil voltage	2. 2700
C.	Primary coil current	3. 450

A. ____________ B. ____________ C. ____________

85. **Statement I** There is always some flux leakage, i.e. not all of the flux due to primary passes through the secondary due to poor design of the core or the air gaps in the core.
Statement II Flux leakage can be reduced by winding the primary and secondary coils, one over the other.
Which of the following statement(s) is/are correct?

(a) Only statement I ☐
(b) Only statement II ☐
(c) Both statements I and II ☐
(d) Neither statement I nor II ☐

Assertion-Reason Questions

Direction (Q. Nos. 1-10) *In the following questions, a statement of Assertion is followed by a corresponding statement of Reason. From the following options, choose the correct one.*

(a) Both Assertion and Reason are correct and Reason is the correct explanation of Assertion.
(b) Both Assertion and Reason are correct but Reason is not the correct explanation of Assertion.
(c) Assertion is correct but Reason is incorrect.
(d) Assertion is incorrect but Reason is correct.

1. **Assertion** (A) Alternating voltage and current in purely resistive circuit, are in the same direction.

Reason (R) The phase angle between the voltage and current is zero.

(a) ☐ (b) ☐ (c) ☐ (d) ☐

***2.** **Assertion** (A) At resonance, *LCR* series circuit have a maximum current.

Reason (R) At resonance in *LCR* series circuit, the current and emf are not in phase.

(a) ☐ (b) ☐ (c) ☐ (d) ☐

3. **Assertion** (A) When AC circuit contains resistor only, its power is maximum.

Reason (R) Power of circuit is independent of phase angle.

(a) ☐ (b) ☐ (c) ☐ (d) ☐

4. **Assertion** (A) Resonance phenomenon is exhibited by a circuit only, if both L and C are present in the circuit.

Reason (R) Voltage across L and C cancel each other and the current amplitude is $\frac{V_m}{R}$.

The total source voltage appearing across R causes resonance.

(a) ☐ (b) ☐ (c) ☐ (d) ☐

***5.** **Assertion** (A) The alternating current leads behind the emf by a phase angle of $\frac{\pi}{2}$, when AC flows through an inductor.

Reason (R) The inductive reactance decreases as the frequency of AC source decreases.

(a) ☐ (b) ☐ (c) ☐ (d) ☐

6. **Assertion** (A) Capacitor serves as a block for DC and offers an easy path to AC.

Reason (R) Capacitor reactance is inversely proportional to frequency.

(a) ☐ (b) ☐ (c) ☐ (d) ☐

7. **Assertion** (A) An inductor acts as a perfect insulator for DC.

Reason (R) DC remains constant in magnitude and direction.

(a) ☐ (b) ☐ (c) ☐ (d) ☐

8. **Assertion** (A) When capacitive reactance is smaller than inductive reactance in LCR circuit, emf leads by the current.

Reason (R) The phase angle is the angle between the alternating emf and alternating current of the circuit.

(a) ☐ (b) ☐ (c) ☐ (d) ☐

9. Assertion (A) An alternating current does not show any magnetic effect.

Reason (R) Alternating current varies with time.

(a) ☐ (b) ☐ (c) ☐ (d) ☐

***10. Assertion** (A) The DC and AC both can be measured by a hot wire instrument.

Reason (R) The hot wire instrument is based on principle of magnetic effect of current.

(a) ☐ (b) ☐ (c) ☐ (d) ☐

Case Based Questions

1 The rate at which electric energy is consumed in an electric circuit is called its power. In a DC circuit, power is given by product of voltage and current. But in an AC circuit, both voltage E and current I vary sinusoidally with time and are generally not in phase.

(i) For a series LCR circuit. The power loss at resonance is

(a) $\dfrac{V^2}{\left[\omega L - \dfrac{1}{\omega C}\right]}$ ☐ (b) $I^2 L\omega$ ☐

(c) $I^2 R$ ☐ (d) $\dfrac{V^2}{C\omega}$ ☐

(ii) In an AC circuit with phase voltage V and current I, power dissipated is

(a) $V.I$ ☐

(b) dependent on phase angle between V and I ☐

(c) $\dfrac{1}{2} \times V.I$ ☐

(d) $\dfrac{1}{\sqrt{2}} \times V.I$ ☐

(iii) In an AC circuit, current flowing $I = 5 \sin\left(100t - \dfrac{\pi}{2}\right) A$ and potential difference $V = 200 \sin(100t) V$. Power consumption is

(a) 20 W ☐ (b) 0 W ☐

(c) 1000 W ☐ (d) 40 W ☐

(iv) In an AC circuit emf (E) and current (I) at any instant are given respectively by $e_o = E_0 \sin \omega t \; i = i_0 \sin(\omega t - \phi)$. Average power in the circuit over one cycle of AC

(a) $E_o I_o$ ☐ (b) $\dfrac{E_o I_o}{2}$ ☐

(c) $\dfrac{E_o I_o}{2} \sin \phi$ ☐ (d) $\dfrac{E_o I_o}{2} \cos \phi$ ☐

2. A transformer is an electrical device for converting an alternating current at law voltage into high voltage and *vice versa*. If it increases the input voltage, it is called step-up transformer and if it decreases the input voltage, it is called step-down transformer.

(i) A step down transformer connected to an ac mains supply of 220V is made to operate at 11 V, 44W lamp. Ignoring power losses in to the transformer, what is the current in primary circuit?

(a) 0.4 A ☐ (b) 2A ☐ (c) 4A ☐ (d) 0.2 A ☐

(ii) A transformer having efficiency of 90% is working on 200V and 3 kW power supply. If current in secondary coil is 6A, voltage across secondary coil and current in primary coil are.

(a) 300 V, 15 A ☐ (b) 450 V, 15 A ☐
(c) 450 V, 13.5 A ☐ (d) 600 V, 15 A ☐

(iii) A 220 V input is supplied to a transformer, the output circuit draws a current of 2 A at 440 V. If the efficiency of transformer is 80% , the current drawn by primary windings of transformer is

(a) 5 A ☐ (b) 3.6 A ☐
(c) 2.8 A ☐ (d) 2.5 A ☐

(iv) A transformer is used to light a 100 W and 110 V lamp from a 220 V mains. If the main current is 0.5 A, efficiency of transformer is approximately.

(a) 50% ☐ (b) 90% ☐
(c) 10% ☐ (d) 30% ☐

COMPETITION EDGE UP

1. *When a coil is connected across a 20 V DC supply, it draws a current of 5 A. When it is connected across 20 V, 50 Hz AC supply, it draws a current of 4 A. The self inductance of the coil is .... mH. (Take, $\pi = 3$)*

[NCERT Pg. 187, JEE Main 2024]

2. *An alternating emf $E = 110\sqrt{2}\sin 100t$ V is applied to a capacitor of 2 μF, the rms value of current in the circuit is .... mA.*

[NCERT Pg. 184, JEE Main 2024]

3. *A series L-C-R circuit is subjected to an AC signal of 200V, 50 Hz. If the voltage across the inductor (L = 10 mH) is 31.4 V, then the current in this circuit is ....*

[NCERT Pg. 187, JEE Main 2024]

(a) 68 A ☐ (b) 10 A ☐
(c) 63 A ☐ (d) 10 mA ☐

4 *A transformer has an efficiency of 80% and works at 10 V and 4 kW. If the secondary voltage is 240 V, then the current in the secondary coil is ....*

[NCERT Pg. 195, JEE Main 2024]

5. *In an ideal transformer, the turns ratio is $\frac{N_p}{N_s} = \frac{1}{2}$. The ratio $V_s : V_p$ is equal to (the symbols carry their usual meaning)*

[NCERT Pg. 195, NEET 2024]

(a) 1 : 2 ☐ (b) 2 : 1 ☐
(c) 1 : 1 ☐ (d) 1 : 4 ☐

6. *A 12 V, 60 W lamp is connected to the secondary of a step down transformer, whose primary is connected to AC mains of 220 V. Assuming the transformer to be ideal, what is the current in the primary winding ?*

[NCERT Pg. 195, NEET 2023]

(a) 2.7 A ☐ (b) 3.7 A ☐
(c) 0.37 A ☐ (d) 0.27 A ☐

7. *In a series L-C-R circuit, the inductance L is 10 mH, capacitance C is 1 μF and resistance R is 100 Ω. The frequency at which resonance occurs is* **[NCERT Pg. 189, NEET 2023]**

(a) 15.9 kHz ☐
(b) 1.59 rad/s ☐
(c) 1.59 kHz ☐
(d) 15.9 rad/s ☐

8. *The peak voltage of the AC source is equal to* **[NCERT Pg. 180, NEET 2022]**

(a) the rms value of the AC source. ☐
(b) $\sqrt{2}$ times the rms value of the AC source. ☐
(c) $1/\sqrt{2}$ times the rms value of the AC source. ☐
(d) the value of voltage supplied to the circuit. ☐

9. *A series L-C-R circuit with inductance 10 H, capacitance 10 μF, resistance 50 Ω is connected to an AC source of voltage, $V = 200\sin(100t)$ V. If the resonant frequency of the L-C-R circuit is ν_0 and the frequency of the AC source is ν, then* **[NCERT Pg. 189, NEET 2022]**

(a) $\nu_0 = \nu = \frac{50}{\pi}$ Hz ☐
(b) $\nu_0 = \frac{50}{\pi}$ Hz, $\nu = 50$ Hz ☐
(c) $\nu = 100$ Hz, $\nu_0 = \frac{100}{\pi}$ Hz ☐
(d) $\nu_0 = \nu = 50$ Hz ☐

10. *A series L-C-R circuit containing 5.0 H inductor, 80 μF capacitor and 40 Ω resistor is connected to 230 V variable frequency AC source. The angular frequencies of the source at which power transferred to the circuit is half the power at the resonant angular frequency are likely to be* **[NCERT Pg. 189, NEET 2021]**

(a) 25 rad/s and 75 rad/s ☐
(b) 50 rad/s and 25 rad/s ☐
(c) 46 rad/s and 54 rad/s ☐
(d) 42 rad/s and 58 rad/s ☐

11. *A step down transformer connected to an AC mains supply of 220 V is made to operate at 11 V, 44 W lamp. Ignoring power losses in the transformer, what is the current in the primary circuit?* **[NCERT Pg. 195, NEET 2021]**

(a) 0.2 A ☐ (b) 0.4 A ☐
(c) 2 A ☐ (d) 4 A ☐

12. *A 40 μF capacitor is connected to a 200 V, 50 Hz AC supply. The rms value of the current in the circuit is, nearly* **[NCERT Pg. 184, NEET (Sep.) 2020]**

(a) 2.05 A ☐ (b) 2.5 A ☐
(c) 25.1 A ☐ (d) 1.7 A ☐

Chapter 8

Electromagnetic Waves

Scan and take Chapter Test

TOPIC 1

Displacement Current

NCERT Pg 202-205

1. Complete the following analogy.
Conduction current : Flow of charges :: Displacement current : ______________

2. The source of the magnetic field is not just the _________ (conduction/displacement) current due to flowing charges, but also time rate of change of _______ (electric/magnetic) field.

3. During charging of a capacitor,

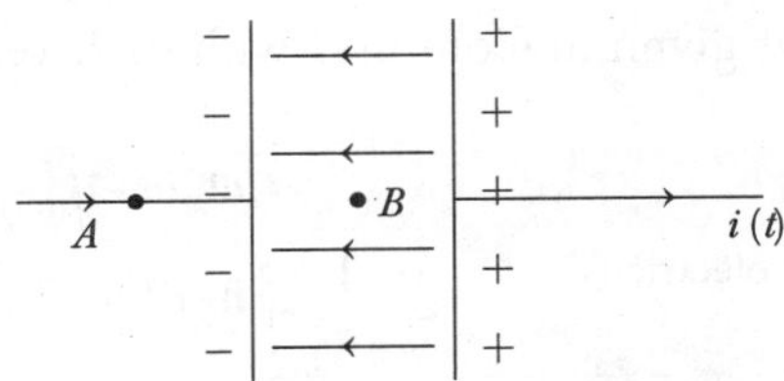

$i = i_c + i_d$ is true for (i_c = conduction current, i_d = displacement current)

(a) point A ☐ (b) point B ☐ (c) Both A and B ☐ (d) None of A and B ☐

4. Consider the conduction current (i_c) and displacement current (i_d). Now, choose correct statements.

(i) $i_c > i_d$ during charging.
(ii) $i_c < i_d$ during discharging.
(iii) $i_c = i_d$ for a capacitor.
(iv) i_c and i_d follow Kirchhoff's rule.

____

***5.** The charge on a parallel plate capacitor varies as $q = q_0 \cos 2\pi\nu t$. The plates are very large and close together (area = A, separation = d), neglecting the edge effects. Find the displacement current through the capacitor.

____

*Concepts of all questions bearing * are important for JEE/NEET/CUET.*

***6.** A parallel plate capacitor is charged to 100×10^{-6} C. Due to radiations falling from a radiating source, the plate gets charged in 10 s at the rate of 2×10^{-7} Cs^{-1}. The magnitude of displacement current is ________ (2×10^{-7} A/50 A).

7. In generalised Ampere's circuital law, the total current passing through any surface of which the closed loop is the perimeter, is the sum of the conduction current and the displacement current.

True ☐ False ☐

8. In a charging capacitor, both conduction and displacement currents may be present in ________ (same/different) region of space.

9. In the given figure, magnetic field exists between the plates of the capacitor at *M* and just outside the plate of capacitor at *P*. Is the field in both cases same ?

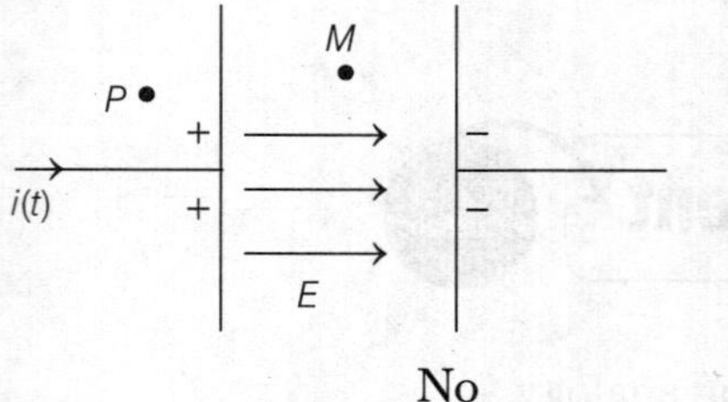

Yes ☐ No ☐

10. Time dependent electric and magnetic fields give rise to each other. Which of the following laws gives a quantitative expression of this statement ?

I. Faraday's law of electromagnetic induction

II. Ampere-Maxwell law

____

***11.** Match the following laws given in Column I with their respective Maxwell's equations given in Column II.

Column I	Column II
A. Gauss' law for electricity	1. $\oint \mathbf{B} \cdot d\mathbf{l} = \mu_0 \left(i_c + \varepsilon_0 \frac{d\phi_E}{dt} \right)$
B. Gauss' law for magnetism	2. $\oint \mathbf{B} \cdot d\mathbf{A} = 0$
C. Faraday's law	3. $\varepsilon_0 \oint \mathbf{E} \cdot d\mathbf{A} = Q$
D. Ampere-Maxwell law	4. $\oint \mathbf{E} \cdot d\mathbf{l} = \frac{-d\phi_B}{dt}$

A. ________ B. ________ C. ________ D. ________

***12.** A parallel plate capacitor is connected as shown below.

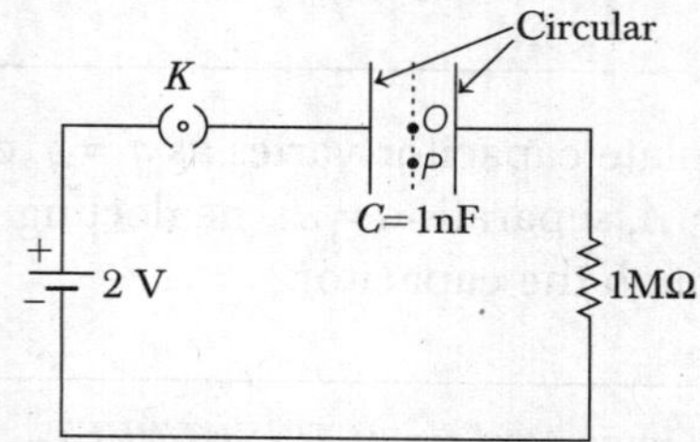

Key K is closed at $t = 0$. Now for a point P ($OP = 0.5$ m) at $t = 10^{-3}$ s; mid-way between plates (q be instantaneous charge and radius of circular plate = 1 m), find

(i) electric field between plates (ii) displacement current.

TOPIC 2

Electromagnetic Waves

13. Out of the following options, which one can be used to produce a propagating electromagnetic wave?

(a) A stationary charge ☐ (b) A chargeless particle ☐

(c) An accelerating charge ☐ (d) A charge moving at constant velocity ☐

***14.** The electric and magnetic fields of an electromagnetic wave are __________ (in phase/out of phase) and __________ (parallel/perpendicular) to each other.

15. Tick (✓/✗) for correct/incorrect statement in given boxes.

I. An electromagnetic wave contains a time varying electric field E and a time varying magnetic field B. ☐

II. **E** and **B** are parallel. ☐

III. $\mathbf{E} \times \mathbf{B}$ points in the direction of propagation of wave. ☐

***16.** The variations of electric and magnetic fields are shown below. What will be the direction of propagation of wave ?

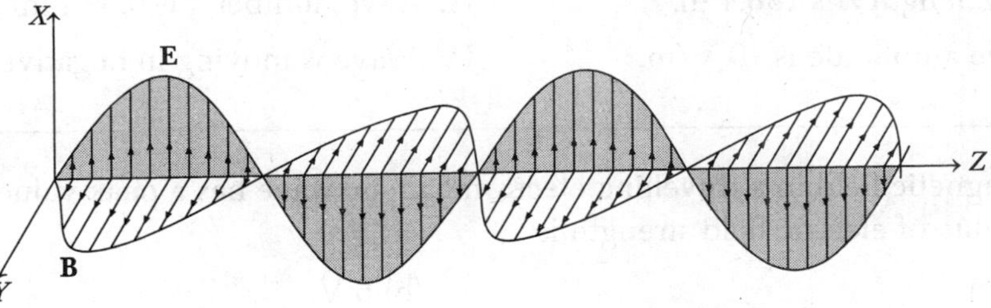

---

17. Time variation of electric and magnetic fields of an electromagnetic wave are

$$E = E_0 \sin(kz - \omega t)$$

$$B = B_0 \sin(kz - \omega t)$$

Tick (✓/✗) for correct/incorrect statement considering above equation.

(i) Electric field vector is parallel to Y-axis. ☐

(ii) Magnetic field vector oscillates along X-axis. ☐

(iii) Wave is moving along positive Z-axis. ☐

(iv) Data is not sufficient to state the direction of motion of wave. ☐

18. Equation for electric field for an electromagnetic wave moving in negative z-direction will be ____________ $[E = E_0 \sin(kz - \omega t)/E = E_0 \sin(kz + \omega t)]$.

19. The direction of k describes

(a) direction of propagation of the wave ☐

(b) opposite direction of propagation of the wave ☐

(c) direction of propagation of electric field ☐

(d) direction of propagation of magnetic field ☐

20. If electric field of an EM wave in vacuum is given by

$$E = 40 \cos(kz - 6 \times 10^8 t)\ \text{V/m}$$

Find the value of wave number k.

____

21. Magnetic field of a plane electromagnetic wave is
$B = 2 \times 10^{-7} \cdot \sin(0.17 \times 10^2 x + 0.5 \times 10^{10} t)$
Wavelength of wave will be ____________ (0.37/3.70) m.

22. A charged particle oscillates about its mean position with a frequency of 10^9 Hz. The electromagnetic waves produced will have

(a) frequency of 10^9 Hz ☐ (b) frequency of 2×10^9 Hz ☐

(c) wavelength of 0.2 m ☐ (d) wavelength of 0.5 m ☐

23. Electric field of an EM wave in space is $\mathbf{E} = 10 \sin(10^7 t + kx)\ \hat{\mathbf{j}}$ V/m. Choose the incorrect statement.

I. Wavelength λ is 188.4 m. II. Wave number k is 0.33 rad/m.

III. Wave amplitude is 10 V/m. IV. Wave is moving in negative x-direction.

____

***24.** The magnetic field in a travelling electromagnetic wave has a peak value of 20 nT. The peak value of electric field strength is

(a) 2 Vm^{-1} ☐ (b) 6 Vm^{-1} ☐

(c) 9 Vm^{-1} ☐ (d) 12 Vm^{-1} ☐

***25.** The amplitude of the magnetic field part of a harmonic electromagnetic wave in vacuum is $B_0 = 510$ nT. What is the amplitude of the electric field part of the wave ?

____

26. Suppose that the amplitude of electric field of an electromagnetic wave is $E_0 = 120\ \text{NC}^{-1}$ and its frequency is $\nu = 50.0$ MHz. The expressions for E will be (if wave travels along X-axis)

(a) $[(120\ NC^{-1})\sin\{(1.05\ rad\ m^{-1})x - (3.14\times 10^{8}\ rads^{-1})t\}]\ \hat{\mathbf{i}}$ ☐

(b) $[(120\ NC^{-1})\sin\{(1.05\ rad\ m^{-1})x - (3.14\times 10^{8}\ rads^{-1})t\}]\ \hat{\mathbf{k}}$ ☐

(c) $[(120\ NC^{-1})\sin\{(1.05\ rad\ m^{-1})x - (3.14\times 10^{8}\ rads^{-1})t\}]\ \hat{\mathbf{j}}$ ☐

(d) $[(120\ NC^{-1})\cos\{(1.05\ rad\ m^{-1})x - (3.14\times 10^{8}\ rads^{-1})t\}]\ \hat{\mathbf{j}}$ ☐

***27.** For a transparent medium, relative permeability and permittivity μ_r and ε_r are 1.0 and 1.44, respectively. The velocity of light in this medium would be

(a) $2.5\times 10^{8}\ ms^{-1}$ ☐ (b) $3\times 10^{8}\ ms^{-1}$ ☐

(c) $2.08\times 10^{8}\ ms^{-1}$ ☐ (d) $4.32\times 10^{8}\ ms^{-1}$ ☐

28. Tick the incorrect statement for the observations shown by Hertz.

I. He showed the existence of electromagnetic waves.

II. He demonstrated that wave having wavelength ten million times that of light waves can be diffracted, refracted but not polarised.

III. He established the wave nature of the radiation.

____

29. In AM radio to receive electric part of signal, the antenna must be ________(horizontal/vertical) and to receive magnetic part, it should be ________ (horizontal/vertical).

30. Amplitude of electric field of an EM wave is 100 V/m. What will be the energy density for wave?

____

31. If μ_E and μ_B are respectively the electric and magnetic energy densities of an electromagnetic wave, then ratio $\frac{u_E}{u_B}$ is equal to ____________ (zero/unity).

32. Which of these pairs are correctly matched?

I. Energy per unit volume → Energy density

II. Energy per unit area per unit time → Radiation pressure

____

33. If a plane electromagnetic wave in free space travelling along *X*-axis, $\mathbf{E} = 6.3\hat{\mathbf{j}}\left(\frac{V}{m}\right)$, then

(a) $\mathbf{B} = 2.1\times 10^{-8}\hat{\mathbf{k}}T$ ☐ (b) $\mathbf{B} = 2.1\times 10^{-8}\hat{\mathbf{i}}T$ ☐

(c) $\mathbf{B} = 2.1\times 10^{-8}(-\hat{\mathbf{k}})T$ ☐ (d) $\mathbf{B} = 2.1\times 10^{-8}(-\hat{\mathbf{i}})T$ ☐

***34.** Light with an energy flux of 18 W/m^2 falls on a non-reflecting surface at normal incidence. If the surface area is 20 m^2, find the average force exerted on the surface during a 30 min time span.

____

***35.** The radiations are coming from a 100 W bulb at a distance of 3 m. Assume that, the efficiency of the bulb is 2.5% and it is a point source.
Match the quantities given in Column I with their respective values given in Column II.

Column I	Column II
A. Intensity (in W/m^2)	1. 2.9
B. E_{rms} (in V/m)	2. 0.022
C. B_{rms} (in T)	3. 9.6×10^{-9}

A. ________ B. ________ C. ________

36. The magnetic field component of intensity of an electromagnetic wave is $4I_0$. If x is the electric field component of intensity, then find the value of x.

____

37. In an electromagnetic wave, energy associated with electric field is much higher than that of magnetic field.

Yes ☐ No ☐

TOPIC 3
Electromagnetic Spectrum

NCERT Pg 208-211

38. Arrange the following electromagnetic radiations in the order of increasing wavelength.

I. Blue light II. Yellow light
III. X-ray IV. Radio wave

____

39. Tick (✓/×) for correct/incorrect statement in given boxes.

(i) Radio waves are produced by the accelerated motion of charges in conducting wires. ☐

(ii) Radio waves are used in radio and television communication systems. ☐

(iii) Cellular phones use radio waves to transmit voice communication in the low frequency range. ☐

(iv) Infrared waves are called heat waves. ☐

(v) Water molecules readily absorbs infrared waves. ☐

***40.** Match the EM waves given in Column I with their respective frequency range given in Column II.

Column I	Column II
A. Radio waves	1. 530 kHz-1710 kHz
B. AM waves	2. 88 MHz-108 MHz
C. TV waves	3. 500 kHz-1000 MHz
D. FM waves	4. 54 MHz-890 MHz

A. ______________ B. ______________ C. ______________ D. ______________

41. Find the wavelength of a radio wave of frequency of 1 MHz.

____

42. The condition under which a microwave oven heats up a food item, containing water molecules, most efficiently is

(a) the frequency of the microwave must match the resonant frequency of the water molecules ☐

(b) the frequency of the microwave has no relation with natural frequency of water molecules ☐

(c) microwave are heat waves, so always produce heating ☐

(d) infrared waves produce heating in a microwave oven ☐

43. The magnetic field of plane electromagnetic wave is given by

$$B_y = 2\times 10^{-7} \sin (0.5\times 10^{3}\, x + 1.5\times 10^{11}\, t)\text{T}$$

To which electromagnetic wave, the above value of magnetic field belong?

____

***44.** **Statement I** Most of harmful UV radiation of sun is absorbed by ozone layer.

Statement II Ozone layer lies in ionosphere.

Which of the following statement(s) is/are correct?

(a) Only statement I ☐ (b) Only statement II ☐

(c) Both statements I and II ☐ (d) Neither statement I nor II ☐

***45.** Welders wear special glass goggles or face masks with glass windows to protect their eyes from large amount of UV radiation produced by welding arcs.

True ☐ False ☐

***46.** Match Column I (electromagnetic wave type) with Column II (its association/application).

Column I	Column II
A. Infrared waves	1. To treat muscular strain
B. Radio waves	2. For broadcasting
C. X-rays	3. To detect fracture of bones
D. Ultraviolet	4. Absorbed by the ozone layer of the atmosphere

A. ______________ B. ______________ C. ______________ D. ______________

47. If v_γ, v_X and v_M are the speeds of γ-rays, X-rays and microwaves respectively in vacuum, then

(a) $v_\gamma > v_M > v_X$ ☐ (b) $v_\gamma > v_X > v_M$ ☐

(c) $v_\gamma = v_X = v_M$ ☐ (d) None of these ☐

Assertion-Reason Questions

Direction (Q. Nos. 1-10) *In the following questions, a statement of Assertion is followed by a corresponding statement of Reason. From the following options, choose the correct one.*

(a) Both Assertion and Reason are correct and Reason is the correct explanation of Assertion.
(b) Both Assertion and Reason are correct but Reason is not the correct explanation of Assertion.
(c) Assertion is correct but Reason is incorrect.
(d) Assertion is incorrect but Reason is correct.

1. **Assertion** (A) Electromagnetic waves are longitudinal in nature.

Reason (R) Electromagnetic waves are produced due to oscillation of a charged particle.

(a) ☐ (b) ☐ (c) ☐ (d) ☐

***2.** **Assertion** (A) Like light radiation, thermal radiations are also electromagnetic radiation.

Reason (R) The thermal radiations require no medium for propagation.

(a) ☐ (b) ☐ (c) ☐ (d) ☐

3. **Assertion** (A) Electromagnetic waves carry energy and momentum.
Reason (R) Electromagnetic waves can be polarised.

(a) ☐ (b) ☐ (c) ☐ (d) ☐

***4.** **Assertion** (A) Electromagnetic waves interact with matter and set up oscillations.
Reason (R) Interaction is independent of the wavelength of the electromagnetic wave.

(a) ☐ (b) ☐ (c) ☐ (d) ☐

5. **Assertion** (A) In electromagnetic wave, the direction of variations of electric and magnetic field are perpendicular to each other and also perpendicular to the direction of wave propagation.
Reason (R) Electromagnetic waves are transverse in nature.

(a) ☐ (b) ☐ (c) ☐ (d) ☐

6. **Assertion** (A) The velocity of electromagnetic waves depends on electric and magnetic properties of the medium.
Reason (R) Velocity of electromagnetic waves in free space is constant.

(a) ☐ (b) ☐ (c) ☐ (d) ☐3

7. **Assertion** (A) The frequency of the electromagnetic wave naturally equals the frequency of oscillation of the charge.

Reason (R) The energy associated with the propagating wave comes at the expense of the energy of the source.

(a) ☐ (b) ☐ (c) ☐ (d) ☐

*8. **Assertion** (A) Infrared radiation plays an important role in maintaining the average temperature of the earth.
Reason (R) Infrared radiations are sometimes referred to as heat waves.

(a) ☐ (b) ☐ (c) ☐ (d) ☐

9. **Assertion** (A) Microwaves are used in microwaves oven for cooking purpose.

Reason (R) The frequency of microwaves is from 10^{14} to 10^{17} Hz.

(a) ☐ (b) ☐ (c) ☐ (d) ☐

10. **Assertion** (A) Ultraviolet radiations of higher frequency wave are dangerous to human being.

Reason (R) Ultraviolet radiations are absorbed by the atmosphere.

(a) ☐ (b) ☐ (c) ☐ (d) ☐

Case Based Questions

1. When EM waves propagate through a medium, electric field (**E**) and magnetic field (**B**) vary sinusoidally. Electric field and magnetic field become maximum at same position and time.

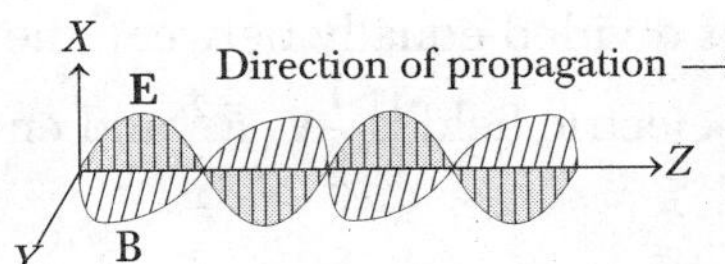

A plane EM wave travelling along Z-axis

Also **E** and **B** are perpendicular to each other as well as to the direction of propagation of the wave (**E** × **B**). In the given figure, electric field is along x-direction, magnetic field is along y-direction and the wave propagates along z-direction.

The EM wave propagating in the positive z-direction may be represented by following equation

Here, $E = E_x = E_0 \sin(kz - \omega t)$

$B = B_y = B_0 \sin(kz - \omega t)$

The magnetic field in a plane electromagnetic wave is given by

$B_y = (2 \times 10^{-7} \text{ T}) \sin (0.5 \times 10^3 x + 1.5 \times 10^{11} t)$

Answer the following questions.

(i) The wavelength of wave is

(a) 12.6 cm ☐ (b) 1.26 cm ☐

(c) 126 cm ☐ (d) 0.126 cm ☐

(ii) The frequency of wave is

(a) 23.6×10^{10} Hz ☐ (b) 238×10^{10} Hz ☐

(c) 2.38×10^{10} Hz ☐ (d) 2.38×10^{12} Hz ☐

(iii) The expression for the electric field is

(a) $(60\ \text{NC}^{-1})\sin(0.5 \times 10^3 x + 1.5 \times 10^{11} t)$ ☐

(b) $(60\ \text{NC}^{-1})\sin(10^3 x + 1.5 \times 10^{11} t)$ ☐

(c) $(60\ \text{NC}^{-1})\sin(0.5x + 1.5 \times 10^{11} t)$ ☐

(d) $(2 \times 10^7\ \text{NC}^{-1})\sin(0.5 \times 10^3 x + 1.5 \times 10^{11} t)$ ☐

(iv) The average energy density corresponding to the electric field is

(a) $\frac{10^{-7}}{4}$ Jm^{-3} ☐ (b) $\frac{10^7}{4\pi}$ Jm^{-1} ☐

(c) $\frac{1}{4\pi}$ Jm^{-3} ☐ (d) $\frac{10^{-7}}{4\pi}$ Jm^{-3} ☐

2. When EM wave travels in free space, then its speed is $c = \frac{1}{\sqrt{\mu_0 \varepsilon_0}}$

where, μ_0 = absolute permeability

ε_0 = absolute permittivity

c = speed of light

The energy in EM waves is divided equally between the electric and magnetic fields. The energy per unit volume of electric field is $\frac{1}{2}\varepsilon_0 E^2$ and energy density of magnetic field is $\frac{1}{2}\frac{B^2}{\mu_0}$.

Answer the following questions.

(i) The amplitude of electric field in a parallel beam of light of intensity 4.0 Wm^{-2} is

(a) 54.87 NC^{-1} ☐ (b) 5.487 NC^{-1} ☐

(c) 548.7 NC^{-1} ☐ (d) 5487 NC^{-1} ☐

(ii) The amplitude of magnetic field in a parallel beam of light of intensity 4.0 Wm^{-2} is

(a) 1.83×10^{-7} T ☐ (b) 18.3×10^{-7} T ☐

(c) 1.83×10^{-8} T ☐ (d) 18.3×10^{-9} T ☐

(iii) Electromagnetic wave's speed in medium is given by

(a) $\frac{1}{\sqrt{\varepsilon}}$ ☐ (b) $\frac{1}{\sqrt{\mu}}$ ☐

(c) $\frac{1}{\sqrt{\mu\varepsilon}}$ ☐ (d) $\sqrt{\mu\varepsilon}$ ☐

(iv) Electric intensity at any point in an electric field is equal to the ……… at that point.

(a) electric flux ☐ (b) magnetic flux density ☐

(c) potential gradient ☐ (d) None of these ☐

COMPETITION EDGE UP

1. A plane EM wave is propagating along x-direction. It has a wavelength of 4 mm. If electric field is in y-direction with the maximum magnitude of 60 Vm^{-1}, the equation for magnetic field is

[NCERT Pg. 206, JEE Main 2024]

(a) $B_z = 2 \times 10^{-7} \sin\left[\frac{\pi}{2} \times 10^3 (x - 3 \times 10^8 t)\right]\hat{k}$ T ☐

(b) $B_x = 60 \sin\left[\frac{\pi}{2} (x - 3 \times 10^8 t\right]\hat{i}$ T ☐

(c) $B_z = 2 \times 10^{-7} \sin\left[\frac{\pi}{2} (x - 3 \times 10^8 t)\right]\hat{k}$ T ☐

(d) $B_z = 60 \sin\left[\frac{\pi}{2} (x - 3 \times 10^8 t)\right]\hat{k}$ T ☐

2. In the given electromagnetic wave $E_y = 600 \sin(\omega t - kx)$ Vm^{-1}, intensity of the associate light beam is (in W/m^2) (Given, $\varepsilon_0 = 9 \times 10^{-12}$ $C^2N^{-1}m^{-2}$)

[NCERT Pg. 207, JEE Main 2024]

(a) 486 ☐ (b) 972 ☐

(c) 243 ☐ (d) 729

3. Match List I with List II.

	List I (EM-Wave)		List II (Wavelength Range)
A.	Infrared	I.	$< 10^{-3}$ nm
B.	Ultraviolet	II.	400 nm to 1 nm
C.	X-rays	III.	1 mm to 700 nm
D.	Gamma rays	IV.	1 nm to 10^{-3} nm

Choose the correct answer from the options given below. **[NCERT Pg. 209, JEE Main 2024]**

(a) A-IV, B-III, C-II, D-I ☐

(b) A-II, B-I, C-IV, D-III ☐

(c) A-III, B-II, C-IV, D-I ☐

(d) A-I, B-III, C-II, D-IV ☐

4. Arrange the following in the ascending order of wavelength.

A. Gamma rays (λ_1)

B. X-rays (λ_2)

C. Infrared waves (λ_3)

D. Microwaves (λ_4)

Choose the most appropriate answer from the options given below.

[NCERT Pg. 209, JEE Main 2024]

(a) $\lambda_2 < \lambda_1 < \lambda_4 < \lambda_3$ ☐

(b) $\lambda_1 < \lambda_2 < \lambda_3 < \lambda_4$ ☐

(c) $\lambda_4 < \lambda_3 < \lambda_1 < \lambda_2$ ☐

(d) $\lambda_4 < \lambda_3 < \lambda_2 < \lambda_1$ ☐

5. If frequency of electromagnetic wave is 60 MHz and it travels in air along z-direction, then the corresponding electric and magnetic field vectors will be mutually perpendicular to each other and the wavelength of the wave (in m) is

[NCERT Pg. 207, JEE Main 2024]

(a) 2 ☐ (b) 2.5 ☐

(c) 10 ☐ (d) 5 ☐

6. A parallel plate capacitor is charged by connecting it to a battery through a resistor. If I is the current in the circuit, then in the gap between the plates.

[NCERT Pg. 203, NEET 2024]

(a) There is no current. ☐

(b) Displacement current of magnitude equal to I flows in the same direction as I. ☐

(c) Displacement current of magnitude equal to I flows in a direction opposite to that of I. ☐

(d) Displacement current of magnitude greater than I flows but can be in any direction. ☐

7. The property which is not of an electromagnetic wave travelling in free space is that **[NCERT Pg. 207, NEET 2024]**

(a) They are transverse in nature ☐

(b) The energy density in electric field is equal to energy density in magnetic field ☐

(c) They travel with a speed equal to $\frac{1}{\sqrt{\mu_0 \varepsilon_0}}$ ☐

(d) They originate from charges moving with uniform speed ☐

8. In a plane electromagnetic wave travelling in free space, the electric field component oscillates sinusoidally at a frequency of 2.0×10^{10} Hz and amplitude 48 V m^{-1}. Then the amplitude of oscillating magnetic field is (Speed of light in free space $= 3 \times 10^8 \text{ m s}^{-1}$) **[NCERT Pg. 207, NEET 2023]**

(a) 1.6×10^{-8} T ☐

(b) 1.6×10^{-7} T ☐

(c) 1.6×10^{-6} T ☐

(d) 1.6×10^{-9} T ☐

9. When light propagates through a material medium of relative permittivity ϵ_r and relative permeability μ_r, the velocity of light, v is given by (c-velocity of light in vacuum) **[NCERT Pg. 207, NEET 2022]**

(a) $v = \sqrt{\frac{\mu_r}{\varepsilon_r}}$ ☐ (b) $v = \sqrt{\frac{\varepsilon_r}{\mu_r}}$ ☐

(c) $v = \frac{c}{\sqrt{\varepsilon_r \mu_r}}$ ☐ (d) $v = c$ ☐

10. The electromagnetic wave with shortest wavelength among the following is **[NCERT Pg 211, NEET (Oct.) 2020]**

(a) UV-rays ☐

(b) X-rays ☐

(c) γ-rays ☐

(d) microwaves ☐

Chapter 9

Ray Optics and Optical Instruments

TOPIC 1

Reflection of Light by Spherical Mirrors

1. Angle of reflection for ray shown will be _________(30/60) degrees.

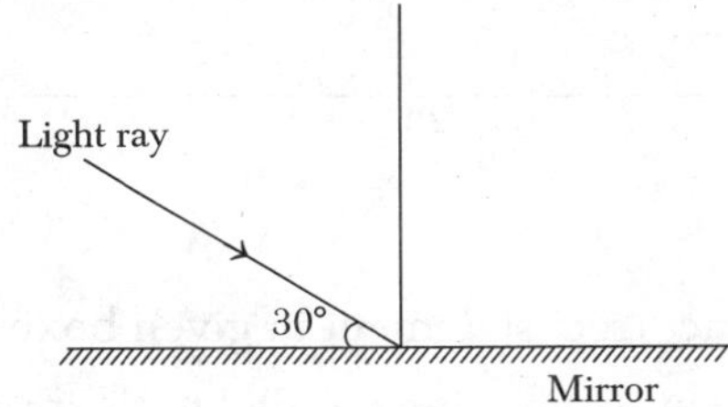

2. A ray of light travelling in XOY-plane is made incident over surface of a plane mirror, then reflected beam cannot be

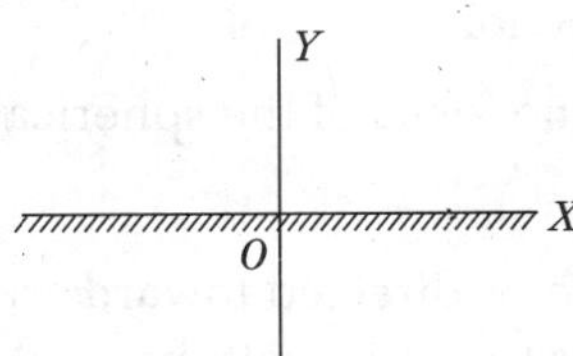

(a) directed along + X-axis ☐ (b) directed along + Y-axis ☐
(c) directed along + Z-axis ☐ (d) directed along – X-axis ☐

3. In given case of image formation using a convex mirror, write the sign of following.

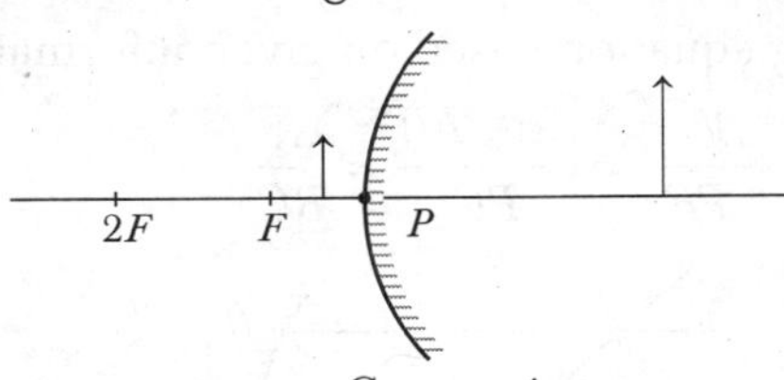

Convex mirror

*Concepts of all questions bearing * are important for JEE/NEET/CUET.*

I. Object distance = ________ II. Image distance = ________

III. Image height = ________ IV. Radius of curvature of mirror = ________

4. In the given figure, what is shown by the shaded portion?

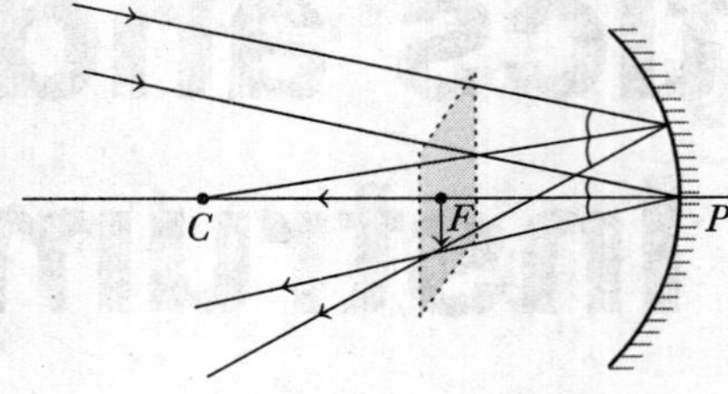

____

5. The following figure shows the reflection of a ray falling at an angle of 10° on the curved surface of a convex mirror. Here, angle α = ________ (10°/20°) and ratio $\frac{CP}{FP}$ = ________ (1 : 2/2 : 1).

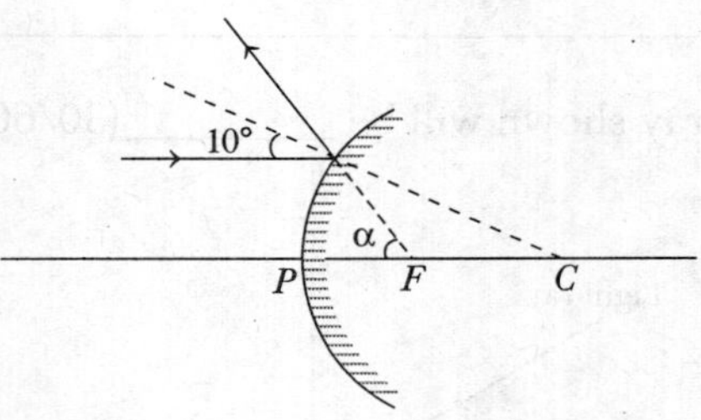

6. Tick (✓/×) for correct/incorrect statement in given boxes.

(i) The ray from a point source moving parallel to the principal axis, passes through the focus of the spherical mirror after reflection. ☐

(ii) The ray passing through the centre of curvature of the spherical mirror, retraces its path after reflection. ☐

(iii) The ray passing through the focus of the spherical mirror passes undeviated through it after reflection. ☐

7. A ray of light passing through or directed towards centre of curvature of a spherical mirror is reflected such that it traces its path back. What is the value of angle of incidence in this case?

____

***8.** In given figure, ΔABC and $\Delta A'B'C$ are similar. Also, $\Delta A'B'F$ and ΔNPF are similar. Complete the following equation based on given information.

$$\frac{B'F}{PF} = \frac{\ldots - FP}{PF} = \frac{\ldots}{BC}$$

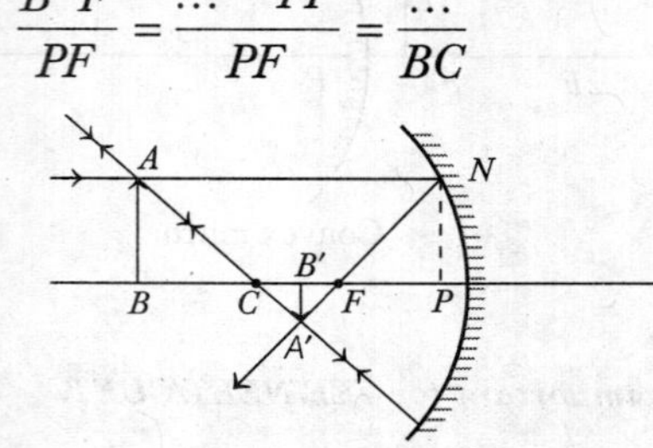

9. Write the nature of image formed in given two cases.

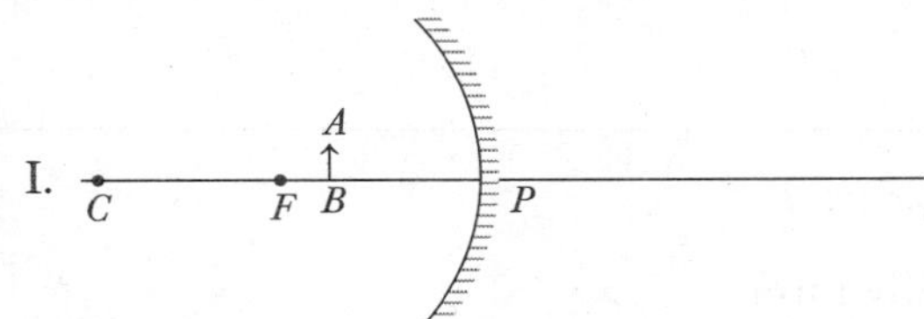

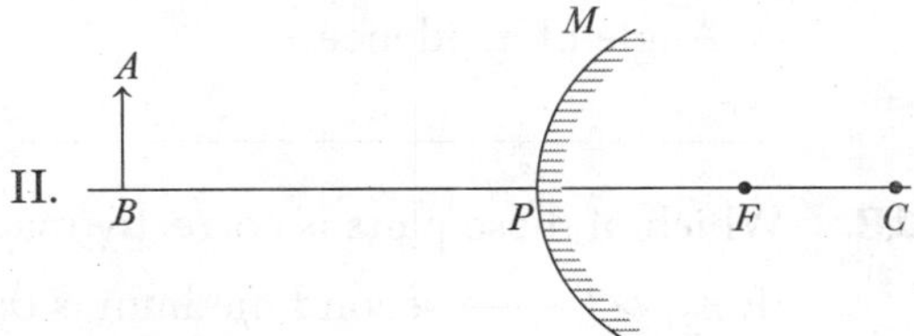

---

10. A real object is placed at a distance f in front of a convex mirror, where f is magnitude of focal length of mirror. Will the image be formed at a finite distance?

Yes ☐ No ☐

***11.** Object is placed 15 cm from a concave mirror of focal length 10 cm, then the nature of image formed will be

(a) magnified and inverted ☐ (b) magnified and erect ☐

(c) small in size and inverted ☐ (d) small in size and erect ☐

***12.** Consider a concave mirror of radius 20 cm. Choose correctly matched pair.

I. Object at 15 cm ⟶ magnification ($m = -2$)

II. Object at 5 cm ⟶ magnification ($m = +1.5$)

---

13. If lower half of a concave mirror is blackened, then the intensity of the image formed will be ________ (high/low).

14. An object is placed at (i) 10 cm (ii) 5 cm in front of a concave mirror of radius of curvature 15 cm. Find the position, nature and magnification of the image in each case.

***15.** Rear view mirror at a car is of radius of curvature $R = 2\,\text{m}$. A jogger approaches car (from behind) at a speed of $5\,\text{ms}^{-1}$. The speed of image (in cms^{-1}) when jogger is 39 m from the mirror is ________________(0.57/0.35).

16. A ray of light strikes an air-glass interface at an angle of incidence ($i = 60°$) and gets refracted at an angle of refraction r. On increasing the angle of incidence ($i > 60°$), the angle of refraction r______________ (increases/decreases).

***17.** From Snell's law, the refractive index of medium is $n = \dfrac{\sin i}{\sin r}$.

On which of the following factors it depends?

A. Characteristics of medium B. Wavelength of light

C. Angle of incidence

---

18. Which of these pairs is correctly matched?

I. $n_{21} > 1 \longrightarrow$ second medium is optically rarer

II. $n_{21} < 1 \longrightarrow$ second medium is optically rarer

---

19. Solve the given analogy.

Mass density: Ratio of mass and volume :: Optical density : ____________

20. Figs. (i) and (ii) show refraction of light from air to glass and from air to water. Find the value of θ in the case of refraction as shown in Fig. (iii).

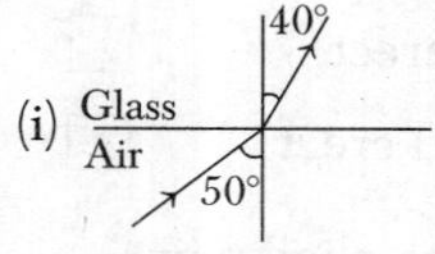

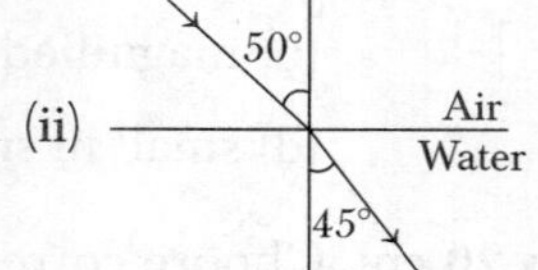

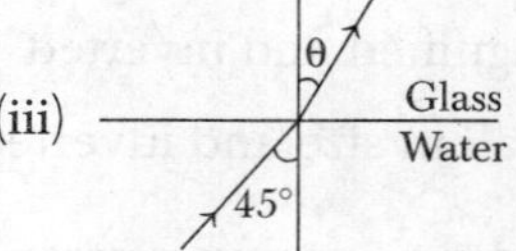

---

21. When an object lying in a denser medium is observed from rarer medium, the real depth of the object is________________ (less/more) than the observed depth.

22. Apparent depth or thickness of a denser medium slab decreases, if observer moves his eyes away from the normal.

True ☐ False ☐

***23.** A boy is in a pool and shines a flashlight towards the level of it at a 35° angle to the vertical. At what angle does the flashlight beam leave the pool ? (The index of refraction of glass is 1.33)

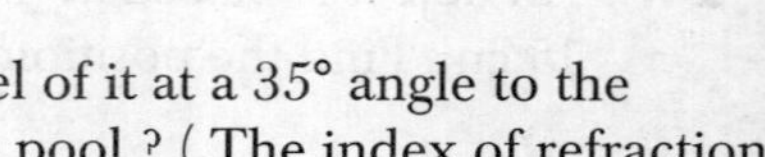

---

24. A lifeguard runs towards a drowning child in a pool along path $A \rightarrow B \rightarrow C$.

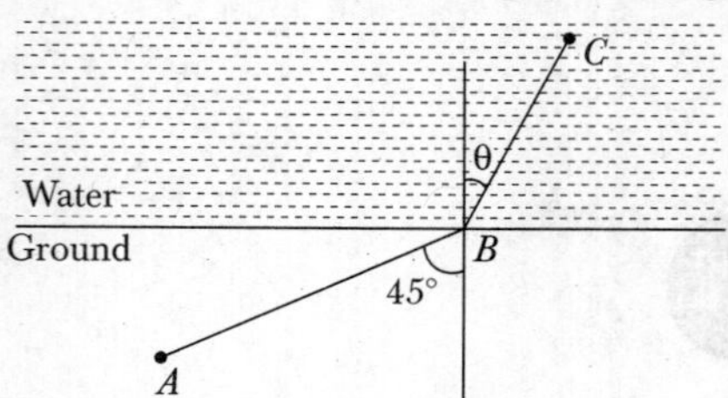

Speed of running of guard on ground is 10 km/h and his speed of swimming in water is 2 km/h. If guard wants to reach child at C in minimum time, then angle θ must be, such that

(a) $\text{cosec}\,\theta = 5\sqrt{2}$ ☐

(b) $\cos\theta = 0.5$ ☐

(c) $\tan\theta = 5\sqrt{2}$ ☐

(d) $\sec\theta = 5\sqrt{2}$ ☐

TOPIC 3

Total Internal Reflection

NCERT Pg 229-232

25. In given case, what will be the value of θ?

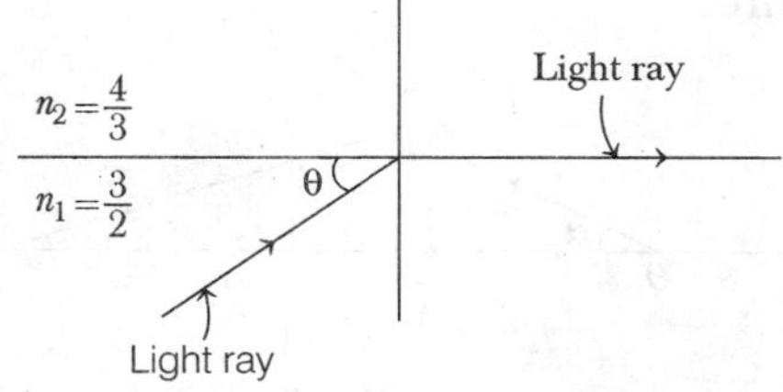

***26.** A ray of light is incident at the glass-water interface at an angle i. If it emerges finally parallel to the surface of water, then the value of n_g would be ________ $\left(\sin i / \frac{1}{\sin i}\right)$.

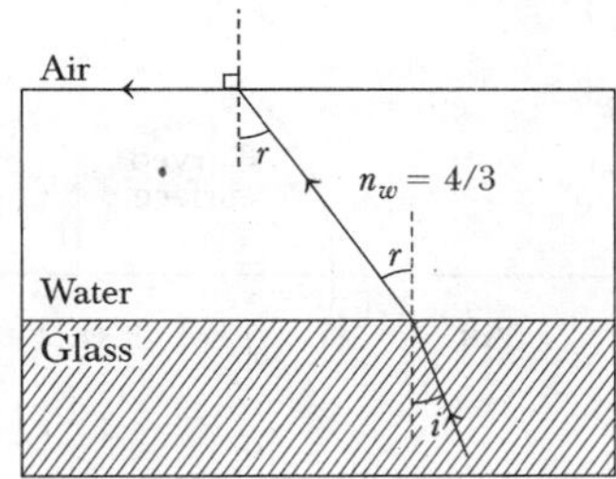

***27.** A light ray is made incident on surface of region II as shown below. Refractive indices of media in regions I, II, III and IV are n_0, $\frac{n_0}{2}$, $\frac{n_0}{6}$ and $\frac{n_0}{8}$, respectively.

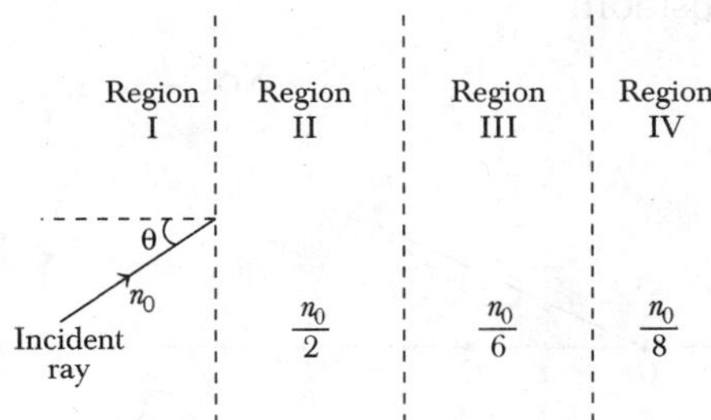

Angle θ for which light ray does not reach region IV is

(a) $\sin^{-1}\left(\frac{3}{4}\right)$ ☐ (b) $\sin^{-1}\left(\frac{1}{8}\right)$ ☐ (c) $\sin^{-1}\left(\frac{1}{4}\right)$ ☐ (d) $\sin^{-1}\left(\frac{1}{3}\right)$ ☐

TOPIC 4

Refraction at Spherical Surfaces and by Lenses

NCERT Pg 232-239

28. Consider the below figure.

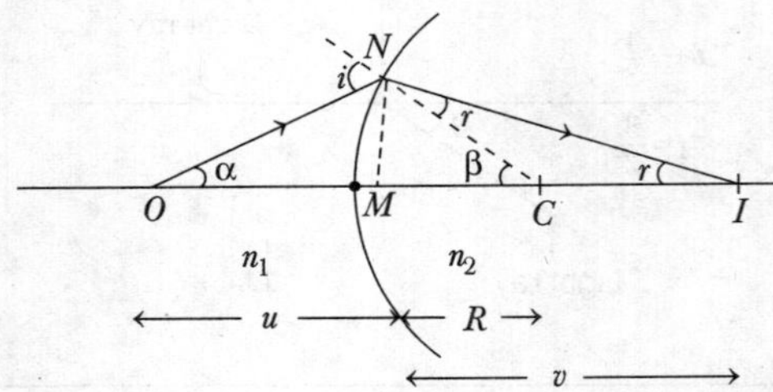

Write the correct relation between object and image distance in terms of refractive index of the medium and the radius of curvature of the curved spherical surface.

29.

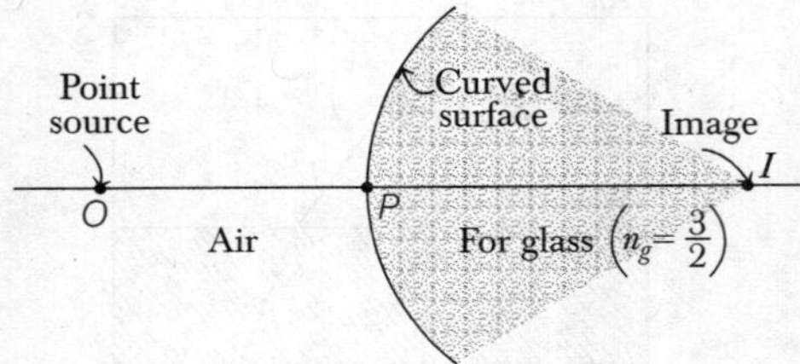

If OP is 100 cm and radius of curvature of surface is 20 cm, then PI is ____________ (100 cm/50 cm).

30. In given case, $PC = 5$ cm and $PO = 10$ cm. Will the distance PI be 7.5 cm ? ($O \to$ object position, $I \to$ image position)

Yes ☐ No ☐

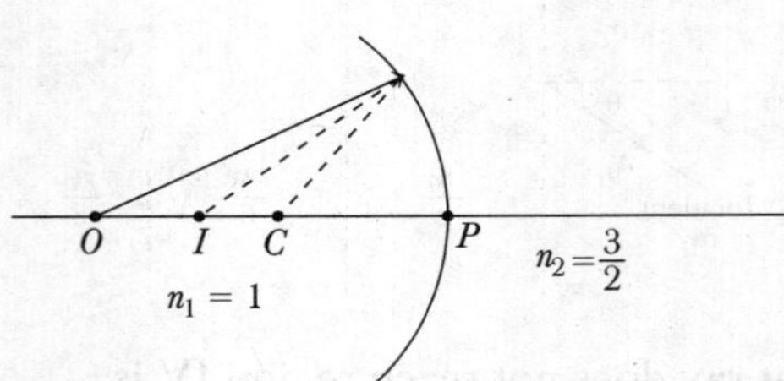

***31.** A parallel beam of light is incident on a solid transparent sphere of a material of refractive index n. If a point image is produced at the back of the sphere as shown in the following figure, then the refractive index of the material of the sphere is ____________ (2/2.5).

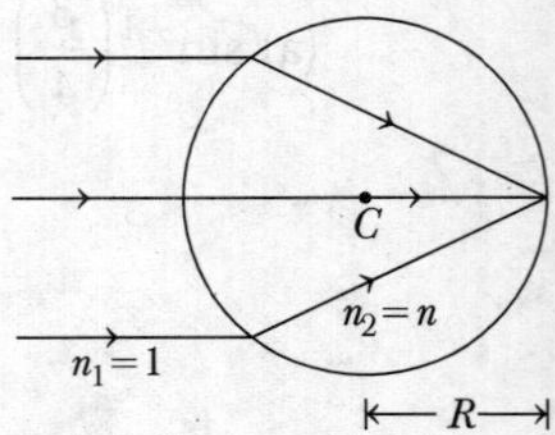

***32.** A double convex lens, made of a material of refractive index n_1 is placed inside two liquids of refractive indices n_2 and n_3 as shown below. $n_2 > n_1 > n_3$. A wide parallel beam of light is incident on the lens from the left. Will the lens give a convergent and a divergent beam?

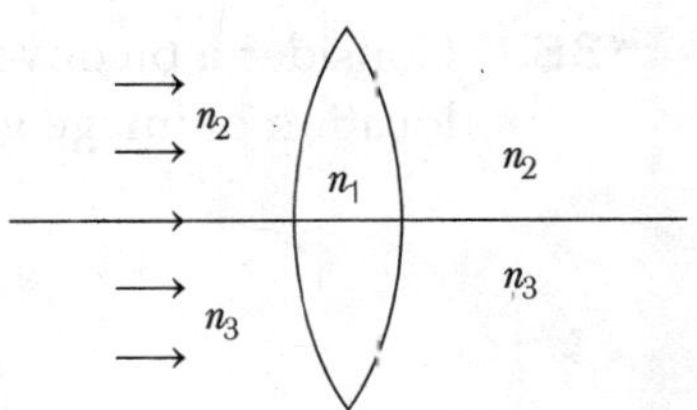

____

33. For rays coming from infinity, two images are formed in the case shown in the following figure.

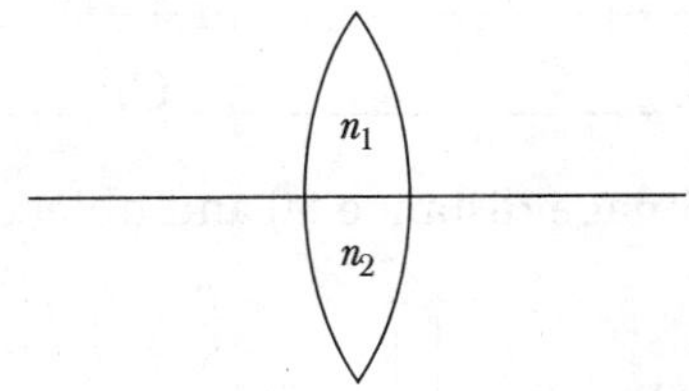

True [ ] False [ ]

***34.** A concave lens made of glass of refractive index 1.5 has both surfaces of same radius of curvature R. On immersion in a medium of refractive index 1.75, it will behave as a __________ (convergent/divergent) lens of focal length __________ ($3R$/$3.5R$).

35. A lens is made of flint glass ($n_g = 1.5$). When the lens is immersed in a liquid of refractive index 1.25, will the focal length of lens increase or decrease?

____

36. Focal length of given lens in water is ______________ (+255/–255) cm.

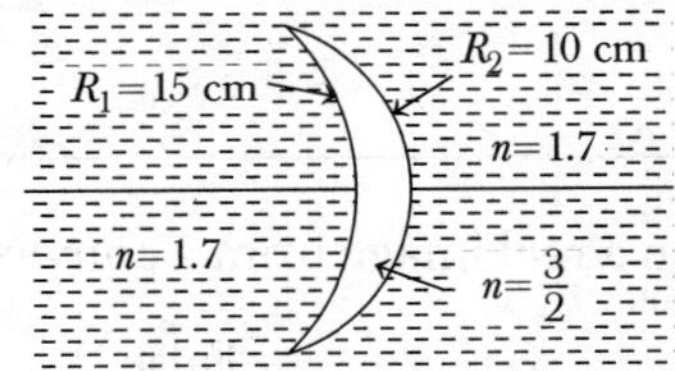

37. Taking radius of curvature R and refractive index of glass 3/2, match the shape of lens with its focal length.

Column I	Column II
A.	1. $f = -2R$
B.	2. $f = -R$
C.	3. $f = 2R$
D.	4. $f = R$

A. ______________ B. ______________ C. ______________ D. ______________

***38.** Consider a biconvex lens and match the location of object given in Column I with the location of image given in Column II.

Column I	Column II
A. $f < u < 2f$	1. $v = 2f$
B. $u = 2f$	2. $v > u$
C. $u < f$	3. $f < v < 2f$
D. $u > 2f$	4. $v > 2f$

A. ________ B. ________ C. ________ D. ________

39. The graph between the image distance (v) and object distance (u) from the convex lens is

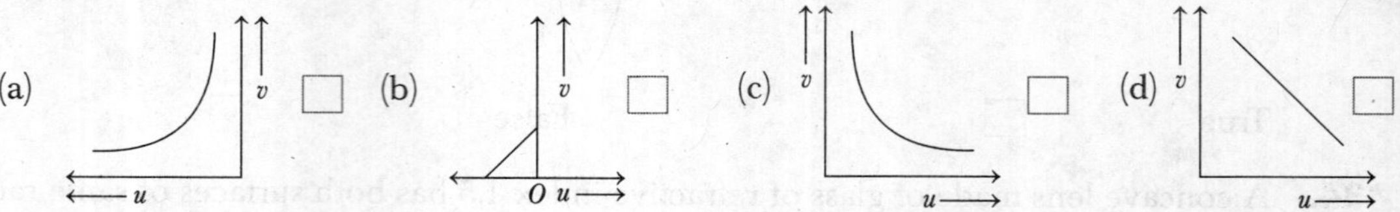

40. Which of these pairs is correctly matched?

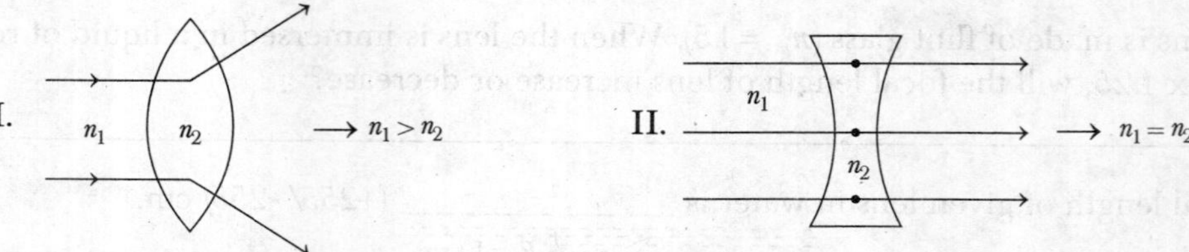

____

41. Minimum distance to obtain a real image from a convex lens (focal length = f) must be $f/4$.

True ☐ False ☐

42. A concave lens of focal length 40 cm is placed at position AB in the path of a beam converging at point P.

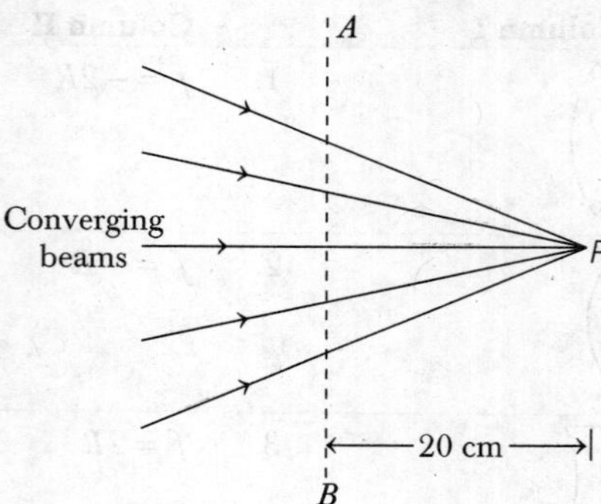

At what distance is the image formed?

____

***43.** In the figure given below, APB is a curved surface of radius of curvature 10 cm separating air and a tranparent material $\left(\mu = \frac{4}{3}\right)$. A point object O is placed in air on the principal axis of the surface 20 cm from P. The distance of the image of O from P will be

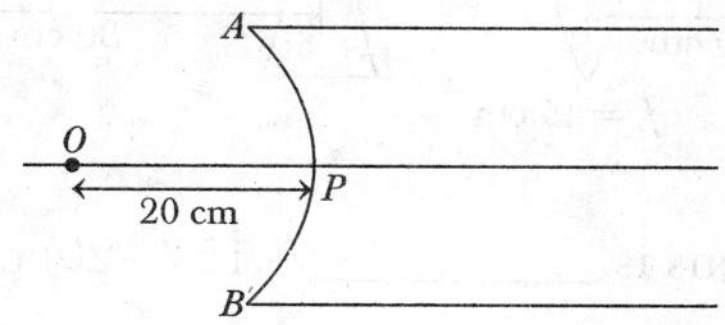

(a) 16 cm left of P in air ☐ (b) 16 cm right of P in water ☐
(c) 20 cm right of P in water ☐ (d) 20 cm left of P in air ☐

44. A wire mesh consisting of very small square is viewed at a distance of 8 cm through a magnifying converging lens of focal length 10 cm, kept close to the eye. The magnification produced by the lens is ________(5/6).

***45.** A glass lens ($n_g = 1.47$) disappears in a liquid (n_l) when dipped in it. Ratio of $\frac{n_l}{n_g}$ is nearly ________ $\left(1/\frac{2}{3}\right)$.

***46.** The power of a biconvex lens is 20 D and the radius of curvature of each surface is 5 cm. Find the refractive index of the material of lens.

____

***47.** Given figures show the arrangements of two lenses. The radii of curvature of all the curved surfaces are same. The ratio of the equivalent focal length of combinations P, Q and R is ________ (1: 2: 3/1: 1: 1).

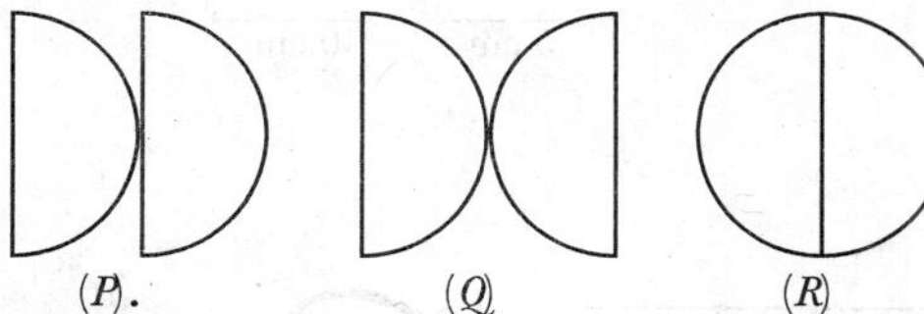

***48.** A convex lens of focal length 40 cm, a concave lens of focal length 40 cm and a concave lens of focal length 15 cm are placed in contact. Find the power of the combination in dioptre.

____

***49.** Ratio of powers of lenses L_1 and L_2 is $\frac{3}{2}$. Their equivalent focal length is 30 cm.

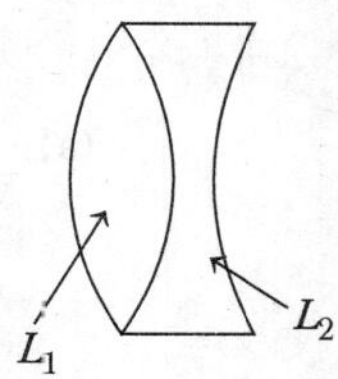

Then, tick the correctly matched pair.

I. $f_1 = 10$ cm II. $f_2 = 15$ cm

____

***50.** Two lenses (as shown) form an image at 30 cm when object is placed at 40 cm.

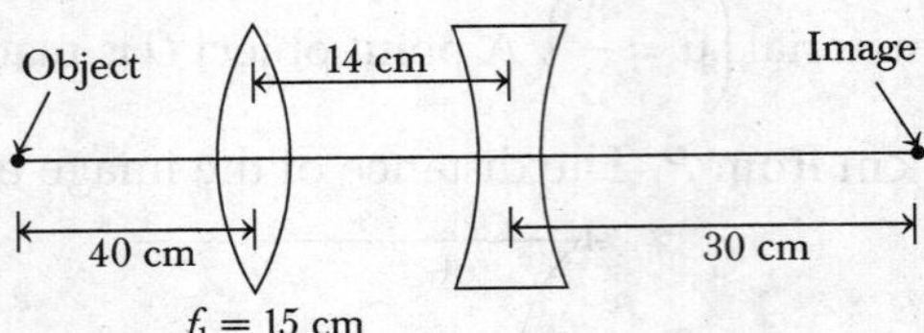

Focal length of concave lens is __________ (–15 / –20) cm.

51. A convex lens of focal length 1 m and a concave lens of focal length 0.25 m are kept 0.75 m apart. A parallel beam of light first passes through the convex lens, then the refracted rays passes through the concave lens.

Tick the correct statement from given below.

I. The final image is formed at 0.5 m away from the concave lens.

II. The final image is formed at focus of the concave lens.

III. The rays after refraction from both the lenses becomes parallel to the principal axis.

IV. The final image is real and formed at 0.75 m from the concave lens.

____

***52.** In given arrangement, image is formed at __________ (30/50) cm to the __________ (left/right) of the third lens.

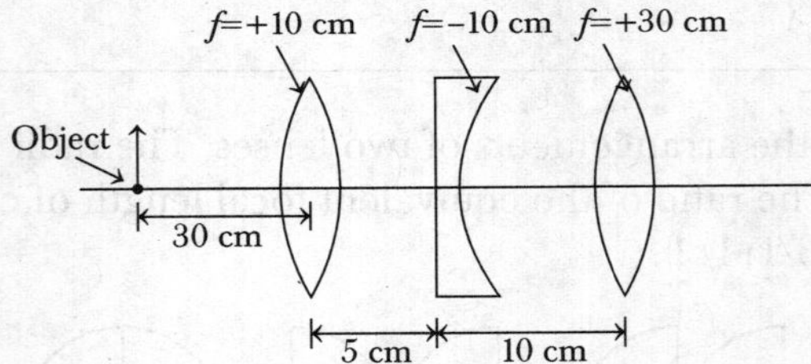

TOPIC 5
Refraction through a Prism

NCERT Pg 239-240

53. The graph between angle of deviation (δ) and angle of incidence (i) for a triangular prism is represented by

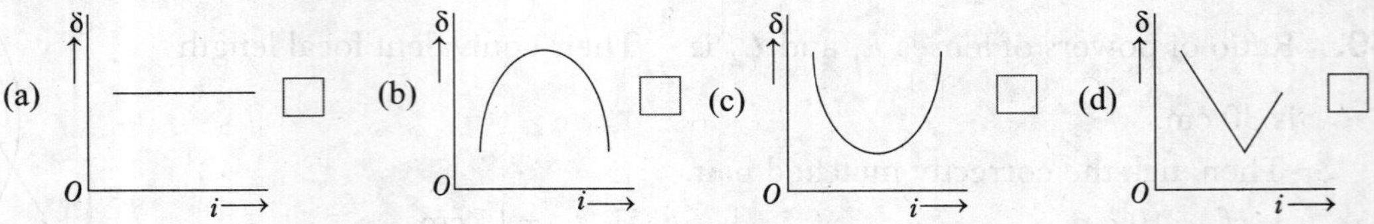

54. In a prism, when angle of incidence is made 3/4th of angle of prism, minimum deviation occurs. Is the angle of deviation become half of angle of prism?

Yes ☐ No ☐

55. Minimum deviation for an equilateral prism is 30°. Calculate the angle of incidence.

56. The refracting angle of a prism is A and refractive index of the material of the prism is cot $(A/2)$. The angle of minimum deviation is

(a) 180°–3A ☐ (b) 180°–2A ☐ (c) 90°–A ☐ (d) 180°+2A ☐

***57.** In following case, angle of incidence will be ________ (30°/45°), if refractive index of prism is $\sqrt{2}$.

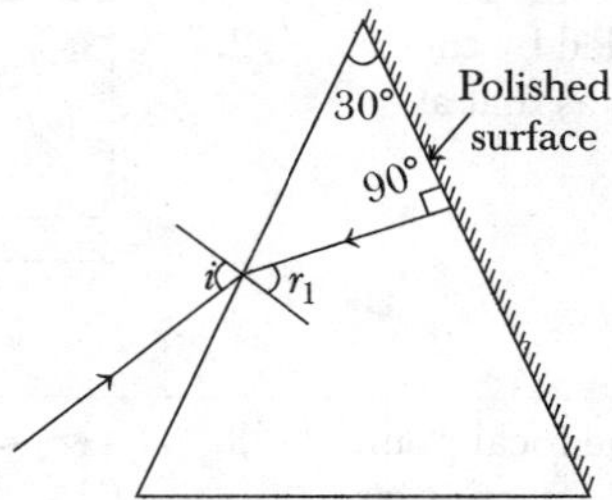

58. A prism (μ = 1.57) gives a deviation of 5.5°. The angle of prism must be 9.64°.

True ☐ False ☐

59. A monochromatic light is incident on the face of the prism at an angle of incidence i = 60°. The ray thus undergoes ________ (deviation/dispersion).

***60.** For the diagram shown below, do we get a spectrum on the screen?

Yes ☐ No ☐

***61.** A thin prism P_1 with angle 4° made from glass of refractive index 1.54 is combined with another thin prism P_2 made from glass of refractive index 1.72 to produce dispersion without deviation. The angle of the prism P_2 is

(a) 5.33° ☐ (b) 4° ☐ (c) 3° ☐ (d) 2.6° ☐

TOPIC 6

Optical Instruments

NCERT Pg 240-246

62. Which of these pairs is correctly matched?

I. 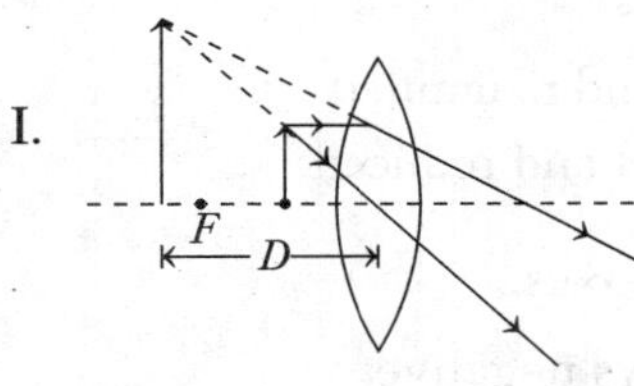

→ Magnification, $m = 1 + \left(\frac{D}{f}\right)$

II. 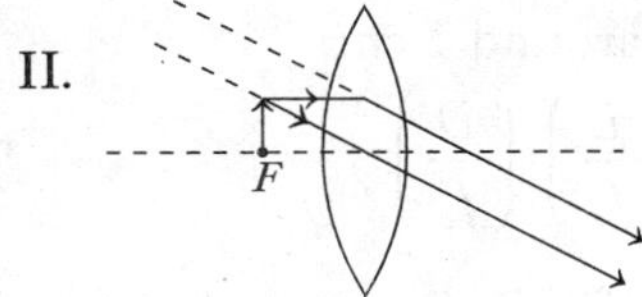

→ Magnification, $m = \left(1 - \frac{D}{f}\right)$

***63.** Match the Column I (different cases of simple microscope) with Column II (ray diagram).

Column I	Column II
A. The magnifying lens is located such that image is at the near point.	1. h, θ_i, f, θ_i; Eye focused at infinity
B. The angle subtended by the object, is the same as that at the near point.	2. Eye focused on near point; D, u
C. The object near the focal point of the lens and the image is far off but closer than infinity.	3. h, θ_0, D

A. ________________ B. ________________ C. ________________

64. The least distance of distinct vision is 25 cm. The focal length of a convex lens is 5 cm. It can act as a simple microscope of magnifying power ________ (5/6).

65. For a simple microscope, difference of maximum magnification and minimum magnification is ________ (1/0).

66. For a compound microscope, choose incorrect statement.

I. $F_{\text{eyepiece}} > F_{\text{objective}}$

II. $P_{\text{eyepiece}} > P_{\text{objective}}$

III. Diameter of eyepiece > Diameter of objective

IV. Magnification of objective > Magnification of eyepiece.

____

67. Considering a compound microscope, complete the following sentences.

I. Length of tube is $v_o + u_e$ when final image is at ________ (D/∞) .

II. Length of tube is $v_o + f_e$ when final image is at ______ (D/∞) .

***68.** In a compound microscope, the intermediate image is

(a) virtual, erect and magnified ☐ (b) real, erect and magnified ☐

(c) real, inverted and magnified ☐ (d) virtual, erect and reduced ☐

69. Tick (✓/✗) for correct/incorrect statement in given boxes.

(i) In a compound microscope, magnification is always negative. ☐

(ii) In any optical instrument, diameter of eyepiece is around 1 cm. ☐

(iii) Magnification of a compound microscope is $m = \left(\frac{L}{f_e}\right)\cdot\left(\frac{D}{f_e}\right)$ ☐

(iv) In a compound microscope, the ratio of diameter of objective to that of eyepiece is equal to unity. ☐

***70.** In a compound microscope, $f_o = 4$ mm, $f_e = 25$ mm and $L = 16$ cm.
If final image is formed at infinity, then magnification obtained will be ____________ (more/less) than 300.

***71.** For an astronomical telescope having objective lens of focal length 10 m and eyepiece lens of focal length 10 cm, telescope's the tube length and magnification respectively are
(a) 20 cm, 1 ☐ (b) 1000 cm, 1 ☐ (c) 1010 cm, 1 ☐ (d) 1010 cm, 100 ☐

72. In a laboratory four convex lenses L_1, L_2, L_3 and L_4 of focal lengths 2, 4, 6 and 8 cm respectively are available. Two of these lenses form a telescope of length 10 cm and magnifying power is 4. Which of the above lenses satisfy the given criteria?

____

73. In a telescope, $f_o = 60$ cm, $f_e = 5$ cm. An object is viewed through it which subtends an angle of 2° at objective. Angle subtended by image at eyepiece will be________ (12°/24°).

***74.** Diameter of moon is 3.5×10^3 km and it is at a distance of 3.8×10^5 km from earth. Focal lengths of objective and eyepiece of a telescope used to view moon are 4 m and 10 cm, respectively. Find the angular diameter of the image (in degree) of the moon.

____

75. In a terrestrial telescope, focal length of objective is 90 cm, focal length of inverting lens is 5 cm and focal length of eyepiece is 6 cm.
If final image is at 30 cm, will the magnification obtained be 18?
Yes ☐ No ☐

76. Reflecting telescopes are used because they have no chromatic aberration, use parabolic reflecting surface and the weight of mirror is much less than that of a lens.
True ☐ False ☐

Assertion-Reason Questions

Direction (Q. Nos. 1-10) *In the following questions, a statement of Assertion is followed by a corresponding statement of Reason. From the following options, choose the correct one.*
(a) Both Assertion and Reason are correct and Reason is the correct explanation of Assertion.
(b) Both Assertion and Reason are correct but Reason is not the correct explanation of Assertion.
(c) Assertion is correct but Reason is incorrect.
(d) Assertion is incorrect but Reason is correct.

1. **Assertion** (A) Reflection makes object visible to eyes when light is incident on the object.
Reason (R) Smooth surfaces cause reflection and reflected rays are received by our eyes.
(a) ☐ (b) ☐ (c) ☐ (d) ☐

2. **Assertion** (A) The concave mirror will always focus incident light on its focus.
Reason (R) The relation between focal length and radius of curvature is $f = \frac{R}{2}$.
(a) ☐ (b) ☐ (c) ☐ (d) ☐

3. **Assertion** (A) Optical density of turpentine is more than that of water.
Reason (R) Turpentine has lesser mass density than that of water

(a) ☐ (b) ☐ (c) ☐ (d) ☐

4. **Assertion** (A) We can use a prism to bend rays by 90° or 180° or to invert image.

Reason (R) Critical angle for glass is less than 45°.

(a) ☐ (b) ☐ (c) ☐ (d) ☐

5. **Assertion** (A) A concave refracting surface cannot form a real image of an object.
Reason (R) Concave surface diverges a parallel beam of light.

(a) ☐ (b) ☐ (c) ☐ (d) ☐

***6.** **Assertion** (A) If several convex lenses of equal power are placed close to each other, their power increases.
Reason (R) The focal length of the combination decreases when convex lenses of equal focal length are placed together.

(a) ☐ (b) ☐ (c) ☐ (d) ☐

7. **Assertion** (A) Angle of deviation depends on the angle of prism.
Reason (R) For thin prism, $\delta = (\mu - 1)A$.

where, δ = angle of deviation, μ = refractive index and A = angle of prism.

(a) ☐ (b) ☐ (c) ☐ (d) ☐

8. **Assertion** (A) In case of minimum deviation, $i = e$ and $r_1 = r_2$.

Reason (R) Light ray passes parallel to base of prism when prism is in minimum deviation position.

(a) ☐ (b) ☐ (c) ☐ (d) ☐

***9.** **Assertion** (A) The magnifying power of a simple microscope increases as the focal length of its lens decreases.
Reason (R) The magnifying power of a simple microscope is inversely proportional to the focal length of its lens.

(a) ☐ (b) ☐ (c) ☐ (d) ☐

10. **Assertion** (A) It is not possible to increase light gathering power of a telescope.

Reason (R) Large lenses are impractical.

(a) ☐ (b) ☐ (c) ☐ (d) ☐

Case Based Questions

1. When two transparent media are separated by a spherical surface, light incident on the surface from one side get refracted into medium on the other side. Spherical surfaces are of two types as shown in figure.

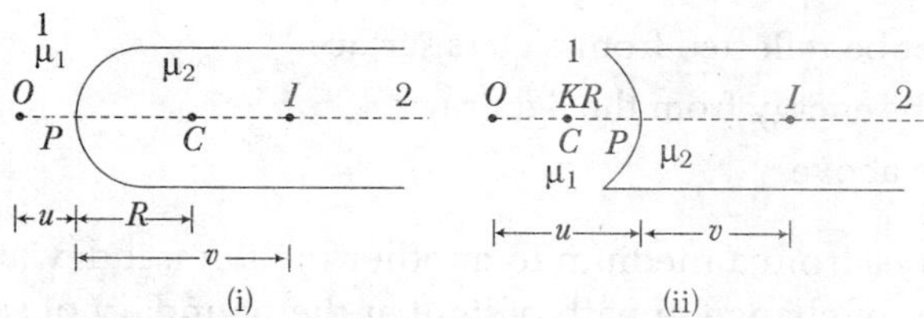

Spherical surface (i) convex (ii) concave

For both surfaces, refraction formula is given by $\frac{\mu_2}{v} - \frac{\mu_1}{u} = \frac{\mu_2 - \mu_1}{R}$

where, μ_1 = refractive index of first medium,

μ_2 = refractive index of second medium,

R = radius of curvature of spherical surfaces,

u = object distance and

v = image distance

Transverse magnification, $m = \frac{h_I}{h_O} = \frac{\mu_1 v}{\mu_2 u}$

(i) If the point C is centre of curvature of the spherical surface, then position of image will be

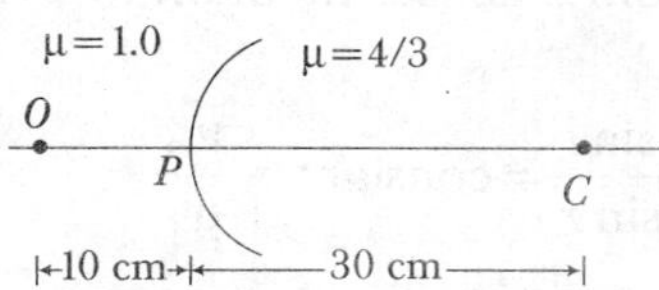

(a) 15 cm left of spherical surface ☐

(b) 15 cm right of spherical surface ☐

(c) 10 cm left of spherical surface ☐

(d) 10 cm right of spherical surface ☐

(ii) A light ray falls from a point source in air on a convex spherical surface of refractive index 1.5 and radius of curvature 20 cm. The distance of light source from the glass surface is 100 cm. The position of the image is.

(a) 50 cm ☐ (b) 75 cm ☐

(c) 100 cm ☐ (d) 60 cm ☐

(iii) A convex refracting surface having radius of curvature 0.2m separates two media of refractive index $\frac{4}{3}$ and 1.6. An object is placed in the first medium $\left(\mu = \frac{4}{3}\right)$ at a distance of 2 m from the refracting surface. The position of the image will be

(a) 2.4 m is rarer medium ☐
(b) 2.4 m in denser medium ☐
(c) 1.6 m in rarer medium ☐
(d) 1.6 m in denser medium ☐

(iv) Rays of light get refracted while passing from air to glass because
(a) Speed of light in glass is less than the speed of light in air. ☐
(b) They cannot be reflected from a glass surface ☐
(c) Glass absorbs energy from the light rays ☐
(d) None of the above ☐

2. When a light passes from a medium to another medium, it deviates from its original path. The phenomenon of change in path of light at the boundary of separation of two medium, as it goes from one medium to another medium called refraction.

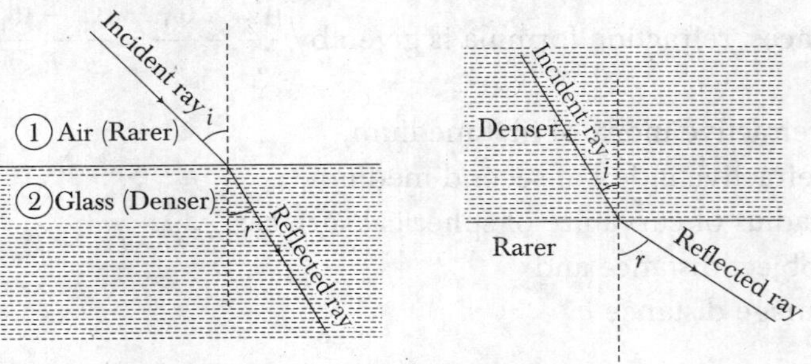

Refraction of light

When ray of light goes from a rarer medium to a denser medium, it bends towards the normal.

When a ray of light goes from a denser medium to a rarer medium, it bends away from the normal.

For two particular media, $\frac{\sin i}{\sin r} = \text{constant} = \frac{\mu_2}{\mu_1}$ ...(i)

This is known as **Snell's law.**

The incident ray, the reflected ray and the refracted ray all lie in the same plane.

(i) Light of wavelength 300 nm in medium A enters into medium B through a plane surface. If frequency of light is 5×10^{14} Hz and $\frac{V_A}{V_B} = \frac{4}{5}$, then ratio of absolute refractive index of medium A to medium B is
(a) $\frac{5}{2}$ ☐ (b) $\frac{2}{5}$ ☐
(c) $\frac{5}{4}$ ☐ (d) $\frac{3}{5}$ ☐

(ii) A ray of light falls on a glass plate of refractive index $\mu = 1.5$ What is the angle of incidence of the ray, if the angle between the reflected and refracted rays is 90°?
(a) $\tan^{-1}(1.2)$ ☐ (b) $\tan^{-1}(1.5)$ ☐
(c) $\sin^{-1}(1.2)$ ☐ (d) $\sin^{-1}(0.5)$ ☐

(iii) When a ray of light passes from one medium to another, then which of the following characteristic remains unchanged.

(a) Frequency ☐ (b) Phase ☐
(c) Amplitude ☐ (d) Frequency and phase both ☐

(iv) Refractive index of glass and water are $\frac{3}{2}$ and $\frac{4}{3}$ respectively. If the speed of light in glass is 2.4×10^8 m/s, then speed of light in water is

(a) 2.7×10^8 m/s ☐ (b) 2.5×10^8 m/s ☐
(c) 3×10^8 m/s ☐ (d) 2×10^8 m/s ☐

COMPETITION EDGE UP

1 The following figure represents two biconvex lenses L_1 and L_2 having focal length 10 cm and 15 cm respectively. The distance between L_1 and L_2 is [NCERT Pg. 238, JEE Main 2024]

L_1 L_2

(a) 15 cm ☐ (b) 10 cm ☐
(c) 35 cm ☐ (d) 25 cm ☐

2 Critical angle of incidence for a pair of optical media is 45°. The refractive indices of first and second media are in the ratio [NCERT Pg. 229, JEE Main 2024]

(a) 1 : 2 ☐ (b) $1 : \sqrt{2}$ ☐
(c) 2 : 1 ☐ (d) $\sqrt{2} : 1$ ☐

3 The refractive index of prism is $\mu = \sqrt{3}$ and the ratio of the angle of minimum deviation to the angle of prism is one. The value of angle of prism (in degree) is .... [NCERT Pg. 239, JEE Main 2024]

4 Given below are two statements.

Statement I When the white light passed through a prism, the red light bends lesser than yellow and violet.

Statement II The refractive indices are different for different wavelengths in dispersive medium.

In the light of the above statements, choose the correct answer from the options given below. [NCERT Pg. 239, JEE Main 2024]

(a) Statement I is true but Statement II is false. ☐
(b) Both Statement I and Statement II are true. ☐
(c) Statement I is false but Statement II is true. ☐
(d) Both Statement I and Statement II are false. ☐

5 If the distance between object and its two times magnified virtual image produced by a curved mirror is 15 cm, the focal length of the mirror must be [NCERT Pg. 225, JEE Main 2024]

(a) −12 cm ☐ (b) (10/3) cm ☐
(c) −10 cm ☐ (d) 15 cm ☐

6 A convex mirror of radius of curvature 30 cm forms an image that is half the size of the object. The object distance is [NCERT Pg. 226, JEE Main 2024]

(a) − 45 cm ☐ (b) 15 cm ☐
(c) 45 cm ☐ (d) −15 cm ☐

7 A small telescope has an objective of focal length 140 cm and an eye piece of focal length 5.0 cm. The magnifying power of telescope for viewing a distant object is [NCERT Pg. 244, NEET 2024]

(a) 34 ☐ (b) 28 ☐
(c) 17 ☐ (d) 32 ☐

8 Two thin lenses are of same focal lengths f, but one is convex and the other one is concave. When they are placed in contact with each other, the equivalent focal length of the combination will be

[NCERT Pg. 238, NEET 2023]

(a) $f/4$ ☐ (b) $f/2$ ☐

(c) infinite ☐ (d) zero ☐

9 A lens of large focal length and large aperture is best suited as an objective of an astronomical telescope, since

[NCERT Pg. 242, NEET 2021]

(a) a large aperture contributes to the quality and visibility of the images ☐

(b) a large area of the objective ensures better light gathering power ☐

(c) a large aperture provides a better resolution ☐

(d) All of the above ☐

10 The power of a biconvex lens is 10 D and the radius of curvature of each surface is 10 cm. Then, the refractive index of the material of the lens is

[NCERT Pg. 234, NEET (Oct) 2020]

(a) $\frac{4}{3}$ ☐ (b) $\frac{9}{8}$ ☐

(c) $\frac{5}{3}$ ☐ (d) $\frac{3}{2}$ ☐

11 A ray is incident at an angle of incidence i on one surface of a small angle prism (with angle of prism A) and emerges normally from the opposite surface. If the refractive index of the material of the prism is μ, then the angle of incidence is nearly equal to

[NCERT Pg. 240, NEET (Sep) 2020]

(a) $\frac{2A}{\mu}$ ☐

(b) μA ☐

(c) $\frac{\mu A}{2}$ ☐

(d) $\frac{A}{2\mu}$ ☐

12 An object is placed on the principal axis of a concave mirror at a distance of $1.5f$ (f is the focal length). The image will be at

[NCERT Pg. 225, NEET (Oct) 2020]

(a) $-3f$ ☐ (b) $1.5f$ ☐

(c) $-1.5f$ ☐ (d) $3f$ ☐

Chapter 10

Wave Optics

Scan and take Chapter Test

TOPIC 1

Huygens' Principle

NCERT Pg 257-258

1. According to corpuscular model of light on refraction, the speed of light would be ____________ (greater/lesser) in the denser medium. While in wave model of light, on refraction, the speed of light would be ____________ (greater/lesser) in the denser medium.

2. Wave theory cannot explain the phenomena of

I. polarisation

II. diffraction

III. compton effect

IV. photoelectric effect

Which of the following is correct?

(a) I and II ☐ (b) II and III ☐

(c) III and IV ☐ (d) IV and I ☐

3. Match the shape of wavefront given in Column I with its possible source given in Column II.

	Column I		Column II
A.	Spherical	1.	Point source at infinite distance
B.	Cylindrical	2.	Point source at finite distance
C.	Plane	3.	Slit or source of finite length

A. ____________ B. ____________ C. ____________

*Concepts of all questions bearing * are important for JEE/NEET/CUET.*

4. A point source S emitting wavefronts A, B ... etc., at phase difference of 2π rad apart are shown below.

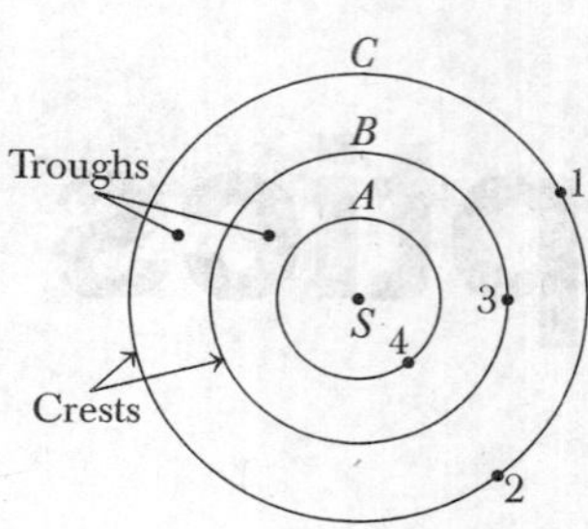

Now, consider points 1, 2, 3, 4 on wavefronts A, B, C. Complete the following blanks.

(i) Phase difference of points 1 and 2 are __________ $(0/2\pi)$ rad.

(ii) Phase difference of points 1 and 4 are __________ $(2\pi/4\pi)$ rad.

5. Does Huygens' principle allow us to determine the shape of wavefront after a small time interval?

Yes ☐ No ☐

***6.** Huygens' principle of __________ (primary/secondary) wavelets may be used to find the new __________ (position/speed) of a wavefront.

7. A wavefront moving with velocity v at $t = 0$ is shown below.

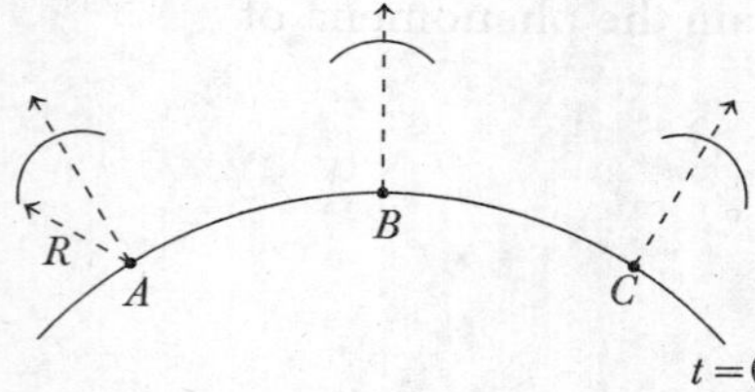

To draw position of a new wavefront after time τ, we draw spheres of radius R from points A, B and C, respectively. What is the value of R here?

____

***8.** Let a wavefront AB of light creates a secondary wavefront CD in air after 1ns.

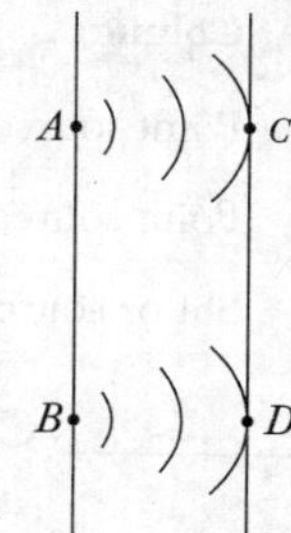

Then, find the distance between wavefronts.

____

TOPIC 2

Refraction and Reflection of Plane Waves Using Huygens' Principle

***9.** The refraction of a plane wavefront from rarer to denser medium is shown below.

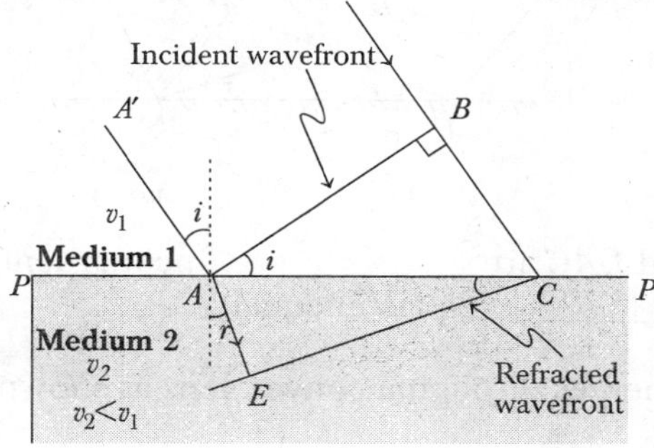

Which of the following is correct about given figure?

I. If the crest from B reaches C in time t, then the crest from A should also reach E in time t.

II. The ratio $\frac{BC}{AE} = \frac{\sin i}{\sin r} = \frac{v_2}{v_1}$

____

***10.** A wavefront is incident over a surface separating two media.
In first medium, speed of wave is 330 m/s and wavelength is 1 m.
In second medium, if wave speed is 1650 ms^{-1}, then the wavelength in second medium will be ________ (1m/5 m).

***11.** A glass slab of thickness 4 cm contains the same number of waves as a 5 cm thick plastic have when same light beam is passed through them. Calculate the refractive index of plastic with respect to glass.

____

12. When a wave gets refracted into a denser medium, the __________ (wavelength / frequency) and __________ (speed/frequency) of propagation decreases but the __________ (wavelength / frequency) remains the same.

13. The refraction of a plane wavefront at a rarer medium is shown below.

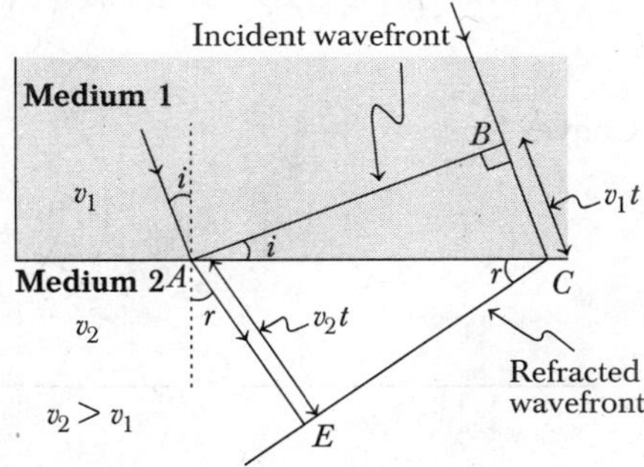

In which medium, the wavefront *CE* will be formed when $i > i_c$ (critical angle)?

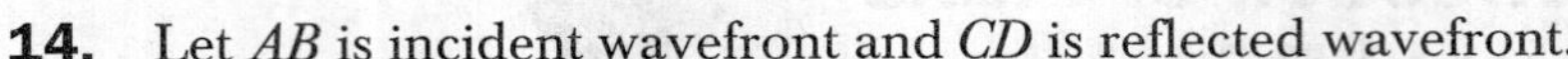

14. Let *AB* is incident wavefront and *CD* is reflected wavefront.

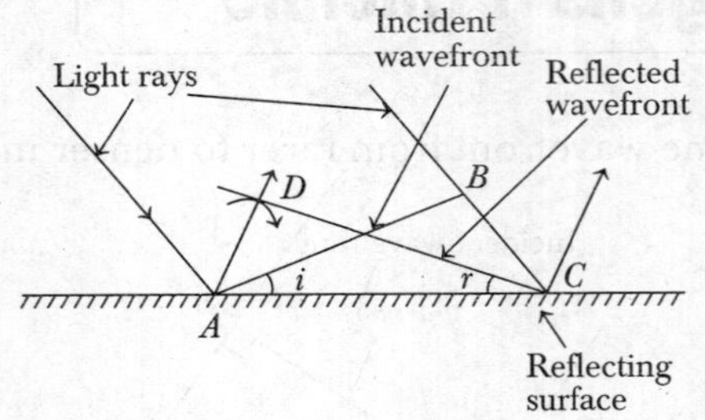

The triangles *BAC* and *DAC* are ____________ (incongruent/congruent) and therefore, angles *i* and *r* are ___________ (equal/unequal).

15. A plane wavefront emerges through a convex lens as shown below.

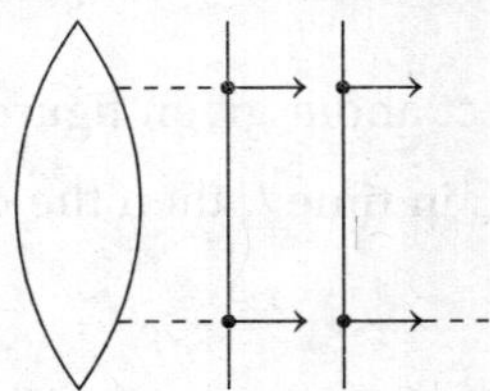

What must be the shape of incident wavefront ?

____

16. A plane wavefront is incident different. Match the material given in Column I with its emergent wavefront shape shown in Column II.

	Column I		Column II
A.	Concave mirror	1.	
B.	Concave lens	2.	
C.	Convex mirror	3.	
D.	Convex lens	4.	

A. _______________ B. _______________ C. _______________ D.

17. **Statement I** When a light ray goes from rarer to denser medium, its intensity decreases.

Statement II Speed of light in denser medium is less than that in rarer medium

Which of the following statement(s) is/are correct?

(a) Only statement I ☐ (b) Only Statement II ☐

(c) Both statement I and II ☐ (d) Neither statement I nor II ☐

TOPIC 3

Coherent and Incoherent Addition of Waves

18. Will the ratio of amplitudes of two waves with intensity ratio $\frac{81}{25}$ be $\frac{9}{5}$?

Yes ☐ No ☐

19. At a particular point in a medium, the resultant displacement produced by a number of waves is the vector sum of the displacement produced by each of the waves. Which principle is described by the above information?

____

20. Let two waves having displacements y_1 and y_2 passes through a point P. Displacement produced at P will be _________ (sum/difference) of displacements.

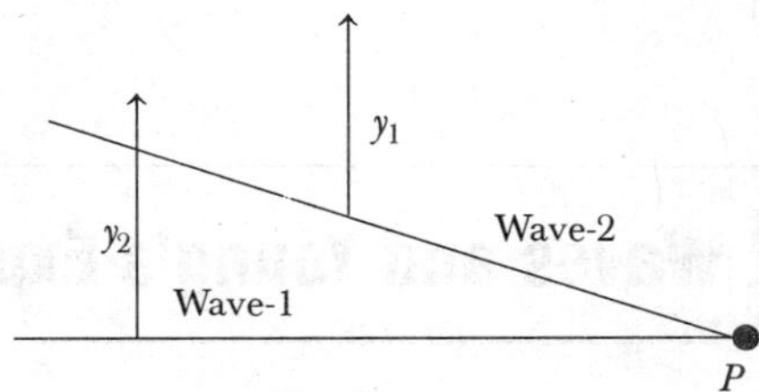

21. Two waves of displacement $y_1 = a\cos\omega t$ and $y_2 = a\cos\omega t$ are produced from a point source P. If I_0 be the intensity produced by each wave, will the resultant intensity be $4I_0$?

Yes ☐ No ☐

22. S_1 and S_2 sources produces waves $y_1 = y_2 = A\cdot\cos\omega t$.

Now, match the value of net displacement y given in Column II with their respective path difference $S_1P - S_2P$ values given in Column I.

Column I	Column II
A. 0	1. $2A\cos\omega t$
B. 2λ	2. 0
C. 2.5λ	

A. __________ B. __________ C. __________

23. Choose the correct statement.

Interference is

I. net effect of combination of two waves

II. destructive when path difference between two waves is $\left(n+\frac{1}{2}\right)\lambda$

III. constructive when path difference between two waves is $n\lambda$

IV. always noticeable

____

24. Match the value of phase difference in Column I with resultant intensity at point P in Column II. Take, intensity of sources S_1 and S_2 as I_0 as shown in figure.

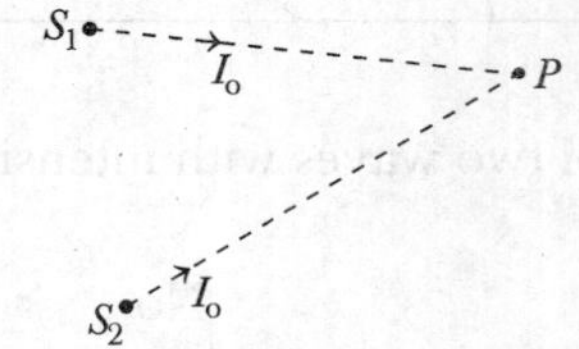

	Column I		Column II
A.	$\pi/3$	1.	$2I_0$
B.	$\pi/2$	2.	I_0
C.	$\frac{2\pi}{3}$	3.	$3I_0$

A. ____________ B. ____________ C. ____________

TOPIC4

Interference of Light Waves and Young's Experiment

25. To observe interference, sodium vapour lamp is preferred because it is nearly monochromatic.

True ☐ False ☐

26. In given YDSE arrangement, path difference $S_2P - S_1P$ is nearly equals to $\frac{xd}{D}$.

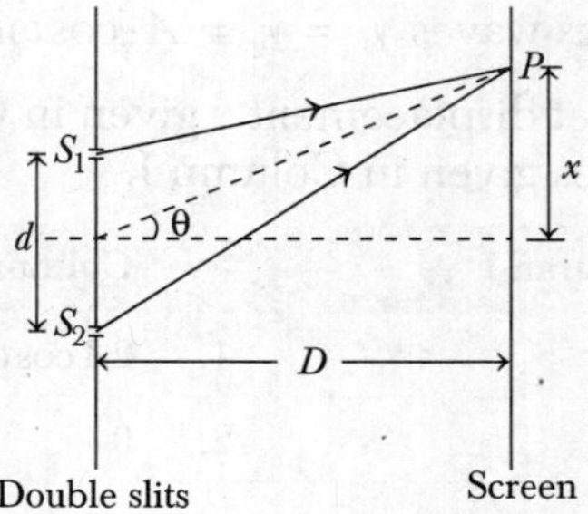

True  False 

27. A YDSE arrangement is given below

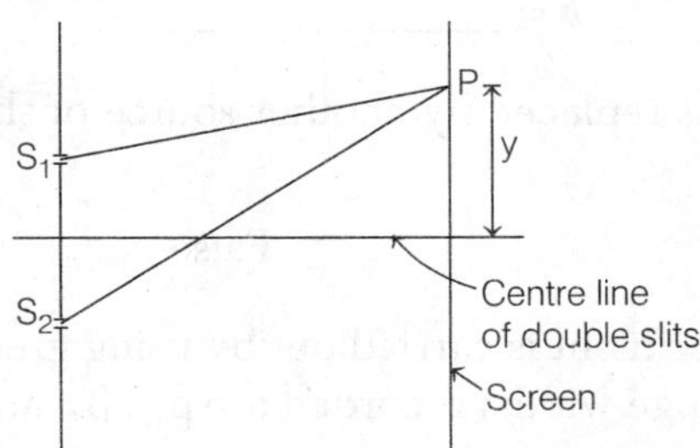

Complete the following equations.

Distance of a bright fringe from centre line, y_n = ____________ $\left(\frac{n\lambda D}{d} / \frac{n\lambda d}{D}\right)$

Distance of a dark fringe from centre line, y_n' = ____________ $\left[(2n-1)\frac{\lambda D}{d} / (2n+1)\frac{\lambda D}{2d}\right]$

***28.** Young's double slit experiment is performed with sodium (yellow) light of wavelength 584.3 nm and the interference pattern is observed on a screen 100 cm away. The 10th bright fringe has its centre at a distance of 12 mm from the central maximum. What will be the separation between the slits?

____

***29.** In Young's experiment, the distance between the two slits is 0.8 mm and the distance of the screen from the slits is 1.2 m. If the fringe width is 0.75 mm, calculate the wavelength of light.

____

***30.** In a Young's double slit experiment, the slit separation is 1 mm and the screen is 1m from the slit. For a monochromatic light of wavelength 500 nm, will the distance of 3rd minima from the central maxima be 1.25 mm?

Yes ☐ No ☐

31. In a Young's double slit experiment, if there is no initial phase difference between the light from the two slits, a point on the screen corresponding to the 5th minimum has path difference

(a) $5\frac{\lambda}{2}$ ☐ (b) $10\frac{\lambda}{2}$ ☐ (c) $9\frac{\lambda}{2}$ ☐ (d) $11\frac{\lambda}{2}$ ☐

32. In YDSE, bright and dark bands on screen called fringes are as shown below.

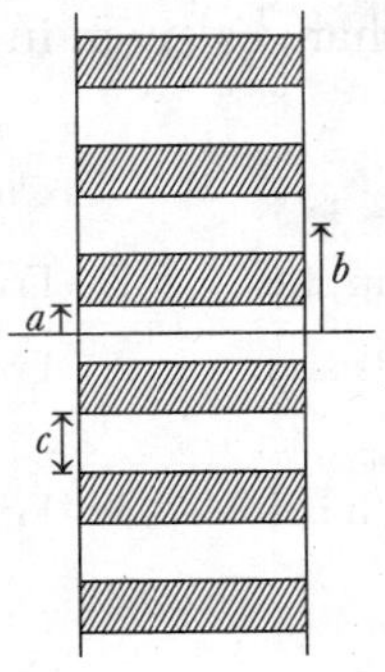

If wavelength of light is λ, distance between slits is d and distance of screen and slits is D, then

$a =$ ______ $b =$ ______ $c =$ ______

33. In YDSE, if the source is replaced by another source of shorter wavelength, then fringe separation increases.

True ☐ False ☐

***34.** Young's double slit experiment is carried out by using green, red and blue lights, one colour at a time. The fringe widths recorded are β_G, β_R and β_B respectively, then

(a) $\beta_G > \beta_B > \beta_R$ ☐ (b) $\beta_B > \beta_G > \beta_R$ ☐ (c) $\beta_R > \beta_B > \beta_G$ ☐ (d) $\beta_R > \beta_G > \beta_B$ ☐

35. When distance of slits and screen (D) is reduced to half, fringe width becomes one-fourth.

True ☐ False ☐

36. If in YDSE, distance between slits is increased 3 times, then fringe width also becomes 3 times.

Yes ☐ No ☐

37. In YDSE with light of wavelength 6000 Å, a fringe width of 0.06 cm is obtained. With a light of wavelength 5000 Å, the fringe width obtained will be ______ (0.06/0.05) cm.

38. Shape of fringes on screen in YDSE is (assuming screen is not very far from slits)

(a) straight lines ☐ (b) parabolas ☐ (c) hyperbolas ☐ (d) Both (b) and (c) ☐

39. In YDSE, if $d = 1\,\text{mm}$, $D = 1\,\text{m}$, $\lambda = 500$ nm, then answer the following questions.

(i) Calculate the central bright fringe width.

______

(ii) Will the distance of 3rd bright fringe from centre of screen be 3 mm?

Yes ☐ No ☐

(iii) Find fringe width for first dark band.

______

(iv) The distance of second dark fringe from centre line is

(a) 1 mm ☐ (b) 0.75 mm ☐ (c) 1.5 mm ☐ (d) 2 mm ☐

40. Considering YDSE, match the changes given in Column I with the effects on fringe width given in Column II.

Column I	Column II
A. Screen is moved away from slits	1. Fringe width decreases
B. Water is filled between slits and screen	2. Fringes becomes less bright
C. Source slit (single slit) width is increased	3. Fringe width increases

A. ______ B. ______ C. ______

41. If a Young's double slit experiment performed with a source of white light, only black and white fringes are observed.

True ☐ False ☐

42. Alternate dark and bright boundaries in the shadow of an opaque object is due to ____________ (interference/diffraction).

43. Consider single slit diffraction for a light beam of wavelength λ and fill the following blanks.

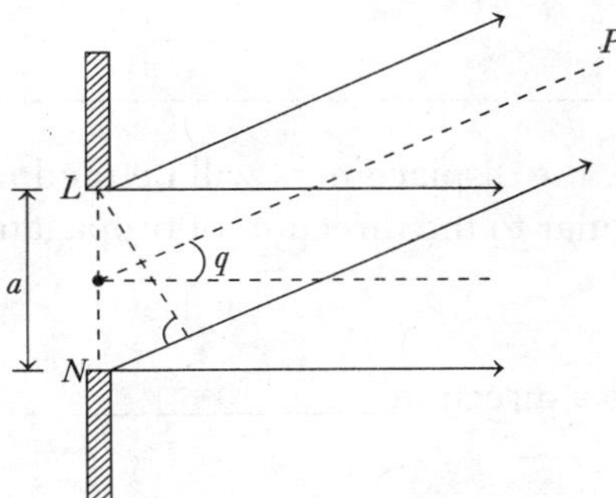

Path difference ΔL between rays LP and NP = ____________

Intensity maxima occurs at angle θ = ____________

Intensity minima occurs at angle θ = ____________

44. A parallel beam of light of wavelength 600Å gets diffracted by a single slit of width 0.3 mm. Find the angular position of the first minima of diffracted light.

____

45. Suppose we observe the single slit diffraction with wavelength λ and slit width *e*, the width of the central maximum is 2θ. Will θ increase on increasing the slit width for the same λ?

Yes ☐ No ☐

46. Interference pattern is a series of equally spaced bright and dark bands, whereas in diffraction pattern central ____________ (bright/dark) maximum is ____________ (half/ twice) as wide as the other maxima.

***47.** In a single slit, first minima occurs at angle $\frac{\lambda}{a}$. Will we observe a maxima at same angular position in the diffraction pattern?

Yes ☐ No ☐

48. The interference phenomenon is consistent with the principle of conservation of energy while the diffraction phenomenon is inconsistent with it.

True ☐ False ☐

***49.** Which of these pairs is correctly matched?

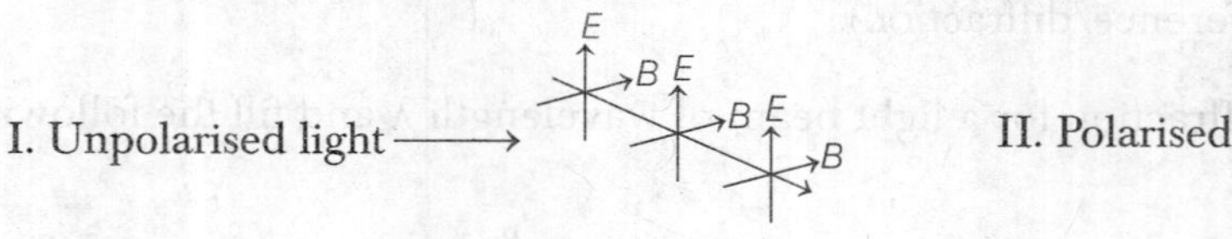

____

50. For an unpolarised wave, the displacement will be randomly changing with time though it will always be perpendicular to the direction of propagation.

True ☐ False ☐

51. In a polaroid, pass axis is a direction ____________ (parallel/perpendicular) to the aligned molecules.

***52.** Match the orientation of polaroids shown in Column I with the behaviour of electric vector shown in Column II.

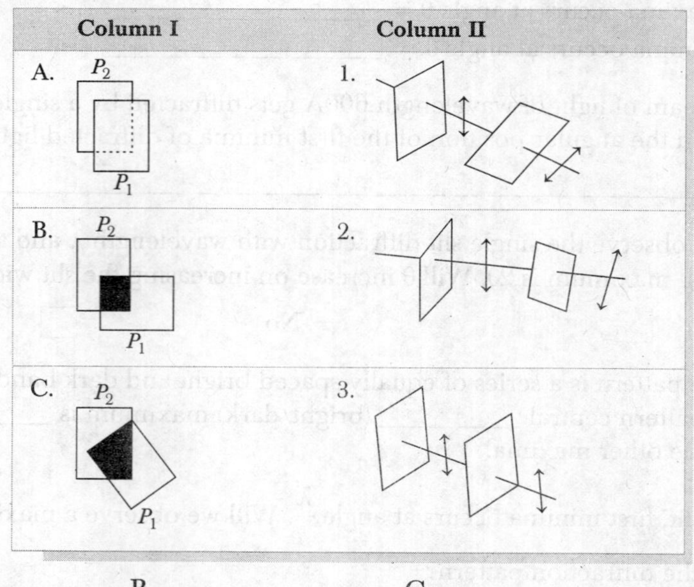

A. ____________ B. ____________ C. ____________

53. If a polarised beam is observed through an analyser, then output intensity is proportional to cosine of angle between plane of polarisation and pass axis of analyser.

True ☐ False ☐

54.

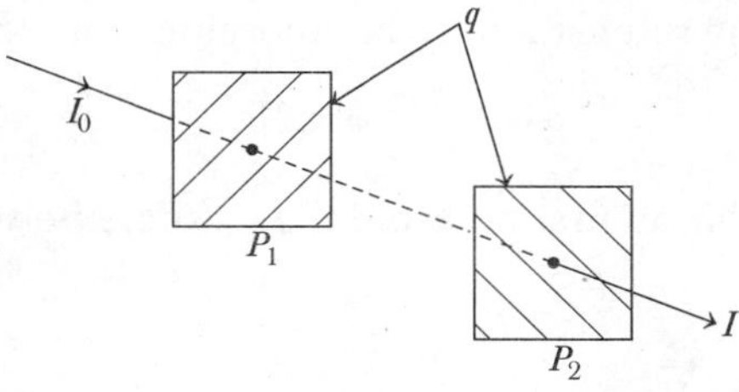

In the given set-up, P_1 is kept fixed and P_2 is rotated. Correct graph of output intensity I with angle θ is

(a) 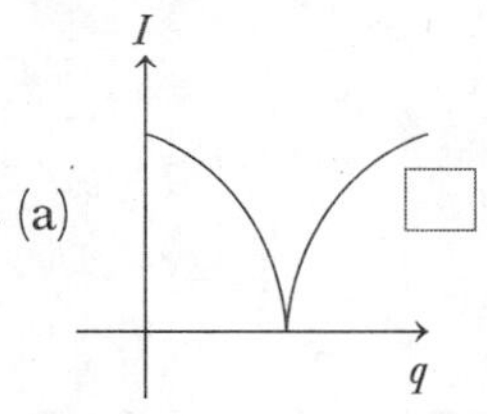

☐ (b) 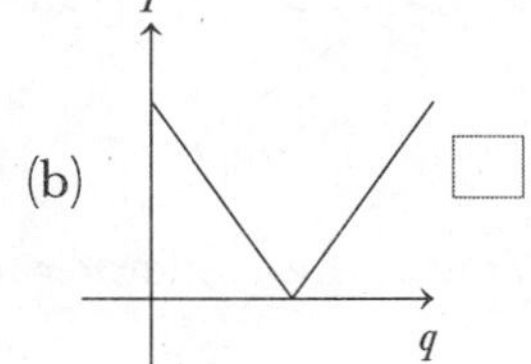

☐ (c) 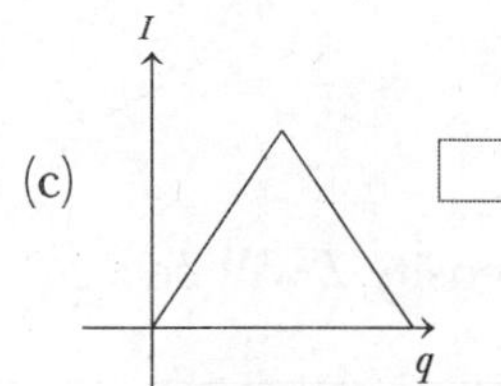

☐ (d) 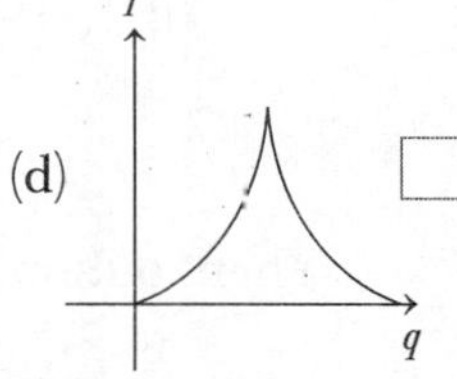

☐

55. An unpolarised light beam of intensity I_0 pass through a polaroid.

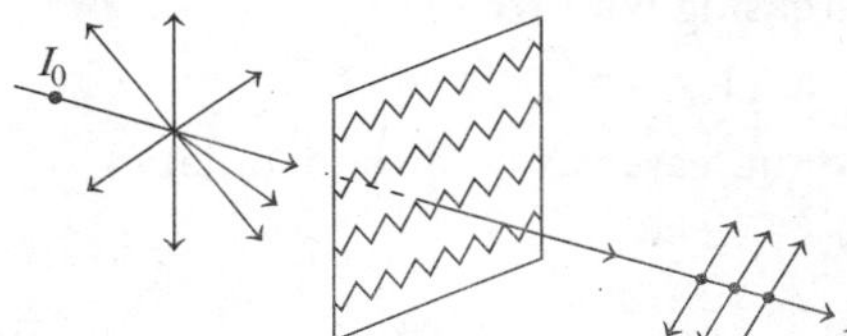

If intensity of transmitted light is I, then find the ratio of $\frac{I_0}{I}$.

____

56. An unpolarised beam of light passes through a polaroid P_1. The transmitted beam is again made to pass through a second polaroid P_2. If θ is angle between pass axis of polaroid P_1 and P_2, then ratio $I_1 : I_2 : I_3$ will be ________ ($1 : 2 : \cos^2\theta / 2 : 1 : \cos^2\theta$).

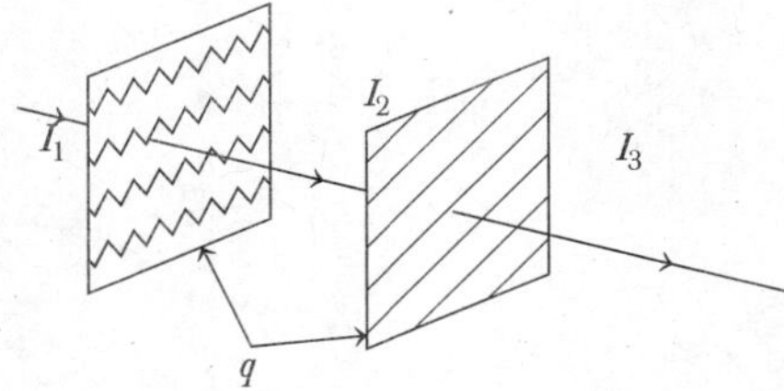

***57.** Two polaroids are oriented with their planes perpendicular to incident light and transmission axis making an angle of 30° with each other. What fraction of incident unpolarised light is transmitted?

(a) $\frac{1}{2}$ ☐ (b) $\frac{3}{4}$ ☐ (c) $\frac{7}{8}$ ☐ (d) $\frac{3}{8}$ ☐

58. At which angle, the intensity of transmitted light is maximum when a polaroid sheet is rotated between two crossed polaroids?

____

59. An unpolarised beam of intensity I_0 is incident on a pair of nicols making an angle of 60° with each other. Will the intensity of light emerging from the pair be $I_0/8$?

Yes ☐ No ☐

***60.** Incident intensity of light on first polaroid is I_0. Angle between any two consecutive pass axes is 30°.

q=30°

I_0 I

q=30° q=30°

Then, output intensity I will be $x\,I_0$. What is the value of x here?

____

61. When sky is observed with a polaroid (which is rotated), we observe

(a) intensity keeps on decreasing with rotation ☐
(b) zero intensity at every angle ☐
(c) intensity decreases and increases as polaroid is rotated ☐
(d) no change in intensity ☐

62. For a good polariser in case of unpolarised light, we will observe no ____________ (transmission/reflection) and total ____________ (transmission/reflection) of light.

COMPETITION CONNECT

Topic Polarisation [NCERT (Old) Pg. 376-381]

1. Write the name of the labelling in the figure given below for polarisation by scattering.

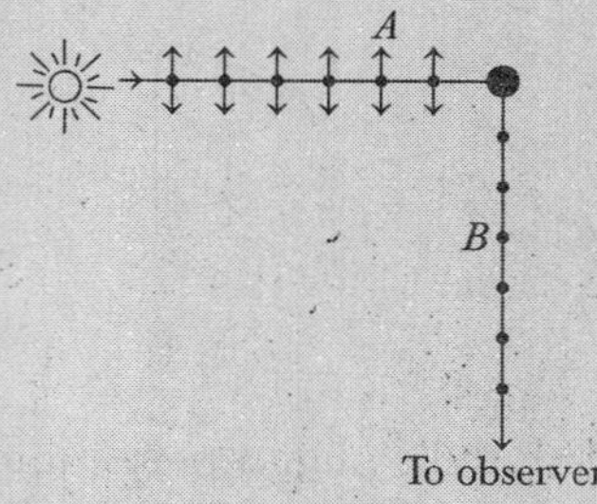

A. ________________ B. ________________

2.

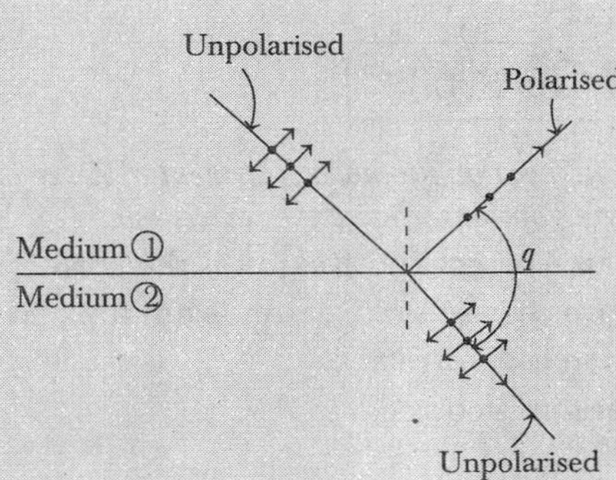

In above situation, angle θ must be________________ (less than/more than/equal to) 90°.

3. Observation of polarisation by reflection are shown below. Fill the following boxes to obtain Brewster's angle.

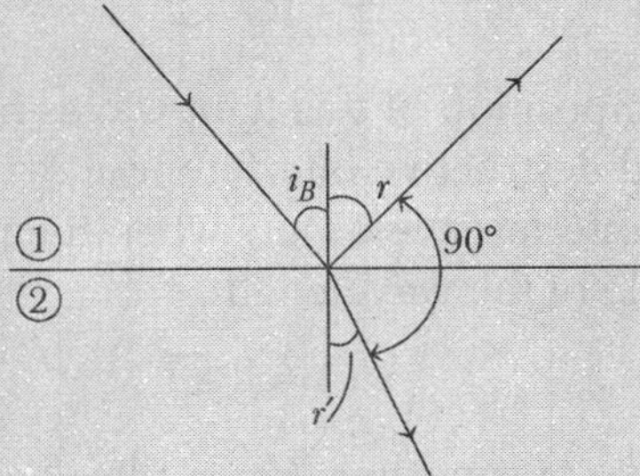

$r + r' = \square$ degrees

$$n_{21} = \frac{n_2}{n_1} = \frac{\sin i_B}{\sin r'} = \square$$

4. Choose the correct option.
(a) Scattered light from air molecules is only partially polarised. ☐
(b) Reflected light is partially polarised. ☐
(c) When reflected and refracted beams are perpendicular, refracted part is partially polarised. ☐
(d) If sum of angle of refraction and reflection is 90°, then reflected beam is totally polarised. ☐

5. Is it possible that under some conditions, a monochromatic beam of light incident on a surface (which is normally reflective), gets completely transmitted with no reflection?

Yes ☐ No ☐

6. Unpolarised light is incident on a plane glass surface. What should be the angle of incidence, so that the reflected and refracted rays are perpendicular to each other?

____

7. The critical angle of a certain medium is $\sin^{-1}\left(\frac{3}{5}\right)$. The polarising angle of the medium is

(a) $\sin^{-1}\left(\frac{4}{5}\right)$ ☐ (b) $\tan^{-1}\left(\frac{5}{3}\right)$ ☐

(c) $\tan^{-1}\left(\frac{3}{4}\right)$ ☐ (d) $\tan^{-1}\left(\frac{4}{3}\right)$ ☐

Assertion-Reason Questions

Direction (Q. Nos. 1-10) *In the following questions, a statement of Assertion is followed by a corresponding statement of Reason. From the following options, choose the correct one.*

(a) Both Assertion and Reason are correct and Reason is the correct explanation of Assertion.
(b) Both Assertion and Reason are correct but Reason is not the correct explanation of Assertion.
(c) Assertion is correct but Reason is incorrect.
(d) Assertion is incorrect but Reason is correct.

1. **Assertion** (A) Huygens' principle is used to derive the laws of reflection.
Reason (R) According to Huygens' principle, the angle of incidence is always equal to the angle of reflection.

(a) ☐ (b) ☐ (c) ☐ (d) ☐

2. **Assertion** (A) The superimposition of two light waves from coherent sources can result in regions of constructive and destructive interference.
Reason (R) Constructive interference occurs when the path difference between the two waves is an integer multiple of the wavelength.

(a) ☐ (b) ☐ (c) ☐ (d) ☐

***3.** **Assertion** (A) The principle of superposition applies only to coherent light sources.
Reason (R) The principle of superposition states that the resultant displacement at any point is the algebraic sum of the displacements due to individual waves.

(a) ☐ (b) ☐ (c) ☐ (d) ☐

4. **Assertion** (A) The fringe width in Young's double-slit experiment decreases, if the distance between the slits is increased.
Reason (R) The fringe width is directly proportional to the distance between the slits in YDSE.

(a) ☐ (b) ☐ (c) ☐ (d) ☐

***5.** **Assertion** (A) In YDSE, if one of the slits is covered with a thin film. the interference pattern shifts.
Reason (R) The thin film introduces an additional phase difference between the two waves from the slits.

(a) ☐ (b) ☐ (c) ☐ (d) ☐

6. **Assertion** (A) The intensity of the bright fringes in YDSE is twice that of the individual slit intensities.

Reason (R) The intensity of the bright fringes is the result of constructive interference. where the amplitude of the waves adds up.

(a) ☐ (b) ☐ (c) ☐ (d) ☐

7. **Assertion** (A) With white light, fringes close to central fringe are red and fringes far away are blue.
Reason (R) Wavelength of red colour is more than that of blue colour.

(a) ☐ (b) ☐ (c) ☐ (d) ☐

8. **Assertion** (A) In YDSE, if a film is introduced in front of the upper slit, then the fringe pattern shifts in the upward direction.
Reason (R) In YDSE, if the slit widths are unequal, the minima will be completely dark.

(a) ☐ (b) ☐ (c) ☐ (d) ☐

9. **Assertion** (A) In a single slit diffraction experiment, the central maximum is twice as wide as the other maxima.
Reason (R) The intensity of the central maximum is higher than that of the other maxima.

(a) ☐ (b) ☐ (c) ☐ (d) ☐

***10.** **Assertion** (A) In single slit diffraction, the angular position of the first minimum is inversely proportional to the wavelength of light used.
Reason (R) The position of the minima in single slit diffraction is given by the condition $a \sin \theta = m\lambda$, where a is the slit width and m is the order of the minimum.

(a) ☐ (b) ☐ (c) ☐ (d) ☐

Case Based Questions

1. One of the first to demonstrate the interference of light was Thomas Young in 1801. In his experimental arrangement (as shown in figure), monochromatic light (single wavelength) from a narrow vertical slit S falls on two other narrow slits S_1 and S_2 which are very close together and equidistant to S. S_1 and S_2 act as two coherent sources (both being derived from S). The emerging beams spread into the region beyond the slits. Superposition occurs in the shaded area, where the beams overlap. Alternate bright and dark equally spaced vertical bands (interference fringes) can be observed on a screen placed at some distance from the slits.

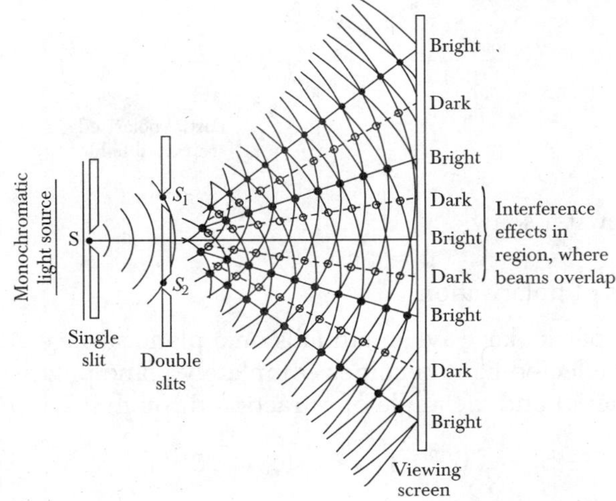

Width of fringes obtained in above experiment is calculated by using $\beta = \frac{D\lambda}{d}$

where, symbols are their usual meanings.

(i) If either of source (S_1 or S_2) is covered with opaque material, then

(a) fringes will disappear □
(b) width of the fringes will increase □
(c) width of the fringes will decrease □
(d) width of the fringes will remain unchanged □

(ii) Two coherent sources, each emitting light of intensity I_0, interfere in a medium at a point where phase difference between them is $\frac{2\pi}{3}$. The resultant intensity at that point would be

(a) $2I_0$ □ (b) I_0 □
(c) $\frac{I_0}{2}$ □ (d) $\frac{3}{2}I_0$ □

(iii) In a Young's double slit experiment using monochromatic light of wavelength λ, the intensity of light at a point, where path difference is 2λ is found to be I_0. What will be the intensity at a point when path difference is $\frac{\lambda}{3}$?

(a) I_0 □ (b) $2I_0$ □ (c) $\frac{I_0}{2}$ □ (d) $\frac{I_0}{4}$ □

(iv) In case of destructive interference, path difference may be

(a) $n\lambda$ □ (b) $(2n+1)\frac{\lambda}{2}$ □ (c) $(n+1)\frac{\lambda}{2}$ □ (d) $(n-1)\frac{\lambda}{2}$ □

2. When a beam of unpolarised light is reflected from a transparent medium (refractive index = μ), then the reflected light is completely plane polarised at a certain angle of incidence (called the angle of polarisation θ_p).
In this case, reflected and refracted waves are perpendicular to each other.

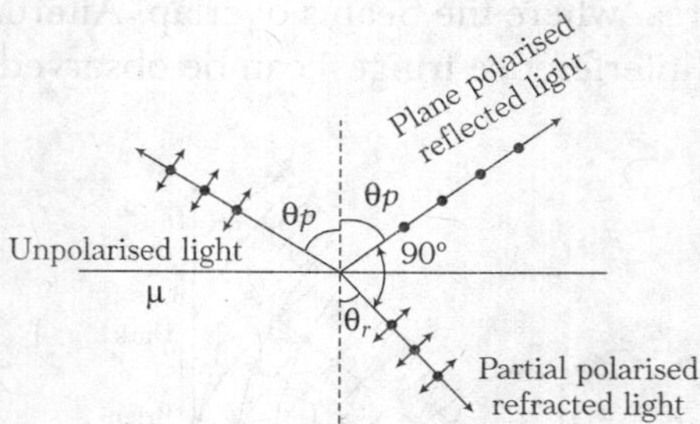

According to Brewster's law,

$$\mu = \tan i_p$$

where, i_p is angle of polarisation.

(i) When light of particular wavelength falls on a plane surface at an angle of incidence 60°, then the reflected light becomes completely plane polarised. The refractive index of surface material and the angle of refraction through it are respectively.

(a) $\sqrt{3}$, 60° □ (b) $\frac{1}{\sqrt{3}}$, 60° □ (c) $\sqrt{3}$, 30° □ (d) $\frac{1}{\sqrt{3}}$, 30° □

(ii) Which of the following cannot polarised ?

(a) Infrared rays ☐ (b) Radiowaves ☐

(c) Ultraviolet rays ☐ (d) Ultrasonic waves ☐

(iii) The angle of polarisation for any medium is 60°, what will be critical angle for this ?

(a) $\sin^{-1}\sqrt{3}$ ☐ (b) $\tan^{-1}\sqrt{3}$ ☐

(c) $\cos^{-1}\sqrt{3}$ ☐ (d) $\sin^{-1}\frac{1}{\sqrt{3}}$ ☐

(iv) The transverse nature of light is shown by

(a) interference of light ☐ (b) refraction of light ☐

(c) polarisation of light ☐ (d) dispersion of light ☐

COMPETITION EDGE UP

1. In a Young's double slit experiment, the intensity at a point is $\left(\frac{1}{4}\right)$th of the maximum intensity the minimum distance of the point from the central maximum is ______ μm. (Given, $\lambda = 600$ nm, $d = 1.0$ mm, $D = 1.0$ m)
[NCERT Pg 266, JEE Main 2024]

2. Two slits are 1 mm apart and the screen is located 1 m away from the slits. A light of wavelength 500 nm is used. The width of each slit to obtain 10 maxima of the double slit pattern within the central maximum of the single slit pattern is ___ $\times 10^{-4}$ m.
[NCERT Pg 266, JEE Main 2024]

3. A microwave of wavelength 2.0 cm falls normally on a slit of width 4.0 cm. The angular spread of the central maxima of the diffraction pattern obtained on a screen 1.5 m away from the slit, will be **[NCERT Pg 267, JEE Main 2024]**

(a) 15° ☐

(b) 30° ☐

(c) 60° ☐

(d) 45° ☐

4. A beam of unpolarised light of intensity I_0 is passed through a polaroid A and then through another polaroid B which is oriented, so that its principal plane makes an angle of 45°, relative to that of A. The intensity of emergent light is
[NCERT Pg 269, JEE Main 2024]

(a) $\frac{I_0}{8}$ ☐ (b) $\frac{I_0}{4}$ ☐

(c) $\frac{I_0}{2}$ ☐ (d) I_0 ☐

5. In Young's double slit experiment, light from two identical sources are superimposing on a screen. The path difference between the two lights reaching at a point on the screen is $\frac{7\lambda}{4}$. The ratio of intensity of fringe at this point with respect to the maximum intensity of the fringe is
[NCERT Pg 266, JEE Main 2024]

(a) $\frac{3}{4}$ ☐ (b) $\frac{1}{3}$ ☐

(c) $\frac{1}{2}$ ☐ (d) $\frac{1}{4}$ ☐

6. If the monochromatic source in Young's double slit experiment is replaced by white light, then
[NCERT Pg 266, NEET 2024]

(a) interference pattern will disappear ☐

(b) there will be a central dark fringe surrounded by a few coloured fringes ☐

(c) there will be a central bright white fringe surrounded by a few coloured fringes ☐

(d) all bright fringes will be of equal width ☐

7. For Young's double slit experiment, two statements are given below

Statement I If screen is moved away from the plane of slits, angular separation of the fringes remains constant.

Statement II If the monochromatic source is replaced by another monochromatic source of larger wavelength, the angular separation of fringes decreases.
[NCERT Pg. 266, NEET 2023]

In the light of the above statements, choose the correct answer from the options given below

(a) Both Statement I and Statement II are false. ☐

(b) Statement I is true but Statement II is false. ☐

(c) Statement I is false but Statement II is true. ☐

(d) Both Statement I and Statement II are true. ☐

8. In a Young's double slit experiment, a student observes 8 fringes in a certain segment of screen when a monochromatic light of 600 nm wavelength is used. If the wavelength of light is changed to 400 nm, then the number of fringes he would observe in the same region of the screen is **[NCERT Pg. 266, NEET 2022]**

(a) 8 ☐ (b) 9 ☐

(c) 12 ☐ (d) 6 ☐

9. In Young's double slit experiment, if the separation between coherent sources is halved and the distance of the screen from the coherent sources is doubled, then the fringe width becomes

[NCERT Pg. 266, NEET (Sep) 2020]

(a) half ☐

(b) four times ☐

(c) one-fourth ☐

(d) double ☐

10. In a Young's double slit experiment, if there is no initial phase-difference between the light from the two slits, a point on the screen corresponding to the fifth minimum has path difference.

[NCERT Pg. 266, NEET (Odisha) 2020]

(a) $5\frac{\lambda}{2}$ ☐ (b) $10\frac{\lambda}{2}$ ☐

(c) $9\frac{\lambda}{2}$ ☐ (d) $11\frac{\lambda}{2}$ ☐

Chapter 11

Dual Nature of Radiation and Matter

Scan and take Chapter Test

TOPIC 1

Electron Emission

NCERT Pg 275-276

1. In the phenomenon of electric discharge through gases at low pressure, the coloured glow in the tube appears as a result of

(a) excitation of electrons in the atoms

(b) collision between the atoms of the gas

(c) collision between the charged particles emitted from the cathode and the atoms of the gas

(d) collision between different electrons of the atoms of the gas

2. A neutral metal surface can emit a single electron. Energy needed to remove the electron will be equal to its ____________ ($\frac{e}{m}$ ratio/work function).

3. Complete the given analogy.

Thermionic emission : Heat : : Photoemission : ____________

4. Which of these processes cannot result in emission of an electron from a metal surface?

(a) Application of a strong electric field

(b) Shining radiation over surface

(c) Bombarding surface with fast moving electrons

(d) Striking surface with a metal stick

***5.** **Statement I** When light falls on a metal surface, some electrons near the surface absorb enough energy from incident radiation to overcome the attraction of positive ions in the surface material.

Statement II After gaining sufficient energy from the incident light, the electrons escape from the metal surface into surrounding space.

Which of the following statement(s) is/are correct ?

(a) Only Statement I

(b) Only Statement II

(c) Both Statements I and II

(d) Neither Statement I nor II

*Concepts of all questions bearing * are important for JEE/NEET/CUET.*

TOPIC 2

Photoelectric Effect & Experimental Study of Photoelectric Effect

6. As per Hertz's experiment, electrons can be easily emitted with the help of incident light.

True ☐ False ☐

7. In following Lenard's experiment, label the following diagram.

A = ______

B = ______

C = ______

D = ______

E = ______

8. Threshold frequency is minimum frequency required for ______ (photoemission/photoabsorption).

9. On which of these factors, threshold frequency does not depend?

(a) Material of surface ☐ (b) Surface finish ☐

(c) Temperature of surface ☐ (d) Thickness of plate ☐

10. Choose the metal in which photoemission occurs by visible light.

Silver, Copper, Halogens, Aluminium, Alkali

______

11. For a light source, which of these following pairs is correctly matched?

I. Intensity ⟶ Brightness II. Wavelength ⟶ Colour

______

12. Which quantity of a light beam remains constant during reflection, refraction, polarisation and diffraction processes?

______

13. While measuring the effect of intensity, collector is maintained at negative potential with respect to emitter.

True ☐ False ☐

14. To observe effect of intensity, ________ (frequency/wavelength) and ________ (anode potential/cathode potential) are kept constant in a photoelectric effect experiment.

***15.** Saturation of photocurrent with increasing anode potential refers to situation when all electrons from ________(emitter/collector) reaches the ________ (emitter/collector) plate.

16. Minimum negative value of collector plate potential at which photocurrent becomes zero is called stopping potential.

Yes ☐ No ☐

17. Tick (✓) in front of correct statement and (×) in front of incorrect statement.

I. All photoelectrons emitted from emitter plate have same kinetic energy. ☐

II. Photocurrent is zero at all negative values of collector plate potential. ☐

III. Stopping potential V_0 and kinetic energy K_{max} of an emitted electron are related as $K_{max} = eV_0$. ☐

IV. For different intensities of incident light, we have different values of stopping potential. ☐

18. Kinetic energy of photoelectrons depends on _______ (intensity/frequency) and _______ (frequency/work function) but it is independent of ________ (intensity/energy).

***19.** In given graph, I indicates the intensity of incident light.

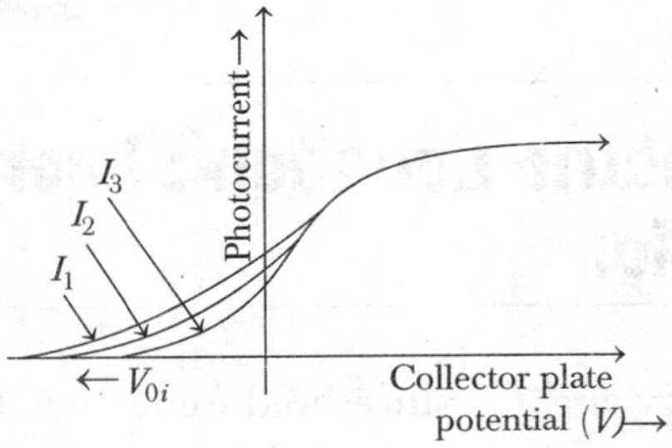

Rank intensities I_1, I_2 and I_3.

____

20. Tick (✓) in front of correct statement and (×) in front of incorrect statement.

I. Maximum KE of photoelectrons depends on the frequency of light. ☐

II. Maximum KE of photoelectrons does not depend on the intensity of light. ☐

III. For frequency lower than threshold frequency, no emission is possible. ☐

IV. Photoemission occurs after a time lag of 10^8 s. ☐

21. When intensity of light is doubled,

(a) both number of emitted electrons and their KE are doubled ☐

(b) number of emitted electrons is doubled ☐

(c) KE of emitted electrons is doubled ☐

(d) no change is observed ☐

***22.** Match the terms given in Column I with the graph given in Column II.

Column I	Column II
A. Variation of photoelectric current with intensity of light	1.
B. Variation of photoelectric current with collector plate potential for different intensities	2.
C. Variation of photoelectric current with collector plate potential for different frequencies	3.
D. Variation of stopping potential with frequency of light	4.

A. ______ B. ______ C. ______ D. ______

TOPIC 3

Einstein's Photoelectric Equation : Energy Quantum of Radiation

23. If f_1 = incident frequency and f_2 = threshold frequency, then write the emitted electron's kinetic energy.

______

24. According to Einstein's photoelectric equation, there is no photoemission when ______ (frequency/intensity) is less than the threshold frequency.

25. Einstein's work on photoelectric effect concludes.

I. $E = h\nu -$ ☐ II. $h\nu = \frac{1}{2} mv^2_{max} +$ ☐

***26.** In graph of frequency f and stopping potential V_0, tick the correct name of the labelling.

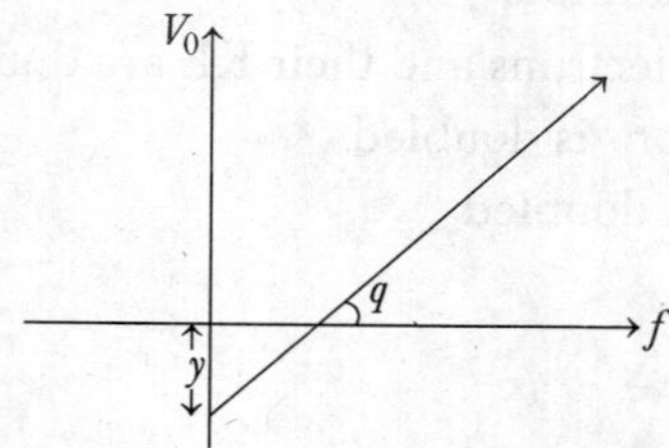

(a) y = Work function ☐ (b) $\tan\theta$ = Planck's constant ☐

(c) $\frac{y}{e}$ = Work function ☐ (d) $e \tan\theta$ = Planck's constant ☐

Here, e = charge of electron.

***27.** A student plots two different graphs for two different metals A and B.

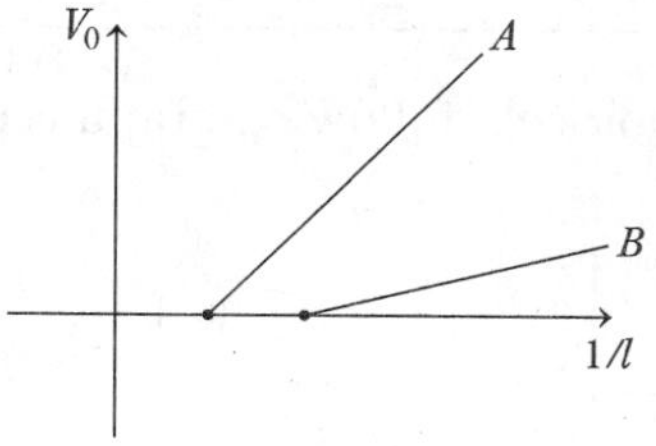

V_0 — $1/\lambda$ (graph with lines A and B)

From these, we can infer that

(a) $\phi_A > \phi_B$ ☐ (b) $(f_0)_A > (f_0)_B$ ☐

(c) $(K_{max})_A > (K_{max})_B$ ☐ (d) Student's data is not correct ☐

28. If a photon beam of energy 3.4 eV is incident over a metal surface having a work function of 2.0 eV, the KE of emitted electrons is equal to x. What is the magnitude of x (in eV) here ?

____

***29.** Work function of sodium metal is nearly________ (1.5/2.5) eV, if its threshold wavelength is 5000 Å.

30. Energy of a photon is nearly 2.5 eV. It can impart a vision of colour ________ (blue/green/red) to our eye.

***31.** The work function of a photosensitive material is 4.0 eV. Find the longest wavelength of light that can cause photon emission from the substance.

____

32. In a photocell, when UV-light of 2000 Å is used, stopping potential is −1.5 V.

Work function of metal is around x eV. Find the value of x here.

____

***33.** Suppose f_0 be the threshold frequency for a metal surface. With incident frequency $2f_0$, velocity of fastest electron is x. What will be the velocity of fastest electron with incident frequency $5f_0$?

____

34. With wavelength λ, stopping potential is V and with wavelength 3λ, stopping potential is $\frac{V}{4}$.

If the threshold wavelength is $n\lambda$, then value of n is __________ (6/9).

35. The cathode of a photoelectric cell is changed such that the work function changes from W_1 to W_2 $(W_2 > W_1)$. If the current before and after are i_1 and i_2, respectively and all other conditions remaining unchanged, then $i_1 = i_2$.

True ☐ False ☐

36. In an experiment with rubidium photocell, the following lines from a mercury source are used $\lambda_1 = 3650$ Å, $\lambda_2 = 4047$ Å, $\lambda_3 = 4358$ Å, $\lambda_4 = 5461$ Å, $\lambda_5 = 6907$ Å and stopping potentials respectively are $V_{01} = 1.28$ V, $V_{02} = 0.95$ V, $V_{03} = 0.74$ V, $V_{04} = 0.16$ V, $V_{05} = 0$ V. Calculate

(i) threshold frequency and (ii) work function of metal.

***37.** In an experiment with a photocell, following graph is obtained.

$V_{stopping}$ V A (6, V) B (5.5, 0) $f (5.5 \times 10^{14} Hz)$

Minimum energy required for photoelectron ejection is

(a) 2.27 eV ☐ (b) 2.59 eV ☐
(c) 1.93 eV ☐ (d) 2.10 eV ☐

***38.** In a photoelectric experiment, wavelength of incident light is changed from 300 nm to 400 nm. Change in stopping potential will be ________ (1.03/1.30)V.

39. A 1 cm metal ball of work function 4.47 eV is irradiated with a radiation of 2500 Å. What will be charge on ball after a long time?

TOPIC 4

Particle Nature of Light : The Photon

NCERT Pg 283-284

40. When radiation interacts with matter, ________ (electron/proton) absorbs a fixed amount of ________ (radiation/energy) of radiation.

***41.** Two sources emit X-rays (1 nm) and visible light (500 nm). If power of each source is 200 W, ratio of number density of photons will be ________ (500 : 1/1 : 500).

***42.** A short wave radio transmitter emits a 300 m wave at 10 kW power. Number of photons emitted by transmitter in 1 min will be ________ $(20/15) \times 10^{30}$.

43. Light of frequency 6.10×10^{14} Hz falls on a surface of work function 1.50 eV.

Emitted electrons can have a maximum speed of ________ $(5 \times 10^5 \text{ ms}^{-1}/6 \times 10^5 \text{ ms}^{-1})$

44. Ultraviolet light of wavelength 99 nm falls on a metal plate of work function 1.0 eV. Maximum KE of emitted electrons will be 1.84×10^{-19} J.

Yes ☐ No ☐

***45.** The 21 cm radio wave emitted by hydrogen in interstellar space is due to the interaction called hyperfine structure of hydrogen atom. The energy of the emitted wave is nearly ________ $(10^{-24} / 7 \times 10^{-8})$ J.

46. The anode voltage of a photocell is kept fixed. The wavelength λ of the light falling on the cathode is gradually changed. Draw the graph of current I of photocell w.r.t. λ.

____

47. Which among the following can be used to obtain wave character associated with a moving particle?

I. Planck's formula of photon energy. ☐

II. Einstein's formula for mass-energy. ☐

III. Equation of conservation of momentum. ☐

IV. Equation of conservation of energy. ☐

48. Mass associated with a photon of frequency ν will be ________ $\left(\frac{h}{c\lambda} / \frac{hc}{\lambda}\right)$.

***49.** If momentum of a photon is 3.3×10^{-29} kg ms^{-1}, it belongs to visible region.

True ☐ False ☐

TOPIC 5

Wave Nature of Matter

NCERT Pg 284-286

***50.** When KE of a particle is doubled, its de-Broglie wavelength changes by a factor of $\frac{1}{\sqrt{2}}$.

True ☐ False ☐

***51.** An electron, a doubly ionised He atom and a proton are given same kinetic energy. Arrange their de-Broglie wavelengths λ_e, λ_{He} and λ_p in increasing order.

____

52. A particle is moving five times as fast of an electron. Ratio of de-Broglie wavelengths of the particle to that of electron is 1.878×10^{-4}. Calculate the mass of particle.

____

53. Wavelength associated with a moving electron which is accelerated by a potential difference of 120 V will be xÅ. What will be the value of x?

____

54. Find the de-Broglie wavelength associated with an electron moving with a speed of 5.4×10^6 ms^{-1}.

____

COMPETITION CONNECT

Topic Wave Nature of Matter [NCERT (Old) Pg. 398-403]

1. Let Δx = uncertainty of position and Δp = uncertainty in momentum, then according to Heisenberg uncertainty principle, order of product $\Delta x \cdot \Delta p$ will be

(a) h ☐ (b) $\frac{h}{2\pi}$ ☐ (c) $2\pi h$ ☐ (d) $\frac{2\pi}{h}$ ☐

2. An electron is confined to a 1 nm wide region. Find the uncertainty in momentum using Heisenberg uncertainty principle. (Take, $h = 6.63 \times 10^{-34}$ J-s)

____

3. Particles x and y collided perfectly inelastically.

If λ_x and λ_y are their initial de-Broglie wavelengths, then the de-Broglie wavelength observed after collision will be $\frac{\lambda_x \lambda_y}{|\lambda_x - \lambda_y|}$.

Yes ☐ No ☐

4. A particle A of mass m and charge q is accelerated by a potential of 50 V. Another particle B of mass 4 m and charge q is accelerated by a potential of 2500 V.
Ratio of de-Broglie wavelengths $\lambda_A : \lambda_B$ is______________ (1:10/10 : 1).

5. Calculate momentum and de-Broglie wavelength of

I. a bullet of mass 0.40 kg travelling with speed of 1.0 kms^{-1}.

____

II. a ball of mass 0.60 kg moving at a speed of 1.0 ms^{-1}.

____

III. a dust particle of mass 1.0×10^{-9} kg drifting with a speed of 2.2 ms^{-1}.

____

6. The wavelength of light from the spectral emission line of sodium is 589 nm. Find the kinetic energy at which

(i) an electron and (ii) a neutron.

Would have the same de-Broglie wavelength?

____

7. A proton and an α-particle are accelerated through the same potential difference. The ratio of de-Broglie wavelengths λ_p to that of λ_α is

(a) $\sqrt{2}:1$ ☐ (b) $\sqrt{4}:1$ ☐ (c) $\sqrt{6}:1$ ☐ (d) $\sqrt{8}:1$ ☐

8. Electrons used in an electron microscope are accelerated by a voltage of 25 kV. If the voltage is increased to 100 kV, then the de-Broglie wavelength associated with the electrons would increases by 2 times.

True ☐ False ☐

Assertion-Reason Questions

Direction (Q. Nos. 1-10) *In the following questions, a statement of Assertion is followed by a corresponding statement of Reason. From the following options, choose the correct one.*

(a) Both Assertion and Reason are correct and Reason is the correct explanation of Assertion.
(b) Both Assertion and Reason are correct but Reason is not the correct explanation of Assertion.
(c) Assertion is correct but Reason is incorrect.
(d) Assertion is incorrect but Reason is correct.

1. **Assertion** (A) Thermionic emission of electrons from a metal surface increases with increasing temperature.

Reason (R) Increasing the temperature provides more energy to the electrons, allowing them to overcome the work function of the metal.

(a) ☐ (b) ☐ (c) ☐ (d) ☐

***2.** **Assertion** (A) Field emission of electrons requires a very high electric field.

Reason (R) The high electric field lowers the potential barrier at the surface of the material, allowing electrons to tunnel through.

(a) ☐ (b) ☐ (c) ☐ (d) ☐

3. **Assertion** (A) Photocurrent increases with intensity of incident light.

Reason (R) Total energy of light beam increases with intensity.

(a) ☐ (b) ☐ (c) ☐ (d) ☐

***4.** **Assertion** (A) Stopping potential remains constant on varying intensity of light.

Reason (R) On increasing intensity, kinetic energy of emitted photoelectron also increases.

(a) ☐ (b) ☐ (c) ☐ (d) ☐

***5.** **Assertion** (A) Stopping potential is more negative for higher frequencies.

Reason (R) Greater the frequency of incident light, greater is the maximum kinetic energy of the photoelectrons.

(a) ☐ (b) ☐ (c) ☐ (d) ☐

6. **Assertion** (A) A monochromatic light contains photons of same energy.

Reason (R) Photon energy depends on wavelength of radiation.

(a) ☐ (b) ☐ (c) ☐ (d) ☐

7. **Assertion** (A) According to wave theory, time lag of hours is required for photoemission.

Reason (R) Energy contained even in an intense light beam is very small.

(a) ☐ (b) ☐ (c) ☐ (d) ☐

8. **Assertion** (A) In a photon-electron collision, the number of photons is always conserved.

Reason (R) The total energy and total momentum are conserved in a photon-particle collision.

(a) ☐ (b) ☐ (c) ☐ (d) ☐

***9.** **Assertion** (A) de-Broglie wavelength associated with a particle decreases as kinetic energy of the particle increases.

Reason (R) Wavelength, $\lambda = \dfrac{h}{\text{KE}}$

(a) ☐ (b) ☐ (c) ☐ (d) ☐

10. **Assertion** (A) The de-Broglie wavelength is significant for macroscopic objects such as a tennis ball.

Reason (R) The momentum of macroscopic objects is very large compared to subatomic particles.

(a) ☐ (b) ☐ (c) ☐ (d) ☐

Case Based Questions

1. An extensive study of photoelectric effect was made by Lenard and RA Millikan. Figure given below shows the experimental arrangement for the study of photoelectric effect. It consists of an evacuated glass or quartz tube which encloses a photosensitive plate C (called emitter) and a metal plate A (called collector). A transparent quartz window is sealed onto the glass tube which permits ultraviolet radiation to pass through it and fall on photosensitive plate C. The electrons are emitted by the plate C and are collected by the plate A. When the collector plate A is positive with respect to the emitter plate C, the electrons are attracted to it and hence photoelectron current is constituted.

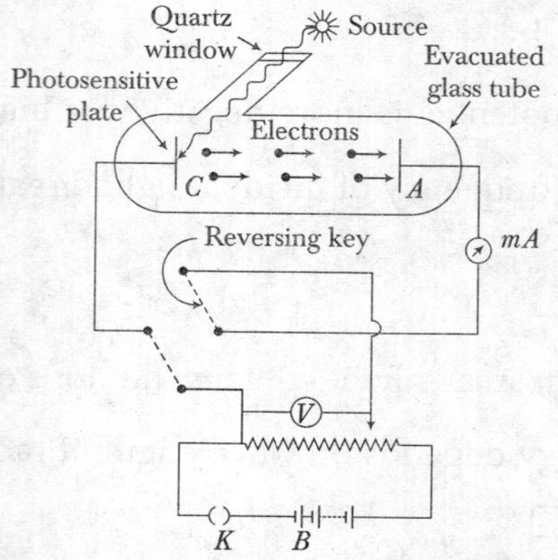

Experimental arrangement for the study of photoelectric effect

Maximum kinetic energy of emitted photoelectrons is given as
$K_{max} = eV_0 = h(\nu - \nu_0)$
where, $V_0 \rightarrow$ cutoff voltage
$\nu_0 \rightarrow$ threshold frequency
$\nu \rightarrow$ frequency of incident light

(i) In an experimental study of photoelectric effect, the stopping potential for a metallic surface is 5.68 V. The maximum velocity of the electrons is

(a) 1.4×10^3 km/s ☐ (b) 2.5×10^4 km/s ☐
(c) 1.7×10^4 km/s ☐ (d) 2.9×10^3 km/s ☐

(ii) The photoelectric cut-off voltage in a certain experiment is 1.5 V. What is the maximum kinetic energy of photoelectrons emitted?

(a) 6.2×10^{-19} J ☐ (b) 2.4×10^{-19} J ☐
(c) 3.5×10^{-19} J ☐ (d) 7.1×10^{-19} J ☐

(iii) Which of the following graph shows correct variation between photoelectric current and intensity of incident light?

(a) 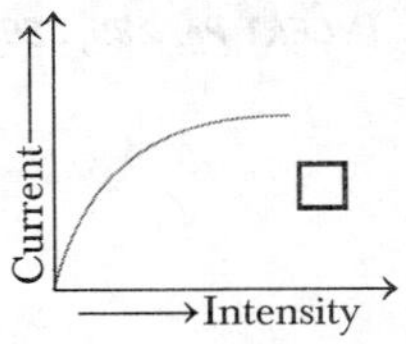 [graph: Current vs Intensity] ☐ (b) 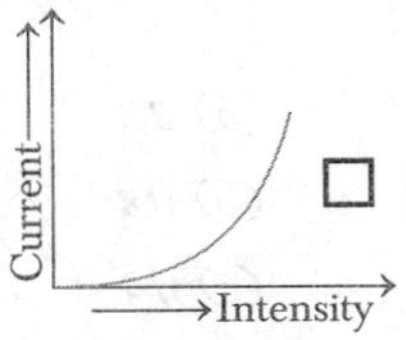 [graph: Current vs Intensity] ☐ (c) 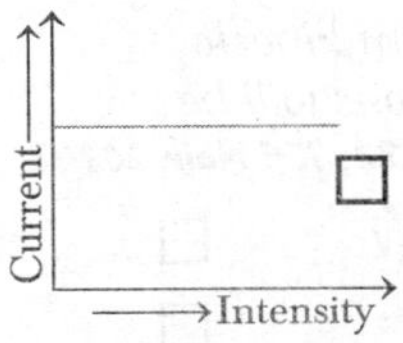 [graph: Current vs Intensity] ☐ (d) 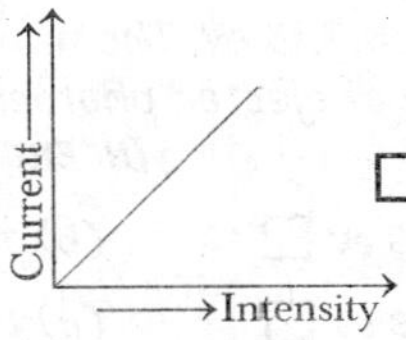 [graph: Current vs Intensity] ☐

(iv) If incident radiation of frequency, ν can emit one electron from a photosensitive material, then number of emitted electron when frequency of emitted electron is increased to double, will be

(a) 1 ☐ (b) 4 ☐
(c) 2 ☐ (d) 3 ☐

2. According to de-Broglie, a wave is associated with moving material particle which controls the particle in every respect.
The wave associated with moving particle is called **matter waves** or **de-Broglie wave** and it propagates in the form of wave packets with group velocity. Wavelength associated with de-Broglie wave is called **de-Broglie wavelength** and is given by $\lambda = \frac{h}{mv} = \frac{h}{p}$ where, m and v are the mass and velocity of the particle respectively and p is momentum of particle and h is Planck's constant.
According to Planck's quantum theory, the energy of the photon is given by $E = h\nu = \frac{hc}{\lambda}$

(i) Which of the following is correct?

(a) Matter wave are electoromagnetic waves ☐
(b) Matter waves are non-mechanical waves ☐
(c) Matter wave can not travel in vacuum ☐
(d) Observation of matter waves is possible only when the de-Broglie wavelength is of the order of size of the particle. ☐

(ii) A particle of mass 1 mg has the same wavelength as an electron moving with a velocity of 3×10^6 ms^{-1}. The velocity of the particle is

(a) 3.25×10^{-16} m/s ☐ (b) 6.25×10^{-18} m/s ☐
(c) 2.7×10^{-18} m/s ☐ (d) 7.8×10^{-12} m/s ☐

(iii) Find out the energy that should be added to an electron in terms of initial energy (E_1) to reduce its de-Broglie wavelengths from 10^{-10} m to 0.5×10^{-10} m.

(a) $2E_1$ ☐ (b) E_1 ☐
(c) $4E_1$ ☐ (d) $3E_1$ ☐

(iv) Which of the following particle will have smallest de-Broglie wavelength moving with same KE?

(a) Proton ☐ (b) Electron ☐
(c) Neutron ☐ (d) None of these ☐

COMPETITION EDGE UP

1. UV light of 4.13 eV is incident on a photosensitive metal surface having work function 3.13 eV. The maximum kinetic energy of ejected photoelectrons will be **[NCERT Pg. 282, JEE Main 2024]**

(a) 3.13 eV ☐ (b) 7.26 eV ☐
(c) 4.13 eV ☐ (d) 1 eV ☐

2. A proton and an electron have the same de-Broglie wavelength. If K_p and K_e be the kinetic energies of proton and electron respectively, then choose the correct relation **[NCERT Pg. 285, JEE Main 2024]**

(a) $K_p = K_e$ ☐ (b) $K_p < K_e$ ☐
(c) $K_p = K_e^2$ ☐ (d) $K_p > K_e$ ☐

3. When UV light of wavelength 300 nm is incident on the metal surface having work function 2.13 eV, electron emission takes place. The stopping potential is(Given, $hc = 1240$ eV-nm) **[NCERT Pg. 282, JEE Main 2024]**

(a) 4 V ☐ (b) 4.1 V ☐
(c) 1.5 V ☐ (d) 2 V ☐

4. The de-Broglie wavelengths of a proton and an α-particle are λ and 2λ, respectively. The ratio of the velocities of proton and α-particle will be **[NCERT Pg. 285, JEE Main 2024]**

(a) 1 : 2 ☐ (b) 1 : 8 ☐
(c) 8 : 1 ☐ (d) 4 : 1 ☐

5. The de-Broglie wavelength of an electron is the same as that of a photon. If velocity of electron is 25% of the velocity of light, then the ratio of KE of electron and KE of photon will be **[NCERT Pg. 285, JEE Main 2024]**

(a) 8/1 ☐
(b) 1/8 ☐
(c) 1/4 ☐
(d) 1/1 ☐

6. The graph which shows the variation of $\frac{1}{\lambda^2}$ and its kinetic energy, E is (where, λ is de-Broglie wavelength of a free particle): **[NCERT Pg. 285, NEET 2024]**

(a) 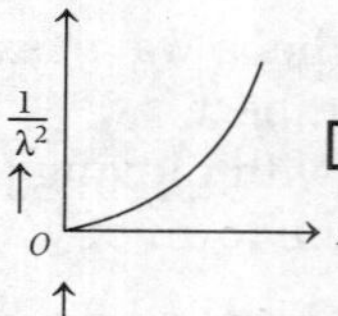 [graph: $\frac{1}{\lambda^2}$ vs E] ☐ (b) 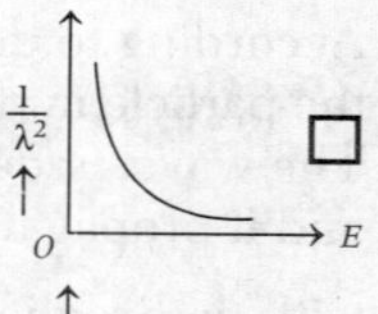 [graph: $\frac{1}{\lambda^2}$ vs E] ☐
(c) 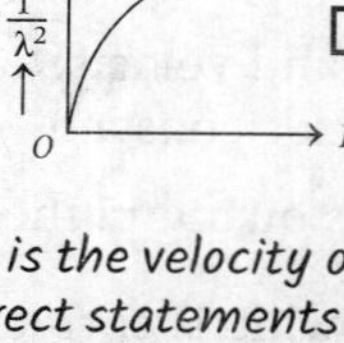 [graph: $\frac{1}{\lambda^2}$ vs E] ☐ (d) 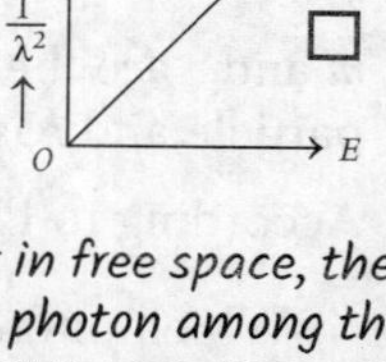 [graph: $\frac{1}{\lambda^2}$ vs E] ☐

7. If c is the velocity of light in free space, the correct statements about photon among the following are: **[NCERT Pg. 283, NEET 2024]**

A. The energy of a photon is $E = h\nu$.
B. The velocity of a photon is c.
C. The momentum of a photon, $p = \frac{h\nu}{c}$
D. In a photon-electron collision, both total energy and total momentum are conserved.
E. Photon possesses positive charge.

Choose the correct answer from the options given below:

(a) A and B only ☐

(b) A, B, C and D only ☐

(c) A, C and D only ☐

(d) A, B, D and E only ☐

8. When two monochromatic lights of frequency, ν and $\nu/2$ are incident on a photoelectric metal, their stopping potential becomes $V_s/2$ and V_s, respectively. The threshold frequency for this metal is **[NCERT Pg. 281, NEET 2022]**

(a) 3ν ☐ (b) $\frac{2}{3}\nu$ ☐

(c) $\frac{3}{2}\nu$ ☐ (d) 2ν ☐

9. An electromagnetic wave of wavelength λ is incident on a photosensitive surface of negligible work function. If m mass is of photoelectron emitted from the surface has de-Broglie wavelength λ_d, then **[NCERT Pg. 285, NEET 2021]**

(a) $\lambda = \left(\frac{2h}{mc}\right)\lambda_d^2$ ☐

(b) $\lambda = \left(\frac{2m}{hc}\right)\lambda_d^2$ ☐

(c) $\lambda = \left(\frac{2mc}{h}\right)\lambda^2$ ☐

(d) $\lambda = \left(\frac{2mc}{h}\right)\lambda_d^2$ ☐

10. The de-Broglie wavelength of an electron moving with kinetic energy of 144 eV is nearly **[NCERT Pg. 285, NEET 2020]**

(a) 102×10^{-3} nm ☐ (b) 102×10^{-4} nm ☐

(c) 102×10^{-5} nm ☐ (d) 102×10^{-2} nm ☐

Chapter 12

Atoms

TOPIC 1

Alpha-Particele Scattering and Rutherford's Nuclear Model of Atom

1. Label the given diagram showing Geiger-Marsden α-particle scattering experiment.

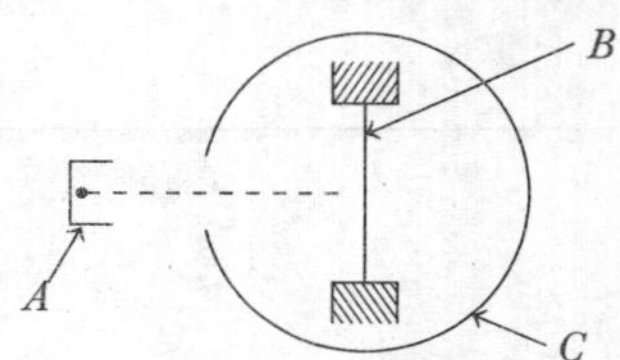

$A =$ ____________ $B =$ ____________

$C =$ ____________

2. Match observation of Geiger-Marsden experiment in Column I with its conclusion in Column II.

	Column I		Column II
A.	Most of α-particles pass straight	1.	Atom contains a positively charged nucleus which contains most of mass of atom.
B.	Few α-particles are deflected at small angles	2.	There is a positive charge at the centre in atom.
C.	Very few α-particles are deflected in backward direction	3.	Most part of atom is empty.

A. ____________ B. ____________ C. ____________

3. Draw the graph of number of scattered particles (N) with respect to scattering angle (θ).

____

4. Let F = force and r = distance between a gold nucleus and an α-particle, then the product of $F \cdot r^2$ is ____________ $(158e^2\ /112e^2) \times 9 \times 10^9$:

*Concepts of all questions bearing * are important for JEE/NEET/CUET.*

5. Mark value of impact parameter for the α-particles shown below.

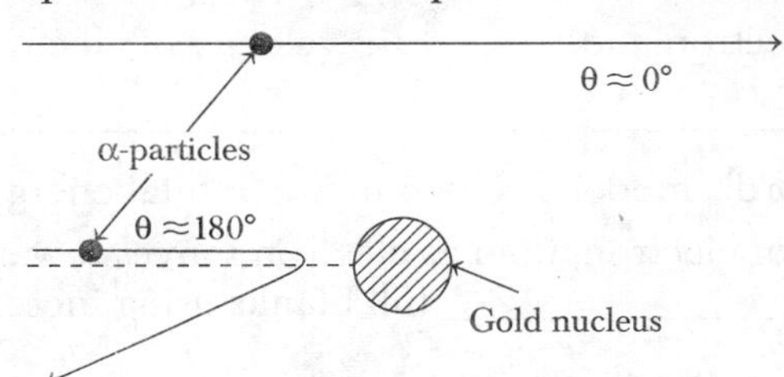

(i) For $\theta = 0°$, b = ____________ (small/large)

(ii) For $\theta = \pi$, b = ____________ (maximum/minimum)

6. In Rutherford's model, size of nucleus is about 10^{-15} m and that of atom is about 10^{-10} m. Radius of sun is about 7×10^{8} m and earth's orbital radius is about 1.5×10^{11} m. If dimensions of the solar system has the same proportions as those of the atom, then size of earth's orbit will be

(a) less than 10 times ☐ (b) less than 100 times ☐

(c) more than 10 times ☐ (d) more than 100 times ☐

***7.** An α-particle is moving for a head-on collision with a gold nucleus having kinetic energy K, so the distance of closest approach is given by d = ____________ $\left(\frac{Ze^2}{4\pi\varepsilon_0 K} / \frac{2Ze^2}{4\pi\varepsilon_0 K}\right)$.

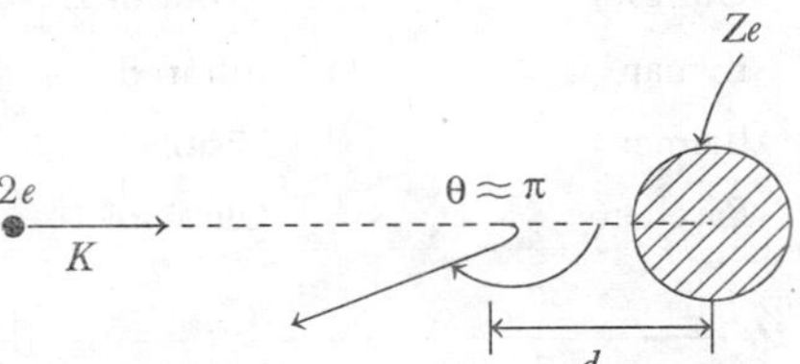

8. With which of the following targets, no large angle scattering of α-particles can be observed?

(a) A thin sheet of gold ☐ (b) A thin sheet of copper ☐

(c) A thin sheet of silver ☐ (d) A thin sheet of solid hydrogen ☐

9. In Rutherford's model, centripetal force for revolving electron is provided by ____________ (coulombian/magnetic) force of nucleus.

10. Considering Rutherford's model, match various energies given in Column I with their respective relation given in Column II.

Column I	Column II
A. Kinetic energy of electron	1. $\frac{-e^2}{8\pi\varepsilon_0 r}$
B. Potential energy of electron	2. $\frac{-e^2}{4\pi\varepsilon_0 r}$
C. Total energy of electron	3. $\frac{e^2}{8\pi\varepsilon_0 r}$

A. ____________ B. ____________ C. ____________

11. In Rutherford's model, the ratio of total energy and kinetic energy of an electron is ______ (1/– 1) and the ratio of potential energy and total energy is ______ (2/3).

12. Total binding energy of an electron in a H-atom is 13.6 eV. Compute
(i) orbital radius of electron and (ii) velocity of electron.

____

13. Considering Rutherford's model of H-atom, if E = total energy, K = kinetic energy and U = potential energy of electron, then as electron moves towards nucleus, E ________, K ________ and U ____________ (fill blanks using increase/decrease).

TOPIC 2

Atomic Spectra

NCERT Pg 296-297

14. When a gas or vapour is excited at a low pressure, the emitted radiation spectrum contains few wavelengths which are different from absorbed wavelengths of white light (when white light is passed through unexcited gas).

True ☐ False ☐

15. Match the spectral series given in Column I with region of electromagnetic spectrum (to which they belong) given in Column II.

	Column I		Column II
A.	Lyman	1.	Infrared
B.	Balmer	2.	Visible
C.	Paschen	3.	Ultraviolet

A. ____________ B. ____________ C. ____________

***16.** An emission line spectrum is observed when
(a) a gas is excited by heating or by passing a electric discharge through it ☐
(b) a gas is excited by applying pressure ☐
(c) a gas under low pressure condition is excited by heating or by passing a electric discharge through it ☐
(d) a gas under high pressure condition is excited by heating or by passing a electric discharge through it ☐

***17.** When white light is passed through an unexcited gas, then transmitted light consists of
(a) few bright lines in dark background ☐
(b) few dark lines in bright background ☐
(c) alternate dark and bright lines ☐
(d) alternate dark and bright bands ☐

TOPIC 3

Bohr Model of the Hydrogen Atom

18. Rutherford's model is not acceptable as electron is losing energy continuously, so it would spiral inward and eventually fall into nucleus.

True ☐ False ☐

19. Frequency of light emitted by revolving electrons in Rutherford's model is equal to twice the frequency of revolution of electron.

Yes ☐ No ☐

***20.** According to classical theory, initial frequency of emitted light by revolving electron of H-atom is ______________ $(6.6 / 3.3) \times 10^{15}$ Hz. (Take, radius = 0.53 Å and velocity = 2.2×10^{6} ms^{-1})

***21.** When an electron in hydrogen atom is excited from its 4th to 5th stationary orbit, the change in angular momentum of electron is ______________ $(3.32/1.05) \times 10^{-34}$ J-s.

22. The graph of radius r_n of electron in nth orbit *versus* atomic number Z is

(a) 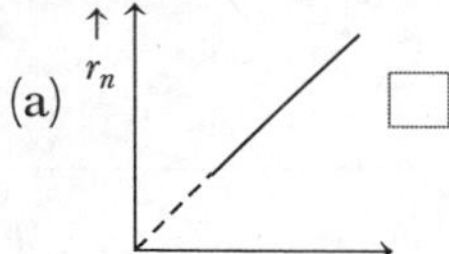

☐

(b) ☐

(c) 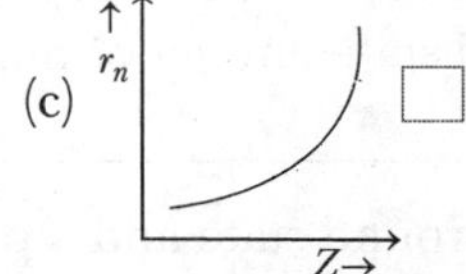

☐

(d) 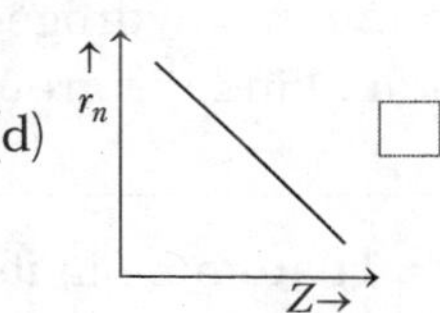

☐

23. In terms of Bohr radius a_0, express the radius of second Bohr orbit of a hydrogen atom.

____

24. The radius of hydrogen atom in its ground state is 5.3×10^{-11} m. After collision with an electron, it is found to have a radius of 21.2×10^{-11} m. What is the principal quantum number n of the final state of the atom?

(a) $n = 4$ ☐ (b) $n = 2$ ☐

(c) $n = 16$ ☐ (d) $n = 8$ ☐

25. Which of the following transitions gives photon of maximum energy?

(a) $n = 1$ to $n = 2$ ☐ (b) $n = 2$ to $n = 1$ ☐

(c) $n = 2$ to $n = 6$ ☐ (d) $n = 6$ to $n = 2$ ☐

***26.** An atom makes a transition from $(n-1)$th level to nth level when a photon of frequency 5.6×10^{14} Hz is absorbed by electron. Difference of energies of these levels is ________ (3.2 eV/2.3 eV).

27. Tick (✓/✗) for correct/incorrect statement.

I. $E_n = \dfrac{-me^4}{8\varepsilon_0^2 h^2} \cdot \dfrac{1}{n^2}$ (J) ☐ II. $E_n = -Rch \cdot \dfrac{1}{n^2}$ (J) ☐

III $E_n = \dfrac{-2.18 \times 10^{-18}}{n^2}$ (J) ☐ IV. $E_n = \dfrac{13.6}{n^2}$ (eV) ☐

***28.** For atomic model of hydrogen atom given by Niels Bohr, match the Column I (quantities) with Column II (proportionalities).

Column I	Column II
A. Angular momentum	1. $1/n$
B. Velocity of electron	2. n^2
C. Radius of electron	3. $1/n^2$
D. Energy of electron	4. n

A. ________ B. ________ C. ________ D. ________

29. If we take orbits elliptical instead of circular as in Bohr's atom, then energy of electron in ground state would be ________ (more than/less than/equal to) 13.6 eV.

30. Total energy of an electron in the first excited state of H-atom is about – 3.4 eV, then find the

(i) kinetic energy of electron and

(ii) potential energy of electron.

____

31. In a muonic hydrogen atom, a negatively charged muon (mass = 207 m_e) orbits around a proton. Find the ground state energy of muonic hydrogen atom.

____

32. Let a H-atom be in its ground state and a photon of energy 10.5 eV is made to fall on this atom, then

(a) electron move to first excited state by absorbing 10.2 eV of energy ☐

(b) electron absorbs 10.5 eV energy, emitting photon of energy 0.3 eVand achieves first excited state ☐

(c) electron absorbs 10.5 eV and moves to intermediate state between $n = 1$ and $n = 2$ ☐

(d) electron does not absorb photon of energy 10.5 eV ☐

33. Once an electron acquires some higher excited state, it remains there till some interatomic collision causes de-excitation.

True ☐ False ☐

34. Write values of energy of excited states in following energy-level diagram for a H-atom.

Total energy
E(eV)

E_∞=0 eV	$n=\infty$
E_5=	n=5
E_4=	n=4
E_3=	n=3
E_2=	n=2
E_1=–13.6 eV	n=1

____

35. The speed of an electron in ground state energy level is $2.6 \times 10^{6}\ \text{ms}^{-1}$, so its speed in third excited state will be $x \times 10^{5}$. What is value of x here?

---

36. Energy of an electron in an excited state of hydrogen atom is – 3.4 eV. Calculate its angular momentum.

---

37. Let r_1 = radius of electron in ground state and r_2 = radius of electron in third excited state, then what will be the ratio $\frac{r_2}{r_1}$?

TOPIC 4

The Line Spectra of the Hydrogen Atom

38. A hydrogen atom in its ground state absorbs a photon and attains third excited state. Wavelength of photon is nearest to __________ (100/200)nm.

***39.** An electron in an excited state in a hydrogen like atom. It has a total energy of –1.5 eV, then the kinetic energyof electron is

(a) 2.5 eV ☐ (b) 1.5 eV ☐

(c) 13.6 eV ☐ (d) 0.85 eV ☐

40. The ground state energy of H-atom is 13.6 eV. Calculate the energy needed to ionise H-atom from its second excited state.

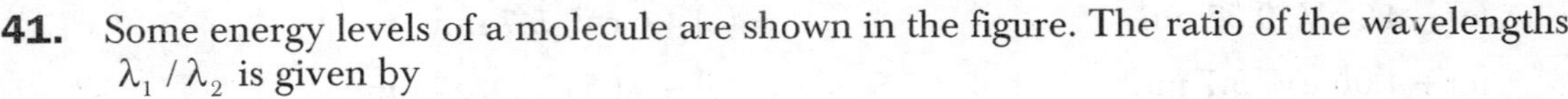

41. Some energy levels of a molecule are shown in the figure. The ratio of the wavelengths λ_1 / λ_2 is given by

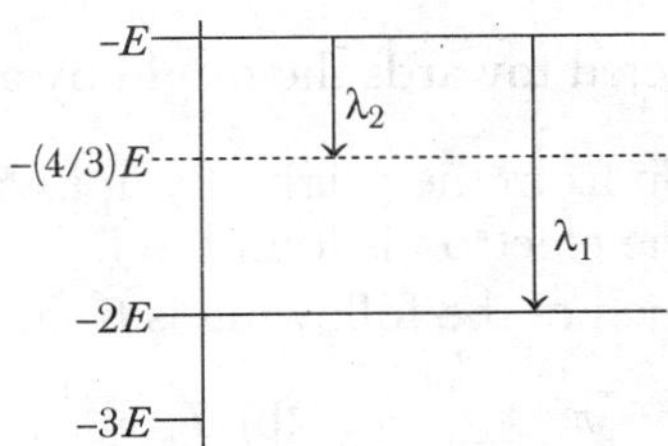

(a) $\frac{2}{3}$ ☐ (b) $\frac{3}{4}$ ☐

(c) $\frac{1}{3}$ ☐ (d) $\frac{4}{3}$ ☐

42. Take value of $hc = 1240$ eV-nm and $Rh = 13.6$ eV and find the values of wavelengths emitted in following transitions.

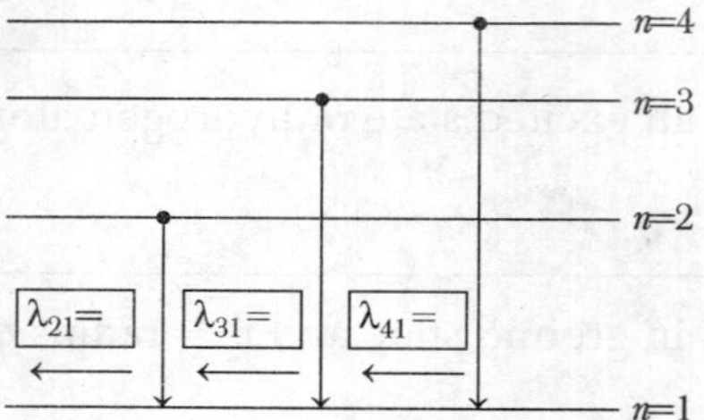

TOPIC 5

de-Broglie's Explanation of Bohr's Second Postulate of Quantisation

43. Which of these electron orbits (dotted) are not possible? (Dark waves are de-Broglie's waves)

I. de-Broglie wave ☐ II. ☐ III. Electron ☐

44. Bohr's model is not applicable to singly ionised helium or doubly ionised lithium.

True ☐ False ☐

***45.** An electron of a hydrogen like atom is in excited state. If total energy of the electron is – 4.6 eV, the kinetic energy and the de-Broglie wavelength of the electron is

(a) – 4.6 eV, 0.57 nm ☐ (b) 4.6 eV, 5.7 nm ☐

(c) + 4.06 eV, 5.7 nm ☐ (d) – 4.06 eV, 0.57 nm ☐

***46.** Suppose an electron is attracted towards the origin by a force $\frac{k}{r}$, where k is a constant and r is the distance of the electron from the origin. By applying Bohr model to this system, the radius of the nth orbital of the electron is found to be r_n and the kinetic energy of the electron to be T_n. Then, which of the following is true?

(a) T_n is independent of n, $r_n \propto n$ ☐ (b) $T_n \propto \frac{1}{n}, r_n \propto n$ ☐

(c) $T_n \propto \frac{1}{n}, r_n \propto n^2$ ☐ (d) $T_n \propto \frac{1}{n^2}, r_n \propto n^2$ ☐

COMPETITION CONNECT

Topic 1. Atomic Spectra [NCERT (Old) Pg. 420-422]

1. Match spectral series (Column I) with minimum wavelength of spectral lines (Column II).

	Column I		Column II
A.	Lyman	1.	$9/R$
B.	Balmer	2.	$16/R$
C.	Paschen	3.	$4/R$
D.	Brackett	4.	$1/R$
E.	Pfund	5.	$25/R$

A. ______________ B. ______________ C. ______________

D. ______________ E. ______________

2. If wavelength of the first line of the Balmer series of hydrogen is 6561Å, the wavelength of the second line of the series should be __________ (3280Å/4860Å).

3. The ratio of wavelengths of the last line of Balmer series and the last line of Lyman series is

(a) 2 ☐ (b) 1 ☐ (c) 4 ☐ (d) 0.5 ☐

4. In Pfund series, ratio of maximum to minimum wavelength of emitted spectral lines is 36 : 11.

True ☐ False ☐

5. In the spectrum of hydrogen, the largest wavelength in the Lyman series is 5 times the largest wavelength in the Balmer series.

Yes No

6. If the series limit frequency of the Lyman series is v_L, then the series limit frequency of the Pfund series is

(a) $25\,\nu_L$ ☐ (b) $16\,\nu_L$ ☐ (c) $\frac{\nu_L}{16}$ ☐ (d) $\frac{\nu_L}{25}$ ☐

Topic 2. The Line Spectra of Hydrogen Atom [NCERT (Old) Pg. 428-430]

7. Choose correct expressions from the following.
R = Rydberg constant, m = mass of electron, e = charge of electron, ε_0 = permittivity of free space, h = Planck's constant, n_i and n_f = initial and final states quantum numbers and ν_{if} = frequency of photon.

I. $R = \frac{me^4}{8\varepsilon_0^2 h^3 c}$ II. $R = \frac{me^4}{8\varepsilon_0^2 h^2 c}$

____

8. Draw all possible emissions corresponding to absorption given below.

____

9. An electron jumps from the 4th orbit to 2nd orbit of the hydrogen atom. Given, Rydberg's constant $R = 10^7 \text{ m}^{-1}$, the frequency of emitted radiation will be $\frac{a}{b} \times 10^{15}$ Hz. What is the value of a and b?

Assertion-Reason Questions

Direction (Q. Nos. 1-10) *In the following questions, a statement of Assertion is followed by a corresponding statement of Reason. From the following options, choose the correct one.*

(a) Both Assertion and Reason are correct and Reason is the correct explanation of Assertion.
(b) Both Assertion and Reason are correct but Reason is not the correct explanation of Assertion.
(c) Assertion is correct but Reason is incorrect..
(d) Assertion is incorrect but Reason is correct.

***1. Assertion** (A) Electrons in an atom are held due to Coulomb forces.
Reason (R) The atom is stable only because the centripetal force due to Coulomb's law is balanced by the centrifugal force.

(a) ☐ (b) ☐ (c) ☐ (d) ☐

***2. Assertion** (A) Angular momentum of single electron in any orbit of hydrogen type atoms is independent of the atomic number of the element.

Reason (R) In ground state angular momentum is minimum.

(a) ☐ (b) ☐ (c) ☐ (d) ☐

3. Assertion (A) The energy of an electron in a hydrogen atom in the first excited state is approximately -5.45×10^{-19} J.

Reason (R) The energy of an electron in a hydrogen atom can be found by $-\frac{m^2 l^2}{8n^2 \varepsilon_0 h^2}$.

where, m is mass of electron, e is elementary charge, n is principal quantum number and h is Planck's constant.

(a) ☐ (b) ☐ (c) ☐ (d) ☐

4. Assertion (A) Highest energy state corresponds with the electron revolving in an orbit closest to the nucleus.

Reason (R) Energies of the excited states come closer and closer together as n increases.

(a) ☐ (b) ☐ (c) ☐ (d) ☐

5. Assertion (A) Energy E_1 is required to remove first electron from helium atom and energy E_2 is to required to remove the second electron. Then, $E_1 < E_2$.

Reason (R) Ionisation energy of single electron of He^+ is 54.4 eV.

(a) ☐ (b) ☐ (c) ☐ (d) ☐

6. Assertion (A) An electron can absorb any photon of energy more than 13.6 eV.

Reason (R) Energy absorbed by an electron is always equal to difference of energy values of two energy levels.

(a) ☐ (b) ☐ (c) ☐ (d) ☐

***7.** **Assertion** (A) It is not essential that all the lines available in the emission spectrum will also be available in the absorption spectrum.

Reason (R) The spectrum of hydrogen atom is only absorption spectrum.

(a) ☐ (b) ☐ (c) ☐ (d) ☐

8. **Assertion** (A) Emission line spectrum of an element serve as a fingerprint of that element.

Reason (R) There is no regular pattern of field lines in an emission spectrum.

(a) ☐ (b) ☐ (c) ☐ (d) ☐

***9.** **Assertion** (A) Energy of 13.6 eV is required to remove an electron from the H-atom to a distance infinitely far away from proton.

Reason (R) Energy of electron in ground state of H-atom is 13.6 eV.

(a) ☐ (b) ☐ (c) ☐ (d) ☐

10. **Assertion** (A) Second orbit circumference of hydrogen atom is two times the de-Broglie wavelength of electrons in that orbit.

Reason (R) de-Broglie wavelength of electron in ground state is minimum.

(a) ☐ (b) ☐ (c) ☐ (d) ☐

Case Based Questions

1. An electron is rotating in a circular path under the influence of a magnetic field of constant magnitude and direction. Assume that Bohr's quantisation of angular momentum is valid for this electron. (Take, h = Planck's constant, q = charge of electron, r = radius of path and B = magnetic field strength)

(i) Radius of nth orbit of electron is

(a) $\sqrt{\frac{2\pi h}{\pi n B q}}$ ☐ (b) $\sqrt{\frac{nh}{2\pi Bq}}$ ☐ (c) $\sqrt{\frac{nqh}{2\pi B}}$ ☐ (d) $\sqrt{\frac{2nh}{\pi Bq}}$ ☐

(ii) The frequency of the electron's revolution in the circular path under the magnetic field is directly proportional to

(a) B ☐ (b) $\frac{1}{B}$ ☐ (c) B^2 ☐ (d) $\frac{1}{B^2}$ ☐

(iii) Kinetic energy of the nth orbit will be

(a) $\frac{nhBq}{4\pi m}$ ☐ (b) $\frac{nhBq}{2\pi m}$ ☐ (c) $\frac{nhB}{4\pi mq}$ ☐ (d) $\frac{nhB}{2\pi mq}$ ☐

(iv) Let the electron makes a transition from second orbit to first orbit and let a photon is emitted in this process, then frequency of emitted photon will be

(a) zero (no emission) ☐

(b) Cannot be found ☐

(c) half of classical revolution frequency ☐

(d) classical revolution frequency ☐

Or

In Bohr's model, if an electron jumps from a higher energy orbit to a lower energy orbit around a nucleus, the energy released is

(a) converted into kinetic energy of the electron ☐
(b) converted into potential energy of the electron ☐
(c) released as electromagnetic radiation ☐
(d) stored as nuclear energy ☐

2. Atomic spectra refer to the unique patterns of light emitted or absorbed by atoms when electrons transition takes place between energy levels. These spectra are crucial in identifying elements and understanding atomic structure. There are three main types of atomic spectra : emission spectra, absorption spectra and continuous spectra.

When an atomic gas or vapour is excited at low pressure, usually by passing an electric current through it, the emitted radiation has a spectrum containing specific wavelengths only.

On the other hand, if white light passes through a gas, we found that the transmitted light consists of some dark lines in the spectrum. These dark lines correspond precisely to those wavelengths which were found in the emission spectrum of gas.

(i) Atomic spectra is obtained when excited electrons in atoms return to lower energy. This spectra is known as

(a) emission spectra ☐ (b) absorption spectra ☐
(c) continuous spectra ☐ (d) diffraction spectra ☐

(ii) The atomic spectra obtained in stars and other hot, dense objects is

(a) emission spectra ☐ (b) absorption spectra ☐
(c) continuous spectra ☐ (d) line spectra ☐

Or

The study of atomic spectra is essential because

(a) it helps to identify chemical reactions ☐
(b) it provides information about atomic composition and energy levels ☐
(c) it explains nuclear reactions ☐
(d) it determines molecular structures ☐

(iii) A sodium lamp emites light primarily in the yellow region of the spectrum at a wavelength of approximate by 589 nm. From this information, we conclude that the energy difference between two energy levels of sodium atom is

(a) 3.37×10^{-19} J ☐ (b) 4.4×10^{-19} J ☐
(c) 2.63×10^{-16} J ☐ (d) 3.59×10^{-20} J ☐

(iv) Hydrogen atom emits light when it changes from $n = 5$ energy level to $n = 2$ level. Which colour of light would the atom emit?

(a) Red ☐ (b) Yellow ☐
(c) Green ☐ (d) Violet ☐

COMPETITION EDGE UP

1. In an alpha particle scattering experiment distance of closest approach for the α-particle is 4.5×10^{-14} m. If target nucleus has atomic number 80. Then, maximum velocity of α-particle is .... $\times 10^5$ m/s approximately.

$\left(\frac{1}{4\pi\varepsilon_0} = 9 \times 10^9 \text{ SI unit, mass of } \alpha\text{-particle} = 6.72 \times 10^{-27} \text{ kg}\right)$

[NCERT Pg. 295, JEE Main 2024]

2. The angular momentum of an electron in a hydrogen atom is proportional to (where, r is the radius of orbit of electron)

[NCERT Pg. 299, JEE Main 2024]

(a) r ☐ (b) $\frac{1}{r}$ ☐

(c) $\frac{1}{\sqrt{r}}$ ☐ (d) $\sqrt{r}$ ☐

3. According to Bohr's theory, the moment of momentum of an electron revolving in 4th orbit of hydrogen atom is

[NCERT Pg. 299, JEE Main 2024]

(a) $\frac{h}{\pi}$ ☐ (b) $2\frac{h}{\pi}$ ☐

(c) $8\frac{h}{\pi}$ ☐ (d) $\frac{h}{2\pi}$ ☐

4. The ratio of the magnitude of the kinetic energy to the potential energy of an electron in the 5th excited state of a hydrogen atom is

[NCERT Pg. 296, JEE Main 2024]

(a) 1 ☐ (b) 1/4 ☐

(c) 1/2 ☐ (d) 4 ☐

5. Given below are two statements.

Statement I Most of the mass of the atom and all its positive charge are concentrated in a tiny nucleus and the electrons revolve around it, is Rutherford's model.

Statement II An atom is a spherical cloud of positive charges with electrons embedded in it, is a special case of Rutherford's model.

[NCERT Pg. 293, JEE Main 2024]

In the light of the above statements, choose the most appropriate from the options given below.

(a) Statement I is true but Statement II is false ☐

(b) Both Statement I and Statement II are false ☐

(c) Both Statement I and Statement II are true ☐

(d) Statement I is false but Statement II is true ☐

6. The radius of third stationary orbit of electron for Bohr's atom is R. The radius of fourth stationary orbit will be

[NCERT Pg. 299, JEE Main 2024]

(a) $\frac{9}{16}R$ ☐ (b) $\frac{3}{4}R$ ☐

(c) $\frac{16}{9}R$ ☐ (d) $\frac{4}{3}R$ ☐

7. Given below are two statements.

Statement I Atoms are electrically neutral as they contain equal number of positive and negative charges.

Statement II Atoms of each element are stable and emit their characteristic spectrum.

In the light of the above statements, choose the most appropriate answer from the options given below. **[NCERT Pg. 290, NEET 2024]**

(a) Both Statement I and Statement II are correct. ☐

(b) Both Statement I and Statement II are incorrect. ☐

(c) Statement I is correct but Statement II is incorrect. ☐

(d) Statement I is incorrect but Statement II is correct. ☐

8. The radius of inner most orbit of hydrogen atom is 5.3×10^{-11} m. What is the radius of third allowed orbit of hydrogen atom ?

[NCERT Pg. 299, NEET 2023]

(a) 1.06 Å ☐ (b) 1.59 Å ☐

(c) 4.77 Å ☐ (d) 0.53 Å ☐

9. The total energy of an electron in the nth stationary orbit of the hydrogen atom can be obtained by **[NCERT Pg. 299, NEET (Oct.) 2020]**

(a) $E_n = \frac{13.6}{n^2}$ eV ☐

(b) $E_n = -\frac{13.6}{n^2}$ eV ☐

(c) $E_n = -\frac{1.36}{n^2}$ eV ☐

(d) $E_n = -13.6 \times n^2$ eV ☐

Chapter 13

Nuclei

TOPIC 1

Atomic Masses and Composition of Nucleus

1. Tick (✓) in front of correct and (×) in front of incorrect statements about nucleus of an atom.

I. Nucleus contains most of the mass (more than 99.9%) of atoms. ☐

II. Radius of atom is nearly equal to 10^4 times of radius of nucleus. ☐

III. Volume of atom is about 10^{12} times of volume of nucleus. ☐

IV. Nucleus contains about 90% of total charge of atom. ☐

V. Atomic masses are generally integral multiple of mass of hydrogen atom. ☐

2. As mass of an atom is very small, we use atomic mass unit (u) to express atomic masses. 1 atomic mass unit is

(a) mass of 1 atom of protium (hydrogen ^1H) ☐

(b) $\frac{1}{16}$th of mass of an oxygen (^{16}O) atom ☐

(c) $\frac{1}{12}$th of mass of a carbon (C^{12}) atom ☐

(d) $\frac{1}{14}$th of mass of a nitrogen (^{14}N) atom ☐

3. Hydrogen atom has three isotopes : Protium (P), deuterium (D) and tritium (T). Match the properties in Column I with order in Column II.

Column I		Column II	
A.	Place in periodic table	1.	$P > D > T$
B.	Increasing order of number of neutrons	2.	$P = D = T$
		3.	$P < D < T$

A. ________________ B. ________________

*Concepts of all questions bearing * are important for JEE/NEET/CUET.*

4. If an element has three isotopes with masses m_1, m_2 and m_3. Also, their percentage abundances are x_1, x_2 and x_3 respectively, then average atomic mass of element is taken as, $\overline{m}$ = ______________ $\left(\dfrac{m_1 + m_2 + m_3}{100} / \dfrac{m_1x_1 + m_2x_2 + m_3x_3}{100}\right)$.

***5.** Masses of three isotopes of hydrogen are: 1.0078 u, 2.0141 u and 3.0160 u. Also, mass of a single electron is 0.00055 u.
Using above data, mass of a proton and a neutron (neglecting mass defect) respectively, are closest to

(a) 1.00725 u and 1.0019 u ☐
(b) 1.00725 u and 1.0063 u ☐
(c) 1.00725 u and 1.0041 u ☐
(d) Cannot be estimated using above data ☐

6. Ratio of masses of nuclei hydrogen, deuterium and tritium is 1 : 2 : 3 but they all contain only one proton. This accounts for

(a) existence of neutral matter in multiples of basic unit of mass ☐
(b) existence of neutral matter not in multiple of basic unit of mass ☐
(c) existence of heavier electrons ☐
(d) existence of heavier photons ☐

7. Arrange electron, proton and neutron in increasing order of stability in free state.

____

***8.** Match the Column I with Column II.

	Column I		Column II
A.	Atoms with same mass number (A)	1.	Isotones
B.	Atoms with same neutron number	2.	Isotopes
C.	Atoms with same number of protons	3.	Isobars

A. ____________ B. ____________ C. ____________

TOPIC 2

Size of the Nucleus

NCERT Pg 309-310

9. When an α-particle with kinetic energy of 5.5 MeV is projected towards a gold nucleus ($Z = 79$) in α-particle scattering experiment, distance of closest approach is nearly around

(a) 4×10^{-15} m ☐ (b) 2×10^{-15} m ☐
(c) 2×10^{-14} m ☐ (d) 4×10^{-14} m ☐

***10.** Ratio of radii of $^{197}_{97}$Au and $^{107}_{47}$Ag is more than 1.5.

True ☐ False ☐

***11.** Two nuclei have mass numbers A and B respectively. The density ratio of the nuclei is

(a) $A : B$ ☐ (b) $\sqrt{A} : \sqrt{B}$ ☐

(c) $A^2 : B^2$ ☐ (d) 1 : 1 ☐

12. Match quantities given in Column I with their respective values (in SI units) given in Column II.

Column I	Column II
A. Nuclear density	1. same for all
B. Ordinary matter density	2. 10^{17}
C. Ratio of nuclear density of $^{210}_{84}$Po and $^{94}_{36}$Kr	3. 10^{-28}

A. ________ B. ________ C. ________

13. Find volume of a neutron star whose mass is 2.3×10^{31} kg.

____

***14.** Surface area of a nucleus (assuming it to be a perfect sphere), is (where, A = mass number)

(a) $(1.8 \times 10^{-29})A^{1/3}$ ☐ (b) $(1.8 \times 10^{-29})A^2$ ☐

(c) $(1.8 \times 10^{-29})A^{2/3}$ ☐ (d) $(1.8 \times 10^{-29})A^3$ ☐

***15.** Mass of iron nucleus is 55.85 u and $A = 56$. Its nuclear density will be (take, $R_0 = 1.2 \times 10^{-15}$ m)

(a) 4.28×10^{17} kg m^{-3} ☐ (b) 2×10^{-3} kg m^{-3} ☐

(c) 2.29×10^{17} kg m^{-3} ☐ (d) 9×10^{10} kg m^{-3} ☐

TOPIC 3

Mass-Energy, Nuclear Binding Energy and Nuclear Force

NCERT Pg 310-314

16. Given, mass of a neutron = 1.00866 u, mass of a proton = 1.00727 u, mass of an electron = 0.00055 u and mass of $^{16}_{8}$O atom = 15.99493 u. Then, find mass defect.

____

17. Energy equivalent of one atomic mass unit (1.66×10^{-27} kg) is ________ (9.315/931.5) MeV.

18. Mass defect for helium nucleus is 0.0303 amu. Calculate binding energy per nucleon (in MeV) for helium.

____

19. Tick (✓) in front of correct and (×) in front of incorrect statements.

I. Average energy per nucleon needed to separate a nucleus into its nucleons is called binding energy per nucleon. ☐

II. BE per nucleon is nearly constant for nuclei of mass number 30 to 170. ☐

III. BE per nucleon is less than 8 MeV for nucleons of mass number less than 30. ☐

IV. BE per nucleon increases linearly with mass number. ☐

***20.** For lighter nuclei ($A < 30$), BE per nucleon continuously increases with mass number.

True ☐ False ☐

21. Let a heavy nucleus $A = 240$ break into two lighter nuclei each with $A = 120$. The type of reaction is __________ (exothermic/endothermic)

***22.** BE per nucleon of a deuteron (^2_1H) is 1.112 MeV and for an α-particle (^4_2He) is 7.047 MeV. What will be the energy released in given fusion reaction?

$$^2_1H + ^2_1H \longrightarrow ^4_2He$$

____

***23.** Observe the following BE per nucleon graph.

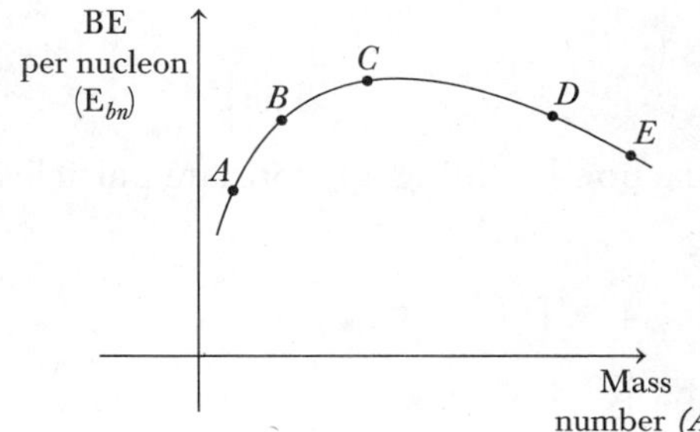

Now, match entries of Column I and Column II correctly.

	Column I		Column II
A.	$A + B \longrightarrow C$	1.	Not possible energetically
B.	$D + E \longrightarrow C$	2.	Energy is liberated
C.	$D \longrightarrow 2B$	3.	Energy is absorbed

A. ______________ B. ______________ C. ______________

***24.** Nuclear energy required to separate all the neutrons and protons of a 3g copper coin is (Take, mass of $^{63}_{29}Cu = 62.92960$ u)

(a) 1.6×10^{16} MeV ☐ (b) 1.6×10^{19} MeV ☐

(c) 1.6×10^{25} MeV ☐ (d) 1.6×10^{31} MeV ☐

25. Select the correct graph showing variation of nuclear force *versus* distance between two nucleons.

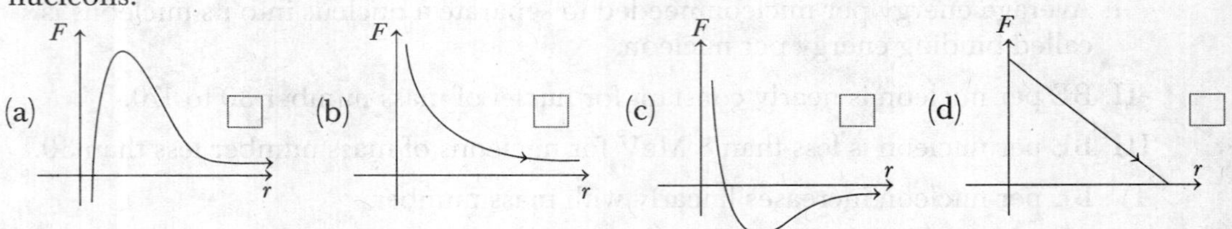

26. Ratio of force between two protons and force between two neutrons inside a nucleus is __________ (greater than/less than/equals to) 1.

TOPIC 4 Radioactivity

NCERT Pg 314

***27.** Alpha decay of a parent nuclei ${}_{Z}^{A}X$ is given by ${}_{Z}^{A}X \rightarrow \square + {}_{2}^{4}\text{He}$

Fill the box with appropriate symbol of daughter nucleus.

***28.** In reaction, ${}_{Z}^{A}X \longrightarrow {}_{Z-2}^{A-4}Y + {}_{2}^{4}\text{He}$. The disintegration energy is given by $Q = (m_X - m_Y) \cdot c^2$

True ☐ False ☐

***29.** Complete the nuclear reaction by filling appropriate particles and elements considering β^+ and β^--decays.

I. ${}_{27}^{60}\text{Co} \longrightarrow {}_{28}^{60}\text{Ni} + \square + \square$

II. ${}_{11}^{22}\text{Na} \longrightarrow \quad + \square + \beta^+ + \nu_e$

III. ${}_{15}^{32}\text{P} \longrightarrow {}_{16}^{32}\text{S} + \square + \overline{\nu}_e$

IV. ${}_{6}^{14}\text{C} \longrightarrow {}_{7}^{14}\text{N} + \square +$

30. Tick (✓) in front of correct and (×) in front of incorrect statements.

I. Half-life of β^--decay is more than that of β^+-decay. ☐

II. Neutrinos are neutral particles with very less mass. ☐

III. If $\frac{N}{Z}$ ratio is more than 1, then nucleus can undergo β^--decay. ☐

IV. If $\frac{N}{Z}$ ratio is less than 1, then nucleus can undergo β^+-decay. ☐

V. A free neutron can decay into a proton. ☐

VI. A free proton can decay into a neutron. ☐

TOPIC 5

Nuclear Energy

NCERT Pg 314-318

31. Consider the following fission.

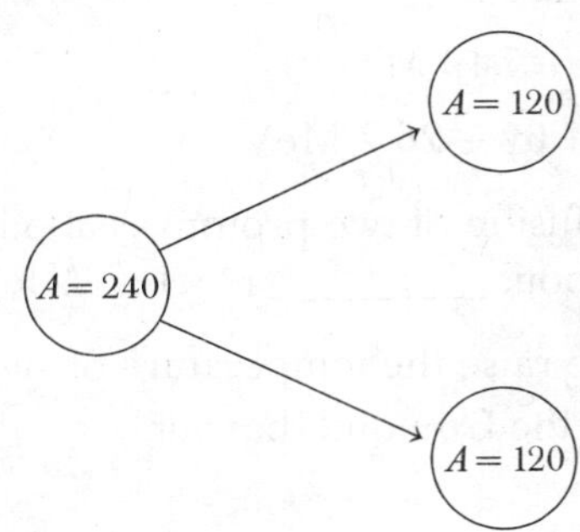

Given, E for parent nuclei is about 7.6 MeV and for daughter nuclei is about 8.5 MeV. Total gain in BE is about ____________ (200/216) MeV.

***32.** Fission of $^{56}_{26}Fe$ can result in two equal fragments of $^{28}_{13}Al$.
[Take, $m(^{56}_{26}Fe) = 55.93494$ u and $m(^{28}_{13}Al) = 27.98191$ u]

True ☐ False ☐

33. Tick (✓) in front of correct and (×) in front of incorrect statements.

I. Fission disintegration energy initially appears as kinetic energy of products. ☐

II. Kinetic energy of products is finally converted into heat by collisions. ☐

III. In nuclear reactor, energy is finally converted into electrical energy. ☐

IV. In a nuclear reactor, energy is released from uncontrolled nuclear fission. ☐

34. In a nuclear bomb, we have an uncontrolled chain reaction, whereas in case of a nuclear reactor, there is no chain reaction.

True ☐ False ☐

35. The efficiency of a nuclear power plant is ________ (more/less/equal) compared to a conventional thermal power plant.

36. If the energy released in a nuclear reaction is E_N and energy released from a chemical source is E_C, then

(a) $E_N \simeq E_C$ ☐ (b) $E_N > E_C$ ☐

(c) $E_N < E_C$ ☐ (d) $E_N = E_C$ ☐

37. Fill the boxes to complete given fusion reactions.

A. ${}_1^1\text{H}+{}_1^1\text{H} \longrightarrow \square + e^+ + \nu + 0.42\text{ MeV}$

B. ${}_1^2\text{H}+{}_1^2\text{H} \longrightarrow \square + {}_0^1n + 3.27\text{ MeV}$

C. ${}_1^2\text{H}+{}_1^2\text{H} \longrightarrow \square + {}_1^1\text{H} + 4.03\text{ MeV}$

D. $e^+ + e^- \longrightarrow \square + 1.02\text{ MeV}$

E. ${}_1^2\text{H}+{}_1^1\text{H} \longrightarrow {}_2^3\text{He} + \square + 5.49\text{ MeV}$

F. $4{}_1^1\text{H} + 2e^- \longrightarrow \square + 2\nu + 6\gamma + 26.7\text{ MeV}$

38. Potential barrier height for fusion of two protons is about ________ (400/500) keV and this requires a temperature of about __________ (3×10^9 /2×10^2) K.

39. In thermonuclear fusion, we raise the temperature of system, so that particles have enough kinetic energy to overcome the Coulomb barrier.

True ☐ False ☐

40. When more of helium is formed, star begins to cool and finally collapse under its own gravity.

Yes ☐ No ☐

41. Tick (✓) in front of correct and (×) in front of incorrect statements.

I. Fusion rate on a star keeps on reducing after reaching a maxima. ☐

II. All higher mass nuclei are formed in stars due to fusion reactions. ☐

III. Age of sun is about 5×10^9 years. ☐

IV. Gravity causes collapse of core to produce high temperatures. ☐

V. Helium-carbon cycle occurs on Red Giant. ☐

42. Which of these conditions are not required for thermonuclear fusion?

A. High temperature B. High fuel density

C. Low pressure D. High fuel volume

(a) A and B ☐ (b) B and C ☐

(c) C and D ☐ (d) B and D ☐

43. At temperatures of range of 10^8 K, the fuel is a mixture of positive ions and electrons. It is known as __________ (plasma/ionic matter).

44. Normal activity of living carbon-containing matter is about ____________ (15/150) decays per minute for every gram of carbon and this activity arises due to ____________ (${}_6^{14}\text{C}$/${}_6^{12}\text{C}$) isotope.

COMPETITION CONNECT

Topic 1. Radioactivity [NCERT (Old) Pg. 446-451]

1. In a spontaneous decay, kinetic energy of products is equal to __________ (mass energy/mass defect).

***2.** We are given with following atomic masses.
$^{238}_{92}U = 238.05079$ u, $^{234}_{90}Th = 234.04363$ u, $^{4}_{2}He = 4.00260$ u

Calculate the energy released during α-decay of $^{238}_{92}U$.

____

3. Match the items given in Column I with the items given in Column II.

Column I	Column II
A. β^--decay	1. Less half-life
B. β^+-decay	2. More half-life
	3. Anti-neutrino
	4. Neutrino

A. __________ B. __________

4. In gamma decay, __________ (parent nucleus/daughter nucleus) radiates excess energy which is acquired during an α or β -decay.

Topic 2. Nuclear Energy [NCERT (Old) Pg. 451-458]

5. In nuclear reactors, we use __________ (moderator/catalyst) to slow down fast moving neutrons.

6. Reactor operation is called __________ for $k = 1$, __________ for $k > 1$ and __________ for $k < 1$.

7. Using safety rods, multiplication factor k can be reduced rapidly to less than one.

True ☐ False ☐

8. Pick odd one out.

Fuel rod, Control rod, Moderator, Coolant

____

9. Complete following reactions by filling the boxes.

I. $^{238}_{92}U + \square \longrightarrow {}^{239}_{92}U \longrightarrow {}^{239}_{93}Np + \square + \bar{\nu}$

II. $^{239}_{93}Np \longrightarrow {}^{239}_{94}Pu + \square + \bar{\nu}$

10. Label the components of nuclear reactor shown here.

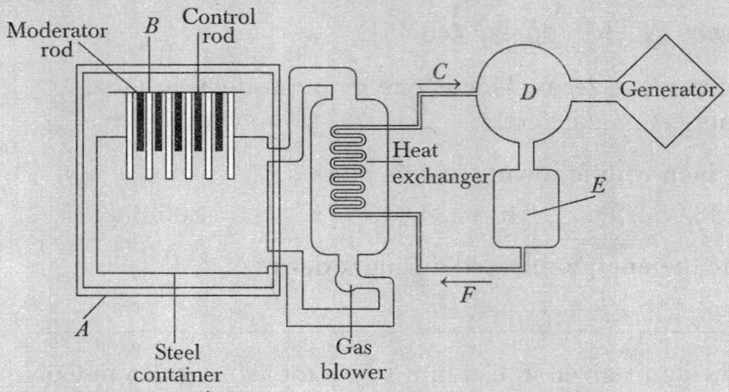

A. __________ *B.* __________ *C.* __________ *D.* __________

E. __________ *F.* __________.

11. Match the components of a nuclear reactor given in Column I with their respective function given in Column II.

	Column I		Column II
A.	Reflector	1.	Steam generation
B.	Core	2.	Carries heat from core
C.	Moderator	3.	Converts KE to heat
D.	Coolant	4.	Contains fuel and control rods
E.	Heat exchanger	5.	Confined neutrons to core
F.	Steam turbine	6.	Generate electrical power

A. __________ B. __________ C. __________ D. __________

E. __________ F. __________

12. Shielding in a nuclear reactor is protection against radioactive emission.

Yes ☐ No ☐

Assertion-Reason Questions

Direction (Q. Nos. 1-10) *In the following questions, a statement of Assertion is followed by a corresponding statement of Reason. From the following options, choose the correct one.*

(a) Both Assertion and Reason are correct and Reason is the correct explanation of Assertion.
(b) Both Assertion and Reason are correct but Reason is not the correct explanation of Assertion.
(c) Assertion is correct but Reason is incorrect.
(d) Assertion is incorrect but Reason is correct.

***1** **Assertion** (A) Nuclear density of heavy atoms is more as compared to nuclear density of lighter atoms.

Reason (R) Number of neutrons in heavier nuclei more than the number of protons.

(a) ☐ (b) ☐ (c) ☐ (d) ☐

2 **Assertion** (A) For an element, generally $N \geq Z$ (N = number of neutrons, Z = atomic number).

Reason (R) Neutrons do not always experience attractive nuclear force.

(a) ☐ (b) ☐ (c) ☐ (d) ☐

3 **Assertion** (A) Nuclide ${}^{30}_{13}Al$ is less stable than ${}^{40}_{20}Ca$.

Reason (R) Nuclides having odd number of protons and neutrons are generally unstable.

(a) ☐ (b) ☐ (c) ☐ (d) ☐

4 **Assertion** (A) Nuclear force between neutron-neutron, proton-neutron and proton-proton is approximately the same.

Reason (R) The nuclear force does not depend on the electric charge.

(a) ☐ (b) ☐ (c) ☐ (d) ☐

***5** **Assertion** (A) Binding energy per nucleon is more for helium ($A = 4$) than lithium ($A = 6$) and also greater for carbon ($A = 12$) than nitrogen ($A = 14$).

Reason (R) Nuclear forces are short range forces.

(a) ☐ (b) ☐ (c) ☐ (d) ☐

***6** **Assertion** (A) ${}^{238}_{92}U$ decays to give ${}^{234}_{90}Th$ emitting an alpha particle.

Reason (R) In α-decay, the mass number of product nucleus decreases by two, while the atomic number decreases by four.

(a) ☐ (b) ☐ (c) ☐ (d) ☐

7 **Assertion** (A) In both fission and fusion processes, energy is released.

Reason (R) BE per nucleon of reactants is less than BE per nucleon of products in both cases.

(a) ☐ (b) ☐ (c) ☐ (d) ☐

***8** **Assertion** (A) In a fusion reaction, two light nuclei combines to form a larger nucleus with release of energy.

Reason (R) Larger nucleus formed is more tightly bound.

(a) ☐ (b) ☐ (c) ☐ (d) ☐

9 **Assertion** (A) Thermonuclear fusion reaction is not possible on earth naturally.

Reason (R) For thermonuclear fusion reaction to take place, extreme condition of temperature and pressure are required.

(a) ☐ (b) ☐ (c) ☐ (d) ☐

10 **Assertion** (A) Thermonuclear fusion is the source of energy in the interior of stars.

Reason (R) Temperature in interior of sun is high enough for fusion of two protons.

(a) ☐ (b) ☐ (c) ☐ (d) ☐

Case Based Questions

1. Nucleus was discovered in the year 1911 by Rutherford and his associates from the study of large angle scattering of alpha particle from the thin metal foil. The experimental result indicate that the size of the nucleus is of the order of 10^{-14} m and it thus 1000 times smaller than the size of atom.

(i) Masses of nuclei of hydrogen, deuterium and tritium are in ratio

(a) 1 : 2 : 3 ☐ (b) 1 : 1 : 1 ☐
(c) 1 : 1 : 2 ☐ (d) 1 : 2 : 4 ☐

(ii) The density of nuclear matter is (approximately)

(a) 2.3×10^{17} kgm^{-3} ☐ (b) 1.7×10^{17} kgm^{-3} ☐
(c) 3.2×10^{16} kgm^{-3} ☐ (d) 4.1×10^{16} kgm^{-3} ☐

(iii) The atoms of an element that have the same number of protons and different number of neutrons are

(a) isobars ☐ (b) isotopes ☐
(c) isotones ☐ (d) None of these ☐

(iv) The ratio of the nuclear radii of the gold isotope $^{197}_{79}$Au and silver isotope $^{107}_{47}$Ag is

(a) 1.23 ☐ (b) 0.216 ☐
(c) 2.13 ☐ (d) 3.46 ☐

2. A heavy nucleus breaks into comparatively lighter nuclei which are more stable compared to the original heavy nucleus. When a heavy nucleus like uranium is bombarded by slow moving neutrons, it splits into two parts releasing large amount of energy. The typical fission reaction of $_{92}U^{235}$ is

$$_{92}U^{235} + {}_0n^1 \rightarrow {}_{56}Ba^{141} + {}_{36}Kr^{92} + 3\,{}_0n^1 + 200 \text{ MeV}$$

The fission of $_{92}U^{235}$ approximately released 200 MeV of energy.

(i) In any fission process, ratio of mass of daughter nucleus to mass of parent nucleus is

(a) less than 1 ☐ (b) greater than 1 ☐
(c) equal to 1 ☐ (d) Both (a) and (b) ☐

(ii) The element used to produce nuclear energy is

(a) palladium ☐ (b) strontium ☐
(c) uranium ☐ (d) Both (a) and (c) ☐

(iii) If 200 MeV energy is released in the fission of a single nucleus of $^{235}_{92}$U. The number of fissions per second required to produce a power of 1 kW is

(a) 3.125×10^{13} ☐ (b) 1.52×10^{9} ☐
(c) 2.26×10^{10} ☐ (d) 3.5×10^{12} ☐

(iv) The energy released per fissioning nucleus in the fission reaction of nuclei like uranium is of the order of

(a) 200 MeV ☐ (b) 320 MeV ☐
(c) 150 MeV ☐ (d) 400 MeV ☐

COMPETITION EDGE UP

1 A nucleus at rest disintegrates into two smaller nuclei with their masses in the ratio of 2 : 1. After disintegration, they will move **[NCERT Pg. 306, JEE Main 2024]**

(a) in opposite directions with speed in the ratio of 1 : 2 respectively ☐

(b) in opposite directions with the same speed

(c) in the same direction with same speed

(d) in opposite directions with speed in the ratio of 2 : 1 respectively ☐

2 If M_0 is the mass of isotope, ${}^{12}_{5}B$, M_p and M_n are the masses of proton and neutron then nuclear binding energy of isotope is **[NCERT Pg. 311, JEE Main 2024]**

(a) $(M_0 - 12M_n)c^2$ ☐

(b) $(5M_p + 7M_n - M_0)c^2$ ☐

(c) $(M_0 - 5M_p - 7M_n)c^2$ ☐

(d) $(M_0 - 5M_p)c^2$ ☐

3 Binding energy of a certain nucleus is 18×10^8 J. How much is the difference between total mass of all the nucleons and nuclear mass of the given nucleus ? **[NCERT Pg. 311. JEE Main 2024]**

(a) 20 μg ☐ (b) 2 μg ☐

(c) 0.2 μg ☐ (d) 10 μg ☐

4 The mass number of nucleus having radius equal to half of the radius of nucleus with mass number 192 is **[NCERT Pg. 309, JEE Main 2024]**

(a) 20 ☐ (b) 32 ☐

(c) 24 ☐ (d) 40 ☐

5 A nucleus has mass number A_1 and volume V_1. Another nucleus has mass number A_2 and volume V_2. If relation between mass number is $A_2 = 4A_1$, then $\frac{V_2}{V_1}$ = ____ . **[NCERT Pg. 309, JEE Main 2024]**

6 The explosive in a Hydrogen bomb is a mixture of ${}_1H^2$, ${}_1H^3$ and ${}_3Li^6$ in some condensed form. The chain reaction is given by

$${}_3Li^6 + {}_0n^1 \longrightarrow {}_2He^4 + {}_1H^3;$$
$${}_1H^2 + {}_1H^3 \longrightarrow {}_2He^4 + {}_0n$$

During the explosion the energy released is approximately

[Given : M (Li) = 6.01690 amu, M $({}_1H^2)$ = 2.01471 amu, M $({}_2He^4)$ = 4.00388 amu, and 1 amu = 931.5 MeV] **[NCERT Pg. 315, JEE Main 2024]**

(a) 12.64 MeV ☐

(b) 28.12 MeV ☐

(c) 22.22 MeV ☐

(d) 16.48 MeV ☐

7 The atomic mass of ${}_6C^{12}$ is 12.000000 u and that of ${}_6C^{13}$ is 13.003354 u. The required energy to remove a neutron from ${}_6C^{13}$, if mass of neutron is 1.008665 u, will be **[NCERT Pg. 311, JEE Main 2024]**

(a) 4.95 MeV ☐

(b) 62.5 MeV ☐

(c) 49.5 MeV ☐

(d) 6.25 MeV ☐

8 Assume that protons and neutrons have equal masses. Mass of a nucleon is 1.6×10^{-27} kg and radius of nucleus is $1.5 \times 10^{-15} A^{1/3}$ m. The approximate ratio of the nuclear density and water density is $n \times 10^{13}$. The value of n is _______ . **[NCERT Pg. 309, JEE Main 2023]**

9 A nucleus of mass number 189 splits into two nuclei having mass number 125 and 64. The ratio of radius of two daughter nuclei, respectively is **[NCERT Pg. 309, NEET 2022]**

(a) 4 : 5 ☐ (b) 5 : 4 ☐

(c) 25 : 16 ☐ (d) 1 : 1 ☐

10 The energy equivalent of 0.5 g of a substance is **[NCERT Pg. 311, NEET (Sep.) 2020]**

(a) 4.5×10^{13} J ☐ (b) 1.5×10^{13} J ☐

(c) 0.5×10^{13} J ☐ (d) 4.5×10^{16} J ☐

Chapter 14

Semiconductor Electronics : Materials, Devices and Simple Circuits

Scan and take Chapter Test

TOPIC 1

Classification of Metals, Conductors and Semiconductors

NCERT Pg 324-327

1. Match the different substances listed in Column I with their respective range of resistivities listed in Column II.

Column I	Column II
A. Metals	1. 10^{-5}-10^{6} Ω-m
B. Semiconductors	2. 10^{11}-10^{19} Ω-m
C. Insulators	3. 10^{-2}-10^{8} Ω-m

A. ____________ B. ____________ C. ____________

2. Resistivity of a pure elemental semiconductor is around

(a) 60 Ω-cm ☐ (b) 6×10^4 Ω-cm ☐

(c) 6×10^{-4} Ω-cm ☐ (d) 6×10^{14} Ω-cm ☐

3. Complete the given analogy.

Germanium : Semiconductor :: Carbon : ____________

4. An electron in a solid can only have energies that fall within ____________ (energy bands/energy gap)

5. In between energy bands, range of energy, where existence of electron is entirely impossible, is known as forbidden energy gap.

Yes ☐ No ☐

6. Tick (✓/×) for correct/incorrect statement in given boxes.

Consider *N* atoms of silicon (Si) or germanium (Ge) in a crystal.

I. Total number of outer electrons in crystal is 4 *N*. ☐

II. Maximum possible number of outermost electrons in crystal is 8 *N*. ☐

*Concepts of all questions bearing * are important for JEE/NEET/CUET.*

III. Conduction band contains 4 N p-states or levels. ☐

IV. Valence band contains 2 N s-states and $2N$ p-states. ☐

V. Energy gap contains 2 N p-states. ☐

7. Label following energy band gap diagram.

A = ______________ B = ______________ C = ______________

8. Which of these pairs are correctly matched?

I. Lowest level of conduction band lies within valence band ⟶ All crystalline solids

II. Some of energy levels of conduction band are occupied by valence electrons ⟶ Semiconductor at room temperature

____

9. Arrange the following materials in the increasing order of their energy band gaps.

(a) Silicon (b) Germanium

(c) Mercury (d) Solid sodium

(e) Gallium arsenide

____

***10.** Match the Column I (approximate energy band diagram) with Column II (type of solid).

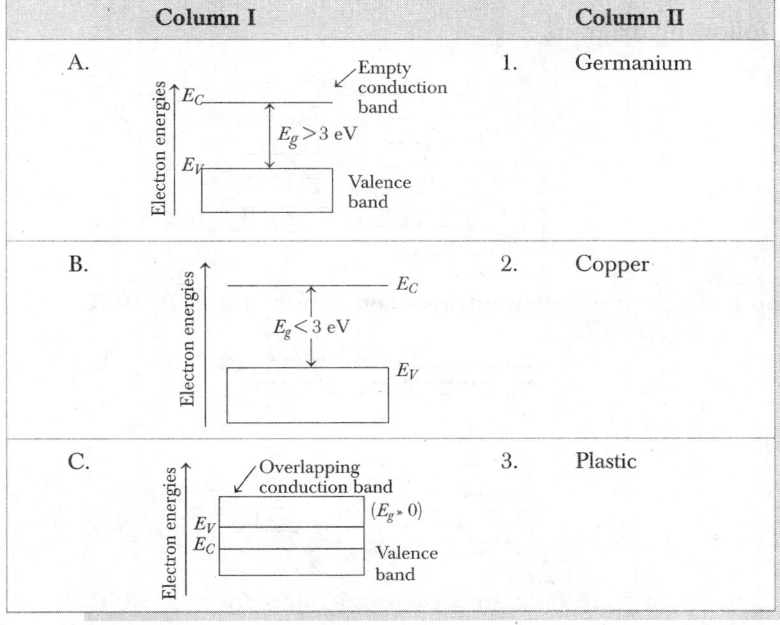

A. ______________ B. ______________ C. ______________

***11.** **Statement I** At room temperature, there are few occupied levels in conduction band of a semiconductor.

Statement II Thermal energy effectively ionises few atoms in crystalline lattice.

Which of the following statement(s) is/are correct ?

(a) Only statement I ☐ (b) Only statement II ☐

(c) Both statements I and II ☐ (d) Neither statement I nor II ☐

TOPIC 2

Intrinsic Semiconductor

NCERT Pg 327-329

12. Intrinsic solids does not have any free charge carriers at ________ (room temperature/ absolute zero)

***13.** In an intrinsic semiconductor, correct relation between number density of holes (n_h) and number density of electrons (n_e) is

(a) $n_e > n_h$ ☐ (b) $n_e < n_h$ ☐

(c) $n_e = n_h$ ☐ (d) $n_e \cdot n_h = 1$ ☐

***14.** In intrinsic semiconductor (at equilibrium), rate of generation of free charges is exactly equal to rate of recombination of holes and electrons.

True ☐ False ☐

15. Pick the odd one out.

Arsenic, Antimony, Phosphorus, Aluminium

____

16. Label the following diagram.

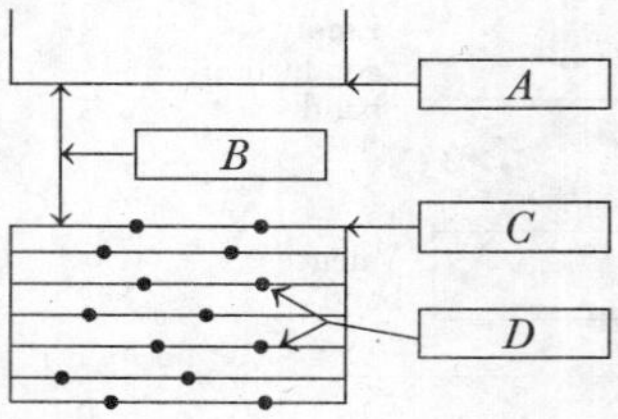

A
B
C
D

Energy gap band diagram of an intrinsic semiconductor at $T = 0$ K

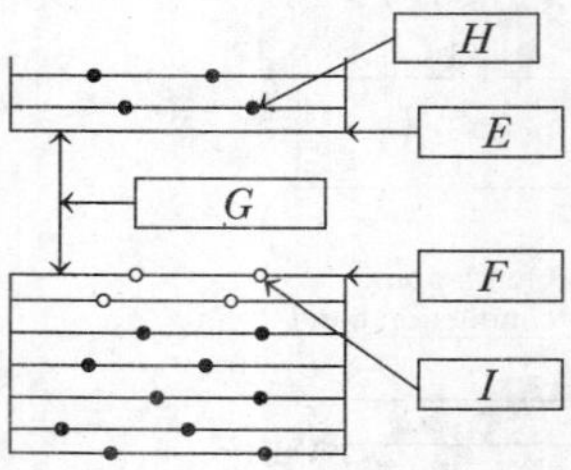

H
E
G
F
I

Energy gap band diagram of an intrinsic semiconductor at $T > 0$ K

A. ________ *B.* ________ *C.* ________ *D.* ________ *E.* ________ *F.* ________ *G.* ________

H. ________ *I.* ________

***17.** If n_1 = number of holes in an intrinsic semiconductor and n_2 = number of holes in same semiconductor after doping with a pentavalent impurity, then ratio of $\frac{n_1}{n_2}$ will be

(a) exactly 1 ☐ (b) less than 1 ☐
(c) more than 1 ☐ (d) depends on impurity element ☐

18. The elements C and Si both have same lattice structure, having 4 bonding electrons in each. However, C is insulator, whereas Si is intrinsic semiconductor. This is because

(a) in case of C, the valence band is not completely filled at absolute zero temperature ☐
(b) in case of C, the conduction band is partly filled even at absolute zero temperature ☐
(c) the four bonding electrons in the case of C lie in the second orbit, whereas in the case of Si, they lie in the third orbit ☐
(d) the four bonding electrons in the case of C lie in the third orbit, whereas for Si, they lie in the fourth orbit ☐

TOPIC 3

Extrinsic Semiconductors

NCERT Pg 329-332

***19.** **Statement I** For higher conductivity, we can use impurities belonging to group 7 or higher.
Statement II Dopant atom must not distort original semiconductor atom size.
Which of the following statement(s) is/are correct ?

(a) Only statement I ☐ (b) Only statement II ☐
(c) Both statements I and II ☐ (d) Neither statement I nor II ☐

20. Complete the given analogy.

I. Pentavalent : Electron :: Trivalent : ________________

II. Pentavalent : Donor : : Trivalent : ________________

21. A pentavalent impurity creates an electron that lies in ____________ (valence/conduction) band.

22. Ionisation energy for an unbonded electron of a pentavalent impurity does not depends on base semiconductor.

True ☐ False ☐

23. Value of energy states of donor impurities is ____________ (lower/higher) than lowest conduction level and value of energy states of acceptor impurities is____________ (lower/higher) than the uppermost level of valence band.

***24.** In a semiconductor, electron concentration is $7 \times 10^{13}\ \text{cm}^{-3}$ and hole concentration is $5 \times 10^{12}\ \text{cm}^{-3}$, then what type of semiconductor it is?

____

***25.** A pure Si crystal has 5×10^{28} atoms m^{-3}. On doping with a pentavalent impurity by 1 ppm concentration, ratio of number of electrons and holes obtained is of the order (Given, $n_i = 1.5 \times 10^{16}\ \text{m}^{-3}$)

(a) 10^{13} ☐ (b) 10^{16} ☐ (c) 10^{22} ☐ (d) 10^{28} ☐

TOPIC 4

p-n Junction and Semiconductor Diode

NCERT Pg 333-337

***26.** Considering formation of *p-n* junction, arrange these processes in correct order.

I. Formation of potential barrier
II. Generation of junction field
III. Diffusion of free charge carriers
IV. Equilibrium state

____

***27.** Diffusion process causes formation of __________ (depletion/diffusion) zone and a junction field is established which points from _________ (*n* to *p* / *p* to *n*) side.

28. Which of these pairs is correctly matched?

I. Diffusion of electron → Ionised donor in depletion region
II. Diffusion of hole → Ionised semiconductor atom in depletion region

____

29. Draw the variation of diffusion (I_d) and drift current (I_b) magnitudes with time during formation of *p-n* junction.

____

***30.** Identify the biasing of these diodes.

I. –5 V ——▷|—— –10 V
II. 5 V ——▷|—— 10 V
III. 5 V ——▷|—— –10 V
IV. –5 V ——▷|—— 10 V

____

31. Considering forward biasing of a *p-n* junction, tick (✓/×) for correct/incorrect statement in given boxes.

I. Depletion layer thickness decreases due to biasing. ☐
II. Potential barrier is opposed by biasing voltage. ☐
III. Diffusion of charge carriers occurs under biasing voltage. ☐
IV. At junction boundary, minority concentration increases. ☐
V. Total diode current is difference of electron current and hole current. ☐

32. Consider potential drop across depletion zone in forward bias.

V_p ① V_n ②

Now, fill the blanks choosing given options.

Plot 1 shows potential drop in ___________ (unbiased/biased) *p-n* junction and plot 2 shows potential drop in_________ (unbiased/biased) condition.

33. Which of the following circuits is used to study forward characteristics of a *p-n* junction diode?

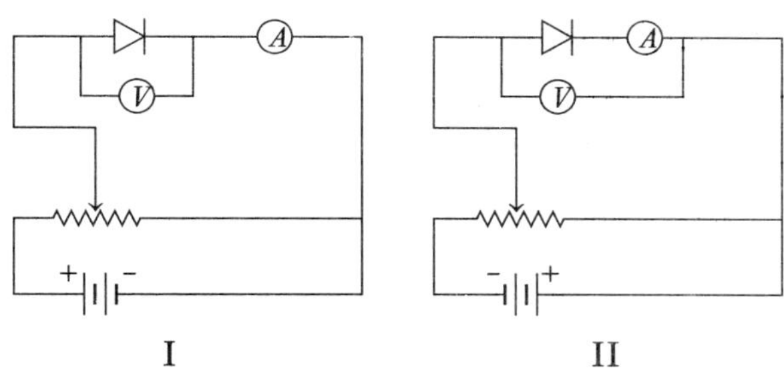

34. Potential drop across points *A* and *B* will be

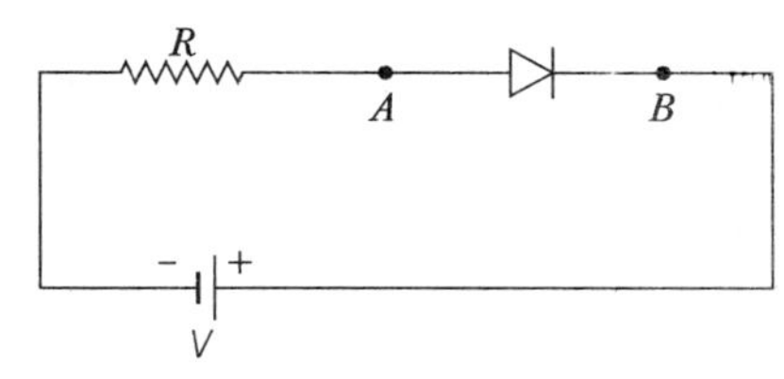

(a) 0 ☐ (b) V ☐ (c) $\frac{V}{2}$ ☐ (d) $2V$ ☐

35. Which of these pairs are correctly matched?

I. Silicon ⟶ 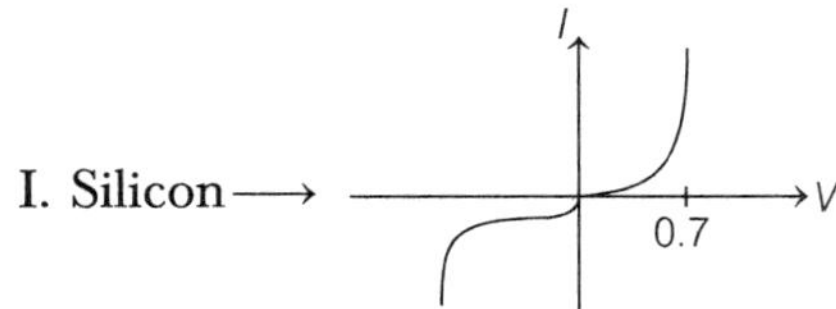

II. Germanium ⟶ 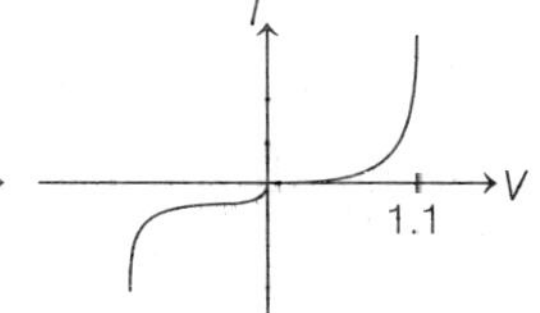

36. Consider characteristics curves of diode given and mark the knee voltage.

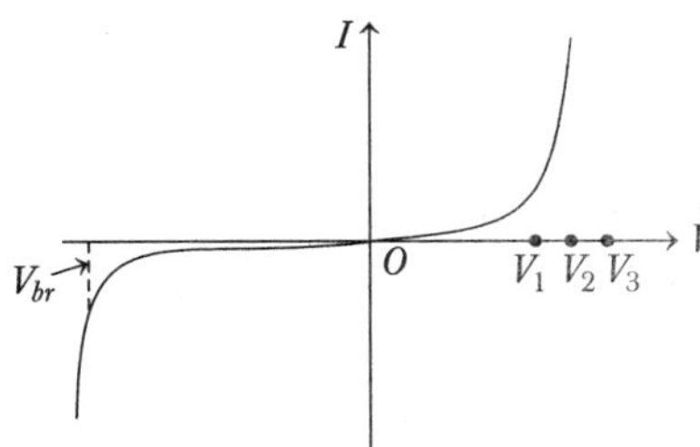

***37.** Consider given *V-I* characteristics of a *p-n* junction.

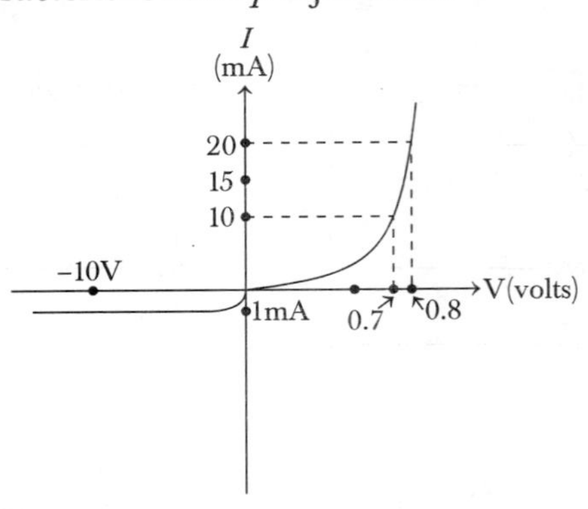

The resistance of diode at $V_D = -10$ V will be around

(a) 10^{-6} Ω ☐ (b) 10^{6}Ω ☐ (c) 10^{-7}Ω ☐ (d) 10^{7}Ω ☐

38. For a given circuit of ideal *p-n* junction diode, which of the following is correct?

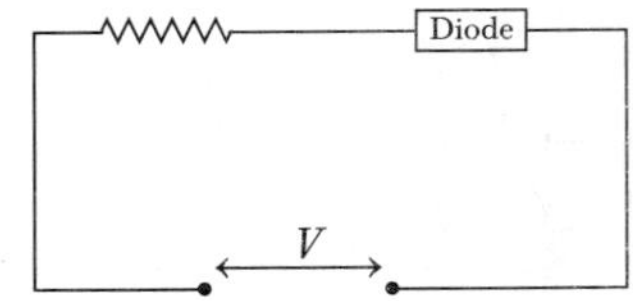

(a) In forward biasing, the voltage across *R* is *V* ☐

(b) In reverse biasing, the voltage across *R* is *V* ☐

(c) In forward biasing, the voltage across *R* is 2*V* ☐

(d) In reverse biasing, the voltage across *R* is 2*V* ☐

***39.** Consider the internal resistance of the cell to be zero. What is the value of current flowing through the given circuit?

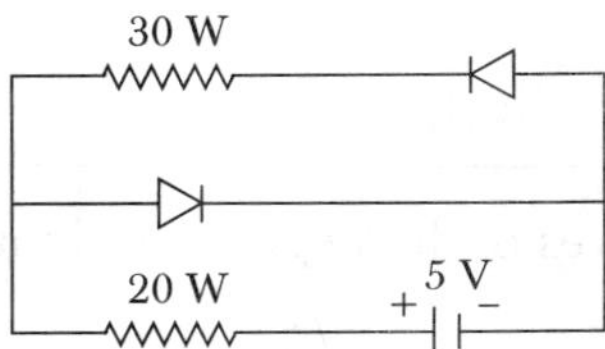

***40** At 0.3 V and 0.7 V, the diodes Ge and Si become conductor, respectively. In given figure, if ends of diode Ge overturned, the change in potential V_o will be

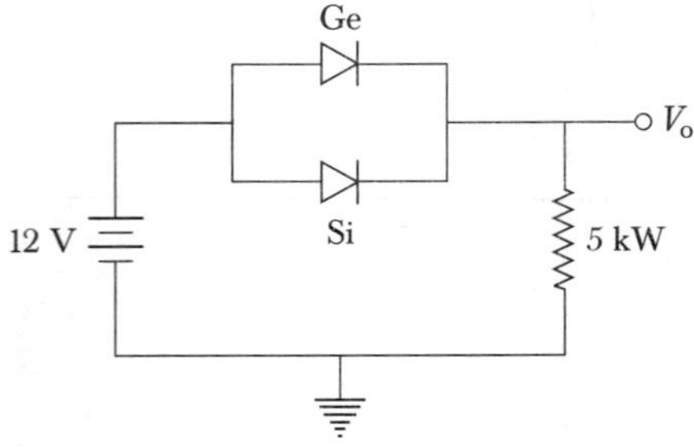

(a) 0.2 V ☐ (b) 0.6V ☐ (c) 0.4 V ☐ (d) 0.8 V ☐

***41.** Find the current i in the network.

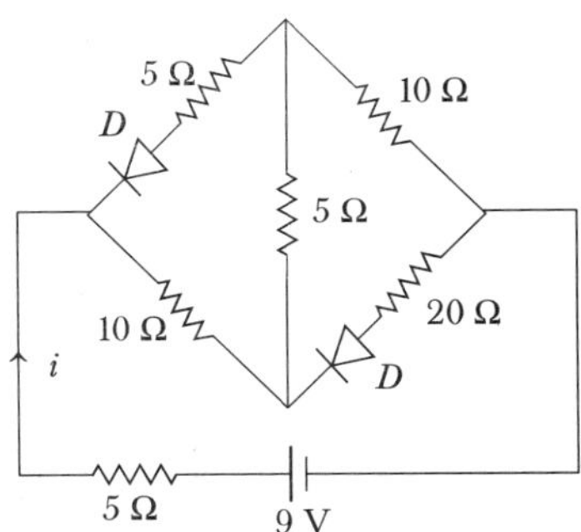

42. The diode used in the circuit shown in the following figure has a constant voltage drop of 0.5 V at all currents and a maximum power rating of 100 mW. The value of maximum current in the circuit is I when voltage across resistance R is V_R. Match the quantities in Column I with the values in Column II.

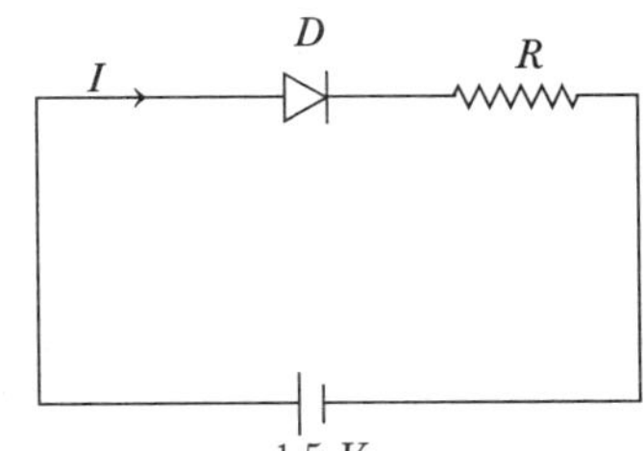

	Column I		Column II
A.	I (in mA)	1.	1
B.	V_R (in V)	2.	200
C.	R (in Ω)	3.	5

A. ______________ B. ______________ C. ______________

TOPIC 5

Application of Junction Diode as a Rectifier

43. Label the circuit given below.

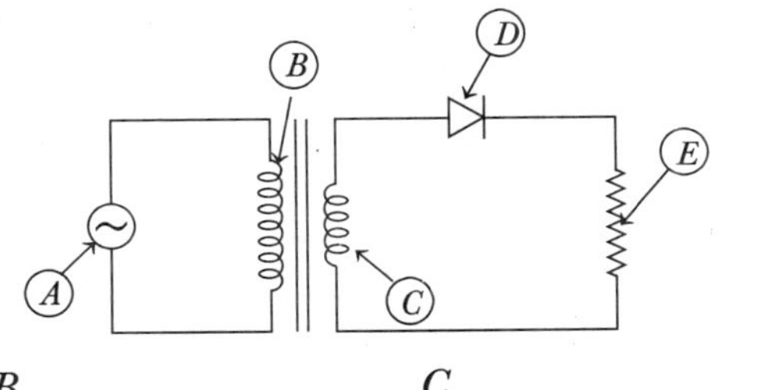

A. ______________ *B.* ______________ *C.* ______________

D. ______________ *E.* ______________

44. Following time varying input is fed to terminal A of diode (shown).

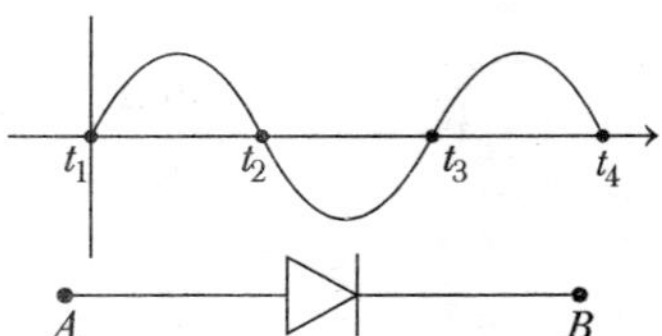

Output obtained at B is

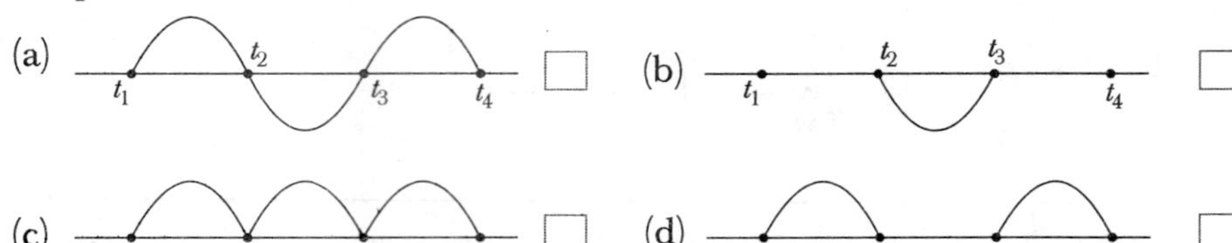

***45.** Shown AC input is given to a half-wave rectifier.

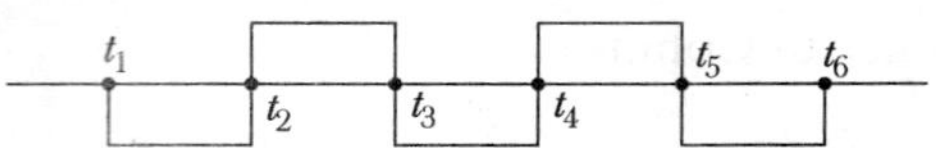

Correct output wave is

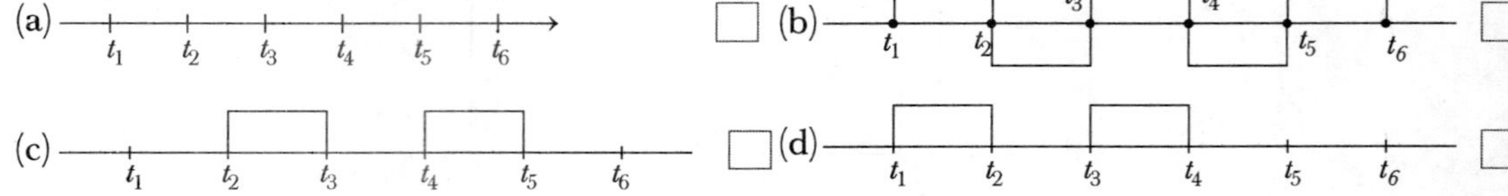

***46.** If in a p-n junction, a square input signal of 10 V is applied as shown below.

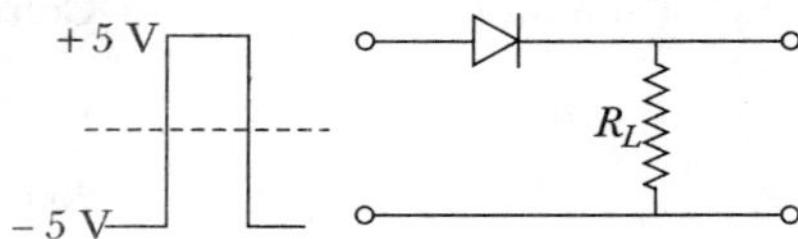

Then, draw the output across R_L.

____

***47.** For a full wave rectifier, if the input frequency is 50 Hz, the output frequency will be

(a) 50 Hz ☐ (b) 100 Hz ☐

(c) 25 Hz ☐ (d) 0 Hz ☐

48. Label the following circuit.

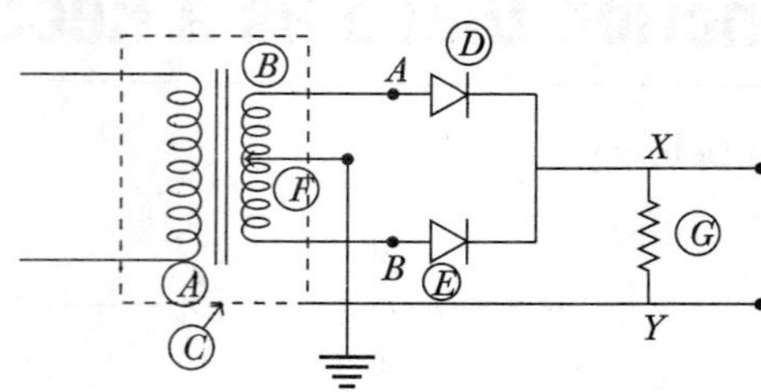

A = __________ B = __________ C = __________

D = __________ E = __________ F = __________

G = __________

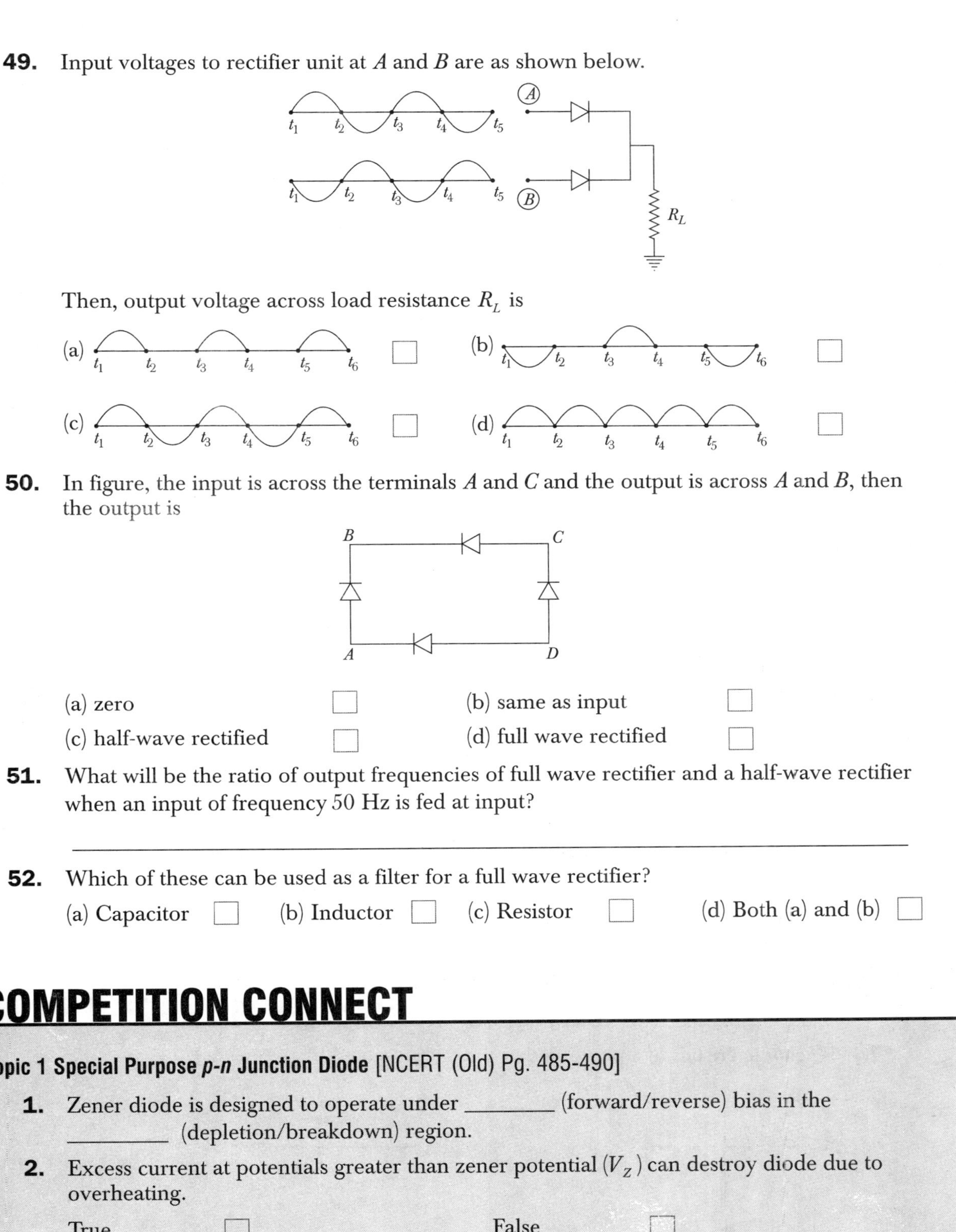

49. Input voltages to rectifier unit at A and B are as shown below.

Then, output voltage across load resistance R_L is

(a) ☐ (b) ☐

(c) ☐ (d) ☐

50. In figure, the input is across the terminals A and C and the output is across A and B, then the output is

(a) zero ☐ (b) same as input ☐

(c) half-wave rectified ☐ (d) full wave rectified ☐

51. What will be the ratio of output frequencies of full wave rectifier and a half-wave rectifier when an input of frequency 50 Hz is fed at input?

____

52. Which of these can be used as a filter for a full wave rectifier?

(a) Capacitor ☐ (b) Inductor ☐ (c) Resistor ☐ (d) Both (a) and (b) ☐

COMPETITION CONNECT

Topic 1 Special Purpose *p-n* Junction Diode [NCERT (Old) Pg. 485-490]

1. Zener diode is designed to operate under ________ (forward/reverse) bias in the ________ (depletion/breakdown) region.

2. Excess current at potentials greater than zener potential (V_Z) can destroy diode due to overheating.

True ☐ False ☐

3. Label the voltage regulator circuit given below.

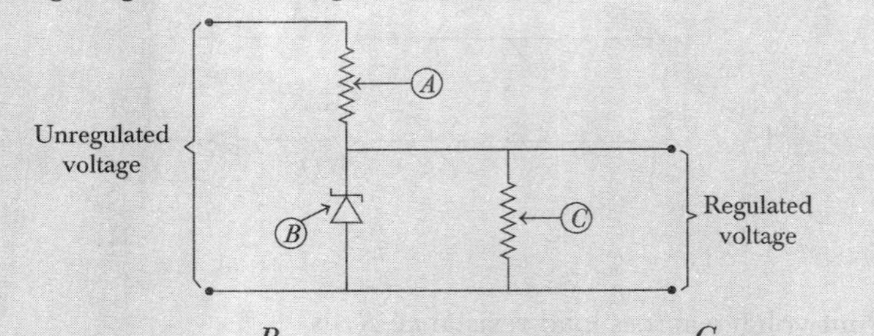

$A =$ ____________ $B =$ ____________ $C =$ ____________

***4.** When unregulated voltage exceeds beyond V_Z, then where does excess voltage is used? Mark region in the given circuit.

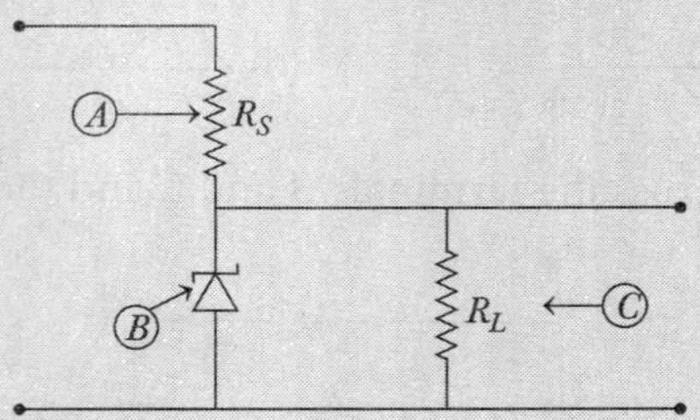

(a) In region A ☐ (b) In region B ☐
(c) In region C ☐ (d) In regions A, B and C ☐

5. In a voltage regulator circuit, let $V_Z = 6.0$ V, load current I_L is 4.0 mA. If unregulated input voltage may reach a maximum of 10.0 V, then series resistance R_S needed in the circuit will be of (Take, $I_{max} = 5I_Z$)

(a) 1.50 Ω ☐ (b) 15.0 Ω ☐
(c) 150 Ω ☐ (d) 15 kΩ ☐

6. Consider operation of a photodiode and choose the correct statement.

I. Photodiode response is zero when used in forward bias.
II. Current through photodiode is more in reverse bias than in forward bias.
III. Photodiode can be used in forward bias.
IV. Change in reverse current is more than that of forward current.

***7.** *V-I* characteristics of a photodiode is best represented by

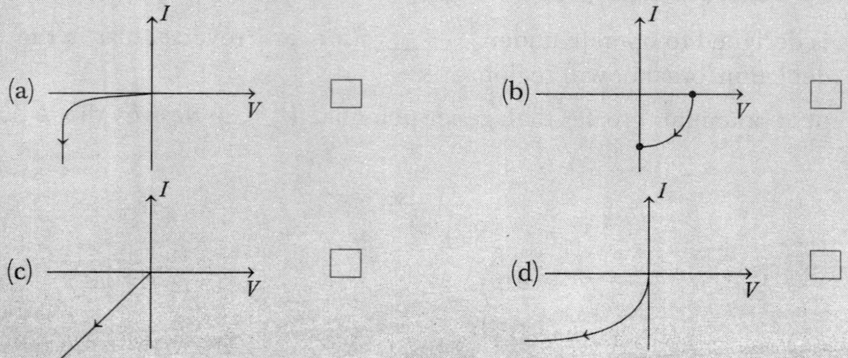

8. A *p-n* junction photodiode is fabricated from a semiconductor with a band gap of 2.8 eV. Upto which wavelength, it can detect?

____

***9.** Label the following graph.

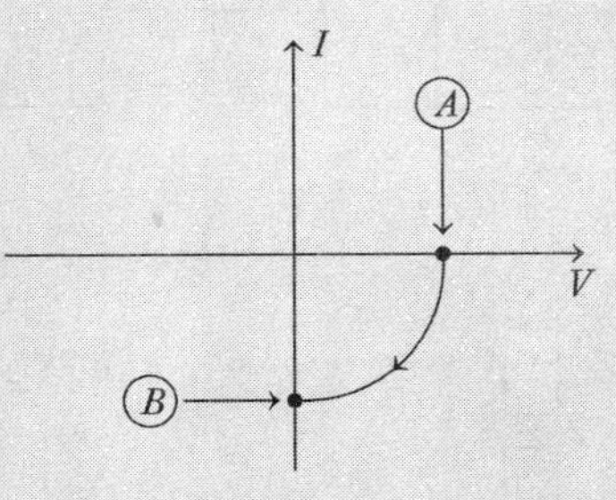

$A =$ __________ $B =$ __________

Topic 2 Digital Electronics and Logic Gates [NCERT (Old) Pg. 501-505]

10. What is the name of the device that follows a certain relationship between input and output voltages?

____

11. Consider given table of input and output voltages of a gate.

Input (in V)	Output (in V)
5	10
10	5

It is obtained from a/an

(a) OR gate ☐ (b) AND gate ☐ (c) NOT gate ☐ (d) NAND gate ☐

12. Consider truth table of OR gate. Match inputs in Column I with outputs in Column II.

Column I	Column II
A. $A = 0, B = 0$	1. 0
B. $A = 0, B = 1$	2. 1
C. $A = 1, B = 0$	
D. $A = 1. B = 1$	

A. __________ B. __________ C. __________ D. __________

13. The correct Boolean operation represented by the circuit diagram drawn is NOR gate.

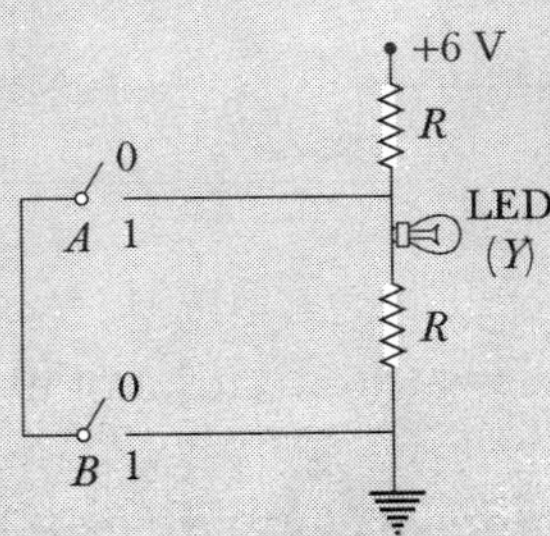

True ☐ False ☐

***14.** Inputs of a NAND gate A and B are shown below.

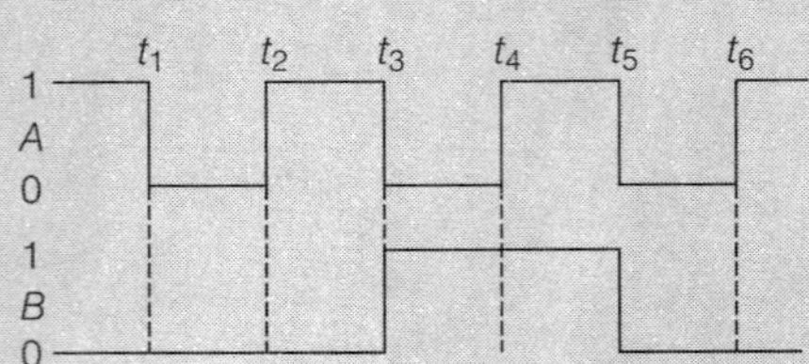

Output of the NAND gate is

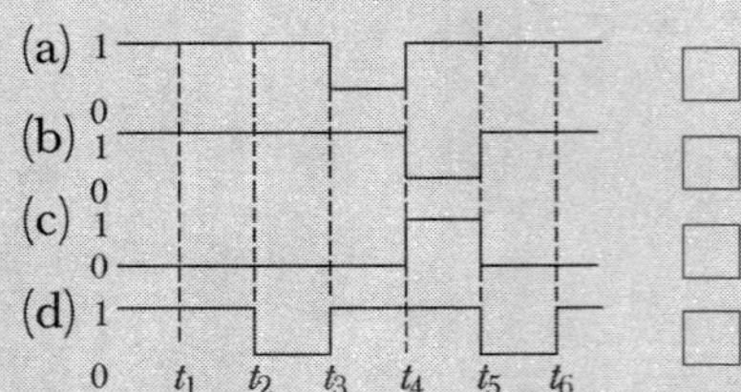

***15.** Given below are the combination of few NAND gates. Write the name of the configuration shown by them.

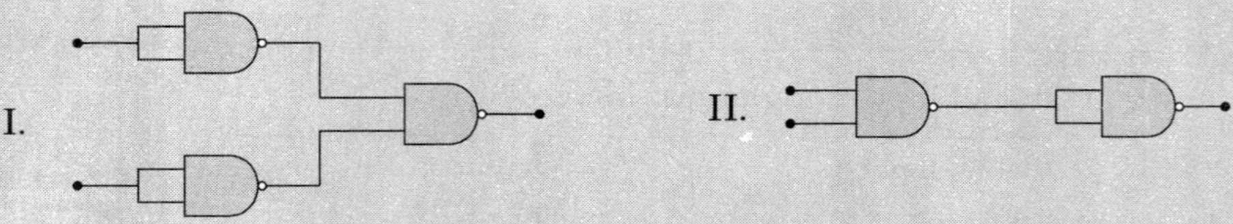

***16.** In the combination of the following gates, find output Y in terms of inputs A and B.

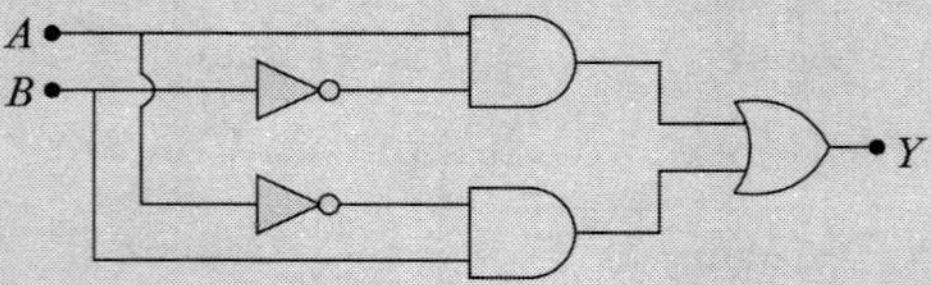

***17.** In the given circuit, value of Y is

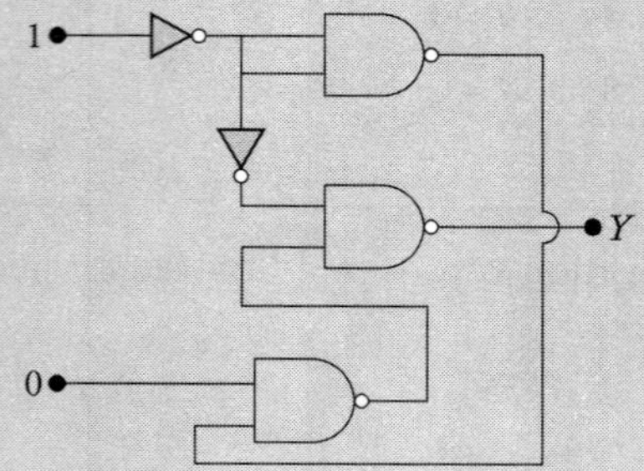

(a) toggles between 0 and 1 ☐ (b) 1 ☐

(c) 0 ☐ (d) not execute ☐

***18.** In given combination,

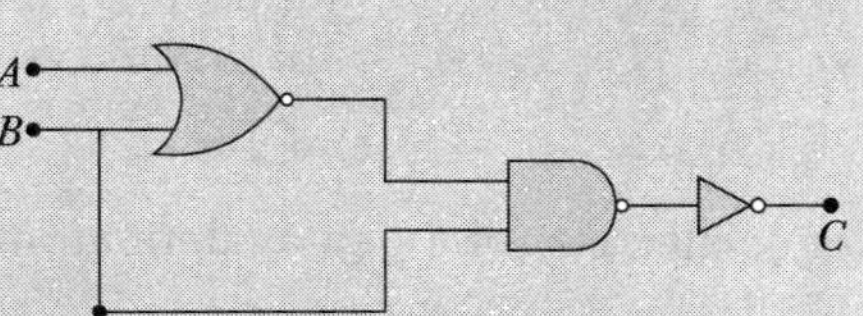

Fill the following truth table.

A	B	C
0	0	–
0	1	–
1	0	–
1	1	–

Assertion-Reason Questions

Direction (Q. Nos. 1-10) *In the following questions, a statement of Assertion is followed by a corresponding statement of Reason. From the following options, choose the correct one.*

(a) Both Assertion and Reason are correct and Reason is the correct explanation of Assertion.
(b) Both Assertion and Reason are correct but Reason is not the correct explanation of Assertion.
(c) Assertion is correct but Reason is incorrect.
(d) Assertion is incorrect but Reason is correct.

1. **Assertion** (A) In a solid, the outer orbits of electrons from neighbouring atoms come very close or even overlap.
Reason (R) The energy of an electron in a solid is affected by the proximity and interaction with electrons from neighbouring atoms.

(a) ☐ (b) ☐ (c) ☐ (d) ☐

2. **Assertion** (A) At absolute zero, the conduction band in Si and Ge crystals is completely empty.
Reason (R) At absolute zero, the valence band in Si and Ge crystals is completely occupied by valence electrons.

(a) ☐ (b) ☐ (c) ☐ (d) ☐

***3.** **Assertion** (A) If the valence band is partially empty, electrons can move to higher levels within the valence band, making conduction possible.
Reason (R) A partially filled valence band means there are available energy states for electrons to move to, facilitating electrical conduction.

(a) ☐ (b) ☐ (c) ☐ (d) ☐

4. **Assertion** (A) In semiconductors, conduction band always contains few electrons.
Reason (R) Energy gap of conduction and valence band in a semiconductor is less than 3 eV.

(a) ☐ (b) ☐ (c) ☐ (d) ☐

5. **Assertion** (A) Intrinsic semiconductors are not used for making electronic devices.
Reason (R) Very high voltage is required to maintain a current in intrinsic semiconductor.

(a) ☐ (b) ☐ (c) ☐ (d) ☐

6. **Assertion** (A) Fifth valence electron of a pentavalent atom has higher energy than four other electrons.
Reason (R) On doping with a pentavalent atom, we get an electron in conduction band.

(a) ☐ (b) ☐ (c) ☐ (d) ☐

7. **Assertion** (A) Conductivity of an *n*-type semiconductor increases exponentially with temperature.
Reason (R) Number of electrons donated by donor atoms does not depend on the temperature.

(a) ☐ (b) ☐ (c) ☐ (d) ☐

*8. **Assertion (A)** In a *p-n* junction diode, minority carriers play a significant role in the reverse saturation current.
Reason (R) The reverse saturation current is due to the minority carriers crossing the junction.

(a) ☐ (b) ☐ (c) ☐ (d) ☐

9. **Assertion** (A) The forward voltage drop of a silicon *p-n* junction diode is approximately 0.7 V.
Reason (R) Silicon has a wider energy band gap compared to germanium.

(a) ☐ (b) ☐ (c) ☐ (d) ☐

*10. **Assertion** (A) In a full-wave rectifier, both positive and negative half cycles of the input AC signal are used.
Reason (R) A full-wave rectifier consists of two or more diodes to convert both halves of the AC cycle into DC.

(a) ☐ (b) ☐ (c) ☐ (d) ☐

Case Based Questions

1. A semiconductor diode [Fig. (a)] is basically a *p-n* junction with metallic contacts provided at the ends for the application of an external voltage. It is a two terminals device. A *p-n* junction diode is represented by the symbol as shown in Fig. (b).

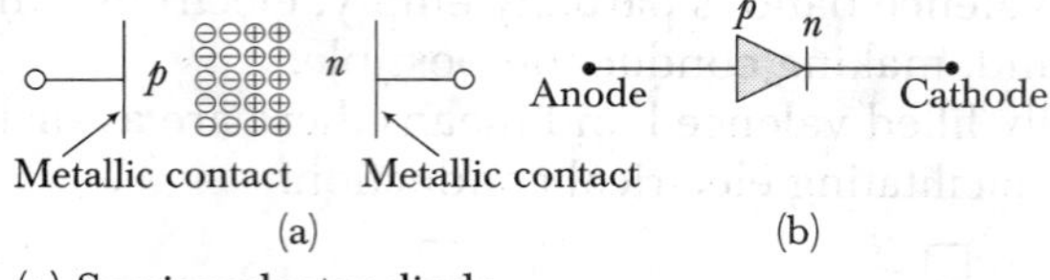

(a) Semiconductor diode,
(b) Symbol for *p-n* junction diode

The direction of arrow indicates the conventional direction of current.

A *p-n* junction diode is said to be in forward biased, if its *p*-side is connected with higher voltage than *n*-side.

(i) A *p-n* junction diode is

(a) electrically neutral ☐ (b) electrically positive ☐

(c) electrically negative ☐ (d) None of these ☐

(ii) Which of the following diode is in reverse bias?

(a) 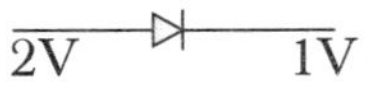 2V —▷|— 1V ☐ (b) 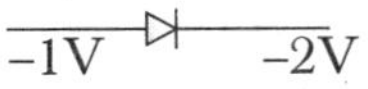 –1V —▷|— –2V ☐

(c) 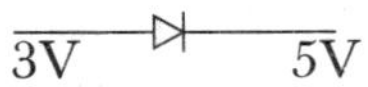 3V —▷|— 5V ☐ (d) 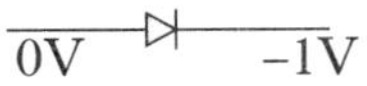 0V —▷|— –1V ☐

(iii) The diode used in the circuit shown in the figure has a constant voltage drop of 0.5 V at all current and a maximum power rating of 200 mW. What should be the value of the resistor R connected in series with the diode, for obtaining maximum current?

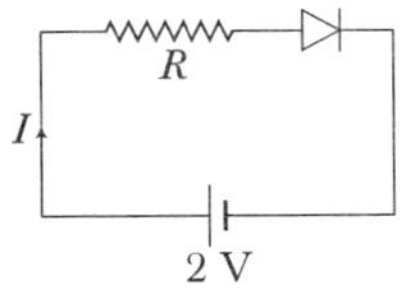

R

I

2 V

(a) 2 Ω ☐ (b) 4.25 Ω ☐

(c) 3.75 Ω ☐ (d) 4.5 Ω ☐

(iv) Current through *p-n* junction diode is due to flow of

(a) electrons only ☐ (b) holes only ☐

(c) both electrons and holes ☐ (d) proton only ☐

2. A rectifier is a device which converts an alternating current (or voltage) into a direct (or unidirectional) current (or voltage).

A *p-n* junction diode can work as an excellent rectifier because it permits current in one direction only.

It offers a low resistance for the current to flow when it is forward biased, but a very high resistance when reverse biased. Thus, it allows current to flow through it in only one direction and acts as a rectifier.

The junction diode can be used either as an half wave rectifier or as a full-wave rectifier.

(i) A full wave rectifier is fed with a AC signal of frequency 60 Hz. The frequency of signal obtained from the output of the rectifier is

(a) 50 Hz ☐ (b) 100 Hz ☐

(c) 60 Hz ☐ (d) 120 Hz ☐

(ii) The output signal obtained from the full wave rectifier is

(a) pure DC ☐ (b) pure AC ☐

(c) both DC and AC ☐ (d) 50% DC and 50% AC ☐

(iii) Which of the following is correct for half wave rectifier?

(a) $I_{DC} = \frac{I_0}{\pi}$ and $I_{rms} = \frac{I_0}{2}$ ☐ (b) $I_{DC} = \frac{I_0}{2}$ and $I_{rms} = \frac{I_0}{\pi}$ ☐

(c) $I_{DC} = \frac{2I_0}{\pi}$ and $I_{rms} = I_0$ ☐ (d) $I_{DC} = I_0$ and $I_{rms} = \frac{I_0}{\pi}$ ☐

COMPETITION EDGE UP

1. A potential divider circuit is connected with a DC source of 20 V, a light emitting diode of glow in voltage 1.8 V and a zener diode of breakdown voltage of 3.2 V. The length (PR) of the resistive wire is 20 cm.
The minimum length of PQ to just glow the LED is .... cm.
[NCERT (Old) Pg. 485, JEE Main 2024]

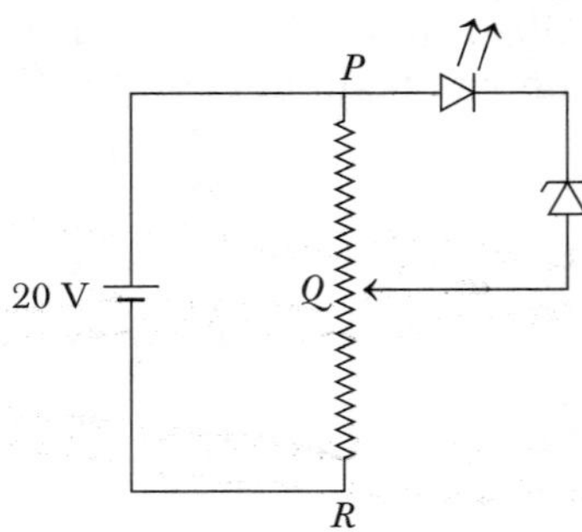

2. The acceptor level of a p-type semiconductor is 6 eV. The maximum wavelength of light which can create a hole would be (Given, $hc = 1242$ eV-nm)
[NCERT Pg. 333, JEE Main 2024]

(a) 414 nm ☐
(b) 207 nm ☐
(c) 407 nm ☐
(d) 103.5 nm ☐

3. Which of the diode circuit shows correct biasing used for the measurement of dynamic resistance of p-n junction diode?
[NCERT Pg. 334, JEE Main 2024]

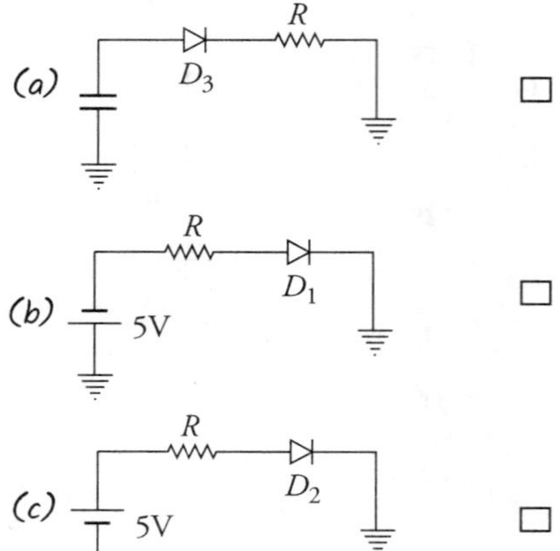

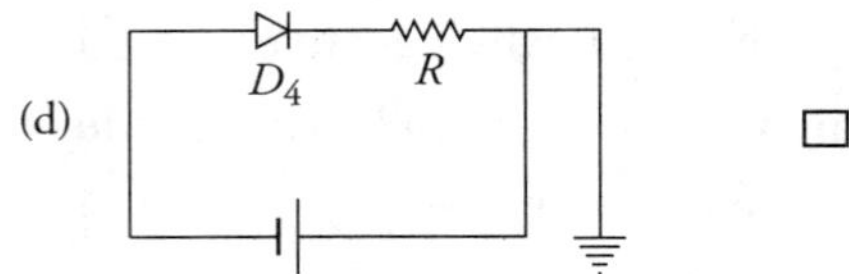

4. In the given circuit, if the power rating of zener diode is 10 mW, the value of series resistance R_s to regulate the input unregulated supply is
[NCERT (Old) Pg. 485, JEE Main 2024]

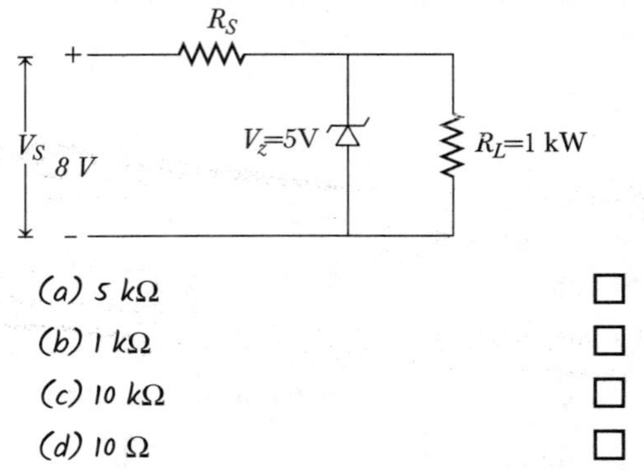

(a) 5 kΩ ☐
(b) 1 kΩ ☐
(c) 10 kΩ ☐
(d) 10 Ω ☐

5. In the given circuit, the voltage across load resistance (R_L) is
[NCERT Pg. 335, JEE Main 2024]

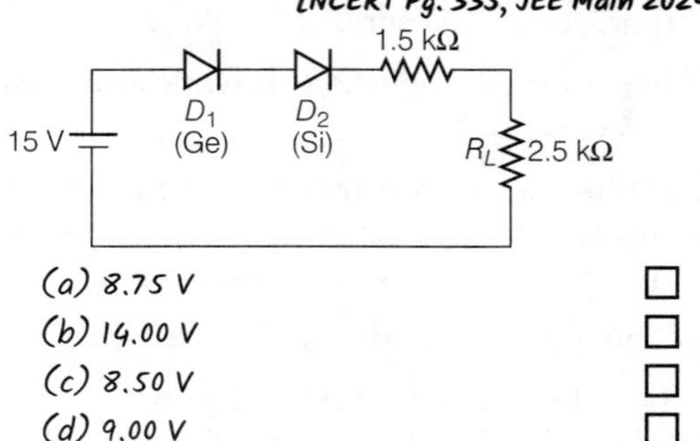

(a) 8.75 V ☐
(b) 14.00 V ☐
(c) 8.50 V ☐
(d) 9.00 V ☐

6. Consider the following statements A and B and identify the correct answer.
[NCERT (Old) Pg. 489, NEET 2024]

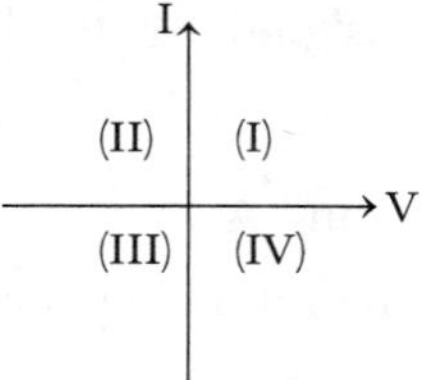

A. For a solar-cell, the I-V characteristics lies in the IV quadrant of the given graph.

B. In a reverse biased p-n junction diode, the current measured in (μA), is due to majority charge carriers.

(a) A is correct but B is incorrect. ☐

(b) A is incorrect but B is correct. ☐

(c) Both A and B are correct. ☐

(d) Both A and B are incorrect. ☐

7. The output Y of the given logic gate is similar to the output of an/a **[NCERT (Old) Pg. 502, NEET 2024]**

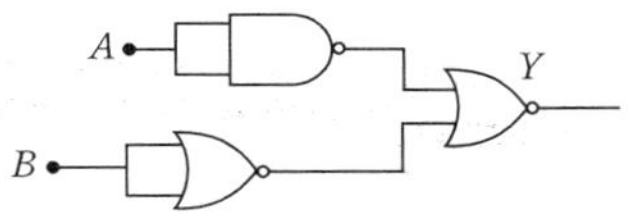

A, B, Y

(a) NAND gate ☐

(b) NOR gate ☐

(c) OR gate ☐

(d) AND gate ☐

8. A full wave rectifier circuit consists of two p-n junction diodes, a centre-tapped transformer, capacitor and a load resistance. Which of these components remove the AC ripple from the rectified output? **[NCERT Pg. 338, NEET 2023]**

(a) p-n junction diodes ☐

(b) Capacitor ☐

(c) Load resistance ☐

(d) A centre-tapped transformer ☐

9. Given below are two statements.

Statement I Photovoltaic devices can convert optical radiation into electricity.

Statement II Zener diode is designed to operate under reverse bias in breakdown region.

In the light of the above statements, choose the most appropriate answer from the options given below. **[NCERT (Old) Pg. 485, NEET 2023]**

(a) Both Statement I and Statement II are incorrect. ☐

(b) Statement I is correct but Statement II is incorrect. ☐

(c) Statement I is incorrect but Statement II is correct. ☐

(d) Both Statement I and Statement II are correct. ☐

10.

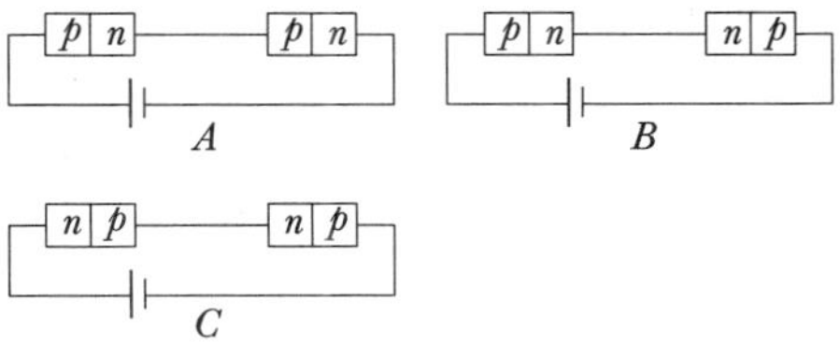

p n, p n — A

p n, n p — B

n p, n p — C

In the given circuits A, B and C the potential drop across the two p-n junctions are equal in **[NCERT Pg. 336, NEET 2022]**

(a) Circuit B only ☐

(b) Circuit C only ☐

(c) Both circuits A and C ☐

(d) Circuit A only ☐

Hints & Solutions

Chapter-1
Electric Charges and Fields

1. Polarity **2.** (*b*)

3. (*b*); When a plastic rod is rubbed with fur, an electic charge is developed on it. On touching this rod to pith balls, these charges are transferred from the rod to the pith ball in contact. As the charge on pith ball is same, so they repel each other.

4. (*d*); Due to friction, a body loses some electrons and other gains them. As charge appearing on both will be equal and opposite, so ratio of $q_1 : q_2 = -1 : 1$.

5. $A \to 3, B \to 1, C \to 2$;

Glass rod on rubbing with silk acquires positive charge, while a plastic rod on rubbing with cat's fur acquires negative charge.

6. (*a*)

7. (*c*); Net charge acquired by cylindrical conductor is zero, as there is only transfer of electrons from one part of body to the other.

8. $(n_2 - n_1)\, e$

9. (No);

By quantisation of charge, $q = ne$

$\therefore$ Number of electrons to be removed from silver dollar,

$$n = \frac{q}{e} = \frac{2.4}{1.6 \times 10^{-19}} = 1.5 \times 10^{19}$$

10. (3.2);

Here, number of electrons removed = number of atoms in 1g

$$\text{or } n = \frac{4 \times 10^{20}}{10^3} = 4 \times 10^{17}$$

$\therefore$ Charge, $q = ne = 4 \times 10^{17} \times 1.6 \times 10^{-19} = 6.4 \times 10^{-2}$ C

Hence, $x = 6.4$ and $y = 2$

$$\Rightarrow \quad x/y = \frac{6.4}{2} = 3.2$$

11. (200);

Time required, $t = \dfrac{Q}{I} = \dfrac{Q}{ne}$

where, n = number of electrons and e = charge of electron.

$$t = \frac{1\text{C}}{1.6 \times 10^{-19} \times 10^9}$$

$$\simeq 6.25 \times 10^9 \text{ s} \simeq 200 \text{ years}$$

12. (*b*); Number of molecules of water, $n = \dfrac{m}{M} \times 6.02 \times 10^{23}$

$$= \frac{250}{18} \times 6.02 \times 10^{23}$$

Total positive charge = Total negative charge $= ne$

$$= \frac{250}{18} \times 6.02 \times 10^{23} \times 1.6 \times 10^{-19} \times 10$$

$$= 1.34 \times 10^7 \text{ C}$$

13. $\dfrac{q}{2}$

14. (*c*); According to Coulomb's law, force between two point charges varies with distance as $F \propto \dfrac{1}{r^2}$.

15. (81);

From Coulomb's law, $F = K\dfrac{q_1 q_2}{r^2}$

$$= 9 \times 10^9 \times \frac{1 \times 1}{(1)^2} = 9 \times 10^9 \text{ N}$$

Hence, $x = 9$ and $y = 9$

$\Rightarrow \quad xy = 9 \times 9 = 81$

16. (*b*) For first case,

$$F = \frac{Kq_1 d_2}{d^2}$$

For second case,

$$F = \frac{K\,(2q_1)\,(2q_2)}{x^2}$$

According to question force must be equal in both case

$$\Rightarrow \quad \frac{Kq_1 d_2}{d^2} = \frac{4Kq_1 d_2}{x^2}$$

$\therefore \quad x = 2d$

17. (16);

From the formula,

$$F = \frac{1}{4\pi\varepsilon_0}\frac{q_1 q_2}{r^2}$$

$$F' = \frac{1}{4\pi\varepsilon_0}\frac{2q_1 \times 2q_2}{(r/2)^2} = \frac{4}{1/4}F$$

$$= 16F$$

$nF = 16F \Rightarrow n = 16$

18. (*a*); Initially, the force between two point charges A and B is given by

$$F = \frac{KQ_A Q_B}{r^2} = \frac{KQ(-Q)}{r^2}$$

$$= -\frac{KQ^2}{r^2} \qquad \text{...(i)}$$

When 25% charge of A is transferred to B, new amount of charge on A and B respectively, becomes

$$Q'_A = \frac{75}{100}(Q_A) = \frac{3}{4}Q$$

$$Q'_B = \left(\frac{25}{100}Q_A + Q_B\right)$$

$$= \left(\frac{1}{4}Q - Q\right) = \frac{-3}{4}Q$$

So, the force between the two charges, now becomes

$$F' = \frac{KQ'_A Q'_B}{r^2}$$

$$= \frac{K\left(\frac{3}{4}Q\right)\left(-\frac{3}{4}Q\right)}{r^2}$$

$$= \frac{-9KQ^2}{16r^2} = \frac{9}{16}F$$

[from Eq. (i)]

19. (a) Yes (b) Yes (c) Yes

20. (*a*); In absence of gravitational effect, due to repulsion, the separation between two spheres will be maximum, i.e. $d = 2L$ and angle between two suspensions and tension will be 180°.

$\therefore$ Tension,

$$T = \frac{1}{4\pi\varepsilon_0}\frac{Q^2}{(2L)^2}$$

21. (1.8 N);

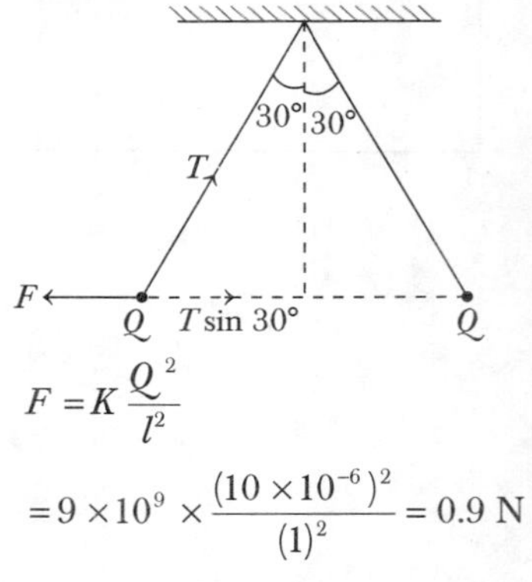

$$F = K\frac{Q^2}{l^2}$$

$$= 9 \times 10^9 \times \frac{(10 \times 10^{-6})^2}{(1)^2} = 0.9 \text{ N}$$

$T \sin\theta = F$

$$\Rightarrow \quad T = \frac{0.9}{\sin 30^\circ} = 1.8 \text{ N}$$

22. (i) (2.4×10^{39});

If m_p and m_e be the masses of proton and electron,

$$\left|\frac{F_e}{F_g}\right| = \frac{1}{4\pi\varepsilon_0}\frac{e^2}{r^2}\times\frac{r^2}{Gm_pm_e}$$

$$= \frac{e^2}{4\pi\varepsilon_0 Gm_pm_e} = 2.4\times 10^{39}$$

(ii) (*b*); Force, $F = \frac{1}{4\pi\varepsilon_0}\frac{e^2}{r^2}$

$$= 9\times 10^9 \times \frac{(1.6\times 10^{-19})^2}{(10^{-10})^2}$$

$$= 2.3\times 10^{-8}\ \text{N}$$

Since, $F = ma$

For electron,

$$a_e = \frac{2.3\times 10^{-8}}{9.1\times 10^{-31}} = 2.5\times 10^{22}\ \text{ms}^{-2}$$

For proton,

$$a_p = \frac{2.3\times 10^{-8}}{1.6\times 10^{-27}} = 1.4\times 10^{19}\text{ms}^{-2}$$

23. $(-Q/4)$;

The given condition is shown in the figure given below.

$x=0$

$+Q$ q $+Q$

$\longleftarrow d/2 \longrightarrow$

$\longleftarrow d \longrightarrow$

Net force on charge Q placed at origin, i.e. at $x=0$ in accordance with the principle of superposition can be given as

$$F = \frac{1}{4\pi\varepsilon_0}\cdot\frac{Q\times q}{\left(\frac{d}{2}\right)^2} + \frac{1}{4\pi\varepsilon_0}\cdot\frac{Q\times Q}{(d)^2}$$

Since, it has been given that, $F = 0$.

$$\Rightarrow \frac{1}{4\pi\varepsilon_0}\cdot\frac{Q\times q}{\left(\frac{d}{2}\right)^2} + \frac{1}{4\pi\varepsilon_0}\cdot\frac{Q\times Q}{(d)^2} = 0$$

$$\Rightarrow \frac{1}{4\pi\varepsilon_0}\cdot\frac{Q\times q}{\left(\frac{d}{2}\right)^2} = -\frac{1}{4\pi\varepsilon_0}\cdot\frac{Q\times Q}{(d)^2}$$

or $q = -\frac{Q}{4}$

24. $\left(\frac{d}{\sqrt{2}+1}\right)$;

Since, net force is zero. If x be the distance of third charge from q, then

$$\frac{KqQ}{x^2} = \frac{2KqQ}{(d-x)^2}$$

$$\Rightarrow (d-x)^2 = 2x^2$$

$$\Rightarrow x = \frac{d}{\sqrt{2}+1}$$

25. (*d*); Net force,

$$F_{\text{net}} = 2F\cos\theta$$

$$= 2\times\frac{1}{4\pi\varepsilon_0}\times\frac{-qQ}{(a^2+2a^2)}\times\frac{2a}{\sqrt{a^2+2a^2}}$$

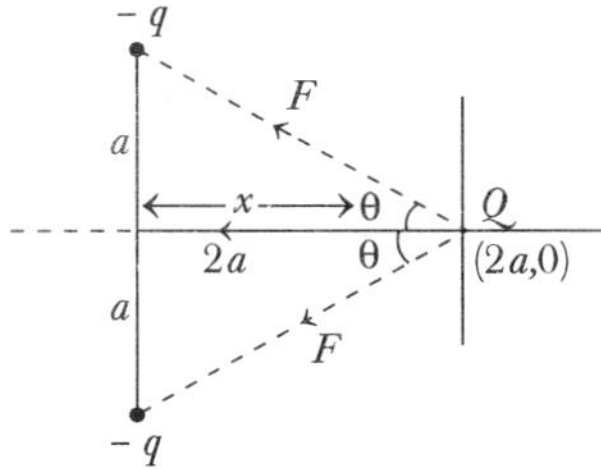

As force is non-linear, so, motion will be oscillatory but not simple harmonic.

26. A → 2, B → 3, C → 4, D → 1

27. (0);

Since, O is centroid, so

$$AO = BO = CO = \frac{l}{\sqrt{3}}$$

$$\therefore F_1 = \frac{3}{4\pi\varepsilon_0}\frac{Qq}{l^2} \text{ along } AO$$

$$F_2 = \frac{3}{4\pi\varepsilon_0}\frac{Qq}{l^2} \text{ along } BO$$

$$F_3 = \frac{3}{4\pi\varepsilon_0}\frac{Qq}{l^2} \text{ along } CO$$

Resultant of F_2 and F_3,

$$F_R = \frac{3}{4\pi\varepsilon_0}\frac{Qq}{l^2} \text{ along } OA$$

$\therefore$ Total force on Q,

$$F = \frac{3}{4\pi\varepsilon_0}\frac{Qq}{l^2}(\hat{\mathbf{r}}-\hat{\mathbf{r}}) = 0$$

28. $\left(F = \frac{q^2}{4\pi\varepsilon_0 l^2}\right)$;

From Coulomb's law, the force of attraction or repulsion on each pair of charges has same magnitude and is given by

$$F = \frac{q^2}{4\pi\varepsilon_0 l^2}$$

29. (*b*); Since, net force on q_1 is along $+X$-axis, so it must be negative and due to addition of positive charge Q at $(x, 0)$, the force on it increases along $+X$-axis.

30. $\frac{kQ}{r^2}$

31. (*c*); Given, electric field,

$$E = Aa \quad \text{...(i)}$$

A charge q contained in a sphere of radius a centred at the origin is shown below.

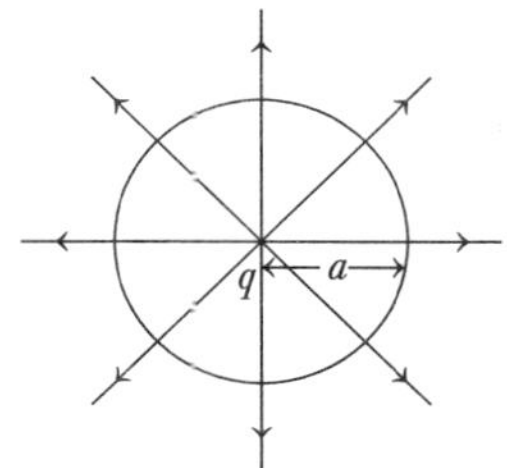

Here, radius, $r = a$

$\therefore$ Electric field,

$$E = \frac{1}{4\pi\varepsilon_0}\cdot\frac{q}{a^2} \quad \text{...(ii)}$$

From Eqs. (i) and (ii), we get

$$\frac{1}{4\pi\varepsilon_0}\cdot\frac{q}{a^2} = Aa \Rightarrow q = 4\pi\varepsilon_0 Aa^3$$

32. (6.6 nC);

Electric field, $E = \frac{KQ}{r^2}$

$$\Rightarrow Q = \frac{Er^2}{K}$$

$$= \frac{1.5\times 10^3\times(20\times 10^{-2})^2}{9\times 10^9}$$

$$= 6.6\ \text{nC}$$

33. Yes **34.** Yes

35. q_n to p, distance

36. (Yes);

The direction of electric fields is as shown in the figure given below.

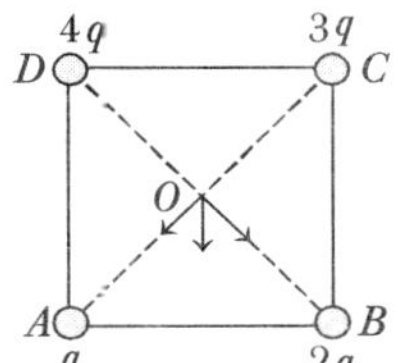

So, the net electric field will be along bisector of angle AOB, which is parallel to CB.

37. (2);

Here, $E_A = E_C$

So, net electric field at M,

$E_{net} = E_B$, i.e. along vector 2.

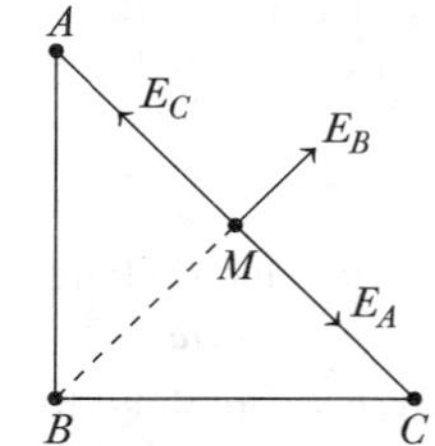

38. (*b*)

39. (2.9×10^{-9}s, 1.3×10^{-7}s);

For electron, $a_e = \frac{F}{m_e} = \frac{eE}{m_e}$

Time of fall, $t_e = \sqrt{\frac{2h}{a_e}} = \sqrt{\frac{2hm_e}{eE}}$

$$= \sqrt{\frac{2\times 1.5\times 10^{-2}\times 9.1\times 10^{-31}}{1.6\times 10^{-19}\times 2\times 10^4}}$$

$= 2.9\times 10^{-9}$ s

Similarly, for proton,

$a_p = \frac{eE}{m_p}$

$\Rightarrow t_p = \sqrt{\frac{2h}{a_p}} = \sqrt{\frac{2hm_p}{eE}}$

$$= \sqrt{\frac{2\times 1.5\times 10^{-2}\times 1.67\times 10^{-27}}{1.6\times 10^{-19}\times 2\times 10^4}}$$

$= 1.3\times 10^{-7}$ s

40. (*b*); At A,

$E_A = E_{1A} + E_{2A} = 2E_{1A}$

$$= 2\times\frac{9\times 10^9\times 10^{-8}}{(0.05)^2}$$

$= 7.2\times 10^4$ NC^{-1}

At B, $E_B = E_{1B} + E_{2B}$

$$= \frac{9\times10^9\times10^{-8}}{(0.05)^2} - \frac{9\times10^9\times10^{-8}}{(0.5)^2}$$

$= 3.2\times 10^4$ NC^{-1}

At C, $E_C = E_{1C}\cos\frac{\pi}{3} + E_{2C}\cos\frac{\pi}{3}$

$= 2E_{1C}\cos\frac{\pi}{3}$

$$= 2\times\frac{9\times 10^9\times 10^{-8}}{(0.10)^2}\times\frac{1}{2}$$

$= 9\times10^3$ NC^{-1}

41. positive, negative

42. (*c*)

43. (i) Yes (ii) Yes (iii) strong, more, weaker, less

44. A $\rightarrow$ 2, B $\rightarrow$ 1, C $\rightarrow$ 4, D $\rightarrow$ 3

45. (i) Yes (ii) Yes (iii) Yes (iv) No

46. II

47. 4

48. (*d*)

49. (*c*) ;

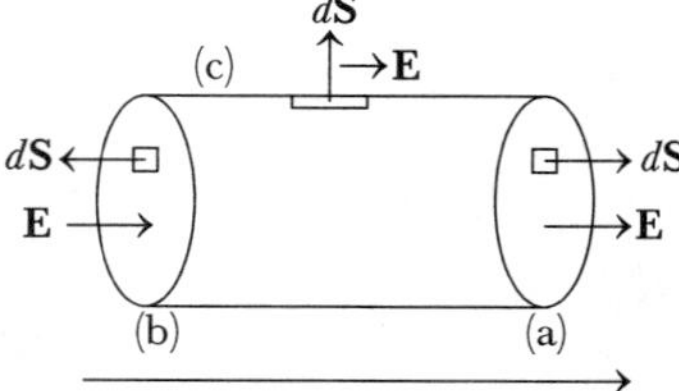

Divide cylinder into three parts, two circular parts (a) and (b) and one cylindrical surface (c).

$\phi = \phi_a + \phi_b + \phi_c$

$$= \int_a \mathbf{E}\cdot d\mathbf{S} + \int_b \mathbf{E}\cdot d\mathbf{S} + \int_c \mathbf{E}\cdot d\mathbf{S}$$

$$= \int^a EdS\cos 0° + \int^b EdS\cos 180° + \int^c EdS\cos 90°$$

$= ES - ES + 0 = 0$

50. (*b*) ;

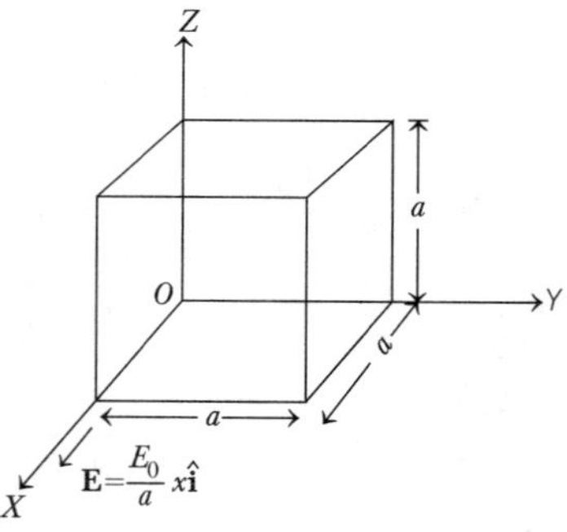

On four faces, electric field and area are perpendicular, hence flux is zero. One face is at origin, i.e. $x = 0$, $E = 0$, flux is zero. On the sixth face, $x = a$.

$$\mathbf{E} = \frac{E_0}{a}x\hat{\mathbf{i}} = E_0\hat{\mathbf{i}}$$

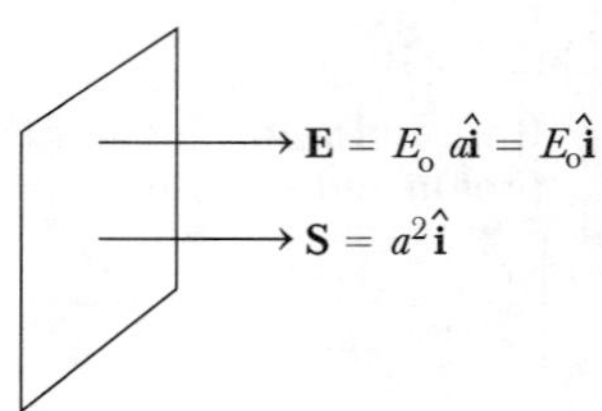

$$\phi = \mathbf{E}\cdot\mathbf{S} = E_0\hat{\mathbf{i}}\cdot a^2\hat{\mathbf{i}} = E_0 a^2$$

51. $-\frac{kp}{r^3}$

52. (i) False (ii) True

53. Yes; As we know,

$$\frac{E_{axis}}{E_{equator}} = \frac{2p/4\pi\varepsilon_0 r^3}{p/4\pi\varepsilon_0 r^3} = \frac{2}{1}$$

54. (180);

Electric field due to dipole

$$= \frac{qd\cos\theta}{2\pi\varepsilon_0 r^2}$$

$$= \frac{4\times10^{-6}\times2\times10^{-2}\times\cos 60°\times4.5\times10^9}{1}$$

$= 8\times10^{-8}\times\frac{1}{2}\times4.5\times10^9$

$= 180$ N/C

55. (2.6×10^5) ;

At an axial point,

$$E = \frac{2p}{4\pi\varepsilon_0 r^3} = \frac{2\times 2a\times q}{4\pi\varepsilon_0 r^3}$$

$$= \frac{2\times 5\times 10^{-3}\times 10^{-5}}{4\pi(8.854\times 10^{-12})(15\times 10^{-2})^3}$$

$= 2.6\times 10^5$ NC^{-1}

56. (1.33×10^5 NC^{-1});

At an equatorial point,

$$E = \frac{p}{4\pi\varepsilon_0 r^3}$$

$$= \frac{5\times 10^{-3}\times 10^{-5}}{4\pi(8.854\times 10^{-12})\times(15\times 10^{-2})^3}$$

$= 1.33\times 10^5$ NC^{-1}

57. (*b*);

+q, p_1, p, $-2q$, p_2, $+q$

$p = \sqrt{p_1^2 + p_2^2}$

$= \sqrt{(qa)^2 + (qa)^2}$

$= \sqrt{2}qa$

58. (*c*); For stable equilibrium, the angle θ should be zero.

E

$-q$ $+q$

$$\tau = pE \sin\theta = 0$$

59. (i) Zero (ii) Yes (iii) Yes (iv) $2qaE \sin\theta$, the direction of the torque is normal to the plane of paper.

60. (*b*); Since, strength of field decreases from left to right, so the dipole experiences a force towards left.

61. (*b*)

62. (2 mC);

Torque,

$$\tau = pE \sin\theta$$
$$= 2a \times Q \times E \sin\theta$$
$$\Rightarrow 4 = 2\times10^{-2} \times Q \times 2 \times 10^5 \times \sin 30^\circ$$
$$\Rightarrow Q = 200\times10^{-5} = 2\,\text{mC}$$

63. (2×10^{-4} N-m);

$\because \tau = pE \sin\theta = q \times 2a \times E \sin\theta$

$\therefore$ Maximum value of τ

$$= 10^{-7}\times2\times10^{-2}\times10^5\times1$$
$$= 2\times10^{-4}\text{ N-m}$$

64. ($\sigma_2 > \sigma_1 > \sigma_3$); Charge density is inversely proportional to the radius of curvature, i.e.

Charge density $\propto \dfrac{1}{\text{Radius of curvature}}$

Therefore, as shown in figure,

$$\sigma_2 > \sigma_1 > \sigma_3$$

65. (1.4×10^{-3}C); Given, radius of sphere,

$$r = \frac{d}{2} = \frac{2.4}{2} = 1.2\,\text{m}$$

Surface charge density,

$$\sigma = 80\,\mu\text{Cm}^{-2} = 80\times10^{-6}\text{ Cm}^{-2}$$

We know that,

$$\sigma = \frac{q}{4\pi r^2} \Rightarrow q = \sigma\times4\pi r^2$$
$$= 80\times10^{-6}\times4\times3.14\times1.2\times1.2$$
$$q = 1.4\times10^{-3}\text{C}$$

66. Yes

67. (*c*)

68. Yes

69. (*c*)

70. (1.88×10^5);

It can be considered as a face of a cube, so electric flux through one face of cube,

$$\phi = \frac{\phi_{\text{total}}}{6} = \frac{1}{6}\frac{q}{\varepsilon_0}$$
$$= \frac{1}{6}\times\frac{10\times10^{-6}}{8.854\times10^{-12}}$$
$$= 1.88\times10^5\text{ N-m}^2\text{C}^{-1}$$

71. $\left(\dfrac{q}{6\varepsilon_0}\right)$; The outside charge does not contribute to the total flux, so flux through face *EFGH*,

$$\phi = \frac{\phi_{\text{total}}}{6} = \frac{q}{6\varepsilon_0}$$

72. (*b*); When a sphere encloses an electric dipole, the situation is as shown below.

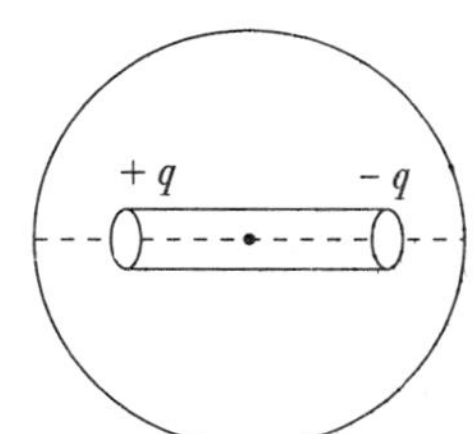

According to Gauss's law,

$$\phi_E = \frac{q_{\text{enclosed}}}{\varepsilon_0} = \frac{q_+ + q_-}{\varepsilon_0}$$
$$= \frac{+3\times10^{-6} - 3\times10^{-6}}{\varepsilon_0} = 0$$

73. Yes

74. (*a*); Using Gauss's law,

$$\phi = \frac{q_{\text{net}}}{\varepsilon_0} = \frac{q_1+q_2+q_3}{\varepsilon_0}$$
$$= \frac{8.85\times10^{-9}}{8.85\times10^{-12}}$$
$$= 10^3\text{ N-m}^2\text{C}^{-1}$$

75. ($1.05, 9.27\times10^{-12}$);
Here, electric field is contributed only due to two shaded faces and given as

$$E_L = \alpha a^{\frac{1}{2}}$$

and $E_R = \alpha(2a)^{\frac{1}{2}}$

$\therefore$ $\phi_L = \mathbf{E}_L\cdot\Delta\mathbf{S} = -E_L a^2$

and $\phi_R = \mathbf{E}_R\cdot\Delta\mathbf{S} = E_R a^2$

Net flux, $\phi_{\text{net}} = \phi_R + \phi_L$

$$= a^2(E_R - E_L)$$
$$= a^2\alpha\left[(2a)^{\frac{1}{2}} - a^{\frac{1}{2}}\right]$$
$$= \alpha a^{\frac{5}{2}}(\sqrt{2}-1)$$
$$= 800(0.1)^{\frac{5}{2}}(\sqrt{2}-1)$$
$$= 1.05\text{ N-m}^2\text{C}^{-1}$$

Using Gauss's law, $\phi = \dfrac{q}{\varepsilon_0}$

$$\Rightarrow q = \phi\varepsilon_0$$
$$= 1.05\times8.854\times10^{-12}$$
$$= 9.27\times10^{-12}\text{ C}$$

76. (i) (1.57 N-m^{2}C^{-1});

$$\phi = \mathbf{E}\cdot\Delta\mathbf{S} = -200\hat{\mathbf{i}}\cdot\Delta\mathbf{S}$$
$$= +200\,\hat{\mathbf{i}}\,\Delta S \quad (\Delta S = -\Delta S)$$
$$= 200\times\pi\times(0.05)^2$$
$$= 1.57\text{ N-m}^2\text{C}^{-1}$$

(ii) (*b*); $\phi = \mathbf{E}\cdot\Delta\mathbf{S}$

$$= E\Delta S\cos 90^\circ = 0$$

(iii) (3.14); Net outward flux through the cylinder

$$= 1.57 + 1.57 + 0$$
$$= 3.14\text{ Nm}^2\text{C}^{-1}$$

(iv) (Yes); $q = \varepsilon_0\phi$

$$= 3.14\times8.854\times10^{-12}$$
$$= 2.78\times10^{-11}\text{ C}$$

77. (1 : 1);

As per Gauss's law, $\phi = \dfrac{Q}{\varepsilon_0}$

$$\therefore \frac{\phi_1}{\phi_2} = \frac{\frac{Q}{\varepsilon_0}}{\frac{Q}{\varepsilon_0}} = 1:1$$

78. A → 2, B → 3, C → 4, D → 1

79. $\left(\dfrac{100Q}{\varepsilon_0}\right)$;

From Gauss's law,

Electric flux, $\phi = \dfrac{q}{\varepsilon_0}$

Charge enclosed by cylindrical surface (length 100 cm) is

$$q = 100Q$$
$$\therefore \phi = \frac{100Q}{\varepsilon_0}$$

80. ($\dfrac{\sigma}{\varepsilon_0}$, normal);

By Gauss's law,

$$\int E\cdot\Delta S = \frac{q}{\varepsilon_0}$$
$$\Rightarrow E\cdot A = \frac{q}{\varepsilon_0}$$
$$\Rightarrow E = \frac{q}{A\varepsilon_0} = \frac{\sigma}{\varepsilon_0}$$ and it is normal to the surface.

81. (*d*);

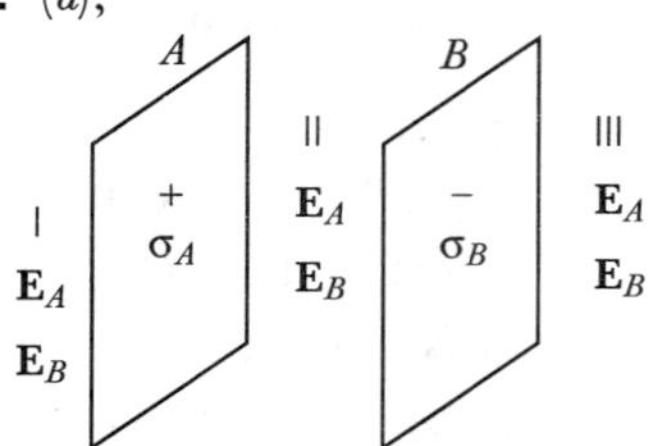

According to Gauss's theorem, if the plates have same surface charge density but having opposite signs, then the electric field in the outer region of the first plate (region I) is zero.

$$\mathbf{E}_I = \mathbf{E}_A + \mathbf{E}_B$$

$$= \frac{\sigma}{2\varepsilon_0} + \left(-\frac{\sigma}{2\varepsilon_0}\right) = 0$$

82. (*b*); Using Gauss's law at outer surface, let charge on dipole be q.

$$\phi = \frac{\Sigma q}{\varepsilon_0} = E \cdot A$$

or $$E = \frac{1}{A\varepsilon_0}\Sigma q = \frac{(+Q + q - q)}{A\varepsilon_0}$$

$$= \frac{Q}{A\varepsilon_0} = \frac{\sigma}{\varepsilon_0} = \text{constant}$$

83. (0); At $r > R$, total charge enclosed is zero. So, from Gauss's law,

$$E \cdot \Delta S = 0 \Rightarrow E = 0$$

84. (*c*); The given situation can be shown as below

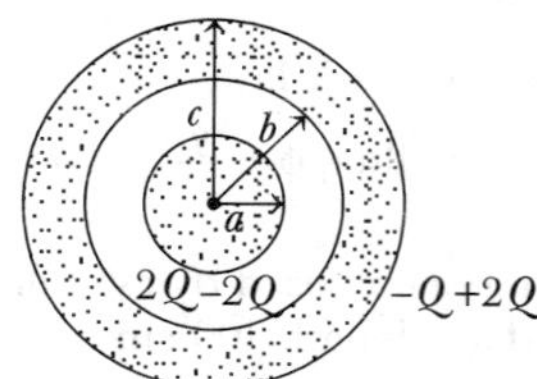

$\therefore$ Surface charge density on inner surface of shell, $\sigma_I = \frac{-2Q}{4\pi b^2}$

and that on the outer surface, is

$$\sigma_0 = \frac{-Q + 2Q}{4\pi c^2} = \frac{Q}{4\pi c^2}$$

85. $(0.29E)$;

Electric field at centre of disc,

$$E = \frac{\sigma}{2\varepsilon_0}$$

At distance x,

$$E' = \frac{\sigma}{2\varepsilon_0}\left(1 - \frac{R}{\sqrt{x^2 + R^2}}\right)$$

$$= \frac{\sigma}{2\varepsilon_0}\left(1 - \frac{R}{\sqrt{R^2 + R^2}}\right) (\because \chi = R)$$

$$= 0.29\ E$$

86. (*d*); Charge inside the sphere of radius R,

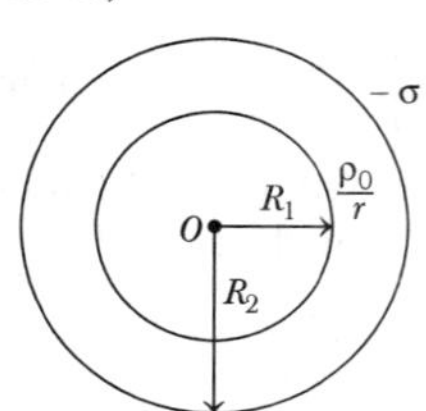

$$Q_1 = \int \rho \cdot 4\pi r^2 dx$$

$$= 4\pi\rho_0 \int_0^{R_1} r dr$$

$$= 2\pi\rho_0 R_1^2$$

Charge on hollow sphere,

$$Q_2 = -\sigma \cdot 4\pi R_2^2$$

Given, $Q_1 + Q_2 = 0$

$$\Rightarrow 2\pi\rho_0 R_1^2 - 4\pi\sigma R_2^2 = 0$$

$$\Rightarrow \frac{R_2}{R_1} = \sqrt{\frac{\rho_0}{2\sigma}}$$

Assertion-Reason Questions

1. (*b*); Coulomb attraction exists even when one body is charged and the other body is uncharged.

2. (*a*); By losing electrons, the body acquires positive charge. So, its mass decreases.

3. (*a*); If the two electric lines of force intersect each other, then at the point of intersection, we can draw two tangents. This mean two directions of electric field lines at the point of intersection, which is not possible.

4. (*a*); The force F on the charge q due to charge Q depends on the particular location of the charge q and so the electric field (F/q) at different positions is different and independent of charge q.

5. (*a*)

6. (*a*)

As net field is zero, the forces must form a cyclic triangle.

7. (*d*); The rate of decrease of electric field is different in the two case. In case of a point charge, it decreases as $\frac{1}{r^2}$ but in the case of electric dipole, it decreases more rapidly, as $1/r^3$.

8. (*b*); As $F = qE$, and charge (q) of an electron and a proton has the same magnitude, therefore force F on each is same.

9. (*d*); By Gauss' law, the net flux is zero. So, number of lines of force terminating on the surface will be equal to the number lines of force leaving it.

10. (*c*); Electric field does not exist inside a hollow shell, so electrostatic shielding is possible. But field lines are not reflected from metal surface.

Case Based Questions

1. (i) (*d*)

(ii) (*d*); Charge on a body, $q = ne$

$\therefore$ Number of electrons present on a body,

$$n = \frac{q}{e} = \frac{1 \times 10^{-9}\ \text{C}}{1.6 \times 10^{-19}\ \text{C}}$$

$$= 6.25 \times 10^9$$

(iii) (*a*) ; $q = ne$

$$q = 2 \times 10^{12} \times 1.6 \times 10^{-19}$$

$$= 3.2 \times 10^{-7}\ \text{C}$$

(iv) (*a*)

2. (i) (*d*); Electric flux,

$$\phi = \mathbf{E} \cdot \mathbf{A} = EA \cos\theta$$

where, $\mathbf{A} = A\hat{\mathbf{n}}$

For electric flux passing through S_6, $\hat{\mathbf{n}}_{S_6} = -i$ (Back)

$\therefore \phi_{S_6} = -(4 \times 10^3)(0.1)^2 \cos 37° = -32\ \text{Nm}^2\,\text{C}^{-1}$

(ii) (*a*); For electric flux passing through S_1,

$$\hat{\mathbf{n}}_{S_1} = -\hat{\mathbf{j}}\ \text{(left)}$$

$$\therefore \phi_{S_1} = -(4 \times 10^3)(0.1)^2 \cos(90° - 37°)$$

$$= -24\ \text{Nm}^2\ \text{C}^{-1}$$

(iii) (*d*); As the field is uniform, the total flux through the cube must be zero, i.e., any flux entering the cube must leave it.

(iv) (*b*); Electric flux is measure of the electric field lines passing through a given surface area. Flux is negative if the field lines are entering the surface.

Competition Edge Up

1. (*a*);

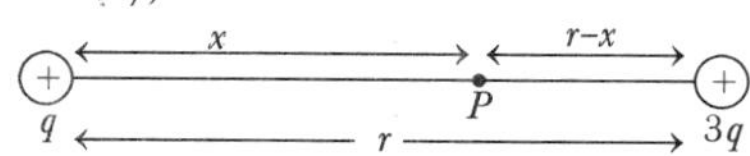

Net electric field at P is zero.

So, $\frac{kq}{x^2} = \frac{k \cdot 3q}{(r-x)^2} \Rightarrow \frac{1}{x} = \frac{\sqrt{3}}{r-x}$

$\Rightarrow \quad x = \left(\frac{1}{1+\sqrt{3}}\right) \cdot r$

2. (*a*); Electric field at a distance r due to infinite long wire,

$$E = \frac{2k\lambda}{r} \quad ...(i)$$

Force on an electron,

$$\Rightarrow \quad F = qE = eE \quad ...(ii)$$

$$F = e\left(\frac{2k\lambda}{r}\right)$$

$$\Rightarrow \quad F = \frac{2k\lambda e}{r} \quad ...(iii)$$

This force will provide the centripetal force,

$\frac{mv^2}{r} = \frac{2k\lambda e}{r} \Rightarrow v = \sqrt{\frac{2k\lambda e}{m}}$

Kinetic energy $\Rightarrow$ KE $= \frac{1}{2}mv^2$

$$\text{KE} = \frac{1}{2}m\left(\frac{2k\lambda e}{m}\right)$$

$= k\lambda e$ (where k is constant)

Kinetic energy will remain constant.

3. (*c*); Total flux $(\phi) = \frac{Q_{\text{enclosed}}}{\varepsilon_0}$

$$= \frac{+5q + q - 2q}{\varepsilon_0} = \frac{4q}{\varepsilon_0}$$

4. (*b*); According to Gauss's law,

$$\oint \mathbf{E} \cdot d\mathbf{A} = \frac{q}{\varepsilon_0}$$

$\Rightarrow \quad EdA \cos 0° = \frac{\sigma dA}{\varepsilon_0} \Rightarrow E = \frac{\sigma}{\varepsilon_0}$

5. (*c*); According to Gauss's law,

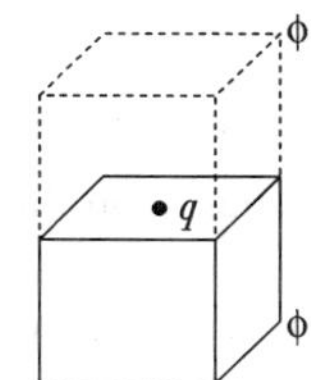

$$2\phi = \frac{q}{\varepsilon_0} \Rightarrow \phi = \frac{q}{2\varepsilon_0}$$

6. (*d*); $\therefore$ Electric flux,

$\phi = \mathbf{E} \cdot \mathbf{A} = (6\hat{\mathbf{i}} + 5\hat{\mathbf{j}} + 3\hat{\mathbf{k}}) \cdot 30\hat{\mathbf{i}}$

$= 180 \text{ N-m}^2/\text{C}$

7. (*d*); Given,

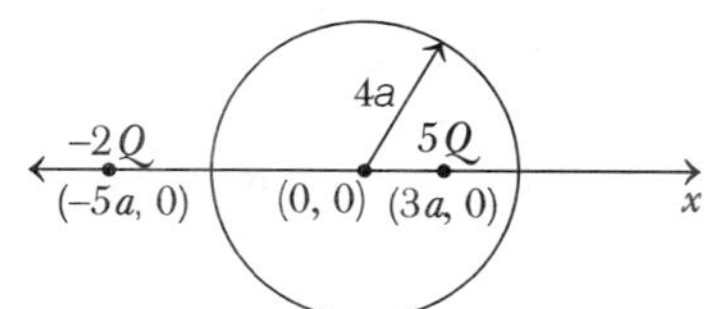

$5Q$ charge is inside the spherical region flux through sphere $= \frac{5Q}{\varepsilon_0}$

8. (*d*); $\therefore \phi_E = \frac{q_{\text{enclosed}}}{\varepsilon_0}$

Flux through cube C_1,
$\phi_1 = 2Q / \varepsilon_0$

Flux through cube C_2,

$$\phi_2 = \frac{2Q + 3Q}{\varepsilon_0} = \frac{5Q}{\varepsilon_0}$$

Ratio, $\frac{\phi_1}{\phi_2} = \frac{2Q/\varepsilon_0}{5Q/\varepsilon_0} = \frac{2}{5}$

9. (*d*); According to Gauss's law, $\oint \mathbf{E} \cdot d\mathbf{S}$ represents total electric flux passing through a closed surface.

If $\oint \mathbf{E} \cdot d\mathbf{S} = 0$, then it signifies that the number of electric flux lines entering the surface must be equal to the number of flux lines leaving the surface.

10. (*a*); The arrangement of charges shown in the figure is an electric dipole. Hence, electric field at point P at a distance $R (R >> L)$ from the dipole is equal to electric field due to electric dipole on axial position.

$-q$ ——— $+q$ ——— P ; $\longleftarrow R \longrightarrow$; $\longleftarrow L \longrightarrow$

i.e., $\quad E = \frac{1}{4\pi\varepsilon_0} \cdot \frac{2p}{R^3}$

where, $p = qL$ (Electric dipole moment)

$\therefore \quad E \propto \frac{1}{R^3}$

11. (*c*); Force of mutual attraction between the electron and proton. (when, $r = 1.6$ Å $= 1.6 \times 10^{-10}$ m) is given as

$$F = 9 \times 10^9 \times \frac{e^2}{r^2}$$

$$= 9 \times 10^9 \times \frac{(1.6 \times 10^{-19})^2}{(1.6 \times 10^{-10})^2}$$

$$= 9 \times 10^{-9} \text{ N}$$

$\therefore$ Acceleration of electron

$$= \frac{F}{m_e} = \frac{9 \times 10^{-9}}{9 \times 10^{-31}} = 10^{22} \text{ m/s}^2$$

12. (*a*); Electric field

$$E = \frac{1}{4\pi\varepsilon_0} \cdot \frac{q}{x^2}$$

$$= 9 \times 10^9 \times \frac{3.2 \times 10^{-7}}{(15 \times 10^{-2})^2}$$

$$= 1.28 \times 10^5 \text{ N/C}$$

Chapter-2

Electrostatic Potential and Capacitance

1. (i) ✓ (ii) ✓

2. Yes;

Since, work done is independent of path and only depends on the initial and final positions.

3. (0); Since, initial and final points are same. Hence, work done is zero.

4. I. Yes II. Yes III. No

5. (15); Since, $V_B - V_A = \frac{W_{AB}}{q_0}$

By external force,

$V - (-10\text{V}) = \frac{100 \text{ J}}{4 \text{ C}} = 25 \text{ V}$

or $\quad V = 25 - 10 = 15 \text{ V}$

6. (*c*);

$\because V \propto \frac{1}{r}$, so correct graph is (c).

7. $(4 \times 10^4 \text{ V})$;

Since, $V = \frac{Kq}{r}$

$$= \frac{9 \times 10^9 \times 4 \times 10^{-7}}{9 \times 10^{-2}}$$

$$= 4 \times 10^4 \text{ V}$$

8. (b); Electric potential due to an dipole in vector form,

$$V = \frac{K\mathbf{p}\cdot\mathbf{r}}{r^3}$$

$$= \frac{9\times10^9 \times(5\hat{\mathbf{i}} - 9\hat{\mathbf{j}} + 3\hat{\mathbf{k}})}{(2^2+2^2+1^2)^{\frac{3}{2}}} \cdot (2\hat{\mathbf{i}} + 2\hat{\mathbf{j}} - \hat{\mathbf{k}})$$

where $\mathbf{r}$ is

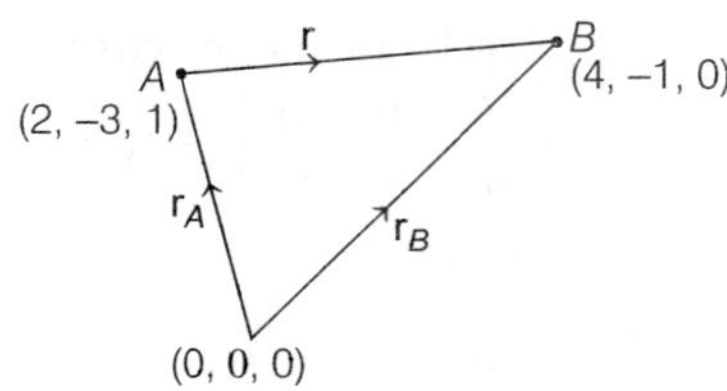

$$\mathbf{r} = \mathbf{r}_B - \mathbf{r}_A$$

$$= (4\hat{\mathbf{i}} - \hat{\mathbf{j}} + 0\hat{\mathbf{k}}) - (2\hat{\mathbf{i}} - 3\hat{\mathbf{j}} + \hat{\mathbf{k}})$$

$$= (2\hat{\mathbf{i}} + 2\hat{\mathbf{j}} - \hat{\mathbf{k}})$$

Hence,

$$V = \frac{9\times10^9\times(10-18-3)}{27}$$

$$= \frac{9\times10^9\,(-11)}{27}$$

$$= -3.66\times10^9 \text{ V}$$

9. (200 V);

Potential due to a dipole at an angular position,

$$V = \frac{Kp\cos\theta}{r^2}$$

$$= 9\times10^9\times\frac{16\times10^{-9}\times\cos60^\circ}{(0.6)^2}$$

$$= 200 \text{ V}$$

10. (i) $\dfrac{2k_e qa}{x^2 - a^2}$;

For a point in figure,

$$V = k_e\,\Sigma\frac{q_i}{r_1}$$

$$= k_e\left(\frac{q}{x-a} - \frac{q}{x+a}\right)$$

$$= \frac{2k_e qa}{x^2 - a^2}$$

(ii) $\dfrac{2k_e qa}{x^2}$;

If point P is far from the dipole, such that $x >> a$, then a^2 can be neglected in the terms, $x^2 - a^2$ and V becomes $V = \dfrac{2k_e\,qa}{x^2}$ $(x >> a)$.

11. (d); Potential at a point due to electric dipole,

$$V = \frac{p\cos\theta}{r^2}$$

If $\theta = 0°$, then V will be maximum and if $\theta = 180°$, then V will be minimum.

12. (b); The potential due to an electric dipole,

$$V = \frac{1}{4\pi\varepsilon_0}\frac{\mathbf{p}\cdot\mathbf{r}}{r^2} = \frac{1}{4\pi\varepsilon_0}\cdot\frac{pr\cos\theta}{r^2}$$

$$= \frac{1}{4\pi\varepsilon_0}\cdot\frac{pr\cos\left(\frac{\pi}{2}\right)}{r^2} \quad \left[\because \theta = \frac{\pi}{2}\right]$$

$$= 0$$

13. (a); If potential at centre is zero, then

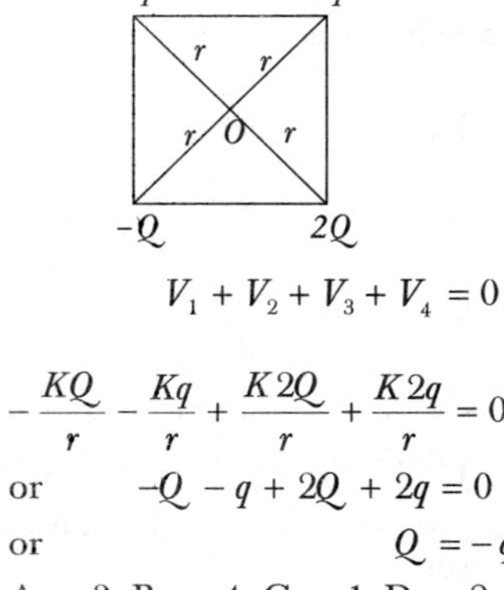

$$V_1 + V_2 + V_3 + V_4 = 0$$

$$-\frac{KQ}{r} - \frac{Kq}{r} + \frac{K2Q}{r} + \frac{K2q}{r} = 0$$

or $\quad -Q - q + 2Q + 2q = 0$

or $\quad Q = -q$

14. A $\to$ 3, B $\to$ 4, C $\to$ 1, D $\to$ 2

15. (i) ✓ (ii) ✓

16. (d) On bringing the conducting spheres in contact, the potential of the system of spheres will become equal

$$\therefore \quad V_1 = V_2$$

$$\Rightarrow \frac{Q_1}{4\pi\varepsilon_0 R_1} = \frac{Q_2}{4\pi\varepsilon_0 R_2}$$

$$\Rightarrow \frac{Q_1}{R_1} = \frac{Q_2}{R_2}$$

17. (b)

18. (b); Potential of B = Potential due to charge on A + Potential due to charge on B + Potential due to charge on C.

$$\therefore \quad V_B = \frac{K(Q_A + Q_B)}{b} + \frac{KQ_C}{c}$$

$$= \frac{1}{4\pi\varepsilon_0}\left[\frac{\sigma 4\pi a^2}{b} - \frac{\sigma 4\pi b^2}{b} + \frac{\sigma 4\pi c^2}{c}\right]$$

$$= \frac{\sigma}{\varepsilon_0}\left(\frac{a^2 - b^2}{b} + \frac{c^2}{c}\right)$$

$$= \frac{\sigma}{\varepsilon_0}\left(\frac{a^2 - b^2}{b} + c\right)$$

19. (9 cm);

O ←— x —→ P A
3×10^{-8} C $\quad -2\times10^{-8}$ C
|←— 15 cm —→|

According to question,

$$\frac{1}{4\pi\varepsilon_0}\left[\frac{3\times10^{-8}}{x\times10^{-2}} - \frac{2\times10^{-8}}{(15-x)\times10^{-2}}\right] = 0$$

$$\Rightarrow \quad \frac{3}{x} - \frac{2}{15-x} = 0$$

which gives $x = 9$ cm

20. (c); For inner surface, $\sigma = \dfrac{q_1}{4\pi R^2}$

$$\Rightarrow q_1 = (4\pi R^2)\sigma$$

For outer surface, $\sigma = \dfrac{q_2}{36\pi R^2}$

$$\Rightarrow \quad q_2 = (36\pi R^2)\sigma$$

$$V_{\text{outer}} = k\left[\frac{q_1}{3R} - \frac{q_2}{3R}\right]$$

$$= k\left[\frac{4\pi R^2\sigma}{3R} - \frac{36\pi R^2\sigma}{3R}\right]$$

$$= \frac{R}{4\varepsilon_0}\left[\frac{4\sigma}{3} - \frac{36\sigma}{3}\right]$$

$$= \frac{-8\sigma R}{3\varepsilon_0}$$

21. (3);

Charge flows from high potential to low potential,

Electric potential on smaller sphere = Electric potential on bigger sphere

$$\frac{KQ_1}{3} = \frac{KQ_2}{1}$$

$$\Rightarrow \quad Q_1 = 3Q_2 \qquad \text{...(i)}$$

$$Q_1 + Q_2 = 4\times10^{-2}$$

$$\Rightarrow \quad 4Q_2 = 4\times10^{-2}$$

$$\Rightarrow \quad Q_2 = 10^{-2} \text{ C} \qquad \text{...(ii)}$$

From Eqs. (i) and (ii), we get the final charge on the bigger sphere,

$$Q_1 = 3\times10^{-2} \text{ C}$$

$$\therefore \quad x = 3$$

22. (*c*)

23. (*b*); The electric field is maximum at *B*, because electric field is directed along decreasing potential $V_B > V_C > V_A$.

Therefore, electric potential is maximum at point *B*.

24. (*a*) **25.** uniform

26. True

27. (3);

For a uniform electric field, the equipotential surfaces are placed at right angles to the field lines.

Here, one point is above and two points are below, the shaded point are at same potential.

28. left and upward;

Electric field lines are perpendicular to the equipotential surface and point in the direction of decreasing potential. So, at point *P*, electric field **E** is to the left and at point *R*, **E** is upward.

29. (*b*); $W = q\Delta V$

Since, ΔV is same in all cases, so *W* is also same.

30. (i) Yes (ii) No **31.** (*c*)

32. (3); As, $E = \frac{V}{r}$

$$\Rightarrow \quad r = \frac{V}{E} = \frac{600}{200} = 3 \text{ m}$$

33. $(-6\hat{\mathbf{i}} - 5\hat{\mathbf{j}} - 2\hat{\mathbf{k}})$;

As, $E = -\frac{dV}{dr}$

$$= \left(\frac{-dV}{dx}\hat{\mathbf{i}} - \frac{dV}{dy}\hat{\mathbf{j}} - \frac{dV}{dz}\hat{\mathbf{k}} \right)$$

$$= -6y\hat{\mathbf{i}} - (6x - 1 + 2z)\hat{\mathbf{j}} - (2y)\hat{\mathbf{k}}$$

At (1, 1, 0),

$$E = (-6\hat{\mathbf{i}} - 5\hat{\mathbf{j}} - 2\hat{\mathbf{k}}) \text{ N/C}$$

34. (*a*); Given, $V = -x^2y - xz^3 + 4$

$$\mathbf{E} = -\frac{\partial V}{\partial r}$$

$$= \left[-\frac{\partial V}{\partial x}\hat{\mathbf{i}} - \frac{\partial V}{\partial y}\hat{\mathbf{j}} - \frac{\partial V}{\partial z}\hat{\mathbf{k}} \right]$$

$$= [(2xy + z^3)\hat{\mathbf{i}} + x^2\hat{\mathbf{j}} + 3xz^2\hat{\mathbf{k}}]$$

35. True **36.** Yes

37. (Zero);

As charges at corners *A* and *B* are at equal distance from 10 μC at the centre. So, potential at corners *A* and *B* due to 10 μC charge are equal and potential difference is zero.

∴ Work done,

$$W_{AB} = q(V_B - V_A) = 0.$$

38. (*d*); Total energy of the charge system is shown in the figure below.

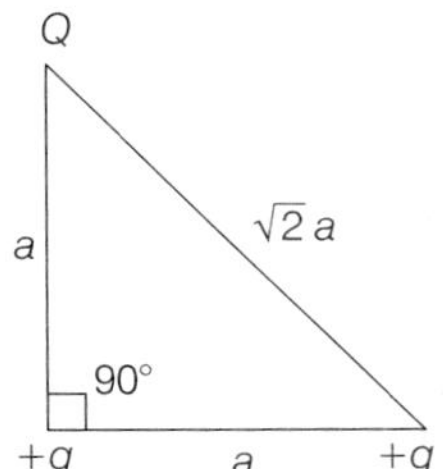

$$U = \frac{Kq^2}{a} + \frac{KQq}{a} + \frac{KQq}{\sqrt{2}a}$$

It is given that, $U = 0$

$$\therefore \quad \frac{Kq}{a}\left[q + Q + \frac{Q}{\sqrt{2}} \right] = 0$$

$$\Rightarrow \quad Q = \frac{-\sqrt{2} \times q}{(\sqrt{2} + 1)}$$

39. A → 3, B → 2, C → 4, D → 1;

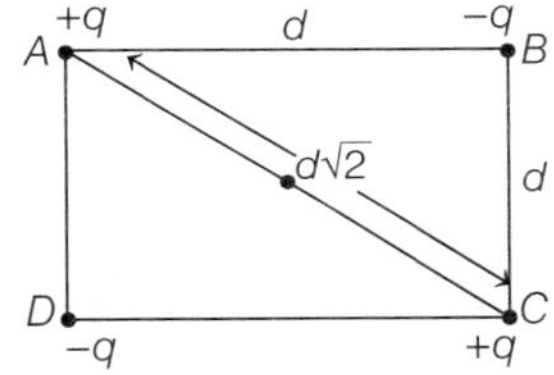

(i) Work needed to bring charge $+q$ to *A* when no charge is present elsewhere is zero. i.e. $W_A = 0$.

(ii) Work needed to bring charge $-q$ to *B* when charge $+q$ is at *A*.

$$W_B = -q \times \left(\frac{q}{4\pi\varepsilon_0 d} \right) = -\frac{q^2}{4\pi\varepsilon_0 d}$$

(iii) Work needed to bring charge $+q$ to *C* when charge $+q$ is at *A* and $-q$ is at *B*.

$$W_C = +q\left(\frac{+q}{4\pi\varepsilon_0 d\sqrt{2}} + \frac{-q}{4\pi\varepsilon_0 d} \right)$$

$$= \frac{-q^2}{4\pi\varepsilon_0 d}\left(1 - \frac{1}{\sqrt{2}} \right)$$

(iv) Work needed to bring charge $-q$ to *D* near charges $+q$ at *A*, $-q$ at *B* and charge $+q$ at *C*.

$$W_D = -q\left(\frac{+q}{4\pi\varepsilon_0 d} + \frac{-q}{4\pi\varepsilon_0 d\sqrt{2}} + \frac{q}{4\pi\varepsilon_0 d} \right)$$

$$= \frac{-q^2}{4\pi\varepsilon_0 d}\left(2 - \frac{1}{\sqrt{2}} \right)$$

40. (i) Negative (ii) Increase

41. (i) -0.7 J;

$$U = K\frac{q_1 q_2}{r} = 9 \times 10^9 \times \frac{7 \times 10^{-6} \times (-2 \times 10^{-6})}{(0.09 + 0.09)}$$

$$= -0.7 \text{ J}$$

(ii) (*a*); $W = U_2 - U_1$

$$= 0 - U = 0.7 \text{ J}$$

(iii) (49.3);

Total electrostatic energy of the system

$$= q_1 V_1 + q_2 V_2 + \frac{Kq_1 q_2}{r_{12}}$$

$$= A\left(\frac{-2 \times 10^{-6}}{0.09} \right) + A\left(\frac{7 \times 10^{-6}}{0.09} \right) + \left(\frac{-9 \times 10^9 \times 7 \times 2 \times 10^{-12}}{0.18} \right)$$

$$= \frac{9 \times 10^5 (5 \times 10^{-6})}{0.09} - 0.7 \text{ J}$$

$$= 50 \text{ J} - 0.7 = 49.3 \text{ J}$$

42. (*c*); Magnitude of torque in external electric field,

$$\tau = pE \sin\theta$$

$$20\sqrt{3} = p \times 10^6 \times \frac{1}{2}$$

So, magnitude of dipole,

$$\Rightarrow p = 40\sqrt{3} \times 10^{-6} \text{ C-m}$$

Now, the potential energy of the dipole, $U = -pE\cos\theta$

$$= -(40\sqrt{3} \times 10^{-6}) \times (10^6) \times \cos 30^\circ$$

$$= -(40\sqrt{3}) \times \frac{\sqrt{3}}{2}$$

$$= -(20 \times 3) = -60 \text{ J}$$

43. (*d*); $U = \mathbf{p} \cdot \mathbf{E} = -pE\cos\theta$

$$= -10^{-29} \times 1000 \times \cos 45^\circ$$

$$U \approx -7 \times 10^{-27} \text{ J}$$

44. (200);

$$\tau = p \times E = pE \sin\theta$$

$$= 2l \times q \times E \sin\theta$$

$$4 = 2 \times 10^{-2} \times q \times 2 \times 10^5 \times \sin 30^\circ$$

$\Rightarrow \quad q = 200$ mC

$\therefore \quad x = 200$

45. (*c*); Total dipole moment of all molecules in 1 mole of substance,

$p = 6 \times 10^{23} \times 10^{-29}$ C-m

$= 6 \times 10^{-6}$ C-m

Initial potential energy,

$U_i = -pE\cos\theta$

$= -6 \times 10^{-6} \times 10^{6} \times \cos 0°$

$= -6$ J

Final potential energy (when $\theta = 60°$),

$U_f = -6 \times 10^{-6} \times 10^{6} \times \cos 60°$

$= -3$ J

$\therefore$ Heat energy $= -\Delta U$

$(\because \Delta U = U_f - U_i)$

$= -3 - (-6) = 3$ J

46. Yes

47. (*a*); When spheres are shorted, the potential become same for both the spheres, i.e.,

$$V_1 = V_2$$

$$\frac{kq_1}{r_1} = \frac{kq_2}{r_2}$$

$$\Rightarrow \frac{q_1}{q_2} = \frac{1}{2}$$

$$\Rightarrow q_2 = 2q_1$$

Total charge $= 150 + 150 = 300\,\mu$C

$q_1 + q_2 = 300$

$\Rightarrow q_1 = 100\,\mu$C, $q_2 = 200\,\mu$C

$50\,\mu$C charge will flow from smaller to bigger sphere.

48. (i) Yes (ii) Yes (iii) (*b*)

49. zero **50.** Yes

51. coincide, permanent, Oxygen, hydrogen, non-polar, no.

52. A $\rightarrow$ 3, B $\rightarrow$ 4, C $\rightarrow$ 2, D $\rightarrow$ 1

53. (*b*)

54. (*b*)

$t = 4$mm; When d increases by 3.2; $\leftarrow d \rightarrow$; $\leftarrow d + 3.2$; $C_1 = \frac{\varepsilon_0 A}{d}$; $C_2 = \frac{\varepsilon_0 A}{d - t + \frac{t}{K}}$; $C_2' = \frac{\varepsilon_0 A}{d + 3.2 - t + \frac{t}{K}}$

$$C_1 = \frac{\varepsilon_0 A}{d}$$

$$C_2 = \frac{\varepsilon_0 A}{d - t + \dfrac{t}{K}}$$

$$C'_2 = \frac{\varepsilon_0 A}{d + 3.2 - t + t}$$

Then, $C'_2 \rightarrow$ becomes equal to C_1 (original)^k

$$\frac{\varepsilon_0 A}{d} = \frac{\varepsilon_0 A}{d + 3.2 - 4 + \dfrac{4}{K}}$$

$$d = d - 0.8 + \frac{4}{K}$$

$$\frac{4}{K} = 0.8 \Rightarrow K = \frac{4}{0.8} = 5$$

55. (*b*); When a dielectric is placed in an electric field, an electric field E_i is induced inside the dielectric in direction, opposite to the external field E, due to polarisation. On account of this, the net electric field E inside the slab is less than the external field as $E = E_0 - E_i$, i.e., the electric field inside the dielectric decrease.

56. (No); Inside the dielectric, the volume element ΔV has not net charge.

57. doubled

58. (i) Parallel plate capacitor

(ii) Zero

(iii) Zero

(iv) $\left(\dfrac{Q}{\varepsilon_0 A}\right)$;

$$E = \frac{\sigma}{2\varepsilon_0} + \frac{\sigma}{2\varepsilon_0} = \frac{\sigma}{\varepsilon_0} = \frac{Q}{\varepsilon_0 A}$$

59. decrease

60. (2);

$$F = \frac{Q^2}{2A\varepsilon_0} = \frac{C^2V^2}{2(Cd)} = \frac{CV^2}{2d}$$

61. (*A*); From the given graphs,

$$\frac{V_B}{V_A} = \frac{Q/C_B}{Q/C_A} = \frac{C_A}{C_B}$$

Since, $V_B > V_A \Rightarrow C_A > C_B$, i.e., the capacitor A has the higher capacitance than B.

62. (*b*); $Q = CV = \dfrac{\varepsilon_0 A}{d} \cdot Ed = \varepsilon_0 AE$

$= 8.85 \times 10^{-12} \times 1 \times 100$

$= 8.85 \times 10^{-10}$ C

63. (*a*);

Charge of capacitor,

$$q = \Delta q_{\text{net}} = \frac{4 - 2}{2} = 1\,\mu\text{C}$$

$\therefore$ Potential difference between capacitor plates,

$$V = \frac{Q}{C} = \frac{1\,\mu\text{C}}{1\,\mu\text{F}} = 1\text{ V}$$

64. high, high

65. (*c*); As, charge on capacitor,

$$Q = CV$$

Since, V is constant, therefore

$$Q \propto C$$

Hence, C becomes

$$\frac{100}{40} = 2.5 \text{ times}$$

$\therefore \quad k = 2.5$

66. (*a*)

67. *KC*

68. (*b*);

As, $E' = \dfrac{\sigma}{K\varepsilon_0}$

$\Rightarrow \sigma = K\varepsilon_0 \times E'$

$= 2.2 \times 8.85 \times 10^{-12} \times 3 \times 10^{4}$

$\approx 5.8 \times 10^{-7}$ Cm^{-2}

69. (*c*); $\dfrac{C_0}{C} = \dfrac{\varepsilon_0 A}{d} \times \dfrac{3d}{K\varepsilon_0 A} = \dfrac{3}{K}$

$\Rightarrow K = \dfrac{3C}{C_0} = \dfrac{3 \times 72}{18} = 12$

70. $\left(\dfrac{4K}{(K+3)} C_0\right)$;

The potential becomes

$V = \left[\begin{array}{l}\text{Potential due to} \\ \text{the empty space left } \left(d - \frac{3}{4}\right)d \\ \text{in between the plates} \\ + \text{Potential due to} \\ \text{the slab between the plates}\end{array}\right]$

$= E_0\left(\dfrac{1}{4}d\right) + \dfrac{E_0}{K}\left(\dfrac{3}{4}d\right)$

$(\because V = E \cdot dS)$

$= E_0 d\left(\dfrac{1}{4} + \dfrac{3}{4K}\right)$

$= V_0 \cdot \dfrac{K + 3}{4K}$

$\therefore$ The capacitance become

$$C = \frac{Q_0}{V} = \frac{4K}{K+3} \cdot \frac{Q_0}{V_0}$$

$$= \frac{4K}{K+3} C_0 \quad \left(\because C_0 = \frac{Q_0}{V_0}\right)$$

71. (*b*); Since, $K = \frac{C'}{C} = \frac{30}{6} = 5$

Also, $K = \frac{\varepsilon}{\varepsilon_0}$

$\Rightarrow \varepsilon = K\varepsilon_0 = 5 \times 8.854 \times 10^{-12}$

$\simeq 0.44 \times 10^{-10}\ C^2N^{-1}m^{-2}$

72. (*c*); As, charge is same in series connection.

$q_1 = q_2$

$\Rightarrow C_1V_1 = C_2V_2$

$\Rightarrow 120C_1 = 200C_2$ or $\frac{C_1}{C_2} = \frac{5}{3}$

73. $\left(\frac{2K\varepsilon_0 A}{(K+1)d}\right)$;

Here, $C_1 = \frac{K\varepsilon_0 A}{d/2}$ and $C_2 = \frac{\varepsilon_0 A}{d/2}$

$\therefore \quad C_{net} = \frac{C_1C_2}{C_1 + C_2}$

$= \frac{\left(\frac{2K\varepsilon_0 A}{d}\right)\left(\frac{2\varepsilon_0 A}{d}\right)}{\left(\frac{2K\varepsilon_0 A}{d} + \frac{2\varepsilon_0 A}{d}\right)}$

$= \frac{2KA\varepsilon_0}{(K+1)d}$

74. (*a*); They are connected in parallel combination, so positive charge will cancel out the negative charge.

75. (3);

It forms three capacitors in parallel connection, so

$C_p = C_1 + C_2 + C_3 = \frac{3\varepsilon_0 A}{d}$

$\therefore \quad n = 3$

76. (i) 10 μF (ii) 4 μF (iii) 13.44 μF

77. Yes;

$C' = 20 + 20 + 20 = 60\ \mu F$

$\therefore \quad \frac{1}{C''} = \frac{1}{C} + \frac{1}{C'}$

$\Rightarrow \quad \frac{1}{30} = \frac{1}{C} + \frac{1}{60}$

$\Rightarrow \quad C = 60\ \mu F$

78. (9090);

Charge, $q = nCV$

$1 = n \times 1 \times 10^{-6} \times 110$

$n = \frac{1}{110 \times 10^{-6}}$

$\Rightarrow \quad n = \frac{100000}{11} \approx 9090$

79. (*b*); The points *C* and *D* will be at same potentials.

$C_1 = \frac{3 \times 6}{3 + 6} = 2\ \mu F$

$C_2 = \frac{4 \times 8}{4 + 8} = \frac{8}{3}\ \mu F$

Resultant capacitance,

$C = C_1 + C_2$

$= 2 + \frac{8}{3} = \frac{14}{3}\ \mu F$

80 (2 μF);

The given combination forms a GP,

$s = 1 + \frac{1}{2} + \frac{1}{4} + \frac{1}{8} + \ldots$

Sum of infinite GP,

$s = \frac{a}{1 - r}$

$\Rightarrow \quad s = \frac{1}{1 - \frac{1}{2}} \Rightarrow s = \frac{1}{\frac{1}{2}}$

$\therefore \quad s = 2$

Hence, capacitance of the combination,

$C_\infty = 2 \times 1\ \mu F = 2\ \mu F$

81. Yes;

$C' = 3 + 6 = 9\ \mu F$

$C = \frac{9 \times 4.5}{9 + 4.5} = 3\ \mu F$

As, $q = CV = 3 \times 12 = 36\ \mu C$

$\therefore$ Potential difference across 4.5 μF,

$V' = \frac{q}{4.5} = \frac{36}{4.5} = 8\ V$

82. A → 1, B → 4, C → 3, D → 2;

A. When *S* is open, then

$C_{eq} = \frac{C_1 C_2}{C_1 + C_2}$

$= \frac{(2\mu F)(3\mu F)}{(2\mu F + 3\mu F)} = \frac{6}{5}\ \mu F$

Charge *q* on both the capacitors will be the same (as these are in series), i.e.

$q = C_{eq}\ V$

$= \left(\frac{6}{5}\ \mu F\right)(30 + 60)\ V$

$= 108\ \mu C$

B. Charge on C_2, i.e.

$q_2 = C_2V_2 = (3\mu F)(60\ V)$

$= 180\ \mu C$

C. When *S* is closed, charge on C_1, i.e.

$q_1 = C_1V_1 = (2\mu F)(30\ V)$

$= 60\ \mu C$

D. Charge on C_1 and C_2

$= 60\ \mu C + 180 = 240\ \mu C$

83. (i) (13.3 μF);

$\frac{1}{C'} = \frac{1}{C_1} + \frac{1}{C_2} + \frac{1}{C_3}$

$= \frac{1}{10} + \frac{1}{10} + \frac{1}{10}$

$\Rightarrow \quad C' = \frac{10}{3}\ \mu F$

$\therefore \quad C = C' + C_4$

$= \frac{10}{3} + 10 = 13.3\ \mu F$

(ii) (5×10^{-3} C);

Charge on C_1, C_2 and C_3 is same, $Q = CV$

$= \frac{10}{3} \times 10^{-6} \times 500$

$= 1.7 \times 10^{-3}\ C$

Charge on C_4,

$Q' = C_4V$

$= 10 \times 10^{-6} \times 500$

$= 5 \times 10^{-3}\ C$

84. (*c*); $U = \frac{1}{2}CV^2 = \frac{1}{2} \times \frac{A\varepsilon_0}{d} \times (Ed)^2$

$= \frac{1}{2}\varepsilon_0 E^2 Ad$

85. (II and IV);

$\because V = \frac{q}{KC}$ and $U = \frac{1}{2}\frac{q^2}{KC}$

86. (4.5×10^{-6} J);

The energy stored by the capacitor $= (1/2)CV^2$

$= 1/2 \times 900 \times 10^{-12} \times (100)^2$

$= 4.5 \times 10^{-6}\ J$

87. (2.25);

Here, $Q' = \frac{Q}{2}$ and $V' = \frac{V}{2}$

$\therefore$ Energy stored

$$= 2 \times \frac{1}{2} Q'V' = \frac{1}{4} \times Q \times V$$

$$= \frac{1}{4} \times CV^2$$

$$= \frac{1}{4} \times 900 \times 10^{-12} \times (100)^2$$

$$= 2.25 \times 10^{-6} \text{ J}$$

$\therefore x = 2.25$

88. (*b*)

89. (50);

When C_1 is connected to voltage source, $U = \frac{1}{2} CV^2$

When key is connected between *b* and *c*, redistribution of charge takes place.

The loss of energy due to redistribution of charge is given by

$$\Delta U = \frac{C_1 C_2}{2(C_1 + C_2)} (V_1 - V_2)^2$$

According to the question,

$$C_1 = C_2 = C = \frac{C \times C}{2(C + C)} (V - 0)^2$$

$$\Delta U = \frac{1}{4} CV^2$$

$$\therefore \text{Percentage loss} = \frac{\Delta U}{U} \times 100$$

$$= \frac{\frac{1}{4} CV^2}{\frac{1}{2} CV^2} \times 100 = 50\%$$

$\therefore \quad n = 50$

Assertion-Reason Questions

1. (*b*); Potential energy of a system of two charges, $U = K \frac{q_1 q_2}{r}$.

$\therefore$ When two positive point charges move away from other then their potential energy decreases and work done by F can always be expressed in terms of a potential energy.

2. (*a*)

3. (*a*); Charge present on a conductor determines its potential. Capacity is a function of size and shape of the conductor and of the surrounding medium.

Capacitance in case of parallel plate capacitor is $C = \frac{K\varepsilon_0 A}{d}$,

where K is dielectric constant of medium, A is area of plates and d is the distance between two plates.

4. (*b*); A conductor has free electrons. As long as electric field is not zero, the free charge carrier would experience force and drift. In the static situation, the free charges have so distributed themselves that the electric field is zero everywhere inside. Hence, electrostatic field is zero inside a conductor.

5. (*a*); Since, $\quad V = \frac{KQ}{R}$

$$\Rightarrow \quad \frac{V_1}{V_2} = \frac{R_2}{R_1} \left(\frac{Q_1}{Q_2} \right)$$

As, $\quad V_1 = V_2$

$$R_1 = R_2$$

$$\Rightarrow \quad Q_1 = Q_2$$

6. (*b*); A material containing polar molecules, they will generally be in random orientations when no electric field is applied. An applied field will polarize the material by orienting the dipole moment of polar molecules.

7. (*a*); The molcules of the dielectric are polarised, which produces an opposite electric field. Thus, the effective field and the potential difference between the plates is reduced and consequently the capacitance is increased.

8. (*b*); $C = \frac{\varepsilon_0 k A}{d}$

$$\Rightarrow \quad C \propto \frac{k}{d}$$

$$\therefore \quad \frac{C_1}{C_2} = \frac{k_1}{d_1} \times \frac{d_1}{k_2}$$

$$= \frac{k}{d} \times \frac{\frac{d}{2}}{3k} = \frac{1}{6}$$

$$C_2 = 6C_1$$

Again for capacity of a capacitor,

$$C = \frac{k\varepsilon_0 A}{d}$$

Therefore, capacity of a capacitor depends upon the medium between two plates of capacitor.

9. (*b*);The quantity of charge that can be given to a capacitor is limited by the fact that every dielectric is limited by the dielectric strength of medium between the plates. The dielectric strength is maximum value of electric field that it can tolerate without breakdown. Beyond this field, the dielectric no more behaves as dielectric but it conduct electricity.

10. (*c*); Energy stored in the capacitor,

$$U' = \frac{1}{2} C' V'^2$$

$$= \frac{1}{2} (KC)(V^2)$$

$$= \left(\frac{1}{2} CV^2 \right) K = KU$$

Surface charge density,

$$\sigma' = \frac{q'}{A} = \frac{C'V'}{A}$$

$$= \frac{KCV}{A}$$

$$= K \cdot \frac{q}{A} = K\sigma$$

Case Based Questions

1. (i) (*b*); Potential due to a charge q at a distance r is,

$$V = \frac{1}{4\pi\varepsilon_0} \cdot \frac{q}{r}$$

Potential at the centre of the square due to four equal charges q at four corners will be,

$$V = \frac{4q}{4\pi\varepsilon_0 \frac{(a\sqrt{2})}{2}}$$

$$= \frac{2q}{\sqrt{2}\, \pi\varepsilon_0 a}$$

$$= \frac{\sqrt{2}q}{\pi\varepsilon_0 a}$$

Work done in carrying a charge $-q$ from its centre to infinity is,

$$W_{0 \to \infty} = -W_{\infty \to 0}$$

$$= -(-q)\, V = \frac{\sqrt{2}\, q^2}{\pi\varepsilon_0 a}$$

(ii) (*c*); Given,

Charge $q = 2\,\mu C = 2 \times 10^{-6}$ C

$r_A = 2$ m and $r_B = 1$ m

$r_A = 2$m $r_B = 1$m

$+2\mu$C

So, the potential difference between points A and B is,

$$V_A - V_B = \frac{q}{4\pi\varepsilon_0}\left[\frac{1}{r_A} - \frac{1}{r_B}\right]$$

$$= 2 \times 10^{-6} \times 9 \times 10^9 \left[\frac{1}{2} - \frac{1}{1}\right]$$

$$\Delta V = -9 \times 10^3 \text{ V}$$

(iii) (*b*); Given, $q_A = +3$ nC and $q_B = +1$ nC

$r_{AB} = 5$ cm $= 5 \times 10^{-2}$ m

Work done = Change in potential energy of the system

$$W = U_f - U_i$$

$$= \frac{q_A q_B}{4\pi\varepsilon_0 r_f} - \frac{q_A q_B}{4\pi\varepsilon_0 r_i}$$

$$= \frac{q_A q_B}{4\pi\varepsilon_0}\left[\frac{1}{r_f} - \frac{1}{r_i}\right]$$

$$\therefore \quad W = 9 \times 10^9 \times 3 \times 10^{-9}) \times 1 \times 10^{-9} \times \left[\frac{1}{4 \times 10^{-2}} - \frac{1}{5 \times 10^{-2}}\right]$$

$$= 27 \times 10^{-7} \times 0.05$$

$$= 1.35 \times 10^{-7}\text{J}$$

(iv) (*d*); $W = qV$

$$= 5 \times 16 = 80 \text{ J}$$

2. (i) (*a*);

$$K = \frac{\text{Capacitance with dielectric}}{\text{Capacitance without dielectric}}$$

$$K = \frac{50\,\mu\text{F}}{5\,\mu\text{F}} = 10$$

(ii) (*d*); Capacitance of the capacitor with air between plates is $C' = \frac{\varepsilon_0 A}{d} = 10$ pF.

With the capacitor is filled with dielectric ($K = 5$) between its plates and the distance between the plates is reduced by half, capacitance become

$$C = \frac{\varepsilon_0 KA}{\frac{d}{2}} = \frac{\varepsilon_0 \times 5 \times A}{\frac{d}{2}}$$

$$= \frac{10\varepsilon_0 A}{d} = 10 \times 10 = 100 \text{ pF}$$

(iii) (*a*); If a dielectric medium of dielectric constant K is filled completely between the plates, then capacitance increases by K times.

(iv) (*c*); We know that, the charge on a capacitor is given as

$$Q = CV$$

For a capacitor charged by a battery with V volts will have the charge as

$$Q_1 = C_1 V \quad \text{...(i)}$$

When dielectric inserted

$$Q_2 = C_2 V \text{ where } C_2 = KC_1 \quad \text{...(ii)}$$

$$Q_1 = Q_2$$

Hence, from Eqs. (i) and (ii), we get

$$V_2 = \frac{V}{K}$$

Competition Edge Up

1. (*d*); Electric potential due to electric dipole is given by

$$V = \frac{1}{4\pi\varepsilon_0} \cdot \frac{p\cos\theta}{r^2}$$

where p is dipole moment.

$$\Rightarrow \quad V \propto \frac{1}{r^2}$$

2. (*b*); Potential due to a point charge, $V = \frac{kq}{r}$.

Here, $OP = \sqrt{(\sqrt{3})^2 + (\sqrt{3})^2} = \sqrt{6}$

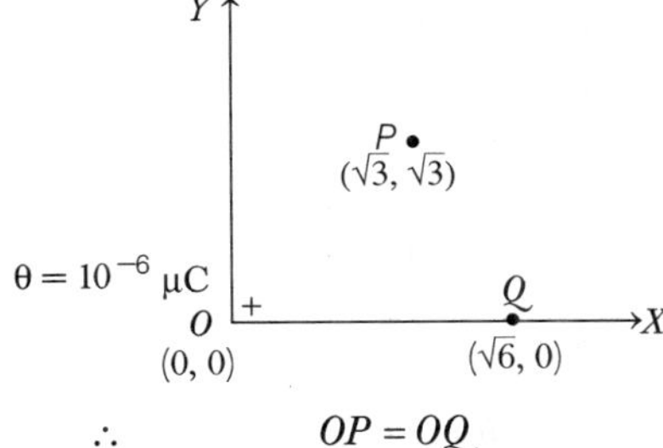

$$\therefore \quad OP = OQ$$

$$\Rightarrow \quad V_P = V_Q$$

Hence, $V_P - V_Q = 0$

3. (*b*);

C, V C, 2V

$$V_C = \frac{Q_1 + Q_2}{C_1 + C_2}$$

$$= \frac{CV + 2CV}{C + C} = \frac{3V}{2}$$

Loss of energy = Initial energy − Final energy

$$= \frac{1}{2}CV^2 + \frac{1}{2}C(2V)^2 - \frac{1}{2}(C + C)\left(\frac{3V}{2}\right)^2$$

$$= \frac{1}{4}CV^2$$

4. (*a*); Given combination of capacitors represent Wheatstone bridge, thus central capacitor can be removed.

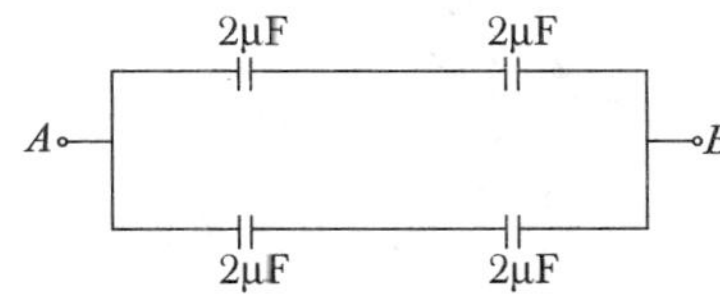

Capacitance of each branch,

$$C = \frac{2}{2} = 1\,\mu\text{F}$$

Capacitance between A and B,

$C_{net} = 1 + 1 = 2\,\mu$F

5. (*d*); Since, there is no electric field inside the shell the potential at any point inside the shell is equal to the potential on the surface of the shell i.e.

$$V = \frac{1}{4\pi\varepsilon_0} \cdot \frac{q}{r}$$

$$V_C - V_P = 0$$

6. (*d*); Equivalent capacitance of the system,

$$C_{AB} = \frac{3 \times (3 + 3)}{3 + (3 + 3)} = \frac{18}{9} = 2\,\mu\text{F}$$

7. (*a*); Potential on the hollow conducting sphere,

$$V = \frac{1}{4\pi\varepsilon_0} \cdot \frac{Q}{R}$$

$$\Rightarrow \quad V \propto \frac{1}{R} \quad \text{[For same charge } Q\text{]}$$

$$\Rightarrow \quad \frac{V_1}{V_2} = \frac{R_2}{R_1}$$

Since, $\quad R_1 > R_2$

$$\therefore \quad \frac{R_2}{R_1} < 1$$

$$\therefore \quad \frac{V_1}{V_2} < 1$$

$$\therefore \quad V_1 < V_2$$

8. (*c*);

C_1 C_2 C_3 C_4

$$C_1 = \frac{K_1\varepsilon_0 A}{3\frac{d}{2}} = \frac{2K_1\varepsilon_0 A}{3d}$$

$$C_2 = \frac{K_2\varepsilon_0 A}{3\frac{d}{2}} = \frac{2K_2\varepsilon_0 A}{3d}$$

$$C_3 = \frac{K_3\varepsilon_0 A}{3\frac{d}{2}} = \frac{2K_3\varepsilon_0 A}{3d}$$

$$C' = C_1 + C_2 + C_3 = \frac{2K_1\varepsilon_0 A}{3d} + \frac{2K_2\varepsilon_0 A}{3d} + \frac{2K_3\varepsilon_0 A}{3d} = \frac{2\varepsilon_0 A}{3d}(K_1 + K_2 + K_3)$$

$$C_4 = \frac{K_4\varepsilon_0 A}{\frac{d}{2}}$$

$$\frac{1}{C_{eq}} = \frac{1}{C'} + \frac{1}{C_4}$$

$$\frac{1}{\frac{K\varepsilon_0 A}{d}} = \frac{1}{\frac{2\varepsilon_0 A}{3d}(K_1 + K_2 + K_3)} + \frac{1}{\frac{K_4\varepsilon_0 A}{\frac{d}{2}}}$$

$$\frac{1}{K} = \frac{3}{2(K_1 + K_2 + K_3)} + \frac{1}{2K_4}$$

$$\frac{2}{K} = \frac{3}{(K_1 + K_2 + K_3)} + \frac{1}{K_4}$$

Option (c) is correct.

Chapter-3

Current Electricity

1. (*d*)

2. (*c*); We have, $i = \frac{dq}{dt} = 3t^2 + 2t + 5$

$$\Rightarrow dq = (3t^2 + 2t + 5)dt$$

$$\therefore q = \int_0^2 (3t^2 + 2t + 5)\, dt = \left(\frac{3t^3}{3} + \frac{2t^2}{2} + 5t\right)^2 = [t^3 + t^2 + 5t]_0^2 = 22\text{ C}$$

3. (*b*); $I = 4 - 0.08\, t$

$$\Rightarrow \frac{dq}{dt} = 4 - 0.08\, t$$

$$\Rightarrow q = \int_0^{50} (4 - 0.08t)\, dt$$

$$\Rightarrow Ne = \left[4t - \frac{0.08t^2}{2}\right]_0^{50} = 100\text{ C}$$

$$\Rightarrow N = \frac{100}{e} = \frac{100}{1.6 \times 10^{-19}} = 6.25 \times 10^{20}$$

4. (i) ✓ (ii) ✓ (iii) ✓

5. (*d*)

6. Yes

7. False

8. (*c*); When slab is cut as per the question, length l remains same, but area of cross-section becomes $\frac{A}{2}$.

Since, $R \propto \frac{l}{A}$. Therefore, resistance of each half,

$$R' \propto \frac{l}{A'}$$

$$\Rightarrow R' \propto \frac{l}{\frac{A}{2}}$$

$$\Rightarrow R' \propto 2\left(\frac{l}{A}\right)$$

$$\Rightarrow R' = 2R$$

9. (*b*); $m_1 = m_2$

$$\Rightarrow \rho_1 V_1 = \rho_2 V_2$$

$$\Rightarrow V_1 = V_2$$

or $A_1 l_1 = A_2 l_2$

According to question,

$$A_1 \times 10 = A_2 \times 20$$

$$\Rightarrow \frac{A_1}{A_2} = \frac{2}{1}$$

Since, $R \propto \frac{l}{A}$

$$\Rightarrow \frac{R_A}{R_B} = \frac{l_1}{A_1} \times \frac{A_2}{l_2} = \frac{l_1}{l_2} \times \frac{A_2}{A_1} = \frac{10}{20} \times \frac{1}{2} = \frac{1}{4}$$

$$\therefore x = 4$$

10. (1 : 1);

According to the question, $R_1 = R_2$

$$\rho\frac{l}{A_1} = \rho\frac{l}{A_2}$$

$$\Rightarrow \frac{A_1}{A_2} = 1:1$$

11. (n^2);

New resistance,

$$R' = n^2 R$$

12. (5);

As we know,

$$J = \sigma E = 5 \times 10^7 \times 10 \times 10^{-3} = 50 \times 10^4 \text{ A/m}^2$$

and $I = J \times \pi r^2$

$$= 50 \times 10^4 \times \pi \times (0.5)^2 \times 10^{-6} = 125\pi \times 10^{-3}\text{ A or } (5)^3\pi \text{ mA}$$

13. electrons, independent, time

14. A → 3, B → 4, C → 1, D → 2

15. (*a*); We know that, $E \propto \frac{1}{r^2}$ ...(i)

and $v_d = \frac{eE\tau}{m}$

or $v_d \propto E$ ...(ii)

From Eqs. (i) and (ii), we can say that, if r decreases, E will increase and due to this, v_d will also increase.

16. (*d*) As the temperatures increases, the KE of electron increases, so the thermal velocity will increase. Due to increase in number of collision the drift velocity will decrease.

17. (1.1 mms^{-1});

Number of copper atoms per m^3,

$$n = \frac{N_A}{\text{atomic mass}} \times \text{density} = \frac{6.0 \times 10^{23}}{63.5 \times 10^{-3}} \times 9.0 \times 10^3 = 8.5 \times 10^{28}$$

$$\therefore v_d = \frac{I}{neA} = \frac{1.5}{8.5 \times 10^{28} \times 1.6 \times 10^{-19} \times 1 \times 10^{-7}} = 1.1 \text{ mm s}^{-1}$$

18. (*c*); $\therefore i = nAev_d$

or $v_d = \frac{i}{nAe}$

Total number of free electrons in the unit length of conductor,

$$N = nA \times 1$$

Total linear momentum of all the free electrons per unit length

$$= (Nm)\, v_d = nAm \times \frac{i}{nAe} = \frac{i}{(e/m)} = \frac{i}{s}$$

19. (c) **20.** Yes

21. False **22.** (a)

23. A → 3, B → 2, C → 1

24. Mobility, $m^2/V\text{-s}$, 10^4

25. I

26. (c); $\mu = \frac{e\tau}{m}$, so μ is independent of E.

27. Electron mobility is given by

$$\mu = \frac{v_d}{E} = \frac{v_d}{\frac{V}{l}} \Rightarrow \mu \propto \frac{1}{V}$$

Hence for the constant length and temperature of conductor, if the potential difference is doubled, mobility will be halved.

28. For good conductor,

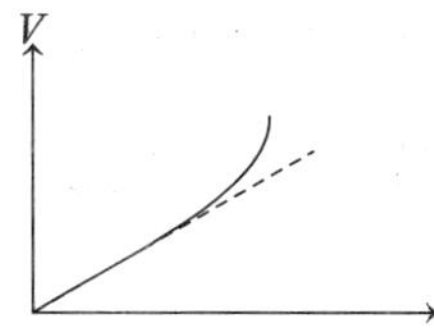

29. CD **30.** No

31. (c) **32.** (d)

33. resistivities, increasing, Metals, low, $10^{-8}\,\Omega\text{-m}$.

34. (d)

35. (1×10^{-7});

Resistivity only depends on the nature of the material.

36. (i) ✓ (ii) ✓

37. (increases);

Resistivity increase in metals with temperature.

38. (b); The resistance will changes as

$$R' = (1.1)^2 R = 1.21R$$

39. (b); Variation of resistance with temperature is given by

$$\Rightarrow \quad R = R_0(1 + \alpha\Delta T)$$

Now,

$$\frac{R_2}{R_1} = \frac{R_0[1 + \alpha\,(T_2 - 0)]}{R_0\,[1 + \alpha\,(T_1 - 0)]} = \frac{(1 + \alpha T_2)}{(1 + \alpha T_1)}$$

Given, $R_2 = 2R_1$ and $T_1 = 0$

So, $\quad 2 = 1 + \alpha T_2 \Rightarrow T_2 = \frac{1}{\alpha}$

$$= \frac{1}{(4 \times 10^{-3})} = 250°\text{C}$$

40. I

41. (a)

42.

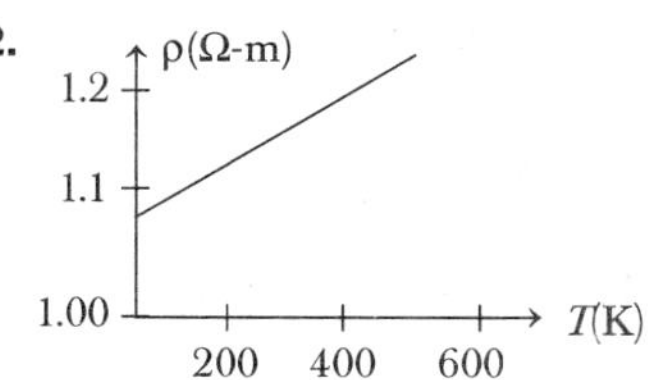

43. (c)

44. semiconductor

45. decrease

46. (b); The equation $R = R_0(1 + \alpha\Delta T)$ is not valid in all the cases.

For $R = R_i(1 + \alpha\Delta T)$ to be true, the temperature change ΔT is small and $\Delta R = (R - R_0) << R_0$.

47. (T_1);

Resistance of metal increases with rise in temperature and the slope of given graph gives inverse of resistance.

$\therefore \quad R_2 > R_1$ and $T_2 > T_1$.

48. (848.8);

As, $R_2 = \frac{230\text{ V}}{2.68\text{ A}} = 85.8\Omega$

Using $R_2 = R_1[1 + \alpha(T_2 - T_1)]$, we get

$$T_2 - T_1 = \frac{85.8 - 75.3}{(75.3) \times 1.7 \times 10^{-4}} = 821.8°\text{C}$$

Therefore, $T_2 = (821.8 + 27)°\text{C}$

$$= 848.8°\text{C}$$

49. (Yes);

We know that, $R_t = R_0(1 + \alpha t)$

$$\Rightarrow \quad t = \frac{R_t - R_0}{R_{100} - R_0} \times 100$$

$$= \frac{5.795 - 5}{5.23 - 5} \times 100$$

$$= 345.65°\text{C}$$

50. (a); Power is given by

$$P = \frac{V^2}{R} = \frac{(200)^2}{100} = 400\text{ W}$$

Energy spent = Power × time

$$= 400 \times 2 = 800\text{Wh}$$

51. (a); Heat produced, $H = \frac{V^2 t}{R}$

$$\Rightarrow H = \frac{V^2 tA}{\rho l} \left(\text{We knows } R = \frac{\rho l}{A}\right)$$

From above equation,

$$\Rightarrow \quad t \propto l \Rightarrow \frac{t_2}{t_1} = \frac{l_2}{l_1}$$

$$\Rightarrow \quad \frac{t_2}{20} = \frac{\frac{7}{4} l_1}{l_1}$$

$$\Rightarrow \quad t_2 = \frac{7}{4} \times 20 = 35\text{ min}$$

52. (c); Power, $P = \frac{V^2}{R}$

$$\therefore \quad R = \frac{V^2}{P} \text{ or } R \propto V^2$$

$$i.e. \ \frac{R_1}{R_2} = \left[\frac{200}{300}\right]^2 = \frac{4}{9}$$

When connected in series, then potential drop and power consumed are in the ratio of their resistances. So,

$$\frac{P_1}{P_2} = \frac{V_1}{V_2} = \frac{R_1}{R_2} = \frac{4}{9}$$

53. (b); $P = \frac{V^2}{R}$

$$\Rightarrow \quad R = \frac{V^2}{P} = \frac{220 \times 220}{100}$$

$$R = 484\ \Omega$$

The voltage drops by 5% of its rated value,

$$V' = 220 - (5\% \text{ of } 220)$$

$$= 220 - \frac{5 \times 220}{100} = 209\text{ V}$$

New power, $P' = \frac{(V')^2}{R}$

$$= \frac{209 \times 209}{484} = 90.25$$

Now, % decrease in power

$$= \frac{(100 - P')}{100} \times 100$$

$$= 100 - 90.25$$

$$= 9.75\% \approx 10\%$$

54. (d); $\therefore$

$$\frac{P_{200}}{P_{800}} = \frac{\frac{V^2}{R_{200}}}{\frac{V^2}{R_{800}}} = \frac{R_{800}}{R_{200}}$$

$$= \frac{R_{200}\,(1 + \alpha\Delta T)}{R_{200}}$$

$\Rightarrow P_{200} = P_{800} \times (1 + 4 \times 10^{-4} \times 600)$

$= 500\,(1 + 4 \times 10^{-4} \times 600)$

$= 620$ W

55. (*b*); Distance between two cities, $d = 150$ km

Fall of potential per km, $V = 8$ V

Average resistance per km, $R = 0.5\,\Omega$

Power loss per km,

$$P_1 = \frac{V^2}{R} = \frac{8^2}{0.5} = 128 \text{ W}$$

$\therefore$ Total power loss in wire

$= P_1 \times d = 128 \times 150$

$= 19200$ W

$= 19.2$ kW

56. (*c*); Resistance of bulb,

$$R = \frac{V^2}{P} = \frac{(230)^2}{100} = 529\ \Omega$$

When the voltage drops to 115 V, heat and light energy produced by the bulb in 20 min is given by

$$W = \frac{V^2}{R}t = \frac{(115)^2}{529} \times 20 \times 60$$

$= 30000$ J

57. two, positive, negative, electrolytic, charges

58. (*c*); $V = E - ir$

$$= E - \left(\frac{E}{R + r}\right) r$$

$$= E\left(\frac{R}{R + r}\right) = \frac{E}{1 + \dfrac{r}{R}}$$

59. (*d*); Equivalent internal resistance of parallel connection,

$$R_{\text{int}} = \frac{r_1 r_2}{r_1 + r_2}$$

$$\therefore R_{\text{int}} = \frac{1 \times 2}{1 + 2} = \frac{2}{3}\ \Omega$$

Equivalent emf of cell in parallel connection,

$$E_{\text{eq}} = \left(\frac{E_1}{r_1} + \frac{E_2}{r_2}\right) R_{\text{int}}$$

$$\therefore E_{\text{eq}} = \left(\frac{2}{1} + \frac{1}{2}\right)\frac{2}{3} = \frac{5}{3}\text{ V}$$

Now, total resistance in the circuit

$R_{\text{Total}} = R_{\text{ext}} + R_{\text{int}}$

$$R_{\text{total}} = \frac{4}{3} + \frac{2}{3} = \frac{6}{3} = 2\ \Omega$$

Current through external resistor,

$$I = \frac{V}{R} = \frac{\frac{5}{3}}{2} = \frac{5}{6}\text{ A}$$

60. True

61. $I = \dfrac{E}{R}$, $R = 0$

62. (*c*); $i = \dfrac{2+2}{1 + 1.9 + 0.9} = \dfrac{4}{3.8}$ A

For cell A, $E = V + ir$

$V = E - ir$

$= 2 - \dfrac{4}{3.8} \times 1.9$

$V = 0$ (zero)

63. (*b*)

64. (Yes); $I = I_1 + I_2$

$V = E_1 - I_1 r_1$

$$I_1 = \frac{E_1 - V}{r_1}$$

Similarly, $I_2 = \dfrac{E_2 - V}{r_2}$

Putting values of I_1 and I_2 in Eq. (i), we get

$$V = \frac{E_1 r_2 + E_2 r_1}{r_1 r_2} - I\left(\frac{r_2 + r_1}{r_1 r_2}\right)$$

65. $\dfrac{E_1 r_2 + E_2 r_1}{r_1 + r_2}$

66. (*c*); Equivalent emf of the combination, $E_{\text{eq}} = nE$

Equivalent internal resistance,

$r_{\text{eq}} = nr$

$$\therefore \text{Current, } I = \frac{E_{\text{eq}}}{r_{\text{eq}}} = \frac{E}{r} = \text{constant}$$

67. (*c*); Out of n cells, two cells will cancel out each others emf. So, net emf $= (n - 2)\,E$

Total resistance $= R + nr$

$$\text{Current, } i = \frac{(n-2)\,E}{nr + R}$$

68. (*d*); Applying Kirchhoff's law at point D, we get

$I_1 = I_2 + I_3$

$$\frac{V_A - V_D}{10} = \frac{V_D - V_B}{20} + \frac{V_D - V_C}{30}$$

$\Rightarrow \quad V_D = 40$ V

$$\Rightarrow \quad i_1 = \frac{70 - 40}{10} = 3\text{ A}$$

$$i_2 = \frac{40 - 0}{20} = 2\text{ A}$$

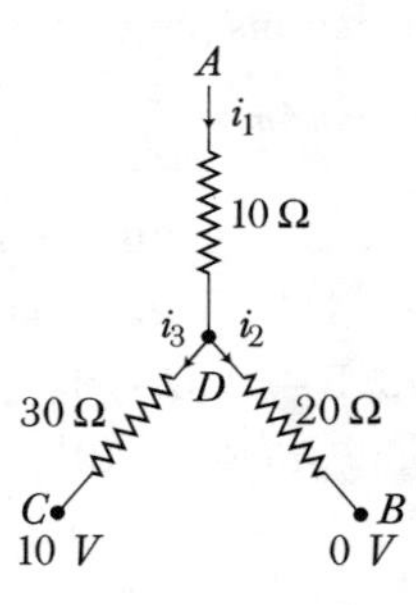

and $\quad i_3 = \dfrac{40 - 10}{30} = 1$ A

69. (0.2);

According to KCL, $\Sigma I = 0$

$0.4 - 0.6 + 0.5 - 0.7 + I + 0.2 = 0$

$\Rightarrow \quad I - 0.2 = 0$

$\Rightarrow \quad I = +\,0.2$ A

70. (*a*); Let the potential at junction C, is V.

Applying Kirchhoff's junction law at C

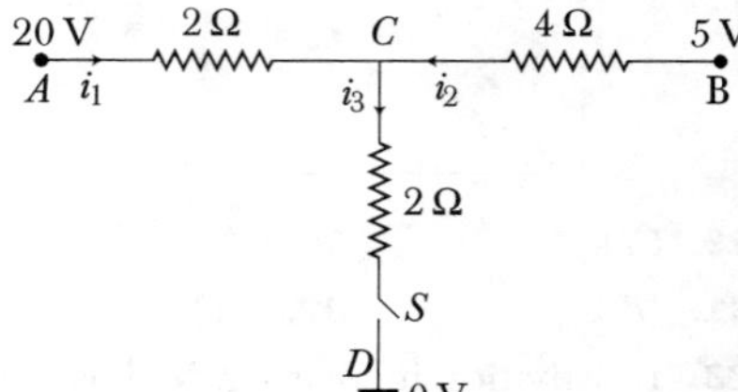

$$\text{or} \quad \frac{V_A - V_C}{4} + \frac{V_B - V_C}{4} = \frac{V_C - V_D}{2}$$

$$\text{or} \quad \frac{20 - V}{4} + \frac{5 - V}{4} = \frac{V - 0}{2}$$

or $\quad 5V = 45$

$\therefore \quad V = 9$ V

$\therefore$ Current through switch S,

$$i_3 = \frac{9}{2} = 4.5\text{ A}$$

71. ($5\,\Omega$, $5\,\Omega$);

In circuit (i),

$1 \times 1 - 10 + 1 \times R + 4 \times 1 = 0$

$\Rightarrow R = 5\,\Omega$

In circuit (ii),

$3 \times 1 - 12 + 1 \times R + 4 \times 1 = 0$

$\Rightarrow R = 5\,\Omega$

72. (1A);

From graph, slope between 3s to 4s is 5

At $t = 3.2$ s,

$$V = 5 + (0.2 \times 5) = 6 \text{ V}$$

Therefore, the circuit diagram is given by

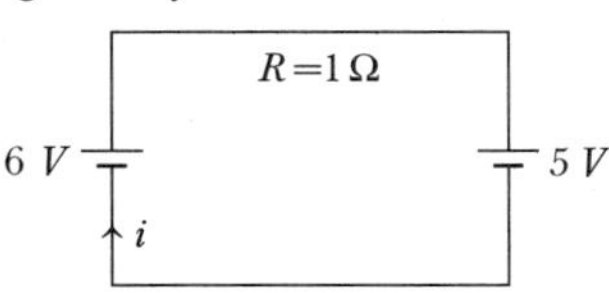

$\therefore$ Current, $i = \dfrac{6\text{ V} - 5\text{ V}}{1\,\Omega} = 1\text{ A}$

73. (1A from a to b through e);

$E_1(10\text{V}) > E_2(4\text{V})$. So, applying KVL in clockwise direction,

$$-1 \times i + 10 - 4 - 2 \times i - 3 \times i = 0$$

$$\Rightarrow i = 1\text{ A}$$

74. (c); In loop 1,

$$+6 - 3i_1 + i_2 - i_1 = 0$$

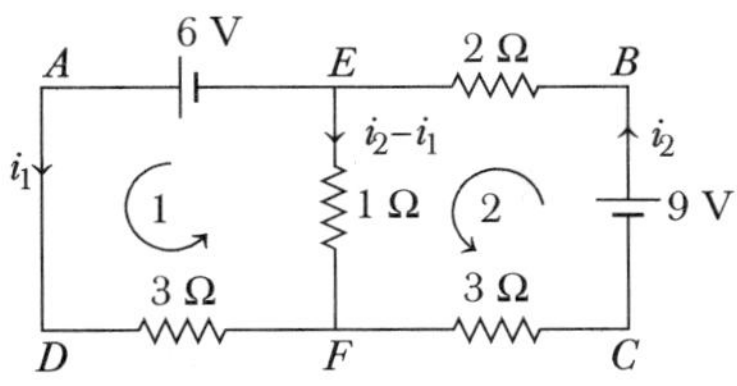

$\Rightarrow 4i_1 - i_2 = 6$ ...(i)

In loop 2, $+9 - 5i_2 - i_2 + i_1 = 0$

$\Rightarrow 6i_2 - i_1 = 9$ ...(ii)

From Eqs. (i) and (ii), we get

$$i_2 = 1.82\text{A}, \; i_1 = 1.955\text{ A}$$

Therefore, current in 1 Ω resistor

$$= 1.955 - 1.82 = 0.13\text{ A}$$

75. (i) $\left(\dfrac{5}{6}R\right)$;

The paths AA', AD and AB are symmetric.

In a closed loop $ABCC'EA$,

$$IR + \frac{1}{2}IR + IR - E = 0$$

$$\Rightarrow 2IR + \frac{IR}{2} = E \Rightarrow E = \frac{5}{2}IR$$

Equivalent resistance (R_{eq})

$$= \frac{E}{3I} = \frac{5}{6}R$$

(ii) (4A);

For $R = 1\Omega$, $R_{eq} = \dfrac{5}{6}\Omega$

and $E = 10$ V

Total current $= 3I = 10\text{V}/\dfrac{5}{6}\,\Omega$

$$= 12\text{ A} \Rightarrow I = 4\text{A}$$

76. $\left(\dfrac{5}{8}\text{A}, 2\dfrac{1}{2}\text{A}, 1\dfrac{7}{8}\text{A}, 0\text{A}, 2\dfrac{1}{2}\text{A}\right)$

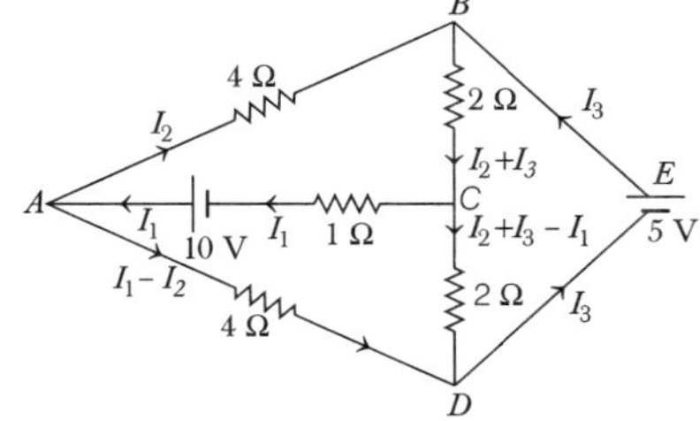

Applying Kirchhoff's second rule in loop $ADCA$,

$$10 - 4(I_1 - I_2) + 2(I_2 + I_3 - I_1) - I_1 = 0$$

$7I_1 - 6I_2 - 2I_3 = 10$ ...(i)

For closed loop $ABCA$,

$$10 - 4I_2 - 2(I_2 + I_3) - I_1 = 0$$

$I_1 + 6I_2 + 2I_3 = 10$ ...(ii)

For closed loop $BCDEB$,

$$5 - 2(I_2 + I_3) - 2(I_2 + I_3 - I_1) = 0$$

$2I_1 - 4I_2 - 4I_3 = -5$ ...(iii)

On solving Eqs. (i), (ii) and (iii), we get

$$I_1 = 2.5\text{ A}, \; I_2 = \frac{5}{8}\text{ A}, \; I_3 = 1\frac{7}{8}\text{ A}$$

The current in various branch of the network are

$$AB = \frac{5}{8}\text{ A}$$

$$CA = 2\frac{1}{2}\text{ A}$$

$$DEB = 1\frac{7}{8}\text{ A}$$

$$AD = 1\frac{7}{8}\text{ A}$$

$$CD = 0$$

$$BC = 2\frac{1}{2}\text{ A}$$

77. (i) Wheatstone bridge

(ii) battery arm

(iii) galvanometer arm

(iv) current

78. (c); For a balanced Wheatstone bridge,

$$\frac{P}{R} = \frac{Q}{X}$$

In first case when $R = 400\,\Omega$, the balancing equation will be

$$\frac{P}{R} = \frac{Q}{X}$$

$$\Rightarrow \frac{P}{400\,\Omega} = \frac{Q}{X}$$

$\Rightarrow P = \dfrac{400 \times Q}{X}$ ...(i)

In second case, P and Q are interchanged and $R = 405\,\Omega$

$$\therefore \frac{Q}{R} = \frac{P}{X}$$

$\Rightarrow \dfrac{Q}{405} = \dfrac{P}{X}$ ...(ii)

Substituting the value of P from Eq. (i) in Eq. (ii), we get

$$\frac{Q}{405} = \frac{Q \times 400}{X^2}$$

$$\Rightarrow X^2 = 400 \times 405$$

$$\Rightarrow X = \sqrt{400 \times 405}$$

$$= 402.5$$

The value of X is close to 402.5 Ω.

79. $\dfrac{R_3}{R_1} = \dfrac{R_4}{R_2}$

80. (b); As no current flows through the middle 8 Ω resistor, the circuit represents a balanced wheatstone bridge.

$$\therefore \frac{X}{18} = \frac{2}{6}$$

$$\Rightarrow X = \frac{18}{3} = 6$$

$$\Rightarrow X = 6\,\Omega$$

81. 4.87;

In the loop $BADB$,

$20I_1 + 3I_g - 12I_2 = 0$ ...(i)

In the loop $BCDB$,

$2I_1 - 6I_g - I_2 = 0$ ...(ii)

In the loop $ADCEA$,

$13I_2 + I_g = 2$ ..(iii)

Solving Eqs. (i), (ii) and (iii), we get

$$I_g = 4.87\text{ mA}$$

82. Four resistance,

$$R_1 = R_2 = R_3 = 3\,\Omega$$

$R_4 = 4\ \Omega$

Resistance R is connecting with $4\ \Omega$,

$$R_{eq} = \frac{4R}{4+R} \quad \ldots(i)$$

For balance bridge

$$\frac{3}{3} = \frac{R_{eq}}{3}$$

$R_{eq} = 3$

From Eq. (i), we get

$$R_{eq} = 3 = \frac{4R}{4+R}$$

$12 + 3R = 4R$

$R = 12\ \Omega$

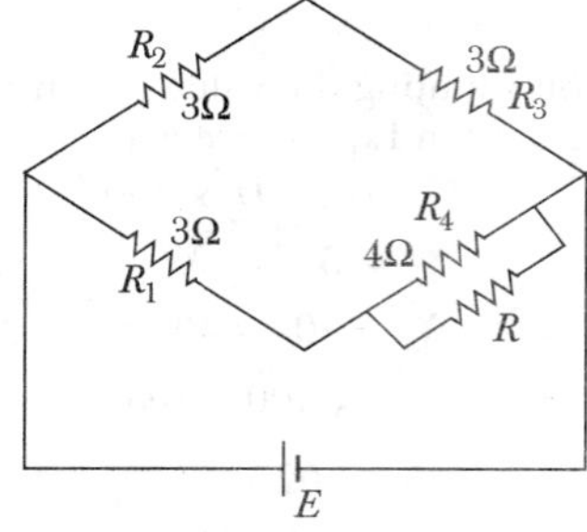

Competition Connect

1. (*b*); By using series and parallel combination of resistor formula,

For parallel combination of resistors,

$$\frac{1}{R_{eq}} = \frac{1}{R_1} + \frac{1}{R_2} \ldots + \frac{1}{R_n}$$

For series combination of resistors,

$$R_{eq} = R_1 + R_2 \ldots + R_n$$

Total resistance between point A and B is 18 Ω.

2. $R_1 + R_2 + R_3$

3. (i) $R\ \Omega$

(ii) 27.5 Ω

(iii) 7.5 Ω

4. (97 m); $R = \dfrac{R_1 R_2}{R_1 + R_2}$

$$3 = \frac{\frac{\rho_1 l}{\pi r_1^2} \cdot \frac{\rho_2 l}{\pi r_2^2}}{\frac{\rho_1 l}{\pi r_1^2} + \frac{\rho_2 l}{\pi r_2^2}}$$

$$3 = \frac{\rho_1 \rho_2 l^2}{\pi r_1^2 \cdot \pi r_2^2} \times \frac{\pi r_1^2 \cdot \pi r_2^2}{\rho_1 l \pi r_2^2 + \rho_2 l \pi r_1^2}$$

$$3 = \frac{\rho_1 \rho_2 l}{\rho_1 \pi r_2^2 + \rho_2 \pi r_1^2}$$

$$3 = \frac{12 \times 10^{-6} \times 10^{-2} \times 51 \times 10^{-6} \times 10^{-2} l}{12 \times 10^{-6} \times 10^{-2}\ \pi\ (10^{-6}) + 51 \times 10^{-6} \times 10^{-2} \times \pi \times 10^{-6}}$$

$$3 = \frac{612 \times 10^{-16}\ l}{63\pi \times 10^{-14}}$$

$$3 = \frac{612 \times 10^{-16}\ l}{63 \times \frac{22}{7} \times 10^{-14}}$$

$$3 = \frac{612 \times 10^{-2}\ l}{198}$$

$$l = \frac{198 \times 3 \times 10^2}{612} = 97\ \text{m}$$

5. (6);

The middle resistor in the lower branch is short-circuited,

therefore circuit can be reduced as

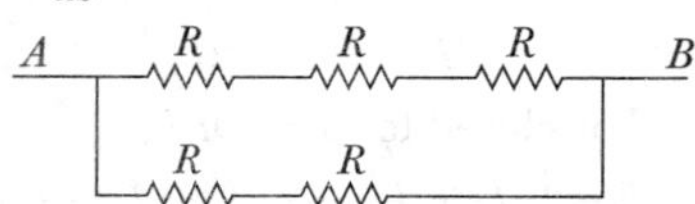

Equivalent resistance is given by

$$\frac{1}{R_p} = \frac{1}{3R} + \frac{1}{2R}$$

$$\Rightarrow R_p = \frac{6R}{5}$$

6. (*d*) The 5 Ω resistance is short-circuited, therefore new circuit can be drawn as

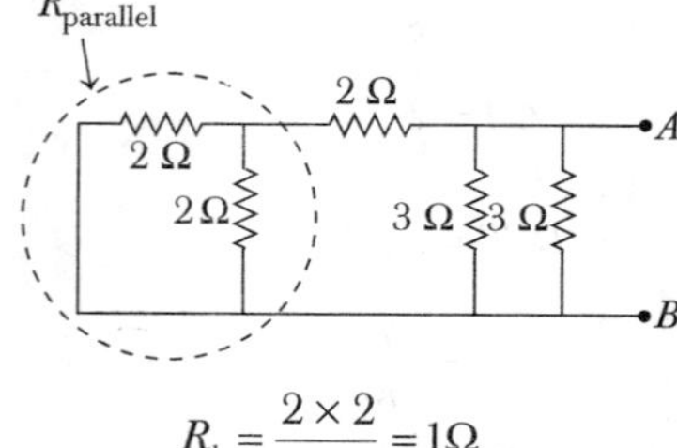

$$R_1 = \frac{2 \times 2}{2+2} = 1\Omega$$

Thus, the circuit can be reduced further as

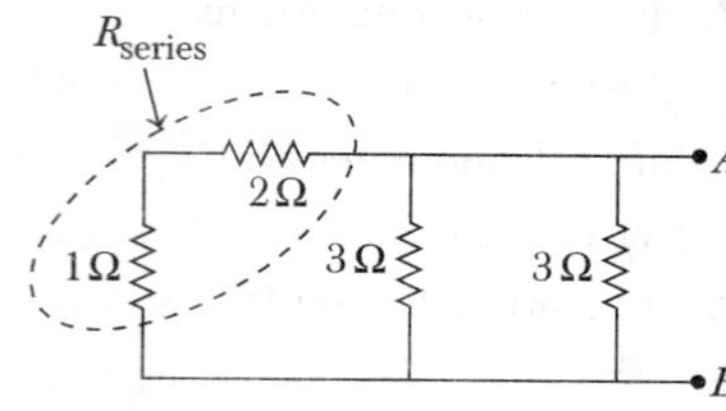

$R_2 = R_1 + 2 = 1 + 2 = 3\ \Omega$

Again, reducing circuit, we get

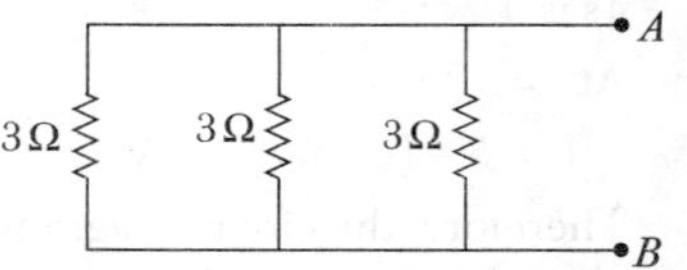

∴ Equivalent resistance is given by

$$\frac{1}{R_{eq}} = \frac{1}{3} + \frac{1}{3} + \frac{1}{3} \Rightarrow R_{eq} = 1\ \Omega$$

7. $\left(\dfrac{r}{3}\right)$;

The effective resistance of each arm of the triangle would be $\dfrac{r \times r}{r + r} = r/2$.

The two arms AB and AC are in series, $R' = (r/2) + (r/2) = r$

∴ Total resistance,

$$\frac{1}{R} = \frac{1}{r} + \frac{2}{r} = \frac{3}{r}$$

$\Rightarrow \quad R = r/3$

8. (1 : 2);

Given, resistance of wire,

$$R_0 = R_1 + R_2 = 12\ \Omega$$

Resistance between A and B,

$$R = \frac{R_1 \times R_2}{R_1 + R_2} = \frac{8}{3}\Omega$$

$$\Rightarrow R_1 R_2 = \frac{8}{3}(R_1 + R_2)$$

$$= \frac{8}{3} \times 12 = 32\ \Omega$$

The possible values of resistances that satisfy the given condition are

$R_1 = 4\ \Omega$ and $R_2 = 8\ \Omega$

As $R \propto l$, then

$$\frac{l_1}{l_2} = \frac{R_1}{R_2} = \frac{4}{8} = \frac{1}{2}$$

9. (*a*); The equivalent resistance between Q and S is given by

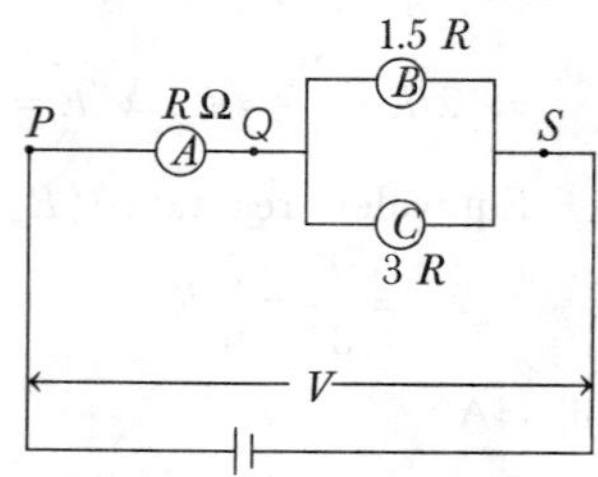

$$\frac{1}{R'} = \frac{1}{1.5R} + \frac{1}{3R} = \frac{2+1}{3R}$$

$\Rightarrow \quad R' = R$

Now, $\quad V_{PQ} = V_A = IR$

Also, $\quad V_{QS} = V_B = V_C = IR$

Hence, $\quad V_A = V_B = V_C$

10. The equivalent resistance of parallel resistors 8Ω, 8Ω and 4Ω,

$$\frac{1}{R_1} = \frac{1}{8} + \frac{1}{8} + \frac{1}{4} = \frac{4}{8}$$

$\Rightarrow R_1 = 2\,\Omega$

∴ Total resistance of upper branch,

$$R_2 = R_1 + 4 = 2 + 4 = 6\,\Omega$$

Now, circuit can be redraw of

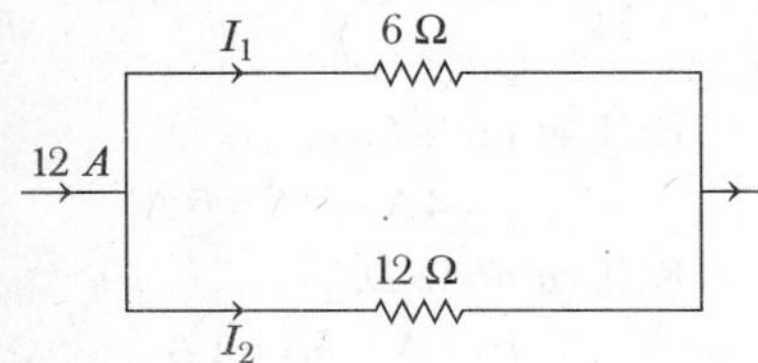

(i) (4 A);

By current division rule, current through 12 Ω resistor,

$$I_2 = \frac{12 \times 6}{12 + 6} = 12 \times \frac{1}{3} = 4\text{ A}$$

(ii) (48 V);

Voltage across 12 Ω resistor,

$$V = I_2R = 4 \times 12 = 48\text{ V}$$

11. (i) (7 Ω);

$$R_1 = \frac{4 \times 4}{4 + 4} = 2\,\Omega$$

$$R_2 = \frac{12 \times 6}{12 + 6} = 4\,\Omega$$

Total resistance

$$= 2 + 1 + 4 = 7\,\Omega$$

(ii) 2A;

Current in the circuit,

$$I = \frac{V}{R + r} = \frac{16}{(7+1)} = \frac{16}{8} = 2\text{ A}$$

12. The balanced meter bridge is given by

$$\frac{l_1}{100 - l_1} = \frac{R}{S}$$

13. (220 Ω);

As we know, $\frac{P}{Q} = \frac{l}{100 - l}$

$$\Rightarrow \quad \frac{55}{R} = \frac{20}{80}$$

$$\Rightarrow \quad R = 55 \times 4 = 220\,\Omega$$

14. (Yes);

As $P \propto l_1$ and $Q \propto l_2$

The condition $\frac{P}{Q} = \frac{l_1}{l_2}$ will remain same after interchanging the cell and galvanometer.

15. (15 cm to the left);

$$\therefore \quad \frac{l}{100 - l} = \frac{20}{30}$$

$$\Rightarrow \quad l = 40\text{ cm}$$

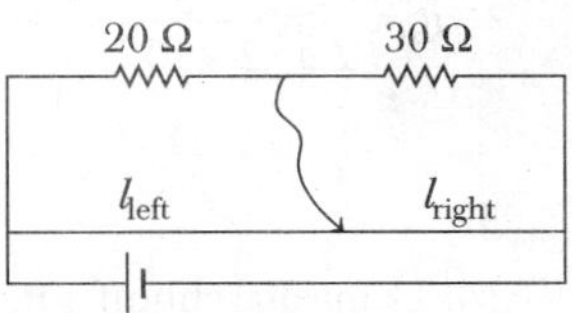

After shutting, resistance is halved.

∴ New length l' will be given as

$$\frac{l'}{100 - l'} = \frac{10}{30}$$

$$\Rightarrow \quad l' = 25\text{ cm}$$

The shift in balancing length,

$$\Delta l = 40 - 25 = 15\text{ cm}$$

to the left

16. (*d*); As $x = R\frac{(100 - l)}{l}$

Therefore, **For** (1) $x \simeq 667$

For (2) $x \simeq 669$

For (3) $x \simeq 656$

For (4) $x \simeq 99$

Hence, (d) is inconsistent.

17. (Yes);

As we know, $\frac{P}{Q} = \frac{l}{100 - l}$

$$\Rightarrow \quad Q = \frac{P(100 - l)}{l}$$

$$\frac{\Delta Q}{Q} = \frac{\Delta(100 - l)}{100 - l} + \frac{\Delta l}{l}$$

(∴ Error is always added)

$$\Rightarrow \frac{\Delta Q}{Q} = \frac{\Delta 100}{100 - l} + \frac{\Delta l}{100 - l} + \frac{\Delta l}{l}$$

$$\Rightarrow \frac{\Delta Q}{Q} = \Delta l\left(\frac{1}{100 - l} + \frac{1}{l}\right)$$

(∴ Δ100 = 0)

Therefore, $\frac{\Delta Q}{Q} \rightarrow$ minimum

when $l = 50$ cm

18. (i); When S changes to S_{eq}, we have

$$S_{eq} = \frac{12S}{S + 12}$$

According to the question,

$$\frac{51.9}{48.1} = \frac{R}{S_{eq}} = \frac{R(S + 12)}{12S}$$

$$\Rightarrow \quad S = 13.5 \quad \text{...(i)}$$

We also know from add values,

$$\frac{R}{S} = \frac{33.7}{66.3}$$

$\Rightarrow \quad R = 6.86\,\Omega$ [using Eq.(i)]

19. (10.6 Ω);

In a balanced Wheatstone bridge condition, We have

$$\frac{X}{10\Omega} = \frac{52 + 1}{48 + 2} = \frac{53}{50}$$

$$\Rightarrow \quad X = 10.6\,\Omega$$

Assertion-Reason Questions

1. (*b*); On increasing temperature of wire the kinetic energy of free electrons increase and collide more rapidly with each other, hence their drift velocity decrease. Also, when temperature increases, resistance increase and resistance is inversely proportional to conductivity of material.

2. (*a*)

3. (*c*); Consider a conductor of length l and cross-section area A. Then time taken by the free electrons to cross the conductor, $t = \frac{l}{v_d}$

Hence, current, $I = \frac{q}{t} = \frac{Al \times ne}{l \times v_d}$

or $\quad I = Anev_d$

or $\quad I \propto v_d$

4. (*b*)

5. (*d*); Resistance of voltmeter is high. If it is connected in series, then current will decrease but circuit will not burn.

6. (*b*); Resistance of wire, $R = \rho\left(\frac{l}{A}\right)$

Here, ρ is resistivity of material which does not depend on the geometry of wire.

7. (*b*); Heater wire must have high resistance and high melting point, because in series current remains same, therefore according to Joule's law $H = \frac{i^2Rt}{4.2}$, heat produced is high if R is high. Melting point must be high so that wire may not melt with increase in temperature.

8. (*b*); When bulbs are connected in series and out of that one get fused then due to this there will be no continuity in the circuit (or resistance offered by fused bulb is infinite) hence no current will flow through the remaining bulbs.

9. (*c*); During charging of the cell, current flows inside the cell from positive to negative, supporting the electrostatic field inside. Therefore, $V > E$.

10. (*d*); Current through a resistance wire flows from higher potential to lower potential. But inside cell it flows from lower to higher potential.

Further, during charging of a battery current flows in the direction shown in above figure.

Case Based Questions

1. (i) (*c*); As current density,

$$J = \frac{I}{A}$$

$$= \frac{1}{2\times10^{-6}}$$

$$= 0.5\times10^{6}\ \text{Am}^{-2}$$

(ii) (*a*); Given, $l_1 = l + \frac{25}{100}l = \frac{5l}{4}$.

Since, volume of wire remains unchanged on increasing length. Hence,

$$\Rightarrow \quad Al = A_1 \times \frac{5l}{4}$$

$$\Rightarrow \quad A_1 = \frac{4A}{5}$$

Given, $R = 100 = \frac{\rho l}{A}$

and $\quad R_1 = \frac{\rho l_1}{A_1}$

$$= \frac{\frac{\rho 5l}{4}}{\frac{4A}{5}} = \frac{25}{16}\frac{\rho l}{A}$$

$$R_1 = \frac{25}{16}\times100$$

$$= \frac{2500}{16} = 156.25\ \Omega$$

(iii) (*b*);

$$R = \frac{V}{I} = \frac{6}{2\times10^{-6}}$$

$$= 3\times10^{6}\ \Omega$$

(iv) (*c*)

2. (i) (*c*); Using Kirchhoff's junction law,

$$(+I) + (4\text{A}) + (2\text{A}) + (-5\text{A}) + (-3\text{A}) = 0$$

$$\Rightarrow \quad I + 6\text{A} - 8\text{A} = 0$$

$$\Rightarrow \quad I - 2\text{A} = 0$$

$$\Rightarrow \quad I = 2\text{A}$$

(ii) (*b*); In the given circuit,

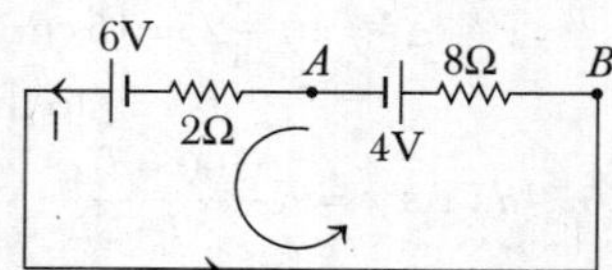

Applying the Kirchhoff's voltage loop rule, we get,

$$\Rightarrow 6 - 8I - 4 - 2I = 0$$

$$\Rightarrow 2 - 10I = 0 \Rightarrow I = \frac{2}{10} = 0.2\ \text{A}$$

So, potential difference between A and B,

$$V_{AB} = 4 + I\times8$$

$$= 4 + 0.2\times8 = 5.6\ \text{V}$$

(iii) (*c*); In loop 1, $i_1 = \frac{5}{10} = \frac{1}{2}\text{A}$

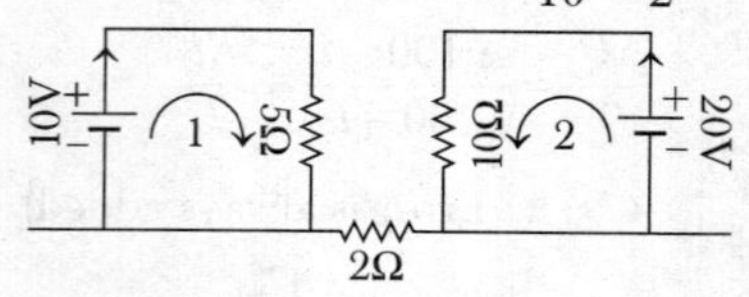

In loop 2, $i_2 = \frac{20}{10} = 2\ \text{A}$

But both currents are confined to separated loops and so current through 2 Ω resistor is zero.

(iv) (*c*);

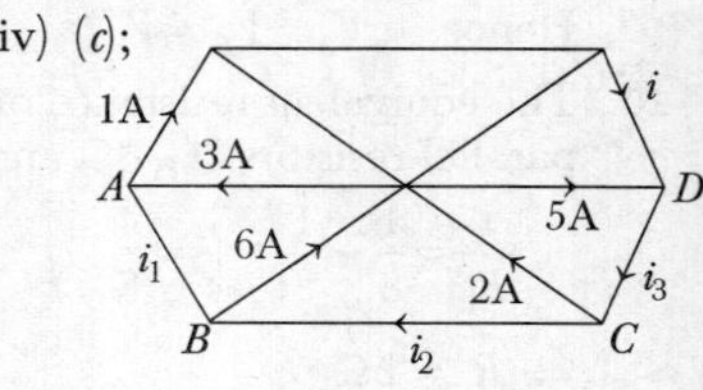

KCL at node A,

$$i_1 + 1\ \text{A} = 3\ \text{A}$$

$$i_1 = 2\ \text{A}$$

KCL at node B,

$$i_2 + 2\ \text{A} = 6\ \text{A}$$

$$i_2 = 4\ \text{A}$$

KCL at node C,

$$i_3 = 4\text{A} + 2\text{A} = 6\ \text{A}$$

KCL at node D,

$$i = 6\text{A} - 5\text{A} = 1\ \text{A}$$

Competition Edge Up

1. (*c*); Let initial resistance is R and length is l.

We know, power $P = \frac{V^2}{R}$ and

$$R = \frac{\rho l}{A}$$

$$\therefore \quad P \propto \frac{1}{l}$$

For case I $t = t_1 = 20$ min

and

For case II $t = t_2 = 15$ min

$$P_1 \propto \frac{1}{t_1} \text{ and } P_2 \propto \frac{1}{t_2}$$

$$\Rightarrow \quad \frac{P_1}{P_2} = \frac{t_2}{t_1} = \frac{15}{20} = \frac{l_2}{l_1}$$

$$\Rightarrow \quad l_2 = \frac{3}{4}l_1$$

2. (*c*); $\therefore I = \frac{P}{V} = \frac{110}{220} = 0.5\ \text{A}$

Since, $I = \frac{ne}{t}$

$$\Rightarrow \quad \frac{n}{t} = \frac{I}{e} = \frac{0.5}{1.6\times10^{-19}}$$

$$= 31.25\times10^{17}\ \text{electrons/second}$$

3. (*d*); For bulb, $P = 50$ W, $V = 200$ V

$\therefore$ Resistance of the bulb,

$$R = \frac{V^2}{P} \quad \left[\because P = \frac{V^2}{R}\right]$$

$$= \frac{200 \times 200}{50} = 800\ \Omega$$

$\therefore$ Power dissipation when bulb is connected with $V' = 100$ V supply,

$$P' = \frac{(V')^2}{R}$$

$$= \frac{100 \times 100}{800} = 12.5\ \text{W}$$

4. (*b*);

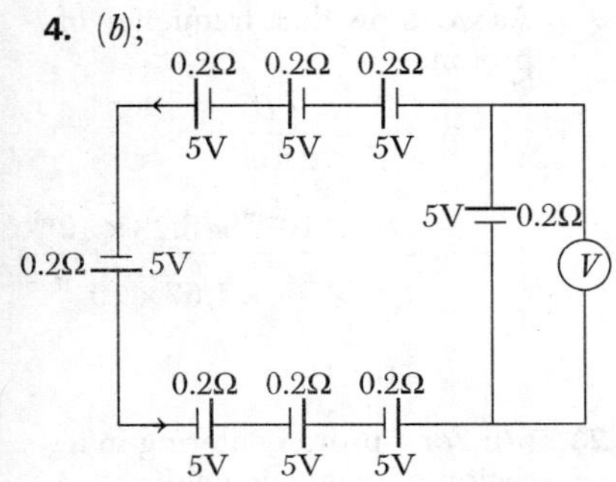

All cells are identical

$r = 0.25\ \Omega$, $V = 5$ V

Above circuit can be reduced to,

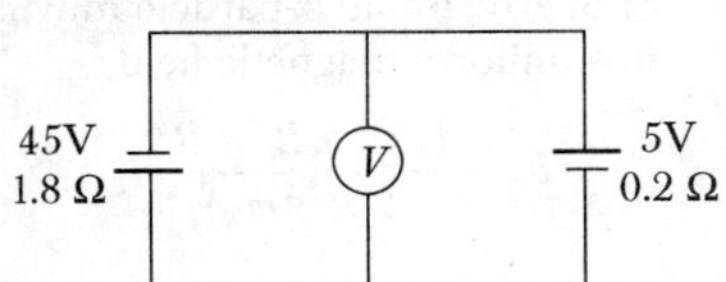

So, potential drop across parallel combination of above cells is,

$$V = \frac{E_2 r_1 - E_1 r_2}{r_1 + r_2}$$

$$= \frac{5 \times 1.8 - 45 \times 0.2}{1.8 + 0.2}$$

$$= 0\ \text{V}$$

5. (*c*); Illumination $\propto$ Power

Now, $P_i = I^2 R$

$$\Rightarrow P_f = \left(\frac{80}{100} I\right)^2 R$$

$$= 0.64 P_i$$

Percentage drop in power (illumination)

$$= \frac{P_i - P_f}{P_i} \times 100$$

$$= \frac{P_i(1 - 0.64)}{P_i} \times 100$$

$$= 0.36 \times 100 = 36\%$$

6. (*c*); Specific resistance does not depend on length of wire. It is depend on the material of wire.

Therefore, specific resistance remain same.

7. (*c*); Given,

EMF, $\varepsilon = 10$ V

Internal resistance, $r = 1\ \Omega$

External resistance, $R = 4\ \Omega$

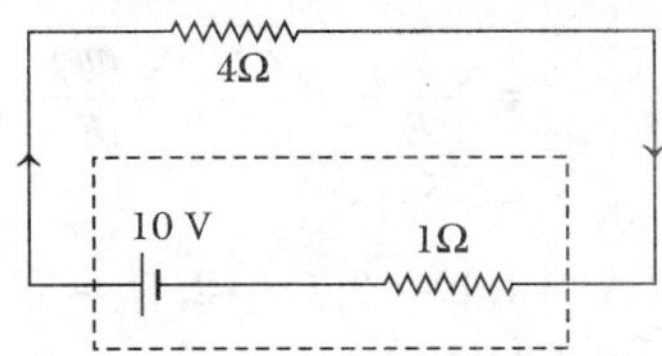

Terminal voltage, $V = \varepsilon - Ir$

and $I = \frac{\varepsilon}{R + r} = \frac{10}{4 + 1} = 2$ A

Thus, $V = 10 - 2 \times 1 = 8$ V

8. (*b*); $P_{\text{Series}} = \frac{P_1 P_2}{P_1 + P_2}$

and $P_{\text{Parallel}} = P_1 + P_2$

According to question,

$$\frac{P_{\text{Series}}}{P_{\text{Parallel}}} = \frac{\frac{1 \times 2}{1 + 2}}{1 + 2} = \frac{2}{3 \times 3} = \frac{2}{9}$$

9. (*b*); Given, $R_0 = 2\ \Omega$

At $t = 80°$C, $R_t = 6.8\ \Omega$

We know that,

$$R_f = R_0 (1 + \alpha t)$$

$$\Rightarrow R_t = R_0 + R_0 \alpha t$$

$$\therefore \alpha = \frac{R_t - R_0}{R_0 t}$$

$$= \frac{6.8 - 2}{2 \times 80}$$

$$= \frac{4.8}{2 \times 80} = 0.03$$

$$= 3 \times 10^{-2}\ °\text{C}^{-1}$$

10. (*b*); The given situation is shown below.

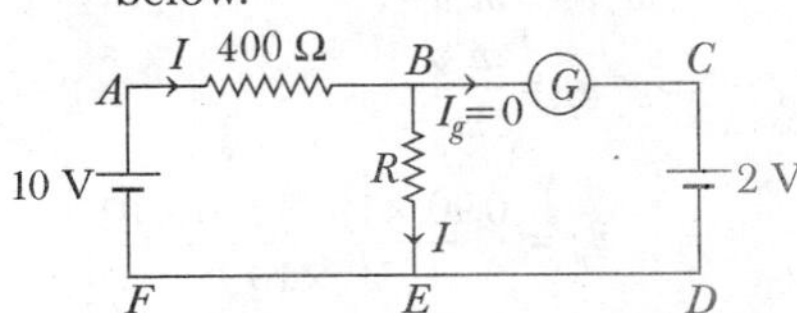

Applying Kirchhoff's voltage law in the loop *ABCDEFA*, we get

$$400I + 2 - 10 = 0$$

$$\Rightarrow I = \frac{8}{400} = \frac{1}{50}\ \text{A}$$

Applying Kirchhoff's voltage law in loop *ABEFA*, we get

$$400I + RI - 10 = 0$$

$$\Rightarrow (400 + R)I = 10$$

$$\Rightarrow (400 + R) \times \frac{1}{50} = 100$$

$$\Rightarrow 400 + R = 500$$

$$\Rightarrow R = 100\ \Omega$$

11. (*a*); The circuit diagram is shown as

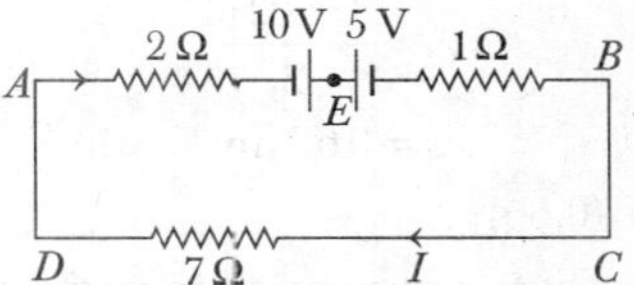

Applying KVL in the closed loop *AEBCDA*,

$$2I - 10 + 5 + I \cdot 1 + 7I = 0$$

$$\Rightarrow 10I = 5$$

$$\Rightarrow I = 0.5\ \text{A}$$

Since, current is positive, hence, direction of current is from *A* to *B* through *E*.

12. (*d*); The current density,

$$j = \sigma E = \frac{E}{\rho} \quad \ldots\text{(i)}$$

So, $\rho = \frac{RA}{l} = \frac{10 \times \pi \times \frac{10^{-4}}{\pi}}{10}$

$$= 10^{-4}\ \Omega\ \text{m}$$

From equation (i), we get

$$j = \frac{10}{10^{-4}} = 10^5\ \text{A/m}^2$$

Chapter-4

Moving Charges and Magnetism

1. (*a*); Net force on the proton,

$$F = B q v \sin\theta$$

$$= 1.5 \times 1.6 \times 10^{-19} \times 2 \times 10^7 \times \sin 30°$$

$$= 2.4 \times 10^{-12}\ \text{N}$$

2. False;

When a charged particle is kept stationary ($v = 0$) in the strong magnetic field, no force acts on the charged particle.

$$F = Bqv = Bq \times 0$$

$$\Rightarrow F = 0$$

3. Zero; $F_E = F_B$ (given)
and the direction of F_E and F_B are opposite to each other.
So, net force will be zero.

4. (*c*)

5. Yes ;
Since, $\mathbf{F} = I\,(\mathbf{l} \times \mathbf{B})$

$$F = IlB \sin\theta$$

$$\Rightarrow \frac{F}{l} = 8 \times 0.15 \times \sin 30^\circ = \frac{8 \times 0.15}{2} = 0.6 \text{ Nm}^{-1}$$

6. (0.65);
During suspension in mid air, the force will be balanced by the weight of the wire.
So, $BIl = mg$

$$\Rightarrow B = \frac{mg}{Il} = \frac{0.2 \times 9.8}{2 \times 1.5} = 0.65 \text{ T}$$

$\therefore \quad x = 0.65$

7. The velocity v of the particle is along the X-axis and the magnetic field is along positive Y-axis. So, the cross product $(v_x \times B_y)$ is along the Z-axis.
(i) Now, for an electron (– ve charge), the force will be in $-Z$-axis direction.
(ii) For a positively charged particle (proton), the force will be along $+Z$-axis direction.

8. True

9. centripetal, circular, perpendicular

10. No

11. Helical

12. (*a*)

13. bigger

14. (*d*); $p_H = p_\alpha = p$

$$r_H = \frac{p}{eB}$$

$$r_\alpha = \frac{p}{2eB}$$

(as α-particle has a charge $2e$)

$$\therefore \frac{r_H}{r_\alpha} = \frac{2}{1}$$

$$r_H : r_\alpha = 2 : 1$$

15. $r_d > r_p = r_\alpha$;
As we know that, radius of circle,

$$r = \frac{mv}{Bq}, \; p = mv \text{ and KE, } E = \frac{p^2}{2m}$$

$$p = \sqrt{2mE}$$

$$\text{So, } r = \frac{\sqrt{2mE}}{qB}$$

Now, $r_d : r_p : r_\alpha$

$$= \frac{\sqrt{2m_d E}}{q_d B} : \frac{\sqrt{2m_p E}}{q_p B} : \frac{\sqrt{2m_\alpha E}}{q_\alpha B}$$

$$= \sqrt{\frac{2m_d}{E}} : \sqrt{\frac{2m_p}{E}} : \sqrt{\frac{4m_p}{2E}}$$

$$= \sqrt{2} : 1 : 1$$

16. A → 4, B → 3, C → 2, D → 1

17. (i) (28×10^{-2} m);

$$\text{Radius, } r = \frac{mv}{qB} = \frac{9 \times 10^{-31} \times 3 \times 10^7}{1.6 \times 10^{-19} \times 6 \times 10^{-4}} = 28 \times 10^{-2} \text{ m}$$

(ii) (17 MHz);

$$\text{Frequency, } \nu = \frac{v}{2\pi r} = \frac{3 \times 10^7}{2 \times 3.14 \times 28 \times 10^{-2}} = 17 \text{ MHz}$$

(iii) (2.5 keV);

$$\text{Energy, } E = \frac{1}{2} mv^2 = \frac{1}{2} \times 9 \times 10^{-31} \times 9 \times 10^{14} = 40.5 \times 10^{-17} \text{ J} = 2.5 \text{ keV}$$

$(\because 1 \text{ J} = 6.242 \times 10^{15} \text{ keV})$

18. (*b*); We know that, $mv = Bqr$
$\therefore B$ and r are same for both electron and proton. Also, q is numerically same for both.

$\therefore \quad mv = \text{constant}$

$$\therefore m_p v_p = m_e v_e$$

$$\Rightarrow v_p = \frac{m_e v_e}{m_p}$$

$$\Rightarrow v_p = \frac{0.90 \times 10^{-30} \times 3 \times 10^6}{1.8 \times 10^{-27}}$$

$$\Rightarrow v_p = 1.5 \times 10^3 \text{ms}^{-1}$$

19. undeflected

20. (*a*); Positron has an electric charge $+e$ and the mass same as an electron.

$$\text{So, } \frac{q}{m} = \frac{+e}{m} = \frac{1.6 \times 10^{-19}}{9.1 \times 10^{-31}} \simeq +2 \times 10^{11} \text{ C kg}^{-1}$$

21. (*a*); $\frac{e}{m} = 1.76 \times 10^{11} \text{ C kg}^{-1}$
Frequency of revolution,

$$\nu = \frac{qB}{2\pi m} \quad [\because q = e]$$

$$= \frac{3.57 \times 10^{-2} \times 1.76 \times 10^{11}}{2\pi} = 1 \text{ GHz}$$

22. (Approx. 10^4 Hz);
As we know that, frequency of proton,

$$\nu = \frac{1}{T} = \frac{qB}{2\pi m} = \frac{1.6 \times 10^{-19} \times 6.28 \times 10^{-4}}{2 \times \frac{22}{7} \times 1.67 \times 10^{-27}} \approx 10^4 \text{ Hz}$$

23. (*d*); For a proton entering in a region of magnetic field,

$$E_1 = \frac{e^2 \times B^2 \times R^2}{2 \times m_p} \quad \ldots\text{(i)}$$

Similarly, for an α-particle moving in a uniform magnetic field,

$$E_2 = \frac{(2e)^2 \times B^2 \times R^2}{2 \times (4m_p)} \quad (\because m_\alpha = 4m_p) \ldots\text{(ii)}$$

Dividing Eq. (ii) by Eq. (i), we get

$$\frac{E_2}{E_1} = \frac{(2e)^2 \times B^2 \times R^2}{2 \times (4m_p)} \times \frac{2 \times m_p}{e^2 \times B^2 \times R^2}$$

$$\Rightarrow \frac{E_2}{E_1} = 1$$

$$\Rightarrow E_2 = E_1 = 1 \text{ MeV}$$

24. (*c*)

25. (*d*) Magnetic field at current carrying wire of radius R, i.e.

$$B_1 = \frac{\mu_0 i}{4\pi R} \times \frac{\pi}{2}$$

Similarly, magnetic field at current carrying of radius R', i.e.

$$B_2 = \frac{\mu_0}{4\pi} \times \frac{i}{R'} \times \frac{3\pi}{2}$$

Net magnetic field at point O, i.e.
$B = B_1 + B_2$

$$B = \frac{\mu_0 i}{4\pi R} \times \frac{\pi}{2} + \frac{\mu_0}{4\pi} \cdot \frac{i}{R'} \times \frac{3\pi}{2}$$
$$= \frac{\mu_0 i}{8}\left(\frac{1}{R} + \frac{3}{R'}\right)$$

26. (True);
$$dB = \frac{\mu_0}{4\pi} \times \frac{Idl \sin\theta}{r^2}$$
For any point on conductor itself, $\theta = 0$ or $180°$

$\therefore \quad dB = 0$

27. (4×10^{-8} T);
The magnitude of magnetic field,
$$B = \frac{\mu_0}{4\pi} \times \frac{Idl \sin\theta}{r^2}$$
$$= \frac{10^{-7} \times 10 \times 10^{-2} \times \sin 90°}{(0.5)^2}$$
$$= 4 \times 10^{-8} \text{ T}$$

28. Yes

29. (*c*); According to Maxwell's right hand thumb rule, it is clear that magnetic field will be in same direction by both the coils.
$$\therefore B = B_1 + B_2 = \frac{\mu_0 IR^2}{2(R^2 + x^2)^{3/2}} + \frac{\mu_0 IR^2}{2(R^2 + x^2)^{3/2}}$$
$$= \frac{\mu_0 I R^2}{(R^2 + x^2)^{3/2}}$$
$$= \frac{\mu_0 \times (7/2) \times (0.1)^2}{[(0.1)^2 + (0.05)^2]^{3/2}}$$
$$= \frac{56\mu_0}{\sqrt{5}} \text{ T}$$

30. $\frac{\mu_0 I}{2R}$

31. (*d*); Magnetic field at centre of circular coil, $B = \frac{\mu_0 I}{2r}$ ...(i)
$$I = \frac{q}{t} = \frac{e}{1/n} \quad \text{...(ii)}$$
From Eqs. (i) and (ii), we get
$$B = \frac{\mu_0 ne}{2r}$$

32. (i) (Zero);
For each straight segments, dr and r are parallel.
So, $\theta = 0° \Rightarrow d\mathbf{l} \times \mathbf{r} = 0$
$\Rightarrow B = 0$ due to straight segments.

(ii) ($B_C = 2B_{SC}$);
Magnetic field due to a semi-circular arc is given by
$$B_{SC} = \frac{\mu_0 I}{4\pi r} \times (\pi)$$
$$= \frac{\mu_0 I}{4r} \text{ (inwards) ...(i)}$$
Now, magnetic field at centre of a circle is
$$B_C = \frac{\mu_0 I}{4\pi r} \times (2\pi) = \frac{\mu_0 I}{2r}$$
(inwards)...(ii)

From Eqs. (i) and (ii), we get
$$B_C = 2B_{SC}$$
(iii) (*a*); Magnitude of B will remain same but opposite in direction.

33. (6.28);
Magnetic field at the centre of the coil B is given by
$$B = \frac{\mu_0 IN}{2r} = \frac{10^{-7} \times 4\pi \times 1 \times 100}{2 \times 0.1}$$
$$= 6.28 \times 10^{-4} \text{ T}$$
$\therefore x = 6.28$

34. (*d*)

35. tangential, $\frac{\mu_0 I}{2\pi r}$

36. True

37. (*b*); For $r > a$,
Length (L) = $2\pi r$ (Amperian loop)

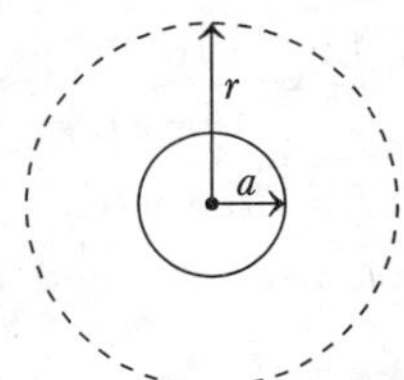

Using the Amperian circuital law,
$$B(2\pi r) = \mu_0 I$$
$$\Rightarrow \quad B = \frac{\mu_0 I}{2\pi r}$$

38. (2);
For $r < a$,
Length of the Amperian loop $= 2\pi r$
Now, the current enclosed will not be equal to I but as we have assumed a uniform distribution, so the enclosed current is given as follows
$$I_e = \frac{I(\pi r^2)}{\pi a^2} = \frac{Ir^2}{a^2}$$
According to Ampere's circuital law,
$$B(2\pi r) = \mu_0 I_e$$
$$\Rightarrow B = \frac{\mu_0}{2\pi r} \times \frac{r^2}{a^2} \times I = \left(\frac{\mu_0 I}{2\pi a^2}\right) r$$
$\therefore \quad x = 2$

39. (*b*) In a hollow cylinder having infinite length and carrying a uniform current per unit length λ along the circumference.
According to Ampere's circuital law, we get

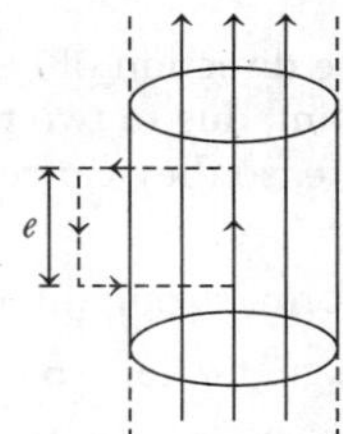

$$\int \mathbf{B} \cdot d\mathbf{l} = \mu_0 \times dI$$
(Linear density i.e. $\lambda = \frac{dI}{dl}$, so $dI = \lambda\, dl$)

i.e. $B = \mu_0 \lambda$
Magnetic field inside the cylinder, i.e.
$$B = \mu_0 \lambda$$

40. (*d*) According to Ampere's circuital law, we have
$$\oint \mathbf{B} \cdot d\mathbf{l} = \mu_0 nl$$
$$\oint_{ABCD} \mathbf{B} \cdot d\mathbf{l} = \oint_{ABCA} \mathbf{B} \cdot d\mathbf{l} + \oint_{CDAC} \mathbf{B} \cdot d\mathbf{l}$$
$$= \mu_0 I_1 + \mu_0 I_2 = \mu_0(I_1 + I_2)$$

41. (*d*) Consider a long straight wire of radius a carries a steady current I.
i.e. $\mathbf{B} = \frac{\mu_0 I}{2\pi a^2} \times r$

***Case* I** Magnetic field at $r = \frac{a}{2}$ is
$$B_1 = \frac{\mu_0 I}{2\pi a^2} \times \frac{a}{2} = \frac{\mu_0 I}{4\pi a} \text{ ...(i)}$$
***Case* II** Magnetic field at $r = 2a$ is
$$B_2 = \frac{\mu_0 I}{2\pi r}$$
$$= \frac{\mu_0 I}{2\pi (2a)} = \frac{\mu_0 I}{4\pi a} \text{ ...(ii)}$$

On dividing Eq. (i) by Eq. (ii), we get

$$\frac{B_1}{B_2} = 1$$

42. (*d*) Take any point *P* inside the thin walled pipe. Consider a circular loop through this point and apply Ampere's circuital law. As, net current inside the loop is zero, the magnetic field at any point inside the loop will be zero.

$$\oint \mathbf{B} \cdot d\mathbf{l} = \mu_0 nI = \mu_0 \times 0 = 0$$

43. Zero;

Because direction of fields in mid-point, due to two field is opposite, so they cancel out the net effect.

44. (i) uniform, strong (ii) Yes

45. (*d*); Magnetic field, $B = \mu_0 nI$

$$\Rightarrow 20 \times 10^{-3} = 4\pi \times 10^{-7} \times 2000 \times I$$

$$\Rightarrow I = \frac{20 \times 10^{-3}}{4\pi \times 10^{-7} \times 2000} \simeq 8 \text{ A}$$

46. (6.28);

$$B = \mu_0 nI$$

where, *n* is the number of turns per unit length

$$= \frac{500}{0.5} = 1000 \text{ turns/m}$$

$$\Rightarrow B = 4\pi \times 10^{-7} \times 1000 \times 5$$

$$= 6.28 \times 10^{-3} \text{ T}$$

$$\therefore x = 6.28$$

47. (2);

The magnitude of force on segment *L* of *b* due to *a*,

$$F_{ba} = B_a I_b L$$

$$F_{ba} = \frac{\mu_0 I_a I_b}{2\pi d} L$$

$$\therefore \quad x = 2$$

48. (8×10^{-5} N);

$$F = \frac{\mu_0}{2\pi} \frac{I_1 I_2}{r} \times L$$

$$= \frac{10^{-7} \times 2 \times 10 \times 2}{0.1} \times 2$$

$$= 8 \times 10^{-5} \text{ N}$$

49. (*a*); Force on a current-carrying wire,

$$F = \frac{\mu_0 I_1 I_2 \, l}{2\pi r}$$

$$= \frac{4\pi \times 10^{-7} \times 4.0 \times 5.0 \times 0.20}{2 \times 3.14 \times 4 \times 10^{-2}}$$

$$= 2 \times 10^{-5} \text{ N (towards } B)$$

50. (Yes);

$$F = \frac{\mu_0 2 I_1 I_2}{4\pi d}$$

$$= \frac{4\pi \times 10^{-7} \times 2 \times 1 \times 1}{4\pi \times 1}$$

$$= 2 \times 10^{-7} \text{ N/m}$$

51. (9 cm);

Consider the given figure,

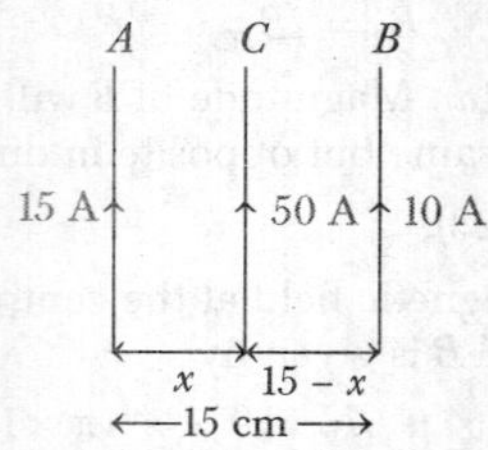

Since, wire *C* is so placed that it experiences no net force,

so $\frac{F_{AC}}{l} = \frac{F_{BC}}{l}$

$$\Rightarrow \frac{\mu_0 2 I_A I_C}{4\pi d} = \frac{\mu_0 2 I_B I_C}{4\pi d'}$$

$$\Rightarrow \frac{\mu_0}{4\pi} \cdot \frac{2 \times 15 \times 50}{x} = \frac{\mu_0}{4\pi} \times \frac{2 \times 10 \times 50}{15 - x}$$

$$\Rightarrow \frac{15}{x} = \frac{10}{(15 - x)} \Rightarrow x = 9 \text{ cm}$$

52. (i) (*a*); $F = BIL \sin \theta$

Force per unit length becomes

$$\frac{F}{L} = BI \sin \theta$$

$$= 3 \times 10^{-5} \times 1 \times \sin 90^\circ$$

$$= 3 \times 10^{-5} \text{ N/m}$$

(ii) (0);

When current will flow from South to North, $\theta = 0^\circ$

$$\Rightarrow \frac{F}{L} = BI \sin 0^\circ = 0$$

$$\therefore \quad x = 0$$

53. (*b*); When a current-carrying closed loop is suspended in a uniform magnetic field $\mathbf{F}_{net} = 0$, only torque acts.

So, if force on one arm is **F**, then force on remaining three arms must be **–F**.

54. (*c*) Torque experienced by loop,

$$\tau = MB$$

$$= il^2 B$$

$$= 10 \times 0.1 \times 0.1 \times 0.2$$

$$= 2 \times 10^{-2} \text{ Nm}$$

55. (True);

Since, $m = IA = 2 \times 2 \times 10^{-3} = 4 \times 10^{-3} \text{ JT}^{-1}$

56. (i) ✓ (ii) ✓ (iii) ✓

57. (Yes);

Here, the circular coil is placed normal to the direction of magnetic field, so the angle between the direction of magnetic moment **m** and magnetic field **B** is zero. Therefore,

$$\tau = mB \sin \theta$$

$$= mB \sin 0^\circ = 0$$

58. (i) (2×10^{-3} T);

$$B = \frac{\mu_0 NI}{2R}$$

$$= \frac{4\pi \times 10^{-7} \times 100 \times 3.2}{2 \times 10 \times 10^{-2}}$$

$$= 2 \times 10^{-3} \text{T}$$

(ii) (10 A-m^2);

$$M = NIA$$

$$= 100 \times 3.2 \times 3.14 \times (0.1)^2$$

$$= 10 \text{ A-m}^2$$

59. (i) (0, 20 N-m);

$$\tau = MB \sin \theta$$

In initial position, $\theta = 0^\circ$

$$\Rightarrow \quad \tau = 0$$

In final position, $\theta = 90^\circ$

$$\tau = MB = 20 \text{ N-m}$$

(ii) (20 rad/s);

Using Newton second law,

$$\frac{I d\omega}{dt} = MB \sin \theta$$

or $I\omega \, d\omega = MB \sin \theta \, d\theta$

Integrating both sides within given limits,

$$I \int_0^{\omega} \omega \, d\omega = MB \int_0^{\pi/2} \sin \theta \, d\theta$$

$$\Rightarrow \frac{I \omega^2}{2} = MB$$

$$\Rightarrow \frac{0.1 \times \omega^2}{2} = 10 \times 2$$

$$\Rightarrow \omega = 20 \text{ rad/s}$$

60. No, because of the fact that in order to turn the loop around itself, the torque should be in the vertical direction.

61. external field

62. (*a*)

63. (*d*); Resistance,

$$R = \frac{R_G r_s}{R_G + r_s} = \frac{70 \times 0.03}{70 + 0.03}$$

$$= 0.02998 = 0.030\ \Omega$$

64. shunt, shunt

65. I. Ammeter II. Voltmeter

66. $A \to 4, B \to 3, C \to 2, D \to 1$

67. (*d*); Consider the given figure.

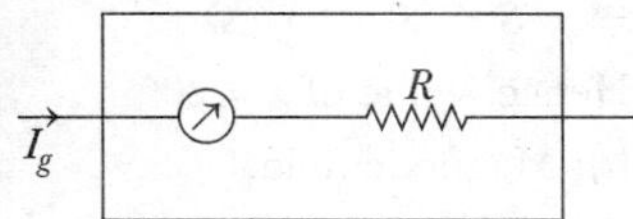

R is the resistance connected in series with galvanometer to convert into voltmeter.

$$\therefore \quad V = I_g (R_g + R)$$

$$25 = 10^{-2} (50 + R)$$

$$[\because I_g = 25 \times 4 \times 10^{-4} = 10^{-2}\ \text{A}]$$

$$\Rightarrow R = \frac{25}{10^{-2}} - 50$$

$$= 2500 - 50$$

$$= 2450\ \Omega \text{ in series}$$

68. $(5 \times 10^6\ \text{A}^{-1})$;

Current sensitivity, $I_S = \dfrac{NBA}{K}$

$$= \frac{100 \times 5 \times 1 \times 10^{-4}}{10^{-8}}$$

$$= 5 \times 10^6\ \text{A}^{-1}$$

69. (*a*); Since, $R_G = \dfrac{I_S}{V_S}$

$$= \frac{5 \times 10^3}{20} = 250\ \Omega$$

70. (doubled, remain same);

Current sensitivity

$$= \frac{\phi}{I} = \frac{NAB}{K}$$

When number of turns are doubled, current sensitivity gets doubled.

Voltage sensitivity

$$= \frac{\phi}{V} = \frac{NAB}{K} \times \frac{1}{R}$$

When $N \to 2N$, $R \to 2N$

So, voltage sensitivity remains the same.

71. (i) (0.048);

$$I = \frac{V}{R + R_G}$$

$$= \frac{3}{3 + 60} = 0.048\ \text{A}$$

$$\therefore x = 0.048$$

(ii) (0.99 A);

When ammeter is shunted, the effective resistance of the galvanometer becomes

$$R_q = \frac{R_G r_s}{R_G + r_s}$$

$$= \frac{60 \times 0.02}{60 + 0.02} = 0.02\ \Omega$$

$$\therefore \quad I = \frac{V}{R + R_q}$$

$$= \frac{3}{3 + 0.02} = 0.99\ \text{A}$$

(iii) (1);

In case of ideal ammeter with zero resistance, $R_q = 0$

$$\therefore \quad I = \frac{V}{R} = \frac{3}{3} = 1\ \text{A}$$

Assertion-Reason Questions

1. (*b*); $F_m = q(\mathbf{v} \times \mathbf{B}) = qvB \sin\theta$

Hence, the force acts in a (side ways) direction perpendicular to both velocity and magnetic field.

When v and B are parallel or anti-parallel, then $\theta = 0°$ or $180°$.

$$\therefore \quad F_m = 0$$

2. (*d*); From the equation $F = qvB \sin\theta$, force on moving charge will be maximum, if direction of velocity of charged particle is perpendicular to direction of magnetic field (when $\theta = 90°$).

3. (*a*); A stationary charge produces electric field only. However, a moving charge which is equivalent to a current produces a magnetic field in the surrounding space and can interacts with external magnetic field.

4. (*c*); As $dB \propto \sin\theta$, where θ is angle between the direction of the flow of current and the line joining the elementary portion to the observation point which is zero in this case, so the magnetic field is also zero because $\sin\theta$ is equal to zero.

5. (*a*)

6. (*c*); The magnitude of the magnetic field produced due to flow of current through a circular loop at a point on its axis is given by

$$B = \frac{\mu_0}{4\pi} \frac{2\pi I a^2}{(a^2 + x^2)^{3/2}}$$

This is maximum at centre of loop, where $x = 0$.

7. (*c*); When current flows through a solenoid, the current in the various turns of the solenoid are parallel and in the same direction. Since, the currents flowing through parallel wires in the same direction lead to force of attraction between them. Hence, the turns of the solenoid will contract.

8. (*b*); The magnetic field of a solenoid is given by

$$B = \frac{1}{2}\mu_0 nI\ [\cos\theta_1 - \cos\theta_2]$$

For a very long current-carrying solenoid, the magnetic field at the end of a very long solenoid is given by putting, $\theta_1 = 90°$ and $\theta_2 = 180°$.

$$\therefore B = \frac{1}{2}\mu_0 nI = \frac{1}{2} \times \text{Magnetic field}$$

at the centre.

9. (*a*)

10. (*d*); Current sensitivity,

$$S_i = \frac{NBA}{k}$$

$$S_i \propto N$$

and voltage sensitivity,

$$S_V = \frac{NBA}{kR}$$

$$S_V \propto \frac{N}{R}$$

So, when S_i is increased by increasing number of turns N, length of wire used also increases and so resistance R increases. Hence, S_V may remain same or decrease, whereas S_i increases.

Case Based Questions

1. (i) (*a*); Let magnetic field B be zero at any arbitrary point $P(x, y)$ in the XY-plane.

For zero magnetic field points,

$$B_x = B_y$$

$$\Rightarrow \frac{\mu_0(30)}{2\pi y} = \frac{\mu_0(10)}{2\pi x}$$

$$\Rightarrow \frac{3}{y} = \frac{1}{x}$$

$$\Rightarrow 3x = y \text{ or } y = 3x$$

(ii) (*a*); Magnetic field due to a long straight wire of radius a carrying current I at a point distant r from the centre of the wire is given as follows

$$B = \frac{\mu_0 Ir}{2\pi a^2}$$

$$\Rightarrow B \propto r \quad (\text{for } r < a)$$

$$B = \frac{\mu_0 I}{2\pi a} \quad (\text{for } r = a)$$

$$B = \frac{\mu_0 I}{2\pi r}$$

$$\Rightarrow B \propto \frac{1}{r} \quad (\text{for } r > a)$$

(iii) (*a*)

(iv) (*d*); Given, $B_1 = 0.8$ T, $d_1 = 0.5$ cm

Current is constant in wire, then

$$B \propto \frac{1}{d}$$

$$\Rightarrow B_1 d_1 = B_2 d_2$$

$$B_2 = \frac{B_1 d_1}{d_2} = 0.4 \text{ T}$$

2. (i) (*d*); A moving coil galvanometer is a sensitive instrument which is used to measure a deflection when a current flows through its coil.

(ii) (*d*); In the galvanometer, shunt resistance is given as

$$S = \frac{i_g G}{(i - i_g)}$$

$$= \frac{2\times10^{-3}\times 3000}{30 - 2\times10^{-3}}$$

$$= \frac{6}{29.998} = 0.2\ \Omega$$

(iii) (*d*)

(iv) (*c*)

Competition Edge Up

1. (*c*); Electrostatic force, $F_1 = qE$ and magnetic force $F_2 = q(\mathbf{v}\times\mathbf{B})$

2. (*a*); As, $F_e = qE$ and $F_B = Bqv$

When $E = 0$ and $B = 0$, there is no force on charged particle.

When $E = 0$ and $\mathbf{v} \parallel \mathbf{B}$, there is no force on charged particle.

When $F_e = F_B$ or $v = \dfrac{E}{B}$, the net force on charged particle is zero.

(A) $E = 0, B = 0$

(B) $E = 0, B \neq 0$

(D) $E \neq 0, B \neq 0$

Option (a) A, B, D correct.

3. (*a*);

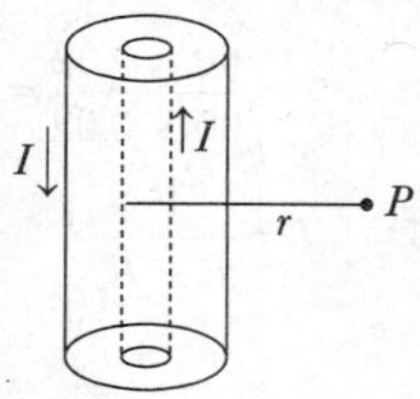

According to Ampere's circuit law,

$$\int \mathbf{B}\cdot d\mathbf{l} = \mu_0 (I_{\text{enclosed}})$$

As $I_{\text{enclosed}} = 0$ (net current)

$$\Rightarrow B = 0$$

Hence, magnetic field outside is zero.

4. (*a*);

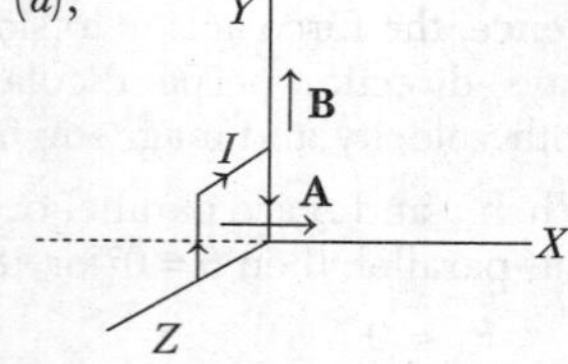

Torque on loop,

$$= \mathbf{m}\times\mathbf{B} = I\mathbf{A}\times\mathbf{B}$$

$$= (5\times0.02\ \hat{i})\times(2\times10^{-3}\ \hat{j})$$

$$= 2\times10^{-4}\ \hat{k} \text{ N-m}$$

5. (*d*); In a galvanometer, $\theta \propto I$

$$\therefore \frac{I_2}{I_1} = \frac{\theta_2}{\theta_1} = \frac{\frac{\pi}{10}}{\frac{\pi}{3}} = \frac{3}{10}$$

$$\Rightarrow I_2 = \frac{3}{10} I_1 = \frac{3}{10}\times 200 = 60\ \mu\text{A}$$

6. (*b*); For a galvanometer;

$$i_g R_g = i_s R_s$$

where, g represent galvanometer and s represent shunt.

$$\because i_g R_g = (i - i_g) R_s$$

Here, $i = 20$ mA, $i_g = 20\ \mu$A

$$\Rightarrow R_s = \left(\frac{20\times10^{-6}}{20\times10^{-3} - 20\times10^{-6}}\right)\times 200$$

$$= \frac{200}{100-1} \simeq 0.20\ \Omega$$

7. (*b*); $I_g = \dfrac{V}{R_g + R_S} = \dfrac{10}{100+400}$

$$\Rightarrow I_g = 20\times10^{-3} \text{ A}$$

$$I_g R_g = (I - I_g)\, S$$

$$20\times10^{-3}\times100 = 10S$$

$$\Rightarrow S = 20\times10^{-2}\ \Omega$$

Hence, value of $x = 20$

8. (*c*); Magnetic field,

$$B = \frac{\mu_0 NI}{2r}$$

$$= \frac{4\pi\times10^{-7}\times100\times7}{2\times10\times10^{-2}}$$

$$\simeq 44\times10^{-4}$$

$$= 4.4\times10^{-3} \text{ T} = 4.4 \text{ mT}$$

9. (*b*); $\mathbf{B} = 2\hat{i} + 3\hat{j} - 4\hat{k}$

$$\therefore \mathbf{F} = I(\mathbf{L}\times\mathbf{B})$$

$$= I\,[L\hat{i}\times(2\hat{i}+3\hat{j}-4\hat{k})]$$

$$= I[2L(\hat{i}\times\hat{i}) + 3L(\hat{i}\times\hat{j}) - 4L(\hat{i}\times\hat{k})]$$

$$= I\,[0 + 3L\hat{k} + 4L\hat{j}]$$

$$= I\,[4L\,\hat{j} + 3L\hat{k}]$$

$$\therefore F = |\mathbf{F}| = \sqrt{(4LI)^2 + (3LI)^2} = 5LI$$

10. (*a*); $\therefore$ Number of turns per metre

$$= \frac{100}{1\times10^{-3}\text{ m}}$$

i.e. $n = 10^5$ turns/m

Current flowing through the solenoid, $I = 1$ A

$\therefore$ Magnetic field strength at the centre of the solenoid, $B = \mu_0 nI$

$$= 4\pi\times10^{-7}\times10^5\times1$$

$$= 4\pi\times10^{-2}\text{ T} = 12.56\times10^{-2}\text{ T}$$

11. (*b*); According to Ampere's circuital law, magnetic field inside the current-carrying long straight wire of circular cross-section is a linearly increasing function of distance $r (r < R)$ upto the boundary of the wire and

magnetic field outside the wire at distance $r(r > R)$ from its axis is decreasing one with $\frac{1}{r}$ dependence as shown in figure.

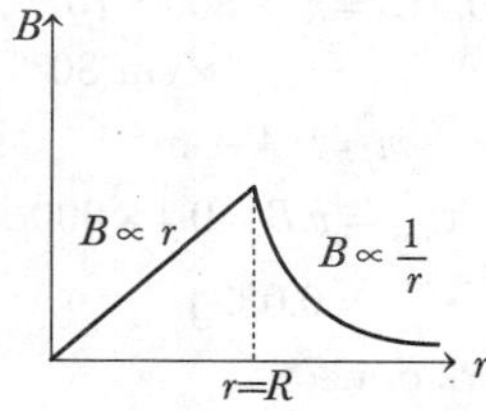

where, R is radius of circular cross-section of wire.

12. (*b*); As we know, $F = q(v \times B)$

Here, $q = 1$ (given)

$\therefore \quad 4\hat{i} - 20\hat{j} + 12\hat{k} = (1)$

$[(2\hat{i} + 4\hat{j} + 6\hat{k}) \times (B\hat{i} + B\hat{j} + B_0\hat{k})]$

$$4\hat{i} - 20\hat{j} + 12\hat{k} = \begin{vmatrix} \hat{i} & \hat{j} & \hat{k} \\ 2 & 4 & 6 \\ B & B & B_0 \end{vmatrix}$$

$\Rightarrow 4\hat{i} - 20\hat{j} + 12\hat{k} = \hat{i}(4B_0 - 6B) - \hat{j}(2B_0 - 6B) + \hat{k}(2B - 4B)$

Comparing the LHS and RHS of the above equation, we get

$4B_0 - 6B = 4 \quad \ldots(i)$

$2B_0 - 6B = 20 \quad \ldots(ii)$

$2B - 4B = 12$

$\Rightarrow \quad B = -6$

From Eq. (ii),

$2B_0 - 6(-6) = 20$

$\Rightarrow \quad B_0 = -8$

Thus, the magnetic field vector,

$B = -6\hat{i} - 6\hat{j} - 8\hat{k}$

Chapter-5

Magnetism and Matter

1. *A*

2. $(B_B < B_A < B_C)$;

Magnitude of the magnetic field increases as the relative closeness between the magnetic field lines increases.

3. False;

Two magnetic field lines do not intersect each other as it will give two directions of line of force at a single point, which is not possible.

4. (*a*)

5. (No);

As we know, magnetic dipole moment, $\mathbf{m} = q_m(2\mathbf{l})$, so a hole in the magnet reduces the effective length of the magnet, hence magnetic moment of magnet with hole is small.

6. (1 : 2 : 6);

As, magnetic moment, $m = q_m \cdot 2l$

$m \propto q_m$

Also, $q_m \propto A$

$\Rightarrow \quad m \propto A$

$\therefore \quad m_1 : m_2 : m_3 = 1 : 2 : 6$

7. (0°); As $\frac{d\tau}{d\theta} = mB\cos\theta$. It will be maximum when $\cos\theta = 1$, i.e. $\theta = 0°$.

8. $\left(\sqrt{\frac{mB}{I}}\right)$;

Time period of compass or magnetic needle in a uniform magnetic field is given by

$$T = 2\pi\sqrt{\frac{I}{mB}}$$

$$\Rightarrow \frac{2\pi}{T} = \sqrt{\frac{mB}{I}}$$

$$\Rightarrow \omega = \sqrt{\frac{mB}{I}} \qquad \left[\because \omega = \frac{2\pi}{T}\right]$$

9. (1.5); As, the time period,

$$T = 2\pi\sqrt{\frac{I}{mB}}$$

or $T \propto \frac{1}{\sqrt{B}} \Rightarrow \frac{T_2}{T_1} = \sqrt{\frac{B_1}{B_2}}$

or $\frac{T_2}{3} = \sqrt{\frac{1}{4}}$ (given)

or $T_2 = 1.5$ s

We can say that, time period reduces to half of its initial value.

10. (i), (ii); Statements (i) and (ii) are incorrect because

(i) Magnetic potential energy U_m is given by

$$U_m = \int mB\sin\theta \, d\theta = -\mathbf{m} \cdot \mathbf{B}$$

which shows that magnetic potential energy is negative.

(ii) Restoring torque is given by $\tau = mB\sin\theta$

11. A → 2, B → 3, C → 1, D → 4

12. (iii) < (i) < (iv) < (ii);

(i) $U = -mB\cos 90° = 0 \quad (\because \cos 90° = 0)$

(ii) $U = -mB\cos 180° = mB \quad (\because \cos 180° = -1)$

(iii) $U = -mB\cos(360° - \theta) = -mB\cos\theta \quad [\because \cos(360° - \theta) = +\cos\theta]$

(iv) $U = -mB\cos(90° + \theta) = mB\sin\theta \quad [\because \cos(90° + \theta) = -\sin\theta]$

13. (ii); Upon cutting a magnet by half, the separated halves also acquires opposite *N-S* poles. Therefore, they oppose or resist to reunification.

So, bar *B* must be a magnet while bar *A* must be made of iron.

14. (1 : 2);

On axial line, $B_A = \frac{\mu_0}{4\pi} \cdot \frac{2m}{r^3}$

and on equatorial line,

$$B_E = \frac{\mu_0}{4\pi} \cdot \frac{m}{r^3} \Rightarrow \frac{B_E}{B_A} = \frac{1}{2}$$

or $B_E : B_A = 1 : 2$

15. True

16. A → 4, B → 3, C → 1, D → 2

17. (*c*); $\Sigma m_i = 0$

As all the dipole moments will cancel out each other when placed in the configuration given below.

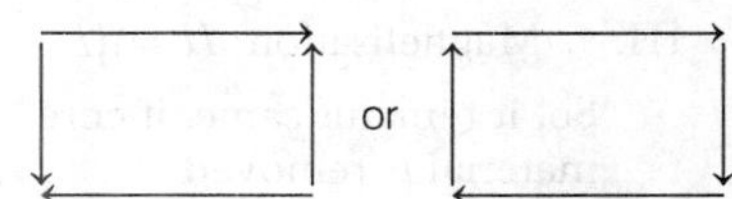

18. (*D*);

For configurations *O* and *D*, the magnetic moment of both dipoles are parallel. Thus, in this configuration, potential energy is lowest.

19. No

20. (zero);

Because magnetic flux through a closed surface is always zero, i.e.

$$\oint_S B \cdot dS = 0$$

21. (*a*); Intensity of magnetisation,

$$I = \frac{M}{V} = \frac{20 \times 10^{-6}}{10^{-6}} = 20 \text{ A/m}$$

Magnetic susceptibility,

$$\chi = \frac{I}{H} = \frac{20}{60 \times 10^3} = 3.33 \times 10^{-4}$$

22. (7.5);

Permeability of iron core,

$$\mu = \mu_0 \mu_r = \mu_0 (1 + \chi_m)$$
$$= (4\pi \times 10^{-7})(1 + 599)$$
$$= 7.5 \times 10^{-4} \text{TmA}^{-1}$$

23. (1431);

$$B = \mu_0 (1 + \chi) H$$
$$\Rightarrow 1.8 = 4\pi \times 10^{-7} (1 + \chi) 1000$$
$$\Rightarrow \chi \simeq 1431$$

24. (2000);

Magnetic intensity, $H = nI$

$$= 1000 \times 2 = 2000 \text{ A/m}$$

25. (*d*); $B = \mu_r \mu_0 H$

$$1 = \mu_r \times 4\pi \times 10^{-7} \times 2000$$
$$\Rightarrow \mu_r = 398 \approx 400$$

26. (I, II);

I. Magnetisation, $M = \frac{(B - \mu_0 H)}{\mu_0}$

$$= \frac{(1 - 4\pi \times 10^{-7} \times 2000)}{4\pi \times 10^{-7}}$$
$$= 8 \times 10^5 \text{ A/m}$$

II. Magnetic field,

$$B = \mu_0 n (i + i_m)$$
$$1 = 4\pi \times 10^{-7} \times 1000 (2 + i_m)$$
$$\left(\because \eta = \frac{H}{I} = \frac{2000}{2} = 1000\right)$$
$$\Rightarrow i_m = 794 \text{ A}$$

III. $\because$ Magnetisation, $H = \eta I$

So, it remains same, if core material is removed.

27. (*b*); Intensity of magnetisation,

$$I = \frac{M}{V} = \frac{M}{\text{mass/density}}$$

Given, mass $= 1 \text{ g} = 10^{-3}$ kg and density $= 5 \text{ g/cm}^3$

$$= \frac{5 \times 10^{-3} \text{ kg}}{(10^{-2})^3}$$
$$= 5 \times 10^3 \text{ kg/m}^3$$

Hence, $I = \frac{6 \times 10^{-7} \times 5 \times 10^3}{10^{-3}}$

$$= 3 \text{A/m}$$

28. (*c*) As, magnetic field on end-on position,

$$B_{\text{axial}} = 9 = \frac{2M}{x^3} \quad \ldots\text{(i)}$$

and magnetic field on broadside

$$B_{\text{equatorial}} = \frac{M}{\left(\frac{x}{2}\right)^3} = \frac{8M}{x^3} \quad \ldots\text{(ii)}$$

On comparing Eqs. (i) and (ii), we get

$$B_{\text{equatorial}} = 36 \text{ gauss}$$

29. (*b*)

30. (Diamagnetic and paramagnetic);

As, $\mu_r < 1$ for substance X, then it must be diamagnetic.

Similarly, $\mu_r > 1$ for substance Y, then it must be paramagnetic.

31. Increases **32.** (*a*)

33. domain

Competition Connect

1. (2A);

Magnetic moment of solenoid,

$$m = NIA$$
$$\Rightarrow 0.40 = 1000 \times I \times 2 \times 10^{-4}$$
$$\Rightarrow I = \frac{0.40 \times 10^4}{1000 \times 2} = 2 \text{ A}$$

2. (*a*); $\tau = \mathbf{m} \times \mathbf{B} = mB \sin\theta$

$$1.6 = m \times 2 \times 10^{-4} \times \sin 45°$$
$$\Rightarrow m = 1.13 \times 10^4 \text{ A-m}^2$$

3. (*d*); Time period of oscillation,

$$T = 2\pi \sqrt{\frac{I}{mB}}$$
$$= 2\pi \sqrt{\frac{7.5 \times 10^{-6}}{6.7 \times 10^{-2} \times 0.01}}$$
$$= 0.665 \text{ s}$$

Hence, time taken for 10 complete oscillations is 6.65 s.

4. (*a*); For unstable equilibrium, **m** is to be anti-parallel to **B**. In this case, $\theta = 180°$, thus

$$U = -mB \cos 180°$$
$$= -mB(-1) = mB$$
$$= (0.32)(0.15) = 4.8 \times 10^{-2} \text{ J}$$

5. (*a*); $B = \frac{4\pi^2 I}{mT^2}$

$$= \frac{4 \times (3.14)^2 \times 7.5 \times 10^{-6}}{6.7 \times 10^{-2} \times (1)^2}$$

$$= 44.14 \times 10^{-4} \text{ T}$$

or 44 G, towards the centre

6. (i) ✓ (ii) ✓ (iii) × (iv) ×

$$\tau = \mathbf{m} \times \mathbf{B} = mB \sin \theta$$
$$\Rightarrow 0.016 = m \times 800 \times 10^{-4} \times \sin 30°$$
$$\Rightarrow m = 0.4 \text{ A-m}^2$$
$$\tau_{\max} = mB = 0.4 \times 800 \times 10^{-4}$$
$$= 0.032 \text{ J}$$

Work done,

$$W = U_m(\theta = 180°) - U_m(\theta = 0°)$$
$$= 2 \times 0.40 \times 800 \times 10^{-4}$$
$$(\because U_m = -mB \cos \theta)$$
$$= 0.064 \text{ J}$$

7. (6.4);

$$B = \frac{\mu_0}{4\pi} \frac{2m}{r^3} = 10^{-7} \times \frac{2 \times 0.40}{(0.5)^3}$$
$$= 6.4 \times 10^{-7} \text{ T}$$

8. (1.6);

$$B_{\text{axial}} = \frac{\mu_0}{4\pi} \frac{2m}{r^3} = 10^{-7} \times \frac{2 \times 50}{(0.4)^3}$$
$$= 1.6 \times 10^{-4} \text{ T}$$
$$\therefore x = 1.6$$

9. $(B_Q < B_R < B_P)$;

$$B_{\text{axial}} = \frac{\mu_0}{4\pi} \frac{2m}{r^3}$$
$$B_{\text{equatorial}} = \frac{\mu_0}{4\pi} \frac{m}{r^3}$$
$$\therefore \quad B_P = \frac{\mu_0}{4\pi} \frac{2m}{(4)^3 \times 10^{-9}}$$
$$= \frac{\mu_0}{4\pi} \frac{m}{32} \times 10^9$$
$$B_Q = \frac{\mu_0}{4\pi} \frac{m}{(6)^3 \times 10^{-9}}$$
$$= \frac{\mu_0}{4\pi} \frac{m}{216} \times 10^9$$
$$B_R = \frac{\mu_0}{4\pi} \frac{m}{(4)^3 \times 10^{-9}}$$
$$= \frac{\mu_0}{4\pi} \frac{m}{64} \times 10^9$$

Therefore, $B_Q < B_R < B_P$

10. (*b*); From Curie's law, $\chi \propto T^{-1}$

$$\frac{\chi_{-173°\text{C}}}{\chi_{-73°\text{C}}} = \frac{T_{-73°\text{C}}}{T_{-173°\text{C}}}$$

$$\frac{\chi_{-173^\circ C}}{0.0060}=\frac{(273-73)}{(273-173)}$$
$$=\frac{200}{100}=2$$
$$\chi_{-173^\circ C}=2\times(0.0060)$$
$$\chi_{-173^\circ C}=0.0120$$

11. $(4.2\times 10^{-2}\ \text{Am}^{-1})$;

Magnetic susceptibility, $\chi \propto \frac{1}{T}$

$$\Rightarrow \chi_1 T_1=\chi_2 T_2$$
$$2.4\times 10^{-5}\times 280=\chi_2\times 320$$
$$\Rightarrow \chi_2=2.1\times 10^{-5}$$

Magnetisation, $M=H\chi_2$
$$=2000\times 2.1\times 10^{-5}$$
$$=4.2\times 10^{-2}\ \text{Am}^{-1}$$

12. I. ✓ II. ✓ III. ✓ IV. ✓

13. Curie temperature

14. A → 2, B → 3, C → 1

A. Diamagnetic materials have negative magnetic susceptibility and it is independent of temperature.

B. In paramagnetic material,
$$\chi\propto\frac{1}{T}$$

C. In ferromagnetic material,
$$\chi\propto\frac{1}{(T-T_C)}$$

15. retentivity **16.** (*a*)

17. (*b*) **18.** True

19. Steel **20.** Soft iron

21. (*a*) **22.** Zero

23. (II);

Hysteresis curve for transformer core must be narrow.

Assertion-Reason Questions

1. (*a*)

2. (*b*); In a ferromagnetic substance, the magnetic moments of the individual atoms are aligned and point in the same direction when placed in an external magnetic field.

3. (*a*)

4. (*a*); When paramagnetic substances are kept in an external magnetic field, then it develops feeble magnetisation in the direction of externally applied magnetic field i.e. magnetic dipoles are weakly aligned along external magnetic field.

5. (*c*); The magnetisation of a paramagnetic material is inversely proportional to the absolute temperatrue T.

$$M=C\frac{B_0}{T}\quad \text{[Curie's law]}$$

where, C = Curie constant.

Thus, a paramagnetic sample displays greater magnetisation (for the same magnetic field) when cooled.

6. (*d*)

7. (*d*); Permeability of a ferromagnetic material depends on the magnetic field.

8. (*b*); The poles of magnet cannot separated by breaking into two pieces.

If a bar magnet is broken into two halves, we get to similar bar magnets with somewhat weaker properties.
As, magnetic moment will be reduced to half because magnetic dipole moment is directly proportional to the length between the poles.

9. (*c*); From the relation, susceptibility of the material is

$$\chi=\frac{M}{H}$$
$$\Rightarrow M=\chi H$$

Thus, it is obvious that greater the value of susceptibility of a material, greater will be the value of intensity of magnetisation, i.e. more easily it can be magnetised.

10. (*d*); For a perfectly diamagnetic substance, permeability is zero.

Case Based Questions

1. (i) (*a*); Magnetic susceptibility χ is negative for diamagnetic.

(ii) (*d*); The magnetic moment of a diamagnetic atom is equal to zero.

(iii) (*a*); χ_m of diamagnetic substance is always negative. It is constant and does not vary with field or temperature.

(iv) (*a*); For protecting a magnetic needle it should be placed in an iron box.

2. (i) (*b*); Above curie temperature ferromagnetic material becomes paramagnetic material.

(ii) (*d*); If temperature is increased beyond curie temp., ferromagnetic substance will show paramagnetism.

(iii) (*a*)

(iv) (*a*)

Competition Edge Up

1. (28); When it is bent in semicircular shape.

$$l=\pi r \text{ or } r=l/\pi$$

Now, the distance between two poles,

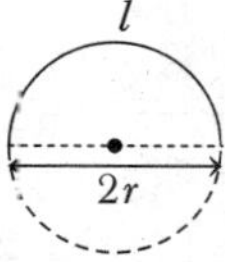

$$2r=2l/\pi$$

Its new magnetic moment is,

$$M'=m\times 2r=m\times\frac{2l}{\pi}$$
$$=\frac{2}{\pi}(m\times l)\quad (\because m\times l=M)$$
$$=\frac{2}{\pi}\times 44=\frac{2}{22}\times 44\times 7$$
$$=7\times 4=28\ \text{Am}^2$$

2. (10); $\therefore\ H=nI=5\times10^3\ \frac{\text{A}}{\text{m}}$

$$\Rightarrow \frac{N}{l}\times I=5\times10^3$$

Here, $N=150$, $l=30\times10^{-2}$ m

$$\Rightarrow \frac{150}{30\times10^{-2}}\times I=5\times10^3$$
$$\Rightarrow I=\frac{5\times10^3\times 30\times10^{-2}}{150}=10\ \text{A}$$

3. (*b*); Paramagnetic substances have a weak net dipole moment of their own.

So, they tend to align with external magnetic field and their susceptibility is a small positive number.

4. (100); Work done in turning coil through 90°

$$=MB(\cos 0^\circ-\cos 90^\circ)$$
$$=MB(1-0)=MB\quad [M=NIA]$$
$$=NIAB$$
$$=100\times1\times10^{-3}\times5\times10^{-3}\times0.2$$
$$=10^{-4}\ \text{J}=100\times10^{-6}\ \text{J}=100\ \mu\text{J}$$

5. (5); Amount of work done,

$W = MB\cos 0° - MB\cos 90°$

$= MB - 0 = MB$

$= NIAB$ $\quad [\because M = NIA]$

$= 200 \times 100 \times 10^{-6} \times 2.5 \times 10^{-4} \times 1$

$= 5\times10^{-6}$ J $= 5$ μJ

6. (*a*); ∴ For most stable state, $\theta_1 = 0°$ and for most unstable stable, $\theta_2 = 180°$

∴ Work done,

$W = MB(\cos 0° - \cos 180°)$

$= 0.5 \times 8 \times 10^{-2}(1+1)$

$= 8 \times 10^{-2}$ J

7. (*a*)

8. (*b*);

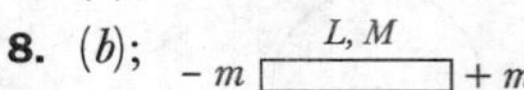

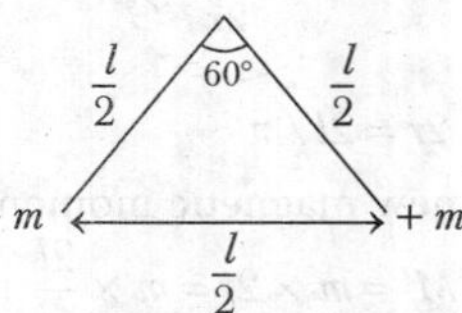

The magnetic moment is given by

$M = m \cdot L$

New magnetic moment,

$M' = m \cdot L' = m \cdot \frac{l}{2} = \frac{ml}{2}$

Thus, $\quad M' = \frac{M}{2}$

9. (*d*); Net magnetic flux through a closed surface is zero because the number of field lines leaving the surface are equal to the number of field lines entering the surface.

10. (*d*); Given, susceptibility, $\chi = 599$

Magnetic field, $B = 1200$ Am^{-1}

Permeability of the material of the rod = ?

As, $\mu_m = \mu_0(1+\chi)$

$= 4\pi \times 10^{-7}(1 + 599)$

$= 2.4\pi \times 10^{-4}$ TmA^{-1}

Chapter-6

Electromagnetic Induction

1. Electromagnetic induction

2. (i) ✓ (ii) ✓ (iii) ✓

3. I < III < II < IV;

Induced current ∝ Speed of magnet

4. Yes

5. False

6. (A → 1, B → 2, C → 3);

A. There is no relative motion between magnet and coil, so no current is induced.

B. The magnet moved towards the coil, so flux or number of field lines increases.

C. The magnet moves away from the coil, so number of field lines decreases.

7. (*b*) Given,

Number of turns, $N = 100$

Radius, $r = 0.01$ m

Resistance, $R = 10\pi^2\Omega$

As we know,

$$\varepsilon = -N\frac{d\phi}{dt}$$

$$\frac{\varepsilon}{R} = -\frac{N\,d\phi}{R\,dt}$$

$$\Delta I = \frac{N\,d\phi}{R\,dt}$$

$$\frac{\Delta}{\Delta t} = -\frac{N\Delta\phi}{R\Delta t}$$

$$\Rightarrow \Delta q = -\left[\frac{N}{R}\left(\frac{\Delta\phi}{\Delta t}\right)\right]\Delta t$$

–ve sign shows that induced emf opposes the change in flux.

$$\Delta q = \frac{\mu_0 n i \pi r^2}{R}$$

$$\Delta q = \frac{4\pi \times 10^{-7} \times 100 \times 4 \times \pi \times (0.01)^2}{10\pi^2}$$

$= 32$ μC

8. increases

9. Faraday's law

10. (*c*); Magnetic flux, $\phi = \mathbf{B}\cdot\mathbf{A}$

$= (\hat{i} + \hat{j} - \hat{k})\cdot(2\hat{i} + 3\hat{j} - 4\hat{k})$

$= 9$ Wb

11. A → 3, B → 1, C → 2;

As, $\phi = \mathbf{B}\cdot\mathbf{A} = BA\cos\theta$

A. $\phi = BA\cos 90° = 0$

B. $\phi = BA\cos 0° = BA$

C. $\phi = BA\cos 37°$

12. 0.02 Wb;

$\phi = BA\cos\theta$

$= B(\pi r^2)\cos\theta$

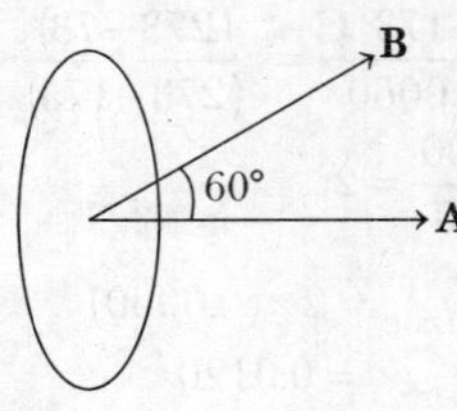

$= \frac{1}{\pi} \times \pi \times (0.2)^2 \cos 60°$

$= 0.02$ Wb

13. (True);

$\phi = BA\cos\theta$

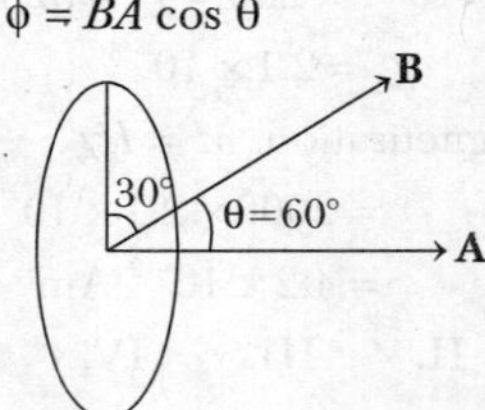

$= 10^4 \times 10 \times 10^{-4} \cos 60°$

$= 5$ Wb

14. True **15.** Yes

16. (No);

It is because emf will be induced across the ends of the pole, as it intercepts neither the horizontal component nor the vertical component of earth's magnetic field.

17. (*b*) **18.** (*c*)

19. (*b*);

Induced current ∝ Relative motion

20. (22);

$\varepsilon\big|_{t=2s} = \frac{d}{dt}(4t^2 + 6t + 9)\Big|_{t=2s}$

$= 8(2) + 6 = 22$ V

21. (16 mV);

$$\varepsilon = \frac{\Delta\phi}{\Delta t} = \frac{(B_2 - B_1)A}{t_2 - t_1}$$

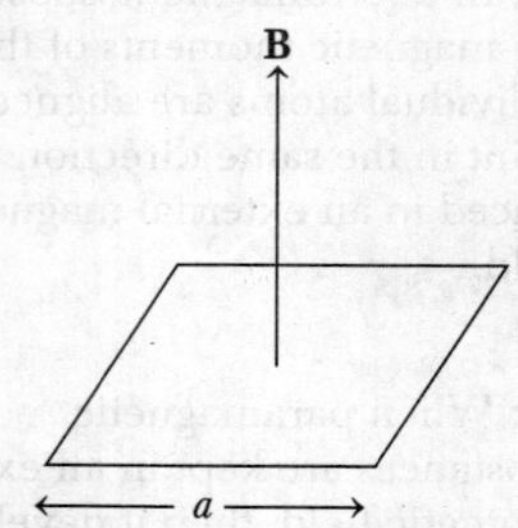

$$= \frac{(0.2-0)\times 0.04}{0.5-0} = 16 \text{ mV}$$

22. (0.2 s);

$$\varepsilon = N \cdot \frac{|\Delta\phi|}{\Delta t} = N \cdot \frac{B \cdot A}{t}$$

$$0.2 = 100 \times \frac{4 \times 10^{-2} \times 10^{-2}}{t}$$

$$\Rightarrow \quad t = 0.2\text{ s}$$

23. (*c*); $\varepsilon = N\dfrac{(\Delta\phi)_{\text{total}}}{\Delta t}$

$$= \frac{(B_2 - B_1) \cdot A \cdot N}{t_2 - t_1}$$

$$\Rightarrow 44 = \frac{(6 \times 10^3 - 10^3) \times \pi \times (0.02)^2 \times N}{4 - 0}$$

$$\Rightarrow N \simeq 28$$

24. (Yes);

$$\varepsilon = \left| -\frac{d\phi}{dt} \right|$$

$$= |-4t + 3|_{t=1} = 1\text{ V}$$

$$\therefore \quad I = \frac{\varepsilon}{R} = 1\text{ A}$$

25. (*a*); $\varepsilon = N\dfrac{|\Delta\phi|}{\Delta t}$

∴ Induced current,

$$I = \frac{\varepsilon}{R} = N \frac{1}{R} \cdot \frac{|\Delta\phi|}{\Delta t}$$

$$= \frac{1}{R} \cdot \frac{(B_2 - B_1) \cdot A \cdot N}{t_2 - t_1}$$

$$= \frac{1}{2} \frac{(10^{-3} - 0) \times (0.1)^2 \times 200}{(10^{-3} - 0)}$$

$$= 1\text{ A}$$

26. (*c*); emf $-\dfrac{d\phi}{dt}$

$$= \frac{-d}{dt}[5t^4 - 100t^2 + 300]$$

$$= -(20t^3 - 200t)$$

At $t = 1$ s, emf

$$= -(20 \times (1)^3 - 200 \times 1)$$

$$= 180\text{ V}$$

27. (*c*); $\left(\dfrac{d\phi}{dt}\right)_{\text{in first case}} = \varepsilon$

$$\left(\frac{d\phi}{dt}\right)_{\text{in second case}} = 4\left(\frac{d\phi}{dt}\right)$$

[∵ relative velocity $4v$]

$$= 4\varepsilon$$

28. (No);

When North pole of a magnet moves towards a coil, the coil will also acquire North polarity and hence, repel the magnet.

29. (*a*)

30. anti-clockwise

31. A → 3, B → 2, C → 4, D → 1;

According to Lenz's law, the direction of induced current is opposite to the cause that produces it.

32. (*c*); The direction of current flow is always opposite to direction of electron flow.

33. A → 2, B → 3, C → 1;

A. The flux in the coil increases, so as per Lenz's law, counter-clockwise current is induced in coil.

B. The flux through the coil decreases, so the current induced will be in clockwise direction.

C. There is no flux change, so no current is induced here.

34. (*a*) **35.** (*b*)

36. True **37.** (*a*)

38. motional emf

39. (True);

$$\varepsilon = Bvl = 1 \times 2 \times 1 = 2\text{ V}$$

40. (2.52 V);

$$\varepsilon = Bvl$$

$$= 0.9 \times 7 \times 0.4 = 2.52\text{ V}$$

41. (8);

Motional emf, $E = Bvl$

$$\Rightarrow \quad A \times 10^{-8} = 2 \times 10^{-6} \times 2 \times 2 \times 10^{-2}$$

$$\therefore \quad A = 8$$

42. As, $\varepsilon = -\dfrac{d\phi}{dt}$

Also, $\varepsilon = Bvl$

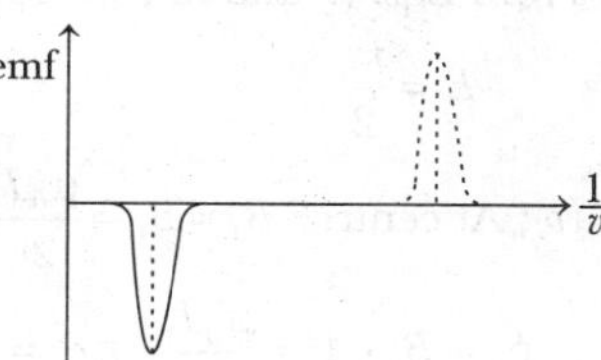

So, when the magnet is approaching the coil, the emf is induced in negative direction, then the flux becomes constant when the magnet is inside it and no emf is induced. Finally when it comes out of it, the emf is induced in positive direction.

43. $\left(I = \dfrac{vBl}{r}\right)$;

$$\varepsilon = \left| -\frac{d\phi}{dt} \right| = \frac{d}{dt}(Blx)$$

$$\therefore \quad \varepsilon = Blv \qquad \left[\because v = \frac{dx}{dt}\right]$$

$$\therefore \quad I = \frac{\varepsilon}{r} = \frac{vBl}{r}$$

44. (True);

$$\varepsilon = Bvl = 0.3 \times 10^{-4} \times 5.0 \times 10$$

$$= 1.5 \times 10^{-3}\text{ V}$$

45. (i) (0.5 V);

Induced emf produced is given by

$$\varepsilon = Blv = 0.4 \times 5 \times 0.25$$

$$= 0.5\text{ V}$$

(ii) (0.1 A);

Current through the 5 Ω resistance, $I = \dfrac{\varepsilon}{R} = \dfrac{0.5}{5} = 0.1$ A

(iii) (From R to S);

According to Lenz's law, the induced current should flow from end R to S through the resistance of 5 Ω.

46. (*a*); $d\varepsilon = Bvdx = B\omega x dx$

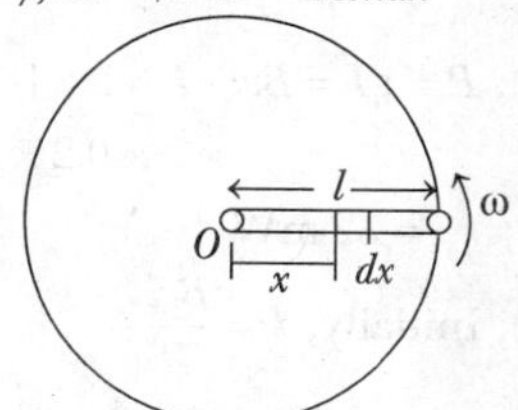

$$\therefore \quad \varepsilon = \int d\varepsilon = B\omega \int_0^l x\,dx = \frac{B\omega l^2}{2}$$

47. – 2;

$$\varepsilon = \frac{B\omega l^2}{2} = \frac{B \times 2\pi f \times l^2}{2}$$

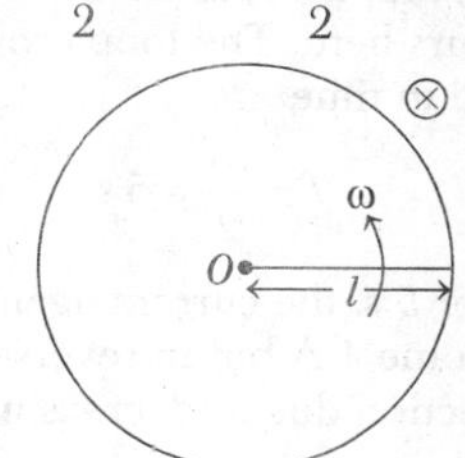

$\Rightarrow 1.5\times 10^{x}$

$$=\frac{0.1\times 2\times \pi \times 20\times \left(\frac{0.1}{2}\right)^2}{2}$$

$\therefore x = -2$

48. (A $\rightarrow$ 2, B $\rightarrow$ 1, C $\rightarrow$ 4, D $\rightarrow$ 3);

A. $E = \frac{1}{2} B\omega l^2$

B. $E = \frac{1}{2} B\omega l^2 - \frac{1}{2} B\omega l^2 = 0$

C. $E = \frac{1}{2} B\omega \left(\frac{l}{2}\right)^2 = \frac{1}{8} B\omega l^2$

D. $E = \frac{1}{2} B\omega \left(\frac{\sqrt{3}l}{2}\right)^2 = \frac{3B\omega l^2}{8}$

49. (*a*); $\varepsilon|_{\text{each spoke}} = \frac{B\omega l^2}{2}$

$$= \frac{B\times 2\pi f \times l^2}{2}$$

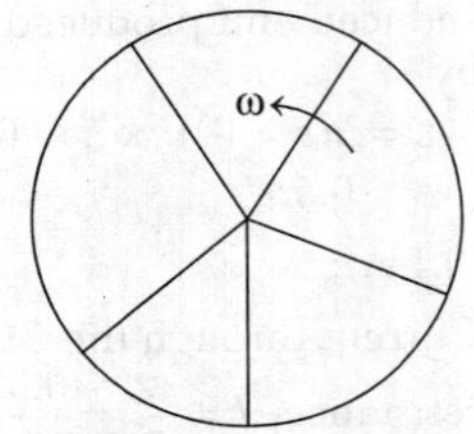

As, 5 spokes are in parallel.

$\therefore \varepsilon_{eq} = \varepsilon$

$$= \frac{10^{-4}\times 2\pi \times 100\times (0.2)^2}{2\times 60}$$

$= 2.09\times 10^{-5}$ V

50. Yes

51. (*a*); $P = \varepsilon I = Bvl \cdot I = 2\times 10^{-3} \times 2\times 0.2\times 40$

$= 32$ mW

52. (*b*); Initially, $I = \frac{Bvl}{R}$

$$= \frac{2\times 2\times 2}{2} = 4\text{A}$$

It remains constant for one second, until the loop is fully inside the field. Then, the current becomes zero, as no flux change occurs here. The loop crosses this field in time

$$t = \frac{10}{2} = 5\text{ s}$$

After 5 s, the current again become 4 A but in reverse direction due to decreasing flux.

The variation is as shown below.

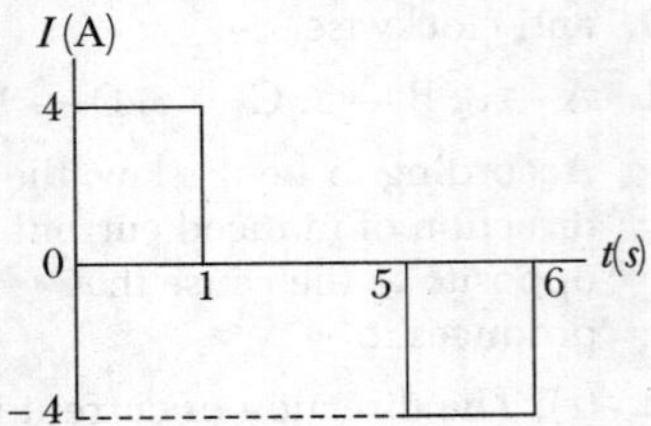

53. (*a*); Flux, $\phi = B\cdot A = Bax$

$\Rightarrow \phi \propto x$ [Slope, $m = Ba$]

where, x is the length of the loop in the field.

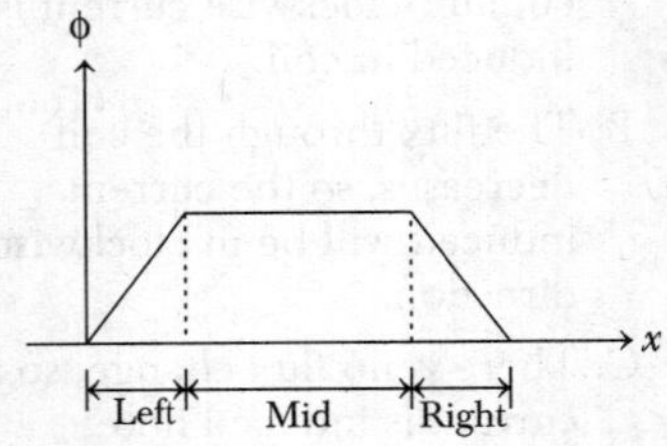

54. (*a*); $B_1 = B_2 = \mu_0 n_2 I_2$

Flux linkage through coil 1,

$N_1\phi_1 = M_{12} I_2$ ...(i)

Also, $N_1\phi_1 = (n_1 l)\cdot \pi r_1^2 \cdot \mu_0 n_2 I_2$ ...(ii)

From Eqs. (i) and (ii), we get

$\Rightarrow M_{12} = \mu_0 n_1 n_2 \pi r_1^2 l$

55. ($rx/2$); Let E be the field strength at any point on the circumference of the ring, then the emf induced

$\varepsilon = \oint \mathbf{E}\cdot d\ell = E 2\pi r$ ...(i)

Also, induced emf

$|\varepsilon| = \frac{d\phi_B}{dt} = \pi r^2 \frac{dB}{dt}$

$= \pi r^2 x$ ...(ii)

From Eqs. (i) and (ii), we get

$$E = \frac{rx}{2}$$

56. (*b*); At centre, $B_2 = B_1 = \frac{\mu_0 I_1}{2r_1}$

$\therefore \phi_2 = B_2 \cdot A_2 = \frac{\mu_0 I_1}{2r_1}\cdot \pi r_2^2 = MI_1$

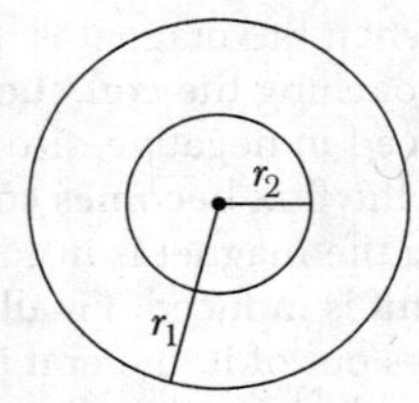

$\Rightarrow M = \left(\frac{\mu_0\pi}{2}\right)\cdot \frac{r_2^2}{r_1}$

$\therefore M \propto \frac{r_2^2}{r_1}$

57. 4H;

$M = \frac{\Delta\phi}{\Delta I} = \frac{4\times 10^{-2}}{10^{-2}} = 4$ H

58. (*b*); ε = induced emf $= \frac{\Delta\phi}{\Delta t}$

$= \frac{M\Delta I}{\Delta t} = \frac{2\times 5}{0.1}$

$= 100$ V

59. (*d*); $L = \frac{\varepsilon\cdot\Delta t}{\Delta I} = \frac{8\times 0.05}{2-(-2)} = 0.1$ H

60. (5 mH);

$L = \frac{\Delta\phi}{\Delta I} = \frac{\varepsilon\cdot\Delta t}{\Delta I}$ $\left[\because \varepsilon = \frac{\Delta\phi}{\Delta t}\right]$

$= \frac{5\times 1\times 10^{-3}}{(3-2)} = 5$ mH

61. (4);

$L \propto n^2 \Rightarrow$ when n is doubled, L becomes 4 times.

62. (1 : 2);

Self-inductance, $L = \frac{\mu_0 N^2 \pi r^2}{l}$

$\Rightarrow \frac{L_1}{L_2} = \left(\frac{r_1}{r_2}\right)^2\left(\frac{l_2}{l_1}\right) = \left(\frac{1}{2}\right)^2 \times \left(\frac{2}{1}\right)$

$\Rightarrow \frac{L_1}{L_2} = \frac{1}{2} = 1:2$

63. (4 mH);

As, $L = \frac{\mu_0 N^2 A}{l}$

$\Rightarrow L = \frac{4\pi\times 10^{-7}\times (10^3)^2\times 10^{-3}}{31.4\times 10^{-2}}$

$= 4$ mH

64. (0.05);

Energy stored,

$E = \frac{1}{2}LI^2 = \frac{1}{2}\times 100\times 10^{-3}\times 1^2$

$= 0.05$ J

65. A $\rightarrow$ 3, B $\rightarrow$ 4, C $\rightarrow$ 1, D $\rightarrow$ 2;

A. $E = \frac{1}{2}LI^2 = \frac{1}{2}\times 2\times (2)^2 = 4$ J

B. $E = \frac{1}{2}\times 3\times 1 = 1.5$ J

C. $E = \frac{1}{2} \times 1 \times 9 = 4.5\text{J}$

D. $E = \frac{1}{2} \times 1 \times 1 = 0.5\text{J}$

66. (ii); $E = NBA\omega \sin \omega t$
$= E_0 \sin 2\pi\nu t$

67. (*b*)

68. (0.314 V);

Maximum voltage emf,

$\varepsilon_{max} = \varepsilon_0 = NBA\omega \sin \omega t$
$= NBA\,(2\pi\nu)$
$[\because \omega = 2\pi\nu, \sin \omega t = 1]$
$= 100 \times 0.01 \times 0.10 \times 2 \times 3.14 \times 0.5$
$= 0.314$ V

Competition Connect

1. (*a*) **2.** eddy current
3. heat **4.** (*a*)
5. True **6.** (*d*)

7. (PVC pipe); Eddy current opposes motion of the magnet in aluminium.

But in PVC due to lack of this current, it requires less time.

Assertion-Reason Questions

1. (*b*)

2. (*a*)

3. (*a*); $L = \frac{-e}{di/dt} \Rightarrow L = 2/4 = 1/2$

On putting values, we get

$\phi = Li \Rightarrow \phi = \frac{1}{2} \times 4 = 2\,\text{Wb}$

4. (*d*); Since, both the loops are identical (same area and number of turns) and moving with a same speed in same magnetic field. Therefore, same emf is induced in both the coils. But the induced current will be more in the copper loop as its resistance wire be lesser as compared to that of the aluminium loop.

5. (*c*); Emf will always induces whenever, there is change in magnetic flux. The current will induced only in closed loop.

6. (*a*); Lenz's law (that the direction of induced emf is always such as to oppose the change that cause it) is direct consequence of the law of conservation of energy.

7. (*a*)

8. (*a*)

9. (*b*); If moving from left to right, current is increasing, then battery $\left(\text{induced emf} = L \cdot \frac{di}{dt}\right)$ will produce right to left current *i.e.*, its positive terminal is on left hand side or $V_A > V_B$.

Further i = constant $\Rightarrow \frac{di}{dt} = 0$ or $V_L = 0$.

10. (*c*); Mutual inductance of two coils depends on the distance between the coils and their orientation and on the magnetic permeability of medium between the coils or nature of material on which two coils are wound.

Case Based Questions

1. (i) (*a*)

Or

(*b*)

(ii) (*b*); $\phi = LI$
$= 5 \times 2.5 = 12.5$ Wb

(iii) (*c*)

(iv) (*b*); $e = -L\frac{di}{dt}$

Given, $L = 10$ H,
$\Delta i = 9 - 4 = 5$ A
$dt = 0.2$ s
$e = 10 \times \frac{5}{0.2} = 250$ V

2. (i) (*b*)

(ii) (*b*); As, charge,

$\Delta Q = \frac{\Delta\phi}{R}$
$= \frac{(10-2)}{2} = 4$ C

(iii) (*b*)

Or

(*d*)

(iv) (*d*); Magnitude of induced emf,

$e = \frac{-d\phi}{dt}$
$e = \frac{-d}{dt}[3t^2 + 4t + 9]$
$= -(6t + 4)$
$= -[6 \times (2) + 4] = -16$ V
$|e| = 16$ V

Competition Edge Up

1. (*3*); Induced emf in loop

$e = \frac{\Delta\phi}{\Delta t} = \frac{NBA}{t}$

Induced power,

$P = \frac{e^2}{R} = \frac{N^2B^2A^2}{t^2 \times R}$

Work done $= P \times t$

$= \frac{N^2B^2A^2}{t^2 \times R} \times t = \frac{N^2B^2A^2}{t \times R}$

$= \frac{10^2 \times \left(\frac{1}{2}\right)^2 \times (3.6 \times 10^{-3})^2}{1 \times 100}$

$\approx 3 \times 10^{-6}$ J

2. (*4*); Given, $I = 3t + 8$

Induced emf, $e = 12$ mV $= 12 \times 10^{-3}$ V

Since, $|e| = L\frac{dI}{dt}$

$\Rightarrow 12 \times 10^{-3} = L \times 3$

$\Rightarrow L = 4 \times 10^{-3}$ H $= 4$ mH

3. (*0*); We know that emf induced across the rotating rod, $\varepsilon = \frac{B\omega l^2}{2}$

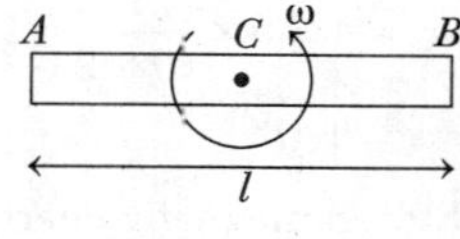

$\therefore$ Induced emf in rod AC = induced emf in rod BC

$= \frac{B\omega(l/2)^2}{2} = \frac{B\omega l^2}{8}$

Also, by symmetry,

$V_A - V_C = V_B - V_C$
$\Rightarrow V_A - V_E = 0$

4. (*2*); Induced current,

$I = -\frac{e}{R} = -\left(\frac{\frac{d}{dt}\phi_B}{R}\right)$

$= -\left(\frac{10t - 36}{8}\right)$

Induced current at $t = 2$s is,

$I = -\left(\frac{10 \times 2 - 36}{8}\right) = 2$ A

5. (*32*); Angular speed, $\omega = 2\pi \times f$
$= \frac{2\pi}{60} \times 1200$ rad/s

$$\omega = 40\pi \text{ rad/s}$$

Induced emf, $\varepsilon = \frac{1}{2} B_V \omega l^2$ ...(i)

$$B_V = B_H \sin\theta$$

$$B_H = 0.5 \text{ G} = 0.5 \times 10^{-4} \text{ T}$$

$$\theta = 30^\circ, \sin 30^\circ = \frac{1}{2}$$

$$B_V = \frac{1}{4} \times 10^{-4}$$

$$\varepsilon = \frac{1}{2} \times \frac{1}{4} \times 10^{-4} \times 40\pi \times (80)^2 \times 10^{-4}$$

$$\varepsilon = 3.2\pi \times 10^{-4} \text{ V} = 32\,\pi \times 10^{-5} \text{ V}$$

6. (*d*); $E_{avg} = \frac{\Delta\phi}{\Delta t} = \frac{BA \cos\theta}{10}$

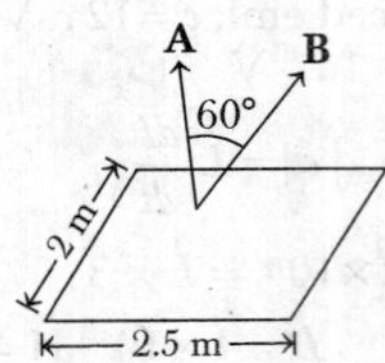

$$= 4 \times 2 \times \frac{5}{2} \times \frac{\cos 60^\circ}{10}$$

$$= 4 \times 5 \times \frac{1}{10 \times 2} = 1 \text{ V}$$

$$= 1 \text{ V}$$

7. (*c*); Stored magnetic energy,

$$U = \frac{1}{2} LI^2$$

$$\therefore \quad U = \frac{1}{2} \times 4 \times 10^{-6} \times 2^2$$

$$= 8 \times 10^{-6} \text{ J} = 8 \text{ μJ}$$

8. (*a*); Magnetic flux passing through the loop,

$$\phi = BA \cos\theta = 0.5 \times 1 \times \cos 0^\circ$$
$$= 0.5 \text{ Wb}$$

9. (*c*); Maximum induced emf

$$= N\omega AB$$

Here area of the circular coil

$$A = \pi r^2$$

$$\varepsilon = N\omega\pi r^2 B$$

$$= 1000 \times 2 \times 3.14 \times (10)^2 \times 2 \times 10^{-5}$$

$$\varepsilon = 12.56 \text{ V}$$

The maximum induced current,

$$i_{max} = \frac{\varepsilon}{R} \Rightarrow i_{max} = \frac{12.56}{12.56} = 1 \text{ A}$$

10. (*d*); Since, both conducting circular loops are in same plane and their centres are coinciding. Hence, magnetic flux,

$$\phi = Mi \quad \text{...(i)}$$

Here, M is the mutual inductance.

Also, the magnetic flux, $\phi = BA$

Here, B is the magnetic field and $A\ (= \pi R_2^2)$ is the area of the inner circular loop. If the current passing through the outer loop is i, then the magnetic field,

$$B = \frac{\mu_0 i}{2R_1}$$

Magnetic flux, $\phi = BA$

$$\Rightarrow \quad \phi = \frac{\mu_0 i}{2R_1} \pi R_2^2 \quad \text{...(ii)}$$

Comparing Eqs. (i) and (ii), we get

$$M = \frac{\mu_0}{2R_1} \pi R_2^2$$

Thus, the mutual inductance is directly proportional to the $\frac{R_2^2}{R_1}$.

11. (*a*); Frequency,

$$f = 12 \text{ rpm} = \frac{120}{60} \text{ rps}$$
$$= 2 \text{ Hz}$$

Induced emf between the axle and rim of the wheel is given as

$$e = \frac{1}{2} B\omega l^2 = \frac{1}{2} B(2\pi f) l^2$$

$$= \pi B f l^2$$

$$= 3.14 \times 0.4 \times 10^{-4} \times 2 \times 1^2$$

$$= 2.51 \times 10^{-4} \text{ V}$$

Chapter-7

Alternating Current

1. AC, $V_m \sin \omega t$ **2.** True

3. (*b*) **4.** zero, zero

5. (*c*); Alternating current keeps changing its polarity periodically. So, for one complete cycle, the average value of alternating current is zero.

6. False

7. Root Mean Square (RMS) current

8. (True); $I = I_1 \cos\omega t + I_2 \sin\omega t$

$$I = \sqrt{I_1^2 + I_2^2 + I_1 I_2 \cos 90^\circ}$$

$$I = \sqrt{I_1^2 + I_2^2} \quad \text{...(i)}$$

$$I_{rms} = \frac{I}{\sqrt{2}} \quad \text{...(ii)}$$

Therefore, from Eqs. (i) and (ii), we get

$$I_{rms} = \frac{1}{\sqrt{2}} \sqrt{I_1^2 + I_2^2}$$

9. (2.5 ms);

$\therefore$ Current

$$(I_{rms}) = \frac{V}{R} = \frac{220 \sin(100\pi t)}{20}$$

$$\Rightarrow \quad I_{rms} = 11 \sin(10\pi t)$$

$$I_{max} = 11 \text{A and } \sin(100\pi t)_{max} = 1$$

$\therefore$ We know that,

$$I_{rms} = \frac{I_0}{\sqrt{2}} = \frac{11}{\sqrt{2}}$$

$$\therefore \quad I_{rms} = 11 \sin(100\pi t)$$

$$\frac{11}{\sqrt{2}} = 11 \sin(100\pi t)$$

$$100\pi t = \sin^{-1}\left(\frac{1}{\sqrt{2}}\right)$$

$$100\pi t = \frac{\pi}{4}$$

$$t = \frac{1}{400} \text{ s} = 2.5 \times 10^{-3} \text{ s}$$
$$= 2.5 \text{ms}$$

10. (198 V);

$$E_{rms} = 220 \text{ V}$$

$$\therefore E_{rms} = \frac{\varepsilon_0}{\sqrt{2}} \Rightarrow \varepsilon_0 = \sqrt{2}\, E_{rms}$$

Average emf over half-cycle

$$= \frac{2}{\pi}\varepsilon_0 = \frac{2}{\pi} \times 220\sqrt{2} = 198 \text{ V}$$

11. (84.8 V);

$$V_{rms} = \frac{V_0}{\sqrt{2}} = \frac{120}{\sqrt{2}}$$

$$V_{rms} = 84.8 \text{ V}$$

12. $(\sqrt{2} \times 220)$;

$$V_{rms} = \frac{V_0}{\sqrt{2}}$$

$$\Rightarrow \quad V_0 = \sqrt{2} V_{rms}$$

$$= \sqrt{2} \times 220 \text{ V}$$

13. (*b*); For peak voltage,

$$V_{peak} = 100 \times \frac{1}{\sqrt{2}} \times \frac{1}{\sqrt{2}}$$

$$V_{peak} = 50 \text{ V}$$

14. (I);

$$V_{rms} = \frac{V_0}{\sqrt{2}} = \frac{240}{\sqrt{2}} = 170 \text{ V}$$

Frequency $(f) = \frac{\omega}{2\pi} = 19$ Hz

15. A → 2, B → 1, C → 3;

Peak voltage,

$$V_0 = \sqrt{2} V_{rms}$$
$$= \sqrt{2} \times 220 = 311 \text{ V}$$

Resistance of bulb,

$$R = \frac{V^2}{P} = \frac{(220)^2}{100} = 484 \ \Omega$$

rms current,

$$I_{rms} = \frac{P}{V_{rms}} = \frac{100}{220} = 0.454 \text{ A}$$

16. (i) ✓ (ii) ✓ (iii) ✓

17. A → 2, B → 3, C → 1

18. current

19. (*d*); As $V = L\frac{-dI}{dt}$, so voltage is a negative constant when the current is linearly increasing (for $t = 0$ to T) and it is a positive constant when the current is decreasing linearly (for $t = \frac{T}{2}$ to T).

It is correctly shown in option (d).

20. (8);

$$I_{min} = \frac{e}{R}$$

$$I_{max} = \frac{e}{R_{eq}}$$

Here, $\frac{1}{R_{eq}} = \frac{1}{R} + \frac{1}{R_{L_1}} + \frac{1}{R_{L_2}}$

$$= \frac{1}{12} + \frac{1}{3} + \frac{1}{4} = \frac{8}{12}$$

$$\therefore \frac{I_{max}}{I_{min}} = \frac{R}{R_{eq}} = \frac{12 \times 8}{12} = 8$$

21. (9.42 Ω);

$$X_L = 2\pi f L$$
$$= 2 \times 3.14 \times 50 \times 30 \times 10^{-3}$$
$$= 9.42 \ \Omega$$

22. (I);

I. $X_L = 2\pi f L \Rightarrow L = \frac{X_L}{2\pi f}$

$$= \frac{120}{2\pi \times 200}$$

$$= \frac{3}{10\pi} \text{ H}$$

II. X_L' (at 60 Hz)

$$= 2\pi \times 60 \times \frac{3}{10\pi}$$
$$= 36 \ \Omega$$

III. $I_{rms} = \frac{V_{rms}}{X_L'} = \frac{240}{36} = 6.66$ A

23. later, one-fourth

24. (7.85 Ω, 28 A);

$$X_L = 2\pi f L$$
$$= 2 \times 3.14 \times 50 \times 25 \times 10^{-3}$$
$$= 7.85 \ \Omega$$
$$I = \frac{V}{X_L} = \frac{220}{7.85} = 28 \text{ A}$$

25. Yes

26. $(\omega C V_m)$; $q = CV_m \sin \omega t$

$$I = \frac{dq}{dt} = \omega C V_m \cos \omega t$$

The maximum amplitude will be

$$I_m = \omega C V_m$$

27. (*a*); $X_C \propto \frac{1}{f}$

When f is doubled, X_C will be halved.

$$I \propto f$$

So, current will be doubled.

28. (i) ✓ (ii) ✓ (iii) ✓

29. earlier, one-fourth

30. A → 2, B → 3, C → 1

31. (I, II);

$$X_C = \frac{1}{\omega C} = \frac{1}{2\pi f C}$$
$$= \frac{1}{2 \times 3.14 \times 60 \times 60 \times 10^{-6}}$$
$$= 44.2 \ \Omega$$
$$\therefore I_{rms} = \frac{E}{X_C} = \frac{110}{44.2} \simeq 2.49 \text{ A}$$

32. (i) (zero);

When DC source is connected, the capacitor is charged but no current flows in the circuit. Therefore, the lamp will not glow.

(ii) (reduced);

Capacitive reactance, $X_C = \frac{1}{\omega C}$ comes into play when the capacitor is connected to AC supply. Therefore, if C is reduced, X_C increases. Hence, the brightness of the lamp is reduced.

33. (A → 1, B → 3, C → 2);

$$X_C = \frac{1}{2\pi f C}$$
$$= \frac{1}{2\pi \times 50 \times 15 \times 10^{-6}} = 212 \ \Omega$$
$$I_{rms} = \frac{V_{rms}}{X_C} = \frac{220}{212} = 1.04 \text{ A}$$
$$I_m = \sqrt{2} I_{rms}$$
$$= \sqrt{2} \times 1.04 = 1.47 \text{ A}$$

34. (20 mA);

$$I_{rms} = \frac{E_{rms}}{X_C} = \frac{E_0}{\sqrt{2}} \times \frac{\omega C}{1}$$
$$= \frac{200\sqrt{2}}{\sqrt{2}} \times 100 \times 10^{-6}$$
$$= 20 \text{ mA}$$

35. $\left(\sqrt{\frac{3}{5}}\right)$;

$$I_{rms} = \frac{V_{rms}}{\sqrt{R^2 + X_C^2}}$$
$$= \frac{V_{rms}}{\sqrt{R^2 + (1/\omega C)^2}} \quad \text{... (i)}$$

When $\omega \to \omega/3$, then

$$\frac{I_{rms}}{2} = \frac{V_{rms}}{\sqrt{R^2 + \left(\frac{3}{\omega C}\right)^2}} \quad \text{... (ii)}$$

Dividing Eq. (ii) by Eq. (i), we get

$$\frac{1}{2} = \frac{\sqrt{R^2 + X_C^2}}{\sqrt{R^2 + 9X_C^2}} \left(\because X_C = \frac{1}{\omega C}\right)$$
$$\Rightarrow \frac{X_C}{R} = \sqrt{\frac{3}{5}}$$

36. $\tan^{-1}\left(\frac{4}{3}\right)$;

$$\tan \phi = \frac{X_L}{R} = \frac{\omega L}{R}$$
$$= \frac{400\pi \times \frac{1}{\pi}}{300} \quad (\because \omega = 2\pi f)$$
$$\Rightarrow \phi = \tan^{-1}\left(\frac{4}{3}\right)$$

37. (i) capacitive, leads (ii) lags

38. large

39. (1×10^6 rad/s);

$$\omega_0=\frac{1}{\sqrt{LC}}=\frac{1}{\sqrt{10^{-3}\times10^{-9}}}$$

$$=1\times10^6 \text{ rad/s}$$

40. (inductive);

$X_L=X_C$ (at resonance)

$X_L\propto\omega$

$X_C\propto\frac{1}{\omega}$

So, $X_L>X_C$

41. (3.98×10^5 Hz, 753.8 m);

$$2\pi f=\frac{1}{\sqrt{LC}}\Rightarrow f=\frac{1}{2\pi}\times\frac{1}{\sqrt{LC}}$$

$$=\frac{1}{2\pi}\frac{1}{\sqrt{8\times10^{-6}\times0.02\times10^{-6}}}$$

$$=3.98\times10^5 \text{ Hz}$$

$$\therefore \lambda=\frac{c}{f}=\frac{3\times10^8}{3.98\times10^5}$$

$$=753.8 \text{ m}$$

42. (A_3);

When the frequency of the power supply is equal to the resonant frequency, the potential difference across the power supply is equal to the potential difference across the inductor and capacitor at all times. In such instance, no current will be flowing through A_3.

43. (250 kV);

Current through R,

$$I=\frac{100}{1}=100 \text{ A}$$

At resonance,

$$V_L=V_C=IX_C$$

$$=100\times\frac{1}{200\times2\times10^{-6}}$$

$$=250 \text{ kV}$$

44. (i) (600 rad/s);

$$\omega_0=2\pi f=2\times3\times100$$

$$=600 \text{ rad/s}$$

(ii) $\left(\frac{1}{36\times10^3}\text{F}\right)$;

$$X_C=\frac{1}{C\omega_0}$$

$$60=\frac{1}{C\times600}$$

$$\Rightarrow C=\frac{1}{36\times10^3}\text{ F}$$

(iii) (0.1 H);

$$\omega_0=\frac{1}{\sqrt{LC}}$$

$$600=\frac{1}{\sqrt{L\left(\frac{1}{36\times10^3}\right)}}$$

$$\Rightarrow L=0.1 \text{ H}$$

45. (*b*)

46. (2.54);

$$Q=\frac{\omega_r L}{R}=\frac{2\pi fL}{R}$$

$$=\frac{2\times\pi\times500\times8.1\times10^{-3}}{10}$$

$$=2.54$$

47. (*c*); Quality factor,

$$Q=\frac{\omega_0 L}{R}=\frac{1}{R}\sqrt{\frac{L}{C}}$$

For option (a), $Q=10.35$

For option (b), $Q=9.42$

For option (c), $Q=22.77$

For option (d), $Q=7.30$

48. (i) ✓ (ii) ✓ (iii) ✓

49. Resonance

50. (1.11×10^3 rad/s);

$$\omega_r=\frac{1}{\sqrt{LC}}$$

$$=\frac{1}{\sqrt{27\times10^{-3}\times30\times10^{-6}}}$$

$$=1.11\times10^3 \text{ rad/s}$$

51. same, same

52. (*a*)

53. ($50\sqrt{2}$ V);

$$V_{CR}=\sqrt{V_C^2+V_R^2}$$

$$=\sqrt{(50)^2+(50)^2}=50\sqrt{2}\text{ V}$$

54. (10 V);

$$E=\sqrt{V_R^2+(V_L-V_C)^2}$$

$$=\sqrt{8^2+(16-10)^2}=10 \text{ V}$$

55. (True);

In an L-C-R series circuit, the voltage across the capacitor and the inductor are in opposite direction.

$$V_L-V_C=0 \text{ V}$$

56. (Yes);

$$V=\sqrt{V_R^2+(V_L-V_C)^2}$$

$$=\sqrt{(40)^2+(60-30)^2}=50 \text{ V}$$

57. (II);

$$X_C=\frac{1}{2\pi fC}$$

$$=\frac{1}{2\times3.14\times50\times15\times10^{-6}}$$

$$=212\ \Omega$$

$$Z=\sqrt{R^2+X_C^2}$$

$$=\sqrt{(200)^2+(212)^2}=291.5\ \Omega$$

$$I_{rms}=\frac{V_{rms}}{Z}=\frac{220}{291.5}$$

$$=0.755 \text{ A}$$

58. (i) (2A);

$$I=\frac{V_{rms}}{\sqrt{R^2+(X_L-X_C)^2}}$$

$$=\frac{10}{\sqrt{(3)^2+(15-11)^2}}=2 \text{ A}$$

(ii) (6 V, 30 V, 22 V);

$V_R=IR=2\times3=6$ V

$V_L=2\times15=30$ V

$V_C=2\times11=22$ V

59. (A → 1, B → 2, C → 4, D → 3);

$$X_L=\omega L=400\times20\times10^{-3}=8 \text{ H}$$

$$X_C=\frac{1}{\omega C}=\left(\frac{1}{400\times625\times10^{-6}}\right)$$

$$=4\ \Omega$$

$$\therefore Z=\sqrt{R^2+(X_L-X_C)^2}$$

$$=\sqrt{(3)^2+(8-4)^2}=5\ \Omega$$

$$\Rightarrow I=\frac{E}{Z}=\frac{300}{5}=60 \text{ A}$$

60. (i) (0.3 A);

Impedance,

$$Z_1=\sqrt{R_1^2+X_C^2}$$

$$=\sqrt{(100)^2+(100)^2}$$

$$\left(\because X_C=\frac{1}{\omega C}=\frac{1}{100\times100\times10^{-6}}\right)$$

$$=100\sqrt{2}\ \Omega$$

$$\text{Current, } I_1=\frac{V}{Z_1}=\frac{20}{100\sqrt{2}}\text{ A} \quad \ldots\text{(i)}$$

$$Z_2=\sqrt{R_2^2+X_L^2}$$

$= \sqrt{(50)^2 + (50)^2}$

$(\because X_L = \omega L = 0.5 \times 100)$

$= 50\sqrt{2}\ \Omega$

$I_2 = \frac{20}{50\sqrt{2}}$ A ...(ii)

Total current,

$I = \sqrt{I_1^2 + I_2^2}$ ...(iii)

From Eqs. (i), (ii) and (iii), we get

$I = \sqrt{\left(\frac{200}{100\sqrt{2}}\right)^2 + \left(\frac{20}{50\sqrt{2}}\right)^2}$

$= \frac{1}{\sqrt{10}} = 0.3$ A

(ii) $(10\sqrt{2}$ V);

Voltage across 100 Ω resistor,

$V_{100} = I_1 R_1 = 10\sqrt{2}$ V

(iii) $(10\sqrt{2}$ V);

Similarly, $V_{50} = I_2 R_2$

$= 10\sqrt{2}$ V

61. (*c*); $\tan \phi = \frac{X_L - X_C}{R}$

$\tan 45^\circ = \frac{X_L - X_C}{R}$

$\Rightarrow \quad X_C = X_L - R$

or $\quad C = \frac{1}{2\pi f(2\pi f L - R)}$

62. (*d*)

63. (Yes);

$\omega = \frac{1}{\sqrt{LC}}$

$2\pi f = \frac{1}{\sqrt{LC}}$

$\Rightarrow f = \frac{1}{2\pi} \times \frac{1}{\sqrt{5 \times 80 \times 10^{-6}}}$

$= \frac{25}{\pi}$ Hz

64. (True);

$f_r = \frac{1}{2\pi\sqrt{LC}}$

As the frequency is unchanged

$f_r = f_r'$

$LC = L'C'$

$L' = \frac{L}{2} \quad (\because C' = 2C)$

65. maximum

66. ($V_3 = 220$ V, $A = 2.2$ A);

The given *L-C-R* circuit is in resonance, as

$V_L = V_C = 300$ V

Therefore, $V_3 = 220$ V

Ammeter reading (A),

$I = \frac{V}{Z} = \frac{220}{100} = 2.2$ A

67. (II);

$\omega = \frac{1}{\sqrt{LC}}$

$= \frac{1}{\sqrt{8 \times 10^{-3} \times 20 \times 10^{-6}}}$

$= 2500$ rad/s

Resonance current,

$I_r = \frac{V}{R} = \frac{220}{44} = 5$ A

68. (zero);

$V = 5 \sin\left(\omega t + \frac{\pi}{2}\right)$ volt

$\left[\because \cos \omega t = \sin\left(\omega t + \frac{\pi}{2}\right)\right]$

and $I = 2 \sin \omega t$ ampere

Angle between voltage and current is $\frac{\pi}{2}$.

$\therefore P = V_{rms} I_{rms} \cos\frac{\pi}{2} = 0$

69. (*d*); $\phi = \frac{\pi}{2}$

$P = V_{rms} I_{rms} \cos\frac{\pi}{2} = 0$

70. (50 W);

$V_{rms} = \frac{200}{\sqrt{2}}$

$I_{rms} = \frac{1}{\sqrt{2}}$

$P = V_{rms} I_{rms} \cos\phi$

$= \frac{200}{\sqrt{2}} \cdot \frac{1}{\sqrt{2}} \cos\frac{\pi}{3} = 50$ W

71. True

72. *L* and *C*

73. (*c*); $P_{avg} = V_{rms} I_{rms} \cos\phi$

$= \frac{100}{\sqrt{2}} \times \frac{20}{\sqrt{2}} \times \cos\frac{\pi}{4}$

$= \frac{1000}{\sqrt{2}}$ W

Wattless current

$= I_{rms} \sin\phi$

$= \frac{20}{\sqrt{2}} \times \sin 45^\circ$

$= 10$ A

74. A → 4, B → 1, C → 3, D → 2

75. Yes

76. (0.80);

$Z = \sqrt{R^2 + (X_C - X_L)^2}$

$= \sqrt{8^2 + (25 - 31)^2}$

$= 10\ \Omega$

$\cos\phi = \frac{R}{Z} = \frac{8}{10} = 0.80$

77. (i) (5 Ω);

$X_L = 2\pi f L = 2 \times \pi \times 50 \times 25.48 \times 10^{-3}$

$= 8\ \Omega$

$X_C = \frac{1}{2\pi f C}$

$= \frac{1}{2\pi \times 50 \times 796 \times 10^{-6}}$

$= 4\ \Omega$

$\therefore Z = \sqrt{R^2 + (X_L - X_C)^2}$

$= \sqrt{3^2 + (8-4)^2} = 5\ \Omega$

(ii) (– 53.1°);

$\phi = \tan^{-1}\left(\frac{X_C - X_L}{R}\right)$

$= \tan^{-1}\left(\frac{4-8}{3}\right) = -53.1^\circ$

(iii) (4805 W);

$P = I^2 R = \left(\frac{I_0}{\sqrt{2}}\right)^2 R$

$= \left(\frac{V_0}{Z\sqrt{2}}\right)^2 \times R$

$= \left(\frac{283}{5\sqrt{2}}\right)^2 \times 3 = 4805$ W

(iv) (0.6);

$\text{PF} = \cos\phi = \cos(-53.1^\circ) = 0.6$

78. (*d*); The Leclanche cell produces direct current. Since, transformers operate on alternating current rather than direct current, the ratio given here won't work. As a result, voltage developed in secondary coil would be zero.

79. (100);

When AC current changes from positive maximum value to negative maximum value, then

Time taken, $dt = \frac{T}{2} = \frac{1}{2v}$

$$= \frac{1}{2 \times 50} = \frac{1}{100} \text{ s}$$

$$e = M\frac{dI}{dt}$$

$$= 0.5 \times \left(\frac{2}{\frac{1}{100}}\right) = 100 \text{ V}$$

80. (400);

$$\frac{V_1}{V_2} = \frac{n_1}{n_2}$$

$$\frac{2300}{230} = \frac{4000}{n_2} \Rightarrow n_2 = 400$$

81. (I);

$$I_s = \frac{E_s}{R_s} = \frac{22}{220} = 0.1 \text{ A}$$

$$\because \quad \frac{E_s}{E_p} = \frac{I_p}{I_s}$$

$$\Rightarrow \quad I_p = 0.01 \text{ A}$$

82. (0.27 A);

It is a step-down transformer, so

$$I_p = \frac{1}{2} \times I_L = \frac{1}{2} \times 0.54$$

$$= 0.27 \text{ A}$$

83. (Yes);

$$\eta = \frac{\text{Power output}}{\text{Power input}} \times 100$$

$$\frac{80}{100} = \frac{120 \times 20}{1000 \times I_1}$$

$$I_1 = 3 \text{ A}$$

84. (A → 2, B → 3, C → 1);

$$I_p = \frac{P_{in}}{V_p} = \frac{3000}{200} = 15 \text{ A}$$

$$\eta = \frac{P_{out}}{P_{in}}$$

$$\frac{90}{100} = \frac{6\, V_s}{3000}$$

$$V_s = 450 \text{ V}$$

$$P_0 = 6 \times 450 = 2700 \text{ W}$$

85. (c)

Assertion-Reason Questions

1. (a)

2. (c); $Z = \sqrt{R^2 + (X_L - X_C)^2}$

$$Z_{min} = R$$

$$\therefore \quad I_{max} = \frac{V}{Z_{min}} = \frac{V}{R}$$

$$\therefore \cos\phi = \frac{R}{Z} = \frac{R}{R} = 1 = \cos 0^\circ$$

$$\phi = 0$$

3. (c); $P = EI\cos\phi$

In case of purely resistive circuit,

$$\phi = 0^\circ$$

$$P_{max} = EI$$

4. (a) **5.** (d) **6.** (a)

7. (d); Conductor for DC $X_L = 2\pi f L$. For DC, it offers zero inductive reactance.

8. (b) **9.** (d) **10.** (c)

Case Based Questions

1. (i) (c); In AC circuit, power loss $P = VI\cos\phi \Rightarrow P = VI = I^2R$ $(\because \quad \phi = 0 \text{ at resonance})$

(ii) (b); Dissipation of power is an AC circuit is $P = VI\cos\phi$

(iii) (b); $\therefore \phi = \frac{\pi}{2} = 90^\circ$

$$P = I_{rms}V_{rms}\cos\phi$$

$$\Rightarrow \quad P = 0 \quad [\because \cos 90^\circ = 0]$$

(iv) (d); Average power in circuit over one cycle

$$< P > = < ei > = \frac{1}{2}E_o I_0 \cos\phi$$

2. (i) (d); For ideal transformer

Input power = Output power

$$V_P I_P = V_s I_s \Rightarrow I_P = \frac{V_S I_S}{V_P}$$

$$\Rightarrow I_P = \frac{44}{220} = \frac{1}{5} = 0.2\text{A}$$

(ii) (b); $\eta = \frac{V_S I_S}{V_P I_P} \Rightarrow 0.9 = \frac{V_S(6)}{3 \times 10^3}$

$$\Rightarrow V_S = 450\text{V}$$

$$V_P I_P = 3000$$

$$\Rightarrow \quad I_P = \frac{3000}{200} = 15\text{A}$$

(iii) (a); $\eta = \frac{V_S I_S}{V_P I_P} = 0.8$

$$\Rightarrow I_P = \frac{440 \times 2}{0.8 \times 220} = 5\text{A}$$

(iv) (b); $\eta = \frac{V_S I_S}{V_P I_P} \times 100$

$$V_S I_S = 100 \text{ W}$$

$$\eta = \frac{100 \times 100}{220 \times 0.5} = 90.9 \cong 90\%$$

Competition Edge Up

1. (10); **Case 1**

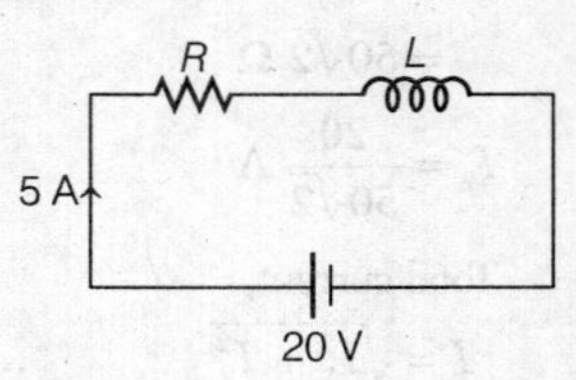

$$i = \frac{20}{R} \Rightarrow 5 = \frac{20}{R} \Rightarrow R = 4\,\Omega$$

Case 2

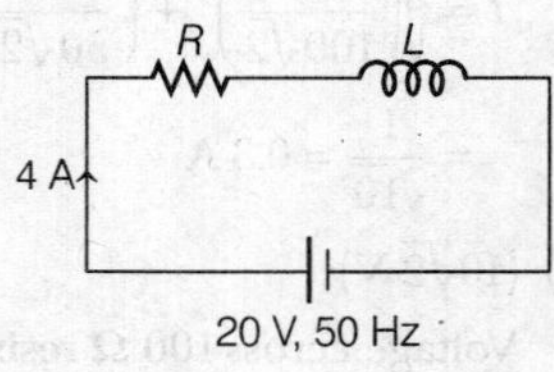

$$i = \frac{20}{Z}$$

$$\Rightarrow 4 = \frac{20}{Z} = \frac{20}{\sqrt{R^2 + X_L^2}}$$

$$\sqrt{R^2 + X_L^2} = 5 \Rightarrow R^2 \times X_L^2 = 25$$

$$(4)^2 + X_L^2 = 25$$

$$X_L^2 = 25 - 16 = 9$$

$$X_L = 3\,\Omega; \; L = \frac{X_L}{2\pi f} = \frac{3}{2\pi \times 50}$$

$$L = \frac{1000}{100} \text{ mH} = 10 \text{ mH}$$

2. (22);

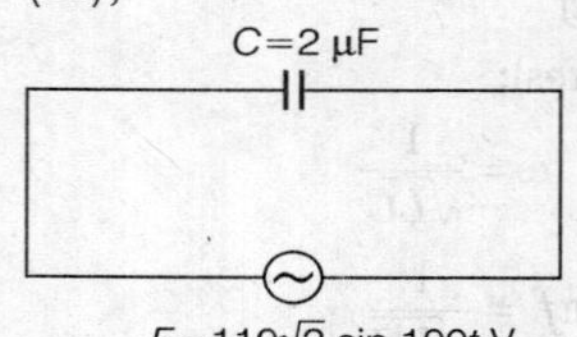

By comparing with standard equation of emf

$$E = E_0 \sin(\omega t)$$

we get, $\omega = 100 \frac{\text{rad}}{\text{s}}$

Capacitive reactance,

$$X_C = \frac{1}{C\omega} = \frac{1}{2 \times 10^{-6} \times 100}$$

$$= \frac{10000}{2} = 5000\,\Omega$$

We know that,

$$I_0 = \frac{E_0}{X_C} \Rightarrow I_0 = \frac{110\sqrt{2}}{5000}$$

$\Rightarrow \quad I_{\text{rms}} = \dfrac{I_0}{\sqrt{2}} = \dfrac{110}{5000}$

$= 2.2 \times 10^{-2}\text{A} = 22 \times 10^{-3}\text{A}$

$= 22 \text{ mA}$

3. (*b*); In a series *L-C-R* circuit,

$V_{\text{rms}} = 200 \text{ V}, f = 50 \text{ Hz},$

$V_L = 31.4 \text{ V}$

$\Rightarrow IX_L = 31.4$

$\Rightarrow \quad I = \dfrac{31.4}{X_L} = \dfrac{31.4}{\omega L} = \dfrac{31.4}{2\pi f L}$

$= \dfrac{31.4}{2 \times 3.14 \times 50 \times 10 \times 10^{-3}}$

$= \dfrac{1}{10^{-1}} = 10 \text{ A}$

4. (13.33 A); Now, efficiency $= \dfrac{P_{\text{out}}}{P_{\text{in}}}$

$\Rightarrow \quad \dfrac{P_{\text{out}}}{P_{\text{in}}} = \dfrac{80}{100}$

$\Rightarrow \quad \dfrac{V_{\text{out}} \cdot I_{\text{out}}}{P_{\text{in}}} = \dfrac{80}{100}$

$\Rightarrow \quad \dfrac{240 \times I_{\text{out}}}{4 \times 1000} = \dfrac{80}{100}$

$\Rightarrow \quad I_{\text{out}} = \dfrac{80 \times 4 \times 1000}{240 \times 100}$

$= 13.33 \text{ A}$

5. (*b*); We know that, transformation ratio, $r = \dfrac{N_s}{N_p} = \dfrac{V_s}{V_p}$

$\because \quad \dfrac{N_p}{N_s} = \dfrac{1}{2} = \dfrac{V_p}{V_s}$

$\Rightarrow V_s : V_p = 2:1$

6. (*d*); According to given situation,

$V_s = 12 \text{ V},$

$\therefore \quad I_s = \dfrac{P}{V_s} = \dfrac{60}{12} = 5 \text{ A}$

$\therefore$ Given, $V_p = 220$ V

For ideal transformer.

$I_p V_p = I_s V_s$

$\Rightarrow \quad I_p = \dfrac{I_s V_s}{V_p} = \dfrac{5 \times 12}{220} = 0.27 \text{ A}$

7. (*c*); In series *L-C-R* circuit,

$L = 10 \text{ mH} = 10^{-2} \text{ H}$

$C = 1\mu\text{F} = 10^{-6} \text{ F}, R = 100\ \Omega$

$\therefore$ Resonance frequency,

$f = \dfrac{1}{2\pi\sqrt{LC}} = \dfrac{1}{2\pi\sqrt{10^{-2} \times 10^{-6}}}$

$= \dfrac{1}{2\pi \times 10^{-4}} = \dfrac{10^4}{2\pi}$

$= 1.59 \times 10^3 \text{ Hz} = 1.59 \text{ kHz}$

8. (*b*); We know that, peak voltage V_0 and rms voltage V_{rms} are related as

$\therefore \quad V_0 = \sqrt{2}\, V_{\text{rms}}$

9. (*a*); Given, in series *L-C-R* circuit,

$L = 10 \text{ H}, C = 10\ \mu\text{F} = 10^{-5}\text{F}$

$R = 50\ \Omega$

Source voltage,

$V = 200 \sin(100\, t)$ V

$\omega = 100$ rad/s

$\therefore 2\pi\nu = 100 \Rightarrow \nu = \dfrac{100}{2\pi} = \dfrac{50}{\pi}$ Hz

Resonance frequency,

$\nu_0 = \dfrac{1}{2\pi\sqrt{LC}} = \dfrac{1}{2\pi\sqrt{10 \times 10^{-5}}}$

$= \dfrac{1}{2\,\pi \times 10^{-2}} = \dfrac{50}{\pi}$ Hz

Hence, $\nu = \nu_0 = \dfrac{50}{\pi}$ Hz

10. (*c*); Given, $L = 5$ H, $R = 40\ \Omega$ and $C = 80\ \mu$F

As, $\omega_r = \dfrac{1}{\sqrt{LC}}$

Substituting the values in the above equation, we get

$\omega_r = \dfrac{1}{\sqrt{5 \times 80 \times 10^{-6}}}$

$= 50$ rad/s

Therefore, the angular frequencies of the source at which power transferred to the circuit is half the power at the resonant angular frequency are

$\omega = \omega_r \pm \Delta\omega \quad \ldots\text{(i)}$

We know that,

$\Delta\omega = \dfrac{R}{2L} \Rightarrow \Delta\omega = \dfrac{40}{2(5)}$

$\Rightarrow \quad \Delta\omega = 4$

Using the Eq. (i), we get

$\omega = \omega_r \pm \Delta\omega$

$\omega = (50 \pm 4)$ rad/s

So, the angular frequency is likely to be 46 rad/s and 54 rad/s.

11. (*a*); The rating of the lamp = 11 V, 44 W

We know that, $P = VI_P \quad \ldots\text{(i)}$

Here, *P* is the power that operates the lamp,

V is the supply line voltage,

I_P is the primary current in the transformer.

From Eq. (i), we get

$\Rightarrow 44 = I_P \times 220 \Rightarrow I_P = 0.2$ A

12. (*b*); As, $X_C = \dfrac{1}{2\pi\nu C}$

$= \dfrac{1}{2\pi \times 50 \times 40 \times 10^{-6}}$

$= \dfrac{250}{\pi}\ \Omega$

$\therefore \quad I_{\text{rms}} = \dfrac{V_{\text{rms}}}{X_C} = \dfrac{200}{\left(\dfrac{250}{\pi}\right)} = 2.5$ A

Chapter-8

Electromagnetic Waves

1. Changing electric field

2. conduction, electric

3. (*c*)

4. (iii) and (iv)

5. $-2q_0\pi\nu\sin(2\pi\nu t)$;

$q = q_0 \cos 2\pi\nu t$

$i_d = \dfrac{dq}{dt}$

$q = q_0 \cos 2\pi\nu t$

$\Rightarrow \quad i_d = \dfrac{d}{dt}(q_0 \cos 2\pi\nu t)$

$= q_0 \times 2\pi\nu\,(-\sin 2\pi\nu t)$

$\therefore \quad i_d = -2q_0\pi\nu \sin 2\pi\nu t$

6. $(2 \times 10^{-7}$ A);

i_d = displacement current

$= i = \dfrac{dq}{dt} = 2 \times 10^{-7}$ A

7. True

8. different

9. Yes

10. (II); $\oint \mathbf{B} \cdot d\mathbf{l} = \mu_0 i_c + \mu_0 \varepsilon_0 \cdot \dfrac{d\phi_E}{dt}$

(Ampere-Maxwell law)

It shows that time dependent electric and magnetic fields are inter-related to each other.

11. A $\rightarrow$ 3, B $\rightarrow$ 2, C $\rightarrow$ 4, D $\rightarrow$ 1

12. (i) (45.29 V/m);

$$q = CV\,(1 - e^{-t/RC})$$
$$= 10^{-9} \times 2\,(1 - e^{-1})$$
$$= 1.26 \times 10^{-9}\ \text{C}$$
$$\oint \mathbf{E} \cdot d\mathbf{A} = \frac{q}{\varepsilon_0}$$
$$\Rightarrow E = \frac{q}{\varepsilon_0 A} = \frac{q}{\varepsilon_0 \pi}$$
$$(\because A = \pi \times 1^2)$$
$$\Rightarrow E = \frac{1.26 \times 10^{-9}}{8.854 \times 10^{-12} \times \pi}$$
$$= 45.29\ \text{V/m}$$

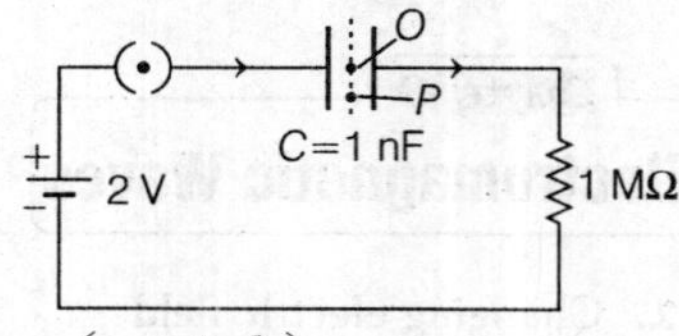

(ii) $\left(i_d = \dfrac{1}{4}\dfrac{dq}{dt} \right)$;

$$i_d = \varepsilon_0 \cdot \frac{d\phi_E}{dt} = \varepsilon_0 \frac{d}{dt}(E \cdot A')$$
$$= \varepsilon_0 \cdot \frac{d}{dt}\left[\frac{q}{\varepsilon_0 \pi} \times \pi \times \left(\frac{1}{2}\right)^2 \right]$$
$$\therefore i_d = \frac{1}{4} \cdot \frac{dq}{dt}$$

13. (c)

14. in phase, perpendicular

15. I. ✓ II. × III. ✓

16. **E** is parallel to *X*-axis, **B** is parallel to *Y*-axis, so electromagnetic wave will be parallel to *Z*-axis.

17. (i) × (ii) × (iii) ✓ (iv) ×

18. $E = E_0 \sin(kz + \omega t)$

19. (a)

20. (2 rad/m);

Wave number,

$$k = \frac{\omega}{c} = \frac{6 \times 10^8}{3 \times 10^8} = 2\ \text{rad/m}$$

21. (0.37); $\lambda = \dfrac{c}{f} = \dfrac{c}{\dfrac{\omega}{2\pi}}$

$$= \frac{2\pi \times 3 \times 10^8}{0.5 \times 10^{10}}$$
$$= 0.37\ \text{m}$$

22. (a); Frequency of electromagnetic waves produced by the charged particle is equal to the frequency of oscillation of the charge,

$\nu = 10^9$ Hz.

Wavelength of electromagnetic wave,

$$\lambda = \frac{c}{\nu} = \frac{3 \times 10^8}{10^9} = 0.3\ \text{m}$$

23. (II);

I. Wavelength, $\lambda = \dfrac{c}{f} = \dfrac{c}{\dfrac{\omega}{2\pi}}$

$$= \frac{3 \times 10^8 \times 2\pi}{10^7} = 188.4\ \text{m}$$

II. Wave number,

$$k = \frac{\omega}{c} = \frac{10^7}{3 \times 10^8}$$
$$= 0.033\ \text{rad/m}$$

III. Wave amplitude,
$E_0 = 10$ V/m

IV. Wave moving in negative *x*-direction.

24. (b); $E_0 = cB_0 = 3 \times 10^8 \times 20 \times 10^{-9}$
$= 6\ \text{Vm}^{-1}$

25. (153 N/C);

$$E_0 = cB_0$$
$$\Rightarrow E_0 = 3 \times 10^8 \times 510 \times 10^{-9}$$
$$\Rightarrow E_0 = 153\ \text{N/C}$$

26. (c); Angular frequency,

$$\omega = 2\pi\nu$$
$$= (2 \times 3.14\ \text{rad})\,(50 \times 10^6\ \text{Hz})$$
$$= 3.14 \times 10^8\ \text{rads}^{-1}$$

Wave constant,

$$k = \frac{\omega}{c} = \frac{3.14 \times 10^8\ \text{rads}^{-1}}{3 \times 10^8\ \text{ms}^{-1}}$$
$$= 1.05\ \text{rad m}^{-1}$$
$$E = E_0 \sin(kx - \omega t)\hat{\mathbf{j}}$$
$$= [120\ \text{NC}^{-1} \sin\{(1.05\ \text{rad m}^{-1})\,x - (3.14 \times 10^8\ \text{rads}^{-1})\,t\}]\,\hat{\mathbf{j}}$$

27. (a); $v = \dfrac{1}{\sqrt{\mu\varepsilon}}$

Also, $\mu = \mu_0\mu_r$ and $\varepsilon = \varepsilon_0\varepsilon_r$.

$$\therefore \quad v = \frac{1}{\sqrt{\mu_r\varepsilon_r\mu_0\varepsilon_0}} = \frac{c}{\sqrt{\mu_r\varepsilon_r}} \quad \left[\because c = \frac{1}{\sqrt{\mu_0\varepsilon_0}}\right]$$
$$= \frac{3 \times 10^8}{\sqrt{1 \times 1.44}} = 2.5 \times 10^8\ \text{ms}^{-1}$$

28. II

29. vertical, horizontal

30. (4.425×10^{-8} J/m^3);

Energy density,

$$\mu_E = \frac{1}{2}\varepsilon_0 E_0^2$$
$$= \frac{1}{2} \times 8.85 \times 10^{-12} \times (100)^2$$
$$= 4.425 \times 10^{-8}\ \text{J/m}^3$$

31. (unity);

As, $u_E = u_B$

$$\therefore \quad \frac{u_E}{u_B} = 1\ \text{(unity)}$$

32. I and II

33. (a); $c = \dfrac{E_0}{B_0}$

$$\Rightarrow B_0 = \frac{6.3}{3 \times 10^8} = 2.1 \times 10^{-8}\ \text{T}$$
$$\therefore B_0 = 2.1 \times 10^{-8}\ \hat{\mathbf{k}}\ \text{T}$$
$$[\because \hat{\mathbf{j}} \times \hat{\mathbf{i}} = \hat{\mathbf{k}}]$$

34. (1.2×10^{-6} N);

Total energy falling on surface,
$U = (18\ \text{W/m}^2) \times (20\ \text{m}^2) \times (30 \times 60) = 6.48 \times 10^5$ J

Total momentum delivered,

$$p = \frac{U}{c} = 2.16 \times 10^{-3}\ \text{kg-m/s}$$

Average force exerted on the surface,

$$F = \frac{p}{t} = \frac{2.16 \times 10^{-3}}{0.18 \times 10^4} = 1.2 \times 10^{-6}\ \text{N}$$

35. (A $\rightarrow$ 2, B $\rightarrow$ 1, C $\rightarrow$ 3);

A. Intensity $= \dfrac{\text{Power}}{\text{Area}}$

$$= \frac{100 \times 2.5\%}{4\pi(3)^2}$$
$$= 0.022\ \text{W/m}^2$$

B. $I_E = \dfrac{\text{Total intensity}}{2} = \dfrac{I}{2}$

$$\Rightarrow \frac{1}{2}\varepsilon_0 E_{\text{rms}}^2 c = \frac{I}{2}$$
$$\Rightarrow \frac{8.85 \times 10^{-12} \times E_{\text{rms}}^2 \times 3 \times 10^8}{2} = \frac{0.022}{2}$$
$$E_{\text{rms}} = 2.9\ \text{V/m}$$

C. $B_{\text{rms}} = \dfrac{E_{\text{rms}}}{c} = \dfrac{2.9}{3 \times 10^8}$

$$= 9.6 \times 10^{-9}\ \text{T}$$

36. $(4I_0)$;

As, $I_E = I_B$

$\therefore \quad x = 4I_0$

37. No

38. III < I < II < IV

39. (i) ✓ (ii) ✓ (iii) × (iv) ✓ (v) ✓

40. A → 3, B → 1, C → 4, D → 2

41. (300 m);

We know that, wavelength,

$$\lambda = \frac{c}{\nu} \qquad (\because c = \nu\lambda)$$

$$= \frac{3\times10^8}{1\times10^6} = 3\times10^2 = 300 \text{ m}$$

42. (*a*)

43. (Microwave);

$$\lambda = \frac{2\pi}{k} = \frac{2\pi}{0.5\times10^3}$$

$$= 0.01256 \text{ m}$$

The wavelength of this wave lies between 10^{-3} to 0.1 m, so the equation represents a microwave.

44. (*a*); Ozone layer lies in stratosphere.

45. True

46. A → 1, B → 2, C → 3, D → 4

47. (*c*)

Assertion-Reason Questions

1. (*d*)

2. (*b*); Thermal radiations are infrared waves. They have wavelengths more than the visible rays because all the waves in infrared zone have the wavelength more than that of visible light. Since, thermal radiations are infrared waves, they follow the properties of light. So, they can propagate through vacuum.

3. (*b*); Consider a plane perpendicular to the direction of propagation of the electromagnetic wave. If electric charges are present in this plane, they will be set and sustained in motion by the electric and magnetic fields of the electromagnetic wave. The charge thus acquires energy and momentum from the wave. This illustrates the fact that an electromagnetic wave like other waves, carries energy and momentum.

4. (*c*); Electromagnetic waves interact with matter via their electric and magnetic fields which is oscillation of charges present in all matter. The detailed interaction and so the mechanism of absorption, scattering, etc. depend on the wavelength of the electromagnetic wave, the nature of the atoms and molecules in the medium.

5. (*a*)

6. (*b*)

7. (*b*)

8. (*b*)

9. (*c*); The frequency range of microwaves is from 10^9 to 10^{11} Hz.

10. (*b*); The wavelength of these waves ranges between 4000 Å to 100 Å that is smaller wavelength and higher frequency. They are absorbed by the atmosphere and convert oxygen into ozone. They cause skin diseases and they are harmful to eye and cause permanent blindness.

Case Based Questions

1. (i) (*b*); Comparing the given equation with the standard equation of electromagnetic wave,

$$B = B_0 \sin(kx + wt)$$

We have, $k = \dfrac{2\pi}{\lambda} = 0.5\times10^3$

$$\lambda = \frac{2\pi}{0.5\times10^3} \text{ m} = 1.26 \text{ cm}$$

(ii) (*a*); $\omega = 2\pi\nu = 1.5\times10^{11}$

$$\nu = \frac{1.5\times10^{11}}{2\pi} \text{ Hz}$$

$$= 23.6\times10^{10} \text{ Hz}$$

(iii) (*a*); $E_0 = B_0 c$

$$= 2\times10^{-7}\times3\times10^8$$

$$= 60 \text{ NC}^{-1}$$

The electric field is perpendicular to both the magnetic field and the direction of propagation of wave. Thus,

$$E_z = (60 \text{ NC}^{-1}) \sin(0.5\times10^3 x + 1.5\times10^{11} t)$$

(iv) (*d*); Average energy density corresponding to electric and magnetic field is given by

$$u_{av} = \frac{1}{4}\varepsilon_0 E_0^2 = \frac{B_0^2}{4\mu_0}$$

Substituting the values,

$$u_{av} = \frac{(2\times10^{-7})^2}{4(4\pi\times10^{-7})}$$

$$= \frac{4\times10^{-14}}{4\times4\pi\times10^{-7}}$$

$$= \frac{1}{4\pi}\times10^{-7} \text{ Jm}^{-3}$$

2. (i) (*a*); The intensity of plane electromagnetic wave s

$$I = \frac{1}{2}\varepsilon_0 E_0^2 c$$

∴ Amplitude of electric field

$$E_0 = \sqrt{\frac{2I}{\varepsilon_0 c}} = 54.87 \text{ NC}^{-1}$$

(ii) (*a*); Amplitude of magnetic field, $B_0 = \dfrac{E_0}{c}$

[E_0 is calculated in above part]

$$= \frac{54.87}{3.0\times10^8}$$

$$= 1.83\times10^{-7} \text{ T}$$

(iii) (*c*)

(iv) (*c*)

Competition Edge Up

1. (*a*); We know that, $\left|\dfrac{E_0}{B_0}\right| = c$

$$\Rightarrow \quad 60 = B_0\times3\times10^8$$

$$B_0 = 2\times10^{-7} \Rightarrow c = f\lambda$$

$$3\times10^8 = f\times4\times10^{-3}$$

$$\Rightarrow \quad f = \frac{3}{4}\times10^{11}$$

$$\omega = 2\pi f = 2\pi\times\frac{3}{4}\times10^{11}$$

$$\omega = \frac{\pi}{2}\times10^3\times3\times10^8$$

$$k = \frac{2\pi}{\lambda} = \frac{2\pi}{4\times10^{-3}} = \frac{\pi}{2}\times10^3$$

$$\therefore B_z = 2\times10^{-7}\sin\left[\frac{\pi}{2}\times10^3(x - 3\times10^8 t)\right]\hat{k} \text{ T}$$

2. (*a*); Intensity, $I = \frac{1}{2}\varepsilon_0 E_0^2 c$

$= \frac{1}{2} \times 9 \times 10^{-12} \times 600^2 \times 3 \times 10^8$

$= 4.86 \times 10^2 = 486 \text{ W/m}^2$

3. (*c*) ;Wavelength range for infrared wave is 1 mm to 700 nm.

Hence, $A \rightarrow III$

Wavelength range for ultraviolet wave is 400 nm to 1 nm.

$\therefore \quad B \rightarrow II$

Wavelength range for X-rays is 1 nm to 10^{-3} nm.

$\therefore \quad C \rightarrow IV$

Wavelength range for Gamma rays is less than 10^{-3} nm.

$\therefore \quad D \rightarrow I$

4. (*b*); $\lambda_{\gamma\text{-rays}} < \lambda_{X\text{-rays}} < \lambda_{\text{infrared}} < \lambda_{\text{microwave}}$

$\Rightarrow \lambda_1 < \lambda_2 < \lambda_3 < \lambda_4$

5. (*d*); Frequency, $f = 60 \times 10^6$ Hz

Velocity, $c = 3 \times 10^8$ m/s

$\text{Wavelength} = \frac{c}{f} = \frac{3 \times 10^8}{60 \times 10^6}$

$= 0.5 \times 10 = 5 \text{ m}$

6. (*b*); When a capacitor is charged through a battery, its opposite plates are charged to a maximum value. There is displacement current as the capacitor is being charged,

$$I_d = \varepsilon \cdot \frac{d\phi_E}{dt}$$

Due to charging, ϕ_E changes and hence displacement current equal to conduction current arises while charging. When capacitor gets fully charged, the displacement current became zero.

7. (*d*); Electromagnetic waves are generated by accelerated charged particles.

Hence, option (d) is incorrect.

8. (*b*) ; As we know, $\frac{|E|}{|B|} = c = \frac{E_0}{B_0}$

where, E_0 = Amplitude of electric field.

B_0 = Amplitude of magnetic field.

$\therefore B_0 = \frac{E_0}{c} = \frac{48 \text{ Vm}^{-1}}{3 \times 10^8 \text{ ms}^{-1}}$

$= 1.6 \times 10^{-7}$ T

9. (*c*); Velocity of light (EM wave) is given by

$$v = \frac{c}{\sqrt{\mu_r \varepsilon_r}}$$

10. (*c*); γ-rays has the shortest wavelength because it has higher frequency than UV-rays, microwaves and X-rays.

Chapter-9

Ray Optics and Optical Instruments

1. 60;

Angle of reflection,

$r = i = 90° - 30° = 60°$

2. (*c*); Incident ray, reflected ray and normal to the reflecting surface lie in the same plane (*xy*-plane).

Hence, reflected beam cannot be directed along + *Z*-axis.

3. I. Negative II. Positive

III. Positive IV. Positive

4. Focal plane

5. (20°, 2 : 1);

$i = r = 10°$

$\alpha = 10° + 10° = 20°$

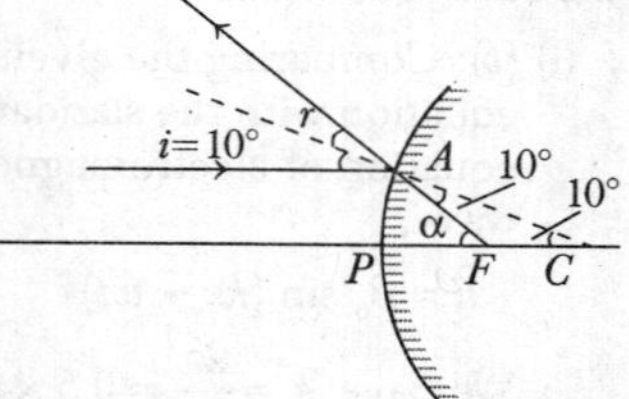

Now, $\frac{CP}{FP} = \frac{R}{f} = \frac{2f}{f} = 2:1$

6. (i) ✓ (ii) ✓ (iii) ×

7. (0°);

Incident ray passes through normal

$\therefore \quad i = r = 0°$

8. ($B'P, B'C$);

$\Delta ABC \sim \Delta A'B'C'$

$\therefore \frac{A'B'}{AB} = \frac{B'C}{BC}$ ...(i)

$\Delta A'B'F \sim \Delta NPF$

$\frac{A'B'}{NP} = \frac{A'B'}{AB} = \frac{B'F}{PF}$ ...(ii)

From Eqs. (i) and (ii), we get

$\frac{B'F}{PF} = \frac{B'P - PF}{PF} = \frac{B'C}{BC}$

9. I. Virtual II. Virtual

10. Yes

11. (*a*); By mirror formula,

$\frac{1}{v} + \frac{1}{u} = \frac{1}{f} \Rightarrow \frac{1}{v} + \frac{1}{(-15)} = \frac{1}{(-10)}$

$\therefore \quad v = -30$ cm

$\therefore \quad m = -\frac{v}{u} = -\frac{(-30)}{(-15)} = -2$

So, image is magnified, real and inverted.

12. (I);

I. $\frac{1}{v} + \frac{1}{u} = \frac{1}{f}$

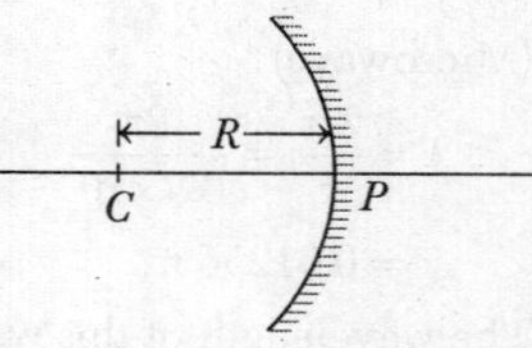

$\Rightarrow \frac{1}{v} + \frac{1}{(-15)} = \frac{1}{(-10)}$

$\Rightarrow v = -30$ cm

$\therefore m = -\frac{v}{u} = -\frac{(-30)}{(-15)} = -2$

II. $\frac{1}{v} + \frac{1}{(-5)} = \frac{1}{(-10)}$

$\Rightarrow v = 10$ cm

$\therefore m = -\frac{v}{u} = -\frac{(10)}{(-5)} = 2$

13. low

14. (i) (– 30 cm, magnified, real and inverted, – 3);

$\frac{1}{v} + \frac{1}{u} = \frac{1}{f}$

$\Rightarrow \frac{1}{v} + \frac{1}{(-10)} = \frac{1}{-\frac{15}{2}}$

$\Rightarrow v = -30$ cm

$\therefore m = -\frac{v}{u} = -\frac{(-30)}{(-10)} = -3$

Image is magnified; real and inverted.

(ii) (15 cm, magnified, virtual and erect, 3);

$\frac{1}{v} + \frac{1}{(-5)} = \frac{1}{-\frac{15}{2}}$

$$\Rightarrow \quad v = 15 \text{ cm}$$

$$\therefore \quad m = -\frac{v}{u}$$

$$= \frac{-15}{-5} = 3$$

Image is magnified, virtual and erect.

15. (0.35);

By mirror formula,

$$\frac{1}{v_I} + \frac{1}{u_I} = \frac{1}{f}$$

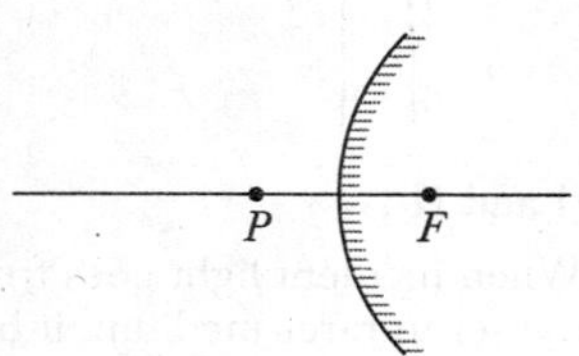

$$\Rightarrow \frac{1}{v_I} + \frac{1}{(-39)} = \frac{1}{1}$$

$$\Rightarrow \quad v_I = \frac{+39}{40} \text{ m}$$

When speed $= 5 \text{ ms}^{-1}$

$\Rightarrow$ In 1s, $\Delta u = 5 \text{ m}$

$\therefore u_F = -(39 - 5) = -34 \text{ m}$

Again by mirror formula,

$$\frac{1}{v_F} + \frac{1}{(-34)} = \frac{1}{1}$$

$$\Rightarrow \quad v_F = +\frac{34}{35} \text{ m}$$

$$\therefore \quad \Delta v = v_I - v_F$$

$$= \frac{39}{40} - \frac{34}{35} = \frac{1}{280} \text{ m}$$

$$\therefore \text{Image speed} = \frac{\Delta v}{\text{Time}}$$

$$= \frac{\left(\frac{1}{280}\right) \times 100}{1}$$

$$= 0.35 \text{ cm s}^{-1}$$

16. increases

17. A and B

18. II

19. Ratio of speed of light in two media

20. (40°);

$$n_{gw} = n_{ga} \times n_{aw}$$

$$\Rightarrow \frac{\sin 45°}{\sin \theta} = \frac{\sin 50°}{\sin 40°} \times \frac{\sin 45°}{\sin 50°}$$

$$\therefore \quad \theta = 40°$$

21. less

22. True

23. (49.72°);

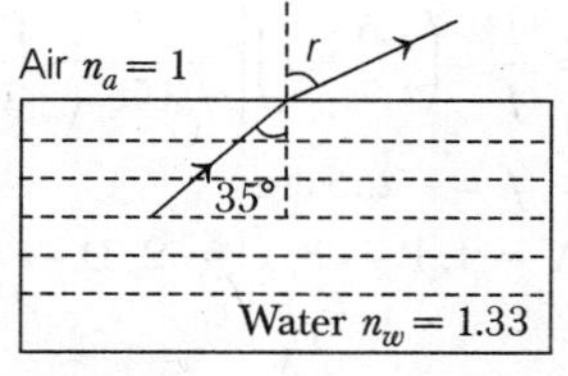

By Snell's law of refraction,

$$\frac{n_a}{n_w} = \frac{\sin i}{\sin r}$$

$$\Rightarrow \quad \frac{1}{1.33} = \frac{\sin 35°}{\sin r}$$

$$\Rightarrow \quad \sin 35° \times 1.33 = \sin r$$

$$\Rightarrow \quad \sin r = 0.7629$$

$$\Rightarrow \quad r = \sin^{-1}(0.7629) = 49.72°$$

24. (*a*) ;

$$\frac{v_g}{v_w} = \frac{\sin 45°}{\sin \theta} \quad \left[\because \mu = \frac{c}{v}\right]$$

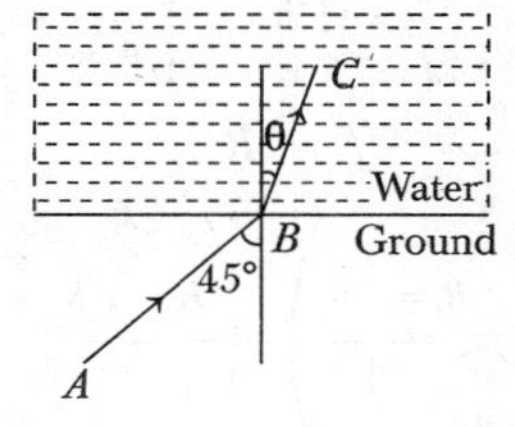

$$\Rightarrow \quad \frac{10}{2} = \frac{\frac{1}{\sqrt{2}}}{\sin \theta}$$

$$\Rightarrow \text{cosec}\,\theta = 5\sqrt{2}$$

25. $\cos^{-1}(8/9)$;

From Snell's law,

$$n_{21} = \frac{\sin i}{\sin r}$$

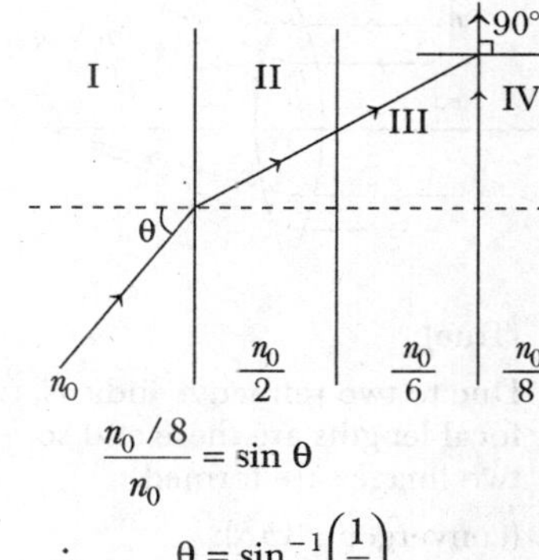

$$\frac{\frac{4}{3}}{\frac{3}{2}} = \frac{\sin(90° - \theta)}{\sin 90°} = \cos \theta$$

$$\Rightarrow \quad \theta = \cos^{-1}\left(\frac{8}{9}\right)$$

26. $\left(\frac{1}{\sin i}\right)$;

$$\frac{n_a}{n_g} = \frac{\sin i}{\sin 90°} \Rightarrow n_g = \frac{1}{\sin i}$$

$[\because n_a = 1]$

27. (*b*); $n_{41} = \frac{\sin \theta}{\sin 90°}$

$$\frac{n_0/8}{n_0} = \sin \theta$$

$$\therefore \quad \theta = \sin^{-1}\left(\frac{1}{8}\right)$$

28. $\frac{n_2}{v} - \frac{n_1}{u} = \frac{n_2 - n_1}{R}$

29. (100 cm);

$$\frac{n_2}{v} - \frac{n_1}{u} = \frac{n_2 - n_1}{R}$$

$$\Rightarrow \frac{1.5}{v} - \frac{1}{(-100)} = \frac{1.5 - 1}{20}$$

$$\therefore v = +100 \text{ cm}$$

30. (Yes);

$$\frac{n_2}{v} - \frac{n_1}{u} = \frac{n_2 - n_1}{R}$$

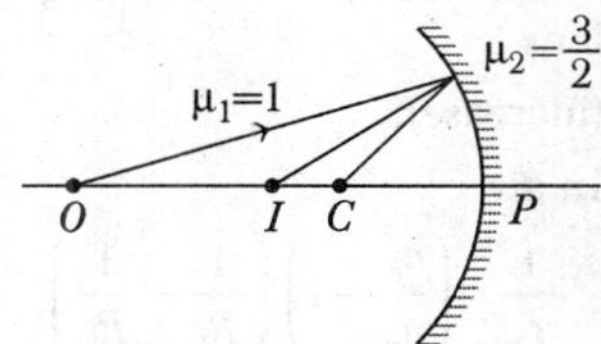

$$\frac{1.5}{v} - \frac{1}{(-10)} = \frac{1.5 - 1}{(-5)}$$

$$\Rightarrow \quad v = -7.5 \text{ cm}$$

$$\therefore \quad PI = 7.5 \text{ cm}$$

31. (2);

$$\frac{n_2}{v} - \frac{n_1}{u} = \frac{n_2 - n_1}{R}$$

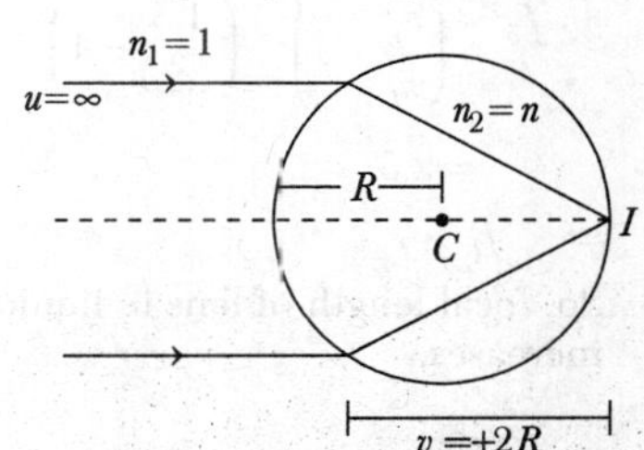

$$\Rightarrow \frac{n}{2R} - \frac{1}{(-\infty)} = \frac{n-1}{R}$$

$$\Rightarrow \quad n = 2n - 2$$

$$\Rightarrow \quad n = 2$$

32. Both convergent and divergent beams are obtained.

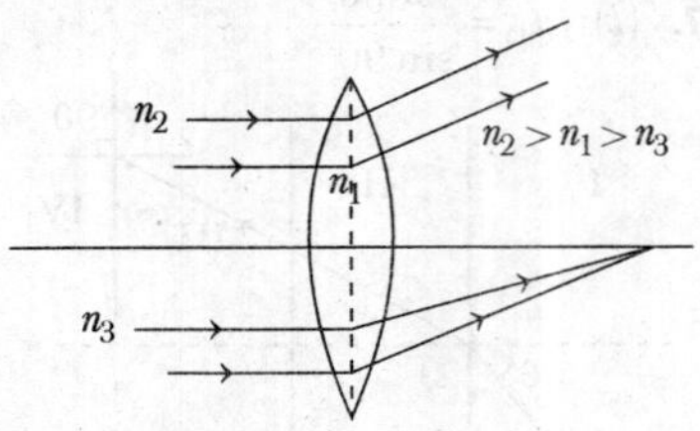

33. (True);

Due to two refractive indices, two focal lengths are there and so, two images are formed.

34. (convergent, $3.5R$);

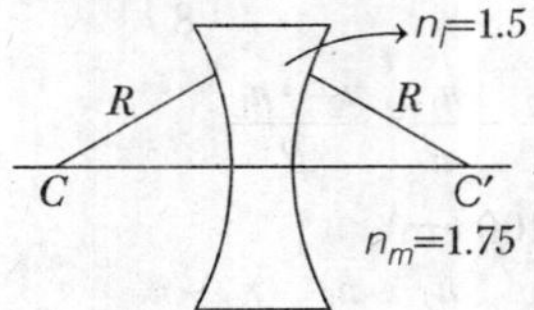

$$\frac{1}{f} = \left(\frac{n_l}{n_m} - 1\right)\left(\frac{1}{R_1} - \frac{1}{R_2}\right)$$

$$= \left(\frac{1.5}{1.75} - 1\right)\left[\frac{1}{-R} - \frac{1}{(+R)}\right]$$

$$\Rightarrow \quad f = +3.5R$$

$\therefore$ Lens behaves as converging lens.

35. (increase);

In air,

$$\frac{1}{f_a} = \left(\frac{n_g}{n_a} - 1\right)\left(\frac{1}{R_1} - \frac{1}{R_2}\right) \quad \text{...(i)}$$

In liquid,

$$\frac{1}{f_l} = \left(\frac{n_g}{n_l} - 1\right)\left(\frac{1}{R_1} - \frac{1}{R_2}\right) \quad \text{...(ii)}$$

Dividing Eq. (i) by Eq. (ii), we get

$$\Rightarrow \frac{f_l}{f_a} = \frac{\left(\frac{n_g}{n_a} - 1\right)}{\left(\frac{n_g}{n_l} - 1\right)} = \frac{\left(\frac{1.5}{1} - 1\right)}{\left(\frac{1.5}{1.25} - 1\right)}$$

$$= 2.5$$

$$\Rightarrow \quad f_l > f_a$$

So, focal length of lens in liquid increases.

36. (-255);

$$\frac{1}{f} = \left(\frac{n_l}{n_m} - 1\right)\left(\frac{1}{R_1} - \frac{1}{R_2}\right)$$

$$\Rightarrow \frac{1}{f} = \left(\frac{1.5}{1.7} - 1\right)\left[\frac{1}{-15} - \frac{1}{(-10)}\right]$$

$$\Rightarrow f = -255 \text{ cm}$$

37. (A → 4, B → 3, C → 2, D → 1);

A.

$R_1 = +R$ $R_2 = -R$ $n_g = 1.5$

$$\therefore \frac{1}{f} = (1.5 - 1)\left(\frac{1}{R} + \frac{1}{R}\right)$$

$$\Rightarrow f = R$$

B.

$R_1 = +\infty$ $R_2 = -R$ $n_g = 1.5$

$$\frac{1}{f} = (1.5 - 1)\left[\frac{1}{+\infty} - \frac{1}{(-R)}\right]$$

$$\Rightarrow \quad f = 2R$$

C.

$R_1 = -R$ $R_2 = +R$

$$\frac{1}{f} = (1.5 - 1)\left(\frac{1}{-R} - \frac{1}{R}\right)$$

$$\Rightarrow \quad f = -R$$

D.

$R_1 = -\infty$ $R_2 = +R$

$$\frac{1}{f} = (1.5 - 1)\left(\frac{1}{-\infty} - \frac{1}{R}\right)$$

$$\Rightarrow f = -2R$$

38. A → 4, B → 1, C → 2, D → 3

39. (*a*);

$$\frac{1}{v} - \frac{1}{u} = \frac{1}{f} \text{ (for lens)}$$

	u	v
1.	0 to $-f$	0 to $-\infty$
2.	$-f$ to $-2f$	$+\infty$ to $+2f$
3.	$-2f$ to $-\infty$	$+2f$ to $+f$

$-\infty$ 2f f O f 2f $+\infty$

$\therefore$ Graph of v-u is

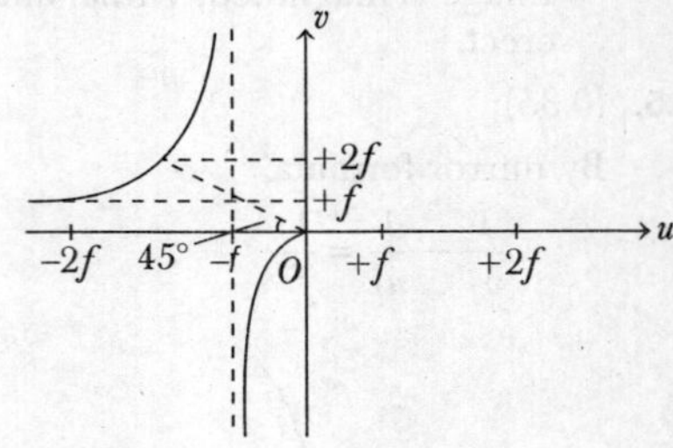

40. (I and II);

When incident light goes from denser to rarer medium, it bends away from normal and *vice-versa.*

41. (False);

Minimum distance to obtain a real image from a convex lens is f.

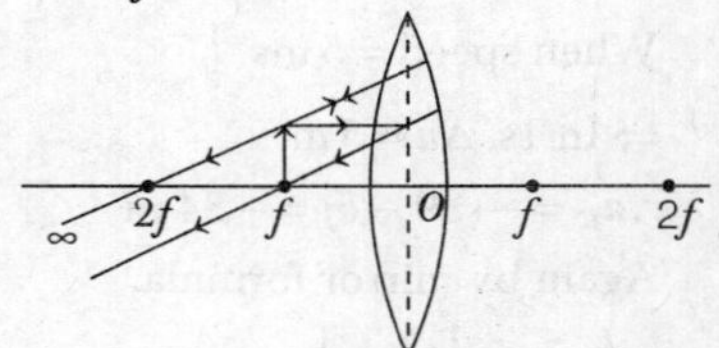

(Real image)

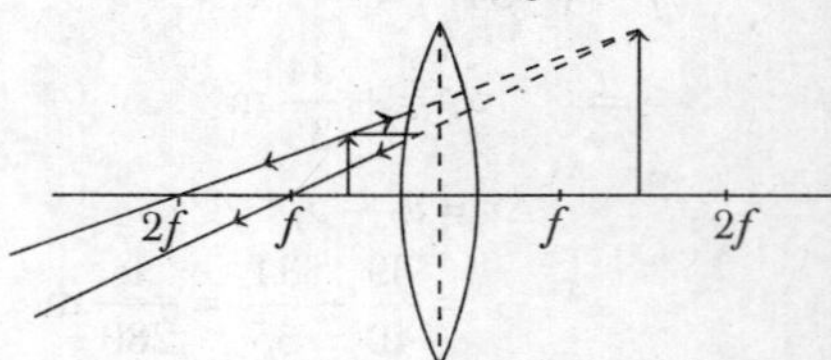

(Virtual image)

42. (40 cm);

Here, P act as virtual object.

$$\therefore \quad \frac{1}{f} = \frac{1}{v} - \frac{1}{u}$$

$$\frac{1}{(-40)} = \frac{1}{v} - \frac{1}{20}$$

$$\Rightarrow \quad v = 40 \text{ cm}$$

43. (*a*); $\frac{\mu_2}{v} - \frac{\mu_1}{u} = \frac{(\mu_2 - \mu_1)}{R}$

$$\frac{4}{3v} - \frac{1}{-20} = \frac{\left(\frac{4}{3} - 1\right)}{-10}$$

$$\frac{4}{3v} = \frac{-1}{30} - \frac{1}{20}$$

$$= \frac{-5}{60} = \frac{-1}{12}$$

$v = -16$ cm, negative sign shows image lies left of the point P. The correct answer is option (a) 16 cm left of P in air.

44. (5);

$$\frac{1}{v} - \frac{1}{u} = \frac{1}{f} \Rightarrow \frac{1}{v} - \frac{1}{(-8)} = \frac{1}{10}$$

$$\Rightarrow \quad v = -40 \text{ cm}$$

$$\therefore m = \frac{v}{u} = \frac{-40}{-8} = 5$$

45. (1);

As, lens disappears in liquid

$n_g = \frac{3}{2}$, $n_l = \frac{3}{2}$

$$\therefore \quad n_g = n_l = \frac{3}{2} \Rightarrow \frac{n_l}{n_g} = 1$$

46. $\left(\frac{3}{2}\right)$;

$$P = \frac{1}{f} = \left(\frac{n_2}{n_1} - 1\right)\left(\frac{1}{R_1} - \frac{1}{R_2}\right)$$

$R_1 = +R$ $R_2 = -R$

$$\frac{20}{100} = (n-1)\left[\frac{1}{5} - \frac{1}{(-5)}\right]$$

$$\Rightarrow \quad n = \frac{3}{2}$$

47. (1 : 1 : 1);

For lens 1,

$R_1 = +\infty$ $R_2 = -R$

$$\frac{1}{f_1} = (n-1)\left(\frac{1}{R_1} - \frac{1}{R_2}\right)$$

$$= (n-1)\left[\frac{1}{+\infty} - \frac{1}{(-R)}\right]$$

$$\Rightarrow f_1 = \frac{R}{(n-1)}$$

For lens 2

$R_1 = +R$ $R_2 = -\infty$

$$\frac{1}{f_2} = (n-1)\left(\frac{1}{R} - \frac{1}{(-\infty)}\right)$$

$$\Rightarrow f_2 = \frac{R}{(n-1)}$$

(i)

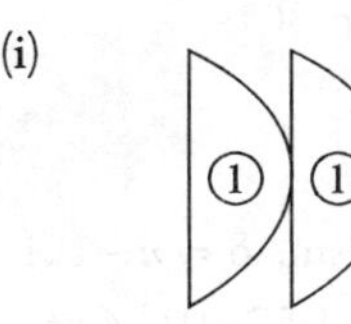

(P)

$$\frac{1}{f_P} = \frac{2}{f_1}$$

$$\therefore \quad f_P = \frac{1}{2} \cdot \frac{R}{(n-1)}$$

(ii)

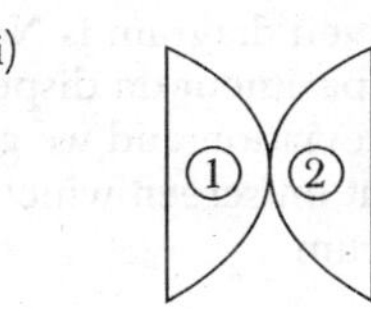

(Q)

$$\frac{1}{f_Q} = \frac{1}{f_1} + \frac{1}{f_2}$$

$$f_Q = \frac{1}{2} \cdot \frac{R}{(n-1)}$$

(iii)

(R)

$$\frac{1}{f_R} = \frac{1}{f_2} + \frac{1}{f_1}$$

$$f_R = \frac{1}{2} \cdot \frac{R}{(n-1)}$$

$$\therefore f_P : f_Q : f_R = 1:1:1$$

48. (− 6.67);

$$\frac{1}{f} = \frac{1}{f_1} + \frac{1}{f_2} + \frac{1}{f_3}$$

$f_1 = 40$ cm $f_2 = -40$ cm $f_3 = -15$ cm

$$= \left(\frac{1}{40} + \frac{1}{(-40)} + \frac{1}{(-15)}\right) \times 100$$

$$= -\frac{100}{15} = -6.67 \text{ D}$$

$\therefore$ Power of combined lens,

$$P = \frac{1}{f} = -6.67 \text{ D}$$

49. (I);

$$\frac{P_1}{P_2} = \frac{\frac{1}{+f_1}}{\frac{1}{-f_2}} \Rightarrow -\frac{f_2}{f_1} = \frac{3}{2}$$

$$\Rightarrow f_2 = -\frac{3}{2} f_1$$

$$\text{Now, } \frac{1}{F} = \frac{1}{f_1} + \frac{1}{f_2} = \frac{1}{f_1} + \frac{2}{(-3f_1)}$$

$$\Rightarrow \frac{1}{30} = \frac{1}{3f_1}$$

$$\Rightarrow f_1 = 10 \text{ cm}, f_2 = -15 \text{ cm}$$

50. (−15);

For convex lens,

$$\frac{1}{v} - \frac{1}{u} = \frac{1}{f_1}$$

$$\Rightarrow \frac{1}{v} - \frac{1}{(-40)} = \frac{1}{15}$$

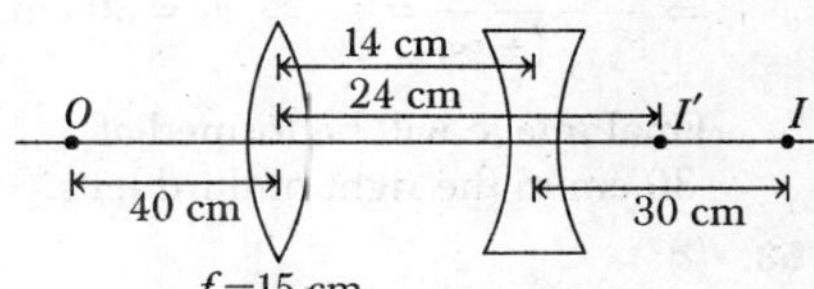

$$\therefore v = 24 \text{ cm}$$

For concave lens,

$$\frac{1}{v} - \frac{1}{u} = \frac{1}{f_2} \Rightarrow \frac{1}{30} - \frac{1}{10} = \frac{1}{f_2}$$

$$\Rightarrow \quad f_2 = -15 \text{ cm}$$

51. (III);

For convex lens,

$$\frac{1}{f} = \frac{1}{v} - \frac{1}{u}$$

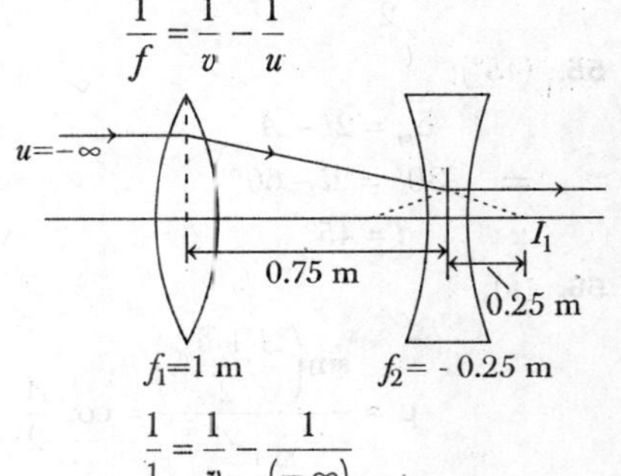

$$\frac{1}{1} = \frac{1}{v} - \frac{1}{(-\infty)}$$

$\Rightarrow \quad v = 1\text{ m}$

For concave lens,

$$\frac{1}{f} = \frac{1}{v} - \frac{1}{u} \Rightarrow \frac{1}{-0.25} = \frac{1}{v} - \frac{1}{0.25}$$

$\Rightarrow \quad v = +\infty$

Rays after refraction from both the lenses becomes parallel to the principal axis.

52. (30, right);

For lens 1,

$$\frac{1}{v_1} - \frac{1}{u_1} = \frac{1}{f_1}$$

$$\Rightarrow \frac{1}{v_1} - \frac{1}{(-30)} = \frac{1}{10}$$

$$\Rightarrow \quad v_1 = 15\text{ cm}$$

For lens 2,

$$\frac{1}{v_2} - \frac{1}{u_2} = \frac{1}{f_2}$$

$$\Rightarrow \frac{1}{v_2} - \frac{1}{(+10)} = \frac{1}{-10}$$

$$(\because u_2 = 15 - 5 = 10\text{ cm})$$

$$\Rightarrow \quad v_2 = +\infty$$

For lens 3,

$$\frac{1}{v_3} - \frac{1}{u_3} = \frac{1}{f_3}$$

$$\Rightarrow \frac{1}{v_3} - \frac{1}{(+\infty)} = \frac{1}{30} \Rightarrow v_3 = 30\text{ cm}$$

Final image will be formed at 30 cm to the right of third lens.

53. (*c*)

54. (Yes);

$\because \quad \delta = i + e - A$

At minimum deviation, $i = e$

$$\therefore \quad \delta = 2i - A = 2\left(\frac{3A}{4}\right) - A \qquad \left(\because i = \frac{3A}{4}\right)$$

$$\therefore \quad \delta = \frac{A}{2}$$

55. (45°);

$$\delta_m = 2i - A$$

$$\Rightarrow \quad 30° = 2i - 60°$$

$$\therefore \quad i = 45°$$

56. (*b*);

$$\mu = \frac{\sin\left(\frac{A+\delta_m}{2}\right)}{\sin\frac{A}{2}} = \cot\frac{A}{2}$$

$$\Rightarrow \cos\frac{A}{2} = \sin\left(\frac{A+\delta_m}{2}\right)$$

$$\therefore \quad \delta_m = 180° - 2A$$

57. (45°);

$$e = r_2 = 0$$

$$\therefore \quad r_1 = A = 30°$$

$$\text{Now, } n = \frac{\sin i}{\sin r_1} \qquad \text{(Snell's law)}$$

$$\Rightarrow \sqrt{2} = \frac{\sin i}{\sin 30°}$$

$$\therefore \quad i = 45°$$

58. (True);

For thin prism, $\delta = (n-1)A$

$\Rightarrow \quad 5.5° = (1.57 - 1)\cdot A \Rightarrow$
$A = 9.64°$

59. (deviation);

Since, light is monochromatic, so it gets only deviation.

60. (No);

As, the given diagram is Newton's classic experiment on dispersion without deviation and we get white light on screen which is not the spectrum.

61. (*c*);

For dispersion without deviation,

$$\delta_1 = \delta_2$$

i.e. $(n_1 - 1)\cdot A_1 = (n_2 - 1)A_2$

$\Rightarrow (1.54 - 1)\times 4° = (1.72 - 1)\times A_2$

$$\therefore \quad A_2 = 3°$$

62. I

63. A $\rightarrow$ 2, B $\rightarrow$ 3, C $\rightarrow$ 1

64. (6);

$$m = \left(1 + \frac{D}{f}\right)$$

$$= 1 + \frac{25}{5} = 6$$

65. 1;

Maximum magnification,

$$M_{\max} = \left(1 + \frac{D}{f}\right)$$

Minimum magnification,

$$M_{\min} = \frac{D}{f}$$

$$\therefore M_{\max} - M_{\min} = 1$$

66. II and III

67. I. D II. ∞

68. (*c*)

69. (i) ✓ (ii) × (iii) × (iv) ×

70. (more);

For compound microscope,

$$m = \left(\frac{L}{f_o}\right)\left(\frac{D}{f_e}\right)$$

$$= \frac{160}{4} \times \frac{250}{25}$$

$$\therefore \quad m = 400$$

71. (*d*); Given, focal length of objective lens = 10 m

Focal length of eyepiece lens = 10 cm = 0.1 m

Telescope's tube length,

$$L = f_{\text{objective}} + f_{\text{eyepiece}}$$

$$L = 10\text{ m} + 0.1\text{ m}$$

$$L = 10.1\text{ m} = 1010\text{ cm}$$

Magnification of the telescope,

$$M = \frac{f_{\text{objective}}}{f_{\text{eyepiece}}} = \frac{10\text{ m}}{0.1\text{ m}} = 100$$

72. (L_4, L_1);

Here, length of telescope,

$$L = f_o + f_e = 10\text{ cm}$$

and magnitude of magnifying power, $m = \frac{f_o}{f_e} = 4.$

Both conditions are satisfied, if $f_o = L_4 = 8$ cm and $f_e = L_1 = 2$ cm.

73. (24°);

For a telescope,

$$m = \frac{f_o}{f_e} = \frac{\beta}{\alpha} \Rightarrow \frac{60}{5} = \frac{\beta}{2}$$

$$\therefore \quad \beta = 24°$$

74. (20);

$$m = \frac{\beta}{\alpha} = \frac{f_o}{f_e} = \frac{400}{10}$$

$$\Rightarrow \beta = \frac{400}{10}\alpha = 40 \times \frac{3.5\times 10^3}{3.8\times 10^5}$$

$$= 0.36\text{ rad} \simeq 20°$$

75. (Yes);

In a terrestrial telescope,

$$m = \frac{f_o}{f_e}\left(1 + \frac{f_e}{v}\right)$$

$$= \frac{90}{6}\left(1 + \frac{6}{30}\right) = 18$$

76. True

Assertion-Reason Questions

1. (c); Both smooth and rough surfaces cause reflection and rough surfaces reflect incident light in all directions which makes objects visible to our eyes.
2. (d); A converging beam will focus before the focal length of concave mirror. Only rays parallel to principal axis focus on focus of mirror.
3. (a); Optical density of turpentine is more than that of water. Optical density is the property of a transparent material that measures the speed of the light through the material.
4. (a) 5. (a)
6. (a)
7. (a); For the prism, angle of deviation depends on the angle of prim.

   Since, $\delta = (\mu - 1) A$
8. (a)
9. (a); We know that, $M = 1 + \frac{D}{f}$ for simple microscope.

   Hence, M increases as f decreases.
10. (a)

Case Based Questions

1. (i) (a); Here, $\mu_1 = 1$, $\mu_2 = \frac{4}{3}$, $u = -10$ cm and $R = 30$ cm

Using the relation,

$$\frac{\mu_2}{v} - \frac{\mu_1}{u} = \frac{\mu_2 - \mu_1}{R}$$

Substituting the values,

$$\Rightarrow \frac{\frac{4}{3}}{v} - \frac{1}{-10} = \frac{\frac{4}{3} - 1}{30}$$

$$\Rightarrow \frac{4}{3v} + \frac{1}{10} = \frac{1}{90}$$

$$\Rightarrow \frac{4}{3v} = \frac{1}{90} - \frac{1}{10} = \frac{-8}{90}$$

$$\Rightarrow \quad v = -15 \text{ cm}$$

The image is formed 15 cm left of spherical surface and is virtual.

(ii) (c); Here

$\mu_1 = 1$, $\mu_2 = 1.5$, $u = -100$ cm

$R = +20$ cm

Using $\frac{\mu_2}{v} - \frac{\mu_1}{u} = \frac{\mu_2 - \mu_1}{R}$

$$\Rightarrow \frac{1.5}{v} - \frac{\mu_1}{u} = \frac{\mu_2 - \mu_1}{R}$$

$$\Rightarrow \frac{1.5}{v} + \frac{1}{100} = \frac{1.5 - 1}{20}$$

$$\Rightarrow \quad v = 100 \text{ cm}$$

(iii) (b); Here,

$\mu_1 = \frac{4}{3}$, $\mu_2 = 1.6$,

$u = -2$ m, $R = 0.2$ m

Since, $\frac{\mu_2}{v} - \frac{\mu_1}{u} = \frac{\mu_2 - \mu_1}{R}$

$$\Rightarrow \frac{1.6}{v} + \frac{\frac{4}{3}}{2} = \frac{1.6 - \frac{4}{3}}{0.2}$$

$\Rightarrow v = 2.4$ m in denser medium.

(iv) (a)

2. (i) (c); As $\mu \propto \frac{I}{v} \Rightarrow \frac{\mu_A}{\mu_B} = \frac{v_B}{v_A} = \frac{5}{4}$

(ii) (b); In the figure, $r = 90 - i$

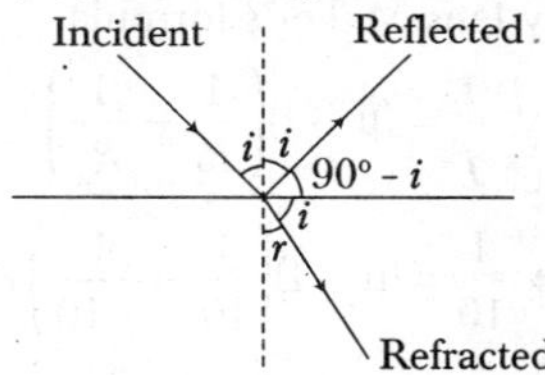

From Snell's law,

$$1.5 = \frac{\sin i}{\sin r} = \frac{\sin i}{\sin(90° - i)} = \tan i$$

$\therefore$ Angle of incidence,

$i = \tan^{-1}(1.5)$

(iii) (d)

(iv) (a); Since,

$$^a\mu_g = \frac{c}{v_g} = \frac{3}{2} \quad \text{...(i)}$$

and $$^a\mu_w = \frac{c}{v_w} = \frac{4}{3} \quad \text{...(ii)}$$

On dividing Eq. (i) by Eq. (iii), we get

$$= \frac{\frac{c}{v_g}}{\frac{c}{v_w}} = \frac{\frac{3}{2}}{\frac{4}{3}} = \frac{9}{8}$$

$$\Rightarrow \frac{v_w}{v_g} = \frac{9}{8}$$

$$\Rightarrow v_w = \frac{9}{8} \times v_g = \frac{9}{8} \times 2.4 \times 10^8$$

$$= 2.7 \times 10^8 \text{ m/s}$$

Competition Edge Up

1. (d); Given, $f_1 = 10$ cm

   $f_2 = 15$ cm

   From the diagram it is clear that rays from lens L_1 converges at a fixed point f_1 and from where the lens L_2 diverges the rays parallel to principal axis.

   i.e. $f_1 + f_2 = 10 + 15 = 25$ cm
2. (d); We are given with following situation,

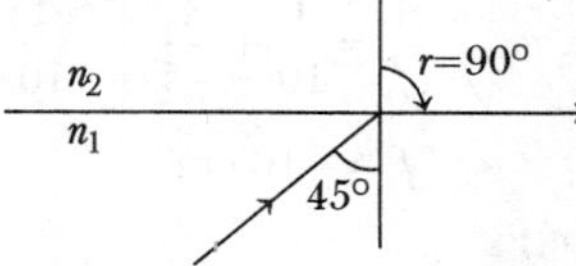

Now, refractive index of medium 2 with respect to medium 1,

$$n = \frac{n_2}{n_1} = \frac{\sin i}{\sin r} = \frac{\sin 45°}{\sin 90°} = \frac{1}{\sqrt{2}}$$

$$\therefore \quad \frac{n_1}{n_2} = \frac{\sqrt{2}}{1}$$

3. (60); Given, $\mu = \sqrt{3}$

$$\Rightarrow \frac{\sin\left(\frac{A + \delta_m}{2}\right)}{\sin A/2} = \sqrt{3}$$

$$\Rightarrow \frac{\sin\left(\frac{A + A}{2}\right)}{\sin A/2} = \sqrt{3}$$

$$[\because \delta_m / A = 1 \Rightarrow \delta_m = A]$$

$$\Rightarrow \frac{\sin A}{\sin A/2} = \sqrt{3}$$

$$\Rightarrow \frac{2 \sin A/2 \cos A/2}{\sin A/2} = \sqrt{3}$$

$$\Rightarrow \cos A/2 = \frac{\sqrt{3}}{2} = \cos 30°$$

$$\Rightarrow \frac{A}{2} = 30° \Rightarrow A = 60°$$

4. (b); When the white light passed through a prism, then red light bends least compared to all other colour of light. As,

   $\lambda_{red} > \lambda_{yellow} > \lambda_{violet}$

   Light ray with longer wavelength bends less. Hence, Statement I is true.

   The refractive indexes are different for different wavelengths of dispersive medium.
5. (c); Given,

   Image distance, $v = 15$ cm

   Here, $m = 2$

i.e., $\frac{-v}{-u} = 2 \Rightarrow v = 2u$

Distance between object and image

$$u + v = 15 \text{ cm}$$

$$u + 2u = 15 \text{ cm} \Rightarrow u = 5 \text{ cm}$$

$$\therefore \quad v = 2 \times 5 = 10 \text{ cm}$$

Using mirror formula,

$$\Rightarrow \frac{1}{f} = \frac{1}{v} + \frac{1}{u}$$

$$\therefore \frac{1}{f} = \frac{1}{10} + \frac{1}{-5} = -\frac{1}{10}$$

$$f = -10 \text{ cm}$$

6. (*d*);

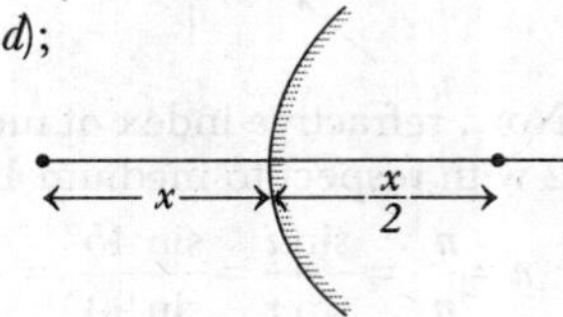

$R = 30$ cm

$$f = \frac{R}{2} = \frac{30}{2} = +15 \text{ cm}$$

Magnification $(m) = \pm \frac{1}{2}$

For convex mirror, virtual image is formed for real object.

Therefore, m is + ve

$$m = \frac{f}{f-u} \Rightarrow +\frac{1}{2} = \frac{f}{f-u}$$

$$\Rightarrow \quad +\frac{1}{2} = \frac{15}{15-u}$$

$$15 - u = 30$$

$$15 - 30 = u \Rightarrow u = -15 \text{ cm}$$

7. (*b*); Magnifying power,

$$M = \left[\frac{f_0}{f_e}\right] = \left[\frac{140}{5}\right] = 28$$

8. (*c*); Focal length of convex lens,

$$f_1 = +f$$

Focal length of concave lens,

$$f_2 = -f$$

When both lenses are kept in contact, then equivalent focal length (F) is given by

$$\frac{1}{F} = \frac{1}{f_1} + \frac{1}{f_2} = \frac{1}{f} + \frac{1}{-f} = 0$$

$$\Rightarrow \quad F = \infty$$

9. (*d*); The objective of an astronomical telescope has large focal length and large aperture.

Because the lens used is a convex lens, the magnification of an astronomical telescope is directly proportional to the focal length of the objective lens.

This large aperture also contributes to the better quality and visibility of the images. Thus, it provides better resolution.

Due to large focal length of the objective, it covers large area which ensures better light gathering power.

Thus, all options (a), (b) and (c) are correct.

10. (*d*); $P = \frac{1}{f} = (\mu - 1)\left(\frac{1}{R_1} - \frac{1}{R_2}\right)$

Power of biconvex lens,

$P = 10$ D

$$\therefore f = \frac{1}{P} = \frac{1}{10} = 0.1 \text{ m} = 10 \text{ cm}$$

$$R_1 = R_2 = 10 \text{ cm}$$

By lens Maker's formula,

$$\frac{1}{f} = (\mu - 1)\left(\frac{1}{R_1} - \frac{1}{R_2}\right)$$

$$\Rightarrow \frac{1}{10} = (\mu - 1)\left(\frac{1}{10} - \frac{1}{-10}\right)$$

$$\Rightarrow \frac{1}{10} = (\mu - 1)\left(\frac{2}{10}\right)$$

$$\Rightarrow 1 = (\mu - 1) \times 2$$

$$\Rightarrow \quad \mu - 1 = \frac{1}{2} \Rightarrow \mu = 1 + \frac{1}{2} = \frac{3}{2}$$

11. (*b*); According to the question, the ray diagram can be shown as

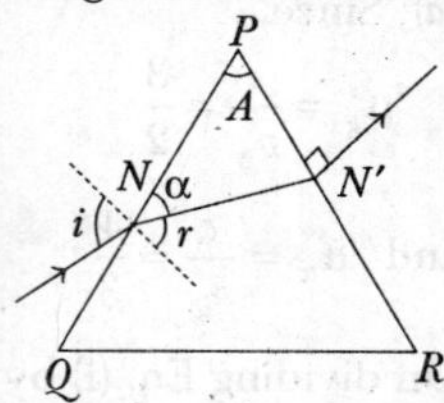

From figure in $\Delta PNN'$,

$$A + \alpha + 90° = 180°$$

$$\Rightarrow \quad \alpha = 90° - A \quad \text{...(i)}$$

Also, $\quad r + \alpha = 90°$

$$\Rightarrow \quad r = 90° - \alpha$$

$$= 90° - (90° - A) = A$$

$[\because$ from Eq. (i)$]$

$$\Rightarrow \quad r = A$$

From Snell's law,

$$\mu_1 \sin i = \mu_2 \sin r \Rightarrow \sin i = \mu \sin A$$

(here, $\mu_1 = 1$ and $\mu_2 = \mu$)

For small angle, $\sin \theta \simeq \theta$

$$\Rightarrow \quad i = \mu A$$

12. (*a*); Object distance, $u = -1.5f$

By mirror formula, $\frac{1}{v} + \frac{1}{u} = \frac{1}{f}$

$$\Rightarrow \frac{1}{v} + \frac{1}{-1.5f} = \frac{1}{-f}$$

$$\Rightarrow \quad \frac{1}{v} = -\frac{1}{f} + \frac{1}{1.5f}$$

$$= \frac{1}{f}\left[-1 + \frac{1}{1.5}\right]$$

$$= \frac{1}{f}\left[-1 + \frac{2}{3}\right]$$

$$\Rightarrow \quad \frac{1}{v} = \frac{1}{f}\left(-\frac{1}{3}\right) \Rightarrow v = -3f$$

Chapter-10

Wave Optics

1. greater, lesser **2.** (*c*)

3. A → 2, B → 3, C → 1

4. (i) 0 (ii) 4π

5. Yes

6. secondary, position

7. Radius (R) = Velocity (v) × Time (t)

8. (0.3 m);

Distance between wavefronts

$$= v\,t = 3 \times 10^8 \times 10^{-9} = 0.3 \text{ m}$$

9. I

10. (5 m);

From Snell's law of refraction,

$$\frac{\lambda_1}{\lambda_2} = \frac{v_1}{v_2}$$

$$\frac{1}{\lambda_2} = \frac{330}{1650} \Rightarrow \lambda_2 = 5 \text{ m}$$

11. $\left(\frac{4}{5}\right)$;

$$n_1 d_1 = n_2 d_2$$

$$\Rightarrow \quad \frac{n_2}{n_1} = n_{21} = \frac{d_1}{d_2} = \frac{4}{5}$$

12. wavelength, speed, frequency

13. Medium 1

14. congruent, equal

15. Spherical

16. A → 2, B → 1, C → 3, D → 4

17. (*c*)

18. (Yes);

$$I \propto a^2$$

or $a \propto \sqrt{I}$

$$\because \quad \frac{a_1}{a_2} = \frac{\sqrt{I_1}}{\sqrt{I_2}} = \frac{\sqrt{81}}{\sqrt{25}} = \frac{9}{5}$$

19. Superposition principle

20. sum

21. (Yes);

$$I = I_1 + I_2 + 2\sqrt{I_1 I_2}\cos\phi$$

$$= I_0 + I_0 + 2\sqrt{I_0 I_0} \quad (\because \phi = 0)$$

$$= 4I_0$$

22. A → 1, B → 1, C → 2

23. (I, II, III);

Interference is only noticeable when the light falls onto a screen and is scattered into our eyes.

24. (A → 3, B → 1, C → 2);

A. $\phi = \frac{\pi}{3}$

As we know,

$$I = 4I_0 \cos^2\left(\frac{\phi}{2}\right)$$

$$I = 4I_0 \cos^2\left(\frac{\pi}{6}\right)$$

$$= 4I_0 \times \frac{3}{4} = 3I_0$$

B. $\phi = \frac{\pi}{2}$

$$I = 4I_0 \cos^2\left(\frac{\pi}{4}\right)$$

$$= 4I_0 \times \frac{1}{2} = 2I_0$$

C. $\phi = \frac{2\pi}{3}$

$$I = 4I_0 \cos^2\left(\frac{\pi}{3}\right) = I_0$$

25. False

26. True

27. $\frac{n\lambda D}{d}, (2n+1)\frac{\lambda D}{2d}$

28. (0.49 mm);

$$x_n = \frac{n\lambda D}{d}$$

$$\Rightarrow \quad d = \frac{n\lambda D}{x_n}$$

$$= \frac{10 \times 584.3 \times 10^{-9} \times 1}{12 \times 10^{-3}}$$

$$= 0.49 \text{ mm}$$

29. (5000Å);

$\because$ We know that, fringe width is given by $\beta = \frac{D\lambda}{d}$

$$\Rightarrow \lambda = \frac{\beta d}{D} = \frac{7.5 \times 10^{-4} \times 8 \times 10^{-4}}{1.2}$$

$$= 5 \times 10^{-7} \text{ m}$$

$$= 5000 \times 10^{-10} \text{m} = 5000 \text{ Å}$$

30. (Yes);

Distance of *n*th minima from central bright fringe is given by

$$x_n = \frac{(2n-1)\lambda D}{2d}$$

For $n = 3$ or 3rd minima,

$$x_3 = \frac{(2 \times 3 - 1) \times 500 \times 10^{-9} \times 1}{2 \times 10^{-3}}.$$

$$= 1.25 \text{ mm}$$

31. (*c*); Path difference $= (2n-1)\frac{\lambda}{2}$

For 5th minimum,

Path difference $= (2 \times 5 - 1)\frac{\lambda}{2}$

$$= \frac{9\lambda}{2}$$

32. $\frac{\lambda D}{2d}, \frac{2\lambda D}{d}, \frac{\lambda D}{d}$

33. (False);

On decreasing wavelength, the fringe separation also decreases as $\beta \propto \lambda$.

34. (*d*); $\beta = \frac{\lambda D}{d}$

As, $\lambda_{Red} > \lambda_{Green} > \lambda_{Blue}$

$\Rightarrow \quad \beta_R > \beta_G > \beta_B$

35. (False);

$$\beta = \frac{\lambda D}{d}$$

$$\Rightarrow \quad \frac{\beta'}{\beta} = \frac{D'}{D} = \frac{1}{2}$$

36. (No);

$$\beta = \frac{\lambda D}{d}$$

$$\Rightarrow \quad \frac{\beta'}{\beta} = \frac{d}{d'} = \frac{1}{3}$$

37. (0.05);

Fringe width, $\beta = \frac{\lambda D}{d}$

As, $\quad \beta \propto \lambda$

$$\Rightarrow \quad \frac{\beta_1}{\beta_2} = \frac{\lambda_1}{\lambda_2}$$

$$\Rightarrow \quad \beta_2 = \frac{5000}{6000} \times 0.06$$

$$\Rightarrow \quad \beta_2 = 0.05 \text{ cm}$$

38. (*c*)

39. (i) (0.5 mm);

$$\beta = \frac{\lambda D}{d}$$

$$= \frac{500 \times 10^{-9} \times 1}{10^{-3}}$$

$$= 0.5 \text{ mm}$$

(ii) (No);

$$x(\text{bright}) = \frac{n\lambda D}{d}$$

$$x_3 = \frac{3 \times 500 \times 10^{-9} \times 1}{10^{-3}}$$

$$= 1.5 \text{ mm}$$

(iii) (0.5 mm);

$$\beta \text{ (dark)} = \frac{\lambda D}{d}$$

$$= \frac{500 \times 10^{-9} \times 1}{10^{-3}}$$

$$= 0.5 \text{ mm}$$

(iv) (*b*); $x \text{ (dark)} = \left(n + \frac{1}{2}\right)\frac{\lambda D}{d}$

$$x_2 = \left(1 + \frac{1}{2}\right) \times 0.5$$

$$= 0.75 \text{ mm}$$

40. A → 3, B → 1, C → 2

41. (False);

In Young's double slit experiment, if source is white light, then the central fringe is white surrounded by coloured fringes.

42. diffraction

43. $a \sin\theta, \left(n + \frac{1}{2}\right)\frac{\lambda}{a}, \frac{n\lambda}{a}$

44. (2×10^{-4} rad);

For first minima, $a \sin\theta = \lambda$

$$0.3 \times 10^{-3} \times \sin\theta = 600 \times 10^{-10}$$

$$\Rightarrow \sin\theta \simeq \theta = 2 \times 10^{-4} \text{ rad}$$

45. (No);

$$2\theta = \frac{2\lambda}{e}$$

$$\Rightarrow \quad \theta \propto \frac{1}{e}$$

So, θ will decrease on increasing the slit width *e*.

46. bright, twice

47. Yes

48. False;

Both interference and diffraction are consistent with the principle of conservation of energy.

49. I

50. True

51. perpendicular

52. A $\rightarrow$ 3, B $\rightarrow$ 1, C $\rightarrow$ 2

53. False

54. (*a*); When unpolarised light of intensity I_0 passes through P_1,

$$I' = I_0/2.$$

When this polarised light passes through P_2,

$$I = \frac{I_0}{2}\cos^2\theta$$

So, correct variation of *I versus* θ is shown below.

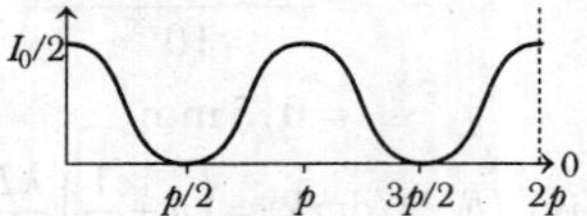

55. (2 : 1);

After passing through a polaroid,

$$I = \frac{I_0}{2}$$

$$\Rightarrow \quad \frac{I_0}{I} = \frac{2}{1} \text{ or } 2:1$$

56. (2 : 1 : $\cos^2\theta$);

According to Malus law, when an unpolarised beam of light passes through a polaroid, the intensity becomes half.

So, $\quad I_2 = \dfrac{I_1}{2}$

When it passes through second polaroid, the intensity will become

$$I_3 = I_2\cos^2\theta = \frac{I_1}{2}\cos^2\theta$$

So, the ratio becomes

$$I_1 : I_2 : I_3 = 2 : 1 : \cos^2\theta$$

57. (*d*); From Malus law,

$$I = \frac{I_0}{2}\cos^2\theta = \frac{I_0}{2}\cos^2 30°$$

$$\therefore \quad \frac{I}{I_0} = \frac{3}{8}$$

58. $\dfrac{\pi}{4}$ or 45°;

Intensity of transmitted light is maximum when the polaroid sheet makes an angle of 45° with the pass axis.

$$I = \frac{I_0}{2}\cos^2 45° = \frac{I_0}{4}$$

59. Yes;

After passing through first nicol,

$$I_1 = \frac{I_0}{2}$$

For second nicol,

$$I = I_1\cos^2\theta$$

$$= \frac{I_0}{2}\cos^2 60° = \frac{I_0}{8}$$

60. 27/128;

After passing the first polaroid P_1,

$$I_1 = \frac{I_0}{2}$$

Now, for P_2, $I_2 = I_1\cos^2 30° = \dfrac{3I_0}{8}$

For P_3, $I_3 = I_2\cos^2 30° = \dfrac{9I_0}{32}$

For P_4, $I_4 = I_3\cos^2 30°$

$$I_4 = I = \frac{27I_0}{128}$$

$$\therefore \quad x = \frac{27}{128}$$

61. (*c*)

62. reflection, transmission

Competition Connect

1. $A \rightarrow$ Incident sunlight (unpolarised)

$B \rightarrow$ Scattered light (polarised)

2. equal to

3. 90, $\tan i_B$

4. (*d*)

5. Yes

6. (57°);

$$\tan i_B = n$$

$$\tan i_B = 1.5$$

$$(\because n = 1.5 \text{ for glass})$$

$$\Rightarrow \quad i_B = 57°$$

7. (*b*); $\quad \mu = \dfrac{1}{\sin C}$

$$= \frac{1}{\sin\left[\sin^{-1}\left(\frac{3}{5}\right)\right]} = \frac{5}{3}$$

By Brewster's law,

$$\tan i_B = \mu$$

$$\Rightarrow \quad i_B = \tan^{-1}\left(\frac{5}{3}\right)$$

Assertion-Reason Questions

1. (*a*) **2.** (*a*)

3. (*d*); A is incorrect because the principle of superposition applies to both coherent and incoherent light sources.

4. (*c*); Fringe width is inversely proportional to the distance between the slits. Hence, Reason is incorrect.

5. (*a*)

6. (*d*); A is incorrect because the intensity of the bright fringes in YDSE is not just twice the individual slit intensities; it is proportional to the square of the resultant amplitude, which can be up to four times the intensity of individual slits.

7. (*a*)

8. (*c*); If a film is introduced in upper slit, the optical path travelled by ray from upper source is more and that travelled by that from lower source, hence some finite path difference exists at the point of earlier central maxima (point equidistant from both sources).

Now to compensate for this extra path difference, ray from upper source needs to travel lesser than ray from lower source. So the central maxima would now be obtained at a point of screen that is closer to the upper source. Hence central maxima shifts upwards, so does the pattern. If slit widths are different, intensity of light from both the sources is different. So the minima would not be dark. Hence, A is correct but R is incorrect.

9. (*b*); In single slit diffraction, the width of the central maximum is twice the width of the secondary maxima. The width is determined by the diffraction pattern formula. Hence, both A and R are correct but R is not the correct explanation of A.

10. (*d*) The angular position of the first minimum is directly proportional to the wavelength of light used. The position of the minima is given by $a \sin\theta = m\lambda$.

Hence, A is incorrect but R is correct.

Case Based Questions

1. (i) (*a*)

(ii) (*b*); Given, phase difference,

$$\phi = \frac{2\pi}{3}$$

and resultant intensity,

$$I = 4I_0 \cos^2\left(\frac{\phi}{2}\right)$$

$$= 4\,I_0 \cos^2\left(\frac{\pi}{3}\right) = I_0$$

(iii) (*d*); We know that,

$$\phi = \frac{2\pi x}{\lambda}$$

Now, phase difference, where path difference is equal to $\lambda/3$ is equal to $\phi = \frac{2\pi}{\lambda} \times \frac{\lambda}{3} = \frac{2\pi}{3}$.

Also, at the point, where path difference = 2λ

Phase difference will be

$$\frac{2\pi}{\lambda} \times 2\lambda = 4\pi$$

Let individual source intensity be I, then

$$I_0 = 4\,I \cos^2 \frac{4\pi}{2} = 4\,I$$

Hence, $I = \frac{I_0}{4}$

Now, at point, where $\phi = \frac{2\pi}{3}$

$$\Rightarrow I' = 4I\cos^2 \frac{2\pi}{3\times 2}$$

$$I' = 4I\cos^2\left(\frac{\pi}{3}\right) = I = \frac{I_0}{4}$$

(iv) (*b*)

2. (i) (*c*); Using Brewster's law,

$$\mu = \tan\theta_p = \tan 60^\circ$$

$$= \sqrt{3}$$

At this condition,

$\theta_p + \theta_r = 90^\circ$

$\therefore \theta_r = 90^\circ - 60^\circ$

Angle of refraction, $\theta_r = 30^\circ$

(ii) (*d*)

(iii) (*d*); By using, $\mu = \tan\theta_p$

$$\Rightarrow \mu = \tan 60^\circ = \sqrt{3}$$

Also, $C = \sin^{-1}\left(\frac{1}{\mu}\right)$

$$\Rightarrow \quad C = \sin^{-1}\left(\frac{1}{\sqrt{3}}\right)$$

(iv) (*c*)

Competition Edge Up

1. (200); We know that,

$$I = I_0 \cdot \cos^2\left(\frac{\Delta\phi}{2}\right)$$

$$\Rightarrow \frac{I_0}{4} = I_0 \cdot \cos^2\left(\frac{\Delta\phi}{2}\right)$$

$$\Delta\phi = 2\pi/3 \quad \ldots\text{(i)}$$

Phase difference $= \frac{2\pi}{\lambda} \times$ path difference

$$\Rightarrow \quad \Delta\phi = \frac{2\pi}{\lambda}\left(\frac{\lambda d}{D}\right)$$

$$= \frac{2\pi}{3}$$

$$y = \frac{\lambda D}{3d} = \frac{600\times10^{-9}\times1}{3\times10^{-3}}$$

$$= 2\times10^{-4}\ \text{m} = 200\,\mu\text{m}$$

2. (2); Width of central maxima

$$\alpha = \frac{2\lambda D}{a},\ a = \text{Slit width}$$

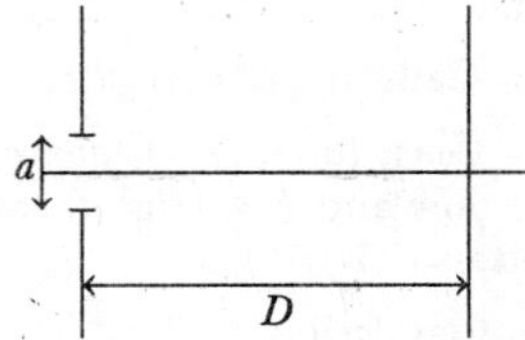

Width of maxima or bright fringe in YDSE is, $\beta = \frac{\lambda D}{d}$

When 10 maxima lies in central maxima then there are 10 minimas also.

$$\therefore \quad \alpha = 10\beta \Rightarrow \frac{2\lambda D}{a} = \frac{10\lambda D}{d}$$

$$d = 5a \Rightarrow a = d/5$$

$$a = \frac{10\times10^{-4}\ \text{m}}{5}$$

$$a = 2\times10^{-4}\ \text{m}$$

3. (*c*) Central maxima lies between two first minimas on either side of centre line.

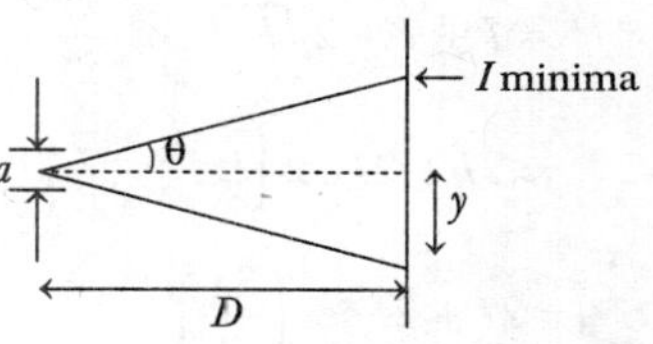

Angular width of central maxima is 2θ

where, $\sin\theta = \frac{\lambda}{a} \Rightarrow \theta = \sin^{-1}\frac{\lambda}{a}$

So, angular width

$$= 2\theta = 2\sin^{-1}\frac{\lambda}{a}$$

$$= 2\sin^{-1}\left(\frac{2}{4}\right) = 2\sin^{-1}\left(\frac{1}{2}\right)$$

$$= 2\times30^\circ = 60^\circ$$

4. (*b*);

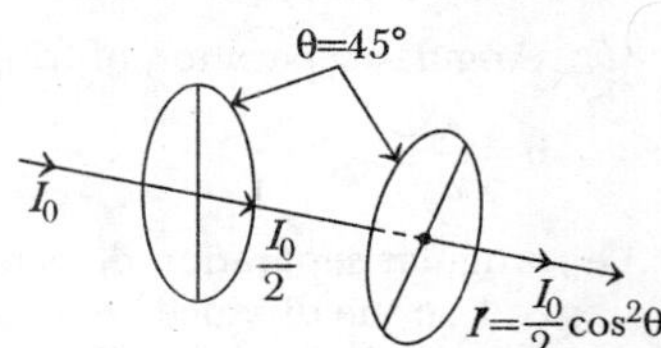

Intensity of light after 1st polaroid

$$= \frac{I_0}{2}$$

By Malus' law,

Intensity of light after second polaroid is,

$$I' = \frac{I_0}{2}\times\cos^2\theta = \frac{I_0}{2}\times\cos^2 45^\circ$$

$$= \frac{I_0}{2}\times\frac{1}{2} = \frac{I_0}{4}$$

5. (*c*); Given,

Path difference,

$$\Delta x = \frac{7\lambda}{4}$$

If I be the intensity of two identical source, then

$$I_{\max} = I_1 + I_2 + 2\sqrt{I_1 I_2}\cos\phi$$

$$= I + I + 2I\cos 0^\circ = 4I$$

When $\Delta x = \frac{7\lambda}{4}$, then

$$\Delta\phi' = \frac{2\pi}{\lambda}\times\Delta x = \frac{2\pi}{\lambda}\times\frac{7\lambda}{4}$$

$$= \frac{7}{2}\pi$$

$\therefore$ Intensity

$$I' = I_1 + I_2 + 2\sqrt{I_1 I_2}\cos\Delta\phi'$$

$$= I + I + 2\sqrt{I \cdot I}\cos\frac{7\pi}{2}$$
$$= 2I + 2I\cos\left(2\pi + \frac{3\pi}{2}\right)$$
$$= 2I + 2I\cos\left(\frac{3\pi}{2}\right)$$
$$= 2I + 2I\cos(\pi + \pi/2)$$
$$= 2I + 2I(-\cos\pi/2) = 2I$$
$$\therefore \quad \frac{I'}{I_{max}} = \frac{2I}{4I} = \frac{1}{2}$$

6. (*c*); When YDSE is performed in white light instead of monochromatic light, all wavelengths shows their maxima and minima in order of their wavelength. Thus, a central bright is observed along with few fringes that will be different colours.

7. (*b*); Angular separation of fringes,
$$\theta = \frac{\lambda}{d}$$
i.e., Angular separation does not depend on the distance between screen and plane of slits. Thus, statement I is correct.

Since, $\theta \propto \lambda$

Thus, if the monochromatic source is replaced by another monochromatic source of larger wavelength, then angular separation of fringes increases. Hence, Statement II is incorrect.

8. (*c*); In Young's double slit experiment, wavelength of light used is inversely proportional to the number of fringes observed.

i.e. $\lambda_1 n_1 = \lambda_2 n_2$
$$n_2 = \frac{n_1\lambda_1}{\lambda_2}$$
Here, $\lambda_1 = 600$ nm $= 6 \times 10^{-7}$ m

$\lambda_2 = 400$ nm $= 4 \times 10^{-7}$ m

$n_1 = 8$
$$\therefore \quad n_2 = \frac{8 \times 6 \times 10^{-7}}{4 \times 10^{-7}} = 12$$

9. (*b*); Fringe width, $\beta = \dfrac{\lambda D}{d}$
$$\therefore \quad \frac{\beta_2}{\beta_1} = \frac{\frac{\lambda_2 D_2}{d_2}}{\frac{\lambda_1 D_1}{d_1}}$$
[As $\lambda_1 = \lambda_2$, $D_2 = 2D_1$ and $d_2 = \dfrac{d_1}{2}$]
$$\therefore \quad \frac{\beta_2}{\beta_1} = \frac{2D_1}{\left(\frac{d_1}{2}\right)} \times \frac{d_1}{D_1} = 4$$
$$\Rightarrow \beta_2 = 4\beta_1$$
i.e., fringe width becomes four times.

10. (*c*); In a YDSE, the path difference for *n* th minima is given by
$$\Delta y = (2n-1)\frac{\lambda}{2}$$
For 5th minima, $n = 5$
$$\therefore \quad \Delta y = [2(5)-1]\frac{\lambda}{2}$$
$$= \frac{9\lambda}{2}$$

Chapter-11

Dual Nature of Radiation and Matter

1. (*a*)
2. work function
3. Light
4. (*d*)
5. (*c*)
6. True
7. A = Cathode, B = Anode, C = Glass tube, D = Quartz window and E = High tension battery
8. photoemission
9. (*d*)
10. Alkali
11. I, II
12. (Frequency);
Frequency of light remains constant during all optical phenomena such as reflection, refraction, polarisation and diffraction.
13. (False);
Collector is the plate, where emitted electrons are gathered. Therefore, it is relatively at high potential than emitter.
14. frequency, cathode potential
15. emitter, collector
16. Yes
17. I. × II. × III. ✓ IV. ×
18. frequency, work function, intensity
19. $I_1 = I_2 = I_3$
20. I. ✓ II. ✓ III. ✓ IV. ×
There is very less time lag ($\sim 10^{-9}$ or less) for photoemission.
21. (*b*)
22. A → 4, B → 3, C → 1, D → 2
23. Kinetic energy of emitted photoelectron,
KE = h (Incident frequency − Threshold frequency)
$$= h(f_1 - f_2)$$
24. frequency
25. I. ϕ_0 or $h\nu_0$ II. ϕ_0 or $h\nu_0$
26. (*d*); $V_0 = \dfrac{h}{e}(f) - \dfrac{\phi}{e}$

Slope of the graph $= \dfrac{h}{e}$

$\Rightarrow \tan\theta = \dfrac{h}{e}$

$\Rightarrow e\tan\theta = h$ (Planck's constant)

27. (*d*); Extrapolating the given graph, we get

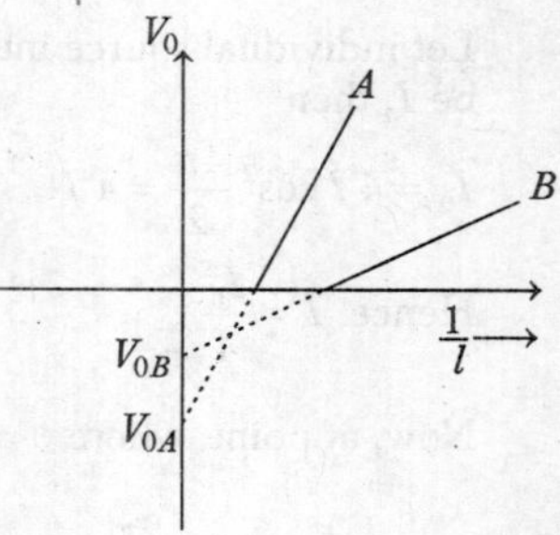

The graph shows that negative potential of A is greater than the negative potential of B.

Therefore, for metal A,
$$\frac{\phi_A}{hc} = \frac{1}{\lambda_1}$$
For metal B, $\dfrac{\phi_B}{hc} = \dfrac{1}{\lambda_2}$

Since, the work function or intensity of both metal is unknown, therefore the data given by student is not sufficient.

28. (1.4 eV);

$K_{max} = (E - \phi_0) = (3.4 - 2)$

$\Rightarrow x = 1.4$ eV

29. (2.5);

$$\phi_0 = \frac{hc}{\lambda_0} = \frac{6.6 \times 10^{-34} \times 3 \times 10^8}{5 \times 10^{-7} \times 1.6 \times 10^{-19}}$$

$\simeq 2.5$ eV

30. (green);

As, $E = h\nu$

$2.5 \times 1.6 \times 10^{-19} = h\nu$

$$\Rightarrow \nu = \frac{2.5 \times 1.6 \times 10^{-19}}{6.626 \times 10^{-34}}$$

$\simeq 6.00 \times 10^{14}$ Hz

which is the frequency of green colour.

31. ($\simeq$ 310 nm);

The work function of material is given by

$$\phi = h\nu = \frac{hc}{\lambda}$$

or $\lambda = \dfrac{hc}{\phi}$

$$= \frac{6.63 \times 10^{-34} \times 3 \times 10^8}{4 \times 1.6 \times 10^{-19}}$$

$= 3.108 \times 10^{-7}$ m $\simeq$ 310 nm

32. (4.68);

Frequency of incident radiation,

$$\nu = \frac{c}{\lambda} = \frac{3 \times 10^8}{2000 \times 10^{-10}}$$

$= 1.5 \times 10^{15}$ Hz

The work function of the metal,

$\phi_0 = h\nu - eV_0$

$= 6.626 \times 10^{-34} \times 1.5 \times 10^{15}$

$- 1.6 \times 10^{-19} \times 1.5$

$= 7.5 \times 10^{-19}$ J or 4.68 eV

($\because 1 \text{ J} = 1.6 \times 10^{-19}$ eV)

$\therefore x = 4.68$

33. (2x);

According to Einstein theory of photoelectric emission,

$K_{max} = h\nu - h\nu_0$

$\Rightarrow \frac{1}{2} mx^2 = 2hf_0 - hf_0$

$\Rightarrow \frac{1}{2} mx^2 = hf_0$ ...(i)

According to question,

$\frac{1}{2} mv^2 = 5hf_0 - hf_0$

$\Rightarrow \frac{1}{2} mv^2 = 4hf_0$ ...(ii)

Dividing Eq. (ii) by Eq. (i), we get

$$\frac{\frac{1}{2} mv^2}{\frac{1}{2} mx^2} = \frac{4hf_0}{hf_0}$$

$\Rightarrow v^2 = x^2 \times 4 \Rightarrow v = 2x$

34. (9);

For case I $\dfrac{hc}{\lambda} - \phi_0 = eV$ ...(i)

For case II $\dfrac{hc}{3\lambda} - \phi_0 = \dfrac{eV}{4}$ ...(ii)

Subtracting Eq. (ii) from Eq. (i), we have

$$\frac{2}{3}\frac{hc}{\lambda} = \frac{3}{4} eV$$

$$\Rightarrow eV = \frac{8}{9}\frac{hc}{\lambda}$$

Putting the value of eV in Eq. (i), we get

$$\frac{hc}{\lambda} - \phi_0 = \frac{8}{9}\frac{hc}{\lambda}$$

$$\Rightarrow \phi_0 = \frac{1}{9}\frac{hc}{\lambda} \Rightarrow \frac{hc}{n\lambda} = \frac{1}{9}\frac{hc}{\lambda}$$

$\therefore n = 9$

35. (True);

Since, photoelectrtic current is independent of work function and depends only on intensity of light. So, it remains same.

36. Frequency of lines can be found by using $\nu = \dfrac{c}{\lambda}$ and they are listed in tabular form as follows

V_0	$\nu \times 10^{14}$ Hz
1.28	8.219
0.95	7.412
0.74	6.884
0.16	5.493
0	4.343

(i) 4.343×10^{14} Hz;

As, at $V_0 = 0$, $\nu = \nu_0$ (threshold frequency)

$\therefore$ From the table, threshold frequency,

$\nu_0 = 4.343 \times 10^{14}$ Hz

(ii) 1.8 eV;

Work function, $\phi_0 = h\nu_0$

$= 6.63 \times 10^{-34} \times 4.343 \times 10^{14}$

$= 36.44 \times 10^{-19}$ J

$$= \frac{36.44 \times 10^{-19}}{1.6 \times 10^{-19}} \approx 1.8 \text{ eV}$$

37. (a);

From Einstein's photoelectric equation, $hf = \phi_0 + eV_0$

For point B,

$6.626 \times 10^{-34} \times 5.5 \times 10^{14}$

$= \phi_0 + 1.6 \times 10^{-19} \times 0$

$\Rightarrow \phi_0 = 36.44 \times 10^{-20}$ J

$$= \frac{36.44 \times 10^{-20}}{1.6 \times 10^{-19}} \text{ eV}$$

$= 2.27$ eV

38. (1.03);

From Einstein's photoelectric equation, we have

$\dfrac{hc}{\lambda_1} = \phi + eV_1$ ...(i)

and $\dfrac{hc}{\lambda_2} = \phi + eV_2$ ...(ii)

From Eqs. (i) and (ii), we get

$$hc\left(\frac{1}{\lambda_1} - \frac{1}{\lambda_2}\right) = e(V_1 - V_2)$$

$$\Rightarrow V_1 - V_2 = \frac{hc}{e}\left(\frac{\lambda_2 - \lambda_1}{\lambda_1 \lambda_2}\right)$$

$$= 1240\left(\frac{100}{300 \times 400}\right) = 1.03 \text{ V}$$

39. (5.5×10^{-13}C); Let the energy of electron be equal to the stopping potential,

i.e. E_i = KE + ϕ.

$\dfrac{hc}{\lambda} = eV + 4.47\ eV$

$\Rightarrow V + 4.47 = \dfrac{12400}{2500}$

$\Rightarrow V = 4.95 - 4.47 = 0.48$

Now, potential due to a sphere is given as

$$V_{\text{sphere}} = \frac{KQ}{r}$$

$$0.48 = \frac{9\times10^9 \times Q}{1\times10^{-2}}$$

$$\Rightarrow \quad Q = 5.5\times10^{-13}\text{ C}$$

40. electron; energy

41. (1 : 500);

Power of given energy source is written as

$$P = (N)\frac{hc}{\lambda}$$

Since, $P_1 = P_2$

Therefore, $\frac{hc}{\lambda_1}(N_1) = (N_2)\frac{hc}{\lambda_2}$

$$\Rightarrow \frac{N_1}{\lambda_1} = \frac{N_2}{\lambda_2} \Rightarrow \frac{N_1}{N_2} = \frac{\lambda_1}{\lambda_2} = \frac{1}{500}$$

42. (15);

Energy of n photons,

$$E = \frac{nhc}{\lambda}$$

$$\Rightarrow \quad n = \frac{E\times\lambda}{hc}$$

$$= \frac{(10\times10^3)\times300}{6.6\times10^{-34}\times3\times10^8}$$

$$= 1.5\times10^{31} \simeq 15\times10^{30}$$

43. (6×10^5 m/s);

$$K_{\max} = \frac{1}{2}mv^2 = h\nu - h\nu_0$$

$$\frac{1}{2}mv^2 = (6.626\times10^{-34}\times6.10\times10^{14}) - (1.50\times1.6\times10^{-19})$$

$$\frac{1}{2}mv^2 = (40.4186\times10^{-20}) - (2.4\times10^{-19})$$

$$\frac{1}{2}mv^2 = 1.6\times10^{-19}\text{J}$$

$$\Rightarrow v^2 = \frac{2\times1.6\times10^{-19}}{9.11\times10^{-31}}$$

$$(\because m = 9.11\times10^{-31}\text{ kg})$$

$$v^2 = 0.3513\times10^{12}$$

$$\Rightarrow \quad v \approx 6\times10^5\text{ m/s}$$

44. (No);

$$\text{KE} = h\nu - h\nu_0$$

$$= \left(\frac{1240}{99} - 1.0\right)\text{eV}$$

$$= (12.525 - 1) = 11.5252\text{ eV}$$

$$= 11.5252\times1.6\times10^{-19}\text{ J}$$

$$= 18.44\times10^{-19}\text{ J}$$

45. (10^{-24});

The energy of the emitted wave,

$$E = \frac{hc}{\lambda} = \frac{6.626\times10^{-34}\times3\times10^8}{21\times10^{-2}}$$

$$= 0.946\times10^{-24}\text{ J} \simeq 10^{-24}\text{J}$$

46.

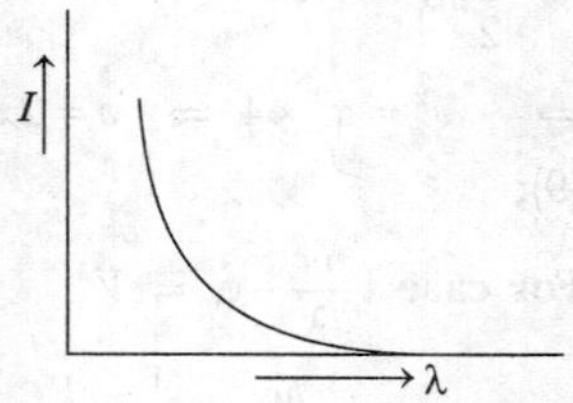

The graph of photoelectric current w.r.t. λ keeping voltage constant.

47. I. × II. × III.✓ IV. ✓

48. $\frac{h}{c\lambda}$

49. (True);

We know that, $p = \frac{h\nu}{c}$

$$\Rightarrow \quad \nu = \frac{3.3\times10^{-29}\times3\times10^8}{6.626\times10^{-34}}$$

$$= 1.49\times10^{13}\text{ Hz}$$

This frequency belongs to visible region.

50. (True);

As we know that, $\lambda = \frac{h}{\sqrt{2m\text{KE}}}$

Therefore, if kinetic energy of a particle is doubled, then its de-Broglie wavelength changes by a factor of $\frac{1}{\sqrt{2}}$.

51. ($\lambda_{\text{He}} < \lambda_p < \lambda_e$);

As we know that, $\lambda \propto \frac{1}{\sqrt{m}}$

We also know that, $m_e < m_p < m_{\text{He}}$

Therefore, $\lambda_{\text{He}} < \lambda_p < \lambda_e$

52. (9.7×10^{-28} kg);

As we know that, $\lambda = \frac{h}{p} = \frac{h}{mv}$

According to question,

$$\frac{\lambda_1}{\lambda_2} = \frac{m_e v_e}{m_p v_p} = 1.878\times10^{-4}$$

$$\Rightarrow m_p = \frac{9.1\times10^{-31}}{5\times1.878\times10^{-4}}$$

$$= 9.7\times10^{-28}\text{ kg}$$

53. (1.12);

$$\lambda = \frac{12.27}{\sqrt{V}}\text{ Å}$$

$\because V = 120$ V

$\Rightarrow \lambda = 1.12$ Å

$\therefore \; x = 1.12$

54. (0.135 nm);

Momentum,

$$p = mv = 9.11\times10^{-31}\times5.4\times10^6$$

$$= 4.92\times10^{-24}\text{ kg-ms}^{-1}$$

de-Broglie wavelength,

$$\lambda = \frac{h}{p}$$

$$= \frac{6.63\times10^{-34}\text{ J-s}}{4.92\times10^{-24}\text{ kg ms}^{-1}}$$

$$= 1.35\times10^{-10}\text{ m}$$

$$= 0.135\text{ nm}$$

Competition Connect

1. (*b*); The product of $\Delta x\cdot\Delta p$ is of order of $\hbar$.

$$\Rightarrow \Delta x\cdot\Delta p = \hbar = \frac{h}{2\pi}$$

2. (1.05×10^{-25} kg ms^{-1});

By Heisenberg uncertainty principle, $\Delta x\cdot\Delta p = \hbar$

$\therefore$ Uncertainty in momentum,

$$\Delta p = \frac{\hbar}{\Delta x} = \frac{h}{2\pi\,\Delta x} \quad \left(\because \hbar = \frac{h}{2\pi}\right)$$

$$= \frac{6.63\times10^{-34}}{2\times\pi\times10^{-9}}$$

$$\approx 1.05\times10^{-25}\text{ kg ms}^{-1}$$

3. (Yes);

We have de-Broglie wavelengths associated with particles are

$$\lambda_x = \frac{h}{p_x} \text{ and } \lambda_y = \frac{h}{p_y}$$

$$\Rightarrow \quad p_x = \frac{h}{\lambda_x}$$

and $p_y = \dfrac{h}{\lambda_y}$

Finally particles collided to form a single particle.

According to conservation of linear momentum,

$$p_p = |p_x - p_y|$$

$$= \left|\frac{h}{\lambda_x} - \frac{h}{\lambda_y}\right|$$

So, de-Broglie wavelength of combined particles is

$$\lambda_p = \frac{h}{|p_p|} = \frac{h}{\left|\frac{h}{\lambda_x} - \frac{h}{\lambda_y}\right|}$$

$$= \frac{\lambda_x \lambda_y}{|\lambda_x - \lambda_y|}$$

4. (10 : 1);

As de-Broglie wavelength is given as $\lambda = \dfrac{h}{\sqrt{2mqV}}$

Therefore,

$$\lambda_A = \frac{h}{\sqrt{2 \times m \times q \times 50}}$$

$$= \frac{h}{\sqrt{100\, me}} \quad \ldots(i)$$

$$\lambda_B = \frac{h}{\sqrt{4m \times q \times 2500}}$$

$$= \frac{h}{\sqrt{10000\, mq}} \quad \ldots(ii)$$

Dividing Eq. (i) by Eq. (ii), we get

$$\frac{\lambda_A}{\lambda_B} = \frac{\frac{h}{\sqrt{100\, mq}}}{\frac{h}{\sqrt{10000\, mq}}} = \frac{10}{1}$$

5. I. (400 kg-ms^{-1}, 1.65 $\times 10^{-36}$ m);

$$p_1 = m_1 v_1 = 0.40 \text{ kg} \times 1 \text{ kms}^{-1}$$

$$= 0.40 \text{ kg} \times 1000 \text{ ms}^{-1}$$

$$= 400 \text{ kg ms}^{-1}$$

$$\Rightarrow \lambda_1 = \frac{h}{p_1}$$

$$= 1.65 \times 10^{-36} \text{ m}$$

II. (0.6 kg-ms^{-1}, 1.1×10^{-33} m);

$$p_2 = m_2 v_2 = 0.60 \text{ kg} \times 1 \text{ ms}^{-1} = 0.6 \text{ kg ms}^{-1}$$

$$\Rightarrow \lambda_2 = \frac{h}{p_2} = 1.1 \times 10^{-33} \text{ m}$$

III. (2.2×10^{-9} kg-ms^{-1}, 3×10^{-25} m);

$$p_3 = m_3 v_3 = 1.0 \times 10^{-9} \text{ kg} \times 2.2 \text{ ms}^{-1}$$

$$= 2.2 \times 10^{-9} \text{ kg ms}^{-1}$$

$$\Rightarrow \lambda_3 = \frac{h}{p_3} = 3 \times 10^{-25} \text{ m}$$

6. Using formula,

$$\lambda = \frac{h}{\sqrt{2\text{KE}_e m_e}}$$

(i) (6.96×10^{-25} J);

Kinetic energy of electron,

$$\text{KE}_e = \frac{h^2}{2\lambda^2 m_e}$$

$$= \frac{(6.63 \times 10^{-34})^2}{2 \times (589 \times 10^{-9})^2 \times 9.1 \times 10^{-31}}$$

$$= 6.96 \times 10^{-25} \text{ J}$$

(ii) (3.82×10^{-28} J);

Kinetic energy of neutron,

$$\text{KE}_n = \frac{h^2}{2\lambda^2 m_n}$$

$$= \frac{(6.63 \times 10^{-34})^2}{2 \times (589 \times 10^{-9})^2 \times 1.67 \times 10^{-27}}$$

$$= 3.82 \times 10^{-28} \text{ J}$$

7. (*d*); As, de-Broglie wavelength,

$$\lambda = \frac{h}{\sqrt{2mqV}}$$

Since, V is same for both the given particles, so

$$\therefore \lambda \propto \frac{1}{\sqrt{mq}} \therefore \frac{\lambda_p}{\lambda_\alpha} = \frac{\sqrt{m_\alpha q_\alpha}}{\sqrt{m_p q_p}}$$

$$= \frac{\sqrt{4m_p \times 2e}}{\sqrt{m_p \times e}} = \sqrt{8} : 1$$

8. (False);

As, $\lambda = \dfrac{12.27}{\sqrt{V}}$

$$\therefore \frac{\lambda_1}{\lambda_2} = \sqrt{\frac{V_2}{V_1}}$$

$$\text{or } \lambda_2 = \lambda_1 \sqrt{\frac{V_1}{V_2}}$$

$$= \lambda_1 \sqrt{\frac{25}{100}} = \frac{\lambda_1}{2}$$

de-Broglie wavelength associated with the electrons decreases by 2 times.

Assertion-Reason Questions

1. (*a*)

2. (*a*)

3. (*b*); As the number of photons increases with increasing intensity, therefore number of photoelectrons also increases. Thus, photocurrent increases with increasing intensity.

4. (*c*); Stopping potential depends on the nature of the material hence, it remains constant on increasing the intensity of light.

On increasing the intensity of light, number of photons increases but their energy remains same hence, kinetic energy of emitted photoelectrons also remains same.

5. (*a*)

6. (*a*)

7. (*a*);Wave theory suggests that the kinetic energy of the photoelectrons should increase with the increase in intensity of light. But energy contained in an intense beam of light is very small.

So, to eject an electron from metal surface, the energy must accumulate sufficiently enough, which may take few hours.

8. (*d*); The number of photons may not be conserved in a collision; photons can be absorbed or created. Total energy and momentum are conserved in such collisions.

9. (*c*); Wavelength,

$$\lambda = \frac{h}{p} = \frac{h}{\sqrt{2m\text{ KE}}}$$

10. (*d*); The de-Broglie wavelength of macroscopic objects is so small that it is insignificant and not observable. The large momentum of macroscopic objects results in an extremely small wavelength.

Case Based Questions

1. (i) (*a*); Stopping potential,

$$V_0 = 5.68 \text{ V}$$

$$m_e = 9.1\times10^{-31} \text{ kg}$$

Maximum KE, $K_{\max}$

$$\Rightarrow \frac{1}{2}mv_{\max}^2 = eV_0$$

$$\Rightarrow v_{\max} = \sqrt{\frac{2eV_0}{m}}$$

$$= \sqrt{\frac{2\times1.6\times10^{-19}\times5.68}{9.1\times10^{-31}}}$$

$$= 1.4\times10^3 \text{ km/s}$$

(ii) (*b*); Maximum kinetic energy of photoelectrons

$$K_{\max} = eV_0$$

where,

$$e = 1.6\times10^{-19} \text{ C}, V_0 = 1.5 \text{ V}$$

$$\therefore K_{\max} = 1.6\times10^{-19}\times1.5$$

$$= 2.4\times10^{-19} \text{ J}$$

(iii) (*d*)

(iv) (*a*)

2. (i) (*b*)

(ii) (*c*); de-Broglie wavelength,

$$\lambda = \frac{h}{mv}$$

As both particle and electron are having same wavelength therefore their momentum will be equal

$$m_p v_p = m_e v_e$$

$$\Rightarrow v_p = \frac{m_e v_e}{m_p}$$

$$= \frac{9.1\times10^{-31}\times3\times10^6}{10^{-6}}$$

$$\Rightarrow v_p = 2.7\times10^{-18} \text{ ms}^{-1}$$

(iii) (*d*); de-Broglie wavelength is given by

$$\lambda = \frac{h}{\sqrt{2mE}}$$

$$\Rightarrow \lambda \propto \frac{1}{\sqrt{E}}$$

$$\frac{\lambda_1}{\lambda_2} = \sqrt{\frac{E_2}{E_1}}$$

$$\Rightarrow \frac{10^{-10}}{0.5\times10^{-10}} = \sqrt{\frac{E_2}{E_1}}$$

$$\Rightarrow E_2 = 4E_1$$

Hence, added energy

$$= E_2 - E_1 = 3E_1$$

(iv) (*c*); de-Broglie wavelength

$$\lambda = \frac{h}{\sqrt{2mKE}}$$

Hence, heaviest particle will have smallest de-Broglie wavelength.

Neutron will have smallest de-Broglie wavelength among given options.

Competition Edge Up

1. (*d*); Energy of UV radiation,

$$E = 4.13 \text{ eV}$$

Work function of metal, $\phi = 3.13$ eV

According of Einstein's photoelectric equation,

$$K_{\max} = E - h\nu_0$$

$$\therefore h\nu_0 = \phi = 4.13 - 3.13 = 1.00 \text{ eV}$$

2. (*b*); de-Broglie wavelength is given by

$$\lambda = \frac{h}{p} = \frac{h}{\sqrt{2mK}}$$

Given, $\lambda_{\text{proton}} = \lambda_{\text{electron}}$

$$\Rightarrow \frac{h}{\sqrt{2m_pK_p}} = \frac{h}{\sqrt{2m_eK_e}}$$

$$\Rightarrow m_pK_p = m_eK_e$$

$$\Rightarrow \frac{K_p}{K_e} = \frac{m_e}{m_p} = \frac{1}{1836}$$

$$\therefore m_p \approx 1836m_e$$

$$\Rightarrow \frac{K_p}{K_e} < 1 \text{ or } K_p < K_e$$

3. (*d*); Given, $\lambda = 300$ nm

$$\phi_0 = 2.13 \text{ eV}$$

According to Einstein's equation,

$$\frac{hc}{\lambda} - \phi_0 = K_{\max}$$

$$\Rightarrow \frac{hc}{\lambda} - \phi_0 = eV_0$$

$$\Rightarrow \left(\frac{1240}{300} - 2.13\right) \text{eV} = eV_0$$

$$\Rightarrow V_0 = 2 \text{ V}$$

4. (*c*); de-Broglie wavelength,

$$\lambda = \frac{h}{p} = \frac{h}{mv}$$

For proton, de-Broglie wavelength,

$$\lambda_1 = \frac{h}{m_p v_p} = \lambda \text{ (given)}$$

For α-particle, de-Broglie wavelength

$$\lambda_2 = \frac{h}{m_\alpha v_\alpha} = 2\lambda \text{ (given)}$$

Dividing, we get

$$\frac{\lambda_1}{\lambda_2} = \frac{m_\alpha v_\alpha}{m_p v_p} = \frac{1}{2}$$

or $$\frac{4\times v_\alpha}{1\times v_p} = \frac{1}{2} \quad \left(\text{As, } \frac{m_\alpha}{m_p} = 4\right)$$

$$\Rightarrow \frac{v_\alpha}{v_p} = \frac{1}{8} \Rightarrow \frac{v_p}{v_\alpha} = \frac{8}{1}$$

5. (*b*); For photon,

$$E_p = \frac{hc}{\lambda_p} \Rightarrow \lambda_p = \frac{hc}{E_p}$$

For electron,

$$\lambda_e = \frac{h}{m_e v_e} = \frac{hv_e}{2K_e} \Rightarrow v_e = 0.25c$$

$$\lambda_e = \frac{h\times0.25c}{2K_e} = \frac{hc}{8K_e}$$

$$\lambda_p = \lambda_e$$

$$\frac{hc}{E_p} = \frac{hc}{8K_e} \Rightarrow \frac{K_e}{E_p} = \frac{1}{8}$$

6. (*d*); We know that $\lambda = \frac{h}{p} = \frac{h}{\sqrt{2mE}}$

Here, E = kinetic energy

Thus, $$\lambda^2 = \frac{h^2}{2mE}$$

$$\Rightarrow \frac{1}{\lambda^2} = \frac{2mE}{h^2} \propto E$$

Hence, option (d) is correct.

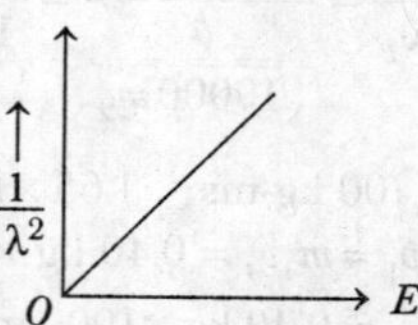

7. (*b*); Photon is quanta of energy. It is a massless and chargeless particle. The rest mass of photon is zero. In free space, it moves with velocity '*c*' and energy of photon is equal to $h\nu$. The momentum of the photon is given by $p = \frac{E}{c} = \frac{h\nu}{c}$.

8. (*c*); Using Einstein's photoelectric equation, $eV' = h\nu' - h\nu_0$

when $\quad \nu' = \nu$

and $\quad V' = V_{s/2}$, then

$$\therefore \quad \frac{eV_s}{2} = h\nu - h\nu_0 \quad \ldots\text{(i)}$$

Again when $\nu' = \dfrac{\nu}{2}$ and $V' = V_s$

then

$$\therefore \quad eV_s = \frac{h\nu}{2} - h\nu_0 \quad \ldots\text{(ii)}$$

Dividing Eq. (i) by Eq. (ii), we get

$$\frac{eV_s/2}{eV_s} = \frac{h\nu - h\nu_0}{\dfrac{h\nu}{2} - h\nu_0}$$

$$\frac{1}{2} = \frac{(\nu - \nu_0)}{\dfrac{\nu}{2} - \nu_0}$$

$$\frac{\nu}{2} - \nu_0 = 2\nu - 2\nu_0$$

$$\Rightarrow \quad \nu_0 = \frac{3}{2}\nu$$

Hence, correct option is (c).

9. (*d*); Since, work function is negligible. Therefore, kinetic energy of emitted electron = Energy of incident photon

i.e., $\dfrac{1}{2}mv^2 = h\nu$

$$\Rightarrow \quad \frac{p^2}{2m} = \frac{hc}{\lambda} \Rightarrow p = \sqrt{\frac{2mhc}{\lambda}}$$

de-Broglie wavelength of emitted electrons is

$$\lambda_d = \frac{h}{p} = \frac{h}{\sqrt{\dfrac{2mhc}{\lambda}}} = \sqrt{\frac{h\lambda}{2mc}}$$

$$\Rightarrow \quad \lambda = \left(\frac{2mc}{h}\right)\lambda_d^2$$

10. (*a*); Kinetic energy of electron,

$K = 144$ eV

$\Rightarrow$ $eV = 144$ eV $\Rightarrow V = 144$ V

$\therefore$ de-Broglie wavelength

$$\lambda = \frac{12.27}{\sqrt{V}}\text{Å} = \frac{12.27}{\sqrt{144}}\text{Å} = \frac{12.27}{12}\text{Å}$$

$$= 1.02\text{Å} = 0.102 \text{ nm}$$

$$= 102 \times 10^{-3} \text{ nm}$$

Chapter-12

Atoms

1. $A \rightarrow$ Source of α-particles

$B \rightarrow$ Gold foil

$C \rightarrow$ Detector plate or screen

2. $A \rightarrow 3$, $B \rightarrow 1$, $C \rightarrow 2$

3.

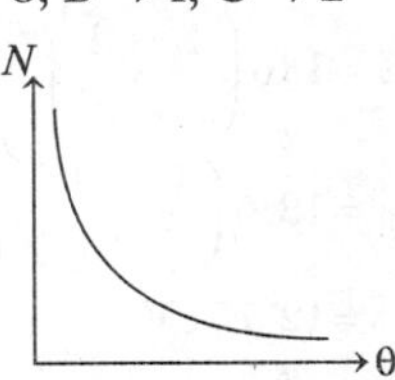

4. ($158\ e^2$);

$$Fr^2 = \frac{2Ze^2}{4\pi\varepsilon_0} = 2 \times 79 \times e^2 \times 9 \times 10^9$$

$$= 158e^2 \times 9 \times 10^9$$

5. (i) large (ii) minimum

6. (*d*); In given case,

Radius of earth's orbit

$$= 7 \times 10^8 \times \frac{10^{-10}}{10^{-15}} = 7 \times 10^{13} \text{ m}$$

which is more than 100 times the actual value of 1.5×10^{11} m.

7. $\dfrac{2Ze^2}{4\pi\varepsilon_0 K}$

8. (*d*)

9. coulombian

10. $A \rightarrow 3$, $B \rightarrow 2$, $C \rightarrow 1$

11. -1, 2

12. (i) (0.53 Å);

$$E = -\frac{e^2}{8\pi\varepsilon_0 r}$$

$$= -13.6 \times 1.6 \times 10^{-19}$$

$$\Rightarrow r = -\frac{(1.6 \times 10^{-19})^2 \times 9 \times 10^9}{2 \times 13.6 \times 1.6 \times 10^{-19}}$$

$$= 0.53 \text{ Å}$$

(ii) (2.2×10^6 ms^{-1});

$$v = \frac{e}{\sqrt{4\pi\varepsilon_0 mr}}$$

$$= \frac{1.6 \times 10^{-19} \times (9 \times 10^9)^{1/2}}{\sqrt{9.1 \times 10^{-31} \times 0.53 \times 10^{-10}}}$$

$$= 2.2 \times 10^6 \text{ ms}^{-1}$$

13. E decrease, K increase, U decrease

14. False

15. $A \rightarrow 3$, $B \rightarrow 2$, $C \rightarrow 1$

16. (*c*); When an atomic gas or vapour under low pressure is excited usually by heating or passing an electric current through it, the emitted radiation has a spectrum which contains certain specific wavelengths only. A spectrum of this kind is termed as emission line spectrum.

17. (*b*); When white light is passed through an unexcited state gas and the transmitted light is analysed using a spectrometer, then it is found that transmitted light consists of few dark lines in bright background. These dark lines correspond precisely to those wavelengths which were found in the emission line spectrum of the gas. This is called the absorption spectrum of the material of the gas.

18. True

19. No

20. (6.6);

Frequency,

$$\nu = \frac{v}{2\pi r} = \frac{2.2 \times 10^6}{2\pi\,(0.53 \times 10^{-10})}$$

$$= 6.6 \times 10^{15} \text{ Hz}$$

21. (1.05);

Change in angular momentum,

$$\Delta L = L_2 - L_1 = \frac{n_2 h}{2\pi} - \frac{n_1 h}{2\pi}$$

$$\Delta L = \frac{h}{2\pi}(n_2 - n_1)$$

$$\Delta L = \frac{6.6 \times 10^{-34}}{2 \times 3.14} \times (5 - 4)$$

$$= 1.05 \times 10^{-34} \text{ J-s}$$

22. (*b*); Radius of electron in nth orbit,

$$r_n = \frac{n^2 h^2 \varepsilon_0}{\pi m Z e^2} \Rightarrow r_n \propto \frac{1}{Z}$$

So, the relation between r_n and Z is correctly depicted in option (b), as the value of Z increases, r_n decreases.

23. ($4a_0$); Since, radius, $r \propto n^2$

$$\therefore \quad \frac{a_2}{a_1} = \left(\frac{2}{1}\right)^2 \Rightarrow a_2 = 4a_0$$

24. (*b*); As we know, $r_n \propto \dfrac{n^2}{Z}$

$$\therefore \quad \frac{r_f}{r_i} = \left(\frac{n_f}{n_i}\right)^2$$

$$\text{or} \quad n_f = \left(\frac{r_f}{r_i}\right)^{1/2} n_i$$

$$= \left(\frac{21.2 \times 10^{-11}}{5.3 \times 10^{-11}}\right)^{1/2} \times 1 = 2$$

25. (*b*); $\Delta E = 13.6\left(\dfrac{1}{n_1^2} - \dfrac{1}{n_2^2}\right)$

$$= 13.6 \times \left(1 - \frac{1}{4}\right) = 10.2 \text{ eV}$$

26. (2.3 eV);

$\Delta E = h\nu$

$= \dfrac{6.626 \times 10^{-34} \times 5.6 \times 10^{14}}{1.6 \times 10^{-19}}$

$= 2.3$ eV

27. I. ✓ II. ✓ III. ✓ IV. ✕

28. A → 4, B → 1, C → 2, D → 3

29. equal to

30. (i) KE = – TE = –(–3.4) = 3.4 eV

(ii) PE = 2TE = 2(–3.4) = – 6.8 eV

31. (– 2.81 eV); As, $E \propto m$

$\therefore E_M = 207\, E_H = 207(-13.6)$

$= -2.81$ keV

32. (*d*)

33. False

34. (– 3.40 eV, – 1.51 eV, – 0.85 eV, 0.54 eV);

$E_2 = -\dfrac{13.6}{(2)^2} = -3.40$ eV

$E_3 = \dfrac{-13.6}{(3)^2} = -1.51$ eV

$E_4 = \dfrac{-13.6}{(4)^2} = -0.85$ eV

$E_5 = \dfrac{-13.6}{(5)^2} = 0.54$ eV

35. (6.5);

According to Bohr's model, velocity of electron,

$v = \dfrac{2\pi K e^2 Z}{nh}$ or $v \propto \dfrac{1}{n}$

$\therefore \quad v_B = v_A \times \dfrac{n_A}{n_B}$

$= 2.6 \times 10^6 \times \dfrac{1}{4}$

$= 6.5 \times 10^5$ ms^{-1}

$\therefore \quad x = 6.5$

36. (2.10×10^{-34} J-s);

Using $E_n = -\dfrac{13.6}{n^2}$

$= -3.4$ eV, we get

$n = \sqrt{\dfrac{13.6}{3.4}} = 2$

$\therefore$ Angular momentum,

$L = \dfrac{nh}{2\pi} = \dfrac{2 \times 6.6 \times 10^{-34}}{2 \times 3.14}$

$= 2.10 \times 10^{-34}$ J-s

37. (16 : 1);

Since, $r \propto n^2$

$\therefore \quad \dfrac{r_2}{r_1} = \left(\dfrac{4}{1}\right)^2 = \dfrac{16}{1}$ or 16 : 1

38. (100);

As, $E = 13.6\left(\dfrac{1}{n_1^2} - \dfrac{1}{n_2^2}\right)$

$= 13.6\left(\dfrac{1}{1^2} - \dfrac{1}{4^2}\right)$

$= 12.75$ eV

$\therefore \quad \lambda = \dfrac{hc}{E}$

$= \dfrac{6.625 \times 10^{-34} \times 3 \times 10^8}{12.75 \times 1.6 \times 10^{-19}}$

$= 97.4 \times 10^{-9}$ m $\simeq 100$ nm

39. (*b*); Kinetic energy

= – (Total Energy)

Kinetic energy = – (–1.5eV)

= 1.5eV

40. (1.51 eV);

As, $E_n \propto \dfrac{Z^2}{n^2}$

$\therefore \quad E_2 = \dfrac{1}{(3)^2} E_0$

$= \dfrac{1}{9} \times 13.6 = 1.51$ eV

41. (*c*); We have,

$\lambda = \dfrac{hc}{\Delta E}$ or $\lambda \propto \dfrac{1}{\Delta E}$

$\therefore \quad \dfrac{\lambda_1}{\lambda_2} = \dfrac{\Delta E_2}{\Delta E_1}$

$\dfrac{\lambda_1}{\lambda_2} = \dfrac{\left(\dfrac{4}{3}E - E\right)}{2E - E} = \dfrac{1}{3}$

42. (1218 Å, 1027 Å, 974.3 Å);

$\lambda_{i1} = \dfrac{0.9134 \times 10^{-7} \times (n_i)^2}{(n_i^2 - 1)}$

$\therefore \lambda_{21} = \dfrac{0.9134 \times 10^{-7} \times (2)^2}{(2^2 - 1)}$

$= 1218$ Å

$\lambda_{31} = \dfrac{0.9134 \times 10^{-7} \times (3)^2}{(3^2 - 1)}$

$= 1027$ Å

$\lambda_{41} = \dfrac{0.9134 \times 10^{-7} \times (4)^2}{(4^2 - 1)}$

$= 974.3$ Å

43. III

44. False

45. (*a*); Given, total energy of electron,

$E = -4.6$ eV

Kinetic energy of electron,

$K = -$ (Total energy, E)

$\Rightarrow K = -E = -(-4.6) = 4.6$ eV

de-Brogile wavelength,

$\lambda = \dfrac{h}{\sqrt{2mK}}$

$= \dfrac{6.6 \times 10^{-34}}{\sqrt{2 \times 9.1 \times 10^{-31} \times 4.61 \times 1.6 \times 10^{-19}}}$

$= 0.57 \times 10^{-9}$ m

$= 0.57$ nm

46. (*a*); According to Bohr theory,

$mvr = n\dfrac{h}{2\pi} \Rightarrow v = \dfrac{nh}{2\pi m r}$

and $\dfrac{mv^2}{r} \propto \dfrac{k}{r} \Rightarrow \dfrac{m}{r}\left(\dfrac{n^2h^2}{4\pi^2 m^2 r^2}\right) \propto \dfrac{k}{r}$

$\Rightarrow \quad r_n \propto n$

Kinetic energy of the electron,

$T = \dfrac{1}{2}mv^2 = \dfrac{1}{2}m\left(\dfrac{n^2h^2}{4\pi^2 m^2 r^2}\right)$

$\Rightarrow \quad T_n \propto \dfrac{n^2}{r^2}$

But as $r \propto n$, therefore $T \propto n^0$.

Competition Connect

1. (A → 4, B → 3, C → 1, D → 2, E → 5);

For minimum wavelength,

$n = 0$

$\therefore \lambda$ (Lyman series) $= \dfrac{1}{R}$

λ (Balmer series) $= \dfrac{2^2}{R} = \dfrac{4}{R}$

λ (Paschen series) $= \dfrac{3^2}{R} = \dfrac{9}{R}$

λ (Brackett series) $= \dfrac{4^2}{R} = \dfrac{16}{R}$

λ (Pfund series) $= \dfrac{5^2}{R} = \dfrac{25}{R}$

2. (4860 Å);

For first line of Balmer series,

$n = 3$

$\Rightarrow \quad \dfrac{1}{\lambda_1} = R\left(\dfrac{1}{2^2} - \dfrac{1}{3^2}\right) = \dfrac{5R}{36}$ ...(i)

For second line, $n = 4$

$\Rightarrow \quad \dfrac{1}{\lambda_2} = R\left(\dfrac{1}{2^2} - \dfrac{1}{4^2}\right) = \dfrac{3R}{16}$ ...(ii)

Dividing Eq. (i) by Eq. (ii), we get

$\therefore \quad \dfrac{\lambda_2}{\lambda_1} = \dfrac{20}{27}$

$\Rightarrow \quad \lambda_2 = \dfrac{20}{27} \times \lambda_1$

$\Rightarrow \quad \lambda_2 = \dfrac{20}{27} \times 6561$

$= 4860$ Å

3. (*c*); For last line of Balmer series, $n_1 = 2$ and $n_2 = \infty$

$$\Rightarrow \frac{1}{\lambda_B} = R\left(\frac{1}{2^2} - \frac{1}{\infty^2}\right) = \frac{R}{4} \quad \dots \text{(i)}$$

Similarly, for last line of Lyman series,

$n_1 = 1$ and $n_2 = \infty$

$$\Rightarrow \frac{1}{\lambda_L} = R\left(\frac{1}{1^2} - \frac{1}{\infty^2}\right) = R \quad \dots \text{(ii)}$$

Dividing Eq. (i) by Eq. (ii), we get

$$\Rightarrow \frac{\lambda_L}{\lambda_B} = \frac{1}{4}$$

$$\Rightarrow \frac{\lambda_B}{\lambda_L} = 4$$

4. (True);

In Pfund series,

Maximum wavelength is given by

$$\frac{1}{\lambda_{max}} = R\left(\frac{1}{5^2} - \frac{1}{6^2}\right)$$

$$= R\left(\frac{11}{900}\right) \quad \dots \text{(i)}$$

Minimum wavelength is given by

$$\frac{1}{\lambda_{min}} = R\left(\frac{1}{5^2} - \frac{1}{\infty}\right)$$

$$= \frac{R}{25} \quad \dots \text{(ii)}$$

Dividing Eq. (ii) by Eq. (i), we get

$$\frac{\lambda_{max}}{\lambda_{min}} = \frac{R/25}{11R/900} = \frac{36}{11}$$

5. (No);

For largest wavelength in Lyman series, $n_1 = 1$ and $n_2 = 2$

$$\frac{1}{\lambda_1} = R\left(\frac{1}{1^2} - \frac{1}{2^2}\right) = \frac{3R}{4} \quad \dots \text{(i)}$$

For largest wavelength in Balmer series, $n_1 = 2$ and $n_2 = 3$

$$\frac{1}{\lambda_2} = R\left(\frac{1}{2^2} - \frac{1}{3^2}\right) = \frac{5R}{36} \quad \dots \text{(ii)}$$

Dividing Eq. (ii) by Eq. (i), we get

$$\frac{\lambda_1}{\lambda_2} = \frac{5}{36} \times \frac{4}{3} = \frac{5}{27}$$

or $\lambda_1 = \frac{5}{27}\lambda_2$

6. (*d*); For Lyman series,

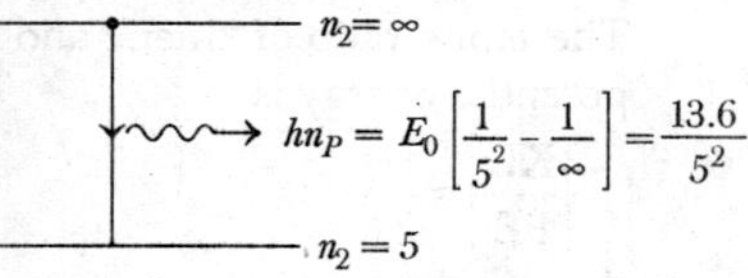

$$h\nu_L = 13.6 \quad \dots \text{(i)}$$

In Pfund series,

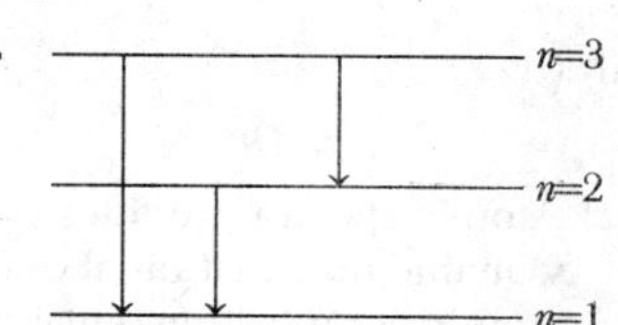

$$h\nu_P = \frac{13.6}{5^2} \quad \dots \text{(ii)}$$

From Eqs. (i) and (ii), we get

$$25h\nu_P = h\nu_L$$

$$\therefore \quad \nu_P = \frac{\nu_L}{25}$$

7. I

8.

$n=3$

$n=2$

$n=1$

9. 9,16;

We know that, frequency,

$$\nu = \frac{c}{\lambda} = c \cdot R\left(\frac{1}{n_1^2} - \frac{1}{n_2^2}\right)$$

$$\left\{\because \frac{1}{\lambda} = R\left(\frac{1}{n_1^2} - \frac{1}{n_2^2}\right)\right\}$$

$$= 3 \times 10^8 \times 10^7 \left(\frac{1}{2^2} - \frac{1}{4^2}\right)$$

$$= \frac{9}{16} \times 10^{15}\text{Hz}$$

$$\therefore \quad a = 9, b = 16$$

Assertion-Reason Questions

1. (*c*); According to postulates of Bohr's atom model, the electron revolves around the nucleus in fixed orbit of definite radii. As long as the electron is in a certain orbit, it does not radiate any energy.

2. (*b*); $L = n\left(\frac{h}{2\pi}\right)$ *i.e.*, $L \propto n$. In ground state, $n = 1$

So, L = minimum.

3. (*c*); The energy of electron in nth orbit of hydrogen atom is,

$$E_n = -\frac{me^4}{8n^2\varepsilon_0^2h^2}$$

$$= \frac{-2.18 \times 10^{-18}}{n^2}$$

For first excited state ($n = 2$)

$$E_2 = -\frac{2.18 \times 10^{-18}}{4}$$

$$= -5.45 \times 10^{-19}\text{J}$$

4. (*d*); The energy of an atom is the least when its electron is revolving in an orbit closest to the nucleus, i.e., the one for which $n = 1$. However, the highest energy state corresponds to $n = \infty$ and has an energy of 0 eV.

Since, $E_n \propto \frac{1}{n^2}$

So, as the value of n increases, energies of excited states comes closer and closer.

5. (*b*); $E_H = 13.6$ eV (ionisation energy)

$$\therefore E_{He^+} = 13.6(Z)^2 = (13.6)(Z)^2$$
$$= 54.4 \text{ eV}$$

6. (*b*); If the electron is free, then it can absorb photon of any energy but if it is bounded then it can absorb only those photons whose energies are equal to the difference of energy values of two energy levels.

7. (*c*); It is not essential that all the lines available in the emission spectrum will also be available in the absorption spectrum.

The spectrum of hydrogen atom may not be absorption spectrum.

8. (*c*)

9. (*c*); Because total energy of electron in ground states of hydrogen atom is −13.6 eV.

10. (*b*); $mv_2r_2 = 2\left(\frac{h}{2\pi}\right)$

$$\therefore 2\pi r_2 = 2\left(\frac{h}{mv_2}\right) = 2\lambda_2$$

Further, $\lambda = \frac{h}{p}$

$\lambda = 2\pi r$

Hence, λ is minimum in ground state.

Case Based Questions

1. (i) (*b*); Force for rotation is provided by magnetic field

$$\Rightarrow \frac{mv^2}{r} = Bqv \text{ (Lorentz force)}$$

$$mvr = \frac{nh}{2\pi} \text{ (Angular momentum quantisation)}$$

Combining, we get $\frac{mvr}{Bq} = r^2$

$$\Rightarrow r = \sqrt{\frac{nh}{2\pi Bq}}$$

(ii) (*a*); The frequency of revolution is given by

$$f = \frac{v}{2\pi r}$$

Radius of revolution is given by $r = \dfrac{mv}{qB}$

On combining the two equations, we get

$$f = \frac{qB}{2\pi m}$$

(iii) (*a*); $\text{KE} = \dfrac{1}{2}mv^2$

$$= \frac{B^2q^2r^2}{2m}$$

$$= \frac{B^2q^2}{2m} \cdot \frac{nh}{2\pi Bq}$$

$$= \frac{Bqnh}{4\pi m} = \frac{nhBq}{4\pi m}$$

(iv) (*d*); A revolving electron is like a current loop. In magnetic field, its potential energy,

$$U = -\mathbf{M} \cdot \mathbf{B} = -MB\cos\theta$$

$$= -(i \cdot A)\, B\cos\theta$$

$$\therefore \text{M} = NIA$$

$$= -(qf\pi r^2)\, B\cos\theta,$$

$$f = \text{frequency} = \frac{1}{T}$$

$$= -\left(q\pi r^2 \cdot \frac{Bq}{2\pi m}\right) B\cos\theta$$

$$\therefore T = \frac{2\pi m}{Bq}$$

$$= -\left(\frac{B^2q^2r^2}{2m}\right) \cdot \cos\theta,\ \theta = 180°$$

$$= \frac{-B^2q^2r^2}{2m} \cdot (-1)$$

or $\text{PE} = U = \text{KE} = \dfrac{Bqnh}{4\pi m}$

So, total energy of electrons in its nth state, $E_n = \dfrac{Bqh}{2\pi m} \cdot n$

In transaction $2 \to 1$,

Energy lost = photon energy

$$= E_2 - E_1 = \frac{Bqh}{2\pi m}(2-1)$$

$$= \frac{Bqh}{2\pi m} = hf$$

or frequency of emitted photon = Classical revolution frequency $= \dfrac{Bq}{2\pi m}$

Or

(iv) (c); The difference of higher and lower energy level is released as electromagnetic wave.

2. (i) (*a*)

(ii) (*c*)

Or

(*b*) Atomic spectra provides valuable information about atomic composition, energy levels and the physical conditions of celestial objects and laboratory samples.

(iii) (*a*); Energy of photon emitted by lamp,

$$E = \frac{hc}{\lambda}$$

$$= \frac{6.626 \times 10^{-34} \times 3.00 \times 10^8}{589 \times 10^{-9}}$$

$$= 3.37 \times 10^{-19}\ \text{J}$$

This energy is equal to the energy difference of two levels of sodium atom.

(iv) (*d*) Energy of electron in nth energy level is given by

$$E_n = -\frac{13.6}{n^2}\ \text{eV}$$

Energy difference between $n = 5$ and $n = 2$ is

$$\Delta E = E_5 - E_2$$

$$= -13.6\left(\frac{1}{25} - \frac{1}{4}\right)\text{eV}$$

Frequency of emitted photon is

$$\nu = \frac{\Delta E}{h}$$

$$= -\frac{13.6}{6.6 \times 10^{-34}}\left(\frac{1}{25} - \frac{1}{4}\right) \times 1.6 \times 10^{-19}$$

$$= 692 \times 10^{12}\ \text{Hz}$$

This frequency corresponds to violet light.

Competition Edge Up

1. (156);

At distance of closest approach, all of kinetic energy becomes potential energy.

$$\Rightarrow \frac{1}{2}mv^2 = \frac{kq_1q_2Z}{r}$$

$$\Rightarrow \left(\frac{1}{2} \times 6.72 \times 10^{-27}\right) v^2$$

$$= \frac{(9 \times 10^9 \times 2 \times 1.6 \times 10^{-19} \times 80 \times 1.6 \times 10^{-19})}{4.5 \times 10^{-14}}$$

$$v^2 = \frac{9 \times 10^9 \times 2 \times 80 \times (1.6 \times 10^{-19})^2 \times 2}{6.72 \times 10^{-27} \times 4.5 \times 10^{-14}}$$

$$= \frac{9 \times 4 \times 80 \times (1.6)^2}{6.72 \times 4.5} \times 10^{-38+9+27+14}$$

$$\Rightarrow v^2 = 243.089 \times 10^{12}$$

or $v = 15.59 \times 10^6$ m/s

$\simeq 156 \times 10^5$ m/s

2. (*d*); Angular momentum,

$$L = \frac{nh}{2\pi} \Rightarrow L \propto n \quad \ldots\text{(i)}$$

Since, $r \propto n^2 \Rightarrow r = Cn^2$

$$\Rightarrow \quad n = \sqrt{\frac{r}{C}} \Rightarrow n \propto \sqrt{r} \quad \ldots\text{(ii)}$$

From Eqs. (i) and (ii), we get

$$L \propto \sqrt{r}$$

3. (*b*); Moment of momentum (or angular momentum) of electron revolving in nth orbit of hydrogen atom, $L_n = nh/2\pi$

For 4th orbit, $n = 4$

$$\therefore \quad L_4 = \frac{4h}{2\pi} = \frac{2h}{\pi}$$

4. (*c*); Relation of kinetic, potential and total energy is given by

$$\text{KE} = |\text{TE}| = \left|\frac{\text{PE}}{2}\right|$$

This relation is in accordance with Bohr's model.

Therefore, ratio of kinetic and potential energy is

$$\left|\frac{\text{KE}}{\text{PE}}\right| = \frac{1}{2}$$

Hence, ratio of magnitudes of KE and PE of an electron is 1/2.

5. (*a*); According to Rutherford model, an atom consists of positively charged particles concentrated at the centre known as nucleus.

The size of nucleus is very small as compared to the size of atom.

Thus, Statement I is true but Statement II is false because it is special case of Thomson's model.

6. (*c*) In Bohr's atom (H-atom), radius of nth orbit is given by

$$R = Kn^2 / Z$$

Let R' = radius of 4th orbit and R = radius of 3rd orbit then,

$$\frac{R}{R'} = \frac{\frac{K(3)^2}{Z}}{\frac{K(4)^2}{Z}}$$

$$\Rightarrow \frac{R}{R'} = \frac{9}{16} \Rightarrow R' = \frac{16}{9}R$$

7. (*c*) Atoms are electrically neutral as they contain equal number of proton and electron. Statement II is incorrect because atom of radioactive elements are not stable.

8. (*c*) Radius of innermost orbit of H-atom

$$r_0 = 5.3 \times 10^{-11} \text{ m}$$

∴ Radius of third allowed orbit of H-atom.

$$r_3 = r_0 n^2 = r_0 (3)^2$$
$$= 9r_0 = 9 \times 5.3 \times 10^{-11}$$
$$= 47.7 \times 10^{-11} = 4.77 \times 10^{-10} \text{ m}$$
$$= 4.77 \text{ Å}$$

9. (*b*) Total energy of an electron in the nth stationary orbit of hydrogen atom is given by

$$E_n = \frac{-Rhc}{n^2} = \frac{-13.6}{n^2} \text{ eV}$$

$[\because Rhc = 13.6 \text{ eV}]$

Chapter-13
Nuclei

1. I. ✓ II. ✓ III. ✓ IV. × V. ×

2. (*c*)

3. A → 2, B → 3

4. $\left(\frac{m_1x_1 + m_2x_2 + m_3x_3}{100}\right)$;

The average atomic mass,

$$\bar{m} = \frac{m_1x_1 + m_2x_2 + m_3x_3}{x_1 + x_2 + x_3}$$
$$= \frac{m_1x_1 + m_2x_2 + m_3x_3}{100}$$

$(\because x_1 + x_2 + x_3 = 100)$

5. (*b*); Mass of proton = Mass of ${}_1^1\text{H}$ − Mass of electron

$$= 1.0078 - 0.00055$$
$$= 1.00725 \text{ u}$$

Mass of neutron = Mass of ${}_1^2\text{H}$ − Mass of electron − Mass of proton

$$= 2.0141 - 0.00055 - 1.00725$$
$$= 1.0063 \text{ u}$$

6. (*a*)

7. neutron < proton < electron

8. A → 3, B → 1, C → 2

9. (*c*); Distance of closest approach,

$$r = \frac{1}{4\pi\varepsilon_0}\frac{Ze^2}{\text{KE}}$$
$$= \frac{9 \times 10^9 \times 79 \times (1.6 \times 10^{-19})^2}{5.5 \times 10^6 \text{ eV}}$$
$$= \frac{9 \times 10^9 \times 79 \times (1.6 \times 10^{-19})^2}{5.5 \times 10^6 \times 1.6 \times 10^{-19}}$$

$(\because 1 \text{ eV} = 1.6 \times 10^{-19} \text{ J})$

$$= 2 \times 10^{-14} \text{ m}$$

10. (False);

Nuclear radius is given by

$$R = R_0(A)^{1/3}$$

$\therefore \quad R_{\text{Au}} = R_0(197)^{1/3}$

$\therefore \quad R_{\text{Ag}} = R_0(107)^{1/3}$

$\because \quad \frac{R_{\text{Au}}}{R_{\text{Ag}}} = \left(\frac{197}{107}\right)^{1/3} = 1.22$

11. (*d*); The density of the nucleus is independent of the mass number. Therefore, the density of the nucleus is the same for every element and hence, the ratio will be 1 : 1.

12. A → 2, B → 3, C → 1

13. $(2.3 \times 10^{14} \text{ m}^3)$;

Mass = Density × Volume

$$2.3 \times 10^{31} = 10^{17} \times \text{Volume}$$
$$\Rightarrow \text{Volume} = \frac{2.3 \times 10^{31}}{10^{17}}$$
$$= 2.3 \times 10^{14} \text{ m}^3$$

14. (*c*); Surface area of nucleus,

$$S_A = 4\pi R^2 = 4\pi\,(R_0 A^{1/3})^2$$
$$= 4\pi R_0^2 \cdot A^{2/3}$$

Substituting constant (R_0) value $= 1.2 \times 10^{-15}$m, we get

$$S_A = 4(3.14)(1.2 \times 10^{-15})^2 A^{2/3}$$
$$= (1.8 \times 10^{-29})\,A^{2/3}$$

15. (*c*); Given, $m_{\text{Fe}} = 55.85$,

$$u = 55.85 \times 1.66 \times 10^{-27} \text{ kg}$$
$$= 9.27 \times 10^{-26} \text{ kg},$$

$A = 26$ and $R_0 = 1.2 \times 10^{-15}$ m

Nuclear density

$$= \frac{\text{Mass}}{\text{Volume}} = \frac{m_{\text{Fe}}}{(4/3)\,\pi R_0^3 A}$$
$$= \frac{9.27 \times 10^{-26}}{(4\pi/3)\,(1.2 \times 10^{-15})^3} \times \frac{1}{56}$$
$$= 2.29 \times 10^{17} \text{ kg m}^{-3}$$

16. (0.13251 amu);

Mass defect = (Number of proton × Mass of proton + Number of neutron × Mass of neutron) − Atomic mass

$$= (Z_p \times m_p + Z_n \times m_n) - A$$
$$= (8 \times 1.00727 + 8 \times 1.00866) - 15.99493$$
$$= 0.13251 \text{ amu}$$

17. (931.5);

$$1 \text{ amu} = 1.66 \times 10^{-27} \text{ kg}$$
$$E = 1.66 \times 10^{-27} \times (3 \times 10^8)^2$$

$(\because E = mc^2)$

$$= 1.66 \times 10^{-27} \times 9 \times 10^{16} \text{ J}$$
$$= \frac{1.66 \times 9 \times 10^{-11}}{1.6 \times 10^{-19}} \text{ eV (approx)}$$
$$\approx 931.5 \text{ MeV}$$

18. (7);

As, $\frac{\text{BE}}{\text{Nucleon}} = \frac{\Delta mc^2}{\text{Number of nucleus}}$

$$= \frac{0.0303 \times 931.5}{4} = \frac{28}{4}$$
$$= 7 \text{ MeV}$$

19. I. ✓ II. ✓ III. ✓ IV. ×

20. False

21. (Exothermic);
As the heavy nuclei breaks, it generates a very high amount of energy and lighter nuclei. Thus, this reaction is exothermic in nature.

22. (23.74 MeV);
Total binding energy of helium nucleus $= 4 \times 7.047$
$= 28.188$ MeV
Total binding energy of each deuteron
$= 2 \times 1.112$
$= 2.224$ MeV
Hence, energy released
$= 28.188 - 2 \times 2.224$
$= 23.74$ MeV

23. $(A \rightarrow 2, B \rightarrow 1, C \rightarrow 3)$;
The element C has the highest BE per nucleon. Thus, $A + B \longrightarrow C$ will liberate energy and form more stable nuclei.
And $(BE)_D \approx (BE)_B$, therefore $D \rightarrow 2B$ by absorbing energy.
And reaction $D + E \longrightarrow C$ is not possible energetically because $(BE)_C > (BE)_D . (BE)_D$

24. (*c*); Number of atoms in 3g coin
$$= \frac{N_A \times 3}{\text{Atomic mass}}$$
$$= \frac{6.023 \times 10^{23} \times 3}{63}$$
$= 2.868 \times 10^{22}$ atoms
Each copper atom has 29 protons and 34 neutrons.
Therefore, mass defect
$= 29 \times 1.00783 + 34 \times 1.00867 - 62.92960$
$= 0.59225$ u
Total mass defect of all atoms
$= 0.59225 \times 2.868 \times 10^{22}$
$= 1.6985 \times 10^{22}$ u
Thus, nuclear energy required
$= 1.6985 \times 10^{22} \times 931$ MeV
$\simeq 1.6 \times 10^{25}$ MeV

25. (*c*)

26. equals to

27. Alpha decay of a parent nuclei is given as
$${}^{A}_{Z}X \longrightarrow {}^{A-4}_{Z-2}Y + {}^{4}_{2}\text{He}$$

28. (False);
For the reaction,
$${}^{A}_{Z}X \longrightarrow {}^{A-4}_{Z-2}Y + {}^{4}_{2}\text{He}$$
The disintegration energy is given by
$$Q = (m_X - m_Y - m_{\text{He}})\, c^2$$

29. I : ${}^{60}_{27}\text{Co} \longrightarrow {}^{60}_{28}\text{Ni} + \beta^- + \bar{\nu}_e$
II : ${}^{22}_{11}\text{Na} \longrightarrow {}^{22}_{10}\text{Ne} + \beta^+ + \nu_e$
III : ${}^{32}_{15}\text{P} \longrightarrow {}^{32}_{16}\text{S} + \beta^- + \bar{\nu}_e$
IV : ${}^{14}_{6}\text{C} \longrightarrow {}^{14}_{7}\text{N} + \beta^- + \bar{\nu}_e$

30. I. × II. ✓ III. ✓
IV. ✓ V. ✓ VI. ✓
Half-life of β^--decay is less than that of β^+-decay

31. (216) ;
Binding energy of one daughter nuclei $= 120 \times 8.5$
Total binding energy of parent nuclei $= 240 \times 7.6$
Hence, energy released
$= 2 \times 120 \times 8.5 - 240 \times 7.6$
$= 216$ MeV

32. (False);
$${}^{56}_{26}\text{Fe} \longrightarrow 2\, {}^{28}_{13}\text{Al}$$
Let $m_1 = 55.93494$ u be atomic mass of Fe and
$m_2 = 27.98191$ u be atomic mass of Al
Q-value $= (m_1 - 2m_2) \times 931.5$ MeV
$= (55.93494 - 2 \times 27.98191) \times 931.5$ MeV
$= -26.902$ MeV
Since, Q is negative the fission is not possible.

33. I. ✓ II. ✓ III. ✓ IV. ×
In a nuclear reactor, energy is released from controlled nuclear fission.

34. (False);
In a nuclear bomb, there is an uncontrolled chain reaction which produces a large amount of energy within a short period of time, whereas in nuclear reactor, there is a controlled chain reaction.

35. more

36. (*b*) In chemical reaction, the energy released is in the range of eV. However, in nuclear reaction the energy release is of the order of MeV. Thus, for the same quantity of matter, nuclear source produce a million times more energy than a chemical source.
$\therefore \quad E_N > E_C$

37. A : ${}^{1}_{1}\text{H} + {}^{1}_{1}\text{H} \longrightarrow {}^{2}_{1}\text{H} + e^+ + \nu + 0.42$ MeV
B : ${}^{2}_{1}\text{H} + {}^{2}_{1}\text{H} \longrightarrow {}^{3}_{2}\text{He} + {}^{1}_{0}n + 3.27$ MeV
C : ${}^{2}_{1}\text{H} + {}^{2}_{1}\text{H} \longrightarrow {}^{3}_{1}\text{H} + {}^{1}_{1}\text{H} + 4.03$ MeV
D : $e^+ + e^- \longrightarrow \gamma + \gamma + 1.02$ MeV
E : ${}^{2}_{1}\text{H} + {}^{1}_{1}\text{H} \longrightarrow {}^{3}_{2}\text{He} + \gamma + 5.49$ MeV
F : $4\,{}^{1}_{1}\text{H} + 2e^- \longrightarrow {}^{4}_{2}\text{He} + 2\nu + 6\gamma + 26.7$ MeV

38. 400, 3×10^9 **39.** True

40. Yes

41. I. ✓ II. × III. ✓
IV. ✓ V. ✓
All higher mass nuclei are formed in the huge explosion of a dying star.

42. (*c*); Thermonuclear fusion requires high temperature and high fuel density.

43. plasma

44. 15, ${}^{14}_{6}\text{C}$

Competition Connect

1. mass energy

2. (4.25 MeV);
According to the reaction,
$${}^{238}_{92}\text{U} \longrightarrow {}^{234}_{90}\text{Th} + {}^{4}_{2}\text{He} + Q$$
$Q = (m_{\text{U}} - m_{\text{Th}} - m_{\text{He}})\, c^2$
$= (238.05079 - 234.04363 - 4.00260) \times 931.5$
$= 4.25$ MeV

3. $A \rightarrow 1, 3, B \rightarrow 2, 4$

4. daughter nucleus

5. moderator

6. For $k = 1$, the chain reaction is called critical.
For $k > 1$, the chain reaction is called super critical.
For $k < 1$, the chain reaction is called subcritical.

7. True

8. (Coolant);
As coolant is only meant to extract energy from the reaction, whereas the other three (i.e. fuel rod, control rod and moderator) helps to sustain the chain reaction.

9. I: $^{238}_{92}U + n \longrightarrow ^{239}_{92}U \longrightarrow ^{239}_{93}Np + e^- + \bar{\nu}$

II : $^{239}_{93}Np \longrightarrow ^{239}_{94}Pu + e^- + \bar{\nu}$

10. *A*–Concrete chamber, *B*–Fuel rod, *C*–Steam, *D*–Turbine, *E*–Condenser, *F*–water

11. A–3, B –4, C–5, D –2, E–1, F –6

12. Yes

Assertion-Reason Questions

1. (*d*);Nuclear density is same for all nuclei.

2. (*d*); For an element, it is not always true that atomic number *Z* is less than or equal to number of neutrons (*N*). e.g. In hydrogen atom, there is no neutron but it has one proton.
Therefore, atomic number of hydrogen atom is greater than number of neutrons.
i.e. $Z > N$, for hydrogen atom.
The force between neutrons in the nucleus is attractive only upto the range of 1 fm. But this attractive force become highly repulsive when neutrons came nearer to about 0.6 to 0.7 fm. Therefore, neutrons do not always experience attractive nuclear force.

3. (*a*); Upto atomic mass of 20, stable nuclei possess neutron to proton ratio $\left(\frac{n}{p}\right) = 1.$

$$\frac{n}{p}(^{30}_{13}Al) = \frac{30-13}{13} = 1.3 > 1,$$

So, Al is unstable.

$$\frac{n}{p}(^{40}_{20}Ca) = \frac{20}{20} = 1, \text{ stable}$$

Also, the oddness of both protons and neutrons tend to lower the nuclear binding energy, making odd nuclei generally less stable.

4. (*b*)

5. (*a*); The nuclear forces are short range force, therefore BE per nucleon is more for helium $(A = 4)$ than that for lithium $(A = 6)$ and also greater for carbon $(A = 12)$ than that for nitrogen $(A = 14)$.

6. (*c*); In α-decay, mass number decreases by 4 and atomic number decreases by 2.

7. (*c*); In case of fission, BE per nucleon for heavier nuclei is less than the BE per nucleon for lighter nuclei, while in case of fusion, BE per nucleon for lighter nuclei is less than the BE per nucleon for heavier nuclei.

8. (*c*); Larger nucleus (having shell type structure) is loosely bound as nuclear forces saturates after a certain distance.

9. (*a*); Thermonuclear reaction are those fusion reactions which are achieved by raising the temperature and pressure of the system, so that particles have enough kinetic energy to overcome the coulomb repulsive barrier.

Since, at earth such conditions are very difficult to attain naturally, so this reaction is not possible.

10. (*c*); Temperature in interior of sun is high enough for thermonuclear reactions.

Case Based Questions

1. (i) (*a*); Since, the nuclei of deuterium and tritium are isotopes of hydrogen, they must contain only one proton each but the masses of the nuclei of hydrogen, deuterium and tritium are in the ration of 1 : 2 : 3, because of presence of neutral matter in deuterium and tritium nuclei.

(ii) (*a*) (iii) (*b*)

(iv) (*a*); Here, $A_1 = 197$ and $A_2 = 107$

$$\therefore \frac{R_1}{R_2} = \left(\frac{A_1}{A_2}\right)^{\frac{1}{3}} = \left(\frac{197}{107}\right)^{\frac{1}{3}}$$

$$= 1.225 = 1.23$$

2. (i) (*a*); In fission process, when a parent nucleus break into daughter nucleus, then some mass lost in the form of energy.
Thus, mass of daughter nucleus < mass of parent nucleus

$$\Rightarrow \frac{\text{Mass of daughter nucleus}}{\text{Mass of parent nucleus}} < 1$$

(ii) (*c*)

(iii) (*a*); Let the number of fission per second be *n*.
Energy released per second

$$= n \times 200 \text{ MeV}$$
$$= n \times 200 \times 1.6 \times 10^{-13} \text{ J}$$

Energy required per second

$$= \text{Power} \times \text{Time}$$
$$= 1 \text{ kW} \times 1 = 1000 \text{ J}$$
$$\therefore n \times 200 \times 1.6 \times 10^{-13} = 1000$$
$$\text{or } n = \frac{1000}{3.2 \times 10^{-11}}$$
$$= 3.125 \times 10^{13}$$

(iv) (*a*)

Competition Edge Up

1. (*a*); $p_{\text{initial}} = p_{\text{final}}$

$$0 = m_1 v_1 + m_2 v_2$$

As, $\frac{m_1}{m_2} = \frac{2}{1}$ given

$$\Rightarrow \frac{v_1}{v_2} = -\left[\frac{1}{2}\right]$$

Thus, the velocity ratio will be 1 : 2 in opposite directions.

2. (*b*); Nuclear BE = Mass defect × c^2

= (Mass of nucleons – mass of nucleus) c^2

$$= (ZM_p + NM_n - M_0)c^2$$

Here, $Z = 5$,
$N = 12 - 5 = 7$

∴ Binding energy is,

$$\text{BE} = (5M_p + 7M_n - M_0)c^2$$

3. (*a*); Binding energy,

$$E = \Delta M \cdot c^2 \quad \ldots\text{(i)}$$

ΔM = mass defect,
$c = 3 \times 10^8$ m/s
$E = 18 \times 10^8$ J

Substituting values in Eq. (i), we get

$$\Delta M = \frac{E}{c^2} = \frac{18\times10^8}{(3\times10^8)^2}$$
$= 2\times10^{-8}$ kg $= 2\times10^{-8}\times10^3$ g
$= 2\times10^{-5}$ g $= 20\times10^{-6}$ g $= 20\,\mu$g

4. (*c*); Radius of nucleus is,
$R = R_0 A^{1/3}$
For nucleus of mass number 192, radius,
$R = R_0\,(192)^{1/3}$ ...(i)
For nucleus of radius $R/2$ let mass number is A', then
$R/2 = R_0 A'^{1/3}$ ...(ii)
Dividing Eq. (i) by Eq. (ii), we get
$2A'^{1/3} = 192^{1/3} \Rightarrow 8A' = 192$
$\Rightarrow A' = 192/8 = 24$

5. (4); Radius of a nucleus,
$R = R_0 A^{1/3}$
So, volume, $V = \frac{4}{3}\pi R_0^3 A$
Now, ratio $\frac{V_2}{V_1}$ is
$$\frac{V_2}{V_1} = \frac{A_2}{A_1} = \frac{4A_1}{A_1} = 4$$

6. (*c*); In given question,
${}_3\text{Li}^6 + {}_0n^1 \rightarrow {}_2\text{He}^4 + {}_1\text{H}^3$
${}_1\text{H}^2 + {}_1\text{H}^3 \rightarrow {}_2\text{He}^4 + {}_0n^1$
So net reaction is,
${}_3\text{Li}^6 + {}_1\text{H}^2 \rightarrow 2({}_2\text{He}^4)$
Energy released in process,
$Q = \Delta mc^2$
$Q = [m(\text{Li}) + m({}_1\text{H}^2) - 2m({}_2\text{He}^4)] \times 931.5$ MeV
$Q = [6.01690 + 2.01471 - 2 \times 4.00388] \times 931.5$ MeV
$Q = 22.216$ MeV, $Q = 22.22$ MeV

7. (*a*) Given, ${}_6\text{C}^{12} = 12.000000$ u
${}_6\text{C}^{13} = 13.003354$ u,
${}_0n^1 = 1.008665$ u
Mass defect,
$\Delta M = [12.000000 + 1.008665] - 13.003354$
$= 0.005311$ u
The required energy,
$\Delta E = 0.005311 \times 931.5$
$= 4.9471 \approx 4.95$ MeV

8. (11) Mass of one nucleon
$= 1.6\times10^{-27}$ kg
Volume of nucleus $= \frac{4}{3}\pi R^3$
$= \frac{4}{3}\pi\,(1.5\times10^{-15})^3 A$
where, A = number of nucleons in nucleus.
So, nuclear density
$$= \frac{\text{Mass}}{\text{Volume}} = \frac{A\times1.6\times10^{-27}}{\frac{4}{3}\pi\times(1.5\times10^{-15})^3\times A}$$
$$= \frac{1.6\times10^{-27}}{\frac{4}{3}\pi\times(1.5)^3\times10^{-45}}\ \text{kg/m}^3$$
$= 1.1\times10^{17}$ kg/m³
Density of water = 1000 kg/m³ will be
$$\frac{\rho_{\text{nucleus}}}{\rho_{\text{water}}} = \frac{1.1\times10^{17}}{1000} = 1.1\times10^{13}$$
$\therefore n\times10^{13} \Rightarrow n = 11$

9. (*b*) We know that, $R = R_0(A^{1/3})$
$$\therefore \frac{R_1}{R_2} = \left(\frac{A_1}{A_2}\right)^{1/3} = \left(\frac{125}{64}\right)^{1/3} = \left[\left(\frac{5}{4}\right)^3\right]^{1/3} = \frac{5}{4}$$
$\therefore R_1 : R_2 = 5:4$

10. (*a*) As, $E = mc^2$
$= 0.5\times10^{-3}\times(3\times10^8)^2$ $(\because c = 3\times10^8)$
$= 4.5\times10^{13}$ J

Chapter-14

Semiconductor Electronics : Materials, Devices and Simple Circuits

1. A→3, B→1, C→2
2. (*b*)
3. Insulator
4. energy bands
5. Yes
6. I. ✓ II. ✓ III. ✓ IV. ✓ V. ×
7. A = Conduction band
B = Valence band
C = Forbidden energy gap
8. II
9. (c) < (d) < (e) < (b) < (a)
10. A→3, B→1, C→2
11. (*a*)
12. absolute zero
13. (*c*)
14. True
15. Aluminium
16. $A\rightarrow E_C$, $B\rightarrow E_g$, $C\rightarrow E_V$, $D\rightarrow$ valence electrons, $E\rightarrow E_C$, $F \rightarrow E_V$, $G\rightarrow E_g$, $H\rightarrow$ conduction electron, $I\rightarrow$ hole
17. (*b*) **18.** (*c*)
19. (*b*)
20. I. Hole II. Acceptor
21. conduction
22. True
23. higher, lower
24. Since, $n_e > n_h$, so it is an *n*-type semiconductor.
25. (*a*);
$$n_e = \frac{5\times10^{28}}{10^6} = 5\times10^{22}$$
$(\because 1\ \text{ppm} = 10^6)$
$$n_h = \frac{n_i^2}{n_e} = \frac{(1.5\times10^{16})^2}{5\times10^{22}}$$
$= 4.5\times10^9$
$$\therefore \frac{n_e}{n_h} = \frac{5\times10^{22}}{4.5\times10^9} \approx 1\times10^{13}$$
26. III, II, I, IV
27. depletion, *n* to *p*
28. I
29.

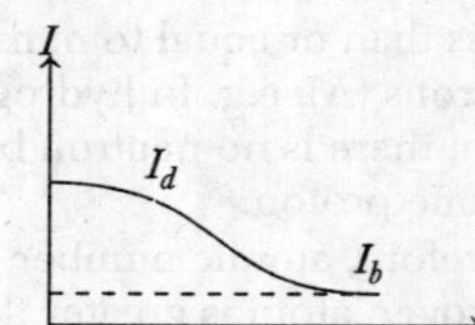

30. I. Forward bias (−5 V > −10 V)
II. Reverse bias (5 V < 10 V)
III. Forward bias (5 V > −10 V)
IV. Reverse bias (−5 V < 10 V)
31. I. ✓ II. ✓ III. ✓ IV. ✓ V. ×
32. unbiased, biased
33. I
34. (*b*); Since, diode is reverse biased. So, it will not conduct the current. Hence, potential difference across A and B will be V same as potential difference across the circuit.
35. I **36.** V_1
37. (*d*);
At $V_D = -10$ V,
$$R = \frac{V_D}{I} = \frac{10}{1\times10^{-6}} = 10^7\,\Omega$$
38. (*a*)
39. $\left(\frac{1}{4}\text{A}\right)$;
Only the diode in middle wire is conducting, so
$$I = \frac{V}{R} = \frac{5}{20} = \frac{1}{4}\ \text{A}$$

40. (*c*); Initially Ge and Si are both forward biased, so current will effectively pass through Ge diode with a voltage drop of 0.3 V.

$\therefore$ Initial output voltage,

$V_O = 12 - 0.3 = 11.7$ V

If Ge is reversed biased, then only Si diode will work.

In this condition, output voltage,

$V_O = 12 - 0.7 = 11.3$ V

$\therefore$ Change in output voltage $= 11.7 - 11.3 = 0.4$ V

41. (0.3 A);

As both diodes are in reverse bias, so given circuit is equivalent to the circuit as shown in the given figure.

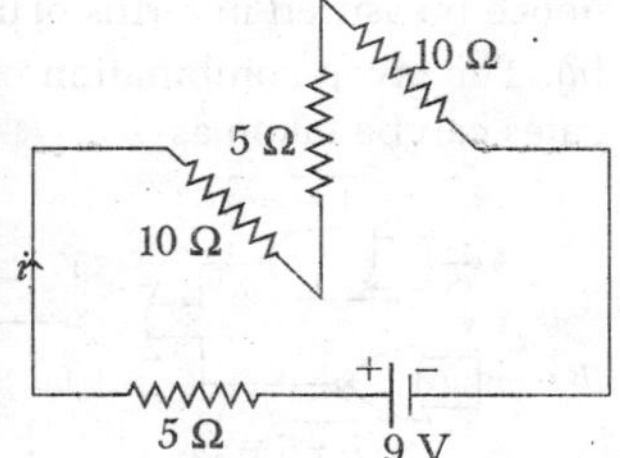

Equivalent resistance of circuit,

$R = 5 + 10 + 5 + 10 = 30\ \Omega$

$\therefore$ Circuit current,

$$I = \frac{V}{R} = \frac{9}{30} = 0.3\text{ A}$$

42. (A → 2, B → 1, C → 3);

Current in circuit,

$$I = \frac{P}{V_d} = \frac{100 \times 10^{-3}}{0.5}$$

$= 200 \times 10^{-3}$ A $= 200$ mA

Voltage across resistance R,

$V_R = 1.5 - 0.5 = 1.0$ V

Thus, resistance, $R = \frac{V_R}{I}$

$$= \frac{1.0}{200 \times 10^{-3}} = 5\ \Omega$$

43. $A \to$ AC input,

$B \to$ Transformer's primary coil,

$C \to$ Transformer's secondary coil,

D → Diode,

$E \to$ Load resistor

44. (*d*) **45.** (*c*)

46. As, the given diode is forward biased, it means, it can only conduct the positive half of the signal.

So, the correct output across R_L is shown below.

47. (*b*); Output frequency is double to that of input frequency. The output frequency of a full-wave rectifier is $2 \times 50 = 100$ Hz.

48. $A \to$ Primary coil,

$B \to$ Secondary coil

$C \to$ Transformer,

$D \to$ First diode (D_1)

$E \to$ Second diode (D_2),

$F \to$ Centre tapping wire

$G \to$ Load resistor

49. (*d*) **50.** (*a*)

51. (2 : 1);

For full wave rectifier,

output frequency = 2 × input frequency

and for half-wave rectifier, output frequency = input frequency.

$\therefore$ Ratio of output frequency of full wave rectifier to half-wave

$$\text{rectifier} = \frac{2 \times 50}{50} = \frac{2}{1}$$

52. (*d*)

Competition Connect

1. reverse, breakdown

2. True

3. $A = R_S$ (Series resistance)

$B =$ Zener diode

$C = R_L$ (Load resistance)

4. (*a*)

5. (*c*);

$$R_S = \frac{V_{\max} - V_Z}{I_{\max} + I_L} = \frac{10 - 6}{(20 + 4) \times 10^{-3}}$$

$$= \frac{4000}{24} = 166\ \Omega \approx 150\ \Omega$$

[nearest option is (c)]

6. IV **7.** (*d*)

8. (4400 A);

As we know that, wavelength,

$$\lambda = \frac{hc}{E_g} = \frac{1240\text{ eV-nm}}{2.8\text{ eV}}$$

$= 440$ nm ≈ 4400 Å

9. $A =$ Open circuit voltage (V_{oc})

$B =$ Short circuit current (I_{sc})

10. Logic gates

11. (*c*)

12. A → 1, B → 2, C → 2, D → 2

13. (False);

$\therefore$ The truth table that can be formed from this circuit diagram is

A	B	C
0	0	1
0	1	1
1	0	1
1	1	0

The output Y is same as that come for NAND gate.

14. (*b*); In case of a NAND gate, the truth table for the given input is

	Input		Output
	A	**B**	**Y**
t_1	0	0	1
t_2	1	0	1
t_3	0	1	1
t_4	1	1	0
t_5	0	0	1
t_6	1	0	1

15. I. $Y = \overline{(\overline{A} \cdot \overline{B})} = A + B =$ OR gate

II. $Y = \overline{\overline{A \cdot B}} = A \cdot B =$ AND gate

16. $A \cdot \overline{B} + \overline{A} \cdot B$;

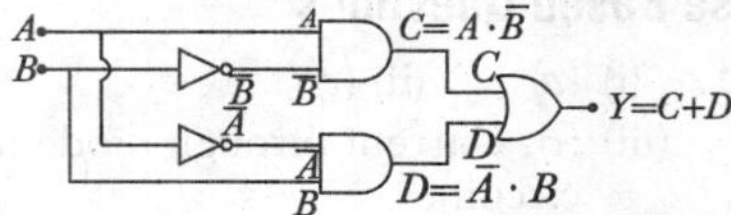

Thus, $Y = C + D = A \cdot \overline{B} + \overline{A} \cdot B$

17. (*c*);

We are showing intermediate outputs on the circuit as given below.

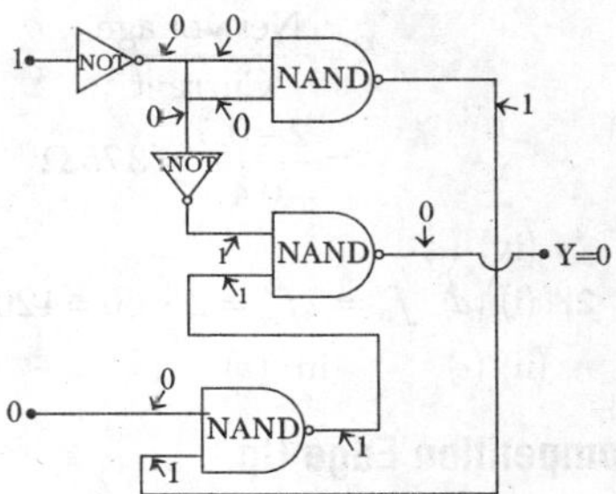

Output of above circuit at given inputs is zero.

18. The output, $C = \overline{(A + B)} \cdot B$, so the output will be as

A	B	C
0	0	0
0	1	0
1	0	0
1	1	0

Assertion-Reason Questions

1. (*a*) **2.** (*a*) **3.** (*a*)

4. (*d*); Assertion is incorrect because conduction band always contains few electrons means electrons can pass from valence band to conduction band without providing any external energy which possible only, if energy gap between conduction band and valence band is zero. But, many materials have non-zero energy gap.

5. (*a*) **6.** (*a*)

7. (*b*); Conductivity of semiconductors is given by,

$$\sigma \propto \exp\left(-\frac{E_g}{2kT}\right)$$

Hence, on increasing temperature conductivity of *n*-type semiconductor increases but, number of electrons donated by donor atoms do not depends on the temperature.

8. (*a*) **9.** (*b*) **10.** (*a*)

Case Based Questions

1. (i) (*a*) (ii) (*c*)

(iii) (*c*); Current through diode (or circuit),

$$I = \frac{\text{Power}}{\text{Voltage}}$$

$$\therefore \quad I = \frac{200\times 10^{-3}}{0.5} = 0.4 \text{ A}$$

and resistance,

$$R = \frac{\text{Net voltage}}{\text{Current}} = \frac{2-0.5}{0.4} = 3.75\,\Omega$$

(iv) (*c*)

2. (i) (*d*); $f_0 = 2f_{in} = 2\times 60 = 120$ Hz

(ii) (*c*) (iii) (*a*)

Competition Edge Up

1. (5); Potential drop across *PQ* length of wire

$$= 1.8 + 3.2 = 5.0 \text{ V}$$

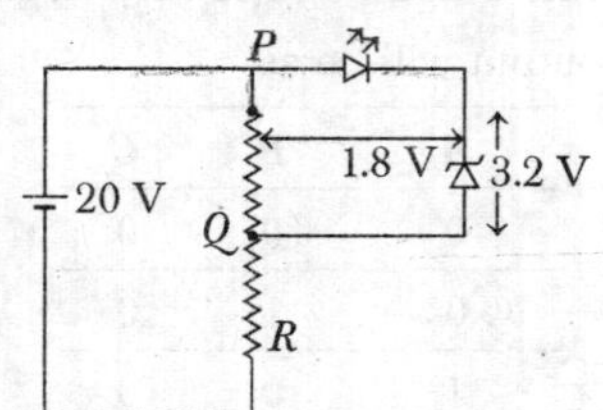

Now, $PR = 20$ cm and $V_{PR} = 20$ V

$\therefore$ Potential drop per unit length

$$\text{(per cm)} = \frac{20 \text{ V}}{20 \text{ cm}} = 1 \text{ V/cm}$$

So, potential drop of 5 V occurs at length *PQ* of 5 cm.

2. (*b*); Given, acceptor energy level,

$$E_g = 6 \text{ eV}$$

$$E = \frac{1242}{\lambda(\text{nm})}$$

$$\Rightarrow \quad \lambda = \frac{1242}{E} = \frac{1242}{6} = 207 \text{ nm}$$

3. (*c*); For the measurement of dynamic resistance of *p-n* junction diode, diode must be connected in forward bias. A diode is said to be forward biased if *p*-side is connected with higher potential than *n*-side. Thus, diode shown in option (c) is connected in forward biased, hence it is used for the measurement of dynamic resistance.

4. (*) Given voltage regulator circuit is,

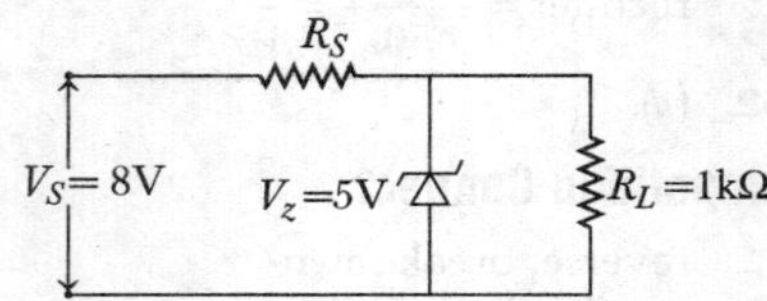

Given, power (rated) for zener,

$$V_z I_z = 10 \text{ mW}$$

Current through zener diode,

$$I_z = \frac{P}{V_z} = \frac{10}{5}\times 10^{-3} = 2\times 10^{-3} \text{ A}$$

Current through load resistor,

$$I_L = \frac{V}{R_L} = \frac{5}{10^3} = 5\times 10^{-3} \text{ A}$$

Current through R_S is,

$$I_S = I_Z + I_L = 7\times 10^{-3} \text{ A}$$

Potential drop across, R_S

$$= 8 - 5 = 3 \text{ V}$$

$$\text{So,} \quad R_S = \frac{V}{I} = \frac{3}{7\times 10^{-3}} = \frac{3000}{7} \approx 428\,\Omega$$

(No option is matching)

5. (*a*);

As both diodes are in forward bias, current will flow. Potential drops of diodes are 0.7 V and 0.3 V in forward bias. So, current in circuit is

$$I = \frac{V}{R} = \frac{15-0.3-0.7}{(2.5+1.5)\times 10^3} = \frac{7}{2}\times 10^{-3} \text{ A} = \frac{7}{2} \text{ mA}$$

So, potential drop across 2.5 kΩ resistor is,

$$V = IR = \frac{7}{2}\times 10^{-3}\times 2.5\times 10^3 = 8.75 \text{ V}$$

6. (*a*); A is correct but B is incorrect. In reverse biased *p-n* junction, the current is due to minority charge carriers, which is very small and hence measured in terms of μA.

7. (*d*); The given combination of gates can be taken as

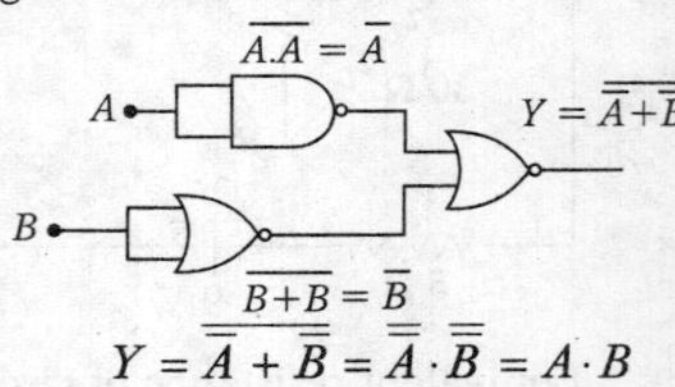

$$Y = \overline{\overline{A} + \overline{B}} = \overline{\overline{A}}\cdot\overline{\overline{B}} = A\cdot B$$

Hence, the output *Y* of the given logic gate is similar to AND gate.

8. (*b*); When AC is converted into DC using a rectifier circuit, then converted DC is an unstable current that includes ripples. A capacitor is used to remove these ripples and maintain a constant voltage across load.

9. (*d*); Photovoltaic devices can convert optical radiation into electricity. The basic example of such device is solar photovoltaic system which converts solar energy directly into electrical energy.

Zener diode is heavily doped *p-n* junction diode operating in reverse biased condition in breakdown region.

10. (*c*); In the circuit diagram *A* and *C*, both the *p-n* junction diodes are in same biasing conditions. So, both diodes offers equal resistances.

Since, both diodes are in series, therefore equal potential will drop across the junction.